THIRD CANADIAN EDITION

Auditing & Assurance Services

A Systematic Approach

William F. Messier, Jr.

Deloitte & Touche Professor
School of Accountancy
Georgia State University

Craig E. N. Emby

Faculty of Business Administration
Institute of Chartered Accountants of British Columbia Research Fellow
Simon Fraser University

Steven M. Glover

PricewaterhouseCoopers Research Fellow
Marriott School of Management
Brigham Young University

Douglas F. Prawitt

Deloitte Research Fellow
Marriott School of Management
Brigham Young University

McGraw-Hill Ryerson

Toronto   Montréal   Boston   Burr Ridge, IL   Dubuque, IA   Madison, WI   New York   San Francisco
St. Louis   Bangkok   Bogotá   Caracas   Kuala Lumpur   Lisbon   London   Madrid   Mexico City
Milan   New Delhi   Santiago   Seoul   Singapore   Sydney   Taipei

This book is dedicated to Teddie, Stacy, Mark, Bob, Brandon, and Zachary.   —William F. Messier, Jr.

This book is dedicated to my wife, Linda, and to my daughter, Cassidy.   —Craig E. N. Emby

This book is dedicated to Tina, Jessica, Andrew, Jennifer, Anna, Wayne, and Penny.   —Steven M. Glover

This book is dedicated to Meryll, Nathan, Matthew, Natalie, Emily, AnnaLisa, Lileah, George, and Diana.   —Douglas F. Prawitt

The McGraw-Hill Companies

McGraw-Hill
Ryerson

Auditing & Assurance Services: A Systematic Approach
Third Canadian Edition

Copyright © 2008, 2005, 2002 by McGraw-Hill Ryerson Limited, a Subsidiary of The McGraw-Hill Companies. Copyright © 2006, 2003, 2000, 1997 by the McGraw-Hill Companies, Inc. All rights reserved. No part of this publication may be reproduced or transmitted in any form or by any means, or stored in a data retrieval system, without the prior written permission of McGraw-Hill Ryerson Limited, or in the case of photocopying or other reprographic copying, a licence from The Canadian Copyright Licensing Agency (Access Copyright). For an Access Copyright licence, visit www.accesscopyright.ca or call toll free to 1-800-893-5777.

ISBN-13: 978-0-07-096476-1
ISBN-10: 0-07-096476-9

1 2 3 4 5 6 7 8 9 10 TCP 0 9 8

Printed and bound in Canada

Care has been taken to trace ownership of copyright material contained in this text; however, the publisher will welcome any information that enables them to rectify any reference or credit for subsequent editions.

Editorial Director: Joanna Cotton
Senior Sponsoring Editor: Rhondda McNabb
Marketing Manager: Joy Armitage Taylor
Developmental Editor: Marcia Luke
Senior Editorial Associate: Christine Lomas
Production Coordinator: Zonia Strynatka
Senior Supervising Editor: Anne Nellis
Copy Editor: Shirley Corriveau
Cover Design: Michelle Losier
Interior Design: Michelle Losier
Cover Image Credit: © Digital Vision/PunchStock
Composition: SR Nova PVT Ltd., Bangalore, India
Printer: Transcontinental Printing Group

Library and Archives Canada Cataloguing in Publication

Auditing & assurance services : a systematic approach /
William F. Messier ... [et al.].—3rd Canadian ed.

Includes bibliographical references and index.
ISBN-13: 978-0-07-096476-1
ISBN-10: 0-07-096476-9

1. Auditing—Textbooks.   I. Messier, William F.
II. Title: Auditing and assurance services.

HF5667.M48 2007   657'.45   C2007-901012-1

About the Authors

Professor William F. Messier, Jr. is the Deloitte & Touche Professor at the School of Accountancy, Georgia State University. He holds a Professor II at the Institute for Accounting & Auditing, Norwegian School of Economics and Business Administration, and he is a visiting faculty member at SDA Bocconi in Milan, Italy. Professor Messier holds a BBA from Siena College, an MS from Clarkson University, and an MBA and DBA from Indiana University. He is a CPA in Florida and has taught at the Universities of Florida and Michigan. Professor Messier is Editor of *Auditing: A Journal of Practice & Theory* and is associate Editor of the *Journal of Accounting Literature*. Professor Messier serves on the AICPA's Auditing Standards Board as Chair of the AICPA's International Auditing Standards Subcommittee. He was formerly Chairperson of the Auditing Section of the American Accounting Association. He has authored or coauthored over 50 articles in accounting, decision science, and computer science journals.

Professor Craig E. N. Emby is a Professor of Accounting and an Institute of Chartered Accountants of British Columbia Research Fellow in the Faculty of Business Administration at Simon Fraser University. He obtained his undergraduate honours degree in commerce from the University of Manitoba, his MBA from the University of British Columbia, and his PhD from the University of Alberta. He is a Chartered Accountant and a member of the Institute of Chartered Accountants of British Columbia.

Professor Emby joined the Faculty of Business Administration at Simon Fraser University in 1987 where he designed and implemented the first auditing course in the BBA program.

Professor Emby's research interests focus on professional judgement in public accounting, particularly judgement and decision making in auditing. He has authored (or coauthored) articles in such journals as *Auditing: A Journal of Practice and Theory*, *Behavioural Research in Accounting*, *Contemporary Accounting Research*, and the *Journal of Accounting Literature*, as well as professional publications and guides to practice.

Professor Emby has been a national examiner in auditing for the Certified General Accountants Association of Canada.

Professor Steven M. Glover is an Associate Professor of Accounting and PricewaterhouseCoopers Research Fellow at the Marriott School of Management, Brigham Young University. Professor Glover is a CPA in Utah and holds a PhD and BS from the University of Washington and an AA in Business from BYU—Idaho. He is a CPA and previously worked as a senior auditor for KPMG LLP and a director in the national office of PricewaterhouseCoopers LLP. Professor Glover sits on the board of advisors for two technology companies and actively consults with public companies and public accounting firms. Professor Glover is on the editorial boards of *Auditing: A Journal of Practice & Theory* and *Accounting Horizons*. He has authored or coauthored over 25 articles and books primarily focused in the areas of auditor decision making, audit education, and audit practice.

Professor Douglas F. Prawitt is a Professor of Accounting and Deloitte Research Fellow at the Marriott School of Management, Brigham Young University. Professor Prawitt is a CPA in Utah and holds a PhD from the University of Arizona, and BS and MAcc degrees from Brigham Young University. He has consulted extensively with several prestigious companies and international and local public accounting firms. Over the past three years he has worked with the Committee of Sponsoring Organizations (COSO) and PricewaterhouseCoopers on the COSO *Enterprise Risk Management Framework* project, which builds on the COSO *Internal Control Integrated Framework*. Professor Prawitt has served in several positions with the American Accounting Association, and is on the editorial boards of *Auditing: A Journal of Practice & Theory* and *Accounting Horizons*. He has authored or coauthored over 25 articles and books, primarily in the areas of auditor judgement and decision making, audit education, and audit practice.

BRIEF CONTENTS

CONTENTS

Preface

The auditing profession in Canada continues to undergo major changes, particularly in its environment. Events surrounding the bankruptcy of companies such as Enron, Worldcom, and Global Crossings, and the demise of Arthur Andersen have resulted in demands that auditors assume more responsibility in society, and in particular, the business world.

The profession is under greater external scrutiny than ever before. The Canadian Public Accountability Board (CPAB), made up of representatives from the profession (industry and securities regulators), oversees the work of audit firms performing audits of publicly listed companies in Canada. A primary function of CPAB is to ensure that firms approved to audit publicly listed companies adhere to appropriate professional standards in the performance of those audits. CPAB has the power to sanction firms and/or individuals within firms for performance, what CPAB deems to be substandard audit work. The results of CPAB's reviews are made public in an annual report.

The most far-reaching changes will come from the profession's convergence with the international auditing standards of the International Federation of Accountants (IFAC). The CICA has issued several documents and timetables covering the period between now and 2011, when complete convergence is scheduled to be achieved. The current form of the Assurance and Auditing Standards as they appear in the *CICA Handbook* will be replaced by Canadian Auditing Standards (CASs), which will be based on the International Standards on Auditing (ISAs) of IFAC, modified as appropriate for the Canadian environment. The Auditing and Assurance Standards Board (AASB) has stated that the new standards will be in place to govern the audits of companies with fiscal years starting in January 2009. At the present time, although the *CICA Handbook* exists as it has in the past, the process has begun and Exposure Drafts incorporating the new format have been issued by the AASB.

Every effort has been made to be as current as possible. The discussion of current auditing standards includes the provisions of those outstanding Exposure Drafts that are likely to be incorporated into the *CICA Handbook* during the preparation of this revision.

To respond to these changes and challenges, the authors continue to believe our students are best served by understanding the basic concepts that underlie the audit process and how to apply those concepts to various audit and assurance services. The Third Canadian Edition of *Auditing & Assurance Services: A Systematic Approach* contains significant changes and revisions that respond to this changing environment. Chapters 1 and 19 contain more detailed coverage of assurance, attestation, and auditing services including discussion of the demand for assurance services and how the provision of such services responds to the need for entities to be accountable to different groups in society.

The new approach to audit risk combines the auditor's assessment of inherent risk and control risk into the assessment of the risk of material misstatement. The CICA has indicated that in assessing the risk of material misstatement it is appropriate to treat inherent risk and control risk globally or separately. Chapters 8 to 14 of Part V, covering applications to specific business processes, follow the latter approach.

As the title indicates, the book takes a *systematic approach* to the audit process by first introducing the three basic concepts underlying that process: *materiality, audit risk,* and *evidence*. These concepts are then applied to each major business process and related account balances using a risk-based approach. For example, each business process chapter starts with an overview of the information system followed by a discussion of inherent risk factors that are relevant for the business process and account balances. The assessment of control risk is then described, followed by discussion of the nature, timing, and extent of audit procedures necessary to obtain sufficient evidence to achieve the appropriate level of detection risk.

In covering these important concepts and their applications, the book focuses on the decision-making processes followed by auditors. Much of auditing practice involves the application of auditor judgement. If a student understands these basic concepts and how to apply them on an audit engagement, he or she will know how to practice in today's dynamic audit environment.

The book can be used in a one-semester introductory auditing or assurance services course, or in a two-course sequence at the undergraduate and graduate levels. It can also be used in introductory professional development courses for external auditors, internal auditors, and government auditors. The sequence of chapter coverage can be modified to suit the instructor's preference. For instance, many instructors wish to introduce the student to auditors' professional responsibilities and the dimensions of legal liability early in their study of auditing. There is no loss of continuity if Chapters 17 and 18 are incorporated early in the course. Likewise, if the instructor wishes to present detailed coverage of audit reporting, including discussion of audit qualifications, Chapter 16 can be incorporated earlier.

Organization

Auditing & Assurance Services: A Systematic Approach is divided into eight parts:

Part	Description	Chapters
I	Introduction to Auditing and Assurance Services	1–2
II	Basic Auditing Concepts: Risk, Materiality, and Evidence	3–4
III	Planning the Audit and Understanding Internal Control	5–6
IV	Audit Testing	7
V	Auditing Business Processes	8–14
VI	Completing the Audit and Reporting Responsibilities	15–16
VII	Professional Responsibilities	17–18
VIII	Accounting Services, Attest Engagements, and Assurance Services	19

important Canadian legal precedent cases. In recognition of the fact that our legal environment has been and continues to be influenced by other jurisdictions, reference is made to important legal cases in both the UK and US, but the emphasis is on the current Canadian environment.

Supplements

CaseWare IDEA Software—Student Version: If practical, hands-on exposure to CaseWare IDEA is important to your course objectives, there is now the option to package a student version of CaseWare IDEA. Integrating the use of this software with the Third Canadian Edition of the text, student exercises requiring the use of CaseWare IDEA have been developed. These are integrated with the text's EarthWear case and are available on the Online Learning Centre.

Online Learning Centre: Numerous complimentary resources are available on the Online Learning Centre (OLC) at:
www.mcgrawhill.ca/olc/messier

By visiting this website, you will find:

- A link to the website of EarthWear's auditor Willis and Adams (featuring a full set of working papers for EarthWear)
- Online appendices
- True/false quizzes
- Multiple-choice questions
- Internet assignments
- UFE Exam Questions
- Glossary
- *The Globe and Mail* headlines
- Up-to-date information on changing standards

Instructor's Online Learning Centre The OLC content is flexible enough to be used with any course management platform currently available. If your department or school is already using a platform, we can help. The OLC includes a password-protected area for Instructors to access downloadable versions of the instructor supplements (except for the test bank which is only available on the Instructor's Resource CD). Also, all of the OLC content is flexible enough to use with any course management platform currently available. For information on our course management services, contact your *i*Learning Sales Specialist.

Instructor's CD-ROM The following instructor supplements are available on the Instructor's Resource CD-ROM:

- **Solutions Manual**, containing thorough up-to-date solutions to the book's end-of-chapter material, is also available from the OLC.
- **Computerized Test Bank**, including additional multiple-choice questions adapted from professional examinations. Professors may use this software to create, edit, and print a variety of tests.
- **PowerPoint® Presentations** to support and organize lectures.

*i***Learning Sales Specialist** Your Integrated Learning Sales Specialist is a McGraw-Hill Ryerson representative who has the experience, product knowledge, training, and support to help you assess and integrate any of the following products, technology, and services into your course for optimum teaching and learning performance. Whether it's helping your students improve their grades, or putting your entire course online, your *i*Learning Sales Specialist is there to help you do it. Contact your local *i*Learning Sales Specialist today to learn how to maximize all of McGraw-Hill Ryerson's resources!

*i***Learning Services** McGraw-Hill Ryerson offers a unique *i*Learning Services package designed for Canadian faculty. Our mission is to equip providers of higher education with superior tools and resources required for excellence in teaching. For additional information visit www.mcgrawhill.ca/highereducation/iservices/.

Teaching, Learning & Technology Conference Series The educational environment has changed tremendously in recent years, and McGraw-Hill Ryerson continues to be committed to helping you acquire the skills you need to succeed in this new milieu. Our innovative Teaching, Learning & Technology Conference Series brings faculty together from across Canada with 3M Teaching Excellence award winners to share teaching and learning best practices in a collaborative and stimulating environment. Preconference workshops on general topics, such as teaching large classes and technology integration, will also be offered. We will also work with you at your own institution to customize workshops that best suit the needs of your faculty.

PageOut McGraw-Hill Ryerson's course management system, PageOut, is the easiest way to create a website for your auditing and assurance course. There is no need for HTML coding, graphic design, or a thick how-to book. Just fill in a series of boxes in plain English and click on one of our professional designs. In no time, your course is online!

Course Management For the integrated instructor, we offer *Auditing & Assurance Services* content for complete online courses. Whatever your needs, you can customize the *Auditing & Assurance Services* Online Learning Centre content and author your own online course materials. It is

WHO USES AUDIT SERVICES?

Jay Johnstone is the owner of a small auto parts distributor. His one-store operation has been very profitable. He financed his current store mainly from personal savings and some borrowings from his family. Mr. Johnstone would like to expand his operations by opening two stores in nearby towns. Mr. Johnstone approached his local bank to request the necessary financing. He provided the loan officer with a set of financial statements that he prepared with the assistance of his bookkeeper. The loan officer informed Mr. Johnstone that because of the amount of the requested financing and his lack of prior credit with the bank, he would have to have his company's financial statements audited by an independent public accountant. The financial statements were audited and an unqualified audit report was issued. Based on the company's financial performance and prospects and the credibility added by the auditor's report, the bank granted the loan.

Sara Thompson, a local community activist, has been operating a not-for-profit centre that provides assistance to abused women and their children. She has financed most of her operations from private contributions. Ms. Thompson has applied to Human Resources Development Canada (HRDC) requesting a large grant to expand her two shelters to accommodate more women. In completing the grant application,

Ms. Thompson discovered that federal law for government grants requires that recipients have their financial statements audited prior to the final granting of funds. Based on the centre's activities, the intended use of the funds, and the auditor's report on the centre's financial statements, the grant was approved.

Conway Computer Company has been a successful wholesaler of computer peripheral products such as disk drives and tape backup systems. The company was started by George and Jimmy Steinbuker five years ago. Two years ago, a venture capital firm provided needed capital for expansion by acquiring 40 percent of the company. Conway Computer has been very successful, with revenues and profits increasing by 25 percent in each of the last two years. The Steinbuker brothers and the venture capital firm are considering taking the company public through a stock sale. They have contacted a number of underwriters about the public offering. The underwriters have informed the company that the company's financial statements will need to be audited by a major public accounting firm before a registration statement can be filed with the Ontario Securities Commission. The company hired a major public accounting firm. Subsequently, the company successfully sold stock to the public.

The situations in the box above show the importance of auditing and audited financial statements to both private and public enterprise. By adding the audit function to each situation, the users of the financial statements have reasonable assurance that the financial statements do not contain material misstatements or omissions.

You will find that the study of auditing is different from any of the other accounting courses you have taken in college, and for good reason. Most other accounting courses focus on learning the rules, techniques, and computations required to prepare and analyze financial information. Auditing focuses on learning the analytical and logical skills necessary to evaluate the relevance and reliability of the systems and processes responsible for recording and summarizing that information, and preparing financial statements, as well as of the information itself. As such, you will find the study of auditing to be more conceptual in nature than your other accounting courses. Learning auditing essentially helps you understand how to gather and assess evidence so you can evaluate assertions made by others.

This text is filled with the tools and techniques used by external auditors. You'll find that the "tool kit" used by auditors consists of a coherent logical framework, filled with tools and techniques useful for analyzing financial data and gathering evidence in a variety of settings from small business to consulting and even executive decision making. An important implication is that learning this framework makes the study of auditing valuable to future accountants and business decision makers, whether or not they plan to become auditors!

While we are convinced the concepts and techniques covered in this book will be useful to you regardless of your career path, our experience is that students frequently fall into the trap of defining auditing in terms of memorized lists of rules, tools, and techniques. The study of auditing and the related rules, tools, and techniques will make a lot more sense to you if you can first build up your understanding of why audits are needed, what an auditor does, and what are the necessary characteristics of audits and auditors. Reliable information is important for managers, investors, creditors, and regulatory agencies to make informed decisions. Auditing helps ensure that information is reliable, credible, relevant, and timely. In fact, you will find that the concepts behind financial statement auditing provide a framework or tool kit that can be used for improving the reliability of information for decision makers of all kinds.

The purpose of this chapter is to provide a context for your study of auditing. The chapter starts by analyzing why there is a demand for auditing and discussing assurance services, attest services, and auditing. Next, the types of audits and auditors are presented. The remainder of this chapter provides information on the public accounting profession and the major organizations that affect the auditing profession. In response to the changing business environment, especially advances in technology, the auditing profession has expanded its scope to offer other assurance services. Chapter 19 discusses some of these other types of professional services that auditors now perform for their clients.

The Demand for Auditing and Assurance[1]

LO 1 > An important question a student might ask is "Why do entities request an audit?" The answer to this question can be found in the economic relationships both within an entity, and between the entity and other parties that have a vested interest in the entity. A historic relationship exists between accounting and auditing in entities. For example, evidence shows that some forms of accounting and auditing existed in early Greece in approximately 500 BC.[2] Until the late 18th and early 19th centuries most

---

[1]See G. L. Sundem, R. E. Dukes, and J. A. Elliott, *The Value of Information and Audits* (New York: Coopers & Lybrand, 1996), for a more detailed discussion of the demand for accounting information and auditing.

[2]G. J. Costouros, "Auditing in the Athenian State of the Golden Age (500–300 bc)," *The Accounting Historians Journal* (Spring 1978), pp. 41–50.

minimum requirements for interest coverage on the debt, may be included in the debt agreement. Again, this arrangement gives rise to a demand for auditing. Ratios and coverages computed using audited financial statement numbers give the debtholders greater confidence that management is abiding by the terms of the restrictive covenants.

This characterization of the demand for auditing may seem quite simplistic given current audit practice. However, it does realistically portray the initial development of auditing. While some have argued that the demand for auditing resulted from events such as the Wall Street collapse of 1929 and from regulations such as the *US Securities Act* of 1933, the *US Securities Exchange Act* of 1934, and the *Canada Business Corporations Act* (CBCA), the empirical evidence does not support this view. A research study showed that in 1926, 82 percent of the companies on the New York Stock Exchange were audited by independent auditors.[4] Additional evidence for the demand for auditing is also provided by the fact that many private companies and municipalities, which are not subject to securities acts, contract for audit services nonetheless.

The purpose of this discussion has been to demonstrate that there is a demand for auditing services in a free market. While regulations account for some demand, they cannot account for all of it. Auditing is demanded because it plays a valuable role in monitoring the contractual relationships between the entity and its shareholders, managers, employees, and debtholders.

The Role of the Auditor

LO 2 > The exponential growth in the amount of information available creates tremendous opportunities for auditors to provide services that add reliability, credibility, relevance, and timeliness to the information. The companion website presents a model of the accountability cycle for a corporation. This model demonstrates how auditors can add value to the various types of information produced by the corporation.

Accounting and Auditing

It must be emphasized that to be a good auditor, one must first be a good accountant. Accounting in a business context consists of identifying, recording, classifying, summarizing, and reporting the effect of economic events in the financial statements. With few exceptions, the financial statements are prepared in accordance with generally accepted accounting principles, which in Canada would be Canadian GAAP. A critical aspect of the auditor's job as monitor is to ensure that the information provided in management's financial statements comply with GAAP. In order to do so he or she must have a comprehensive knowledge of GAAP to be able to evaluate the information in the financial statements, including how it was recorded, analyzed, summarized, and classified for reporting.

The auditor must collect and evaluate audit evidence in order to assess the representations in the financial statements to ensure that they comply

---

[4]G. J. Benston, "The Value of the SEC's Accounting Disclosure Requirements," *The Accounting Review* (July 1969), pp. 515–532.

with GAAP. However, the auditor does more than just consider whether the financial statement information complies with GAAP. The auditor carefully exercises his or her professional judgement to evaluate whether financial statement information reflects the intent of GAAP (the "spirit of the law") and not just the literal interpretation of GAAP (the "letter of the law"). It is the exercise of professional judgement that is the hallmark of the auditor.

The following section provides examples of various types of services that auditors can provide.

Assurance, Attest, and Audit Services

LO 3> Figure 1–2 shows the relationship among assurance, attestation, and auditing. Auditing services are a subset of attest services, which are in turn a subset of assurance services. The remainder of this section explains each of these forms of services in more detail.

Assurance

The broadest perspective on the role of the independent public accountant is conveyed by the term "assurance." An assurance engagement is defined in section 5025 of the *Handbook* of the Canadian Institute of Chartered Accountants (*CICA Handbook*) as:

> an engagement where, pursuant to an accountability relationship between two or more parties, a practitioner is engaged to issue a written communication expressing a conclusion concerning a subject matter for which the accountable party is responsible.

The breadth of the previous definition of assurance services may include dimensions such as the relevance and timeliness of information, as well as the reliability and credibility of both financial and nonfinancial information.

FIGURE 1–2

The Relationship among Auditing, Attest, and Assurance Services

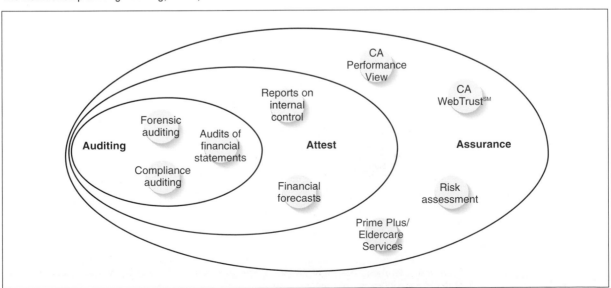

Some examples of assurance services include the following:

- *Electronic commerce*—assurance that systems and tools used in electronic commerce provide appropriate data integrity, security, privacy, and reliability—an example of this type of assurance service is CA*WebTrust*.[SM]
- *Information system reliability*—assurance that an entity's internal information systems provide reliable information for operating and financial decisions—an example of this type of assurance service is CA*WebTrust*.[SM]
- *Performance measurement*—assurance that an entity is measuring the critical success factors that will allow it to assess progress being made in achieving specific targets linked to the entity's vision—an example of this type of assurance service is CA *Performance View*.
- *Risk assessment*—assurance that the entity's profile of business risks is comprehensive and evaluation of whether the entity has appropriate systems in place to effectively manage those risks.
- *CA ElderCare*—assurance that specified goals regarding the elderly are being met by various caregivers.

Chapter 19 provides extended coverage of assurance services, including discussion of the standards for assurance services in the *CICA Handbook*, section 5025.

Attest

Attest engagements are a subset of assurance engagements and the standards for attest engagements are subsumed under the standards for assurance engagements. The term "attest engagements" is used to describe those engagements where an auditor issues a written communication expressing a conclusion *regarding a written assertion* prepared by a party responsible for that assertion.

Some examples of engagements that belong in this category are as follows:

- reports on internal control[5]
- reports on financial information other than financial statements
- reports on future-oriented financial information
- reports on compliance with statutory, regulatory, or contractual obligations

Chapter 19 provides extended coverage of some of the attest engagements that may be offered by public accountants.

Auditing

Since a company's annual financial statements are a written assertion by management, audits are a special subset of attest engagements. However the audit predates the other two types of engagements, both of which can be said to have evolved from it.

[5]See H. M. Hermanson, "An Analysis of the Demand for Reporting on Internal Control," *Accounting Horizons* (September 2000), pp. 325–342, for a survey of user groups on the demand for reporting on internal control.

One of the best general definitions of auditing is provided by the Committee on Basic Auditing Concepts of the American Accounting Association:

> **Auditing** is a systematic process of objectively obtaining and evaluating evidence regarding assertions about economic actions and events to ascertain the degree of correspondence between those assertions and established criteria and communicating the results to interested users.[6]

A number of phrases in this definition require additional explanation. The phrase *systematic process* implies that there should be a well-planned approach for conducting an audit. This plan involves *objectively obtaining and evaluating evidence.* Two activities are involved here. The auditor must *objectively search for* and *evaluate* the relevance and validity of evidence. While the type, quantity, and reliability of evidence may vary between audits, this process of gathering and evaluating evidence makes up most of the auditor's activities on an audit.

The evidence gathered by the auditor must relate to *assertions about economic actions and events.* For example, financial statements prepared by management contain numerous assertions. If the balance sheet contains an amount of $10 million for property, plant, and equipment, management is asserting that the company owns the assets, that it uses them in the production of goods and services, and that this amount represents their undepreciated historical cost. The auditor compares the evidence gathered to assertions about economic activity in order to assess *the degree of correspondence between those assertions and established criteria.* While numerous sets of criteria are available for measuring the degree of correspondence, generally accepted accounting principles (GAAP) are normally used for preparing financial statements.

The last important phrase, *communicating the results to interested users,* is concerned with the type of report the auditor provides to the intended users. The type of communication will vary depending on the type and purpose of the audit. In the case of financial statement audits, very specific types of reports communicate the auditor's findings. For other types of audits, the content and form of the reports vary with the circumstances, and the intended users.

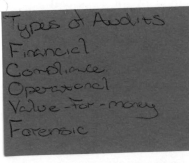

Table 1–1 summarizes the relationship among assurance, attestation, and auditing services. Notice that the definitions included in Table 1–1 progress from very general for assurance services to very specific for auditing services. This text focuses on one type of auditing, financial statement audits, because it represents the major service offered by public accounting firms. However, in many instances, the approach, methods, and techniques used for financial statement audits also apply to attest and assurance service engagements.

Types of Audits

LO 4 While there are many types of audits, five types are generally referred to: *financial statement audits, compliance audits, operational audits,*

---

[6]American Accounting Association, Committee on Basic Auditing Concepts, "A Statement of Basic Auditing Concepts" (Sarasota, FL: AAA, 1973).

Table 1–1	Relationships among the Assurance, Attestation, and Auditing Services	

Service	Characteristics of Information Reported On	Definition of Service
Assurance	Reliability Credibility Relevance Timeliness	A service in which a professional accountant is engaged to issue a written communication expressing a conclusion regarding a subject matter for which the accountable party is responsible.
Attestation	Reliability Credibility	A written communication regarding the reliability of a written assertion of another responsible party.
Auditing	Reliability Credibility	A service in which an auditor issues a written opinion on the correspondence between the information on the financial statements and the criteria established for reporting on economic events.

value-for-money audits, and *forensic audits.* Each of these types of audits will now be explained briefly. Excellent textbooks and articles are available that provide detailed coverage of these different types of audits.

Financial Statement Audits

A financial statement audit determines whether the overall financial statements present fairly in accordance with specified criteria. This type of audit usually covers the basic set of financial statements (balance sheet, income statement, statement of retained earnings, and a statement of cash flows), and *generally accepted accounting principles* (GAAP) serve as the criteria. Figure 1–3 graphically presents a simplified overview of the audit function for a financial statement audit. The auditor gathers evidence about the business transactions that have occurred (economic activity and events) and about management (the preparer of the report). The auditor uses this evidence to compare the assertions contained in the financial statements to the criteria chosen by the user and the auditor's report communicates to the user whether the assertions are consistent with the criteria.

In deciding where to focus audit effort and attention, the auditor often uses the strategic systems approach.[7] The strategic systems approach is consistent with the profession's new standards emphasizing the risk-based approach to auditing. The auditor focuses on those systems in an entity that are critical to the entity's success and to the attainment of its strategic goals. Audit effort is concentrated in those areas (*key business processes*) which, because of their strategic importance, are more sensitive.

The auditor seeks assurance that the key business processes are functioning properly and are free of material misstatement. An example of a

---

[7]For more information see T. Bell, F. Marrs, I. Solomon, and H. Thomas, *Auditing Organizations Through A Strategic-Systems Lens* (KPMG Peat Marwick LLP, Montvale, NJ: 1997) and D. Leslie, *Audit Methodologies of Large Firms* (Stephen Austin & Sons Ltd, Claxton Hill, UK: 2000).

FIGURE 1–3

An Overview of the Financial Statement Audit Process

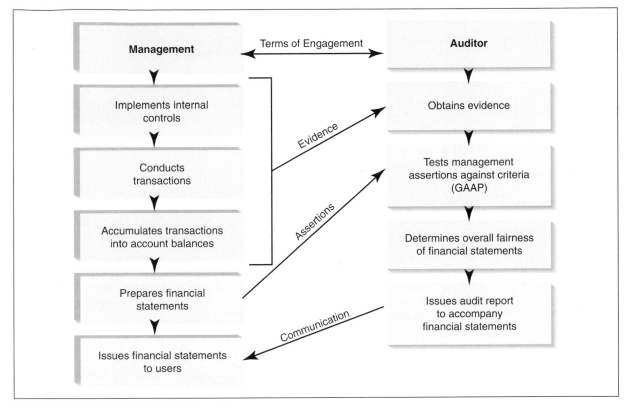

key business process could be the revenue recognition process for an entity in the high-technology software sector. This approach requires that the auditor understand the entity, the entity's strategic goals and initiatives, and be able to identify the key business processes which need to be examined in that context. Strategic Systems Auditing will be discussed in more detail in subsequent chapters.

Compliance Audits

A compliance audit determines the extent to which rules, policies, laws, covenants, or governmental regulations are followed by the entity being audited. For example, a company may have auditors determine whether corporate rules and policies are being followed by departments within the organization. The corporate rules and policies serve as the criteria for measuring the departments' compliance. Another example is examination of tax returns of individuals and companies by the Canada Revenue Agency (CRA) for compliance with the tax laws. In this example, the *Income Tax Act* provides the criteria for measuring compliance.

Operational Audits

An operational audit involves a systematic review of an organization's activities, or a part of them, in relation to the *efficient* and *effective* use of resources. The purpose of an operational audit is to assess performance, identify areas for improvement, and develop recommendations. Sometimes this type of audit is referred to as a *performance audit* or *management audit*. Operational audits are generally more difficult to conduct than financial statement audits or compliance audits because it can be very difficult to identify objective, measurable criteria that can be used to assess effectiveness and efficiency.

Operational auditing has increased in importance in recent years, and it is likely that this trend will continue. With entities restructuring and downsizing, many aspects of the entity's operations are being evaluated. For example, in the public sector, an operational audit may be undertaken to assess the effectiveness and efficiency of the disbursement of grants by Human Resources Development Canada. In the private sector, an operational audit could be performed to assess the efficiency and effectiveness of the entity's use of IT resources.

Value-for-Money Audits

Value-for-money auditing is a "made in Canada" development, primarily in the public sector. Former Auditor General of Canada, James J. MacDonnell, characterized the audits performed by his office as having three interrelated components.

The components, which together were termed a comprehensive audit, are a value-for-money audit, which is similar to an operational audit but considers economy as well as efficiency and effectiveness; a traditional financial statement audit; and a compliance audit.[8]

Forensic Audits

A forensic audit's purpose is the detection or deterrence of a wide variety of fraudulent activities. The use of auditors to conduct forensic audits has grown significantly, especially where the fraud involves financial issues. Some examples where a forensic audit might be conducted include

- business or employee fraud[9]
- criminal investigations
- shareholder and partnership disputes
- business economic losses
- matrimonial disputes

For example, in a business fraud engagement, an audit might involve tracing funds or asset identification and recovery. An employee fraud investigation might involve the existence, nature, extent, and identification of the perpetrator of asset misappropriation. A forensic audit can also be conducted to trace and locate assets in a divorce proceeding. Exhibit 1–1 describes a recent forensic audit conducted by a major accounting firm for the board of directors of Lernout & Hauspie Speech Products NV. Some public accounting firms specialize in forensic audit services.

---

[8]Canadian Comprehensive Auditing Foundation. *Comprehensive Auditing: Concepts, Components and Characteristics* (Ottawa: CCAF, 1980).

[9]See J. T. Wells, *Occupational Fraud and Abuse* (Austin, TX: Obsidian, 1997), for an excellent discussion of various types of business fraud.

EXHIBIT 1–1

PricewaterhouseCoopers Issues Report on Fraudulent Activities at Lernout & Hauspie

Lernout & Hauspie Speech Products NV (L&H), headquartered in Leper, Belgium, was a leader in speech translation software. L&H went public in late 1995 on the NASDAQ stock exchange and at one time had a market capitalization of nearly $US 6 billion. In 2000, the highflying company came under a SEC probe for reported revenues in Asia. Subsequently, the company filed for bankruptcy in both Belgium and the United States.

At the request of the company's new management, PricewaterhouseCoopers (PwC) was hired to conduct a forensic audit of the accounting fraud. Their audit discovered that most of the fraud occurred in L&H's Korean unit. In an effort to obtain bonuses based on sales targets, the managers of the Korean unit went to great lengths to fool L&H's auditor, KPMG. The PwC auditors reported that the Korean unit used two types of schemes to perpetrate the fraud. One involved factoring of receivables with banks to obtain cash to disguise the fact that the receivables were not valid. L&H Korea gave the banks side letters that provided that the money would be given back if the banks could not collect them. These side letters were concealed from KPMG. The second scheme arose after KPMG questioned why L&H Korea was not collecting more of its outstanding receivables. L&H Korea had its customers transfer their contracts to third parties who then took out bank loans to pay L&H Korea. L&H Korea provided the collateral for the loans. PwC reported that nearly 70 percent of the $160 million in sales booked in the Korean unit of L&H were fictitious.

Source: M. Maremont, J. Eisinger, and J. Carreyrou, "How High-Tech Dream at Lernout & Hauspie Crumbled in a Scandal," *The Wall Street Journal* (December 7, 2000), AI, A18; J. Carreyrou and M. Maremont, "Lernout Unit Engaged in Massive Fraud to Fool Auditors, New Inquiry Concludes," *The Wall Street Journal* (April 6, 2001), A3; and J. Carreyrou, "Lernout Unit Booked Fictitious Sales, Says Probe," *The Wall Street Journal* (April 9, 2001), B2.

Types of Auditors

LO 5 > There are a number of different types of auditors; however, they can be classified under four headings: *external auditors, internal auditors, government auditors,* and *forensic auditors.* Each type of auditor will be discussed briefly. One important requirement of each type of auditor is independence, in some manner, from the entity being audited.

External Auditors

External auditors are often referred to as *independent auditors* or *public accountants*. Such auditors are called "external" because they are not employed by the entity being audited. External auditors audit financial statements for publicly traded and private companies, partnerships, municipalities, individuals, and other types of entities. They may also conduct compliance, operational, and forensic audits for such entities. An external auditor may practice as a sole proprietor or as a member of a public accounting firm.

In Canada, there are three professional accounting bodies, Chartered Accountants (CAs) (members of the Canadian Institute of Chartered Accountants), Certified General Accountants (CGAs) (members of the Certified General Accountants Association of Canada), and Certified Management Accountants (CMAs) (members of the Society of Management Accountants of Canada). Currently, as the designation would suggest, the majority of CMAs are employed in private industry, although CMAs do have the right to perform the attest audit function in some provinces.

Although each of the three is distinct, there are similarities across the three organizations. Each institute or association is comprised of provincial bodies responsible for such elements as student education, professional conduct, and continuing professional development. The provincial bodies have delegated some of their functions to the above-mentioned national organizations, which ensures uniform standards for professional designation (e.g., the Uniform Evaluation in the case of the CICA, and the national examinations in the case of the CGA-Canada), and the development and promulgation of professional standards (e.g., the *CICA Handbook*). The website addresses of each of the three national organizations are as follows:

- Canadian Institute of Chartered Accountants (CICA): www.cica.ca. See also *CAMagazine* at www.camagazine.com
- Certified General Accountants Association of Canada (CGA-Canada): www.cga-canada.org. See also *CGA Magazine* at www.cga-canada.org/eng/magazine/default.htm
- Society of Management Accountants of Canada (CMA Canada): www.cma-canada.org. See also *Management* magazine at www.managementmag.com

For other related auditing and assurance services websites, visit the text's website under "Auditing Web Links."

Professional standards require that external auditors maintain their objectivity and independence when providing auditing or other attest services for clients. Later in the text, independence and objectivity will be discussed in depth.

Internal Auditors

Auditors employed by individual companies, partnerships, government agencies, individuals, and other entities are called internal auditors.[10] In major corporations, internal audit staffs may be very large, and the director of internal auditing (sometimes called the chief audit executive, or CAE) is usually a major job title within the entity.

The Institute of Internal Auditors (IIA) is the primary organization representing internal auditors with over 120,000 members in internal auditing governance and internal control, IT audit, education, and security from more than 100 countries.[11]

The IIA defines internal auditing as "an independent, objective assurance and consulting activity designed to add value and improve an organization's operations" with a view to "help[ing] an organization accomplish its objectives by bringing a systematic, disciplined approach to evaluate and improve the effectiveness of risk management, control, and governance processes." Internal auditing reviews the reliability and integrity of information, compliance with policies and regulations, the safeguarding of

---

[10]See D. Galloway, *Internal Auditing: A Guide for the New Auditor*, 2nd ed. (Altamonte Springs, FL: The Institute of Internal Auditors, 2001).

[11]See the IIA's home page (www.theiia.org) for more information on the IIA and the certified internal auditor program.

assets, the economical and efficient use of resources, and established operational goals and objectives. Internal audits encompass financial activities and operations including systems, production, engineering, marketing, and human resources.

The IIA has developed a set of standards that should be followed by internal auditors and has established a certification program. An individual meeting the certification requirements set up by the IIA, which include passing a uniform written examination, can become a certified internal auditor (CIA). Many internal auditors are also CAs or CGAs.

Like external auditors, internal auditors must be objective and independent. To help ensure the objectivity and independence of internal auditors, the IIA suggests that the director of internal auditing report directly to either the board of directors or the audit committee of the board or have free access to the board. If the internal auditors report to the chief financial officer or a similar financial officer within the organization, a conflict of interest may arise. Internal auditors may not be objective and independent when evaluating certain organizational functions if they are direct subordinates of the same individuals whose stewardship they are reporting on.

Internal auditors can be involved in all types of audits. They may conduct compliance, operational, and forensic audits within their organizations; they may assist the external auditors with the annual financial statement audit. Internal auditors may also be involved in assurance and consulting engagements for their entities.

Government Auditors

Government auditors are employed by federal, provincial, and local agencies. At the federal level is the Office of the Auditor General of Canada (www.oag-bvg.gc.ca/domino/oag-bvg.nsf/html/menue.html). Each province has a provincial counterpart (e.g., The Office of the Provincial Auditor of Ontario—www.auditor.on.ca/). It is the offices of the Auditor General that perform comprehensive audits on the financial information of government agencies and Crown corporations, both federally and provincially. Such examinations are mandated at least every five years. Similar requirements exist at provincial and municipal or local levels of government. The addition of economy to the effectiveness and efficiency criteria of an operational audit (the three together are termed a value-for-money audit) reflect the fact that these agencies and Crown corporations are supported in whole or in part by public (taxpayer) funds and therefore have a responsibility to use those funds wisely.

Another group of government auditors are those employed by the Canada Revenue Agency (www.cra-arc.gc.ca/) (formerly the Canada Customs and Revenue Agency). Their job is to audit the books and records of individuals and organizations to ensure adherence to tax laws, including income tax, sales tax, and GST. These audits are typically compliance audits.

Forensic Auditors

Forensic auditors are employed by corporations, government agencies, public accounting firms, and consulting and investigative services firms. They are trained in detecting, investigating, and deterring fraud and white-collar crime. Some examples of situations where forensic auditors have been involved include

- analyzing financial transactions involving unauthorized transfers of cash between companies
- reconstructing incomplete accounting records to settle an insurance claim over inventory valuation
- proving money-laundering activities by reconstructing cash transactions
- embezzlement investigation and documentation, and negotiation of insurance settlements

The Association of Certified Fraud Auditors (ACFE) is the primary organization supporting forensic auditors. The ACFE (www.cfenet. com/home.asp) is a 28,000-member professional organization dedicated to educating Certified Fraud Examiners (CFE), who are trained in the specialized aspects of detecting, investigating, and deterring fraud and white-collar crime.

The ACFE offers a certification program for individuals to become CFEs. An individual interested in becoming a CFE must pass the Uniform CFE Examination, which covers four areas: (1) financial transactions, (2) legal elements of fraud, (3) fraud investigation, and (4) criminology and ethics. CFEs are required to follow the association's Code of Professional Ethics and meet certain continuing education requirements.[12] CFEs come from various professions, including auditors, accountants, fraud investigators, loss prevention specialists, lawyers, educators, and criminologists. The CICA also offers the opportunity for its members, once they have obtained the CA designation, to specialize in this area. Such CA specialists are known as CA·IFA (Investigative and Forensic Accountant).

The Public Accounting Profession

LO 6 > As this text focuses on financial statement audits and assurance services, both of which are conducted by external auditors, this section provides an overview of the public accounting profession.

Public Accounting Firms

Public accounting firms may be organized as proprietorships or partnerships. Typically, local public accounting firms are organized as proprietorships or partnerships. Regional, national, and international firms are normally structured as partnerships. Structuring public accounting firms as proprietorships and partnerships offers additional protection for users of their services because such organizational structures, unlike a corporation, do not provide limited liability for the owners or partners. Thus, users can seek recourse not only against the public accounting firm's assets but also against the personal assets of individual partners. This lends additional credibility to the services provided to the public because the individuals are willing to risk the loss of their personal wealth.

---

[12]See the Association of Certified Fraud Examiners home page (www.acfe.org) for more information on the association and the CFE program.

Regional, national, or international firms may also be structured as limited liability partnerships (LLPs), a form of organization that offers somewhat more individual financial protection, and is allowed by some provinces. An LLP is generally governed by the laws applicable to general partnerships. This organizational structure offers accounting firms the ability to preserve the partnership structure, culture, and taxation but provides more personal protection against lawsuits. Under an LLP, partners are not personally responsible for firm liabilities arising from other partners' and most employees' negligent acts. However, the assets of the partnership are available for settlements of lawsuits resulting from other partners' or employees' acts.

Public accounting firms can be categorized by size. The four largest international public accounting firms in the world, all of which have Canadian partnerships, are Deloitte & Touche, KPMG, Pricewaterhouse-Coopers, and Ernst & Young.[13] In Canada, most audits of public companies are performed by one of the Big 4 plus Grant Thornton and BDO Dunwoody. Together, they audit the majority of the 1,000 largest companies in Canada. In 2006 their gross revenues ranged from a low of $261 million to a high of $1,151 million.[14] A significant advantage of internationalization is the ability to serve the increasing number of multinational clients.

Another group of firms, often referred to as national firms, have offices in most major cities and international affiliations. This allows them to compete with the Big 4 domestically and internationally and offer basically the same range of services. The gross revenues of these firms ranged from $34 million to $115 million in 2006.[15]

Local or regional firms may be quite large in scope either through having a number of offices in different locations or through membership in an association of public accounting firms, or they may have only one or a few offices. These firms provide audit, tax, and accounting services, generally to smaller organizations.

Audits are usually conducted by teams of auditors. The typical audit team is composed of, in order of authority, a partner, a manager, a senior, and staff members. Staff members are typically responsible for conducting portions of the audit work assigned to them by the senior. The senior or in-charge auditor participates in the planning, conduct, and supervision of the audit work. The senior also reviews the staff members' work prior to reviews by the manager and partner. In addition to reviewing the staff and senior's work, the manager and partner have various administrative responsibilities related to the audit engagement, such as scheduling the engagement and billing the client. The partner has the final authority and decision-making responsibility for accounting and auditing matters, including the issuance of the audit report. Table 1–2 summarizes the duties performed by each member of the audit team.

---

[13]Subsequent to the Enron crisis, the firm of Arthur Andersen & Co., which had been one of the Big 5, ceased to continue. Many of the individual partners and employees of Arthur Andersen & Co. are now with other public accounting firms.

[14]"The Annual Top 30 Survey of Canadian Accounting Firms," *The Bottom Line* (April 2006), p. F3.

[15]Ibid, p. F3.

Table 1–2	Selected Duties of Audit Team Members
Audit Team Member	*Selected Duties*
Partner	• Reaching agreement with the client on the scope of the service to be provided.
	• Ensuring that the audit is properly planned.
	• Ensuring that the audit team has the required skills and experience.
	• Supervising the audit team, reviewing the working papers, and quality control.
	• Signing the audit report.
Manager	• Ensuring that the audit is properly planned, including scheduling of staff.
	• Supervising the preparation and approving the audit program.
	• Reviewing the working papers, financial statements, and audit report.
Senior/Auditor-in-charge	• Assisting in the development of the audit plan.
	• Preparing budgets.
	• Assigning audit tasks to staff and directing the day-to-day performance of the audit.
	• Supervising and reviewing the work of the staff.
Staff	• Performing the audit procedures assigned to them.
	• Preparing adequate and appropriate working papers.
	• Informing the senior about any auditing or accounting problems encountered.

Other Types of Services Offered by Public Accounting Firms

In addition to auditing and assurance services, public accounting firms perform three broad categories of services.

Tax Services   Clients of public accounting firms are required to pay various types of federal, provincial, and local taxes. Public accounting firms have tax departments that assist clients with preparing and filing tax returns, provide advice on tax and estate planning, and may provide assistance on tax issues before the Canada Revenue Agency or tax courts.

Management Advisory Services   Management advisory services (MAS) are consulting activities that may involve providing advice and assistance concerning an entity's organization, personnel, finances, operations, systems, or other activities. Because of concerns regarding potential impairment of independence and other issues, a number of the major firms have sold their consulting practices. The consulting practice of KPMG is now BearingPoint, the consulting practice of PriceWaterhouseCoopers (PWC) is now part of IBM Global Services, and the consulting practice of Ernst & Young (EY) is now part of Cap Gemini. Consulting practices that are still associated with audit firms are prohibited from providing certain kinds of management advisory services, in particular IT consulting and internal audit services to their publicly listed audit clients.

Accounting and Review Services   Public accounting firms perform a number of accounting services for their non-audit or nonpublic clients. These services may include bookkeeping, payroll processing, and preparing financial statements. When accounting services for financial statements are provided for nonpublic companies, either a compilation or a review is performed. These forms of services provide less assurance on the correspondence between assertions and established criteria than a financial statement audit does. A *compilation* presents financial statement information that is the representation of management, and the compilation report issued by the public accountant does not provide any assurance on the compiled financial statements. A *review,* on the other hand, provides limited assurance that no material modifications are necessary in order for the financial statements to conform to established criteria. In contrast, an audit provides reasonable assurance that the financial statements conform to established criteria. Accounting services are discussed in more detail in Chapter 19.

Issues and Challenges Currently Affecting the Profession

This section briefly discusses some of the important issues currently confronting the auditing and assurance profession. You are encouraged to examine the references cited for further details.

Expanded Services   In recent years there has been a growing demand for external auditors to expand their services beyond the traditional financial statement audit. The list of assurance services discussed earlier in this chapter is evidence of this demand for expanded services by external auditors. Other types of auditors are also being asked to perform assurance services. Internal and governmental auditors are conducting assurance services that go beyond their traditional activities of compliance and operational audits. The IIA's definition of internal auditing recognizes this fact. Forensic auditors are also performing assurance services that involve investigations beyond their traditional work related to thefts of assets.

All of the major accounting organizations (e.g., CICA, CGA-Canada, CMA, AICPA, IIA, ACFE) that support auditing have taken actions to create an environment where their members can develop their competencies to perform these expanded services. For example, the CICA has developed a number of specialization streams for members. In addition to the CA·IFA previously mentioned in connection with forensic accounting, a CA may choose to specialize in Information Technology (CA·IT), business valuations (CA·CBV), Internal Auditing (CA·CIA), information systems auditing (CA·CISA), or insolvency and restructuring (CA·CIRP). At the time of writing, specializations in corporate finance and in taxation are also under development. More information about these specializations is available on the CICA website.

Globalization   More and more business entities are involved with either the manufacture or distribution of products around the world. One public accounting firm has noted the following about the global business environment:[16]

---

[16]T. B. Bell, F. O. Marrs, I. Solomon, and H. Thomas, *Auditing Organizations Through a Strategic-Systems Lens: The KPMG Business Measurement Process* (New York: KPMG Peat Marwick LLP, 1997).

In today's world, distance is no longer a barrier to market entry, technologies are rapidly replicated by competitors, and information and communications technologies are shaping a new economic order. To manage their business risks effectively, organizations must now view their playing field as the whole global economy (pp. 26–27).

This firm also stated that

Today's global economy and the business organizations operating within it, however, have become so complex and interdependent that new approaches to auditing must be developed (p. 1).

The public accounting profession is being affected by the globalization of business. While most of the major public accounting firms have international operations, the need to deliver many different services worldwide to clients has led to mergers among the major firms. Smaller firms have found it necessary to establish international affiliations or associations in order to service their clients' foreign operations. Issues have also been raised about the diversity of accounting and auditing standards between countries. As a consequence of this problem, we have seen the establishment of international accounting and auditing standards.

Litigation   Recent years have seen an increase in litigation against auditors, most frequently for negligence. Although the auditor's exposure to legal liability in Canada is not as extreme as that in the United States, nor, in the opinion of at least one expert, is it likely to become so, it is instructive to keep abreast of developments there.[17]

The most dramatic recent example of litigation against an auditor is the prosecution in the United States of the firm of Arthur Andersen in relation to its involvement in the events surrounding the Enron bankruptcy in the fall of 2001. In June 2002, Arthur Andersen was found guilty of obstruction of justice. The official sanction was that Arthur Andersen was legally prevented from performing audits of publicly listed clients. However, the unofficial outcome was the almost complete erosion of its client base resulting in the demise of Arthur Andersen as a firm.[18] (Other consequences of the Enron affair are discussed in the following section on Organizations that Affect Financial Statement Audits and more detailed coverage of the legal issues will be provided in Chapter 18.)

Even before Enron, litigation settlements by audit firms in the United States were in the hundreds of millions of dollars. For example, Table 1–3 shows some recent settlements by US auditors. While the numbers in Canada are substantially smaller, litigation is a major concern for the profession. In Canada, the Ontario government, as part of Bill 198, has passed legislation that may both hurt and help auditors of OSC-listed companies. On one hand, the new legislation makes it easier for third parties to sue the auditor for negligence, but on the other hand it puts a cap on the maximum amount of the auditor's liability. Legal liability for auditors in Canada, including Bill 198, is discussed in detail in Chapter 18.

---

[17]M. Paskell-Meade, "What Liability Crisis," *CAMagazine* (May 1994), pp. 42–43.

[18]The 2002 conviction by Arthur Andersen was overturned by the US Supreme Court on May 31, 2005, but by that time the firm had long ceased to exist, except as a name.

Table 1–3	Recent Litigation Settlements by Auditors in the United States	
Auditor	**Company Audited**	**Settlement Amount**
Ernst & Young	Cendant	$335 million
Andersen	Waste Management	75 million
Andersen	Sunbeam	110 million
PricewaterhouseCoopers	Microstrategy	51 million
Ernst & Young	Savings & Loans*	400 million
Deloitte	YBM Magnex International	76 million
KPMG	Rite Aid	125 million

*Various Savings & Loans, including Lincoln and Silverado.

Source: M. Maremont, "KPMG, Former Auditor of L&H, May Draw Investor Ire," *The Wall Street Journal* (January 18, 2001); N. Harris, "Andersen to Pay $110 Million to Settle Sunbeam Accounting-Fraud Lawsuit," *The Wall Street Journal* (May 2, 2001); J. Weil, "Pricewaterhouse Agrees to Settle Microstrategy Suit for $51 Million," *The Wall Street Journal* (May 10, 2001); securities.stanford.edu/news-arhive/2002; and www.philly.com/mld/inquirer.

Independence Issues   Independence is fundamental to the credibility of auditing and assurance services. One of the biggest challenges currently facing the profession is restoring its reputation for independence. In the wake of Enron, the entire profession's reputation suffered serious harm, and confidence in auditors' independence on the part of government, regulators, and the investing public was significantly impaired. In the post-Enron era, there have been initiatives in both Canada and the United States to strengthen auditor independence. The Public Interest and Integrity Committee (PIIC) of the CICA proposed new rules of professional conduct regarding independence, which have been adopted by the provincial institutes.

In Canada, the three professional accounting bodies have all responded by increasing their oversight of auditor independence. In Canada, both the CICA and CGA-Canada have amended their rules of professional conduct to address *independence in fact*, where the auditor is able to maintain an unbiased attitude to the client throughout the audit, and *independence in appearance*, which is concerned with an external observer's view and interpretation of the auditor's relationship with the client. If independence in appearance is lost to observers, even if the auditor does maintain independence in fact, the value added by the audit function is negated.

The rules of professional conduct require the auditor to consider, before accepting, and throughout the audit, five specific threats to independence.

- *Self-interest threat* may arise from a financial interest in the client or its financial results.
- *Self-review threat* may arise where the auditor is in the position of auditing his or her own work (hence the prohibition of MAS for audit clients).

- ***Familiarity threat*** may arise where it may be difficult for the auditor to exercise professional scepticism during the audit (potentially arising as a result of long auditor tenure with a client, or family membership).
- ***Intimidation threat*** may arise where actual or perceive threats from the client may deter the auditor from acting objectively with respect to the conduct of the audit and/or the content of the audit report.
- ***Advocacy threat*** may arise when an individual on the audit team promotes an assurance client's position (e.g., choice of accounting policy) to the point where objectivity is, or appears to be, impaired.

Specific prohibitions relate financial or business relationships, and family relationships. The rules of professional conduct are discussed further in Chapter 17.

Organizations That Affect Financial Statement Audits

Professional Accounting Associations in Canada

LO 7 ⟩

The oldest professional accounting organization in Canada is the CICA. Auditing standards as stated in the *CICA Handbook* must be followed by all public accountants performing audits of companies chartered either federally or provincially. This authority comes from the federal *Canadian Business Corporations Act* and the various provincial corporations acts under which companies are chartered. The standards, issued by the Auditing and Assurance Standards Board (AASB) of the CICA, are codified as "Assurance and Related Services Recommendations" and make up the italicized portions of sections 5000 to 9200 of the *CICA Handbook*. The Auditing and Assurance Standards Oversight Council (AASOC) was established in 2002 by the CICA to oversee the AASB to provide strategic direction and to ensure the inclusion of the user's perspective into the setting of auditing and assurance standards.

In addition, the AASB issues Assurance and Related Services Guidelines. These guidelines (AuGs) may be interpretations of the *CICA Handbook* recommendations or guidance concerning a specific matter. They may be withdrawn or incorporated into the *Handbook* as recommendations. At present there are approximately 40 Audit and Related Services Guidelines outstanding, some of which relate to either auditing in an EDP environment or auditing using EDP techniques.

AASB recommendations relating to auditing in the public sector (i.e., government) appear in sections PS5000 and PS6000 of the *Handbook*. Many of the recommendations concern value-for-money audits for various levels of federal, provincial, and territorial governments.

The usual process by which new recommendations are incorporated into the *Handbook* is through the issuance by the AASB of exposure drafts (EDs). These exposure drafts are available on their website and comments are solicited from interested parties. As a result of their responses, an ED may be amended as the AASB thinks appropriate. It may or may not be issued again as a re-exposure draft. When the AASB is satisfied with the form and content of the ED, it is incorporated into the *Handbook*.

CGA-Canada and SMAC have the same governance role for their members as does the CICA for chartered accountants. They set educational policy and standards, undertake research, and publish materials for their members. However, they are bound by the recommendations of the *CICA Handbook* in their professional practice.

Professional Accounting Organizations Outside Canada

Besides the direct influence of the professional accounting bodies in Canada, professional accounting bodies outside Canada indirectly influence Canadian standards governing financial statement audits. Two of these in particular are the International Federation of Accountants (IFAC, www.ifac.org/) and the American Institute of Certified Public Accountants (AICPA, www.aicpa.org/index.htm).

For Canadian auditors, an important external professional organization is the International Federation of Accountants (www.IFAC.org). IFAC is made up of the professional associations of its member countries. In Canada, the CICA, CGA-Canada, and SMAC are all members of IFAC. The objective of IFAC is to harmonize auditing standards on an international basis through the issuance of International Standards on Auditing (ISAs) and International Auditing Practice Statements. Currently, the Auditing and Assurance Standards Board (AASB) of the CICA is in the process of harmonizing Canadian standards with international standards on auditing.

Complete convergence is to be achieved by 2008, to coincide with the International Auditing and Assurance Standards Board's target completion of its Clarity Project, a major initiative to ensure that the ISAs are based on clear objectives, and are unambiguous and readable. The AASB will continue the process of incorporating ISAs into the existing structure of the *CICA Handbook* until complete convergence is achieved, at which time the sections of the *Handbook* will be renumbered to be consistent with the numbering of the ISAs.

Organizations External to the Profession

A major influence in Canada is the Canadian Public Accountability Board (CPAB), which was formed jointly in 2002 by the Office of the Superintendent of Financial Institutions (a federal regulator), the Canadian Securities Administrators (representing the provinces), and the CICA. CPAB oversees auditors of public companies in Canada and involves such activities as more rigorous inspection of auditors of public companies, tougher auditor independence rules, and new quality control requirements for firms auditing public companies. To date, CPAB has issued three annual reports on the results of its inspections. They can be accessed through its website, www.cpab-ccrc.ca.

CPAB is comprised of 11 members, including professional accountants and representatives from the regulatory agencies. Also, in Canada, any companies that issue securities must adhere to the rules established by their respective securities commissions. The securities exchanges of B.C., Alberta, Saskatchewan, Manitoba, Ontario, and Quebec belong to the Canadian Securities Administration (CSA). The CSA has stated that its members require the use of the *CICA Handbook* GAAP for companies issuing securities under their members' jurisdictions. Because the Toronto Stock Exchange (TSE) is the senior exchange in Canada, the regulations of the Ontario Securities Commission (OSC) are particularly important.

Shares of many Canadian companies are traded on one of the exchanges in the United States (NYSE, AMEX, NASDAQ). Those companies must meet the requirements of the US Securities Exchange Commission (SEC). The SEC is a US federal government agency that administers the *Securities Act* of 1933 which regulates information disclosure in a registration statement for an initial public offering, and the *Securities Exchange Act* of 1934 which regulates ongoing reporting by companies whose securities are listed and traded on a US exchange. The *Securities Exchange Act* of 1934 gives the SEC authority to establish accounting and auditing standards. Since Canadian auditors audit Canadian companies listed on a US exchange, it is important for Canadian public accountants with US-listed clients to be familiar with the SEC.

A number of other US organizations affect auditing standards and practice in the US (and thereby indirectly influence the Canadian environment). The Financial Accounting Standards Board (FASB) is a privately funded body, with membership from the profession, industry, government and academe, whose mission is to establish standards for financial accounting and reporting through the issuance of Statements of Financial Accounting Standards (SFAS). The Government Accounting Standards Board (GASB) is similar in makeup to FASB and operates in the public sector.

In 2002, in response to Enron and other dramatic business events, the US Congress passed the *Sarbanes-Oxley Act* (which will be discussed in more detail in Chapter 18). This Act places many new requirements on auditors and the public companies they audit, but most relevant to this discussion is the fact that the *Sarbanes-Oxley Act* created the Public Company Accounting Oversight Board (PCAOB). PCAOB is a private non-profit corporation funded principally by fees from public companies, made up of representation from a cross-section of public interests. The mandate of PCAOB is to protect the public interest by ensuring that public company financial statements are audited according to the highest standards of quality, independence, and ethics. Public accounting firms are required to register with PCAOB and conform to its rules which are administered and enforced by the SEC, in order to be eligible to perform audits of publicly listed companies.

REVIEW QUESTIONS

LO 1 > **1-1** Discuss why there is a demand for auditing services in a free-market economy. What evidence suggests that auditing would be demanded even if it were not required by government regulation?

1,2 > **1-2** Why is studying auditing different from studying other accounting topics? How might understanding auditing concepts prove useful for consultants, business managers, and so forth?

1> **1-3** What is meant by the statement "The agency relationship between absentee _____ conflict of interest"?

1,2> **1-4** Why is in _____ auditors? How does _____ ip between owners an _____

1,3,4> **1-5** The Com _____ d a widely cited def _____ *systematic process* m _____

3> **1-6** Define au _____ two examples of ea _____

4> **1-7** Identify a _____

4> **1-8** Give three examples each of compliance, operational, and forensic audits.

5> **1-9** List the various types of auditors.

4,5> **1-10** What types of audits are typically conducted by government and CRA auditors?

6> **1-11** What forms of organizations can be used by public accounting firms? What is a limited liability partnership?

6,7> **1-12** What are the issues currently affecting the public accounting profession?

2,5> **1-13** What types of services are commonly offered by public accounting firms?

6> **1-14** What professional accounting organizations inside and outside Canada influence the Canadian public accounting profession?

7> **1-15** What organizations external to the profession inside and outside Canada influence the Canadian public accounting profession?

[Handwritten note: Ch 1 / ✓ All multiple choice / ✓ All review questions / ~ Problems: 22, 23, 24, 26]

MULTIPLE-CHOICE QUESTIONS FROM PROFESSIONAL EXAMINATIONS

Unless otherwise indicated, these multiple-choice questions were adapted from the CPA examinations, courtesy of the American Institute of Certified Public Accountants.

1,2,3> **1-16** An audit aids in the communication of economic data because the audit

a. Confirms the accuracy of management's financial representations.

b. Lends credibility to the financial statements.

c. Guarantees that financial data are fairly presented.

d. Assures the readers of financial statements that any fraudulent activity has been corrected.

4> **1-17** Operational auditing is oriented primarily toward

a. Future improvements to accomplish the goals of management.

b. The accuracy of data reflected in management's financial records.

c. Verification that a company's financial statements are fairly presented.

d. Past protection provided by existing internal control.

4> **1-18** Which of the following is least likely to be a component of a comprehensive audit performed in the public sector?

a. Compliance audit.

b. Value-for-money audit.

c. Financial audit.

d. Tax audit.

(CGA-Canada, adapted. Extract from *Auditing 2*, published by the Certified General Accountants Association of Canada, © CGA-Canada, 1995 to 2006, reproduced with permission. Because of *Tax Act* updates and/or changes to the *CICA Handbook*, the contents of these examinations may be out of date; therefore the currency of the contents is the sole responsibility of the user.)

6> **1-19** Which of the threats to independence identified in the Rules of Professional Conduct may be created by deliberately underbidding to obtain an audit engagement?

a. Self-review threat.

b. Familiarity threat.

c. Advocacy threat.

d. Self-interest threat.

e. Intimidation threat.

(CGA-Canada, adapted)

6,7> **1-20** The International Standards on Auditing (ISAs) issued by the International Auditing and Assurance Standards Board of the International Federation of Accountants can best be described by which of the following statements?

a. ISAs are written to supplement Canadian and other domestic auditing standards by filling in areas not covered by these standards.

b. ISAs have little influence and are rarely used either in Canada or internationally.

c. ISAs are a set of standards that are adopted in whole or in part by many countries around the world, including Canada.

d. ISAs are currently an effective substitute for Canadian auditing standards, and an auditor can choose to audit a domestic company either in accordance with the *CICA Handbook* or the ISAs.

(CGA-Canada, adapted)

PROBLEMS

1,2,3> **1-21** Felix Potvine, the sole owner of a small hardware business, has been told that the business should have financial statements reported on by an independent auditor. Potvine, having some bookkeeping experience, has personally prepared the company's financial statements and does not understand why such statements should be examined by an auditor. Potvine discussed the matter with Steve Barber, an auditor, and asked Barber to explain why an audit is considered important.

Problems continue on page 27

EarthWear

2 0 0 6

COMPANY HISTORY AND OPERATIONS EarthWear Clothiers was founded in Calgary, Alberta, by James Williams and Calvin Rogers in 1974 to make high-quality clothing for outdoor sports, such as hiking, skiing, fly-fishing, and whitewater kayaking. Over the years, the company's product lines have grown to include casual clothing, accessories, shoes, and soft luggage. EarthWear offers its products through three retailing options: catalogues, retail outlets, and its website.

The company strives to provide excellent, high-quality products at reasonable prices. EarthWear has a commitment to excellence in customer service and an unconditional guarantee. The company is also conscious of its environmental responsibilities. All company facilities are insulated, recycle, and conserve power. The company continuously monitors the environmental impact of its products. The company believes that many of its customers share this concern for the environment.

The company offers its products principally through regular mailings of its monthly catalogues in Canada, the United States (its major market), the United Kingdom, Germany, and Japan. EarthWear has five Canadian outlet stores, four in the US, four in the UK, two in Germany, and two in Japan. During 2006, EarthWear expanded its global presence by launching sites in France, Italy, Ireland, and several eastern European countries. The company also offers its products over the Internet. Currently, revenue from catalogue sales, retail outlets, and the website are 20 percent, 5 percent, and 75 percent, respectively. Internet sales have grown significantly in the past few years, although the company still distributes catalogues to inform customers of EarthWear's products.

EarthWear was incorporated in Alberta in 1976 and became a Canadian federally incorporated company in 1987 when it went public.

COMPANY

HISTORY AND BACKGROUND

COMPANY GROWTH STRATEGY EarthWear's growth strategy has three elements. First, the company attempts to increase sales by expanding its customer base and by increasing sales to existing customers through improved product offerings. Second, the company seeks to generate additional sales by targeted mailings of special issues of its catalogues and by offering its products through its website. Third, the company is pursuing additional opportunities to expand its merchandising skills internationally.

CATALOGUES AND SALES OPERATIONS During 2006 the company mailed 12 issues of its regular monthly catalogue with an average of 75 pages per issue from its Canadian operations. Worldwide, the company mailed approximately 160 million full-price catalogues. EarthWear views each catalogue issue as a unique opportunity to communicate with its customers. Products are described in visual and editorial detail, and the company uses such techniques as background stories and distinctive covers to stimulate the readers' interest.

Each issue of the regular catalogue offers certain basic product lines for men and women. The regular catalogue also offers seasonal merchandise. In addition, EarthWear mails two end-of-season clearance catalogues. The company mails its catalogues to prospective customers who are identified based on lists of magazine subscribers and lists of households meeting certain demographic criteria. In addition, the company identifies prospective new customers through its national advertising campaign.

In 1991 the company introduced its first business specialty catalogue, which offered its products to groups and companies for corporate incentive programs. EarthWear's embroidery capabilities allow for the design and monogram of unique logos or emblems for groups and companies. In 2006 the company mailed five issues of its corporate sales catalogues.

The international business segment includes operations in Japan, Germany, and the United Kingdom, and various Internet sites. Catalogues mailed in those countries are written in the local languages and denominated in local currencies. In the spring of 2006, EarthWear launched local websites in each of these countries in their respective languages and currencies.

CUSTOMER DATABASE A principal factor in the company's success has been the development of its own list of active customers. At the end of 2006 the company's mailing list consisted of about 21.1 million persons, approximately 7 million of whom were viewed as customers because they had made at least one purchase from the company within the last 24 months. The company routinely updates and refines the database before mailing catalogues to monitor customer interest as reflected in criteria such as the regency, frequency, dollar amount, and product type of purchases.

EarthWear believes that its customer database has desirable demographic characteristics and is well suited to the products offered in the company's catalogues. A survey conducted by the company in Canada and the United States during 2005 indicated that approximately 50 percent of its customers were in the 35–54 age group and had median incomes of $62,000.

The company advertises nationally to build its reputation and to attract new customers. In 2006 this advertising campaign appeared in about 40 national magazines, as well as on five national cable television networks. In addition, the company advertises in approximately 75 national, regional, and local publications in Canada, the United Kingdom, Germany, and Japan. EarthWear also advertises on a number of Internet search engines and websites.

PRODUCT DEVELOPMENT
EarthWear concentrates on clothing and other products that are aimed at customers interested in outdoor activities. The company products are styled and quality crafted to meet the changing tastes of the company's customers rather than to mimic the changing fads of the fashion world. At the same time, the company seeks to maintain customer interest by developing new products, improving existing core products, and reinforcing its value positioning.

The company continues to incorporate innovations in fabric, construction, and detail that add value and excitement and differentiate EarthWear from the competition. In order to ensure that products are manufactured to the company's quality standards at reasonable prices, product managers, designers, and quality assurance specialists develop the company's own products.

EarthWear deals directly with its suppliers and seeks to avoid intermediaries. All goods are produced by independent manufacturers except for most of its soft luggage, which is assembled at the company's facilities. During 2006 the company purchased merchandise from more than 50 domestic and foreign manufacturers. However, no single manufacturer accounted for more than 10 percent of company purchases in each of the last three years. In 2006 nearly 75 percent of the company's merchandise was imported. The remaining 25 percent was purchased through Canadian suppliers, who may source portions of their production through programs in Central America. The company will continue to take advantage of worldwide sourcing without sacrificing customer service or quality standards.

ORDER ENTRY, FULFILLMENT, AND DELIVERY EarthWear has toll-free telephone numbers that customers can call 24 hours a day, seven days a week (except Christmas Day) to place orders or to request a catalogue. Approximately 90 percent of catalogue orders are placed by telephone. Telephone calls are answered by the company's well-trained sales representatives, who utilize online computer terminals to enter customer orders and to retrieve information about product characteristics and availability. The company has two Canadian telephone-order centres, one located in Calgary, Alberta and one in Mississauga, Ontario. The company's two US telephone centres are located in Boise, Idaho and Canton, Ohio. International telephone centres are located in London, England; Tokyo, Japan; and Mannheim, Germany.

The company's order entry and fulfillment system permits shipment of in-stock orders on the following day, but orders requiring monogramming or inseaming typically require one or two extra days. The company's sales representatives enter orders into an online order entry and inventory control system. Customers using the company's Internet site see colour photos of the products, their availability, and prices. When ordering a product over the Internet, the customer completes a computer screen that requests information on product code, size, colour, and so on. When the customer finishes shopping for products, he or she enters delivery and credit card information into a computer-based form. EarthWear provides assurance through CAWebTrust™ that the website has been evaluated and tested to meet CAWebTrust™ principles and criteria. This assurance service is provided by the company's auditors, Willis & Adams, LLP.

Computer batch processing of orders is performed each night, at which time shipping tickets are printed with bar codes for optical scanning. Inventory is picked based on the location of individual products rather than orders, followed

by computerized sorting and transporting of goods to multiple packing stations and shipping zones. The computerized inventory control system also handles the receipt of shipments from manufacturers, permitting faster access to newly arrived merchandise, as well as the handling of customer return items.

Orders are generally shipped by Canada Post or United Parcel Service (UPS) at various tiered rates that depend on the total dollar value of each customer's order. Other expedited delivery services are available at additional charge. Domestically, the company utilizes two-day Canada Post or UPS service at standard rates, enhancing its customer service. Comparable services are offered in international markets.

MERCHANDISE LIQUIDATION
Liquidations (sales of overstock and end-of-season merchandise at reduced prices) were approximately 12 percent, 11 percent, and 8 percent of net sales in 2006, 2005, and 2004, respectively. Most liquidation sales were made through catalogues and other print media. The balance was sold principally through the company's outlet retail stores.

COMPETITION
The company's principal competitors are retail stores, including specialty shops, department stores, and other catalogue companies. Direct competitors include Eddie Bauer, Land's End, L. L. Bean, Patagonia, and Roots. The company may also face increased competition from other retailers as the number of television shopping channels and the variety of merchandise offered over the Internet increase. The apparel retail business in general is intensely competitive. EarthWear competes principally on the basis of merchandise value (quality and price), its established customer list, and customer service, including fast order fulfillment and its unqualified guarantee.

EarthWare is one of the leading catalogue companies in Canada. The company attributes the growth in the catalogue industry to many factors, including customer convenience, widespread use of credit cards, the use of toll-free telephone lines, customers having less time to shop in stores, and purchasing of products over the Internet. At the same time, the catalogue business is subject to uncertainties in the economy, which result in fluctuating levels of overall consumer spending. Due to the lead times required for catalogue production and distribution, catalogue retailers may not be able to respond as quickly as traditional retailers in an environment of rapidly changing prices. Future growth in e-commerce should reduce lead times that are required by catalogues and decrease operating costs in creating, printing, and distributing catalogues.

TRADEMARKS
The company uses the trademarks of "EarthWear" and "EWC" on products and catalogues.

SEASONALITY OF BUSINESS
The company's business is highly seasonal. Historically, a disproportionate amount of the company's net sales and most of its profits have been realized during the fourth quarter. If the company's sales were materially different from seasonal norms during the fourth quarter, the company's annual operating results could be materially affected. Accordingly, results for the individual quarters do not necessarily indicate results to be expected for the entire year. In 2005, 37 percent of the company's total revenue came in the fourth quarter.

EMPLOYEES
The company believes that its skilled and dedicated workforce is one of its key resources. Employees are not covered by collective bargaining agreements, and the company considers its employee relations to be excellent. As a result of the highly seasonal nature of the company's business, the size of the company's workforce varies, ranging from approximately 3,500 to 5,300 individuals in 2006. During the peak winter season of 2006, approximately 2,700 of the company's 5,300 employees were temporary employees.

EXECUTIVE OFFICERS OF THE COMPANY
James G. Williams, 65, is chairman of the board and former chief executive officer. Mr. Williams was one of the two original founders of EarthWear. He stepped down as chief executive officer in December 1999.

Calvin J. Rogers, 57, is president and chief executive officer of the company. Mr. Rogers was one of the two original founders of the company. He assumed his present position in December 1999.

Dominique DeSantiago, 56, is executive vice president and chief operating officer. Mr. DeSantiago joined the company as chief operating officer in June 1992. He was promoted to vice president in October 1995. Mr. DeSantiago was previously employed by Eddie Bauer in various capacities.

Linda S. McDaniel, 45, is senior vice president of sales. She joined the company in July 1997. Ms. McDaniel served as divisional vice president, merchandising, with Patagonia between 1987 and 1991. Ms. McDaniel was the president and chief executive officer for Mountain Goat Sports from 1991 until 1997. She has been serving as a director of the company since November 1997.

James C. ("JC") Watts, 45, is senior vice president and chief financial officer. Mr. Watts joined the company in May 1997, assuming his current position. He was previously employed by Federated Department Stores.

Mary Ellen Tornesello, 47, is senior vice president of operations. Ms. Tornesello joined the company in 1995 as operations manager. She served as vice president of operations from 1996 until 1998, at which time she assumed her present position.

Market Information The common stock of the company is listed and traded on the Toronto Stock Exchange under the symbol EWCC. The high and low prices of the company's common stock for 2006 were $52.50 and $21.75 per share. The closing price of the company's stock on December 31, 2006, was $40.25 per share.

Shareholders As of December 31, 2006, the number of shareholders of record of common stock of the company was 2,236. This number excludes shareholders whose stock is held in nominee or street name by brokers.

Independent Auditors The company has been audited by Willis & Adams since incorporation in 1976.

06

2006

EARTHWEAR CLOTHIERS

Consolidated Statements of Operations

(In thousands, except per share data)

	For the period ended December 31		
	2006	2005	2004
Net Sales	**$ 950,484**	$ 857,885	$ 891,394
Cost of sales	**$ 546,393**	$ 472,739	490,530
Gross Profit	**$ 404,091**	$ 385,146	400,864
Selling, general, and administrative expenses	**$ 364,012**	$ 334,994	353,890
Nonrecurring charge (credit)	-	(1,153)	8,190
Income from operations	**40,079**	51,305	38,784
Other income (expense):			
Interest expense	**(983)**	(1,229)	(5,027)
Interest income	**1,459**	573	10
Other	**(4,798)**	(1,091)	(1,593)
Total other income (expense), net	**(4,322)**	(1,747)	6,609
Income before income taxes	**35,757**	49,559	32,175
Income tax provision	**13,230**	18,337	11,905
Net income	**$22,527**	$ 31,222	$ 20,270
Basic earnings per share	**1.15**	1.60	1.02
Diluted earnings per share	**1.14**	1.56	1.01
Basic weighted average shares outstanding	**19,531**	19,555	19,806
Diluted weighted average shares outstanding	**19,774**	20,055	19,996

CONSOLIDATED
FINANCIAL STATEMENTS

EARTHWEAR CLOTHIERS

Consolidated Balance Sheets

(In thousands)

	December 31	
Assets	**2006**	2005
Current Assets:		
Cash and cash equivalents	$ 48,978	$ 49,668
Receivables, net	12,875	11,539
Inventory (see Note 1)	122,337	105,425
Prepaid advertising	11,458	10,772
Other prepaid expenses	6,315	3,780
Future income tax benefits	7,132	6,930
Total current assets	209,095	188,115
Property, plant, and equipment, at cost		
Land and buildings	70,918	66,804
Fixtures and equipment	67,513	66,876
Computer hardware and software	64,986	47,466
Leasehold improvements (see Note 1)	3,010	2,894
Total property, plant, and equipment	206,426	184,040
Less accumulated amortization (see Note 1)	85,986	76,256
Property, plant and equipment, net	120,440	107,784
Intangibles, net (see Note 1)	423	628
Total assets	$ 329,959	$ 296,527
Liabilities and shareholders' equity		
Current liabilities:		
Lines of credit (see Note 8)	$ 11,011	$ 7,621
Accounts payable	62,509	48,432
Reserve for returns (see Note 1)	5,890	5,115
Accrued liabilities	26,738	28,440
Accrued profit sharing	1,532	1,794
Income taxes payable	8,588	6,666
Total current liabilities	116,268	98,067
Future income taxes	9,469	5,926
Shareholders' equity (see Note 2):		
Common shares, 26,121 shares issued	261	261
Contributed surplus	5,460	5,460
Additional paid-in capital	20,740	19,311
Deferred compensation	(79)	(153)
Accumulated other comprehensive income	3,883	1,739
Retained earnings	317,907	295,380
Treasury shares, 6,546 and 6,706 shares at cost, respectively	(143,950)	(129,462)
Total shareholders' equity	204,222	192,535
Total liabilities and shareholders' equity	$ 329,959	$ 296,527

EARTHWEAR CLOTHIERS

Consolidated Statements of Cash Flows

(In thousands)

	For the period ended December 31		
Cash flows from (used for) operating activities:	**2006**	2005	2004
Net income	**$22,527**	$ 31,222	$ 20,270
Adjustments to reconcile net income to net cash flows from operating activities:			
Non-recurring charge (credit)		(1,153)	8,190
Amortization	**$15,231**	13,465	12,175
Deferred compensation expense	**$75**	103	424
Future income taxes	**$3,340**	5,376	(3,866)
Loss on disposal of fixed assets	**$284**	602	381
Changes in assets and liabilities excluding the effects of divestitures:			
Receivables, net	**($1,336)**	2,165	(3,666)
Inventory	**($16,912)**	37,370	13,954
Prepaid advertising	**($686)**	3,110	(1,849)
Other prepaid expenses	**($2,534)**	1,152	(1,628)
Accounts payable	**$14,078**	(8,718)	2,716
Reserve for returns	**$775**	439	692
Accrued liabilities	**($709)**	(4,982)	4,545
Accrued profit sharing	**($262)**	328	(1,320)
Income taxes payablc	**$1,923**	(2,810)	(3,834)
Tax benefit of stock options	**$1,429**	1,765	349
Other	**$2,144**	437	733
Net cash from (used for) operating activities	**$39,367**	79,871	48,269
Cash flows from (used for) investing activities:			
Cash paid for capital additions	**(28,959)**	(18,208)	(30,388)
Net cash flows used for investing activities	**(28,959)**	(18,208)	(30,388)
Cash flows from (used for) financing activities:			
Proceeds from (payment of) short-term debt	**3,390**	(17,692)	4,228
Purchases of treasury shares	**(18,192)**	(2,935)	(23,112)
Issuance of treasury shares	**3,704**	4,317	1,199
Net cash flows used for financing activities	**(11,097)**	(16,310)	(17,685)
Net increase (decrease) in cash and cash equivalents	**(690)**	45,352	197
Beginning cash and cash equivalents	**49,668**	4,317	4,120
Ending cash and cash equivalents	**$ 48,978**	$ 49,668	$ 4,317
Supplemental cash flow disclosures:			
Interest paid	**$ 987**	$ 1,229	$ 5,000
Income taxes paid	**6,278**	13,701	18,107

EARTHWEAR CLOTHIERS

Consolidated Statements of Shareholders' Equity

(In thousands)

	Comprehensive Income	Common Stock	Donated Capital	Additional Paid-In Capital	Deferred Compensation	Accumulated Other Comprehensive Income	Retained Earnings	Treasury Stock	Total
Balance, December 31, 2003		$ 261	$5,460	$17,197	($681)	$569	$243,888	($108.931)	$157,763
Purchase of treasury shares								(23,112)	(23,112)
Issuance of treasury shares								1,199	1,199
Tax benefit of stock options exercised				349					349
Deferred compensation expense					424				424
Comprehensive income:									
Net income	$20,270						20,270		20,270
Foreign currency translation adjustments	733					733			733
Comprehensive income	$21,003								
Balance, December 31, 2004		$ 261	$5,460	$17,546	($257)	$1,302	$264,158	($130,844)	$157,626
Purchase of treasury shares								(2,935)	(2,935)
Issuance of treasury shares								4,317	4,317
Tax benefit of stock options exercised				1,765					1,765
Deferred compensation expense					103				103
Comprehensive income:									
Net income	$31,222						31,222		31,222
Foreign currency	60					60			60
translation adjustments	377					377			377
Comprehensive income	$31,659								
Balance, December 31, 2005		$ 261	$5,460	$19,311	($154)	$1,739	$295,380	($129,463)	$192,534
Purchase of treasury shares								(18,192)	(18,192)
Issuance of treasury shares								3,704	3,704
Tax benefit of stock options exercised				1,429					1,429
Deferred compensation expense					75				75
Comprehensive income:									
Net income	$22,527						22,527		22,527
Foreign currency translation adjustments	(1,151)					(1,151)			(1,151)
Unrealized gain on forward contracts	3,295					3,295			3,295
Comprehensive income	$24,671								
Balance, December 31, 2006		$ 261	$5,460	$20,740	($79)	$3,883	$317,907	($143,950)	$204,222

EARTHWEAR CLOTHIERS

Five-Year Consolidated Financial Summary (unaudited)

(In thousands, except per share data)

	For the period ended December 31				
	2006	2005	2004	2003	2002
Income statement data:					
Net Sales	**950,484**	857,885	891,394	821,359	503,434
Pretax Income	**35,757**	49,559	32,175	66,186	38,212
Percent of net sales	**3.8%**	5.8%	3.6%	8.1%	7.6%
Net income	**22,527**	31,222	20,270	41,698	22,929
Per share of common stock:					
Basic earnings per share	**1.15**	1.60	1.02	2.01	1.54
Diluted earnings per share	**1.14**	1.56	1.01	2.00	1.53
Common shares outstanding	**19,531**	19,555	19,806	20,703	14,599
Balance sheet data:					
Current assets	**209,095**	188,115	191,297	194,445	122,418
Current liabilities	**116,268**	98,067	133,434	118,308	65,505
PPE and intangibles	**120,863**	108,412	105,051	87,312	46,658
Total assets	**329,959**	296,527	296,347	281,757	170,121
Noncurrent liabilities	**9,496**	5,926	5,286	5,686	4,211
Shareholders' equity	**204,222**	192,535	157,627	157,763	100,405
Other data:					
Net working capital	**92,827**	90,048	57,863	76,136	56,913
Capital expenditures	**28,959**	18,208	30,388	31,348	8,316
Depreciation and amortization expense	**15,231**	13,465	12,175	9,833	6,101
Return on average shareholders' equity	**11%**	18%	13%	28%	24%
Return on average assets	**7%**	11%	7%	16%	15%

NET INCOME

NET SALES

NET INCOME PER SHARE

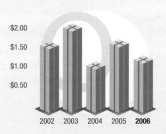

NOTES TO THE FINANCIAL STATEMENTS

NOTE 1: SUMMARY OF SIGNIFICANT ACCOUNTING POLICIES

NATURE OF BUSINESS EarthWear markets high quality clothing for outdoor sports, casual clothing, accessories, shoes, and soft luggage. The Company sells its products primarily in Canada and the United States; other markets include Europe and Japan.

PRINCIPLES OF CONSOLIDATION The consolidated statements include the accounts of the company and its subsidiaries after elimination of intercompany accounts and transactions.

USE OF ESTIMATES The preparation of financial statements in conformity with Canadian generally accepted accounting principles requires management to make estimates and assumptions that affect the reported amounts of assets and liabilities and disclosure of contingent assets and liabilities at the date of the financial statements and the reported amounts of revenues and expenses during the reporting periods. Actual results may differ from these estimates.

REVENUE RECOGNITION The company records revenue at the time of shipment for catalogue and e-commerce sales and at the point of sale for stores.

ADVERTISING The company expenses the costs of advertising for magazines, television, radio, and other media the first time the advertising takes place, except for direct-response advertising, which is capitalized and amortized over its expected period of future benefits. Direct-response advertising consists primarily of catalogue production and mailing costs, which are generally amortized within three months from the date catalogues are mailed.

AMORTIZATION Amortization expense is calculated using the straight-line method over the estimated useful lives of the assets, which are 20 to 30 years for buildings and land improvements and 5 to 10 years for leasehold improvements and furniture, fixtures, equipment, and software. The company allocates one half year of amortization to the year of addition or retirement.

INTANGIBLES Intangible assets, consisting primarily of goodwill, are reviewed annually for appropriateness of valuation.

RESERVE FOR LOSSES ON CUSTOMER RETURNS At the time of sale, the company provides a reserve equal to the gross profit on projected merchandise returns, based on prior returns experience.

FINANCIAL INSTRUMENTS WITH OFF-BALANCE-SHEET RISK The company uses import letters of credit to purchase foreign-sourced merchandise. The letters of credit are primarily US dollar-denominated and are issued through third-party financial institutions to guarantee payment for such merchandise within the agreed-upon time periods. At December 31, 2005, the company had outstanding letters of credit of approximately $23 million, all of which had expiration dates of less than one year.

FOREIGN CURRENCY TRANSLATIONS AND TRANSACTIONS Financial statements of the foreign subsidiaries are translated into Canadian dollars. Translation adjustments are accumulated in a separate component of shareholders' equity.

NOTE 2: SHAREHOLDERS' EQUITY

COMMON SHARES The company currently is authorized to issue 70 million shares of $0.01 par value common shares.

TREASURY SHARES The company's board of directors has authorized the purchase of a total of 12.7 million shares of the company's common stock. A total of 6.5 million and 6.7 million had been purchased as of December 31, 2006 and 2005, respectively.

STOCK AWARDS AND GRANTS The company has a restricted stock award plan. Under the provisions of the plan, a committee of the company's board may award shares of the company's common stock to its officers and key employees. Such shares vest over a 10-year period on a straight-line basis.

The granting of these awards has been recorded as deferred compensation based on the fair market value of the shares at the date of the grant. Compensation expense under these plans is recorded as shares vest.

STOCK OPTIONS The company has 3.5 million shares of common stock that may be issued pursuant to the exercise of options granted under the company's stock option plan. Options are granted at the discretion of a committee of the company's board of directors to officers and key employees of the company. No option may have an exercise price less than the fair market value per share of the common stock at the date of the grant.

NOTE 3: LINES OF CREDIT

The company has unsecured domestic lines of credit with various Canadian banks totalling $150 million. There were $23.4 million amounts outstanding at December 31, 2006 compared to $20.2 million outstanding at December 31, 2005. In addition, the company has unsecured lines of credit with foreign banks totalling the equivalent of $30 million for its wholly owned subsidiaries. At December 31, 2006, $11 million was outstanding at interest rates averaging 4.7 percent, compared with $7.6 million at December 31, 2005.

NOTE 4: LONG-TERM DEBT

There was no long-term debt at December 31, 2006 and 2005.

NOTE 5: LEASES

The company leases store and office space and equipment under various lease arrangements. The leases are accounted for as operating leases.

NOTE 6: RETIREMENT PLANS

The company has a retirement plan that covers most regular employees and provides for annual contributions at the discretion of the board of directors.

MANAGEMENT'S DISCUSSION AND ANALYSIS:

The year 2006 was a year during which we've seen the results of our strategic initiatives of the last two years take hold. Sales momentum picked up towards the end of the third quarter and continued strongly through our all-important holiday season, and we reported a double-digit increase in both revenue and earnings for the fourth quarter. This success enabled us to complete the year with an annual 3.2 percent increase in total revenue, but a 27.8 percent decrease in earnings, mainly due to the weakness of the first nine months. Our strong finish for the year was gratifying in the face of a difficult economy.

MANAGEMENT'S DISCUSSION AND ANALYSIS: RESULTS OF OPERATIONS FOR 2006 COMPARED TO 2005

TOTAL REVENUE INCREASED BY 3.2 PERCENT
Total revenue for the year just ended was $950.5 million, compared with $857.9 million in the prior year, an increase of 3.2 percent. Seasonally strong sales resulted in a higher level of backorders during the fourth quarter and a first-time fulfillment rate of 85 percent for the year as a whole, slightly below the prior year's rate. Overall merchandise sales growth was primarily attributable to changes in circulation, which included adding back our post-Thanksgiving catalogue and our January full-price catalogue, shifting the timing of our fall/winter

mailings, increased page circulation and improved merchandise selection and creative presentations.

NET INCOME DECREASED Net income for 2006 was $22.5 million, down 27.8 percent from the $31.2 million earned in 2005. Diluted earnings per share for the year just ended were $1.14, compared with $1.56 per share for the prior year. The diluted weighted average number of common shares outstanding was 19.8 million for 2006 and 20.0 million for 2005.

GROSS PROFIT MARGIN Gross profit for the year just ended was $404 million, or 42.5 percent of total revenue, compared with $385 million, or 41.6 percent of total revenue, for the prior year. Liquidations were about 11 percent of net merchandise sales in 2006, compared with 12 percent in the prior year. In 2006, the cost of inventory purchases was down 2.0 percent, compared with deflation of 2.7 percent in 2005. This reduction was a result of improved sourcing. As a result, the LIFO inventory reserve was reduced by $2.8 million and $3.8 million in 2006 and 2005, respectively.

SELLING, GENERAL, AND ADMINISTRATIVE EXPENSES Selling, general and administrative (SG&A) expenses increased 9.2 percent to $364 million in 2006, compared with $334 million in the prior year. As a percentage of sales, SG&A was 38.3 percent in 2006 and 36.2 percent in the prior year. The increase in the SG&A ratio was primarily the result of higher catalogue costs associated with increased page circulation, as well as higher information services expenses as we continue to invest in the Internet and upgrade systems capabilities. The cost of producing and mailing catalogues represented about 39 percent and 38 percent of total SG&A in 2006 and 2005, respectively.

CREDIT LINES AND CAPITAL EXPENDITURES Interest expense on lines of credit was down in 2006 due to lower average borrowing levels. Interest expense decreased to $1.0 million in 2006, compared to $1.2 million in 2005. We spent $29 million in cash on capital expenditures, which included $20 million for computer hardware and software. In addition, the company acquired a new airplane by exchanging two of its own aircraft in 2006. Also, we purchased about $18 million in treasury stock. No long-term debt was outstanding at year-end 2006. Amortization expense was $15.2 million, up 13.1 percent from the prior year, mainly due to computer software. Rental expense was $10.4 million, up 3.4 percent from 2005, primarily due to additional computer hardware.

Responsibility for the Consolidated Financial Statements

The management of EarthWear Clothiers and its subsidiaries has the responsibility for preparing the accompanying financial statements and for their integrity and objectivity. The statements were prepared in accordance with Canadian generally accepted accounting principles applied on a consistent basis. The consolidated financial statements include amounts that are based on management's best estimates and judgements. Management also prepared the other information in the annual report and is responsible for its accuracy and consistency with the consolidated financial statements.

The company's consolidated financial statements have been audited by Willis & Adams, chartered accountants. Management has made available to Willis & Adams all the company's financial records and related data, as well as the minutes of shareholder's and directors' meetings. Furthermore, management believes that all representations made to Willis & Adams during the audit were valid and appropriate.

Management of the company has established and maintains a system of internal control that provides appropriate division of responsibility, reasonable assurance as to the integrity and reliability of the consolidated financial statements, the protection of assets from unauthorized use or disposition, the prevention and detection of fraudulent financial reporting, and the maintenance of an active program of internal audits. Management believes that, as of December 31, 2006, the company's system of internal control is adequate to accomplish the objectives discussed herein.

Two directors of the company, not members of management, serve as the audit committee of the board of directors and are the principal means through which the board supervises the performance of the financial reporting duties of management. The audit committee meets with management, the internal audit staff, and the company's independent auditors to review the results of the company and to discuss plans for future audits. At these meetings, the audit committee also meets privately with the internal audit staff and the independent auditors to ensure its free access to them.

Calvin J. Rogers

President and Chief
Executive Officer

James C. Watts

Senior Vice President and
Chief Financial Officer

To the Shareholders of EarthWear Clothiers Inc.

We have audited the consolidated balance sheets of EarthWear Clothiers as of December 31, 2006 and 2005, and the consolidated statements of operations, shareholders' equity, and cash flows for the years then ended. These financial statements are the responsibility of the company's management. Our responsibility is to express an opinion on these financial statements based on our audits.

We conducted our audits in accordance with Canadian generally accepted auditing standards. Those standards require that we plan and perform the audit to obtain reasonable assurance whether the financial statements are free of material misstatement. An audit includes examining, on a test basis, evidence supporting the amounts and disclosures in the financial statements. An audit also includes assessing the accounting principles used and significant estimates made by management, as well as evaluating the overall financial statement presentation.

In our opinion, these consolidated financial statements present fairly, in all material respects, the financial position of EarthWear Clothiers Inc. as of December 31, 2006 and 2005, and the results of its operations and its cash flows for the years then ended in accordance with Canadian generally accepted accounting principles.

Willis & Adams

Willis & Adams, Chartered Accountants

Calgary, Alberta
February 15, 2007

AUDITOR'S REPORT

Required:

a. Describe the objectives of an audit.

b. Identify five ways in which an audit may be beneficial to Potvine.

(Reprinted with permission of AICPA; Copyright © 1970–1999 by American Institute of Certified Public Accountants.)

1,2>   **1-22**   Greenbloom Garden Centres is a small, privately held corporation that has two stores in London, Ontario. The Greenbloom family owns 100 percent of the company's shares, and family members manage the operations. Sales at the company's stores have been growing rapidly, and there appears to be a market for the company's sales concept—providing bulk garden equipment and supplies at low prices. The controller prepares the company's financial statements, which are not audited. The company has no debt but is considering expanding to other cities in Ontario. Such expansion may require long-term borrowings and is likely to reduce the family's day-to-day control of the operations. The family does not intend to sell shares in the company to the public.

Required:

Discuss the factors that may make an audit necessary for the company.

4>   **1-23**   Audits can be categorized into five types: (1) financial statement audits, (2) compliance audits, (3) operational audits, (4) forensic audits, and (5) value-for-money audits.

Required:

For each of the following descriptions, indicate which type of audit (financial statement audit, compliance audit, operational audit, forensic audit, or value-for-money audit) best characterizes the nature of the audit being conducted. Also indicate which type of auditor (external auditor, internal auditor, government auditor, or forensic auditor) is likely to perform the audit engagement.

a. Examine the financial records of the Health Protection Branch and evaluate the policies and procedures of the Health Protection Branch in terms of bringing new drugs to the market.

b. Determine the fair presentation of Ajax Chemical's balance sheet, income statement, and statement of cash flows.

c. Review the payment procedures of the Accounts Payable Department for a large manufacturer.

d. Examine the financial records of a division of a corporation to determine if any accounting irregularities have occurred.

e. Evaluate the feasibility of forecasted rental income for a planned low-income public housing project.

f. Evaluate a company's Computer Services Department in terms of the efficient and effective use of corporate resources.

g. Audit the partnership tax return of a real estate development company.

h. Investigate the possibility of payroll fraud in a labour union pension fund.

1,2 >   **1-24**   You recently attended your five-year university reunion. At the main reception, you encountered an old friend, Lee Beagle, who recently graduated from law school and is now practising with a large law firm in town. When you told him that you were an auditor and employed by a regional public accounting firm, he made the following statement and snickered. "You know, if a statutory and requirement did not exist, no one would be interested in having an audit performed. You auditors are just creatures of regulations." Since you did not wish to cause a scene at the reunion, you let his comment pass. You and Lee agreed to have lunch the following week to talk over old times. However, you were still upset over Lee's comment.

Required:

In preparation for your luncheon with Lee, draft a memo that highlights your thoughts about why auditors are not "creatures of regulations." Cite any relevant evidence of a demand for auditing services in your memo. Focus on the value that auditing provides.

DISCUSSION CASES

1,2,3,6,7 >   **1-25**   Four years ago, the International Cultural Club (ICC) was formed in an effort to create a united social group out of several separate regional clubs in the vicinity of the city of Burlington, located in central Canada. The purpose of the group is to combine resources to meet the recreational, cultural, and social needs of its collective members. ICC was formed through the collaboration of 10 clubs including Russians, Italians, Portuguese, Greeks, Germans, and others.

ICC's board of governors has spent the last four years planning and preparing for its operation. They expect the club's community centre to be fully completed next year. The facilities of the club will include a multi-purpose building to house banquets, meetings, and arts activities; hiking trails; indoor/outdoor tennis facilities; bicycle trails; baseball diamonds; an indoor/outdoor pool, and a soccer field.

The multi-purpose building is 75 percent complete, and ICC's treasurer has stated that it is "approximately within budget" of the total $3.5 million cost. The two hectares of land on which the facility is built were provided by the provincial government by way of a five-year lease at $1 a year. The adjacent land of 24 ha was contributed to the club by a private donor. Previously, this land had been leased to a farmer for $54,000 a year. The 26 ha will be used for the previously mentioned activities, incurring estimated annual operating costs of $2 million. Estimated additional operating and administrative costs are $900,000.

William Cznoro, the newly elected president of the club, recognizes the importance of starting out on a sound footing. He has approached your firm to prepare a report providing recommendations on accounting, finance, and internal control issues. He has also asked you to prepare a presentation for the next meeting of the board of governors identifying the merits of an audit for ICC, and potential problems that might exist.

Required:

Prepare a presentation to the board of governors explaining why it would be beneficial to ICC to have a public accounting firm provide recommendations on accounting, finance, and internal control issues. In your memo, include a discussion of the advantages to ICC of having an audit conducted and identify other assurance services that could be of benefit to ICC now or in the future.

(CICA, adapted)

1,2,3,7⟩   **1-26**   You have been invited to make a presentation to a "Town and Gown" symposium for the members of the business faculty of your university and representatives of the local business community, to be held at the downtown campus of your university. The faculty has invited representatives from industry, the investment community, and the banking community and you, a professional accountant in public practice, to sit on the panel. In light of the current sluggish economy and the precipituous drop in the equity markets, one of the topics on the agenda is the usefulness of the financial statement auditor and the auditor's report. You have noted the following excerpts from presentations by the other participants.

Mr. John Wilton, Vice-President, Finance, Casablanca Industries:

The annual audit has become an unnecessary evil. Our audit fees, in my opinion, are already far too high for the value we receive from the audit. I believe you should reconsider the need for increased auditor involvement. If the auditor's role is to be expanded, something must be done to reduce the costs and maximize the benefits.

Ms. Irene Wong, Financial Analyst:

We are increasingly sceptical of the relevance of audited financial statements to the decisions we have to make. As they are based on the past, we find them of limited value as information for the decisions we need to make. I would be more comfortable if the independent auditor attested to business viability, management credibility, and future-oriented data.

Mr. Ravi Puri, Senior Corporate Loan Officer:

I agree with Irene. In addition to historical-cost financial statements, we need financial statements that portray current values, and prospective information on which to base our decision. We would like more assurance from the auditor than is presently conveyed with the financial statement audit that the company will be able to turn its assets into profits. In order to make loan decisions we need current and future information, not information about events that have already occurred.

Required:

Draft your presentation.

(CICA, adapted)

INTERNET ASSIGNMENTS

1,6,7❭ **1-27** Using an Internet browser, identify five Internet sites that contain accounting resources. For each site identified, prepare a brief summary of the types of information that are available. For example, IFAC's website (www.IFAC.org) contains extensive information on the organization's activities.

3❭ **1-28** Visit the CICA's website and identify three new assurance services that are being developed by the CICA.

1,2,3❭ **1-29** Visit the website for The Royal Bank of Canada (www.royalbank.com) and view the most recent annual report. Does the site contain any other financial or nonfinancial information that might be helpful to potential investors?

EarthWear **1,2**❭ **1-30** EarthWear Clothiers makes high-quality clothing for outdoor sports and sells most of its products through mail order. Use the Internet to obtain information about the mail-order retail industry.

An Overview of Financial Statement Auditing

Chapter 2

Learning Objectives

Upon completion of this chapter, you will be able to

1 Explain how auditing takes place in a context that is shaped by the client's business.

2 Understand a high-level model of a business entity, including the elements of corporate governance, objectives, strategies, processes, controls, transactions, and financial statements.

3 Describe a five-component model of business processes that auditors often use in organizing the audit into manageable components.

4 Outline the eight generally accepted auditing standards (GAAS).

5 Discuss the International Federation of Accountants and International Statements on Auditing.

6 Explain generally accepted accounting principles as audit criteria.

7 Describe the relationships among financial statements, management assertions, and audit procedures.

8 Develop a preliminary understanding of how the concepts of materiality, audit risk, and evidence apply to the audit process.

9 Describe the conceptual basis of auditing.

10 Identify the major phases of the audit process.

11 Grasp the basic elements of audit reporting.

RELEVANT ACCOUNTING AND ASSURANCE PRONOUNCEMENTS

CICA Handbook, **section 5025**, Standards for assurance engagements

CICA Handbook, **section 5095**, Reasonable assurance and audit risk

CICA Handbook, **section 5100**, Generally accepted auditing standards

CICA Handbook, **section 5141**, Understanding the entity and its environment and assessing the risk of material misstatement

CICA Handbook, **section 5142**, Materiality

CICA Handbook, **section 5143**, The auditor's procedures in response to assessed risks

CICA Handbook, **section 5300**, Audit evidence

CICA Handbook, **section 5400**, The auditor's standard report

Assurance and Related Services Guideline AuG-41, Applying the concept of materiality in conducting an audit

This chapter provides an overview of a financial statement audit. For those readers who have relatively little knowledge about the conduct of an audit engagement, this overview is intended to introduce the important concepts and material presented in subsequent chapters. References to chapters where the concepts and material are covered in more depth are provided throughout this chapter.

The chapter covers the following topics:

- the business context of financial statement auditing

- generally accepted auditing standards
- generally accepted accounting principles as an audit criterion
- management assertions
- three fundamental concepts in conducting an audit
- the conceptual basis of auditing

The last two sections of the chapter present an overview of the audit process and an introduction to audit reporting.

The Context of Financial Statement Auditing

Business as the Primary Context of Auditing

LO 1>

The context with which an auditor is concerned on a day-to-day basis is the industry or business of his or her audit client(s). In studying subsequent chapters, you will be building your auditing tool kit. How you apply auditing tools on any particular engagement will depend greatly on the nature of the client's business. For example, if you are auditing a computer hardware manufacturer, one of your concerns will be whether your client has inventories that are not selling quickly and are becoming obsolete due to industry innovation. Such inventory might not be properly valued on the client's financial records. If you are auditing a jeweller, on the other hand, you will probably not be overly concerned with whether the client possesses warehouses full of obsolete diamonds—the possibility of a competitor producing a "new model" of diamond is probably not a serious threat in the diamond business. However, you would be interested in inventory valuation. You may need to hire a diamond appraiser to provide objective evidence, and you would certainly want to keep up on the dynamics of the international diamond market. The point is that the context provided by the client's business greatly impacts the auditor and the audit, and is thus a primary component of the environment in which financial statement auditing is conducted. While every business is different, business organizations can be conceptualized or modelled in common ways. The next section describes the essential characteristics of a business: governance, objectives, strategies, processes, risks, controls, and reporting.

A Model of Business

LO 2>

Business organizations exist to create value for their stakeholders. To form a business enterprise, entrepreneurs decide on an appropriate organizational form (e.g., corporation or partnership) and hire managers to manage the resources that have been made available to the enterprise through investment or lending.

Corporate Governance

Due to the way resources are invested and managed in the modern business world, a system of *corporate governance* is necessary, through which managers are overseen and supervised. Simply defined, corporate governance consists of all the people, processes, and activities in place to help ensure the proper stewardship over an entity's assets. Corporate governance is the implementation and execution of processes to ensure that those managing an entity properly utilize their time, talents, and available resources in the best interest of absentee owners. Good corporate governance creates a system that ensures proper stewardship over invested capital and faithfully reports the economic condition and performance of the enterprise. The body primarily responsible for management oversight in Canadian corporations is the *board of directors*. The *audit committee,* consisting of independent members of the board, oversees the internal and external auditing work done for the organization. Through this link, and through the audit of financial statements (which can be seen as a form of stewardship report), auditors play an important role in facilitating effective corporate governance.

Objectives, Strategies, Processes, Controls, Transactions, and Reports

Management, with guidance and direction from the board of directors, decides on a set of *objectives*, along with *strategies* designed to achieve those objectives. The organization then undertakes certain *processes* in order to implement its strategies. The organization must also assess and manage risks that may threaten achievement of its objectives. While the processes implemented in business organizations are as varied as the different types of businesses themselves, most business enterprises establish processes that fit in five broad *process categories*, sometimes known as *cycles*. The five categories that characterize the processes of most businesses are the *revenue process*, the *purchasing process*, the *human resource management process*, the *inventory management process*, and the *financing process*. Each process involves a variety of important transactions. The enterprise must design and implement *accounting information systems* to capture the details of those transactions and must design and implement a *system of internal control* to ensure that the transactions are handled and recorded appropriately and that its resources are protected. The accounting information system must be capable of producing financial reports, which summarize the effects of the organization's transactions on its account balances and which are used to establish management accountability to outside owners. The next section provides a brief overview of the five process categories. Auditors often rely on this process model to divide the audit of a business's financial statements into manageable pieces. Chapters 9 to 15 go into considerable detail regarding how these processes typically function and how they are used to organize an audit.

A Model of Business Processes: Five Components

LO 3> Figure 2–1 illustrates the five basic business processes in context with the overall business model presented in the previous section. Chapters 8 to 14 discuss auditing these business processes.

The Revenue Process

Businesses generate revenue through sales of goods or services to customers, and collect the proceeds of those sales in cash, either immediately or through collections on receivables. For example, EarthWear retails high-quality clothing for outdoor sports. To create value for its customers, employees,

An Overview of Business

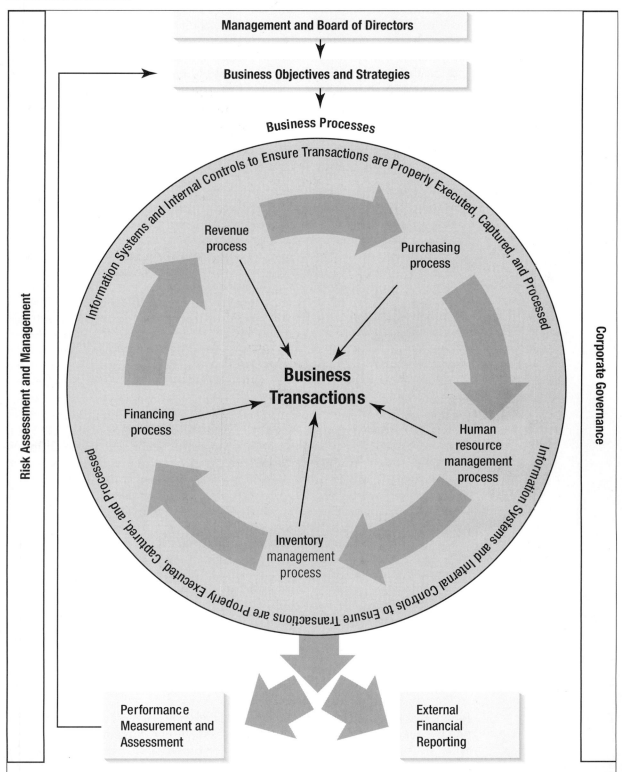

and owners, EarthWear must successfully process orders for, and deliver its clothing to customers. It must also collect cash on those sales, either at the point of sale or through later billing and collection of receivables. Management establishes controls to ensure that sales and collection transactions are appropriately handled and recorded.

The Purchasing Process

Businesses must acquire goods and services to support the sale of their own goods or services. For example, EarthWear must purchase inventory for sale to customers. The company must also purchase office supplies, needed services, and many other items to support its activities.

The Human Resource Management Process

Business organizations hire personnel to perform various functions in accordance with the enterprise's mission and strategy. For example, at EarthWear this process starts with the establishment of sound policies for hiring, training, evaluating, counselling, promoting, compensating, and terminating employees. The main transaction that affects the financial statement accounts in this process is a payroll transaction, which usually begins with an employee performing a job, and ends with payment being made to the employee.

The Inventory Management Process

This process varies widely between different types of businesses. Service providers (such as auditors) rarely have significant inventories to manage, since their primary resources typically consist of information, knowledge, and the time and effort of people. Manufacturers, wholesalers, and retailers, including EarthWear, all typically have significant, numerous, and often complex transactions falling in the inventory management process. While the actual purchasing of finished goods or raw materials inventories is included in the purchasing process (see above), the inventory management process for a manufacturer includes the cost accounting transactions to accumulate and allocate costs to inventory.

The Financing Process

Businesses obtain capital through borrowing or soliciting investments from owners and typically invest in assets such as land, buildings, and equipment in accordance with their strategies. As part of this process, businesses also need to repay lenders and provide a return on owner investments. These types of transactions are all part of the financing process. For example, while EarthWear tends not to rely on long-term debt financing, it primarily uses capital provided by shareholders to invest in such long-term assets as its headquarters building, retail stores, and various order and distribution centres across the Canada and United States and in Japan, Germany, and the United Kingdom.

Relating the Process Components to the Business Model

Management establishes processes in the five categories discussed above to implement the organization's strategies and achieve its objectives. Management then identifies risks, or possible threats to the achievement of established objectives (including compliance with applicable laws and regulations and reliable external reporting), and ensures that the organization's system of internal control mitigates those risks to acceptable

Table 2–1	**Generally Accepted Auditing Standards**

General Standard

The examination should be performed and the report prepared by a person or persons having adequate technical training and proficiency in auditing, with due care and with an objective state of mind.

Examination Standards

1. The auditor should plan and perform the audit to reduce audit risk to an acceptably low level that is consistent with the objective of an audit. The auditor should plan the nature, timing, and extent of direction and supervision of engagement team members and review of their work.

2. The auditor should obtain an understanding of the entity and its environment, including its internal control, sufficient to identify and assess the risks of material misstatement of the financial statements whether due to fraud or error, and sufficient to design and perform further audit procedures.

3. The auditor should obtain sufficient appropriate audit evidence to be able to draw reasonable conclusions on which to base the audit opinion.

Reporting Standards

1. The report should identify the financial statements and distinguish between the responsibilities of management and the responsibilities of the auditor.

2. The report should describe the scope of the auditor's examination.

3. The report should contain either an expression of opinion on the financial statements or an assertion that an opinion cannot be expressed. In the latter case, the reasons therefore should be stated.

4. Where an opinion is expressed, it should indicate whether the financial statements present fairly, in all material respects, the financial position, results of operations and cash flows in accordance with Canadian generally accepted accounting principles. The report should provide adequate explanation with respect to any reservation contained in such opinion.

levels. The organization's accounting information system must be capable of reliably measuring the performance of the business to assess whether objectives are being met and to comply with external reporting requirements. Financial statements represent an important output of the entity's efforts to measure the organization's performance and an important form of external reporting and accountability.

Generally Accepted Auditing Standards

LO 4

Auditing standards are the measures of the quality of the auditor's performance. The CICA first issued generally accepted auditing standards (GAAS) approximately 40 years ago and has periodically modified them to meet changes in the auditor's environment. GAAS *found in paragraph 5100.02 of the CICA Handbook,* are composed of three categories of standards: *the general standard, examination standards,* and *reporting standards.* Table 2–1 contains the eight GAAS.

General Standard

The general standard is concerned with the auditor's qualifications and the quality of his or her work. The first part of the general standard recognizes that an individual must have adequate training and proficiency as an auditor. This is gained through formal education, continuing education programs, and experience. It should be recognized that this training is ongoing with a requirement on the part of the auditor to stay up-to-date with current accounting and auditing pronouncements. Auditors should also be aware of developments in the business world that may affect the auditing profession.

Due care is the focus of the second part of the general standard. In simple terms, due care means that the auditor plans and performs his or her duties with a degree of skill commonly possessed by others in the profession. The requirement of due care imposes an obligation on the members of the audit team to observe the standards of field work and reporting, and to perform the work at the same level as any other professional auditor who offers such services to clients.

The second part of the general standard also requires that the auditor always be independent. Independence precludes relationships that may impair the auditor's objectivity. A distinction is often made between *independence in fact* and *independence in appearance.* An auditor must not only be independent in fact but also avoid actions that may appear to affect independence. If an auditor is perceived as not being independent, users may lose confidence in the auditor's ability to report truthfully on financial statements. For example, an auditor might have a financial interest in an auditee but still be objective. Third parties, however, may assume that the auditor was not independent because the financial interest could have prevented the auditor from maintaining objectivity during the audit. Public confidence is impaired if an auditor is found to lack independence. Rules governing professional conduct identify actions, such as financial or managerial interests in clients, that are believed to impair the auditor's appearance of independence.

Examination Standards	The examination standards relate to the actual conduct of the audit. These three standards provide the conceptual background for the audit process. The first standard of field work deals with planning and performance. Proper planning leads to a more effective audit that is more likely to detect material misstatements if they exist. Proper planning also assists in completing the engagement in a reasonable amount of time.

The second examination standard requires that the auditor gain sufficient understanding of the auditee's internal control to plan an audit and to properly assess the risks that fraud or error could lead to the risk of a material misstatement. Internal control is the process, effected by an entity's board of directors, management, and other personnel, that is designed to provide reasonable assurance regarding the achievement of the following objectives: (1) optimization of the use of resources, (2) prevention and detection of fraud and error, (3) safeguarding assets, and (4) maintaining a reliable information system. If the auditor decides to rely on the entity's system of internal control he or she must document the evidence on which that decision is based.

Sufficient appropriate audit evidence is the focus of the third examination standard. Most of the auditor's work involves the search for and evaluation of evidence to support management's assertions in the financial statements. The auditor uses various audit procedures to gather this evidence. For example, if the balance sheet shows an amount for accounts receivable of $1.5 million, management asserts that this amount is the net realizable value, or the amount expected to be collected from customers, for those receivables. The auditor can send confirmations to customers and examine subsequent payments by customers as audit procedures to gather sufficient appropriate audit evidence on the existence and proper valuation of accounts receivable.

Reporting Standards

The four reporting standards specify what is to be contained in the auditor's report: (1) the financial statements reported upon, and the responsibilities of management and the auditor, (2) the scope of the auditor's examination, (3) the requirement to either express an opinion or to explain why an opinion cannot be expressed, and (4) the opinion should state whether the financial statements are in accordance with "an appropriate disclosed basis of accounting" which, except in rare circumstances, is GAAP. Chapter 16 will cover the auditor's report in detail.

The Structure of the Assurance and Related Services Recommendations Section of the *CICA Handbook*

The Assurance and Related Services Recommendations are classified as:

5000	General Assurance and Auditing
6000	Specific Items
7000	Specialized Areas
8000	Review Engagements
9000	Related Services

The bulk of this text will deal with the topics in section 5000, General Assurance and Auditing; however, each of the other sections listed will be covered in more detail in later chapters.

International Standards on Auditing

LO 5 The globalization of business and the influence of international organizations such as the North American Free Trade Agreement (NAFTA) and the European Economic Union (EU) have all increased the pressure to harmonize auditing standards internationally. An increasingly influential organization in the development and harmonization of world-wide auditing standards is the International Federation of Accountants (IFAC). The CICA, CGA-Canada and SMAC are all members of IFAC. The International Auditing and Assurance Standards Board (IAASB) of IFAC develops and issues International Standards on Auditing (ISAs), authoritative pronouncements for the guidance of auditors in member organizations. As discussed in Chapter 1, the IAASB is undertaking major steps to clarify and strengthen its standards (ISAs), with the objective of producing higher quality audits. At the time of writing, a number of the ISAs have been incorporated into the *CICA Handbook*, with only minor amendments to maintain continuity and consistency with existing *Handbook* sections. This process is ongoing. The Auditing and Assurance Standards Board (AASB) of the CICA has issued an exposure draft and tentative timetable indicating that by 2008 there will be complete convergence between the ISAs and the *CICA Handbook*. At that time the numbering of the *CICA Handbook* will be restructured to be consistent with the numbering of the ISAs. During this time period, the AASB has indicated that it will develop implementation guidance for the application of the ISAs in a Canadian context.[1]

---

[1] See also J. Middlemiss, "Going GLOBAL," *CAMagazine* (June/July 2006), pp.27–33.

At present, Canadian generally accepted accounting principles should be followed, except when the financial statements:

- are prepared as described in the *CICA Handbook*, section 5600, Auditor's report on financial statements prepared using a basis of accounting other than generally accepted accounting principles, or
- are financial statements of a federal, provincial, territorial, or local government, and the auditor is required to express an opinion . . . in accordance with a disclosed basis of accounting, when the auditor would refer to audit of government financial statements, section PS 5200, for guidance.

The report should provide adequate explanation with respect to any reservation contained in such opinion.

Clearly, the trend towards international harmonization of auditing standards is increasing. A Canadian auditor may be engaged to conduct an examination in accordance with International Standards on Auditing. In such cases he or she should consult the most current version of the *IFAC Handbook* for the complete ISAs. Many large firms having an international practice possess extensive libraries of documentation reflecting international practice.

Generally Accepted Accounting Principles as an Audit Criterion

LO 6⟩ The demand for auditing arises from the potential conflict of interest that exists between owners (shareholders) and managers. The contractual arrangement between these parties normally requires that management issue a set of financial statements that purports to show the financial position, results of operations, and cash flows of the entity. In order to properly evaluate the financial statements, the parties to the contract must agree on a benchmark or criterion to measure performance. Without an agreed-upon criterion, it is impossible to measure the fair presentation of the financial statements.

Generally accepted accounting principles (GAAP) have, over time, become the primary criteria used to prepare financial statements. As the term implies, these principles are generally accepted by the diverse users of financial statements. The authority for using GAAP as the benchmark comes from generally accepted auditing standards (GAAS). The fourth reporting standard requires that the auditor's report indicate whether the financial statements are presented in accordance with GAAP. The auditor's standard audit report states that "the financial statements ... present fairly ... in accordance with generally accepted accounting principles." In making this statement in the audit report, the auditor judges whether (1) the accounting principles have general acceptance, (2) the accounting principles are appropriate in the circumstances, (3) the financial statements, including the footnotes, contain adequate disclosure, (4) the information in the financial statements is classified and summarized in a reasonable manner, and (5) the financial statements reflect the underlying transactions and events in a manner that presents the financial position, results of operations, and cash flows stated within a range of acceptable limits.

In judging the proper accounting treatment for a transaction or event, the auditor should always consider whether the substance of the transaction differs from its form. Transactions should be recorded to reflect their economic substance. For example, if a company enters into a lease transaction in which the substance of the transaction is the purchase of the asset with debt, the transaction should be recorded as a capital lease rather than an operating lease.

It is important to consider how GAAP and GAAS are related in the audit function. Figure 1–3 in Chapter 1 presented an overview of the audit function for a financial statement audit. Management and their accountants record business transactions through the entity's accounting system in accordance with GAAP. Therefore, the financial statements that are prepared based on the entity's operations should also be in accordance with GAAP. GAAS, on the other hand, guide the auditor on how to gather evidence to test management's assertions to determine if they are in accordance with GAAP. If the auditor has gathered sufficient evidence to provide reasonable assurance that the financial statements present fairly in accordance with GAAP, an unqualified report can be issued.

Canadian companies registered with the US Securities Exchange Commission (there are approximately 500 Canadian companies registered with US stock exchanges) can apply to the Canadian Securities administrator's (CSA) for an exemption to permit them to file their financial statements for Canada using US standards. In order for a company to qualify, it must demonstrate that it has the necessary expertise to prepare financial statements in accordance with the standards of the Public Company Accounting Oversight Board (PCAOB) and must also show that its auditor is knowledgeable about US GAAS.

Financial Statements, Management Assertions, and Audit Procedures

LO 6 >   In Chapter 1, we introduced the concept that the financial statements issued by management contain explicit and implicit assertions. Table 2–2 reproduced from the information in *CICA Handbook*, paragraph 5300.21, summarizes and explains management assertions. Take a few minutes to examine and understand these assertions—you will see over the next several chapters that this simple conceptual tool is actually quite powerful and underlies much of what auditors do. Assertions are evaluated within three categories: transactions, account balances, and presentation and disclosure. For example, management asserts among other things that *transactions* relating to inventory actually *occurred*, that they are *complete* (i.e., no valid transactions were left out), that they are classified properly (e.g., as an asset rather than an expense), and that they are recorded accurately and in the correct period. Similarly, management asserts that the inventory represented in the inventory account balance *exists*, that the entity *owns* the inventory, that the balance is *complete*, and that the inventory is properly *valued*. Finally, management asserts that the financial statements properly *classify* and *present* the inventory (e.g., inventory is appropriately listed as a current asset on the balance sheet) and that all required *disclosures* having to do

Table 2–2	**Summary of Management Assertions by Category**

Assertions about classes of transactions and events for the period under audit:

- **Occurrence**—transactions and events that have been recorded have occurred and pertain to the entity.
- **Completeness**—all transactions and events that should have been recorded have been recorded.
- **Accuracy**—amounts and other data relating to recorded transactions and events have been recorded appropriately.
- **Cutoff**—transactions and events have been recorded in the correct accounting period.
- **Classification**—transactions and events have been recorded in the proper accounts.

Assertions about account balances at the period end:

- **Existence**—assets, liabilities, and equity interests exist.
- **Rights and obligations**—the entity holds or controls the rights to assets, and liabilities are the obligations of the entity.
- **Completeness**—all assets, liabilities, and equity interests that should have been recorded have been recorded.
- **Valuation and allocation**—assets, liabilities, and equity interests are included in the financial statements at appropriate amounts and any resulting valuation or allocation adjustments are appropriately recorded.

Assertions about presentation and disclosure:

- **Occurrence and rights and obligations**—disclosed events, transactions, and other matters have occurred and pertain to the entity.
- **Completeness**—all disclosures that should have been included in the financial statements have been included.
- **Classification and understandability**—financial information is appropriately presented and described, and disclosures are clearly expressed.
- **Accuracy and valuation**—financial and other information are disclosed fairly and at appropriate amounts.

Source: CICA Handbook, section 5300.21.

with inventory (e.g., a note to the financial statements indicating that the company uses the FIFO inventory method) are included appropriately, accurately, and clearly.

Although all balance-related assertions apply to every account, the assertions are not equally important for each account. Recognizing the assertions that deserve the most emphasis depends on an understanding of the business and of the particular type of account being audited. For example, for liability accounts the completeness assertion is typically the most important assertion for two reasons. First, when all obligations are not properly included in the liability account, the result is often an overstatement of net income. Second, it is expected that usually management is more likely to have an incentive to understate a liability than to overstate it.

Figure 2–2 graphically represents the relationships among management assertions, audit procedures, and audit evidence. Chapter 4 contains more detailed coverage.

Three Fundamental Concepts in Conducting an Audit

LO 8>   A financial statement audit requires an understanding of three fundamental concepts: *materiality, audit risk,* and *evidence*. The auditor's judgement of materiality and audit risk establishes the type and amount of the audit work to be performed (referred to as the *scope* of the audit). In establishing

FIGURE 2–2

The Relationships among
Management's Assertions,
Audit Procedures, and Audit
Evidence

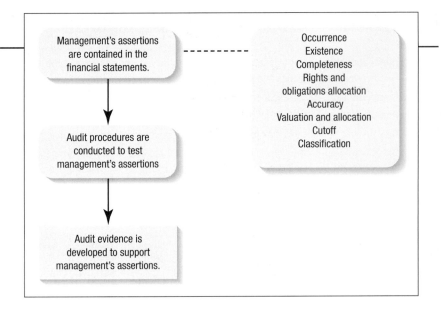

the scope of the audit, the auditor must make decisions about the nature, extent, and timing of evidence to be gathered. This section briefly discusses each of these concepts. The next two chapters cover these concepts in greater depth.

Materiality

CICA Handbook, section 5142, "Materiality," and Assurance and Related Services Guideline AuG-41, "Applying the concept of materiality in conducting an audit," both stress that the auditor's consideration of materiality should be a matter of *professional judgement* and is affected by what the auditor perceives as the view of a reasonable person who is relying on the financial statements. Paragraph 5142.04 of the *CICA Handbook* defines materiality as follows:

> A misstatement or the aggregate of all misstatements in financial statements is considered to be material if, in light of surrounding circumstances, it is probable that the decision of a person who is relying on the financial statements, and who has a reasonable knowledge of business and economic activities (the user), would be changed or influenced by such misstatement or the aggregate of all misstatements.

AuG-41 suggests using quantitative guidelines for the initial assessment of materiality. For example, for a profit-oriented entity, AuG-41 suggests 5 percent of after-tax income from continuing operations, for a not-for-profit entity, 1/2 percent to 2 percent of total revenues or total expenses.

The focus of the definition of materiality is on the users of the financial statements. In planning the engagement, the auditor assesses the magnitude of a misstatement that may affect the users' decisions. Materiality is used by the auditor to *design* the planned audit work and to *evaluate* the auditor's findings. By establishing materiality level, the auditor is focusing on *material misstatements,* where a misstatement is the difference between what management asserts is the balance and the balance based on the auditor's findings.

As you shall see later in this chapter, the wording of the auditor's standard audit report includes the phrase "the financial statements present fairly *in all material respects.*" This is the manner in which the auditor communicates the notion of materiality to the users of the auditor's report. Further, there is no guarantee that the auditor will uncover *all* material misstatements. The auditor can only provide reasonable assurance that all material misstatements are detected. The notion of *reasonable assurance* leads to the second concept.

Audit Risk

The second major concept involved in auditing is *audit risk.*

> **Audit risk** is the risk that the auditor expresses an inappropriate audit opinion when the financial statements are materially misstated.[2]

As mentioned previously, an audit does not guarantee or provide absolute assurance that all misstatements will be detected. The auditor's standard report states that the audit provides only reasonable assurance that the financial statements do not contain material misstatements. The term *reasonable assurance* implies some risk that a material misstatement could be present in the financial statements and the auditor will fail to detect it. In conducting an audit, the auditor decides what level of audit risk he or she is willing to accept and plans the audit to achieve that level of audit risk. The auditor controls the level of audit risk by the nature, timing, and extent of the audit work conducted. The more effective and extensive the audit work, the lower the risk that the misstatement will go undetected and the auditor will issue an inappropriate report. Nevertheless, as discussed previously, an auditor could conduct an audit in accordance with GAAS and issue an unqualified opinion, and the financial statements might still contain material misstatements. The auditor's responsibility with respect to misstatements that might arise from fraudulent activity or illegal acts is covered in detail in Chapter 3.

Evidence

Most of the auditor's work in arriving at an opinion on the financial statements consists of obtaining and evaluating audit evidence. Evidence supporting the financial statements consists of the underlying accounting records and source documents available to the auditor.

In designing a audit program to obtain evidence about management's assertions contained in the financial statements, the auditor selects specific audit procedures that relate to each management assertion (see Figure 2–2). In conjunction with the assessment of materiality and audit risk, the auditor considers the relevant management assertions to determine the nature, extent, and timing of evidence to be gathered. Once the auditor has obtained sufficient appropriate evidence that the management assertions are valid, reasonable assurance is provided that the financial statements are fairly presented.

In searching for and evaluating evidence, the auditor is concerned with the relevance and reliability of the evidence. *Relevance* refers to whether the evidence relates to the specific management assertion being tested.

---

[2]*CICA Handbook,* paragraph 5095.08.

If the auditor relies on evidence that relates to a different management assertion from the one being tested, an incorrect conclusion may result. For example, suppose the auditor wants to test whether the client owns certain property. If the auditor physically examines the property, this would not be relevant evidence. It is possible, for example, that the client is leasing the property the auditor examined. Relevant audit evidence for the management assertion of ownership would be an independently obtained, certified copy of the document showing that the entity holds legal title to the property.

Reliability refers to the diagnosticity of the evidence. In other words, can a particular type of evidence be relied upon to signal the true state of the assertion or audit objective? Suppose an auditor has the choice of gathering evidence from an independent, competent source *outside* the client or from a source *inside* the client. For example, evidence provided by a lawyer on the likely outcome of a lawsuit against the client would be considered more reliable than the controller's assessment of the likely outcome. In this instance, the external source, the lawyer, would be chosen because evidence from the outside source would be viewed as independent and thus more reliable.

The auditor seldom has absolute evidence about the true state of a management assertion. In most situations, the auditor obtains enough evidence to be persuaded that the management assertion is fairly stated. The nature of the evidence obtained by the auditor seldom provides absolute assurance about a management assertion because the types of evidence have different degrees of reliability. Additionally, for many parts of an audit, time and cost constraints mean that the auditor can examine only a sample of the transactions processed during the period. Chapter 8 details the use of sampling techniques by the auditor to obtain audit evidence.

Conceptual Basis of the Audit

LO 9> This section provides a brief introduction to the conceptual approach the auditor employs in the performance of the audit examination. The steps in that process are detailed in the section following. This section describes the risk-based approach that guides those steps. The risk-based approach is consistent with the concepts of the Strategic Systems Approach to auditing,[3] and with the increased emphasis on audit risk in the professional literature, for example, CICA Assurance and Related Services Guideline AuG-41, "Applying the concept of materiality in conducting an audit," *CICA Handbook*, sections 5095, "Reasonable assurance and audit risk," 5141, "Understanding the entity and its environment and assessing the risks of material misstatement," and 5143, "The auditor's procedures in response to assessed risks."

---

[3]See T. B. Bell, F. O. Mapps, I. Solomon, and H. Thomas, *Auditing Organization Through a Strategic Lens: The KPMG Business Measurement Process* (New York: KPMG Peat Marwick, LLP, 1997); see also, T.B. Bell, and I. Solomon (eds.), *Cases in Strategic Systems Auditing* (University of Illinois: KPMG and University of Illinois at Urbana—Champaign Business Measurement and Case Development Program, 2002).

An Overview

The auditor should plan and conduct an audit so that audit risk (the risk that the auditor may unknowingly fail to appropriately modify his or her opinion on financial statements that are materially misstated) will be limited to an acceptable level. Figure 2–3 presents an overview of the audit process.

Obtain and Support an Understanding of the Entity and Its Environment   The auditor starts by obtaining an understanding of the entity and its environment sufficient to plan the audit and to determine the scope (nature, timing, and extent) of the audit procedures to be performed (see Figure 2–3). The auditor's understanding of the entity and its environment should include information on each of the following categories:

- nature of the entity
- industry, regulatory, and other external factors
- management
- governance
- objectives and strategies
- measurement and performance
- business processes

Because the understanding of the entity and its environment is used to assess the risk of material misstatement and to set the scope of the audit, the auditor should perform appropriate procedures to support that understanding. Such procedures might include enquiry of client personnel, observation of activities, analytical procedures, reading business plans and strategies, and other procedures considered necessary in the circumstances.

Identify Risks That May Result in Material Misstatement at the Fianancial Statement Level   Section 5143 of the *CICA Handbook*, "The auditor's procedures in response to assessed risks," identifies two separate dimensions of the risk of material misstatement. The first dimension is the risk of material misstatement at the financial statement level. These risks arise from threats to the entity's ability to achieve its objectives. Most entities face a collection of business risks that may result in material misstatement in the financial statements. Some examples of conditions that may indicate the existence of business risks include significant changes in the entity such as a major reorganization, significant changes in the entity's industry, or significant changes in the information technology (IT) environment. To demonstrate how such risks can result in material misstatements in the financial statements, consider the effect of changes in an entity's industry. Suppose that the entity's industry is subject to rapid technological product changes. If the entity does not manage changing product technology well, it may overstate net income due to its failure to write down the value of obsolete inventory. Based on the auditor's understanding of the entity and its environment, the auditor should identify risks that may result in material misstatement whether due to error or fraud.

FIGURE 2–3

An Overview of the Audit Process

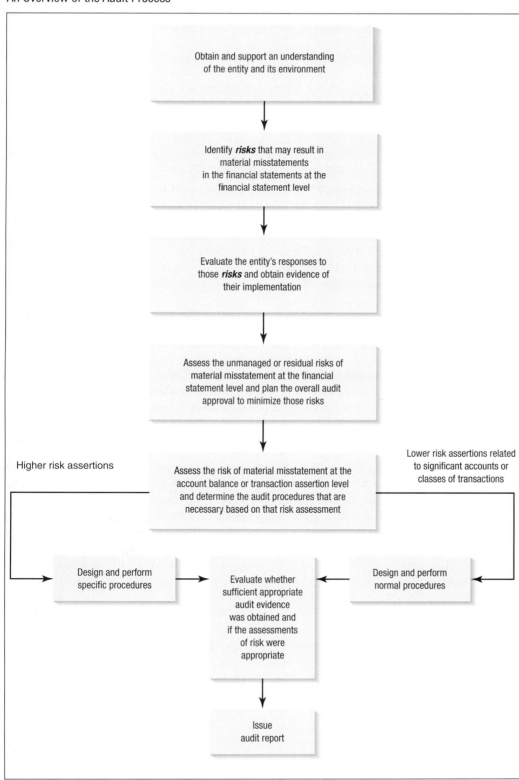

Evaluate the Entity's Response to the Risk of Material Misstatement at the Fianancial Statement Level   Management has a responsibility to strive to attain the entity's objectives. Therefore, management should establish a risk assessment process that identifies, analyzes, assesses, and manages risks that may affect the entity's objectives. This was emphasized in the discussion of the accountability cycle in Chapter 1. For those risks identified as possibly resulting in material misstatement, the auditor should evaluate the entity's responses to those risks and obtain evidence of their implementation. The auditor should perform this step because the entity's responses, or nonresponses, affect audit risk. If, in the auditor's opinion, there are still risks of material misstatement at the financial statement level, section 5143 of the *CICA Handbook* directs the auditor to exercise extra diligence and care in the overall performance of the audit. Specific directions include emphasizing to the audit team the need to maintain professional scepticism in gathering and evaluating audit evidence, ensuring that specialists are used in any phases of the audit requiring specialized knowledge, and adding additional elements of unpredictability in the selection of further audit procedures to be performed (an example could be surprise inventory observations at offsite locations). As discussed in Chapter 6, this evaluation may provide a basis for the auditor's planned level of control risk.

Assess the Risk of Material Misstatement at the Account Balance or Transaction Assertion Level   While the auditor expresses an opinion on the financial statements taken as a whole, the auditor needs to assess audit risk at the individual account balance level (e.g., accounts receivable, inventory, etc.). The auditor assesses audit risk at the *account balance level* because it assists with determining the scope of the audit procedures. The auditor will assess the risk of material misstatement at the *assertion level*, the second dimension of the risk of material misstatement identified in *CICA Handbook* section 5143, (refer to the earlier discussion of management assertions) and determines the specific audit procedures that are necessary based on that risk assessment. Thus, when considering the risks faced by the entity, the auditor should use a "top-down" approach to risk assessment. Risks identified at the entity level may "filter" down and affect the accounts contained in the financial statements. The type of risk identified at the account balance level is likely to affect specific assertions in the account balance. As discussed later in the text, the auditor normally has to test individual transactions that make up the account balance in order to obtain evidence on the assertions. Consider the industry example present above. At the entity level, the risk was changing technology in the industry. That risk filtered down to possible misstatements in inventory due to obsolescence. The potential inventory obsolescence of inventory affects the valuation assertion and hence net income.

Design and Perform Audit Procedures   In Figure 2–3, a distinction is made between higher-risk and lower-risk assertions. For *high-risk* assertions, the auditor should consider how material misstatements may occur and design and perform specific audit procedures to specifically address

Table 2–3	Procedures for Evaluating a Prospective Client

1. Obtain and review available financial information (annual reports, interim financial statements, income tax returns, etc.).

2. Enquire of third parties about any information concerning the integrity of the prospective client and its management. (Such Enquiries should be directed to the prospective client's bankers and lawyers, credit agencies, and other members of the business community who may have such knowledge.)

3. Communicate with the predecessor auditor about whether there were any disagreements about accounting principles, audit procedures, or similar significant matters.

4. Consider whether the prospective client has any circumstances that will require special attention or that may represent unusual business or audit risks, such as litigation or going-concern problems.

5. Determine if the firm is independent of the client and able to provide the desired service.

6. Determine if the firm has the necessary technical skills and knowledge of the industry to complete the engagement.

7. Determine if acceptance of the client would violate the Rules of Professional Conduct.

Prospective Client Acceptance   Public accounting firms should investigate a prospective client prior to accepting an engagement.[5] Table 2–3 lists procedures that a firm might conduct to evaluate a prospective client. Performance of such procedures would normally be documented in a memo or by completion of a client acceptance questionnaire or checklist.

When the prospective client has previously been audited, the successor auditor is required by provincial and national codes of conduct, and by acts of incorporation such as the CBCA, to make certain enquiries of the predecessor auditor before accepting the engagement. The successor auditor should request permission of the prospective client before contacting the predecessor auditor. Because the rules governing professional conduct do not allow an auditor to disclose confidential client information without the client's consent, the prospective client must authorize the predecessor auditor to respond to the successor's requests for information. The successor auditor's communications with the predecessor auditor may include questions related to the integrity of management; disagreements with management over accounting and auditing issues; communications with audit committees or an equivalent group regarding fraud, illegal acts, and internal-control-related matters; and the predecessor's understanding of the reason for the change in auditors. Such enquiries of the predecessor auditor may help the successor auditor determine whether to accept the engagement. The predecessor auditor should respond fully to the successor's requests unless an unusual circumstance (such as a lawsuit) exists. If the predecessor's response is limited, the successor auditor must be informed that the response is limited.

In the unusual case where the prospective client refuses to permit the predecessor to respond, the successor auditor should have reservations about accepting the client. Such a situation should raise serious questions about management's motivations and integrity.

After accepting the engagement, the successor auditor may need information on beginning balances and consistent application of GAAP in order

---

[5]See H. F. Huss and F. A. Jacobs, "Risk Containment: Exploring Auditor Decisions in the Engagement Process," *Auditing: A Journal of Practice and Theory* (Fall 1991), pp. 16–32, for a description of the client acceptance process of the Big 5 firms.

to issue an unqualified report. The successor auditor should request that the client authorize the predecessor auditor to permit a review of his or her working papers. In most instances, the predecessor auditor will allow the successor auditor to make copies of any working papers of continuing interest (for example, details of selected balance sheet accounts).

If the client has not previously been audited, the public accounting firm should complete all the procedures listed in Table 2–3, except for the communication with the predecessor auditor. The auditor should review the prospective client's financial information and carefully assess management integrity by communicating with the entity's bankers and lawyers, as well as other members of the business community. In some cases, the public accounting firm may even hire an investigative agency to check on management's background.

Client Continuance   Public accounting firms need to evaluate periodically whether to retain their current clients. This evaluation may take place at or near the completion of an audit or when some significant event occurs. Conflicts over accounting and auditing issues or disputes over fees may lead a public accounting firm to disassociate itself from a client.

Establish the Terms of the Engagement

The auditor should establish an understanding with the client regarding the services to be performed. For small, privately held entities, the auditor normally negotiates directly with the owner-manager. For larger private or public entities, the auditor will normally be appointed by a vote of the shareholders after recommendation by the audit committee of the board of directors. In all cases, an engagement letter should document the terms agreed to by the auditor and client. Such terms would include, for example, the responsibilities of each party, the assistance to be provided by client personnel and internal auditors, and the expected audit fees. Chapter 5 provides an example of an engagement letter and discusses the audit committee and internal auditors.

Preplanning

There are generally two preplanning activities: (1) determining the audit engagement team requirements and (2) ensuring the independence of the audit team and audit firm. The engagement partner or manager should ensure that the audit team is composed of team members who have the appropriate audit and industry experience for the engagement. The partner or manager should also determine whether the audit will require IT or other types of specialists (e.g., actuaries or appraisers). The second issue that needs to be addressed during preplanning is independence of the team members and the firm from the client. An audit cannot be undertaken if the audit firm is not independent. Chapter 5 addresses this phase of the audit process in more detail.

Establish Materiality and Assess Risks

In order to properly plan the audit, the audit team must establish a preliminary judgement about materiality and make a preliminary assessment of the client's business risks. The materiality judgement and risk assessment are used to set the scope for the audit. Chapter 3 explains both of these concepts in detail.

Reservations in the Auditor's Report

During the course of an audit engagement, circumstances may exist or events may occur that preclude the auditor from issuing an unqualified opinion. These circumstances or events may be related to some aspect or aspects of the client's financial statements' nonconformance with GAAP, or they may be related to the auditor's inability to obtain sufficient appropriate audit evidence to confirm management's assertions about information in the financial statements. In such cases the auditor may need to issue a report containing a *reservation of opinion*. Chapter 16 provides detailed coverage of the auditor's reporting options when a standard unqualified opinion cannot be issued, including examples of the other types of reports.

REVIEW QUESTIONS

LO 2 **2-1** Briefly discuss the essential components of the high-level model of business described in the chapter. Why might understanding the characteristics of a client's business in each of these areas be important for a financial statement auditor?

2,3 **2-2** What roles do information systems and systems of internal control play in the high-level model of business discussed in the chapter, and why might it be important for an auditor to understand these roles?

4 **2-3** List the three categories of GAAS.

4 **2-4** Why are objectivity and independence such important standards for auditors? How do objectivity and independence relate to the agency relationship between owners and managers?

6 **2-5** The auditor normally uses GAAP as a benchmark to measure management's reporting of economic activity and events. The auditor's report states that "the financial statements ... present fairly ... in accordance with generally accepted accounting principles." In making this statement, what judgements does the auditor make concerning GAAP?

7 **2-6** How do management assertions relate to the financial statements? To audit procedures?

8,9 **2-7** What is meant by *client business risk,* and why is it important for the auditor to properly assess this risk?

9 **2-8** Define *materiality.* How is this concept reflected in the auditor's report?

9 **2-9** Define *audit risk.* How is this concept reflected in the auditor's report?

9 **2-10** Describe what is meant by the *relevance* and *reliability* of audit evidence.

9 **2-11** What types of enquiries about a prospective client should an auditor make to third parties?

11 **2-12** Identify the elements of the auditor's standard unqualified report.

11 **2-13** What three important facts are contained in the introductory paragraph of the standard unqualified audit report?

11 **2-14** What is the significance of the audit report date?

MULTIPLE-CHOICE QUESTIONS FROM PROFESSIONAL EXAMINATIONS

Unless otherwise indicated, these multiple-choice questions were adapted from the CPA examinations, courtesy of the American Institute of Certified Public Accountants.

2,3〉   **2-15**   Which of the following best describes the relationship between business objectives, strategies, processes, controls, and transactions?

a. To achieve its objectives, a business formulates strategies and implements processes, which are carried out through business transactions. The entity's information and internal control systems must be designed to ensure that the transactions are properly executed, captured, and processed.

b. To achieve its strategies, a business formulates objectives and implements processes, which are carried out through the entity's information and internal control systems. Transactions are conducted to ensure that the processes are properly executed, captured, and processed.

c. To achieve its objectives, a business formulates strategies to implement its transactions, which are carried out through business processes. The entity's information and internal control systems must be designed to ensure that the processes are properly executed, captured, and processed.

d. To achieve its business processes, a business formulates objectives, which are carried out through the entity's strategies. The entity's information and internal control systems must be designed to ensure that the entity's strategies are properly executed, captured, and processed.

4〉   **2-16**   Which of the following best describes what is meant by the term *generally accepted auditing standards*?

a. Procedures to be used to gather evidence to support financial statements.

b. Measures of the quality of the auditor's performance.

c. Pronouncements issued by the Auditing and Assurance Standards Board.

d. Rules acknowledged by the accounting profession because of their universal application.

4〉   **2-17**   To exercise due professional care, an auditor should

a. Attain the proper balance of professional experience and formal education.

b. Design the audit to detect all instances of illegal acts.

c. Critically review the judgement exercised by those assisting in the audit.

d. Examine all available corroborating evidence supporting management's assertions.

4 >   **2-18**   What is the general theme of the three generally accepted auditing standards classified as examination standards?

a. The competence, independence, and professional care of persons performing the audit.

b. Criteria for the content of the auditor's report on financial statements and related footnote disclosures.

c. Criteria for audit planning and evidence gathering.

d. The need to maintain an independence of mental attitude in all matters relating to the audit.

8,9 >   **2-19**   Prior to beginning the field work on a new audit engagement in which an auditor does *not* possess expertise in the industry in which the client operates, the auditor should

a. Reduce audit risk by lowering the preliminary levels of materiality.

b. Design special substantive tests to compensate for the lack of industry expertise.

c. Engage financial specialists who are familiar with the nature of the industry.

d. Obtain a knowledge of matters that relate to the nature of the entity's business.

10 >   **2-20**   Before accepting an audit engagement, a successor auditor should make specific enquiries of the predecessor auditor regarding the predecessor's

a. Awareness of the consistency in the application of generally accepted accounting principles between periods.

b. Evaluation of all matters of continuing accounting significance.

c. Opinion of any subsequent events occurring since the predecessor's audit report was issued.

d. Understanding as to the reasons for the change of auditors.

11 >   **2-21**   Which of the following statements best describes management's and the external auditor's respective levels of responsibility for a public company's financial statements?

a. Management and the external auditor share equal responsibility for the fairness of the entity's financial statements in accordance with GAAP.

b. Neither management nor the external auditor has significant responsibility for the fairness of the entity's financial statements in accordance with GAAP.

c. Management has the primary responsibility to ensure that the company's financial statements are prepared in accordance with GAAP, and the auditor provides reasonable assurance that the statements are free of material misstatement.

d. Management has the primary responsibility to ensure that the company's financial statements are prepared in accordance with GAAP, and the auditor provides a guarantee that the statements are free of material misstatement.

11> **2-22** An auditor's responsibility to express an opinion on the financial statements is

a. Implicitly represented in the auditor's standard report.

b. Explicitly represented in the opening paragraph of the auditor's standard report.

c. Explicitly represented in the scope paragraph of the auditor's standard report.

d. Explicitly represented in the opinion paragraph of the auditor's standard report.

6,11> **2-23** For an entity's financial statements to be presented fairly in accordance with generally accepted accounting principles, the principles selected should

a. Be applied on a basis consistent with those followed in the prior year.

b. Be approved by the Auditing Standards Board.

c. Reflect transactions in a manner that presents the financial statements within a range of acceptable limits.

d. Match the principles used by most other entities within the entity's particular industry.

9> **2-24** Analysis is a technique that is often used in the planning phase of an audit. In what other phases of the audit could the auditor use analysis?

a. The testing phase.

b. The final review phase.

c. Analysis can be used in all phases of the audit.

d. Analysis is not useful in any other phase of the audit.

(CGA-Canada, adapted)

11> **2-25** The use of standardized wording has been the subject of considerable debate among auditors. Which of the following is the strongest argument in favour of using standardized wording?

a. It facilitates the international harmonization of auditing standards.

b. Standardized wording is not confusing to readers of the auditor's report.

c. It is more informative than a non-flexible standard.

d. The type of opinion is less likely to be misinterpreted by readers when standardized wording is used.

(CGA-Canada, adapted)

PROBLEMS

9,10> **2-26** John Josephs, an audit manager for Tip, Acanoe, & Tylerto, was asked to speak at a dinner meeting of the local Small Business Administration Association. The president of the association has suggested that he talk about the various phases of the audit process. John has asked you, his trusted assistant, to prepare an outline for his speech. He suggests that you answer the following:

a. List and describe the various phases of an audit.

b. Describe how the results of work completed in certain phases provide feedback to earlier-completed phases. Give an example.

c. One of the phases involves understanding an entity's internal control. Why might the members of the association be particularly interested in the work conducted by auditors in this phase of the audit?

9> **2-27** Sheri Shannon was recently hired by the firm of Honson & Hansen LLP. Within two weeks, Sheri was sent to the first-year staff training course. The instructor asked her to prepare answers for the following questions:

a. How is audit evidence defined?

b. How does evidence relate to management assertions, and to the audit report?

c. What characteristics of evidence should an auditor be concerned with when searching for and evaluating evidence?

4> **2-28** Dale Baker, the owner of a small electronics firm, asked Sally Smith, a professional accountant, to conduct an audit of the company's records. Baker told Smith that the audit was to be completed in time to submit audited financial statements to a bank as part of a loan application. Smith immediately accepted the engagement and agreed to provide an auditor's report within one month. Baker agreed to pay Smith her normal audit fee plus a percentage of the loan if it was granted.

Smith hired two recent accounting graduates to conduct the audit and spent several hours telling them exactly what to do. She told the new hires not to spend time reviewing the internal control but instead to concentrate on proving the mathematical accuracy of the general and subsidiary ledgers and summarizing the data in the accounting records that supported Baker's financial statements. The new hires followed Smith's instructions, and after two weeks gave Smith the financial statements excluding footnotes. Smith reviewed the statements and prepared an unqualified auditor's report. The report, however, did not refer to generally accepted accounting principles. Additionally, no audit procedures were conducted to verify the year-to-year application of such principles.

Required:

Briefly describe each of the generally accepted auditing standards and indicate how the action(s) of Smith resulted in a failure to comply with *each* generally accepted auditing standard.

(AICPA, adapted)

2,3,4,9> **2-29** The role of the auditor is changing. Increasingly, financial statement users want more from auditors than just a GAAS audit of

GAAP financial statements. They want assurances as to whether an enterprise has met its stated corporate and social objectives, complied with codes of conduct, and used its resources effectively.

Required:

Discuss the implications for external auditors of expanding the auditor's role to include the kind of assurances identified above.

(ICABC, adapted)

8,9,10 > **2-30** It has been stated that "internal and external auditors serve different clients and operate from different perspectives. With mutual understanding and discussion they can make allowances for their differences and realize their potential for reliance."

Required:

a. Analyze the above statement, pointing out areas of agreement and disagreement.

b. An entity's internal auditors often provide assistance to the external auditors in the annual financial statement audit. Given that the competence and independence of the internal auditors has been established, what kinds of matters should the internal and external auditors discuss prior to the internal auditors commencing work? Why?

(ICABC, adapted)

11 > **2-31** The following auditors' report was drafted by Moore, a staff accountant of Tyler & Tyler, at the completion of the audit of the financial statements of Park Publishing Company, Inc., for the year ended September 30, 2007. The report was submitted to the engagement partner, who reviewed the audit working papers and properly concluded that an unqualified opinion should be issued. In drafting the report, Moore knew that Tyler & Tyler had previously audited the financial statements for the year ended September 30, 2006, and expressed an unqualified opinion.

Independent Auditor's Report

To the Board of Directors of Park Publishing Company, Inc.:

We have audited the accompanying balance sheet of Park Publishing Company, Inc., as of September 30, 2007, and the related statements of income and cash flows for the year ended then. These financial statements are the responsibility of the company's management.

We conducted our audits in accordance with generally accepted auditing standards. Those standards require that we plan and perform the audit to obtain reasonable assurance about whether the financial statements are fairly presented. An audit includes examining, on a test basis, evidence supporting the amounts and disclosures in the financial statements. An audit also includes assessing significant estimates made by management, as well as evaluating the overall financial statement presentation. We believe that our audits provide a basis for determining whether any material modifications should be made to the accompanying financial statements.

In our opinion, the financial statements referred to above present fairly, in all material respects, the financial position of Park Publishing Company, Inc., as of September 30, 2007, and the results of its operations and its cash flows for the year then ended in conformity with generally accepted accounting principles.

Tyler & Tyler,
November 5, 2007

Required:

Identify the deficiencies in the auditors' report as drafted by Moore. Group the deficiencies by paragraph and in the order in which the deficiencies appear. Do *not* redraft the report.

(AICPA, adapted)

DISCUSSION CASES

1,2,3,4 >   **2-32**   **Merry-Go-Round** (MGR), a clothing retailer located primarily in shopping malls, was founded in 1968.[6] By the early 1990s, the company had gone public and had expanded to approximately 1,500 stores, 15,000 employees, and $1 billion in annual sales. The company's locations in malls targeted the youth and teen market. The company was listed by *Forbes* magazine as one of the top 25 companies in the late 1980s. However, in the early 1990s, the company faced many challenges. One of its cofounders died, and the other left to pursue unrelated business interests. The company faced stiff competition from other retailers (e.g., The Gap and Banana Republic), fashion trends changed, and mall traffic declined. Sales fell, and experts speculated that MGR failed to anticipate key industry trends and lost sight of its customer market. To try to regain its strong position, the company acquired Chess King, Inc., a struggling chain of men's clothing stores located in malls, in 1993.

     The company's sales continued to fall, and later in 1993, it brought back one of its cofounders to manage the company and wrote down a significant amount of inventory. However, this inventory write-down caused the company to violate loan covenants. Facing bankruptcy, the company, based on the advice of its newly hired law firm Swidler and Berlin, hired turnaround specialists from Ernst and Young (E&Y) to help overcome the financial crisis and develop a long-term business plan. However, the company's decline continued, and it filed for Chapter 11 reorganization in 1994. In 1996, the remaining assets were sold for pennies on the dollar.

---

[6]The following articles were sources for the information in the case: E. MacDonald, "Ernst & Young Will Pay $185 Million to Settle Claims of Merry-Go-Round," *The Wall Street Journal*, April 29, 1999; and E. McDonald and S. J. Paltrow, "Merry-Go-Round: Ernst & Young Advised the Client, but Not about Everything—It Didn't Reveal Business Ties Alleged to Pose Conflict with Its Consulting Job—Settlement for $185 Million," *The Wall Street Journal*, August 8, 1999, p. A1.

Subsequently, a group of 9,000 creditors (including former employees and shareholders) began litigation against parties it deemed responsible for their losses. These parties included E&Y, which the creditors sued for $4 billion in punitive and compensatory damages (E&Y's fees from MGR totalled $4.5 million).

The lawsuit alleged that E&Y's incompetence was the main cause of MGR's decline and demise. The lawsuit alleged in part that

- The turnaround team did not act fast enough.
- The leader of the team took an eight-day vacation at a critical point during the engagement.
- The cost-cutting strategy called for only $11 million in annual savings, despite the fact that the company was projected to lose up to $200 million in 1994.
- While store closings were key to MGR's survival, by 1995 only 230 of 1,434 stores had been closed and MGR still operated two stores in some malls.
- The turnaround team included inexperienced personnel—a retired consultant, a partner with little experience in the United States and with retail firms, and two recent college graduates.
- E&Y charged exorbitant hourly rates and charged unreasonable expenses (e.g., charges included reimbursement for a dinner for three of the consultants totalling in excess of $200).
- E&Y denied any wrongdoing but in April 1999 agreed to pay $185 million to settle with the injured parties.

Required:

a. Although this was not an audit engagement for E&Y, some of the allegations against the firm can be framed in terms of the eight generally accepted auditing standards. Which of the eight GAAS was E&Y alleged to have violated?

b. Should there be specific professional standards for independent auditors who consult? Given that non-auditors who consult do not have formal professional standards, describe the advantages and disadvantages that result from such standards.

6,11 >   **2-33**   The opinion paragraph of the standard auditor's report uses the phrase "present fairly in accordance with Canadian GAAP." However, the idea that following GAAP produces fairness in reporting has been questioned by some. The *Handbook* recognizes this potential dilemma by stating "the auditor should exercise professional judgement as to the appropriateness of the selection and application of principles to the particular circumstances of an entity and as to the overall effect on the financial statements of separate decisions made in their preparation."

Required:

a. Provide examples of circumstances you feel might cause a conflict between reporting according to GAAP and fair presentation.

b. What other sources of information might the auditor consult in attempting to resolve this conflict.

(CICA, adapted)

INTERNET ASSIGNMENTS

2-34   Visit EarthWear Clothiers' website (www.mcgrawhill.ca/college/ messier/earthwear) and become familiar with the type of information contained there.

2-35   Willis & Adams are the auditors of EarthWear. Visit Willis & Adams' website (www.mcgrawhill.ca/college/messier/willisand-adams) and become familiar with the information contained there.

2-36   Use an Internet search engine to do the following:

a. Visit the websites of Rogers Communications (www.rogers.ca) (listed on the TSE), Microsoft (www.microsoft.com) (listed on NASDAQ), and Telus (www.telus.com) (cross-listed on both the TSE and NASDAQ) and review their financial statements, including auditors' reports. Prepare a brief analysis of their similarities and differences.

b. Search for the website of a non-Canadian company and review its financial statements, including its auditor's report. For example, BMW's website (www.bmwgroup.com) allows a visitor to download the financial statements as a pdf file. The auditor's report on BMW's financial statements is based on German auditing standards.

c. Compare the standard Canadian report with the audit reports for non-Canadian companies from parts (a) and (b). Prepare a brief analysis of their similarities and differences.

Part II BASIC AUDITING CONCEPTS: RISK, MATERIALITY, AND EVIDENCE

| Risk and Materiality

 Chapter **3**

Learning Objectives

Upon completion of this chapter, you will be able to

1 ▸ Describe the relationship between risk and materiality.

2 ▸ Describe the concept of materiality.

3 ▸ Identify the steps for determining and applying materiality in an audit.

4 ▸ Apply the materiality steps to a detailed example (EarthWear).

5 ▸ Explain the concepts of audit risk and the risk of material misstatement.

6 ▸ Explain the auditor's responsibility to consider fraud.

7 ▸ Explain the auditor's responsibility for communication regarding fraud and error.

8 ▸ Explain the auditor's responsibility for illegal acts.

RELEVANT ACCOUNTING AND ASSURANCE PRONOUNCEMENTS

CICA Handbook, **section 5090,** Audit of financial statements—an introduction

CICA Handbook, **section 5095,** Reasonable assurance and audit risk

CICA Handbook, **section 5135,** The auditor's responsibility to consider fraud

CICA Handbook, **section 5136,** Misstatements—Illegal acts

CICA Handbook, **section 5141,** Understanding the entity and its environment and assessing the risks of material misstatement

CICA Handbook, **section 5142,** Materiality

CICA Handbook, **section 5143,** The auditor's procedures in response to assessed risks

CICA Handbook, **section 5150,** Planning

CICA Handbook, **section 5750,** Communication with management of matters identified during the financial statement audit

CICA Handbook, **section 5751,** Communications with those having oversight responsibility for the financial reporting process

AuG-41, Applying the concept of materiality in conducting an audit

Risk Management and Governance Board, *Learning about Risk: Choices, Connections and Competencies*

THE RISE AND FALL OF ENRON

In 1985, following industry deregulation, Kenneth Lay formed Enron Corp. by the merger of two natural gas pipeline companies. To generate profits and cash flow, Enron devised a new and innovative business strategy—it created a "gas bank" in which it would buy gas from a network of suppliers and sell it to a network of consumers, guaranteeing the supply and the price. Enron had such market power that it could predict future prices with great accuracy, guaranteeing profits. In addition, Enron charged fees for each transaction.

In 1996, Enron, under Jeffrey Skilling, the new COO, began to extend the gas bank model to other industries, trading in tangible products such as coal and steel and intangibles such as weather and electronic commodities (e.g., network capacity or bandwidth). To finance this expansion, Enron needed more and more capital. In order to present as attractive a picture as possible of their financial health, maintain their investment grade credit rating, and boost their return on assets (ROA) numbers, they resorted to numerous "innovative" financing techniques to keep debt off their books. Chief among these techniques was the use of Special Purpose Entities (SPEs) such as limited partnerships with outside parties. Through a series of complex transactions, Enron, under the leadership of CFO Andrew Fastow, used SPE financing to turn large amounts of debt into equity and to park troubled assets such as its struggling broadband operation and stock in failing overseas energy facilities. Two of the SPEs, LJM Cayman LP and LJM2 Co-Investment LP, were run by Fastow himself and paid him in excess of $30 million in management fees.

Throughout the spring and summer of 2001, numerous risky deals that Enron had made in underperforming investments of various kinds started to unravel, resulting in a huge cash shortfall. At the same time, it was becoming apparent to analysts and others, the extent of Enron's true debt and shaky financial position. By the fall of 2001, Enron announced a quarterly loss of $1 billion, and on October 22, Enron announced restatement of its financial statements back to 1997. By November 30,

the stock, which had traded on the NYSE at $90 per share in August 2000, was selling at 26 cents per share, and on December 2, 2001, Enron declared bankruptcy.

The ensuing investigations revealed that during this time, in fact since August of 2000, while senior management was reassuring anyone who would listen that Enron was healthy and completely safe, Lay, Skilling, Fastow, and other senior management were selling massive amounts of their own Enron holdings, pocketing hundreds of millions of dollars in the process.

The legal consequences of this massive financial coverup have been extensive. Fastow was convicted of criminal fraud and sentenced to six years in prison. Lay and Skilling were convicted of fraud and conspiracy; Skilling was sentenced to 24 years in prison; Kenneth Lay died in the fall of 2006. In total over 40 individuals connected directly or indirectly with Enron have been criminally prosecuted for their involvement in this scandal.

This chapter discusses materiality, audit risk, and special concerns when material misstatements may be due to fraud or illegal acts. The audit of Enron involved both of these. In particular, it can be argued that the auditors (Arthur Andersen, whose involvement with Enron proved to be their demise) did not give sufficient attention to the many factors present that significantly increased the risks of material misstatement, did not properly address those risks in their audit and as a result did not identify material misstatements that had a cumulative effect of overstating Enron's net income by hundreds of millions of dollars. This chapter will provide you with an understanding of the vital importance of risk and materiality to the planning and performance of an audit in accordance with generally accepted auditing standards.

Sources: www.businessweek.com:/print/magazine/content01_51/b3762001.htm?mz; www.dushkin.com/test-data/articles/32559/body.pdf; www.enronfraud.com; www.llrx.com/features/enron.htm#litigation; www.chron.com/news/specials/enron.

Materiality versus Audit Risk

LO 1> Materiality and risk are highly interconnected concepts. The profession has placed great emphasis on the importance of thoroughly understanding and assessing the elements that give rise to audit risk. However, the concept of risk implies that there is a risk "of something." In this case the "something" is material misstatement(s) in the financial statements. Therefore, before discussing the responsibility of the auditor as it relates to risk, we first cover the concept of materiality.

The Concept of Materiality

LO 2> The auditor's consideration of materiality on an audit is a matter of *professional judgement*. As discussed in Chapter 2, materiality is assessed in terms of the potential effect of a misstatement on decisions made by a reasonable user of the financial statements. Paragraph 5142.04 of the *CICA Handbook* provides the following definition:

> A misstatement or the aggregate of all misstatements in financial statements is considered to be material if, in light of surrounding circumstances, it is probable that the decision of a person who is relying on the financial statements, and who has a reasonable knowledge of business and economic activities (the user), would be changed or influenced by such misstatement or the aggregate of all misstatements.

Simply stated, materiality is an account or fact that would affect decisions made by users relying on the financial statements. This perspective requires that the auditor assess the amount of misstatement that could affect a reasonable user's decisions.

Section 5142 of the *CICA Handbook* discusses materiality at a conceptual level and AuG-41, "Applying the concept of materiality in conducting an audit," provides the auditor with guidance in applying those concepts. For instance, in establishing a judgement about preliminary materiality, AuG-41 suggests bases that may be appropriate for determining materiality in different circumstances. AuG-41 also provides additional guidance on qualitative aspects that the auditor may consider when determining materiality.

In establishing materiality for an audit, the auditor should consider both quantitative and qualitative aspects of the engagement. Although materiality may be estimated initially using a quantitative approach, the qualitative aspects of misstatements of small amounts may also materially affect the users of financial statements. For example, a client may illegally pay a commissioned agent to secure a sales contract. While the amount of the illegal payment may be immaterial to the financial statements, the disclosure of the illegal act may result in loss of the contract and substantial penalties that may be material. The next section presents an approach for determining and applying materiality, which is then followed by a detailed example.

Steps in Determining and Applying Materiality in an Audit

LO 3> Figure 3–1 presents the three major steps in the application of materiality to an audit. Step 1 is normally performed early in the engagement as part of planning the audit (see Figure 2–3 in Chapter 2). Step 2 occurs

FIGURE 3–1

Steps in Determining and
Applying Materiality on an
Audit

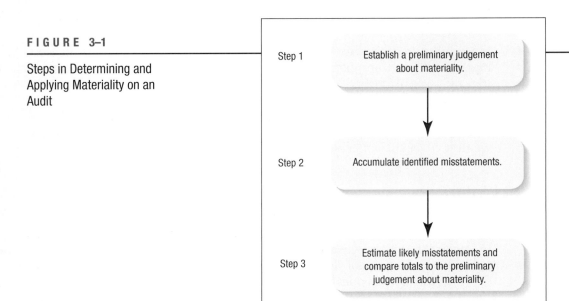

throughout the course of the audit and Step 3 is performed when the
auditor evaluates the evidence at the completion of the audit to determine
if it supports the fair presentation of the financial statements (again, refer
to Figure 2–3).

Step 1: Establish a Preliminary Judgement about Materiality   *CICA
Handbook*, section 5150, directs the auditor to establish a preliminary
judgement about materiality (called *planning materiality*) as part of planning the audit. While auditing standards do not explicitly require that the
auditor quantify and document this judgement, quantifying materiality
allows the audit team to better plan the scope of the audit and evaluate the
results of the audit tests.

The preliminary judgement about materiality is the maximum amount
by which the auditor believes the financial statements could be misstated
and still *not* affect the decisions of reasonable users. Materiality is a relative, not an absolute, concept. For example, $5,000 might be considered
highly material for a small sole proprietorship, but this amount would
clearly be immaterial for a large multinational corporation. Thus, the relative size of the company being audited affects the preliminary judgement
about materiality.

In specifying materiality, an auditor should establish a base (or bases)
that, when multiplied by a percentage factor, determines the initial quantitative judgement about materiality. The resulting materiality amount can
then be adjusted for any qualitative factors that may be relevant to the
engagement. Table 3–1 lists quantitative factors, as identified in assurance
guideline AuG-41, that may be useful in the preliminary determination of
materiality.[1] In some cases AuG-41 suggests a multiplicative factor or range

---

[1]See also D. A. Leslie, *Materiality: The Concept and Its Application to Auditing* (Toronto: CICA,
1985).

Table 3–1	**Common Bases and Qualitative Factors for Establishing Materiality**

Common Quantitative Bases for Establishing Materiality
- 5% of (normalized) net income after taxes (for for-profit entities)
- 1/2% to 2% of expenses or revenues (for not-for-profit entities)
- 1/2% to 2% of net assets (for entities in the mutual fund industry)
- 1% of revenue (for entities whose income is from real estate)
- total equity
- gross profit
- cash flow from operations

Selected Qualitative Factors for Assessing Materiality
- misstatements that may be due to fraud or illegal acts
- amounts that might violate contractual covenants
- amounts that might affect the trend in earnings
- misstatements that have the effect of increasing management compensation
- amounts that may cause the entity to miss forecasted revenue on earnings.

(e.g., 5%; 1/2% to 2%) and in some cases it simply identifies a possible base (e.g., total equity).

For for-profit entities, some form of net income is frequently used by auditors when establishing materiality. Difficulties may arise in using net income as a base when the entity is close to breaking even or experiencing a loss. For example, suppose that an entity has net income after taxes of $3,000,000 one year and the auditor decides that 5 percent of that amount ($150,000) would be material. The scope of the audit in that year would be based on a preliminary judgement about materiality of $150,000. Suppose, in the following year, the entity's net income after taxes falls to $250,000 due to a temporary decrease in sales prices for its products. If the auditor uses the 5 percent factor, the preliminary judgement about materiality would be $12,500 ($250,000 × 0.05), and a much more extensive audit would be required. An advantage of using total assets or total revenues is that for many companies these factors are more stable from year to year than net income before taxes.

It should be stressed that the initial quantitative calculation is only the first step. In the auditor's judgement, it may be that the initial quantitative estimate of planning materiality should be increased or decreased based on qualitative factors that are relevant to the audit. Table 3–1 also includes examples from AuG-41 of qualitative factors that may be relevant in the determination of materiality.[2] For example, planning materiality may be increased based on favourable qualitative factors, such as past audit history (few misstatements in prior years, no illegal acts, no violations of debt covenants), strong financial condition, or sound economic conditions in the entity's industry. Conversely, unfavourable qualitative factors, such

---

[2]AuG-41 identifies a total of 18 qualitative factors that the auditor may consider in the determination of materiality.

as numerous misstatements in prior years, depressed industry conditions, or possible violations of debt covenants, may result in a decrease in planning materiality.

Although AuG-41 provides some explicit guidance in the assessment of materiality, it is important to emphasize that the final determination of materiality requires the auditor to exercise his or her professional judgement. Paragraph 8 of AuG-41 concludes with the statement that materiality "… should reflect, in the auditor's judgement, the measures financial statement users are most likely to consider important."

Step 2: Document Misstatements Identified During the Audit Examination   During the course of the audit examination, the auditor keeps a record of misstatements discovered in the client's financial statements. AuG-41 calls these *identified misstatements* (IM). They are the actual misstatements discovered in the items and samples the auditor has tested. Typically, these identified misstatements are accumulated on a working paper, often called the schedule of proposed adjustments or proposed adjustments schedule.

Step 3: Estimate Likely Misstatements and Compare Totals to the Preliminary Judgement about Materiality   Step 3 is completed near the end of the audit, when the auditor evaluates all the evidence that has been gathered. Based on the results of the audit procedures conducted, the auditor has aggregated identified misstatements from each account or class of transactions. At this time, the auditor will consider another quantity defined by AuG-41, *likely misstatements* (LM). Likely misstatements are the projection to the population of the misstatements identified during audit testing. The exact amount of LM is an estimate, but its existence is fairly certain—it is based on the reasonable assumption that the sample tested by the auditor is representative of the population and that therefore, errors discovered in the sample exist in similar proportion in the population. The sum of likely misstatements in the financial statements is called the *likely aggregate misstatement* (LAM) and includes the effect of unadjusted LM carried forward from the prior period. The auditor compares the likely aggregate misstatement to the preliminary judgement about materiality established in Step 1. If the auditor's judgement about materiality at the planning stage (Step 1) was based on the same information available at the evaluation stage (Step 3), materiality for planning and evaluation would be the same. However, information may come to light during the course of the audit that causes a revision (usually downwards) to the preliminary judgement about materiality—for example, if the auditor feels that as a result of some audit adjustments the client may be in danger of violating a restrictive covenant, or, less benignly, if the auditor becomes aware of management actions which appear to attempt to manipulate the financial statements. Thus, the preliminary judgement about materiality may differ from the materiality judgement used in evaluating the audit findings. When this occurs, the auditor should carefully document the reasons for revising the preliminary judgement about materiality.

When the likely misstatements are less than the auditor's judgement about materiality, the auditor can generally conclude that the financial

Table 3–2	**Qualitative Factors for Evaluating Materiality**

Evaluating the materiality of unadjusted misstatements

- Whether the misstatement masks a change in earnings or trends.
- Whether the misstatement hides a failure to meet analysts' consensus expectations.
- Whether the misstatement changes a loss into income or vice versa.
- Whether the misstatement concerns a segment or other portion of the business that has been portrayed as playing a significant role in the operations or profitability of the entity.
- Whether the misstatement affects compliance with regulatory requirements.
- Whether the misstatement affects compliance with loan covenants or other contractual requirements.
- Whether the misstatement increases management's compensation.
- Whether the misstatement involves the concealment of an unlawful transaction.
- Whether the misstatement may result in a significant positive or negative market reaction.
- Whether small intentional misstatements are part of actions to "manage" earnings.

statements are fairly presented. Conversely, when the likely misstatements are greater than the judgement about materiality, the auditor should request that the client adjust the financial statements. If the client refuses to adjust the financial statements for the likely misstatements, the auditor will issue a reservation of opinion because the financial statements do not present fairly in conformity with GAAP (see Chapter 2, LO 11).

Note that, just as in the determination of planning materiality, qualitative considerations are also important in the auditor's evaluation of misstatements. Table 3–2 lists some of the qualitative factors identified in AuG-41 that the auditor should consider in evaluating the effect of misstatements on the financial statements.

Before illustrating this process with an example, there is one more related concept to consider. AuG-41 briefly discusses one other quantity that the auditor may wish to factor into his or her deliberations at this stage. That quantity is *further possible misstatements* (FPM). The sum of LAM plus FPM is called the *maximum possible misstatement* (MPM). FPM exist because the auditor's testing is done on a sample basis. FPM may exist in addition to LM because of (1) sampling error—the sample may not be representative of the population, or (2) non-sampling error—the auditor may misinterpret the evidence and come to the wrong conclusion about the population.

AuG-41 implicitly recognizes that due to the uncertainty surrounding both the estimate of, and the likelihood of existence of, FPM, it is problematic for the auditor to request the client to make an adjustment if FPM, but not LAM, exceeds the materiality threshold.

An Example of Determining and Applying Materiality

LO 4 In this example, the three steps for applying materiality are discussed. Exhibit 3–1 contains aggregated financial information for EarthWear Clothiers for the year ended December 31, 2006. This financial information is taken from the case illustration included in Chapter 1 and serves as the basis for the example.

EXHIBIT 3–1

Address: http://www.mcgrawhill.ca/college/messier

Financial Information for Estimating Materiality

EarthWear

EARTHWEAR CLOTHIERS
Consolidated Balance Sheet
December 31, 2006
(In thousands)

Assets

Cash and cash equivalents	$ 48,978
Receivables	12,875
Inventory	122,337
Prepaid advertising	11,458
Other prepaid expenses	6,315
Future income tax benefits	7,132
Property, plant, and equipment, net	120,440
Intangibles, net	423
Total assets	$ 329,959

Liabilities and Shareholders' Investment

Lines of credit	$ 11,011
Accounts payable	62,509
Reserve for returns	5,890
Accrued liabilities	26,738
Accrued profit sharing	1,532
Income taxes payable	8,588
Future income taxes	9,469
Common shares	21,001
Contributed surplus	5,460
Less: Future compensation	(79)
Accumulated other comprehensive income	3,883
Retained earnings	317,907
Less: Treasury shares	(143,950)
Total liabilities and shareholders' investment	$ 329,959
Net sales	$ 950,484
Net income before taxes	$ 35,757
Net income after taxes	$ 22,527

EXHIBIT 3–2

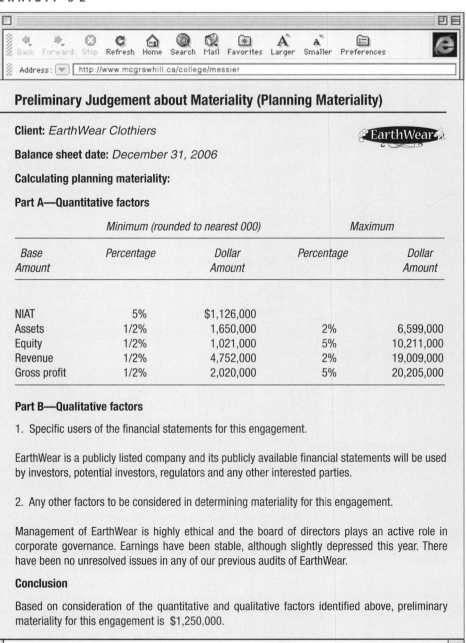

Preliminary Judgement about Materiality (Planning Materiality)

Client: *EarthWear Clothiers*

Balance sheet date: *December 31, 2006*

Calculating planning materiality:

Part A—Quantitative factors

Base Amount	Minimum (rounded to nearest 000)		Maximum	
	Percentage	Dollar Amount	Percentage	Dollar Amount
NIAT	5%	$1,126,000		
Assets	1/2%	1,650,000	2%	6,599,000
Equity	1/2%	1,021,000	5%	10,211,000
Revenue	1/2%	4,752,000	2%	19,009,000
Gross profit	1/2%	2,020,000	5%	20,205,000

Part B—Qualitative factors

1. Specific users of the financial statements for this engagement.

EarthWear is a publicly listed company and its publicly available financial statements will be used by investors, potential investors, regulators and any other interested parties.

2. Any other factors to be considered in determining materiality for this engagement.

Management of EarthWear is highly ethical and the board of directors plays an active role in corporate governance. Earnings have been stable, although slightly depressed this year. There have been no unresolved issues in any of our previous audits of EarthWear.

Conclusion

Based on consideration of the quantitative and qualitative factors identified above, preliminary materiality for this engagement is $1,250,000.

 Step 1: Determine the Preliminary Judgement about Materiality   The calculation of potential materiality figures is shown in Exhibit 3–2. Since EarthWear is a for-profit enterprise, following AuG-41, the most appropriate initial quantitative estimate of materiality, shown first, is based on 5% of NIAT. The other amounts in Exhibit 3–2, derived from the bases and rates suggested in Table 3–1, are generally for other types of entities and are shown here to illustrate the range of values. To make a final determination of the appropriate amount for materiality, the auditor should consider

whether any qualitative factors are relevant for this engagement (see also, Table 3–1). In our example, let us assume that after having done so, the auditor has determined that $1,250,000 will be used for the preliminary judgement of materiality.

Step 2: Document Misstatements Identified in the Audit Examination   During the course of the audit examination, the auditor has identified four misstatements in the client's financial statements. Two have been identified as a result of sampling, and must be projected to the population, and two are based on 100 percent examination and do not require projection to the population. The four identified misstatements are:

1. an error in the accrual of payroll expense (the amount of the accrual was insufficient)
2. an overstatement error in the valuation of inventory (based on a statistical sample)
3. an overstatement error in the valuation of accounts receivable (based on a statistical sample)
4. an error in the sales cutoff at year-end (a sale in 2007 recorded in 2006)

A Schedule of Unadjusted Misstatements working paper is shown in Exhibit 3–3.

Step 3: Estimate the Likely Misstatement and Compare to Materiality   The first column in the working paper shown in Exhibit 3–3 gives the reference to the working paper where the information regarding the misstatement is detailed. The second column provides a brief description of the nature of the misstatement. The third column gives the amount of the identified misstatement and the fourth column projects this to the likely misstatement. Note in the case of items (1) and (4) that the projected amount is the same as the identified amount since they are the result of 100 percent examination. In the case of inventory, the auditors tested items making up one-half of the total account balance. The identified error of $60,000 was projected on a pro rata basis to be $120,000 in the total population. In the case of accounts receivable, the auditors tested items making up 80 percent of the total account balance. The identified error of $10,000 was projected on a pro rata basis to be $12,500 in the total population. Columns five through nine contain the proposed adjusting entries to correct the LMs.

The effect of the LAM would be to reduce NIBT by $178,550 ($22,350 + $156,200). Since preliminary materiality was established at $1,200,000 it would appear that the financial statements are not materially misstated. However, before making a final decision, the auditor considers further possible misstatements that may be due to sampling errors, non-sampling errors and misstatements that carry forward from the prior year. If the maximum possible misstatement was in excess of the materiality limit, the auditor may consider requesting the client to make one or more of the proposed adjusting entries. In our example, the client may be willing, in the interest of accuracy, to make adjustments for the identified errors

EXHIBIT 3–3

Example Working Paper for Estimating Likely Misstatements

EarthWear

EARTHWEAR CLOTHIERS
Schedule of Unadjusted Misstatements
12/31/06

Working Paper Ref.	Identified Misstatement Description	Amount	Likely Misstatement	Assets	Liabilities	Proposed Adjustment Dr(Cr) Equity	Revenues	Expenses
N10	under accrual of payroll liabilities	36,200	36,200		(36,200)			36,200
F20	overstatement of inventory	60,000	120,000	(120,000)				120,000
R10	overstatement of accounts receivable	10,000	12,500	(12,500)			12,500	
R15	sales cutoff error	9,850	9,850	(9,850)			9,850	
				(142,350)	36,200		22,350	156,200

Conclusion: Based on the above analysis, the account balances for EarthWear Clothiers are fairly stated in accordance with GAAP.

in accruals and cutoff, and for the identified portion of the errors in inventory and accounts receivable. Even if the client does not make the adjustments, the value of MPM is clearly below the materiality limit, and the auditor is able to conclude, as is noted on the bottom of the working paper, that the account balances are fairly stated in accordance with GAAP.

Another reason for the client to make adjustments to correct non-material misstatements is that any errors not adjusted will be brought forward to the next year where their amount will be cumulated with identified and projected misstatements from that year's audit to determine whether the total of unadjusted misstatements is material.

Allocating Materiality

The *CICA Handbook* discusses materiality from an overall perspective, as it applies to the financial statements as a whole. However, the auditor must, at least implicitly, consider materiality as it applies at the level of the individual account, group of accounts, or class of transactions. In our example, suppose that there was a likely aggregate misstatement of $900,000, all in the inventory account. While that amount is below the threshold of materiality for the financial statements as a whole, without even considering further possible misstatements, it is a very significant item in relation to the inventory account. To assist the auditor, many firms have developed methods for allocating materiality to individual accounts, groups of accounts, or classes of transactions. This allocated materiality is called "tolerable misstatement." The allocation is done taking into consideration such factors as the magnitude of the account relative to the financial statements as a whole, the expectation of error, and the relative cost to audit the account balance or class of transactions.

The process of allocation may be done judgementally or quantitatively. One straightforward method is to allocate materiality for balance sheet accounts in proportion to the size of the account relative to the sum of balance sheet assets and liabilities. It is not necessary to allocate any portion of total materiality to items that will be audited 100 percent. This would typically include liabilities such as bank loans outstanding or lines of credit and most equity accounts (which are a result of calculations). Such items are excluded from the sum. Retained earnings is excluded because it is a residual amount. Other, more sophisticated models have been proposed in the literature as well.[3]

Audit Risk and the Risk of Material Misstatement

LO 5>   Risk is the second fundamental concept that underlies the audit process. The overall risk faced by an auditor engaged to audit a set of financial statements is *audit risk*, which is defined by the *CICA Handbook* in paragraph 5095.08, as follows:

> [Audit risk is] the risk that the auditor expresses an inappropriate audit opinion when the financial statements are materially misstated.

[3]For example see G. R. Zuber, R. K. Elliot, W. R. Kinney Jr., and J. J. Leisenning, "Using Materiality in Audit Planning," *Journal of Accountancy* (March 1983), pp. 42–55.

In simple terms, audit risk is the risk that an auditor will issue an unqualified opinion on materially misstated financial statements. Audit risk is discussed throughout the remainder of this chapter.

Before discussing audit risk, one additional form of risk that should be mentioned is *auditor business risk,* which can be defined as follows:

> Auditor business risk is the auditor's exposure to loss or injury to his or her professional practice from litigation, adverse publicity, or other events arising in connection with financial statements audited and reported on.

Auditor business risk relates to an auditor's exposure to financial loss and damage to his or her professional reputation. For example, an auditor may conduct an audit in accordance with GAAS and still be sued by the client or a third party. Although the auditor has complied with professional standards and may ultimately win the lawsuit, his or her professional reputation may be damaged in the process by the negative publicity. Auditor business risk cannot be directly controlled by the auditor, although some control can be exercised through the careful acceptance and retention of clients. *Client business risk* is broader than inherent risk and encompasses more than the risk of material misstatement of the financial statements. Recent events, such as the collapse of Enron, WorldCom, and Global Crossings, and the demise of the Arthur Andersen firm, have provided a dramatic illustration of the potential negative consequences of both dimensions of business risk. These events will be discussed in more detail in Chapter 18, "Legal Liability."

The auditor should plan the engagement so that audit risk will be at an acceptably low level before issuing an opinion on the financial statements. The determination of audit risk requires considerable judgement on the part of the auditor.

The auditor's first step in determining an acceptably low level of audit risk is to assess the risk of material misstatement in the financial statements. Figure 3–2 shows that the assessment of the risk of material misstatement is a function of the two dimensions of *inherent risk* (IR) and *control risk* (CR). Inherent risk is defined in section 5095 of the *CICA Handbook* as "… the susceptibility of an assertion to a misstatement that could be material, … assuming that there are no related controls." Inherent risk may be due to internal factors (for example an estimate that is the result of a complex, rather than simple, calculation) or external factors (for example, technological developments in the client's industry leading to product obsolescence and consequently overstatement of inventory value). Control risk is defined as "… the risk that a misstatement that could occur in an assertion and that could be material, … will not be prevented, or detected and corrected, on a timely basis by the entity's internal control."

The *CICA Handbook* contains two major sections that deal with the auditor's assessment of, and response to, risk. The first is section 5141, "Understanding the entity and its environment and assessing the risks of material misstatement." The three main risk assessment procedures identified are enquiries of management and others within the entity, analysis, and observation and inspection. With respect to enquiries, examples of identified groups are internal audit personnel, employees involved in initiating, processing, or recording complex or unusual transactions, and those with governance responsibilities. The objective of the auditor in this process

FIGURE 3–2

The Relationship of the Risk of Material Misstatement Due to Error or Fraud to the Determination of Audit Risk

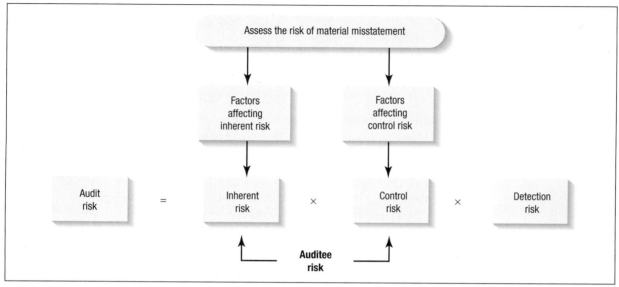

is to identify the extent of enquiries, and the individuals within the entity to whom those enquiries should be directed, that would help the auditor to identify the risks of material misstatement.

With respect to analysis, the section reinforces the requirement for the auditor to use analytical procedures as part of the planning process, and reinforces the value of analytical procedures in identifying the risk of material misstatement.

Observation and inspection relates to entity activities and operations, business plans and strategies, and documents, records, and manuals. "Walk-throughs" (tracing transactions through the information systems relevant to financial reporting from beginning to end) may be appropriate. Reference to outside sources such as industry-related information may also be appropriate.

There is also an explicit requirement for the members of the audit team to discuss the susceptibility of the entity to material misstatement of the financial statements. Major benefits of such discussion are, first, that they provide an opportunity for more experienced and knowledgeable audit team members to share their insights about the entity, and second, the sharing among team members of information obtained throughout the audit may affect assessment of the risks of material misstatement and the selection of audit procedures performed to address those risks.

A final point is that in an ongoing auditor–client relationship, if the auditor intends to use information about the entity obtained in prior periods, the auditor needs to ensure that such information is still relevant in the current audit. Being alert for changes, rather than assuming constancy, is an important step in assessing the risk of material misstatement.

The second part of section 5141 focuses on the importance of understanding the entity and its environment. Understanding the nature of the entity encompasses such things as:

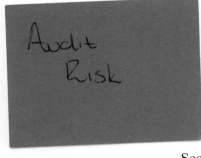

- understanding the entity's application of accounting policies
- considering whether the accounting policies are appropriate
- understanding the entity's strategies, objectives, and related business risks
- understanding the entity's process of identifying and responding to business risks
- understanding the entity's process for measuring and reviewing its financial performance

Section 5141 requires the auditor to perform risk assessment procedures to obtain an understanding of the components of internal control. The understanding of internal control forms the basis for the auditor to identify types of potential misstatements, consider factors that affect the risk of material misstatement, and design the nature, extent, and timing of further audit procedures.

Internal controls that pertain to the objective of preparing financial statements that present fairly in all material respects, are broken down into five components:

- control environment
- entity's risk assessment process
- information system and related business processes
- control procedures
- monitoring of controls

The components of internal control are discussed in detail in Chapter 6; including a brief discussion of internal control in an IT environment.

The third major part of the section addresses the auditor's responsibilities for assessing the risk of material misstatement at the financial statement level, and at the assertion level for classes of transactions, account balances, and disclosures. In order to assess the risks of material misstatement, the auditor should use the information gathered as a result of performing risk assessment procedures, and:

- identify risks by considering the entity and its environment, including relevant controls that relate to the risks, and by considering the classes of transactions, account balances, and disclosures in the financial statements
- relate the identified risks to what can go wrong at the assertion level
- consider whether the risks are of a magnitude that could result in a material misstatement of the financial statements
- consider the likelihood that the risks will result in a material misstatement of the financial statements

Finally, the auditor is required to consider which of the risks identified in the process of the assessment of the risk of material misstatement may require special audit consideration. Some of the characteristics that may indicate significant risks requiring special consideration are:

- whether the risk is a risk of fraud
- the possibility that the risk may give rise to multiple misstatements
- the complexity of transactions or number of non-routine transactions that may give rise to the risk
- whether the risk involves significant transactions that are outside the normal course of business for the entity, or that otherwise appear to be unusual given the auditor's understanding of the entity and its environment
- greater management intervention
- significant related party transactions

In order to substantiate compliance with the requirements of the section, the auditor should document:

- discussion among the audit team regarding the susceptibility of the entity's financial statements to material misstatement due to error or fraud, including how and when the discussion occurred, the audit team members who participated, and the subject matter discussed
- understanding obtained regarding the characteristics of the entity and its environment, including the characteristics of the internal control components, to assess the risk of material misstatement in the financial statements; the sources of information from which the understanding was obtained; and the risk assessment procedures
- controls evaluated
- results of the risk assessment both at the financial statement level and at the assertion level

CICA Handbook, section 5143, "The auditor's procedures in response to assessed risks," requires the auditor to determine an overall response to the risks of material misstatement at the financial statement level and it provides guidance for the auditor in determining the nature, extent, and timing of audit procedures to respond to assessed risks at the assertion level to reduce audit risk to an acceptably low level. It emphasizes that it may not be possible to reduce the risk of material misstatement at the assertion level with evidence derived from substantive tests only.

The lower bottom right corner of Figure 3–2 shows the third component of audit risk, known as *detection risk* (DR). Detection risk is defined in the *CICA Handbook* as "… the risk that the auditor's procedures will not detect misstatements that exist … that could be material." As is shown in Figure 3–2, audit risk can be considered to be a multiplicative function of inherent risk, control risk, and detection risk. Since the auditor cannot do anything to change the risk of material misstatement due to inherent and/or control factors, the objective of the standard is to provide guidance for the auditor in determining the nature, timing, and extent of substantive audit procedures in order to reduce the likelihood, to the extent practicable, of not discovering material misstatements in the financial statements. Thus the appropriate amount of substantive testing (see Chapter 2, LO 9) for the auditor to employ is a result of the auditor's assessment of the risk of

FIGURE 3–3

Substantive Work-Level Matrix

		Auditor's assessment of control risk is		
		High	Moderate	Low
Auditor's assessment of inherent risk is	High	High	High	Moderate
	Moderate	High	Moderate	Low
	Low	Moderate	Low	Low

material misstatement discussed in the standard. The acceptable level of detection risk is that which, when combined with the assessed risk of material misstatement resulting from the application of the above standard, results in the overall level of audit risk being reduced to an acceptably low level. The matrix in Figure 3–3 illustrates one approach the auditor could use in determining the appropriate amount of substantive testing.

The work levels are intended to be illustrative only—each of the levels refers to a range of work effort and the ranges may overlap, particularly where the work level is indicated as being moderate.

In summary, auditing standards have moved away from the traditional "audit risk model," used for risk assessment by the profession for many years. The dimensions of IR, CR, and DR are still present but now the emphasis is on consideration of a more broadly defined inherent risk (which includes elements of business risk) and control risk. However, it is also clear that the concept of audit risk as being composed of inherent risk, control risk, and detective risk will be central to the profession for the foreseeable future.

The Auditor's Responsibility to Consider Fraud

LO 6 〉 A misstatement of the financial statements[4] may consist of any of the following:

- A difference between the amount, classification, or presentation of a reported financial statement element, account, or item and the amount, classification, or presentation that would have been reported under generally accepted accounting principles.
- The omission of a financial statement element, account, or item.
- A financial statement disclosure that is not presented in accordance with generally accepted accounting principles.
- The omission of information required to be disclosed in accordance with generally accepted accounting principles.

The auditor has a responsibility to plan and perform the audit to obtain reasonable assurance about whether the financial statements are free of material misstatement, whether caused by error or fraud. *Errors* are

---

[4]See A. Eilifsen and W. F. Messier, Jr., "Auditor Detection of Misstatements: A Review and Integration of Empirical Research," *Journal of Accounting Literature* 2000 (19), pp. 1–43 for a detailed review of research studies that have examined auditor-detected misstatements.

The Fraud Risk Identification Process

Figure 3–4 presents a diagram of the fraud risk identification process. The first part of the process is the inputs—the sources of information used to identify risks. Within this first part of the process the auditor should perform the following steps to obtain information to identify the risks of material misstatement due to fraud:

- Discussion among the audit team members regarding the risks of material misstatement due to fraud.
- Enquire of management and others about their views on the risks of fraud and how it is addressed.
- Consider any unusual or unexpected relationships that have been identified in performing analytical procedures in planning the audit.
- Understand the client's period-end closing process and investigate unexpected period-end adjustments.
- Consider whether one or more fraud risk factors exist that should be considered in evaluating the risk of material misstatement due to fraud.
- Consider any other information that might indicate the possibility of fraud.

unintentional misstatements or omissions of amounts or disclosures and may involve

- mistakes in gathering or processing data from which financial statements are prepared
- unreasonable accounting estimates arising from oversight or misinterpretation of facts
- mistakes in the application of accounting principles relating to amount, classification, manner of presentation, or disclosure

Section 5135 of the *CICA Handbook*, "The auditor's responsibility to consider fraud," covers in detail the auditor's responsibility with respect to the detection of fraud in the financial statements. *Fraud*, from the auditor's perspective, involves intentional misstatements that can be classified into two types: (1) misstatements arising from fraudulent financial reporting and (2) misstatements arising from misappropriation of assets. Thus, the primary distinction between errors and fraud is whether the misstate-

Table 3–3	**Risk Factors Relating to Incentives/Pressures**

a. Financial stability or profitability is threatened by economic, industry, or entity operating conditions, such as (or as indicated by)
- High degree of competition or market saturation, accompanied by declining margins.
- High vulnerability to rapid changes, such as changes in technology, product obsolescence, or interest rates.
- Significant declines in customer demand and increasing business failures in either the industry or overall economy.
- Operating losses making the threat of bankruptcy, foreclosure, or hostile takeover imminent.
- Recurring negative cash flows from operations or an inability to generate cash flows from operations while reporting earnings and earnings growth.
- Rapid growth or unusual profitability, especially compared with that of other companies in the same industry.
- New accounting, statutory, or regulatory requirements.

b. Excessive pressure exists for management to meet requirements or expectations of third parties due to
- Profitability or trend level expectations of investment analysts, institutional investors, significant creditors, or other external parties (particularly expectations that are unduly aggressive or unrealistic) including expectations created by management in, for example, overly optimistic press releases or annual report messages.
- Need to obtain additional debt or equity financing to stay competitive—including financing of major research and development or capital expenditures.
- Marginal ability to meet exchange listing requirements or debt repayment or other debt covenant requirements.
- Perceived or real adverse effects of reporting poor financial results on significant pending transactions, such as business combinations or contract awards.

c. Management or the board of directors' personal financial situation is threatened by the entity's financial performance arising from the following:
- Significant financial interests in the entity.
- Significant portions of their compensation (e.g., bonuses, stock options) being contingent upon achieving aggressive targets for stock price, operating results, financial position, or cash flow.
- Personal guarantees of significant debts of the entity.

d. There is excessive pressure on management or operating personnel to meet financial targets set up by the board of directors or management, including sales or profitability incentive goals.

Fraudulent Financial Reporting   Tables 3–3 to 3–6 present the risk factors related to each category of conditions for the potential for fraudulent financial reporting. Table 3–3 contains numerous risk factors that, if present, may suggest that management and others have incentives to manipulate financial reporting. For example, the entity may be facing increased competition that results in declining profit margins. Similarly, in the high-technology sector, rapid changes in technology can affect the profitability and the fair market value of products. Entities that have recurring operating losses and negative cash flow from operations may face bankruptcy, foreclosure, or takeover. In each of these situations, management may have incentives to manipulate reported earnings. Management (or the board of directors) may also be facing pressures to maintain the entity's reported earnings to meet analysts' forecasts because their bonuses or personal wealth is tied to the entity's stock price (see Exhibit 3–4).

Management must also have the opportunity to commit the fraud. Table 3–4 lists the opportunities that may be available to management

EXHIBIT 3–4

Nortel Networks Terminates CEO, CFO, and Controller

On April 28, 2004, Nortel Networks fired its CEO, CFO, and controller "with cause." The SEC had been looking into Nortel's use of reserve accounts and trying to determine if Nortel released those reserves back into earnings for legitimate reasons. Speculation suggests that Nortel's problems may have arisen as employees sought ways to participate in a bonus program tied to Nortel's 2003 turnaround after years of heavy losses. Known within the company as the "Return to Profitability" bonus program, Nortel paid out $300 million in employee bonuses in 2003, with approximately $80 million paid to senior executives. One analyst stated that management was too aggressive with accounting accruals in order to show profitability and receive bonuses.

Sources: Nortel Networks, News Release, "Nortel Networks Announces William Owens as New President and CEO" (www.nortelnetworks.com); and M. Heinzl, D. Solomon, and J. S. Lublin, "Nortel Board Fires CEO and Others," *The Wall Street Journal* (April 29, 2004), pp. A3, A6.

Table 3–4	Risk Factors Relating to Opportunities

a. The nature of the industry or the entity's operations provide opportunities to engage in fraudulent financial reporting due to

  • Significant related-party transactions not in the ordinary course of business or with related entities not audited or audited by another firm.

  • A strong financial presence or ability to dominate a certain industry sector that allows the entity to dictate terms or conditions to suppliers or customers that may result in inappropriate or non-arm's-length transactions.

  • Assets, liabilities, revenues, or expenses based on significant estimates that involve subjective judgements or uncertainties that are difficult to corroborate.

  • Significant, unusual, or highly complex transactions, especially those close to year-end that pose difficult "substance over form" questions.

  • Significant operations located or conducted across international borders where differing business environments and cultures exist.

  • Significant bank accounts or subsidiary or branch operations in tax-haven jurisdictions for which there appears to be no clear business justification.

b. There is ineffective monitoring of management due to

  • Domination of management by a single person or small group (in a non-owner-managed business) without compensating controls.

  • Ineffective board of director or audit committee oversight over the financial reporting process and internal control.

c. There is a complex or unstable organizational structure as evidenced by—

  • Difficulty in determining the organization or individuals that have controlling interest in the entity.

  • Overly complex organizational structure involving unusual legal entities or managerial lines of authority.

  • High turnover of senior management, counsel, or board members.

d. Internal control components are deficient due to

  • Inadequate monitoring of controls, including automated controls and controls over interim financial reporting (where external reporting is required).

  • High turnover rates or employment of ineffective accounting, internal audit, or information technology staff.

  • Ineffective accounting and information systems including situations involving reportable conditions.

Where are its major locations?	Calgary, Alberta, is the main corporate location. EarthWear also has phone and distribution centres in the United Kingdom, Germany, Japan, and the United States.	No. None of these country locations poses threats to EarthWear as a result of expropriation or limits on repatriation of earnings.
What are the entity's major assets?	The major assets of the company are inventory; property, plant, and equipment; and its customer mailing list.	No.

(continues)

Table 3–10	**Examples of Circumstances or Information Encountered During the Audit That May Indicate Illegal Acts**

- Unauthorized transactions, improperly recorded transactions, or transactions not recorded in a complete or timely manner.
- Unusually large cash receipts or payments, transfers to numbered bank accounts or accounts in financial institutions with which the entity normally does not do business.
- Unsupported or unexplained payments to consultants, affiliates, employees, or government officials.

(continued)

Risk Factors	Description/Response	Any Remaining Risk
Assignment of Authority and Responsibility		
Does adequate computer systems documentation indicate the controls for authorizing transactions and approving systems changes?	Yes.	No.
Is there adequate documentation of data processing controls?	Yes.	No.
Communications		
Does management communicate employees' duties and control responsibilities in an effective manner?	Yes.	No.
Does communication flow across the organization adequately to enable people to discharge their responsibilities effectively?	Yes.	No.

CLIENT NAME: EARTHWEAR CLOTHIERS
Entity and Environment Category: Measurement and Performance
Year ended: December 31, 2006

Completed by: _____
Reviewed by: _____

Risk Factor	Description/Response	Any Remaining Risk
Does the entity have a performance measurement system?	Yes. The company manages performance through a business plan and a strong budgeting process. Senior management meets at least monthly to discuss the budget and corporate performance.	No.
If so, what key performance indicators (KPIs) are used by management to measure performance?	Profitability, ROI, variances from budgets.	
Does the entity benchmark its performance against its industry and major competitors?	Yes.	
Does the entity consider financial analysts' research and earnings reports?	Yes.	No.
Does the information system give management the necessary reports on the entity's performance relative to established objectives, including internal and external information?	Yes.	No.
How often are performance reports prepared?	Weekly.	No.
Is the information provided to the right people in sufficient detail and in time to enable them to carry out their responsibilities?	Yes.	No.
Are communication channels established for people to report suspected improprieties?	Yes.	No.
Does the entity have an internal audit function?	Yes.	No.
Are recommendations made by the internal and external auditors implemented?	Yes.	No.

REVIEW QUESTIONS

LO 1,2 | **3-1** | The opinion paragraph contains the term *in all material respects*. How should users of the audit report interpret this term?

1,2,3 | **3-2** | Why is it important for audit firms to develop policies and procedures for establishing materiality?

3 | **3-3** | List and describe the three major steps in applying materiality to an audit.

2,3,4 | **3-4** | Discuss why total assets or revenues might be better bases for determining materiality than net income after taxes.

2,3,4 | **3-5** | Give three examples of qualitative factors that might affect the preliminary judgement about materiality.

2,3 | **3-6** | List four qua... ...er when evaluating th...

5 | **3-7** | Explain the t...

5 | **3-8** | Distinguish b...

5 | **3-9** | Define each c...

5 | **3-10** | Discuss the r... ...isk.

5 | **3-11** | How does cli... ...ment of the risk of ma...

5 | **3-12** | What type of... ...assess client busines...

6 | **3-13** | Distinguish b... ...each.

6 | **3-14** | List the three ... ...that affect the auditor's assessment of the presence of material misstatements in the financial statements due to fraudulent financial reporting, and give examples from each group.

6 | **3-15** | List the three groups of factors that relate to the misappropriation of assets. Give examples from each group.

MULTIPLE-CHOICE QUESTIONS FROM PROFESSIONAL EXAMINATIONS

Unless otherwise indicated, these multiple-choice questions were adapted from the CPA examinations, courtesy of the American Institute of Certified Public Accountants.

2,3 | **3-16** | In considering materiality for planning purposes for a for-profit entity, an auditor believes that misstatements aggregating $10,000 would have a material effect on an entity's income statement but that misstatements would have to aggregate $20,000 to materially affect the balance sheet. Ordinarily, it would be appropriate to design auditing procedures that would be expected to detect misstatements that aggregate

a. $10,000.

b. $15,000.

c. $20,000.

d. $30,000.

b. What are some common relationships and other considerations used by the auditor in judging materiality?

c. Identify how planning the scope of an audit might be affected by the auditor's concept of materiality.

(AICPA, adapted)

1,2,5 > 3-27 The auditor should consider audit risk and materiality when planning and performing an examination of financial statements in accordance with generally accepted auditing standards. Audit risk and materiality should also be considered together in determining the nature, timing, and extent of auditing procedures and in evaluating the results of those procedures.

Required:

a. 1 Define *audit risk*.

2. Describe its dimensions of inherent risk, control risk, and detection risk.

3. Explain how these components are interrelated.

b. 1. Define *materiality*.

2. Discuss the factors affecting its determination.

3. Describe the relationship between materiality for planning purposes and materiality for evaluation purposes.

(AICPA, adapted)

2,3 > 3-28 Jim Johnson, an audit manager, is planning the audit for Commodore Container Corporation (CCC), a major producer of containerboard and corrugated boxes. At December 31, 2006, CCC's unaudited balances for accounts receivable, inventory, and plant assets (net) are $102.5 million, $65.3 million, and $591 million, respectively. Total assets amount to $823.9 million. Unaudited net income is $4.5 million on revenues for the year of $778 million. Total current liabilities are $43.6 million, and long-term debt is $670 million.

Required:

a. Make a preliminary judgement about materiality for CCC using the bases included in Exhibit 3–1.

b. Allocate the preliminary judgement about materiality to the accounts, using their relative size.

1,2,3,5 > 3-29 Relco is a high-technology company, which, over its 13-year history, has grown rapidly. Relco operates in an industry characterized by heavy expenditures in research and development and products that are regularly updated and revised. Despite aggressive competition, by the end of 2005 its total assets had reached $250 million, revenues had reached $500 million, and net income was $50 million.

During the second quarter of 2006, Relco acquired a major division from another company in exchange for $150 million in cash, stock, and debt. The transaction was accounted for as a purchase with $100 million attributed to identifiable assets such as inventory ($30 million) and property, plant, and equipment ($70 million), and the remainder to goodwill. The acquisition represents an effort by Relco to broaden its product line in order to compete more effectively with its main rival in the industry. The acquired division develops and manufactures a product, Wordup, which, while distinct from Relco's current offerings, can be bundled with Relco's existing products.

The Wordup product has historically yielded a 30 percent return on assets. However, recent innovations by Relco's rival, which were made public late in the third quarter of 2006, suggest that the industry is headed into a period of intense competition. In the past Relco has developed its major products internally and this purchase represents the first time Relco has acquired significant technology from another company. For the end of 2006 Relco's trial balance shows total assets of $420 million (including $45 million of Wordup inventory), revenues of $700 million, and net income of $60 million. These results include the eight months of 2006 following the Wordup acquisition. You have been assigned to make some of the risk assessments for the 2006 audit of Relco.

Required:

a. Based on the above facts, identify three balance sheet accounts with at least one "red flag" that the auditor should consider as indicating a high inherent risk. Describe the red flags for each account and the type of misstatements about which the auditor would be concerned.

b. Make a preliminary assessment of materiality for this audit and justify your conclusion.

c. The Wordup inventory is to be used as security for a loan and is the subject of a special report. Make a materiality assessment for the Wordup inventory.

(CGA-Canada, adapted)

1,2,3> 3-30 You are the senior in charge of the audit engagement of Valve Control Ltd. ("Valve"), a company that sells valves to the pulp and paper industry. Valve is a publicly listed company that has a September 30 year-end.

In order to prepare for the audit you have obtained the financial statements (see Exhibit 1). Through discussions with the controller and review of the financial statements, you discover that due to low demand in the pulp market, Valve's 2006 business is significantly lower than the previous year.

The materiality level for the previous year was $75,000.

Required:

a. Estimate the preliminary materiality for the Valve audit. Provide both quantitative and qualitative analysis.

b. Assuming the 2006 materiality is lower than the previous year, what additional procedures will be required?

c. Discuss whether quantitative guidelines should be published to assist auditors in determining materiality.

(ICABC, adapted)

b. Close-Moor Stores has experienced slower sales during the last year. There is a new vice president of finance and a new controller. Mr. Musiciak, president of the company, has a reputation for hard-nosed business tactics, and he is always concerned with meeting forecast earnings.

c. MaxiWrite Corporation is one of several companies engaged in the manufacture of high-speed, high-capacity disk drives. The industry is very competitive and subject to quick changes in technology. MaxiWrite's operating results would place the company in the second quartile in terms of profitability and financial position. The company has never been the leader in the industry, with its products typically slightly behind the industry leader's in terms of performance.

d. The Pond City Credit Union has been your client for the past two years. During that period you have had numerous arguments with the president and the controller over a number of accounting issues. The major issue has related to the credit union's reserve for loan losses and the value of collateral. Your prior audits have indicated that a significant adjustment is required each year to the loan loss reserves.

5> **3-35** Bart Green is considering audit risk at the financial statement level in planning the audit of National Federal Bank's (NFB) financial statements for the year ended December 31, 2006. Audit risk at the financial statement level is influenced by the risk of material misstatements, which may be indicated by a combination of factors related to management, the industry, and the entity. In assessing such factors Green has gathered the following information concerning NFB's environment.

Company Profile

NFB is a federally insured bank that has been consistently more profitable than the industry average by marketing mortgages on properties in a prosperous rural area, which has experienced considerable growth in recent years. NFB packages its mortgages and sells them to large mortgage investment trusts. Despite a recent volatility in interest rates, NFB has been able to continue selling its mortgages as a source of new lendable funds.

NFB's board of directors is controlled by Smith, the majority shareholder, who also acts as the chief executive officer. Management at the bank's branch offices has authority for directing and controlling NFB's operations and is compensated based on branch profitability. The internal auditor reports directly to Harris, a minority shareholder, who also acts as chairman of the board's audit committee.

The accounting department has experienced little turnover in personnel during the five years Green has audited NFB. NFB's formula consistently underestimates the allowance for loan losses, but its controller has always been receptive to Green's suggestions to increase the allowance during each engagement.

Recent Developments

During 2006, NFB opened a branch office in a suburban town 30 miles from its principal place of business. Although this branch is not yet profitable due to competition from several well-established regional banks, management believes that the branch will be profitable by 2007.

Also during 2006, NFB increased the efficiency of its accounting operations by installing a new, sophisticated computer system.

Required:

Based only on the information given, describe the factors that most likely would affect the risk of material misstatements. Indicate whether each factor increases or decreases the risk. Use the following format:

Environmental Factor	Effect on Risk of Material Misstatements
Branch management has authority for directing and controlling operations.	Increase

(AICPA, adapted)

DISCUSSION CASES

6 **3-36** **Cendant Corporation (Cendant).** On December 17, 1997, CUC International merged with HFS Incorporated to form Cendant. Cendant operated primarily in three business segments—alliance marketing, travel, and real estate services. Cendant franchises included Century 21, Coldwell Banker, Avis, Days Inn, and Ramada Inn. Cendant, headquartered in Stamford, CT, and Parsippany, NJ, had nearly 40,000 employees, operated in over 100 countries, and made more than 100 million customer contacts annually.

In April 1998, Cendant issued a press release stating that CUC had committed a massive accounting fraud. The press release stated that 1997 earnings were overstated by as much as $115 million. Cendant's audit committee hired Arthur Andersen (AA) to investigate the fraud. AA's report, issued in August 1998, revealed that CUC's chief executive officer (CEO) and chief operating officer (COO) created a culture that accepted fraudulent accounting activities and failed to implement appropriate controls and procedures that might have deterred or detected the fraud. Additional details from AA's report are summarized below:[5]

- In the three years 1995–97, CUC's operating income before taxes was improperly inflated by $500 million, which was more than one-third of its reported pretax income for those years.
- Though many of the improprieties occurred in CUC's biggest subsidiary, Comp-U-Card, they reached to 16 others as well. No fewer than 20 employees participated in the wrongdoing.

---

[5]C. J. Loomis, "Lies, Damned Lies, and Managed Earnings," *Fortune*, August 2, 1999, pp. 74–92.

Required:

In groups of two or three students, prepare a report (five to seven pages) on Enron. The report should include the following:

- An overview of Enron, including the company's business risks.
- A description of the problems(s) that occurred at Enron.
- An analysis of what went wrong and why the auditors did not detect/report the problems.

Audit Evidence: Types of Evidence and Working Paper Documentation

Chapter **4**

Learning Objectives

Upon completion of this chapter, you will be able to

1 Explain the relationship between audit evidence and the auditor's report.

2 Describe management assertions about components in the financial statements.

3 Describe the three major purposes of performing audit procedures.

4 Analyze the relationship between management assertions and audit procedures.

5 Outline the basic concepts of audit evidence.

6 Identify and define the types of audit evidence.

7 Describe the reliability of the types of evidence.

8 Explain the relationship of types of evidence to management assertions and audit activities.

9 Develop an understanding of the contents, types, and ownership of audit working papers.

RELEVANT ACCOUNTING AND ASSURANCE PRONOUNCEMENTS

CICA Handbook, **section 5141,** Understanding the entity and its environment and assessing the risks of material misstatement

CICA Handbook, **section 5142,** Materiality

CICA Handbook, **section 5143,** The auditor's procedures in response to assessed risks

CICA Handbook, **section 5145,** Documentation

CICA Handbook, **section 5150,** Planning

CICA Handbook, **section 5300,** Audit evidence

CICA Handbook, **section 5301,** Analysis

CICA Handbook, **section 5303,** Confirmation

CICA Handbook, **section 5305,** Audit of accounting estimates

SHOW ME THE EVIDENCE

One of the biggest scams of the 1980s, costing investors and creditors, by some estimates, over $100 million, was ZZZZ Best. ZZZZ Best, started by 16-year-old Barry Minkow, began as a small, one-man, carpet cleaning business and in the space of two years grew to be a major player in commercial building restoration, with a market capitalization of more than $200 million. The problem was that the restoration company never existed. Minkow and his co-conspirators, created a multimillion dollar company on paper, and were able to convince the SEC, a major Wall Street investment brokerage house, a prestigious law firm, and last but not least, an international public accounting firm, that the company was real. Minkow and his cronies were able to perpetrate this massive fraud by fabricating documentary evidence such as contracts and invoices, obtaining the collusion of individuals outside the company to provide evidence on their behalf, and misleading the auditors regarding the physical evidence observed. Minkow finally stretched things too far and

his elaborate scheme collapsed. He was tried and convicted on fifty-seven counts of securities fraud and sentenced to twenty-five years in prison. When the scheme came unravelled and the truth about ZZZZ Best came to light, the auditors were roundly criticized for their overwillingness to accept evidence provided by Minkow and other company personnel without subjecting its truthfulness to any critical scrutiny.

These events sent a strong wake-up call to the profession. Had the auditors really made the connection between the evidence they obtained and the different claims that were explicit and implicit on the financial statements of ZZZZ Best, they might have realized that the evidence was highly incomplete and lacking in credibility. That is the focus of this chapter—the different *management assertions* about the accounts and items in the financial statements, the *audit procedures* that may be employed to confirm or disconfirm those assertions and the connections between them.

The Relationship of Audit Evidence to the Audit Report

LO 1 ▷ *CICA Handbook,* section 5300, provides the basic framework for the auditor's understanding of evidence and its use to support the auditor's opinion on the financial statements. In reaching an opinion on the financial statements, the auditor gathers evidence by conducting audit procedures to test the relevant management assertions. The evidence gathered from the audit procedures is used to determine the fairness of the financial statements and the type of audit report to be issued. Figure 4–1 presents an overview of the relationships among the financial statements, management assertions about components of the financial statements, audit procedures, and the audit report. More specifically, there is a top-down relationship from the financial statements to the audit procedures. The financial statements reflect management's assertions about the various financial statement components. The auditor identifies the relevant management assertion(s) for the component and then conducts audit procedures to gather evidence to test whether the assertions are valid. The application of audit procedures provides the evidence that supports the auditor's report.

Auditors typically divide financial statements into components or segments in order to manage the audit. A component can be a financial

FIGURE 4–1

An Overview of the
Relationships among
the Financial Statements,
Management Assertions,
Audit Procedures,
and the Audit Report

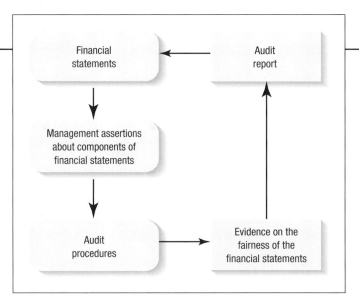

statement account or a business process. As indicated in Chapter 2, the basic processes of most businesses are the *revenue process*, the *purchasing process*, the *human resource management process*, the *inventory management process*, and the *financing process*. Each process involves a variety of important transactions. Business processes also support functions such as sales and postsales services, materials acquisition, production and distribution, and treasury management. Sometimes business processes are referred to as transaction cycles (e.g., revenue cycle or purchasing cycle).

This text focuses on business processes and their related financial statement accounts. Examining business processes and their related accounts allows the auditor to gather evidence by examining the processing of related transactions through the information system from their origin to their ultimate disposition in the accounting journals and ledgers. Later chapters in this text cover each of the major business processes that auditors typically encounter on an engagement. The following two sections expand the discussion of management assertions and audit procedures.

Management Assertions

LO 2>   Management is responsible for the fair presentation of the financial statements. Assertions are expressed or implied representations by management that are reflected in the financial statement components. For example, when the balance sheet contains a line item for accounts receivable of $5 million, management asserts that those receivables exist and have a net realizable value of $5 million. Implicitly, management also asserts that the accounts receivable balance arose from selling goods or services on credit in the normal course of business. In general, the assertions relate to the requirements of generally accepted accounting principles.

Management assertions fall into the following categories:

- Assertions about classes of transactions and events for the period under audit.
- Assertions about account balances at the period end.
- Assertions about presentation and disclosure.

Table 4–1 reproduces the information in section 5300 of the *CICA Handbook* and summarizes the relevant management assertions. The assertions are categorized into those relating to transactions and events during the period under audit, account balances at period end, and those relating to presentation and disclosure. The first category relates primarily to the income statement and the second category to the balance sheet, although there is overlap (for instance the completeness assertion appears in both categories). The third category relates to all of the financial statements.

Assertions about Classes of Transactions and Events during the Period

Occurrence   The occurrence assertion relates to whether all recorded transactions and events have occurred and pertain to the entity. For example, management asserts that all revenue transactions recorded during the period were valid transactions. Occurrence is sometimes also referred to as validity.

Table 4–1   Summary of Management Assertions by Category

Assertions about classes of transactions and events for the period under audit:
- **Occurrence**—transactions and events that have been recorded have occurred and pertain to the entity (sometimes referred to as validity).
- **Completeness**—all transactions and events that should have been recorded have been recorded.
- **Accuracy**—amounts and other data relating to recorded transactions and events have been recorded appropriately.
- **Cutoff**—transactions and events have been recorded in the correct accounting period.
- **Classification**—transactions and events have been recorded in the proper accounts.

Assertions about account balances at the period end:
- **Existence**—assets, liabilities, and equity interests exist.
- **Rights and obligations**—the entity holds or controls the rights to assets, and liabilities are the obligations of the entity.
- **Completeness**—all assets, liabilities and equity interests that should have been recorded have been recorded.
- **Valuation and allocation**—assets, liabilities, and equity interests are included in the financial statements at appropriate amounts, and any resulting valuation or allocation adjustments are appropriately recorded.

Assertions about presentation and disclosure:
- **Occurrence and rights and obligations**—disclosed events, transactions, and other matters have occurred and pertain to the entity.
- **Completeness**—all disclosures that should have been included in the financial statements have been included.
- **Classification and understandability**—financial information is appropriately presented and described, and disclosures are clearly expressed.
- **Accuracy and valuation**—financial and other information are disclosed fairly and at appropriate amounts.

Completeness   The completeness assertion relates to whether all transactions and events that occurred during the period have been recorded. For example, if a client fails to record a valid revenue transaction, the revenue account will be understated. Note that the auditor's concern with the completeness assertion is opposite the concern for occurrence. Failure to meet the completeness assertion results in an understatement in the related account, while invalid recorded amounts result in an overstatement in the related account.

Accuracy   The accuracy assertion addresses whether amounts and other data relating to recorded transactions and events have been recorded appropriately. Generally accepted accounting principles establish the appropriate method for recording a transaction or event. For example, the amount recorded for the cost of a new machine includes its purchase price plus all reasonable costs to install it.

Cutoff   The cutoff assertion relates to whether transactions and events have been recorded in the correct accounting period. The auditor's procedures must ensure that transactions occurring near year-end are recorded in the financial statements in the proper period. For example, the auditor may want to test proper cutoff of revenue transactions at December 31, 2007. The auditor can examine a sample of shipping documents and sales invoices for a few days before and after year-end to test whether the sales transactions are recorded in the proper period. The objective is to determine that all 2007 sales and no 2008 sales have been recorded in 2007. Thus, the auditor examines the shipping documents to ensure that no 2008 sales have been recorded in 2007 and that no 2007 sales are recorded in 2008.

Classification   The classification assertion is concerned with whether transactions and events have been recorded in the proper accounts. For example, management asserts that all direct cost transactions related to inventory have been properly classified in either inventory or as part of cost of sales.

Assertions about Account Balances at the Period End

Existence   The assertion about existence addresses whether assets, liabilities, and equity interests exist at the date of the financial statements. For example, management asserts that inventory shown on the balance sheet exists and is available for sale.

Rights and Obligations   The assertions about rights and obligations address whether the entity holds or controls the rights to assets, and that liabilities are the obligations of the entity. For example, management asserts that the entity has legal title or rights of ownership to the inventory shown on the balance sheet. Similarly, amounts capitalized for leases reflect assertions that the entity has rights to leased property and that the corresponding lease liability represents an obligation of the entity.

Completeness   The assertion about completeness addresses whether all assets, liabilities and equity interests that should have been recorded have been recorded. For example, management implicitly asserts that the amount shown for accounts payable on the balance sheet includes all such liabilities as of the balance sheet date.

Valuation and Allocation   Assertions about valuation or allocation address whether assets, liabilities, and equity interests are included in the financial statements at appropriate amounts and any resulting valuation or allocation adjustments are appropriately recorded. For example, management asserts that inventory is carried at the lower of cost or market value on the balance sheet. Similarly, management asserts that the cost of property, plant, and equipment is systematically allocated to appropriate accounting periods by recognizing amortization expense.

Assertions about Presentation and Disclosure

This category of assertions relates to presentation of information in the financial statements and disclosures in the notes to the financial statements that are directly related to a specific transaction or account balance (e.g., disclosure related to property and equipment) and those that apply to the financial statements in general (e.g., the note for the summary of significant accounting policies).

Occurrence and Rights and Obligations   The assertions about occurrence and rights and obligations address whether disclosed events, transactions, and other matters have occurred and pertain to the entity. For example, when management presents capitalized lease transactions on the balance sheet as leased assets, the related liabilities as long-term debt, and the related note, it is asserting that a lease transaction occurred, it has a right to the leased asset, and it owes the related lease obligation to the lessor. In addition, there is a note disclosure that provides additional information on the lease such as future payments.

Completeness   The completeness assertion relates to whether all disclosures that should have been included in the financial statements have been included. Therefore, management asserts that no material disclosures have been omitted from the notes and other disclosures accompanying the financial statements.

Classification and Understandability   The assertions related to classification and understandability address whether the financial information is appropriately presented and described and disclosures are clearly expressed. For example, management asserts that the portion of long-term debt shown as a current liability will mature in the current year. Similarly, management asserts, through note disclosure, that all major restrictions on the entity resulting from debt covenants are disclosed.

Accuracy and Valuation   The accuracy and valuation assertions address whether financial and other information are disclosed fairly and at appropriate amounts. For example, when management discloses the fair value of financial instruments, it is asserting that these financial instruments are properly valued in accordance with GAAP. In addition, management may disclose in a note other information related to financial instruments.

Before we discuss important characteristics of evidence available to the auditor, pause for a moment to consider the usefulness of the sets of management assertions we have just discussed. The assertions collectively provide a road map for the auditor in determining what evidence to collect regarding various transactions, account balances, and required financial statement disclosures. They also guide the auditor in designing audit procedures to collect the needed evidence, as well as assisting the auditor in evaluating the competence and sufficiency of the evidence. For example, once the auditor is comfortable that he or she has enough good-quality evidence relating to each balance-related assertion for the accounts payable account, the auditor can be satisfied that no important aspect of that account has been neglected. The management assertions help the auditor focus his or her attention on all the various aspects of transactions, account balances, and required disclosures that need to be considered—they help the auditor ensure that "all the bases are covered." As such, the three sets of management assertions constitute a powerful conceptual tool in the auditor's tool kit.

Audit Procedures

LO 3> Audit procedures are specific acts performed by the auditor to gather evidence to determine if specific assertions are being met. Audit procedures are performed to

- Obtain an understanding of the entity and its environment, including its internal control in order to assess the risks of material misstatement at the financial statement and assertion levels. Such audit procedures are referred to as *risk assessment procedures*. These procedures were discussed in Chapter 3.
- Test the operating effectiveness of controls in preventing, or detecting and correcting, material misstatements at the assertion level. Audit procedures performed for this purpose are referred to as *tests of controls*. Tests of controls are discussed in Chapters 5 and 6.
- Detect material misstatements at the assertion level. Such audit procedures are referred to as *substantive procedures*. Substantive procedures include tests of details of transactions, account balances, and disclosures and substantive analytical procedures. Substantive procedures are discussed in detail in Chapter 5 and in each business process chapter.

A set of audit procedures prepared to test assertions for a component of the financial statements is usually referred to as an *audit program*. The reader should note that there is *not* a one-to-one relationship between assertion and audit procedures. In some instances more than one audit procedure is required to test an assertion. Conversely, in some cases an audit procedure provides evidence for more than one assertion. Note that the assertions do not change whether information is processed manually or electronically. However, the methods of applying audit procedures may be influenced by the method of information processing.

How Audit Procedures Relate to Management Assertions

LO 4 ⟩ The following sections highlight the relationship between management assertions and audit procedures in more detail. Some firms identify *audit objectives* as an intermediate step between management assertions and audit procedures. However, following the approach of the *CICA Handbook*, the approach taken in the discussion below proceeds directly from the management assertions to examples of appropriate audit procedures. The identification of audit objectives will be illustrated in later chapters covering the audit of specific business processes.

Audit Procedures Related to Existence and Occurrence

To test the existence of assets, auditors may rely on observation. For example, the auditor may observe the client's physical inventory count to verify that inventory exists. Observation may also be applied to assets such as equipment or fixed assets. As an example of an audit procedure that may be applied to non-physical assets, the auditor may confirm accounts receivable balances directly with the client's customers (the accounts receivable confirmation process will be covered in detail in Chapter 8). As well as providing direct evidence regarding the existence of the asset, confirmation of accounts receivable also provides evidence relating to the occurrence of the sales transactions and associated revenue in the income statement.

The auditor may also use cutoff tests to verify whether the transactions recorded in the account are recorded in the proper period. For example, the auditor can examine a sample of shipping documents and sales invoices for a few days before and after year-end. Since the auditor is usually concerned with overstatement of assets and revenues, the main objective is to ensure, for example, that no 2008 sales have been recorded in 2007. With respect to liabilities and expenses, the auditor's concern focuses on understatement. Thus, the objective of the cutoff test for purchases is to ensure that all 2007 purchases have been properly included in 2007.

Audit Procedures Related to Completeness

To test the completeness assertion for an asset such as accounts receivable, the auditor could compare the total of accounts receivable in the subledger accounts to the accounts receivable control account in the general ledger. If the totals do not agree, for instance if the total of the subledger accounts is greater than the total in the general ledger, some accounts receivable, and the related sales transactions, may not have been properly included in the client's records.

However, the auditor's major concern with regard to completeness relates to the potential understatement of liabilities and expenses. Testing the completeness of liabilities requires the auditor to be more ingenious. For example, to test the completeness of accounts payable, it may not be enough to send confirmation requests to vendors listed in the client's accounts payable subledger accounts. What if the client has simply left the vendor out of the accounts payable? The auditor may wish to review the client's transactions with vendors for the past year to ensure that all important vendors are contacted, even if the client does not show any current accounts payable to them. A most important audit procedure is the search for unrecorded liabilities, a procedure whereby the auditor reviews selected payments made by the client shortly after the year-end to ensure that if the payments were made for goods or services provided prior to year-end, the amount is included in liabilities (e.g., accounts payable) at year-end.

Audit Procedures Related to Rights and Obligations

The management assertion of ownership of an asset may be different from existence and may need to be tested independently. For example, the field-work phase of the audit provides "observation" of a client's premises, but does the client own the land on which the premises are located? To verify the ownership assertion, the auditor may do a title search by requesting a copy of the legal title to the land from the city or municipal authority (or from a company that will contact the relevant authority for its customers). The confirmation of accounts receivable provides partial evidence of ownership as well as existence. The debtor entity is acknowledging their obligation and the right of the auditor to the account. However, note that it is only partial—the debtor would not know it the receivable had been sold or factored.

Audit Procedures Related to Valuation

Testing the valuation assertion for assets, liabilities and shareholders' equity, and the corresponding measurement assertion for revenues and expenses often requires the exercise of substantial professional judgement on the part of the auditor. One example is the valuation of the balance sheet contra account, allowance for doubtful accounts, and the corresponding measurement of bad debt expense. The auditor evaluates management's estimates and assesses the reasonableness of those estimates based on past experience, knowledge of the business and industry, and general economic factors. The results of accounts receivable confirmation requests may also provide information that is relevant to the auditor's assessment of management's estimation. Similarly, the auditor will review management's valuation of inventory to ensure it is carried at the lower of cost or market. For example, inventory obsolescence may be a concern with respect to software manufacturers where new generations of software programs replace older versions in such rapid succession.

In the case of specialized inventory, the auditor may engage the assistance of a specialist to review the valuation. For example, if the client is in the oil and gas industry and its inventory is the value of oil and gas reserves to which it holds legal rights, the auditor may need to engage an independent specialist from that industry for assistance in assessing management's valuation of those reserves.

Audit Procedures Related to Statement Presentation and Disclosure

There are two aspects to proper statement presentation, classification and disclosure. The classification aspect requires that transactions be included in the correct amount and be properly presented in the financial statements. For example, in auditing accounts receivable, the auditor examines the listing of accounts receivable to ensure that receivables from affiliates, officers, directors, or other related parties are classified separately from trade receivables. If some portion of the long-term debt is payable within the next year, that amount should be reclassified to current liabilities.

To audit the disclosure aspect of statement presentation assertion, the auditor can review the financial statements to ensure that all required financial statement and note disclosures are made. For example, if accounts receivable are pledged as security for debt, such information should be disclosed in the financial statements. Similarly, if a long-term debt agreement contains major covenants, that information should be disclosed in the notes to the financial statements.

In conclusion, Tables 4–2 and 4–3 provide examples of the links between management assertions and audit procedures for the audit of accounts receivable, a balance sheet account (Table 4–2) and for the audit of sales revenue, an income statement account (Table 4–3).

Table 4–2	**Management Assertions and Illustrative Audit Procedures for Accounts Receivable**
Management Assertion	*Sample Audit Procedures for Accounts Receivable*
Existence	Confirm accounts receivable.
Rights and obligations	Enquire of management whether receivables have been sold.
Completeness	Agree total of accounts receivable subsidiary ledger to accounts receivable control account.
Valuation and allocation	Trace selected accounts from the aged trial balance to the subsidiary accounts receivable records for proper amount and aging.
	Test the adequacy of the allowance for doubtful accounts.

Table 4–3	**Management Assertions and Illustrative Audit Procedures for Sales Revenue**
Management Assertion	*Sample Audit Procedures*
Occurrence	Confirm accounts receivable
Completeness	Match shipping documents with sales invoices. Account for the numerical sequence of shipping documents and sales orders.
Accuracy	Agree a sample of the daily postings in the sales journal to the Accounts Receivable subsidiary ledger. Review the client's periodic reconciliation of the Accounts Receivable subsidiary ledger to the general ledger control account.
Cutoff	Examine large sales invoices for five days before and after year-end to ensure recording of sales in proper period.
Classification	Ensure proper classification of any instalment sales, contingent sales, etc.

Basic Concepts of Audit Evidence

LO 5 From an audit perspective, audit evidence consists of the underlying accounting data and all corroborating information available to the auditor. Auditing standards discuss the following concepts:

- the nature of audit evidence
- the sufficiency of audit evidence
- the appropriateness of audit evidence
- the evaluation of audit evidence

The Nature of Audit Evidence

Accounting data that can be used as evidence to test audit objectives include the books of original entry (such as general and subsidiary ledgers), related accounting manuals, and records such as worksheets and spreadsheets that support amounts in the financial statements. Many times these data are in electronic form. Corroborating audit evidence includes both written and electronic information such as cheques, records of electronic transfers, invoices, contracts, minutes, confirmations, and written representations. Corroborating evidence also includes information obtained by the auditor through enquiry, observation, inspection, and physical examination.

For some entities, accounting data and corroborating audit evidence may be available only in electronic form.[1] Thus, source documents such as purchase orders, bills of lading, invoices, and cheques are replaced with electronic messages or electronic images. Two common examples are Electronic Data Interchange (EDI) and image processing systems.[2] A client that uses EDI may process sales or purchase transactions electronically. For example, the client's EDI system can contact a vendor electronically when supplies of a part run low. The vendor will then ship the goods to the client and send an invoice electronically. The client can authorize its bank to make an electronic payment directly to the vendor's bank account. In an image processing system, documents are scanned and converted to electronic images to facilitate storage and reference, and the source documents may not be retained after conversion. In such systems, electronic evidence may exist at only a certain point in time and may not be retrievable later. This may require the auditor to select sample items several times during the year rather than at year-end.

The Sufficiency of Audit Evidence

The sufficiency of audit evidence relates to the quantity of evidence that the auditor requires to observe in order to validate the relevant management assertion. In most instances, the auditor relies on evidence that is *persuasive* rather than *convincing* in forming an opinion on a set of financial statements. This occurs for two reasons. First, because an audit must be completed in a reasonable amount of time and at a reasonable cost,

---

[1]See A. L. Williamson, "The Implications of Electronic Evidence," *Journal of Accountancy* (February 1997), pp. 69–71, and Canadian Institute of Chartered Accountants, Electronic *Audit Evidence* (Toronto: CICA, 2003). See Appendix C on the OLC for a discussion of EDI.

[2]*Electronic Audit Evidence* (CICA, 2003), discusses the issues faced by auditors when a client uses electronic document management.

the auditor examines only a sample of the transactions that compose the account balance or class of transactions. Thus, the auditor reaches a conclusion about the account or class based on a subset of the available evidence.

Second, due to the nature of evidence, auditors must often rely on evidence that is not perfectly reliable. As discussed in the next section, different types of audit evidence have different degrees of reliability, and even highly reliable evidence has weaknesses. For example, an auditor can physically examine inventory, but such evidence will not normally ensure that obsolescence is not a problem. Therefore, the nature of the evidence obtained by the auditor seldom provides absolute assurance about management assertions.

The *amount* and *type* of audit evidence are determined by the auditor's professional judgement. In judging the sufficiency of evidence, the auditor relies on the materiality and audit risk for the account balance or class of transactions to determine the scope of the audit. For example, when the account balance is significant, the auditor has to collect more audit evidence than for accounts with smaller balances. Determining the sufficiency of evidence is one of the more critical decisions the auditor faces on an engagement.

The Appropriateness of Audit Evidence

Evidence, regardless of its form, is considered appropriate when it provides information that is both *relevant* and *reliable*.

Relevance   The evidence must be relevant to the management assertion being tested. If the auditor relies on evidence that is unrelated to the management assertion, he or she may reach an incorrect conclusion. For example, suppose the auditor wants to check the completeness assertion for recording sales transactions; that is, are all goods shipped to customers recorded in the sales journal in the appropriate accounting period? A normal audit procedure for testing this assertion is to trace a sample of shipping documents (such as bills of lading) to the related sales invoices and entries in the sales journal. If the auditor samples the population of sales invoices issued during the period, the evidence would not relate to the completeness assertion (that is, the auditor would not detect shipments made that are not billed or recorded). The auditor should check the log of prenumbered bills of lading, after ascertaining that such documents were issued for all customer shipments. Any conclusion based on the population of sales invoices would not be based on evidence relevant to testing the completeness objective.

Reliability   *Reliability* refers to whether a particular type of evidence can be trusted to signal the true state of an assertion. Because of varied circumstances on audit engagements, it is difficult to generalize about the reliability of various types of evidence. However, the auditor should consider the following general factors when assessing the reliability or validity of evidence.

  • ***Independence of the source of the evidence.*** Evidence obtained
    directly by the auditor from an independent source outside the entity
    is usually viewed as more reliable than evidence obtained solely from

within the entity. Thus, a confirmation of the client's bank balance received directly by the auditor would be viewed as more reliable than examination of the cash receipts journal and cash balance as recorded in the general ledger. Additionally, evidence that is obtained from the client, but that has been subjected to verification by an independent source, is viewed as more reliable than evidence obtained solely from within the entity. For example, a cancelled cheque held by the client would be more reliable than a duplicate copy of the cheque because the cancelled cheque would be endorsed by the payee and cleared through the bank—that is, verified by an independent source.

- *Effectiveness of internal control.* A major objective of a client's internal control is to generate reliable information to assist management decision making. As part of the audit, the effectiveness of the client's internal control is assessed. When the auditor assesses the client's internal control as effective (that is, low control risk), evidence generated by that accounting system is viewed as reliable. Conversely, if internal control is assessed as ineffective (that is, high control risk), the evidence from the accounting system would not be considered reliable. Thus, the more effective the client's internal control, the more assurance it provides about the reliability of audit evidence.

- *Auditor's direct personal knowledge.* Evidence obtained directly by the auditor is generally considered to be more reliable than evidence obtained indirectly by other means. For example, an auditor's physical examination of a client's inventory is considered to be relatively reliable because the auditor has direct personal knowledge regarding the inventory. There are, of course, exceptions to this general rule. For example, an auditor may competently examine an inventory composed of pagers; however, if the inventory is composed of diamonds or speciality computer chips, the auditor may lack the competence to assess the validity and valuation of such inventory items. In such cases, the auditor may need the skill and knowledge of a specialist to assist with the inventory audit.

The Evaluation of Audit Evidence

The ability to evaluate evidence is another important skill an auditor must develop. Proper evaluation of evidence requires that the auditor understand the types of evidence that are available and their relative reliability or diagnosticity. The auditor must be capable of assessing when a sufficient amount of appropriate evidence has been obtained in order to determine whether specific audit objectives have been achieved.

In evaluating evidence, an auditor should be *thorough* in searching for evidence and *unbiased* in its evaluation. For example, suppose an auditor decides to mail accounts receivable confirmations to 50 customers. Suppose further that the client has a total of 500 customer accounts receivable. In auditing the 50 customers, the auditor must gather sufficient evidence on *each* of the 50 accounts. In evaluating evidence, the auditor must remain objective and must not allow the evaluation of the evidence to be biased by other considerations. For example, in evaluating a client's response to an audit enquiry, the auditor must not allow any personal factors to influence the evaluation of the client's response.

Types of Audit Evidence

LO 6> Section 5300 of the *CICA Handbook,* "Audit evidence," identifies various types of audit evidence that the auditor may examine. For the following discussion, evidence is categorized into the following types:

- Inspection of records or documents.
- Inspection of tangible assets.
- Reperformance.
- Recalculation.
- Scanning.
- Enquiry.
- Observation.
- Confirmation.
- Analytical procedures.

Inspection of Records or Documents

Inspection consists of examining internal or external records or documents that are in paper form, electronic form, or other media. On most audit engagements, inspection of records or documents makes up the bulk of the evidence gathered by the auditor. Two issues are important in discussing inspection of records or documents: the reliability of such evidence and its relationship to specific assertions.

Reliability of Records or Documents   A previous section noted the independence of the source of evidence as a factor that affected the reliability of audit evidence. In particular, evidence obtained from a source outside the entity was generally considered more reliable than evidence obtained solely from within the entity. Typically a distinction is made between internal and external documents. *Internal documents* are generated and maintained within the entity; that is, these documents have not been seen by any party outside the client's organization. Examples include duplicate copies of sales invoices and shipping documents, materials requisition forms, and worksheets for overhead cost allocation. *External documents* are of two forms: documents originating within the entity but circulated to independent sources outside the entity and documents generated outside the entity but included in the client's accounting records. Examples of the first include remittance advices returned with cash receipts from customers and payroll cheques, while examples of the second include bank statements and vendors' invoices.

In general, such external documentary evidence is viewed as more reliable than internal evidence because a third party either initiated or reviewed it. This difference in reliability between internal and external documents is, however, relative. Internal documents generated by good internal controls are likely to be highly reliable. Conversely, external documents may be manipulated or withheld by client personnel. If this is likely on an engagement, the auditor would discount the reliability of the external documents in the client's possession. In such a situation, the auditor would also discount the reliability of the internal documents. In summary, determining the reliability of documentary evidence involves a good deal of auditor judgement.

Documentary Evidence Related to Assertions   The second issue concerning records or documents relates directly to the occurrence and completeness assertions and to the *direction of testing* taken when documentary evidence is examined. Figure 4–2 presents an overview of this relationship.

The direction of testing between the accounting records and source documents (such as sales invoices or shipping documents) is important when testing the occurrence and completeness assertions. *Vouching* refers to first selecting an item for testing from the accounting journals or ledgers and then examining the underlying source document. Thus, the direction of testing is from the journals or ledgers back to the source documents. This approach provides evidence that items included in the accounting records have *occurred* (or are valid transactions). For example, an auditor may want to examine a sample of sales transactions from the sales journal to ensure that sales are not fictitious. If adequate source documents exist for each sales transaction selected from the sales journal, the auditor can conclude that each sale was valid. *Tracing* refers to first selecting an accounting transaction (a source document) and then following it into the journal or ledger. The direction of testing in this case is from the source documents to the journals or ledgers. Testing in this direction ensures that transactions that occurred are recorded (*completeness*) in the accounting records. For example, if the auditor selects a sample of shipping documents and traces them to the related sales invoices and then to the sales journal, he or she would have evidence on the completeness of sales.

Inspection of Tangible Assets

Inspection of tangible assets consists of physical examination of the assets. Inspection is a relatively reliable type of evidence that involves the auditor inspecting or counting a *tangible* asset. An audit engagement includes many situations in which the auditor physically examines an entity's assets. Some examples might be counting cash on hand, examining inventory or marketable securities, and examining tangible fixed assets. This type of evidence primarily provides assurance that the asset exists. In some instances, such as examining inventory, physical examination may provide evidence on valuation by identifying obsolete or slow-moving items. However, physical examination provides little or no assurance on the rights and obligations assertions.

F I G U R E   4–2

Direction of Testing for
Validity and Completeness

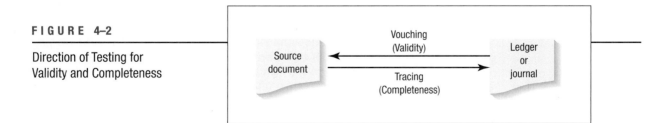

Reperformance

Reperformance is the auditor's independent execution of procedures or controls that were originally performed as part of the entity's internal control, either manually or through the use of computer-assisted audit techniques (CAATs). For example, the auditor may reperform the aging of accounts receivable. Because the auditor creates this type of evidence, it is normally viewed as highly reliable.

Recalculation

Recalculation consists of checking the mathematical accuracy of documents or records. Recalculation can be formed through the use of information technology (e.g., by obtaining an electronic file from the entity and using CAATs to check the accuracy of the summarization of the file). Specific examples of this type of procedure include recalculation of depreciation expense on fixed assets and recalculation of accrued interest. Recalculation also includes footing, crossfooting, reconciling subsidiary ledgers to account balances, and testing postings from journals to ledgers. Because the auditor creates this type of evidence, it is normally viewed as highly reliable.

Scanning

Scanning is the review of accounting data to identify significant or unusual items. This includes the identification of anomalous individual items within account balances or other client data through the scanning or analysis of entries in transaction listings, subsidiary ledgers, general ledger control accounts, adjusting entries, suspense accounts, reconciliations, and other detailed reports. Scanning includes searching for large and unusual items in the accounting records (e.g., nonstandard journal entries), as well as reviewing transaction data (e.g., expense accounts, adjusting journal entries) for indications of errors that have occurred. It might be used in conjunction with analytical procedures but also as a stand-alone procedure. Scanning can be performed either manually or through the use of CAATs.

Enquiry

Enquiry consists of seeking information of knowledgeable persons (both financial and nonfinancial) throughout the entity or outside the entity. Enquiry is an important audit procedure that is used extensively throughout the audit and often is complementary to performing other audit procedures.[3] For example, much of the audit work conducted to understand the entity and its environment including internal control involves enquiry.

Enquiries may range from formal written enquiries to informal oral enquiries. Evaluating responses to enquiries is an integral part of the enquiry process. Table 4–4 provides guidance for conducting and evaluating enquiries.

Responses to enquiries may provide the auditor with information not previously possessed or with corroborative audit evidence. Alternatively, responses might provide information that differs significantly from other information that the auditor has obtained, for example, information

[3]See also Canadian Institute of Chartered Accountants, *Audit Enquiry: Seeking More Reliable Evidence from Audit Enquiry* (Toronto: CICA, 2000).

Table 4–4	**Techniques for Conducting and Evaluating Enquiries**

In conducting enquiry, the auditor should

- Consider the knowledge, objectivity, experience, responsibility, and qualifications of the individual to be questioned.
- Ask clear, concise, and relevant questions.
- Use open or closed questions appropriately.
- Listen actively and effectively.
- Consider the reactions and responses and ask follow-up questions.
- Evaluate the response.

regarding the possibility of management override of controls. The reliability of audit evidence obtained from responses to enquiries is also affected by the training, knowledge, and experience of the auditor performing the enquiry, because the auditor analyzes and assesses responses while performing the enquiry and refines subsequent enquiries according to the circumstances. In some cases, the nature of the response may be so significant that the auditor requests a written representation from the source.

Enquiry alone ordinarily does not provide sufficient audit evidence, and the auditor will gather additional corroborative evidence to support the response. For example, enquiry will not provide sufficient appropriate audit evidence for testing the operating effectiveness of controls. Additionally, when enquiring about management intent, the information available to support management's intent may be limited. In this case, understanding management's past history of carrying out its stated intentions may provide relevant information about management's intent.

Observation

Observation consists of looking at a process or procedure being performed by others. The actions being observed typically do not leave an audit trail that can be tested by examining records or documents. Examples include observation of the counting of inventories by the entity's personnel and observation of the performance of control activities. Observation provides audit evidence about the performance of a process or procedure but is limited to the point in time at which the observation takes place. It is also limited by the fact that the client personnel may act differently when the auditor is not observing them. Observation is generally not considered very reliable and generally requires additional corroboration by the auditor. Corroborating evidence includes data or documents from the accounting records and other documentary information (e.g., contracts and written confirmations).

Students often confuse the technical auditing definition of the term *observation* with the common usage of the word. As a result, students will use the term *observation* to describe such audit procedures as inspection of tangible assets or documents and records. However, as we discussed above, "observation" in the auditing sense consists of looking at a *process or procedure being performed by others*. Technical terms or jargon serve an important role in the efficient communication of professionals, and you will want to develop the proper vocabulary. Just as technical accounting terms such as revenue and income are not used interchangeably by professional accountants, professional auditors do not use "observation" and "inspection" interchangeably.

Confirmation

CICA Handbook, section 5303, defines confirmation as the process of obtaining and evaluating a direct communication (preferably written) from a third party in response to a request for information about a particular item affecting financial statement assertions.

The reliability of evidence obtained through confirmations is directly affected by factors such as

- The form of the confirmation.
- Prior experience with the entity.
- The nature of the information being confirmed.
- The intended respondent.

Confirmations are used extensively on audits; they generally provide reliable evidence for the existence assertion and, in testing certain financial statement components (such as accounts payable), can provide evidence about the completeness assertion. Evidence about other assertions can also be obtained through the use of confirmations. For example, an auditor can send a confirmation to a consignee to verify that a client's inventory has been consigned. The returned confirmation provides evidence that the client owns the inventory (rights and obligations assertion). Table 4–5 lists selected amounts and information confirmed by auditors. Accounts receivable, accounts payable, and bank confirmations are discussed in more detail in later chapters.

Analysis

"Analysis" is the term used in the *CICA Handbook*, section 5301, to refer to the application of analytical procedures. Analytical procedures are an important type of evidence on an audit. They consist of evaluations of financial information made by a study of plausible relationships among

Table 4–5   Amounts and Information Frequently Confirmed by Auditors

Amounts or Information Confirmed	Source of Confirmation
Cash balance	Bank
Accounts receivable	Individual customers
Inventory on consignment	Consignee
Accounts payable	Individual vendors
Bonds payable	Bondholders/trustee
Common shares outstanding	Registrar/transfer agent
Insurance coverage	Insurance company
Collateral for loan	Creditor

both financial and nonfinancial data. For example, the current-year accounts receivable balance can be compared to the prior-year balance after adjusting for any increase or decrease in sales and other economic factors. Similarly, the auditor might compare the current-year gross margin percentage to the gross margin percentage for the previous five years. The auditor makes such comparisons either to identify accounts that may contain material misstatements and require more investigation or as a reasonableness test of the account balance. Analytical procedures are an effective and efficient form of evidence.

The reliability of analytical procedures is a function of (1) the availability and reliability of the data used in the calculations, (2) the plausibility and predictability of the relationship being tested, and (3) the precision of the expectation and the rigour of the investigation. Because of the importance of this type of evidence in auditing, analytical procedures are covered in greater detail in Chapter 5.

Reliability of the Types of Evidence

LO 7> Table 4–6 presents a hierarchy of the reliability of the types of evidence. Physical examination and reperformance are generally considered of high reliability because the auditor has direct knowledge about them. Documentation, confirmation, and analytical procedures are generally considered to be of medium reliability. The reliability of documentation depends primarily on whether a document is internal or external, and the reliability of confirmation is affected by the four factors listed previously. The reliability of analytical procedures may be affected by the availability and reliability of the data. Finally, enquiries of client personnel or management and observation are generally low-reliability types of evidence because both require further corroboration by the auditor.

You should understand, however, that the levels of reliability shown in Table 4–6 are general guidelines. The reliability of the types of evidence

Table 4–6	Hierarchy of the Reliability of Types of Evidence
Level of Reliability	*Type of Evidence*
High	Inspection of tangible assets
	Reperformance
	Recalculation
Medium	Inspection of records and documents
	Scanning
	Confirmation
	Analytical procedures
Low	Enquiry
	Observation

FIGURE 4–3

Summary of Audit Team, Evidence, and Activities

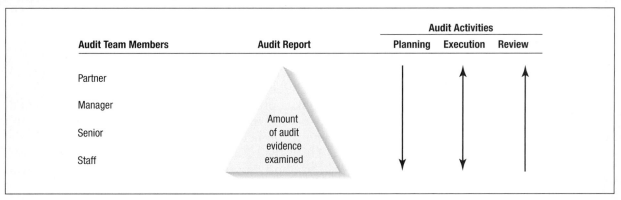

may vary considerably across entities, and it may be subject to a number of exceptions. For example, in some circumstances, confirmations may be viewed as a highly reliable source of evidence. This may be true when a confirmation is sent to an independent third party who is highly qualified to respond to the auditor's request for information. Enquiries of client personnel or management provide another example. Audit research has shown that, in certain situations, enquiries of client personnel or management are relatively effective in detecting material misstatement.[4]

Relationship of Audit Evidence, Management Assertions, and Audit Activities

LO 8> Each of the nine types of evidence discussed in the previous section is used for different management assertions. Recall for example, that while physical examination is generally used to provide evidence on existence and completeness, it can also provide evidence on the measurement and valuation assertions, but not necessarily the ownership assertion. Similarly, analytical procedures can provide evidence on all assertions except ownership. Auditors must understand which management assertions are tested by the various types of evidence in order to properly plan and evaluate audit tests.

Figure 4–3 presents a summary of the audit team and its evidence-related audit activities. In general, most audit evidence is developed by the audit staff and audit senior, while a smaller amount is created by the manager and partner. Three activities—*planning, execution,* and *reviewing*—encompass the main activities related to audit evidence. Planning for the audit starts at the partner level and proceeds downward through the other team members. All members of the team execute the audit. Finally,

---

[4]See A. Eilifson and W. F. Messier, Jr., "Auditor Detection of Misstatements: A Review and Integration of Empirical Research," *Journal of Accounting Literature 2000* (19), pp. 1–43, for a detailed review of research studies that have examined auditor-detected misstatements.

the review of working papers that contain the audit evidence proceeds upward through the audit team.

Working Papers

Objectives of Audit Working Papers

LO 9>

Working papers are the auditor's record of the work performed and the conclusions reached on the audit. The quantity, type, and content of the working papers are a function of the circumstances of the specific engagement. *CICA Handbook,* section 5145, "Documentation," stipulates that working papers have three functions: (1) to demonstrate compliance with the relevant provisions of the *CICA Handbook*, (2) to provide support for the auditor's report, and (3) to demonstrate the agreement between the underlying accounting records and the financial statements.[5]

When the engagement is complete, the auditor must decide on the appropriate type of report to issue. The basis for this decision rests in the audit evidence gathered and the conclusions reached and documented in the working papers. The working papers also document that the scope of the audit was adequate for the report issued. Information on the correspondence of the financial statements with GAAP is also included in the working papers.

Contents of Working Papers

Personal computers and audit software are increasingly being used to prepare and store working papers. Whatever medium they exist is, papers are the principal record of auditing procedures applied, evidence obtained, and conclusions reached by the auditor in the engagement. Working papers should include a written audit program (or set of audit programs) for the engagement. The audit program should set forth in reasonable detail the auditing procedures that the auditor believed necessary to accomplish the objectives of the audit. Working papers should be sufficient to show that standards of fieldwork have been followed and should enable a reviewer with relevant knowledge and experience to understand

- the nature, timing, extent, and results of auditing procedures performed
- the evidence obtained
- the engagement team member(s) who performed and reviewed the work

The auditor should consider the following factors when determining the nature and extent of the working papers for a particular audit area or auditing procedure:

- risk of material misstatement associated with the assertion, account, or class of transactions
- extent of judgement involved in performing the work and evaluating the results

---

[5]See also Canadian Institute of Chartered Accountants, *Assurance Engagement Working Papers* (Toronto: CICA, 1997)

- significance of the evidence obtained to the assertion being tested
- nature and extent of exceptions identified
- the need to document a conclusion or the basis for a conclusion not readily determinable *from* the documentation of the work performed

When documenting the extent of auditing procedures that involve inspection of documents or confirmation of balances, the working papers should include an identification of the items tested and, where appropriate, abstracts or copies of documents such as significant contracts or agreements. Most audit firms maintain working papers in two types of files: permanent and current. *Permanent files* contain historical data about the client that are of continuing relevance to the audit. *Current files,* on the other hand, include information and data related specifically to the current year's engagement. Table 4–7 contains examples of the types of information included in each type of file.

Types of Working Papers

Working papers come in a variety of types. The more common working papers include the audit plan and programs, working trial balance, account analysis and listings, audit memoranda, and adjusting and reclassification entries. Working papers may be in paper form, electronic form, or other media.

Audit Plan and Programs   The audit plan contains the strategy to be followed by the auditor in conducting the audit. This document outlines the auditor's understanding of the client and the potential audit risks.

Table 4–7	**Examples of Information Included in Permanent and Current Files**

Permanent File:
- Copies of, or excerpts from, the corporate charter.
- Chart of accounts.
- Organizational chart.
- Accounting manual (excerpts).
- Copies of important contracts (pension contracts, union contracts, leases, etc.).
- Documentation of internal control (e.g., flowcharts).
- Terms of share and bond issues.
- Prior years' analytical procedure results.

Current File:
- Copy of financial statements and auditor's report.
- Audit plan and audit programs.
- Copies of, or excerpts from, minutes of important committee meetings.
- Working trial balance.
- Adjusting and reclassification journal entries.
- Working papers supporting financial statement accounts.

It contains the basic framework for how the audit resources (budgeted audit hours) are to be allocated to various parts of the engagement. The audit programs contain the audit procedures that will be conducted by the auditor. Generally, each transaction cycle and account balance has a separate audit program.

Working Trial Balance   The working trial balance links the amounts in the financial statements to the audit working papers. Exhibit 4–1 illustrates a partial working trial balance for EarthWear Clothiers. In addition to a column for account name, the trial balance contains columns for working paper references, the prior year's balances, the unadjusted current-year balances, and columns for adjusting and reclassification entries. The last column would agree to the amounts contained in the financial statements after combining common account balances. A lead schedule is then used to show the detailed general ledger accounts that make up a financial statement category (cash, accounts receivable, and so on). For example, the trial balance would contain only one line for "cash and cash equivalents" and the "C lead" schedule would list all general ledger cash accounts. This approach is described in more detail later in the chapter.

Account Analysis and Listings   Account analysis working papers generally include the *activity* in a particular account for the period. For example, Exhibit 4–2 shows the analysis of legal and audit expense for EarthWear Clothiers for the year ended December 31, 2006. Listings represent a schedule of items remaining in the ending balance of an account and are often called *trial balances*. For example, the auditor may obtain a listing of all amounts owed to vendors that make up the accounts payable balance as of the end of the year. This listing would represent a trial balance of unpaid vendors' invoices.

Audit Memoranda   Much of the auditor's work is documented in written memoranda. These include discussions of items such as internal controls, inventory observation, errors identified, and problems encountered during the audit.

Adjusting and Reclassification Entries   The working papers also include documentation for the adjusting and reclassification entries identified by the auditor or client. Adjusting entries are made to correct errors in the client's records. For example, if the auditor discovered that certain inventory items were improperly valued, an adjusting entry would be proposed to correct the dollar error. Adjusting entries are posted in both the client's records and the working trial balance.

Reclassification entries are made to properly present information on the financial statements. A reclassification entry affects income statement accounts or balance sheet accounts, but not both. For example, a reclassification entry might be necessary to present as a current liability the current portion of long-term debt. Reclassification entries are not posted to the client's records.

EXHIBIT 4–1

An Example of a Partial Working Trial Balance

EarthWear

EARTHWEAR CLOTHIERS
Partial Working Trial Balance
December 31, 2006

Account Description	W/P Ref.	Balance 12/31/05	Balance 12/31/06	Adjustments DR	Adjustments CR	Adjusted T/B	Reclassification DR	Reclassification CR	Financial Statements
Cash and cash equivalents	C lead	$ 49,668	$ 48,978						
Receivables	E lead	11,539	12,875						
Inventory	F lead	105,425	122,337						
Prepaid advertising	G lead	10,772	11,458						
. . .									

EXHIBIT 4–2

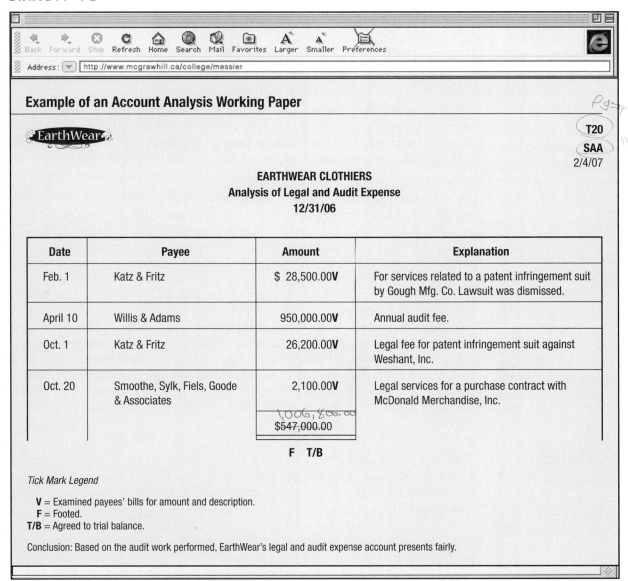

Example of an Account Analysis Working Paper

EarthWear

Pg-7

T20
SAA
2/4/07

EARTHWEAR CLOTHIERS
Analysis of Legal and Audit Expense
12/31/06

Date	Payee	Amount	Explanation
Feb. 1	Katz & Fritz	$ 28,500.00**V**	For services related to a patent infringement suit by Gough Mfg. Co. Lawsuit was dismissed.
April 10	Willis & Adams	950,000.00**V**	Annual audit fee.
Oct. 1	Katz & Fritz	26,200.00**V**	Legal fee for patent infringement suit against Weshant, Inc.
Oct. 20	Smoothe, Sylk, Fiels, Goode & Associates	2,100.00**V**	Legal services for a purchase contract with McDonald Merchandise, Inc.
		1,006,800.00 ~~$547,000.00~~	

F   T/B

Tick Mark Legend

V = Examined payees' bills for amount and description.
F = Footed.
T/B = Agreed to trial balance.

Conclusion: Based on the audit work performed, EarthWear's legal and audit expense account presents fairly.

Format of Working Papers

Audit working papers should clearly and concisely communicate the auditor's work. While the formatting of working papers may differ from firm to firm, three general characteristics should be recognized.

Heading   All working papers should have a proper heading. The heading should include the name of the client, the title of the working paper, and the client's year-end date. Exhibit 4–2 shows a working paper with a proper heading.

Indexing and Cross-Referencing   Working papers must be organized so that members of the audit team or firm can find relevant audit evidence. Some firms use a lettering system; other firms use some type of numbering system. For example, the general working papers may be labelled "A," internal control systems working papers "B," cash working papers "C," and so on. When the auditor performs audit work on one working paper and supporting information is obtained from another working paper, the auditor cross-references the information on each working paper. This process of indexing and cross-referencing provides a trail from the financial statements to the individual working papers that a reviewer can easily follow. Indexing and cross-referencing are discussed further in the next section.

Tick Marks   Auditors use tick marks to document work performed. Tick marks are simply notations that are made by the auditor near, or next to, an item or amount on a working paper. The tick mark symbol is typically explained or defined at the bottom of the working paper, although many firms use a standard set of tick marks. Exhibit 4–2 shows some examples of tick marks. On this working paper, the tick mark "V" indicates that the auditor examined the bills sent to the client by the payee for proper amount and description.

Many CA firms document their conclusions about an individual account or component of the financial statements in the working papers. Exhibit 4–2 shows an example of how an auditor might document a conclusion about an individual account and the link to Willis and Adams: Auditors, in the associated website (www.mcgrawhill.ca/olc/messier), provides many more examples of working papers for the audit of Earth-Wear.

Organization of Working Papers

The auditor's working papers need to be organized so that any member of the audit team (and others) can find the audit evidence that supports each financial statement account. While no specific guidelines dictate how this should be accomplished, although the CICA has provided a model in its research study, *Assurance Working Papers*, the following discussion presents a general approach that should assist in understanding working paper organization.[6]

The financial statements contain the accounts and amounts covered by the auditor's report. These accounts come from the working trial balance, which summarizes the general ledger accounts contained on each lead schedule. Each lead schedule includes the general ledger accounts that make up the financial statement account. Different types of audit working papers (account analysis, listings, confirmations, and so on) are then used to support each of the general ledger accounts. Each of these working papers is indexed, and all important amounts are cross-referenced between working papers.

Figure 4–4 presents an example of how working papers could be organized to support the cash account. Note that each Shaded Square represents a separate page in the working papers. The $15,000 shown on

---

[6]Ibid.

the balance sheet agrees to the working trial balance. The "A lead" schedule in turn contains the three general ledger accounts that are included in the $15,000 balance. Audit working papers then support each of the general ledger accounts. For example, the working papers indexed "A2"

FIGURE 4–4

An Example of Working Paper Organization

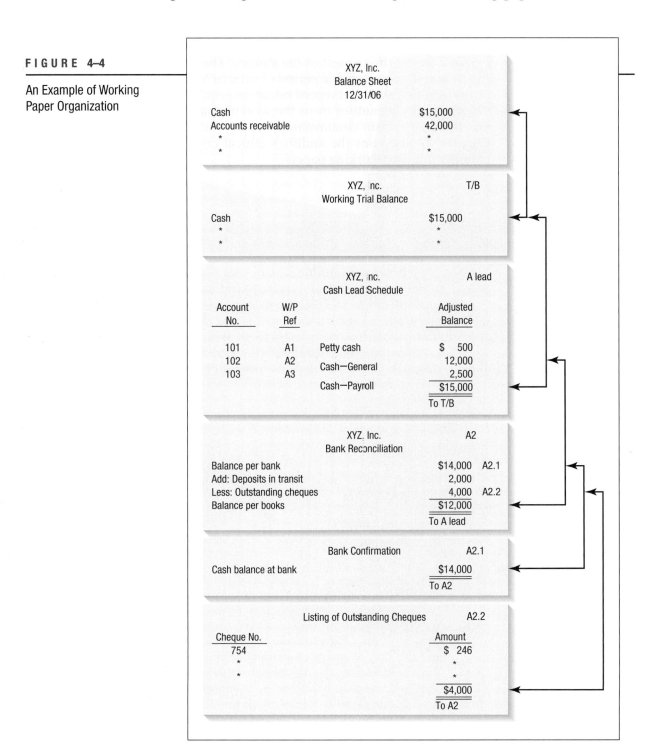

provide the audit evidence supporting the general cash balance of $12,000. Also note that each important amount is cross-referenced. For example, the balance per bank of $14,000 on "A2" is referenced ~~ A2.1" and the cash balance on "A2.1" is referenced back ~~ "

Ownership of Working Papers

The working pa~~   des not only working papers ~~   rs prepared by the client at i~~   etain working papers for a ~~   eeds of his or her practice an~~

Although the ~~   oe shown, except under certa~~   consent. Chapter 17 discus. ~~   ning the confidentiality of w

(handwritten notes:) Ch 4 — ✓ All multiple choice — ✓ All review questions ~ Problems: 32, 33, 34, 36, 37, 39, 40, 43, 44

REVIEW QUESTIONS

LO		
1	4-1	Explain why the auditor divides the financial statements into components or segments in order to test management's assertions.
2	4-2	List and define the management assertions about account balances at the period end.
2	4-3	List and define the management assertions about classes of transactions and events for the period under audit.
3	4-4	Describe the three major purposes of performing audit procedures.
4	4-5	Define audit evidence. Give three examples of corroborating evidence.
7	4-6	Evidence is considered appropriate when it is both reliable and relevant. What is meant by the terms *relevant* and *reliable*?
7	4-7	List and discuss the three general factors that the auditor should consider when assessing the reliability of audit evidence.
8	4-8	Explain why in most instances audit evidence is persuasive rather than convincing.
1,5	4-9	What actions should the auditor take when doubt exists about major assertions?
1,4,8	4-10	How do management assertions relate to the financial statements and audit procedures?
6	4-11	List and define eight types of audit evidence.
6,7	4-12	Distinguish between internal and external forms of documentary evidence. Discuss the relative reliability of each.
8	4-13	When using documentation as a type of evidence, distinguish between vouching and tracing in terms of the direction of testing and the management assertions being tested.
6,7	4-14	Why is it necessary to obtain corroborating evidence for enquiries of client personnel and management and for observation?
7	4-15	Discuss the relative reliability of the different types of evidence.
9	4-16	Define the two major types of working paper files. Give two examples of information contained in each type of file.
9	4-17	Who owns the audit working papers?

MULTIPLE-CHOICE QUESTIONS FROM PROFESSIONAL EXAMINATIONS

Unless otherwise indicated, these multiple-choice questions were adapted from the CPA examinations, courtesy of the American Institute of Certified Public Accountants.

2,4,8> 4-18 On which of the following procedures would an auditor most likely rely to verify management's assertion of completeness?

a. Reviewing standard bank confirmations for indications of kiting.

b. Comparing a sample of shipping documents to related sales invoices.

c. Observing the client's distribution of payroll cheques.

d. Confirming a sample of recorded receivables by direct communication with the debtors.

6,7> 4-19 Which of the following procedures would provide the most reliable audit evidence?

a. Enquiries of the client's internal audit staff held in private.

b. Inspection of prenumbered client purchase orders filed in the vouchers payable department.

c. Analytical procedures performed by the auditor on the entity's trial balance.

d. Inspection of bank statements obtained directly from the client's financial institution.

5,6> 4-20 Which of the following statements concerning audit evidence is correct?

a. Sufficient appropriate audit evidence should be either persuasive or relevant but need *not* be both.

b. The measure of the validity of audit evidence lies in the auditor's judgement.

c. The difficulty and expense of obtaining audit evidence concerning an account balance is a valid basis for omitting the test.

d. A client's accounting data may be sufficient audit evidence to support the financial statements.

5> 4-21 Which of the following statements is generally correct regarding audit evidence?

a. The auditor's direct personal knowledge, obtained through observation and inspection, is more persuasive than information obtained indirectly from independent outside sources.

b. Sufficient appropriate audit evidence must be either valid or relevant but need *not* be both.

c. Accounting data alone may be considered sufficient appropriate audit evidence to issue an unqualified opinion on financial statements.

d. Sufficiency of evidence refers to the amount of corroborative evidence to be obtained.

7> 4-22 An auditor would be *least* likely to use confirmations in connection with the examination of

a. Inventory.

b. Refundable income taxes.

c. Long-term debt.

d. Shareholders' equity.

6,7 ⟩   **4-23**   Which of the following types of audit evidence is the *least* persuasive?

a. Prenumbered purchase order forms.

b. Bank statements obtained from the client.

c. Test counts of inventory performed by the auditor.

d. Correspondence from the client's lawyer about litigation.

6,7 ⟩   **4-24**   Audit evidence can come in different forms with different degrees of persuasiveness. Which of the following is the *most* persuasive type of evidence?

a. Bank statements obtained from the client.

b. Computations made by the auditor.

c. Prenumbered client sales invoices.

d. Vendors' invoices.

6,7 ⟩   **4-25**   In testing the existence assertion for an asset, an auditor ordinarily works from the

a. Financial statements to the potentially unrecorded items.

b. Potentially unrecorded items to the financial statements.

c. Accounting records to the supporting evidence.

d. Supporting evidence to the accounting records.

9 ⟩   **4-26**   An auditor's working papers should

a. Not be permitted to serve as a reference source for the client.

b. Not contain critical comments concerning management.

c. Show that the accounting records agree or reconcile with the financial statements.

d. Provide the primary support for the financial statements being audited.

2,4,8 ⟩   **4-27**   In testing the completeness assertion for a liability, the auditor ordinarily works from the

a. Accounting records to the supporting evidence.

b. Supporting evidence to the accounting records.

c. Potentially unrecorded items and subsequent transactions to the accounting records.

d. Financial statements to the potentially unrecorded items.

(CGA-Canada, adapted)

9 ⟩   **4-28**   The current file of the auditor's working papers should generally include

a. A flowchart of the accounting system.

b. Organization charts.

c. A copy of the financial statements.

d. Copies of bond and note indentures.

9 ⟩   **4-29**   The permanent file section of the working papers that is kept for each audit client most likely contains

a. Review notes pertaining to questions and comments regarding the audit work performed.

b. A schedule of time spent on the engagement by each individual auditor.

c. Correspondence with the client's lawyers concerning pending litigation.

d. Narrative descriptions of the client's accounting system and control procedures.

2,4,8>   **4-30**   If a client is artificially inflating revenues by practicing "bill and hold" (i.e., generating invoices and recording sales for merchandise that has not been shipped), an audit procedure that would obtain relevant evidence would be to:

a. Select a sample of recorded sales invoices and vouch (compare information on the sales invoices) to the related shipping documents.

b. Select a sample of shipping documents and trace to the related recorded sales invoices.

c. Compare the total of the individual accounts in the Accounts Receivable subsidiary files with the balance of the Accounts Receivable in the general ledger.

d. Attend the client's end-of-year inventory count.

(CGA-Canada, adapted)

9>   **4-31**   An audit working paper that reflects the major components of an amount reported in the financial statements is referred to as a(n)

a. Lead schedule.

b. Supporting schedule.

c. Audit control account.

d. Working trial balance.

PROBLEMS

2>   **4-32**   Management makes assertions about components of the financial statements. Match the management assertions shown in the following left-hand column with the proper description of the assertion shown in the right-hand column.

Management Assertion	Description
a. Existence	1. The accounts and transactions that should be included are included; thus, the financial statements are complete.
b. Completeness	2. Assets, liabilities, equity revenues, and expenses are appropriately valued and are allocated to the proper accounting period.
c. Rights and Obligations	3. Amounts shown in the financial statements are properly presented and disclosed.
d. Valuation or allocation	4. The assets are the rights of the entity, and the liabilities are its obligations.
e. Statement presentation and disclosure	5. The assets and liabilities exist, and the recorded transactions have occurred.

6>   **4-33**   For each of the following audit procedures, indicate which type of evidence is being gathered: (1) physical examination,

(2) reperformance, (3) documentation, (4) confirmation, (5) analytical procedures, (6) enquiries of client personnel or management, or (7) observation.

a. Sending a written request to the client's customers requesting that they report the amount owed to the client.

b. Examining large sales invoices for a period of two days before and after year-end to determine if sales are recorded in the proper period.

c. Agreeing the total of the accounts receivable subsidiary ledger to the accounts receivable general ledger account.

d. Discussing the adequacy of the allowance for doubtful accounts with the credit manager.

e. Comparing the current-year gross profit percentage with the gross profit percentage for the last four years.

f. Examining a new plastic extrusion machine to ensure that this major acquisition was received.

g. Watching the client's warehouse personnel count the raw materials inventory.

h. Performing test counts of the warehouse personnel's count of the raw material.

i. Obtaining a letter from the client's lawyer indicating that there were no lawsuits in progress against the client.

j. Tracing the prices used by the client's billing program for pricing sales invoices to the client's approved price list.

4,6 ▷ **4-34**   For each of the audit procedures listed in Problem 4-33, identify the category (assertions about classes of transactions and events or assertions about account balances) and the relevant management assertion being tested.

2,4 ▷ **4-35**   Consideration of the components of audit risk is one of the principal means by which auditors plan engagements and organize their work. Audit risk is a function of inherent risk, control risk, and detection risk. When planning an engagement, the auditor will choose an appropriate level of audit risk, will assess inherent and control risks, and will thereby determine the necessary level of detection risk. In addition, more and more attention is being paid to client business risk.

Required:

Audit tests and procedures are normally designed to verify specific management assertions, rather than the financial statements as a whole. Explain how management assertions are incorporated into the application of the components of audit risk.

(CGA-Canada, adapted)

6,7 ▷ **4-36**   Inspection of records and documents relates to the auditor's examination of client accounting data and corroborating evidential matter. One issue that affects the reliability of documentary evidence is whether the documents are *internal* or *external*. Following are examples of documentary evidence:

1. duplicate copies of sales invoices I
2. purchase orders   I
3. bank statements E
4. remittance advices E
5. vendors' invoices   E
6. materials requisition forms I
7. overhead cost allocation sheets I
8. shipping documents
9. payroll cheques E
10. long-term debt agreements E

Required:

a. Classify each document as internal or external evidence.

b. Classify each document as to its reliability (high, moderate, or low).

6,7 **4-37** Evidence comes in various types and has different degrees of reliability. Following are some statements that compare various types of evidence that the auditor may obtain in different circumstances.

a. A bank confirmation versus observation of the segregation of duties between cash receipts and recording payment in the accounts receivable subsidiary ledger.

b. An auditor's recalculation of depreciation versus examination of raw material requisitions.

c. A bank statement included in the client's records versus shipping documents.

d. Physical examination of common stock certificates versus physical examination of inventory components for a personal computer.

Required:

For each situation, indicate whether the first or second type of evidence is more reliable. Provide a rationale for your choice.

6,7 **4-38** The confirmation process is defined as the process of obtaining and evaluating a direct communication from a third party in response to a request for information about a particular item affecting financial statement assertions.

Required:

a. List and describe the factors that affect the reliability of confirmations.

b. Refer back to EarthWear Clothiers' financial statements included in Chapter 1. Identify any information on EarthWear's financial statements that might be verified through the use of confirmations.

6,7 **4-39** In the course of their examination, as well as reviewing written documentary evidence, auditors ask many questions of client officers and employees.

Required:

a. Describe the factors that the auditor should consider in evaluating oral evidence provided by client officers and employees.

b. Discuss the validity and limitations of oral evidence.

6,7,8>   **4-40**   In connection with the audit of the annual financial statements of a manufacturing company, the auditor is observing the physical inventory of finished goods, which consists of expensive, highly complex electronic equipment.

Required:

Discuss the validity and limitations of the audit evidence provided by this procedure in relation to the relevant management assertions.

9>   **4-41**   Working papers are the auditor's record of work performed and conclusions reached on an audit engagement.

Required:

a. What are the purposes of working papers?

b. List and describe the various types of working papers in the current file.

c. What factors would affect the auditor's judgement about the quantity, type, and content of working papers for a particular engagement?

DISCUSSION CASES

4,5,6,7,8>   **4-42**   **Part I.** Lernout & Hauspie (L & H) was the world's leading provider of speech and language technology products, solutions, and services to businesses and individuals world-wide. Both Microsoft and Intel invested millions in L & H. However, accounting scandals and fraud allegations sent the company's stock crashing, and forced the firm to seek bankruptcy protection in Belgium and the United States. The following selected information pertains to L & H's sales and accounts receivable:

- Consolidated revenue increased 184 percent from the 1997 fiscal year to the 1998 fiscal year.
- Revenue in South Korea, which has a reputation as a difficult market for foreign companies to enter, increased from $97,000 in the first quarter of 1999 to approximately $59 million in the first quarter of 2000.
- In the second quarter of 2000, sales grew by 104 percent but accounts receivable grew by 128 percent.
- Average days outstanding increased from 138 days in 1998 to 160 days for the six-month period ended June 30, 2000.

Required:

a. Based on the above information, which management assertion(s) for sales should the auditor be most concerned with? Why?

b. Based on the above information, which management assertion(s) for accounts receivable should the auditor be most concerned with? Why?

c. What audit evidence should the auditor gather to verify the management assertion(s) for sales and accounts receivable? Be specific as to how each type of evidence relates to the assertions you mentioned in parts a and b of this question.

Part II. L & H's auditor did not confirm accounts receivable from customers in South Korea. However, *The Wall Street Journal* contacted 18 of L & H's South Korean customers and learned the following:

- Three out of 18 customers listed by L & H stated that they were not L & H customers.

- Three others indicated that their purchases from L & H were smaller than those reported by L & H.

Required:

a. If L & H's auditor had confirmed these receivables and received such responses, what additional evidence could they have gathered to try to obtain an accurate figure for sales to and accounts receivable from customers in South Korea?

b. If you were L & H's auditor and you had received such responses from South Korean customers, how likely would you be to use enquiry of the client as an audit procedure? Why?[7]

5,6,7   **4-43**   Bentley Bros. Book Company publishes more than 250 fiction and nonfiction titles. Most of the company's books are written by West Coast authors and typically focus on subjects popular in the region. The company sells most of its books to major retail stores such as Indigo.

Your firm was just selected as the new auditors for Bentley Bros., and you have been appointed as the audit manager for the engagement based on your prior industry experience. The prior auditors were removed because the client felt that it was not receiving adequate business advice. The prior auditors have indicated to you that the change in auditors did not result from any disagreements over accounting or auditing issues.

Your preliminary review of the company's financial statements indicates that the allowance for return of unsold books represents an important account (that is, high risk) because it may contain material misstatements. Consistent with industry practice, retailers are allowed to return unsold books for full credit. You know from your prior experience with other book publishers that the return rate for individual book titles can range from 30 to 50 percent. The client develops its allowance for return of unsold books based on

---

[7]M. Maremont, J. Eisinger, and J. Carreyrou, "How High-Tech Dream at Lernout & Hauspie Crumbled in a Scandal," *The Wall Street Journal* (December 7, 2000), pp. A1, A18; J. Carreyrou and M. Maremont, "Lernout Unit Engaged in Massive Fraud to Fool Auditors, New Inquiry Concludes," *The Wall Street Journal* (April 6, 2001), p. A3; and J. Carreyrou, "Lernout Unit Booked Fictitious Sales, Says Probe," *The Wall Street Journal* (April 9, 2001), p. B2.

internally generated records; that is, it maintains detailed records of all book returns by title.

Required:

a. Discuss how you would assess the reliability of the client's records for developing the allowance for return of unsold books.

b. Discuss how you would determine the return rate for relatively new titles.

c. Consider whether any external evidence can be obtained that would provide additional evidence on the reasonableness of the account.

2,3,4   **4-44**   Alec Goshen has been the auditor of The Gentlemen's Stores Ltd. (TGS), a medium-sized retailer of men's clothes, for several years. TGS has six stores in Ontario. Invoices for inventory purchases are paid by a central office and are approved for payment only after they are matched with receiving slips sent in from the stores.

Each year Alec has verified TGS's accounts receivable by direct communication (written requests for accounts receivable confirmation to TGS's customers). This year he plans to confirm accounts payable also. Sandra Woo, the manager and principal shareholder in TGS, has never been happy about Alec's direct communication with TGS's customers. When Alec informed her that he intended to communicate with the company's creditors also, she was very displeased. "Why," she said, "do you want to communicate with creditors when you have statements representing 75 percent of the dollar value of our payables? You've asked us to keep the statements that we receive and we've gone out of our way to do so but now you're saying they're not good enough. I've gone along with your writing to our debtors because they don't send out statements, but our creditors do. What you're proposing would only serve to remind them that we owe them money and there are some I don't want to remind because then we'll have to pay them faster. Anyway, I understand that your main purpose in verifying accounts payable is to detect unrecorded liabilities, not that there would be any, and surely communicating with existing creditors is not going to help you do that—you're looking at our subsequent payments as it is. I can see why you have to verify accounts receivable this way, but accounts payable are completely different. Besides, it'll cost me more money because it will take you more time to do the audit."

Required:

State the points that Alec would make in replying to Ms. Woo. Cover both theoretical and practical points.

(CICA, adapted)

INTERNET ASSIGNMENT

5,6,7>   **4-45**   Use an Internet browser to search for the following terms:

- Electronic data interchange (EDI)
- Image-processing systems
- Prepare a memo describing EDI and image-processing systems.
- Discuss the implication of each for the auditors consideration of audit evidence.

Part III PLANNING THE AUDIT AND UNDERSTANDING INTERNAL CONTROL

Audit Planning and Types of Audit Tests

Chapter **5**

Learning Objectives

Upon completion of this chapter, you will be able to

1. Explain the auditor's requirements for client acceptance and retention.
2. Explain the steps in establishing the terms of an engagement.
3. Outline the steps that are involved in preplanning for the audit engagement.
4. Describe the steps that are performed in planning an audit engagement.
5. Outline the types of audit procedures.
6. Describe the purposes of analysis and types of analytical procedures.
7. Explain the audit testing heirarchy.

RELEVANT ACCOUNTING AND ASSURANCE PRONOUNCEMENTS

CICA Handbook, **section 3840,** Related party transactions

CICA Handbook, **section 5049,** Use of specialists in assurance engagements

CICA Handbook, **section 5050,** Using the work of internal audit

CICA Handbook, **section 5110,** Terms of the engagement.

CICA Handbook, **section 5141,** Understanding the entity and its environment and assessing the risks of material misstatement

CICA Handbook, **section 5142,** Materiality

CICA Handbook, **section 5143,** The auditor's procedures in response to assessed risks

CICA Handbook, **section 5150,** Planning

CICA Handbook, **section 5301,** Analysis

CICA Handbook, **section 5751,** Communications with those having oversight responsibility for the financial reporting process

CICA Handbook, **section 6010,** Audit of related party transactions

PLANNING FOR THE AUDIT OF EARTHWEAR

EarthWear By the time the members of the engagement team from Willis & Adams arrive at the offices of EarthWear, they will already have spent a good deal of time planning the audit. The very first consideration is whether Willis & Adams wishes to retain EarthWear as an audit client. In the case of EarthWear, Willis & Adams would have few qualms—EarthWear is a financially strong company with experienced, competent, ethical management. Assuming the client retention decision is positive, there are a number of internal decisions that Willis & Adams must address, such as deciding precisely which firm members will be on the engagement team and when they will schedule the actual field-work at EarthWear's premises. They may also need to determine whether or not they will need to obtain the services of any specialists to assist them with any facets of the audit. For example, although EarthWear does not have an outstanding pension obligation to its employees, a not-uncommon occurrence is that the services of an independent actuary may be needed to confirm a company's valuation of its pension obligation, or perhaps to assist with the valuation of highly specialized inventory.

As part of the planning process, the partner and manager on the engagement will use the preliminary financial information of EarthWear to determine a preliminary figure for materiality. They will also learn as much as they can about EarthWear's strategies and business processes in order to identify any areas where they feel there may be a heightened risk of material misstatement and consequently a requirement for more audit attention. At this time Willis & Adams will also prepare an engagement letter to be signed by the senior management of EarthWear explicitly identifying each party's obligations and responsibilities in this engagement. One of the important terms of the engagement that may be specified in the letter is that amount of assistance that may be provided by EarthWear's own internal audit staff. Under stringent conditions, Willis & Adams may use the work of EarthWear's internal auditors.

The last step in planning the audit we will mention here is the important step of analysis. The audit team from Willis & Adams will use this year's financial information from EarthWear, in conjunction with other information from external sources, such as industry information, and internal sources such as prior years and budgets, to critically analyze the information in EarthWear's financial statements. The purpose behind doing this at the planning stage of the audit is to identify areas that may seem different from expectations and therefore merit additional audit attention.

This chapter discusses the steps such as those above, and other steps not mentioned above, that Willis & Adams will go through in planning for the audit of EarthWear. All this preliminary effort has two goals, first to deliver an effective audit, one in which Willis & Adams is satisfied that the risk of material misstatement is kept to an acceptably low level, and two, to deliver an efficient audit so that EarthWear receives the most benefit for their audit fee.

Client Acceptance and Retention

LO 1 The first phase of the audit process that relates to audit planning is client acceptance and retention (see Figure 5–1). The extent of effort that goes into evaluating a new client is normally much greater than the decision to continue an existing client. With a continuing client the auditor possesses extensive knowledge about the entity and its environment.

FIGURE 5–1

The Phases of an
Audit That Relate
to Audit Planning

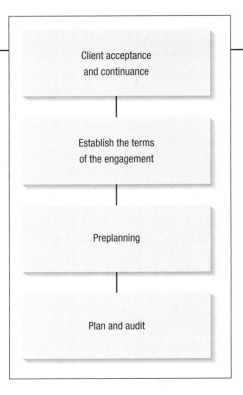

Client acceptance
and continuance

Establish the terms
of the engagement

Preplanning

Plan and audit

Prospective Client Acceptance

Public accounting firms should investigate a prospective client prior to accepting an engagement.[1] Table 5–1 lists procedures that a firm might conduct to evaluate a prospective client. Performance of such procedures would normally be documented in a memo or by completion of a client acceptance questionnaire or checklist.

When the prospective client has previously been audited, the successor auditor is required by the Rules of Professional Conduct to make certain enquiries of the predecessor auditor before accepting the engagement. The successor auditor should request permission of the prospective client before contacting the predecessor auditor. Because the Rules of Professional Conduct do not allow an auditor to disclose confidential client information without the client's consent, the prospective client must authorize the predecessor auditor to respond to the successor's requests for information. The successor auditor's communications with the predecessor auditor should include questions related to the integrity of management; disagreements with management over accounting and auditing issues; communications with audit committees or an equivalent group regarding fraud, illegal acts, and internal-control-related matters; and the predecessor's understanding of the reason for the change in auditors.

---

[1]See H. F. Huss and F. A. Jacobs, "Risk Containment: Exploring Auditor Decisions in the Engagement Process," *Auditing: A Journal of Practice and Theory* (Fall 1991), pp. 16–32, for a description of the client acceptance process of the Big 5 firms.

Table 5–1	**Procedures for Evaluating a Prospective Client**

1. Obtain and review available financial information (annual reports, interim financial statements, income tax returns, etc.).

2. Enquire of third parties about any information concerning the integrity of the prospective client and its management. (Such enquiries should be directed to the prospective client's bankers and lawyers, credit agencies, and other members of the business community who may have such knowledge.)

3. Communicate with the predecessor auditor about whether there were any disagreements about accounting principles, audit procedures, or similar significant matters.

4. Consider whether the prospective client has any circumstances that will require special attention or that may represent unusual business or audit risks, such as litigation or going-concern problems.

5. Determine if the firm is independent of the client and able to provide the desired service.

6. Determine if the firm has the necessary technical skills and knowledge of the industry to complete the engagement.

7. Determine if acceptance of the client would violate any applicable regulatory agency requirements or the Rules of Professional Conduct.

Such enquiries of the predecessor auditor may help the successor auditor determine whether to accept the engagement. The predecessor auditor should respond fully to the successor's requests on a timely basis unless an unusual circumstance (such as a lawsuit) exists. If the predecessor's response is limited, the successor auditor must be informed that the response is limited.

The successor auditor may need information on beginning balances and consistent application of GAAP in order to issue an unqualified report. The successor auditor should request that the client authorize the predecessor auditor to permit a review of his or her working papers. In most instances, the predecessor auditor will allow the successor auditor to make copies of any working papers of continuing interest (for example, details of selected balance sheet accounts).

In the unusual case where the prospective client refuses to permit the predecessor to respond, the successor auditor should have reservations about accepting the client. Such a situation should raise serious questions about management's motivations and integrity.

If the client has not previously been audited, the public accounting firm should complete all the procedures listed in Table 5–1, except for the communication with the predecessor auditor. The auditor should review the prospective client's financial information and carefully assess management integrity by communicating with the entity's bankers and lawyers, as well as other members of the business community. In some cases, the public accounting firm may hire an investigative agency to check on management's background.

Continuing Client Retention

Public accounting firms need to evaluate periodically whether to retain their current clients. This evaluation may take place at or near the completion of an audit or when some significant event occurs. Conflicts over accounting and auditing issues or disputes over fees may lead a public accounting firm to disassociate itself from a client.

Establishing the Terms of the Engagement

LO 2〉 The auditor and the client must agree on the terms of the engagement, including the type, scope, and timing of the engagement. This understanding reduces the risk that either party may misinterpret what is expected or required of the other party. The terms of the engagement, which are documented in the engagement letter, should include the objectives of the engagement, management's responsibilities, the auditor's responsibilities, and the limitations of the engagement. In establishing the terms of the engagement,[2] three topics are discussed below: (1) the engagement letter, (2) using the work of internal auditors, and (3) the audit committee.

The Engagement Letter

An *engagement letter* is a very important document that is signed by both the auditor and the client. It formalizes the arrangement reached between the auditor and the client. This letter serves as a contract, outlining the responsibilities of both parties and preventing misunderstandings between the two parties. Exhibit 5–1 shows a sample engagement letter.[3]

In addition to the items mentioned in the sample engagement letter in Exhibit 5–1, the engagement letter may include:

- arrangements involving the use of internal auditors or specialists
- any limitation of the liability of the auditor or client, such as indemnification to the auditor for liability arising from knowing misrepresentations to the auditor by management (Note that regulatory bodies, such as the OSC or SEC, may restrict or prohibit such liability-limiting arrangements.)
- additional services to be provided relating to regulatory requirements
- arrangements regarding other services (for example, assurance or tax services)

Internal Auditors

When the client has internal auditors, the auditor may request their assistance in conducting the audit. This is dealt with in *CICA Handbook*, section 5050, "Using the work of internal audit." The decision process the auditor follows is outlined in Figure 5–2. The major issue for the independent auditor is assessing the *competence* and *objectivity* of the internal auditors and the effect of their work on the audit. Table 5–2 presents factors that the auditor should consider when assessing the competence and objectivity of the internal auditors.

The internal auditors' work may affect the nature, timing, and extent of the audit procedures performed by the independent auditor. For example, as part of their regular work, internal auditors may review, assess, and monitor the entity's controls that are included in the various accounting cycles. Similarly, part of their work may include confirming receivables or observing certain physical inventories. If the internal auditors are

---

[2]See *CICA Handbook*, section 5110, "Terms of the engagement," for a full discussion.

[3]The Appendix to *CICA Handbook* section 5110 provides a template for Canadian auditors in the preparation of an engagement letter.

EXHIBIT 5–1

A Sample Engagement Letter

Willis & Adams
Calgary, Alberta

April 1, 2007

Mr. Calvin J. Rogers, President and Chief Executive Officer
EarthWear Clothiers
P.O. Box 787
Calgary, Alberta T3T 3T3

Dear Mr. Rogers:

This will confirm our understanding of the arrangements for our audit of the financial statements of EarthWear Clothiers for the year ending December 31, 2006.

Services and Related Report

We will audit the company's financial statements of the year ending December 31, 2006, for the purpose of expressing an opinion on the fairness with which they present, in all material respects, the financial position, results of operations, and cash flows in conformity with generally accepted accounting principles. Upon completion of our audit, we will provide you with our audit report on the financial statements referred to above. As part of our engagement for the year ending December 31, 2006, we will also review the federal income tax return for EarthWear Clothiers.

Our Responsibilities and Limitations

We will conduct our audit in accordance with Canadian generally accepted auditing standards. Those standards require that we obtain reasonable, rather than absolute, assurance that the financial statements are free of material misstatement, whether caused by error or fraud. Accordingly, a material misstatement may remain undetected. Also, an audit is not designed to detect error or fraud that is immaterial to the financial statements; therefore, the audit will not necessarily detect misstatements less than this materiality level that might exist due to error, fraudulent financial reporting, or misappropriation of assets. If, for any reason, we are unable to complete the audit or are unable to form or have not formed an opinion, we may decline to express an opinion or decline to issue a report as a result of the engagement.

While an audit includes obtaining an understanding of internal control sufficient to plan the audit and to determine the nature, timing, and extent of audit procedures to be performed, it is not designed to provide assurance on internal control. However, we are responsible for ensuring that the audit committee (or others with equivalent authority or responsibility) is aware of any significant weaknesses in internal control that come to our attention.

Management's Responsibilities

The financial statements are the responsibility of the company's management. Management is also responsible for (1) establishing and maintaining effective internal control over financial reports, (2) identifying and ensuring that the company complies with the laws and regulations applicable to its activities, (3) making all financial records and related information available to us, and (4) providing to us at the conclusion of the engagement a representation letter that, among other things, will confirm management's responsibility for the preparation of the financial statements in conformity with generally accepted accounting principles, the availability of financial records and related data, the completeness and availability of all minutes of the board and committee meetings, and, to the best of its knowledge and belief, the absence of fraud involving management or those employees who have a significant role in the entity's internal control.

Fees

Our fees will be billed as work progresses and are based on the amount of time required at various levels of responsibility, plus actual out-of-pocket expenses. Invoices are payable upon presentation. We will notify you immediately of any circumstances we encounter that could significantly affect our initial estimate of total fees.

If this letter correctly expresses your understanding, please sign the enclosed copy and return it to us.

We appreciate the opportunity to serve you.

Very truly yours,

Willis & Adams

M. J. Willis
_____
M. J. Willis, Partner

APPROVED:

By _*Calvin J. Rogers*_____ Chief Executive Officer

Date _April 3, 2007_____

FIGURE 5–2

The Auditor's Consideration of the Internal Audit Function in an Audit of Financial Statements

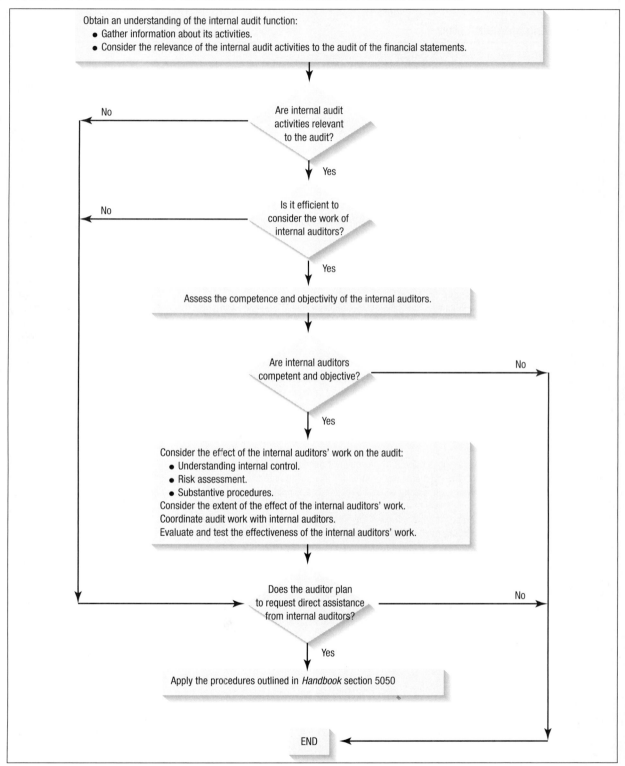

Table 5–2	**Factors for Assessing the Competence and Objectivity of Internal Auditors**

Competence:

- Educational level and professional experience.
- Professional certification and continuing education.
- Audit policies, procedures, and checklists.
- Practices regarding their assignments.
- The supervision and review of their audit activities.
- The quality of their working paper documentation, reports, and recommendations.
- Evaluation of their performance.

Objectivity:

- The organizational status of the internal auditor responsible for the internal audit function (for example, the internal auditor reports to an officer of sufficient status to ensure that the audit coverage is broad and the internal auditor has access to the board of directors or the audit committee).
- Policies to maintain internal auditors' objectivity about the areas audited (for example, internal auditors are prohibited from auditing areas to which they have recently been assigned or are to work upon completion of responsibilities in the internal audit function).

competent and objective, the independent auditor may use the internal auditors' work in these areas to reduce the scope of audit work. The materiality of the account balance or class of transactions and its related audit risk may also determine how much the independent auditor can rely on the internal auditors' work. When internal auditors provide direct assistance, the auditor should supervise, review, evaluate, and test their work.

The Audit Committee[4]

In Canada, all companies incorporated under the *Canada Business Corporations Act* (CBCA) whose shares are widely held are required by the Act to create a special committee of the board of directors called the audit committee. In addition to legislated requirements, the major exchanges (e.g., TSX, NYSE, AMEX) require their listees to have an audit committee. Factors that may affect the effectiveness of the audit committee include the following:

- its independence from management
- the experience and stature of its members
- the extent of its involvement with and scrutiny of the entity's activities
- the appropriateness of its actions

---

[4]See PricewaterhouseCoopers, *Audit Committees: Good Practices for Meeting Market Expectations* (New York: PricewaterhouseCoopers, 1999); PricewaterhouseCoopers, *Audit Committees: Best Practices for Protecting Shareholder Interests* (New York: PricewaterhouseCoopers, 1999); PricewaterhouseCoopers, *Audit Committees: Update* (New York: PricewaterhouseCoopers, 1999); and Criteria of Control Board, *Guidance for Directors— Governance Processes for Control* (Toronto: CICA, 2000); Canadian Securities Administrators, Multilateral Instrument 52-100, *Audit Committees* (Toronto: CSA, 2007).

- the degree to which difficult questions are raised and pursued with management
- its interaction with the internal and external auditors

The audit committee's sole legislated responsibility under the CBCA is to review the audited financial statements before they are issued. However, the requirements of multilateral instrument 52-110 require the audit committee to be involved throughout the audit process. Some of the typical responsibilities of the audit committee include:

- direct responsibility for the appointment, compensation, and oversight of the work of the company's auditors
- review of the parameters and scope of the audit
- preapproval of all audit and non-audit services provided by the auditor
- continuing liaison with the auditors, including resolution of any disputes between the auditors and management
- establishing procedures for the receipt, retention, and treatment of complaints received by the company regarding accounting, internal control, and auditing
- obtaining independent legal advice, if and as necessary to carry out its duties

The audit committee should also interact with the internal audit function. An ideal arrangement for establishing the independence of the internal audit function is for the head of internal auditing to report either directly or indirectly to the audit committee.

The audit committee will meet with the external auditor even before the start of the engagement to discuss the auditor's responsibilities and the company's significant accounting policies. At the beginning of the engagement, the audit committee will review the scope and costs of the auditor's planned work, and even provide input into the scope of the auditor's work such as requesting that the auditor visit certain locations or conduct special investigations into certain matters. The auditor is entitled to attend meetings of the audit committee and even call such meetings during the course of the audit if he or she deems it necessary. Recall from Chapter 3, section 5751 of the *CICA Handbook's* recommendations regarding the auditor's communications with the audit committee both during and after the audit engagement. Thus, the audit committee acts as a liaison and a buffer between company management and the auditor.

Preplanning for the Audit Engagement

LO 3>   There are generally two preplanning activities: (1) determining the audit engagement team requirements, and (2) ensuring the independence of the audit firm and audit team.

Determine the Audit Engagement Team Requirements

Public accounting firms need to ensure that their engagements are completed by auditors having the proper degree of technical training and proficiency given the circumstances of the clients. Factors that should be considered in determining staffing requirements include engagement size and complexity, level of risk, any special expertise, personnel availability, and timing of the work to be performed. For example, if the engagement involves a high level of risk, the firm should staff the engagement with more experienced auditors. Similarly, if the audit involves a specialized industry (banking, insurance, and so on) or if the client uses sophisticated computer processing, the firm must ensure that members of the audit team possess the requisite expertise. Generally, a time budget is prepared in order to assist with the staffing requirements and to schedule the field work.

When the auditor is determining the audit engagement team require-ments in the planning phase, two "special cases" may arise. The first is that in some instances, the audit may require consulting with an outside specialist. In the large majority of audits, the auditors' knowledge of the client's busi-ness provides them with sufficient expertise, but if the client is in a highly specialized industry and produces a highly specialized product, an outside specialist might be used. *CICA Handbook*, section 5049, "Use of specialists in assurance engagements," which provides guidance in this area, characterizes a *specialist* as a person or firm possessing significant expertise in a field other than accounting or auditing. This would include individuals such as actuar-ies, appraisers, attorneys, engineers, and geologists. Such specialists may assist the auditor with valuation issues, determination of physical quantities, amounts derived from specialized techniques, or interpretations of regula-tions or agreements. For example, an auditor might consult an actuary to determine the amount of the client's pension obligations or a geologist to esti-mate a client's oil and gas reserves.[5] The most important point to remember is that the ultimate responsibility for the audit report rests with the auditor. Paragraph 5049.24 of the *Handbook* contains the following recommendation:

> Before accepting an [audit], the [auditor] should consider whether his or her involvement in the [audit] and understanding of the subject matter is sufficient to enable the auditor to discharge his or her responsibilities.

The second special case is when a *primary* auditor will be incor-porating the results of a *secondary* auditor's work in his or her audit. Section 6930 of the *Handbook* addresses reliance by a primary auditor on the report and work of a secondary auditor when the primary auditor is reporting on financial statements that include financial information from financial statements reported on by the secondary auditor. A frequent example would be when the auditor of a parent company requires the financial statements of a subsidiary company for consolidation purposes and those financial statements are audited by another auditor. In such cases the primary auditor bears the ultimate responsibility for all of the work that goes into his or her report on the parent. The *Handbook* suggests several steps that the primary auditor should take, including:

- considering the professional qualifications, competence, and integrity of the secondary auditor
- communicating with the secondary auditor to ensure that the secondary auditor conducted his or her audit in a manner such that the primary auditor can rely on the report and has advised the primary auditor of any matters that could affect the opinion of the primary auditor

---

[5] See also D. C. Selley, *Use of Specialists in Assurance Engagements* (Toronto: CICA, 2000).

In both of these special cases it is clearly important that the auditor be aware of such circumstances early so as to allow sufficient time to plan for the need to incorporate the work of a specialist or another auditor into the engagement.

Assess Objectivity and Independence

The third part of the general standard requires that the auditor perform the audit with an objective state of mind. There are two aspects to objectivity—objectivity in *fact* and objectivity in *appearance*. Since external observers such as financial analysts, investors, or creditors cannot know an auditor's state of mind (objectivity in fact), they infer objectivity in fact from objectivity in appearance. The most widely scrutinized component of objectivity is independence from the client, in financial and managerial relationships. As an example, Rule 204, incorporated in the Rules of Professional Conduct by all of the provincial institutes of CAs, focuses on independence and identifies activities and relationships between auditors and their clients that could impair independence, or could be perceived by an external observer to do so. The flavour of the rule can be discerned from the requirement for the auditor to consider independence and threats to independence before and throughout each assurance engagement. Rule 204 is covered in more detail in Chapter 17.

The interpretation and application of the rule is spelled out in the associated "Council Interpretation of Rules" in the Member's Handbook of the provincial institutes. (Recall that each province has its own Rules of Professional Conduct, although they are similar across all provinces.) Council interpretations provide examples of activities or relationships that would not be in compliance with the rules. For example, according to the interpretations of Rule 204, neither the auditor, nor his or her partner(s), nor his or her family, may hold direct or indirect investment in a client (including shares, bonds, mortgages, etc.), nor may they hold a position such as director, officer, or employee of the client. It is a common practice among the large firms to have all personnel complete an annual questionnaire regarding financial or managerial relationships with the firm's clients.

The foregoing interpretation of Rule 204 adopts the perspective of the auditor's indebtedness to the client, (e.g., a mortgage with a bank client) but another area of concern may be unpaid client fees. If an account receivable from a client takes on the characteristics of a loan, it may bring into question the auditor's ability to maintain financial independence and hence objectivity. Many public accounting firms adopt a policy of not completing the current audit until all of the prior year's fees have been paid.

The provision of consulting services by auditors to their audit clients has long been a contentious issue. The potential impairment of objectivity and independence has been highlighted by recent events. Current standards in Canada and the United States now prohibit audit firms from offering all but tax services to their audit clients.

Planning the Audit

LO 4> Engagement planning involves all the issues the auditor should consider in developing an overall strategy for conducting the audit. The objective of the audit plan is to conduct an effective and efficient audit. Basically, this means that the audit is to be conducted in accordance with auditing standards and that the risk of material misstatements is reduced to an acceptably low level. The audit plan should also consider how to conduct the engagement in a cost-effective manner.

Additional steps to be performed include

- obtain knowledge of the client's business and industry, and assess inherent risk
- establish materiality and consider audit risk
- assess a preliminary level for control risk
- assess the possibility of fraud, errors, and illegal acts
- identify related parties
- conduct preliminary analytical procedures
- develop an overall audit strategy and prepare audit programs

Some of these steps have been discussed previously (such as materiality and audit risk). They are included briefly again here briefly to show their place in the sequence of audit planning. While these steps are listed in the order in which they are usually performed, an audit of financial statements is a cumulative and iterative process that often dictates that these steps be performed concurrently and that the results obtained from one step may result in a reassessment of results from another step.

Obtain Knowledge of the Client's Business and Industry and Assess Inherent Risk: The Strategic Systems Approach

Section 5141 of the *CICA Handbook*, "Understanding the entity and assessing the risk of material misstatement," emphasizes that knowledge of the entity's business is fundamental to planning and executing audit procedures. It provides the auditor with a basis for:

- assessing inherent risk
- obtaining a sufficient understanding of internal control
- identifying the nature and sources of audit evidence available
- designing audit procedures
- understanding the substance of transactions
- assessing whether sufficient appropriate audit evidence has been obtained
- assessing the appropriateness of management's selection of accounting principles
- assessing management's overall financial statement presentation

Figure 5–3 schematically presents this top-down approach.

As shown in Figure 5–3, which illustrates the top-down audit planning process, the auditor starts by identifying and obtaining an understanding of the entity, particularly its objectives and strategies, and key business processes. The auditor also needs to obtain an understanding of such aspects of the entity and its environment as management, governance, measurement and performance, and industry, regulatory and other external factors, particularly as they may either facilitate or pose risks that threaten the entity's achievement of its strategic objectives. Some examples

FIGURE 5–3

An Overview of the Audit Planning Processes

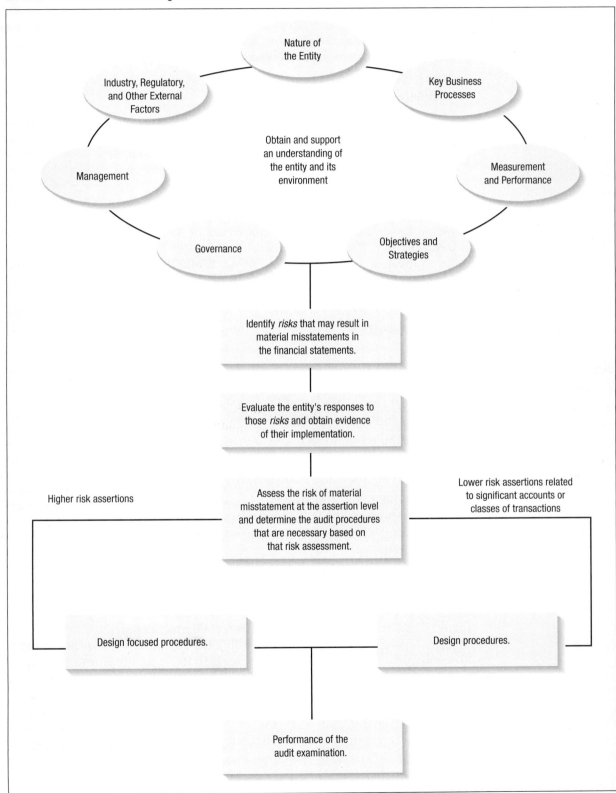

of conditions that may indicate the existence of business risks include significant changes in the entity such as a major reorganization, significant changes in the entity's industry, or significant changes in the information technology (IT) environment.

An understanding of the key business processes of the entity and of its environment is necessary to allow the auditor to assess the risk of material misstatement and to set the scope of the audit. Accordingly, the auditor should perform sufficient appropriate procedures to support that understanding. Such procedures might include enquiry of client personnel, observation of activities, analytical procedures and reading business plans and strategies. Information about the client's industry can be obtained from sources such as trade publications, periodicals, and textbooks. As well, there may be specialized industry-specific training programs, which the auditor can attend.

The auditor should thoroughly understand the client's business processes and its organization. This includes such elements as types of products or services, capital structure, number of locations, and so on. In particular the auditor must be knowledgeable about the key business processes (physical production, distribution, financial and accounting) that the client relies on to achieve its strategic objectives and control its risks. This will assist the auditor in planning a more efficient and effective audit.

Another component is for the auditor to evaluate the entity's own response to risks. Management has a responsibility to strive to attain the entity's objectives. Therefore, management should establish a risk assessment process that identifies, analyzes, assesses, and manages risks that may affect the entity's objectives. For those risks identified as possibly resulting in material misstatement, the auditor should evaluate the entity's responses to those risks and obtain evidence of their implementation. The auditor should perform this step because the entity's responses, or non-responses, affect the design and operation of key business processes, and thereby affect audit risk. For example, in understanding the entity and its environment, the auditor should obtain information on the entity's risk assessment process and whether it is operating effectively. If the entity's response to the identified risk is adequate, the risk of material misstatement may be reduced. However, if the entity's response to the identified risk is inadequate, the auditor's assessment of the risk of material misstatement may increase. As will be discussed in Chapter 6, this evaluation may provide a basis for the auditor's planned level of control risk.

While the auditor expresses an opinion on the financial statements taken as a whole, the auditor needs to assess audit risk at the individual account balance level (e.g., accounts receivable, inventory, etc.). The auditor assesses audit risk at the *account balance level* because it assists with determining the scope of the audit procedures. Based on the knowledge obtained in evaluating the entity's responses to business risks, the auditor assesses the risk of material misstatement at the *assertion level* (refer to the earlier discussion of management assertions) and determines the specific audit procedures that are necessary based on that risk assessment. Risks identified at the entity level may "filter" down and affect the accounts contained in the financial statements. The type of risk identified at the account balance level is likely to affect specific assertions in the account balance. As discussed later in the text, the auditor normally tests individual transactions that make up the account balance in order to obtain evidence on the assertions. Consider the example of changing technology in an industry. The risk posed by changing technology could result in possible misstatements in inventory due to obsolescence. The potential inventory obsolescence of inventory affects the valuation assertion.

In Figure 5–3, a distinction is made between high risk and low risk assertions. For *high risk* assertions, the auditor should consider how material misstatements may occur, and design *focused* audit procedures to specifically address the potential misstatements. Examples of items that may require focused audit procedures include non-routine or unsystematically processed transactions, significant accounting estimates and judgements, or highly complex transactions. Such special procedures are used in the case of significant identified risks and are designed to reduce the risk of undetected material misstatements to a low level. For *low risk* assertions, the auditor should design procedures to address the normal risks of material misstatement. Usually, low risk assertions relate to routine processing of significant transactions whose characteristics often allow highly automated processing by IT with little or no manual intervention. Such transactions are likely to be recurring, objectively measurable, and processed in a similar way.

Establish Materiality and Consider Audit Risk

Materiality and audit risk are major concepts that affect the scope of the audit and therefore must be considered when the auditor plans the engagement. Chapter 3 covered the decision processes followed by the auditor in establishing materiality and audit risk. The reader should return to Chapter 3 and review the important issues related to these concepts.

Assess a Preliminary Level for Control Risk

Control risk is the risk that material misstatements will not be prevented or detected by internal controls. The auditor evaluates the effectiveness of internal control for preventing material misstatements in the financial statements and prepares a preliminary assessment of control risk. A preliminary assessment of control risk is necessary for the auditor to plan the nature, timing, and extent of testing. A primary concern at this point is the extent to which information technology is used in processing accounting information. In evaluating the effect of information technology on the client's accounting systems, the auditor needs information on the following:

- the extent to which information technology is used in each significant accounting system
- the complexity of the client's computer operations
- the organizational structure of the information technology activities
- the availability of data
- the need for information technology–assisted techniques to gather data and conduct audit procedures

The presence of complex information technology may require the use of a computer audit specialist. Chapter 6 covers these issues in more detail.

Assess the Risk of Fraud, Errors, and Illegal Acts

Fraud and Error   The auditor has a responsibility to plan and perform the audit to obtain reasonable assurance that the financial statements are free from material misstatement, whether caused by fraud or error. As discussed in Chapter 3, *errors* are *unintentional* misstatements or omissions of amounts or disclosures in financial statements whereas *fraud* refers to *intentional* misstatements that include management fraud and defalcation. (Refer to Chapter 3 for more detailed coverage of the auditor's responsibility for fraud and errors and see Exhibit 5–2 for an example of management fraud.) It is important for the auditor to exercise due care and professional scepticism to achieve reasonable assurance that both fraud and material errors are detected. *Professional scepticism* means that the auditor should remain objective and unbiased by not assuming that management is either honest or dishonest.

During the conduct of the audit, certain conditions or circumstances that may indicate the presence of fraud may come to the auditor's attention. If the auditor suspects or detects fraud, he or she should, in addition to considering whether it has a material effect on the financial statements, also consider what its potential implications are for other parts of the audit.

Illegal Acts   Recall from Chapter 3 that the term *illegal acts* refers to violations of laws or governmental regulations (see also Table 3–10). In some instances, fraud as described in the previous section may also consist of illegal acts.

If an illegal act has occurred or is likely to have occurred, the auditor should consider its implications for other aspects of the audit, particularly the reliability of management representations. The auditor should ensure that those in charge of corporate governance, such as the audit committee, or other body or person with equivalent authority and responsibility,

EXHIBIT 5–2

Livent—Accounting Irregularities and Restated Earnings

Livent (a contraction of Live Entertainment) was formed in 1990 from a division of Cineplex Odeon. When Livent went public in 1993, its shares were first listed on the Toronto Stock Exchange, and later on NASDAQ in the US as well. The company successfully produced such shows as *Joseph and the Amazing Technicolor Dreamcoat*, *Kiss of the Spider Woman*, and *The Phantom of the Opera*. Livent also owned several theatres in Canada and the US. Following the infusion of needed new capital and a change of management in mid-1998, Livent announced that it had uncovered significant accounting irregularities involving the improper recognition of revenue and the failure to record certain expenses. Following a comprehensive review by KPMG/Peat Marwick, the company restated its financial statements for 1996, reducing 1996 net income from a gain of $11.1 million to a loss of $18.0 million (a $29.1 million reduction) and reducing 1997 net income from a loss of $44.1 million to a loss of $98.7 million (a $54.6 million reduction). It was alleged that the former senior management concealed the manipulations from the auditors and signed false and misleading letters of representation. In June 1999 two of the former senior management were sued in civil court by the SEC and were also indicted by the US federal court for fraud and insider trading. In 2002, the RCMP charged them with 19 counts each of fraud over $5,000. It is estimated that investors lost about $100 million in the wake of the financial turmoil and the subsequent fall in share price.

is adequately informed about significant illegal acts. The auditor should also recognize that, under the circumstances noted previously, he or she may have a duty to notify parties outside the client. In such circumstances, or if the auditor is considering resigning from the engagement, the auditor should seek legal advice.

Identify Related Parties

CICA Handbook, section 3840, "Related party transactions," identifies the types of relationships that give rise to related parties. Some of the relationships are:

- an entity that directly or indirectly controls, is controlled by, or is under common control with the reporting entity
- an entity that is subject to significant influence by the reporting entity
- management
- an individual who directly or indirectly controls the reporting entity
- an individual having an ownership interest that results in significant influence
- an investor or investee, when the investment is accounted for by either the equity method or the proportionate consolidation method

It is important that the auditor attempt to identify all related parties during the planning phase of the audit because transactions between the entity and related parties may not be "at arm's length." For example, the client may lease property from an entity owned by the chief executive officer at lease rates in excess of prevailing market rates. The auditor can identify related parties by evaluating the client's procedures for identifying related parties, requesting a list of related parties from management, and reviewing filings with a securities commission such as the OSC, and other regulatory agencies. Once related parties have been identified, audit personnel should be provided with the names so that transactions with such parties are identified and investigated. Audit procedures that may identify transactions with related parties include:

- enquire of management regarding related-party transactions
- review the minutes of the board of directors and executive or operating committees for information about material transactions authorized or discussed at their meetings
- review conflict-of-interest statements obtained by the company from management
- review the extent and nature of business transacted with major customers, suppliers, borrowers, and lenders for indications of previously undisclosed relationships
- review accounting records for large, unusual, or nonrecurring transactions or balances, paying particular attention to transactions recognized at or near the end of the reporting period
- review confirmations of loans receivable and payable for indications of guarantees (If guarantees are identified, determine their nature and the relationships of the guarantor to the entity.)

Refer to the appendix of *CICA Handbook,* section 6010, "Audit of related party transactions," for additional guidance on searching for and reporting on related parties.

Conduct Preliminary Analytical Procedures

Analytical procedures consist of evaluations of financial information made by a study of plausible relationships among both financial and nonfinancial data. This standard requires that the auditor apply analytical procedures at the planning phase for all audits. The main objectives of analytical procedures at this point are (1) to understand the client's business and transactions and (2) to identify financial statement accounts that are likely to contain errors. By identifying where errors are likely, the auditor can allocate more resources to investigate those accounts. For example, consider the inventory turnover, computed as follows:

$$\text{Inventory turnover} = \frac{\text{Cost of goods sold}}{\text{Inventory}}$$

Suppose that the auditor's analysis of inventory turnover for EarthWear for the past five years showed the following trend, which would be compared to industry data:

	2002	*2003*	*2004*	*2005*	*2006*
Client	8.9	8.8	8.5	8.0	7.9
Industry	8.8	8.7	8.8	8.6	8.6

The inventory turnover ratio in this case has declined steadily over the five-year period, while the industry turnover ratio shows only a minor decline over the same period. The auditor might suspect that the client's inventory contains slow-moving or obsolete inventory. The auditor would then plan additional testing for selected assertions such as valuation, completeness, and existence.

Develop an Overall Audit Strategy and Prepare Audit Programs

Once these planning steps have been completed, the auditor develops an overall audit strategy. This involves decisions about the *nature, timing,* and *extent,* of audit tests. At this stage, the auditor would use his or her accumulated knowledge about the client's business objectives, strategies, and related business and audit risks. One way is for the auditor to record how the client is managing its risks (i.e., through internal control processes) and document the effect of the risks and controls on the planned audit procedures. Auditors can ensure that they have addressed the risks they identified in their understanding–risk assessment processes by documenting the linkage from the client's business objectives and strategy to audit plans. A simple illustration using EarthWear might look as follows:

Business Objectives and Strategy	Business Risks	Account(s): (Assertions)	Audit Risks	Controls	Effect on Audit Plan
Increase market share through sales at new international locations (e.g., during the current year websites were developed for France, Italy, Ireland, and several eastern European countries)	Since EarthWear is in a non-EU country, trade laws may affect sales tactics. Strong consumer protection laws in European countries.	Revenue: accuracy and valuation	Overstated due to pricing issues.	EwC has installed a special group to track compliance with local and international laws.	Observe and test group's policies and procedures (see workpaper R-11).
	Political instability in less developed countries (LDCs).	Reserve for returns: completeness	Understated due to failure to properly track returns in new locations.	EwC has placed more frequent review of returns in new locations.	Extend audit work on EwC's return tracking with emphasis on new locations (see workpaper R-15).
	Foreign currency risks.	Gains/losses from currency hedging: valuation and accuracy	Gains/losses not properly calculated or accrued on hedging activity.	EwC has strong controls in the Treasury Department to account for hedging activities.	Increase the number of hedging contracts tested with particular emphasis on contracts in currencies from LDCs (see work-paper S-14).

The audit strategy is normally documented in an audit plan. Audit programs containing specific audit procedures are also prepared. Exhibit 5–3 presents a partial audit program for substantive tests of accounts receivable. The types of audit tests are discussed later in this chapter.

Consider Additional Value-Added Services

As part of the planning process, the auditor should look for opportunities to recommend additional value-added services. With auditors taking a more global view of the client and its business and industry, there are new opportunities to provide valuable services for the client. For example, the new assurance services (introduced in Chapter 1 and discussed in more detail in Chapter 19) include risk assessment, business performance measurement (benchmarking), and electronic commerce. The auditor also can provide recommendations based on the assessment of client business risk. With the knowledge gathered through assessing client business risk, the auditor can provide important feedback to management and the board of directors on the strengths and weaknesses of business processes, strategic planning, and emerging trends. Proper consideration of

EXHIBIT 5–3

A Partial Audit Program for Substantive Tests of Accounts Receivable

Audit Procedures	W/P Ref.	Completed by	Date
1. Obtain the December 31, 2006, aged accounts receivable trial balance and	_____	_____	_____
a. Foot the trial balance and agree total to accounts receivable control account.	_____	_____	_____
b. Judgementally select 15 accounts from the aged trial balance; agree the information per the aged trial balance to the original sales invoice and determine if the invoice was included in the appropriate aging category.	_____	_____	_____
2. Confirm accounts receivable	_____	_____	_____
a. For all responses with exceptions, follow up on the cause of the error.			
b. For all nonresponses, examine subsequent cash receipts and/or supporting documents.	_____	_____	_____
c. Summarize the confirmation results.	_____	_____	_____
3. Test sales cutoff by identifying the last shipping advice for the year and examining five large sales for three days before and after year-end.	_____	_____	_____
4. Test the reasonableness of the allowance for doubtful accounts by the following:	_____	_____	_____
a. Test the reasonableness using past percentages on bad debts.	_____	_____	_____
b. For any large account in the aged trial balance greater than 90 days old, test for subsequent cash receipts.	_____	_____	_____
c. For the following financial ratios, compare the current year to prior year and internal budgets:			
• Number of days outstanding in receivable.	_____	_____	_____
• Aging of receivables.	_____	_____	_____
• Write-offs as a percentage of sales.	_____	_____	_____
• Bad debt expense as a percentage of sales.	_____	_____	_____
5. Prepare a memo summarizing the tests, results, and conclusions.	_____	_____	_____

value-added services during the planning process should alert the audit team to proactively identify opportunities to improve client service. Of course, if the auditor's client is a public company, as mentioned previously, auditing standards impose limitations on the types of consulting services the auditor can provide to it.

Types of Audit Procedures

LO 5 >   There are three general types of audit procedures:

- risk assessment procedures
- tests of controls
- substantive tests

Risk Assessment Procedures

Risk assessment procedures are used by the auditor to obtain an understanding of the entity and its environment, including its internal control. Risk assessment procedures include enquiries of management and others, analytical procedures, and observation and inspection. Such procedures are used to assess the risks of material misstatement at the financial statement and assertion levels. Risk assessment procedures were discussed in depth in Chapter 3.

Tests of Controls

Tests of controls consist of procedures directed toward the evaluation of the effectiveness of the *design* and *operation* of internal controls. When tests of controls look at design issues, the auditor evaluates whether the control has been properly designed to prevent or detect material misstatements. Tests of controls directed toward the operational effectiveness of a control are concerned with how the control is applied, the consistency of its application during the period, and by whom it is applied. The following audit procedures are examples of tests of controls:

- inspection of documents, reports, and electronic media indicating performance of the control
- observation of the application of specific controls
- walkthroughs, which involve tracing a transaction from its originating point to its inclusion in the financial statements through a combination of audit procedures including enquiry, observation, and inspection
- reperformance of the application of the control by the auditor

Table 5–3 provides examples of internal controls that are normally present in a revenue cycle and tests of controls that the auditor might use to test the operation of the controls.

Substantive Tests

Substantive tests detect material misstatements (that is, monetary errors) in an account balance, transaction class, and disclosure component of the financial statements. There are two categories of substantive tests: (1) *substantive tests of details of classes of transactions, and events account balances, and disclosures* and (2) *analysis*.

Substantive Tests of Transactions   Substantive tests of transactions test for fraud or errors in individual transactions. Examining individual transactions provides the auditor with evidence on the occurrence, completeness, and accuracy assertions. For example, an auditor may examine

Table 5–3	**Examples of Internal Controls and Tests of Controls**

Internal Controls	Test of Controls
Create a separation of duties between the shipping function and the order entry and billing functions.	Observe and evaluate whether shipping personnel have access to the order entry or billing activities.
Credit Department personnel initial sales orders, indicating credit approval.	Inspect a sample of sales orders for presence of initials of Credit Department personnel.
Billing Department personnel account for the numerical sequence of sales invoices.	Enquire of Billing Department personnel about missing sales invoices numbers.
Agree sales invoices to shipping document and customer order for product types, price, and quantity.	For a sample of sales invoices, check for agreement to shipping documents and to customer order. Recompute the information.

a large purchase of inventory by testing that the cost of the goods included on the vendor's invoice is properly recorded in the inventory and accounts payable accounts. As discussed in the next section, substantive tests of transactions are often conducted along with tests of controls as a dual-purpose test.

Tests of Account Balances   Tests of details of account balances and disclosures concentrate on the *details* of amounts contained in an account balance. These important tests establish whether any material misstatements are included in the accounts or disclosures included in the financial statements. For example, the auditor may want to test accounts receivable. To test the details of the accounts receivable account, the auditor can send confirmation requests to a sample of the individual debtor accounts that make up the ending balance in accounts receivable. In examining the confirmation replies, the auditor is concerned with testing the existence, rights and obligations, and valuation assertions.

Substantive Analytical Procedures

Because of the importance of analysis, it is discussed in more detail later in the chapter.

Dual-Purpose Tests

Tests of controls look for errors in the design and application of controls, while substantive tests of transactions are concerned with monetary errors. However, some audit tests are both a test of controls and a substantive test of transactions. For example, in Table 5–3, the last control procedure shown is agreement of sales invoices to shipping documents and customer orders for product type, price, and quantity. The test of controls shown is to recompute the information on a sample of sales invoices. While this test primarily checks the effectiveness of the control, it also provides evidence on whether the sales invoice contains the wrong quantity, product type, or price. Dual-purpose tests can also improve the efficiency of the audit.

This text discusses tests of controls within each cycle when the assessment of control risk is covered. Substantive tests of transactions are discussed along with the other substantive tests when the financial statement accounts affected by the business process are discussed. The reader should remember, however, that in many audit situations substantive tests of transactions are conducted at the same time as tests of controls.

Analysis

LO 6 > *CICA Handbook,* section 5301, "Analysis," describes analytical procedures as consisting of evaluations of financial information made by a study of plausible relationships among both financial and nonfinancial data.[6] Because analytical procedures focus on the financial statement information itself, rather than the process by which the information gets there, they are also classified as substantive tests.

The strategic systems approach stresses the importance of the auditor's possessing a thorough understanding of the client's environment, strategies, business risks, and business processes. Analysis can be an effective tool to assist the auditor in obtaining this understanding. The strategic systems approach is reflected in the standards in the *CICA Handbook*'s discussion of the use of analysis as an audit planning technique. Paragraphs 5301.03 to 5301.05 outline the use of analysis in the planning stages to identify components, e.g., financial statement items or amounts contained therein, transactions or adjustments, and underlying data. Such identification should help the auditor to gain a better understanding of the client and its activities, and to plan a more efficient and effective audit.

Analytical procedures may range from the use of simple comparisons to the use of complex models. The main techniques of analytical procedures are (1) trend analysis—the examination of changes in an account over time, (2) ratio analysis—the comparison, across time or to a benchmark, of relationships between financial statement accounts or between an account and nonfinancial data, and (3) reasonableness analysis—development of a model to form an expectation using financial data, nonfinancial data, or both, to test account balances or changes in account balances between accounting periods. Table 5–4 provides additional information about each technique. The use of more advanced techniques such as regression analysis is covered in advanced auditing texts.[7] Proper application of analytical procedures requires that the auditor have knowledge of the client's business and industry. Without such knowledge, the auditor may be unable to develop appropriate analytical procedures or properly evaluate the results of such tests.

---

[6]See also D. G. Smith, *Analytical Review* (Toronto: CICA, 1983); and C. Emby and S. Spector, *Analytical Procedures: A Guide for Practitioners*, revised edition (Vancouver: CGA-Canada, 2006).

[7]See A. D. Bailey, Jr., *Statistical Auditing: Review, Concepts, and Problems* (New York: Harcourt Brace Jovanovich, 1981), chap. 10, for a detailed discussion of regression analysis applied to auditing.

Table 5–4	**Definitions of the Main Techniques of Analytical Procedures***

Trend analysis is the analysis of changes in an account over time. Simple trend analyses compare last year's account balance (the "expectation") with the current balance. Trend analysis can also encompass multiple time periods and includes comparing recorded trends with budget amounts and with competitor and industry information. The number of time periods used is a function of predictability and desired precision. The more stable the operations over time, the more predictable the relationship and the more appropriate the use of multiple periods. Generally, the more time periods used and the more disaggregated the data, the more precise the expectation. Because trend analysis relies on a single predictor (i.e., prior period information for an account balance), it does not normally yield as precise an expectation as the other two types.

Ratio analysis is the comparison, across time or to a benchmark, of relationships between financial statement accounts (e.g., return on equity) or between an account and nonfinancial data (e.g., cost per square foot or sales per item). Ratio analysis also includes "common-size" analysis, which is the conversion of financial statement amounts to percentages. Industry or competitor ratios are often used to benchmark the client's performance. The advanced module to this chapter illustrates selected financial ratios useful in analytical procedures. Ratio analysis is often more effective at identifying risks and potential misstatements than trend analysis because comparisons of relationships between accounts and operating data are more likely to identify unusual patterns than is an analysis only focused on an individual account. As with trend analysis, to gather substantive evidence effectively, ratio analysis should be performed on disaggregated data (e.g., by product, location, or month) over multiple periods where applicable.

Reasonableness analysis involves forming an expectation using a model. In many cases, a simple model may be sufficient. For example, ticket revenue can be modelled by taking average attendance by average ticket price. Similarly, depreciation expense can be modelled by taking book value divided by average useful life for a class of assets. Because it forms an explicit expectation, reasonableness analysis typically forms a more precise expectation than trend or ratio analysis. Of course the precision of an expectation formed with a reasonableness test depends on the other factors influencing precision (i.e., disaggregation, predictability and reliability).

*Regression analysis is another type of analytical procedure. Because it involves relatively complex statistical modelling in audit settings, we do not discuss it in this text. See footnote 7 for further information.

Techniques for Analytical Procedures

Before discussing the use of analytical procedures further, the following section describes the application of some of the commonly used techniques.

Comparison of Current-Year Financial Information with Comparable Prior Period(s) After Consideration of Known Changes. This is perhaps the most commonly used analytical procedure. The comparison of financial statement amounts can be done using absolute amounts (i.e., trend analysis) or by converting the financial statement amounts to "common-size" financial statements (ratio analysis). Exhibit 5–4 presents an example of common-size financial statements for EarthWear for 2006 and 2005. An auditor may compare the amounts shown on this year's trial balance with the prior year's audited balances and investigate those amounts that differ from expectations by some predetermined cutoff percentage or absolute amount. For example, the auditor can compare the current-year inventory balance with the prior year's balance after adjusting for the change in sales during the current period. In the EarthWear example, inventory has increased in absolute amounts from $105.4 million to $122.3 million and, as a percentage of total assets, from 35.6 to 37.0 percent. Because this type of analytical procedure is typically performed on the aggregated

EXHIBIT 5–4

Common-Size Financial Statements for EarthWear Clothiers (in thousands)

	December 31			
	2006		2005	
Assets				
Current assets:				
Cash and cash equivalents	$ 48,978	14.84%	$ 49,668	16.75%
Receivables, net	12,875	3.90%	11,539	3.89%
Inventory	122,337	37.08%	105,425	35.55%
Prepaid advertising	11,458	3.47%	10,772	3.63%
Other prepaid expenses	6,315	1.91%	3,780	1.27%
Deferred income tax benefits	7,132	2.16%	6,930	2.34%
Total current assets	209,095	63.37%	188,115	63.44%
Property, plant, and equipment, at cost				
Land and buildings	70,918	21.49%	66,804	22.53%
Fixtures and equipment	67,513	20.46%	66,876	22.55%
Computer hardware and software	64,986	19.70%	47,466	16.01%
Leasehold improvements	3,010	0.91%	2,894	0.98%
Total property, plant, and equipment	206,426	62.56%	184,040	62.07%
Less: accumulated amortization	85,986	−26.06%	76,256	−25.72%
Property, plant, and equipment, net	120,440	36.50%	107,784	36.35%
Intangibles, net	423	0.13%	628	0.21%
Total assets	$329,959	100.00%	$296,527	100.00%
Liabilities and shareholder's investment				
Current liabilities:				
Lines of credit	$ 11,011	3.34%	$7,621	2.57%
Accounts payable	62,509	18.94%	48,432	16.33%
Reserve for returns	5,890	1.78%	5,115	1.72%
Accrued liabilities	26,738	8.10%	28,440	9.59%
Accrued profit sharing	1,532	0.46%	1,794	0.61%
Income taxes payable	8,588	2.60%	6,666	2.25%
Total current liabilities	116,268	35.24%	98,067	33.07%
Future income taxes	9,469	2.87%	5,926	2.00%
Shareholders' investment:				
Common stock, 26,121 shares issued	261	0.08%	261	0.09%
Contributed surplus	5,460	1.65%	5,460	1.84%
Additional paid-in capital	20,740	6.29%	19,311	6.51%
Deferred compensation	(79)	−0.02%	(153)	−0.05%
Accumulated other comprehensive income	3,883	1.18%	1,739	0.59%
Retained earnings	317,907	96.35%	295,380	99.61%
Treasury stock, 6,546 and 6,706 shares at cost,				
respectively	(143,950)	−43.63%	(129,462)	−43.66%
Total shareholders' investment	204,222	64.76%	192,535	66.93%
Total liabilities and shareholders' investment	$329,959	100.00%	$296,527	100.00%
Net Sales	$950,484	100.00%	$857,885	100.00%
Cost of sales	546,393	57.49%	472,739	55.11%
Gross Profit	404,091	42.51%	385,146	44.89%
Selling, general and administrative expenses	364,012	38.30%	334,994	39.05%
Nonrecurring charge (credit)	—		(1,153)	−0.13%
Income from operations	40,079	4.29%	51,305	5.98%
Other income (expense):				
Interest expense	(983)	−0.10%	(1,229)	−0.14%
Interest income	1,459	0.15%	573	0.07%
Other	(4,798)	−0.50%	(1,091)	−0.13%
Total other income (expense), net	(4,322)	−0.45%	(1,747)	−0.20%
Income before income taxes	35,757	3.76%	49,559	5.78%
Income tax provision	13,230	1.39%	18,337	2.14%
Net income	$22,527	2.37%	$ 31,222	3.64%
Basic earnings per share	1.15		1.60	
Diluted earnings per share	1.14		1.56	
Basic weighted average shares outstanding	19,531		19,555	
Diluted weighted average shares outstanding	19,774		20,055	

Source: Dun & Bradstreet, Inc.

companywide financial statements, the expectation is relatively imprecise. Thus, it is typically used for planning and final review purposes, but is not considered particularly useful for providing substantive evidence about a particular account balance or class of transactions. At planning, the auditor would investigate this increase in inventory and adjust the planned audit procedures to address risks associated with the increase. The observed increase in inventory may be indicative of a misstatement or it may be reasonable since sales are up in the current period. It is difficult to obtain useful audit evidence from high-level companywide analytical procedures because the expectations are typically not sufficiently precise. In other words, whether or not the auditor observes a significant difference using a year-to-year comparison may be useful for planning purposes, but it would provide little or no audit evidence because of the imprecision of the expectation.

Comparison of Current-Year Financial Information with Budgets, Projections, and Forecasts. This type of analytical procedure is usually performed using trend analysis and is similar to the previous type except that the current-year actual results are compared to the client's planned activity. For example, the auditor can test the reasonableness of selected income and expense accounts by comparing their current-year amounts to the client's budget and investigating accounts that are not consistent with the auditor's expectations.

Relationships among Elements of Financial Information within the Current Period. There are many examples of one element in the financial statements relating to another element. This is particularly true for the relationship between certain balance sheet accounts and their related income or expense accounts. For example, there should be a relationship between the balance for long-term debt and interest expense. The auditor can test this relationship by multiplying the average long-term debt for the period by the average interest rate. This estimate of interest expense can be compared to the balance of interest expense shown on the trial balance. See the example of an interest expense reasonableness test for EarthWear Clothiers later in the chapter.

Comparison of the Client's Financial Information with Industry Data. The auditor can, for example, compare the client's financial ratios (receivable turnover, inventory turnover, and so on) to industry averages. Industry information can be a very valuable benchmark for assessing how well the client's financial position and performance compare with other companies in the industry. Robert Morris Associates, Dun & Bradstreet, and Standard & Poor's publish this type of industry data. Exhibit 5–5 contains an extract of industry data from Industry Norms & Key Business Ratios, published by Dun & Bradstreet, Inc.

Relationships of Financial Information to Nonfinancial Information. The auditor may have relevant nonfinancial information available for comparison purposes or for developing estimates of the client's financial information. This might include items such as the number of employees,

EXHIBIT 5–5

An Example of Industry Data Available from Published Sources

SIC 5961
CTLG, ML-ORDER HSES
(No Breakdown)
(451 Establishments)

	$	%
Cash	101,474	16.6
Accounts receivable	94,139	15.4
Notes receivable	3,668	0.6
Inventory	236,570	38.7
Other current	48,292	7.9
Total current	**484,142**	**79.2**
Capital assets	82, 524	13.5
Other noncurrent	44,624	7.3
Total assets	**611,291**	**100.0**
Accounts payable	125,315	20.5
Bank loans	1,834	0.3
Notes payable	14,671	2.4
Other current	97,195	15.9
Total current	**239,015**	**39.1**
Other long-term	59,907	9.8
Deferred credits	—	
Net worth	312,370	51.1
Total liab and net worth	**611,291**	**100.0**
Net sales	2,386,410	100.0
Gross profit	925,927	38.8
Net profit after tax	78,752	3.3
Working capital	245,127	—

RATIOS	UQ	MED	LQ
Solvency:			
Quick ratio (times)	1.6	0.8	0.3
Current ratio (times)	3.9	2.1	1.4
Curr liab to nw (%)	25.1	68.6	142.6
Curr liab to inv (%)	45.8	92.0	146.8
Total liab to nw (%)	29.7	84.1	178.9
Fixed assets to nw (%)	9.3	22.3	49.4
Efficiency:			
Coll period (days)	4.4	14.1	34.1
Sales to inv (times)	14.6	7.9	5.3
Assets to sales (%)	21.2	31.2	47.3
Sales to nwc (times)	19.6	8.6	4.4
Acct pay to sales (%)	3.8	6.2	9.3
Profitability:			
Return on sales (%)	6.9	2.9	0.6
Return on assets (%)	21.2	7.4	1.2
Return on nw (%)	47.7	17.5	4.9

Source: Dun & Bradstreet, Inc.

FIGURE 5–4

An Illustration of a Monthly Plot of Ending Inentory (in millions)

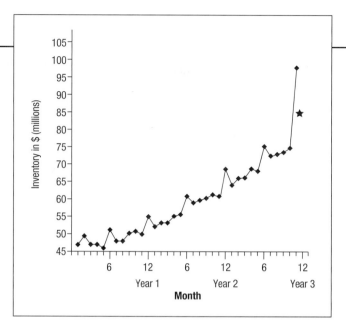

hours worked, and so on. For example, the auditor can multiply commissioned sales by the average commission rate and compare this estimate to the client's recorded commission expense. Another example would be the number of automobiles in service for a company that leases automobiles. This number can be multiplied by the average lease rate to test the total automobile leasing revenue.

Using nonfinancial information in analytical procedures can be an effective way to identify potential frauds because while perpetrators of fraud can manage financial numbers, it is difficult or impossible to manage nonfinancial data (e.g., square feet, days in the calendar year, number of employees).

Plotting Trends over Multiple Periods. It can be very beneficial to plot or graph trends over several periods. Figure 5–4 provides a monthly plot of ending inventory for a three-year period. Suppose the auditor is auditing year-ending inventory for year 3 and that years 1 and 2 have been previously audited. The pattern of previously audited financial information suggests some inventory "spikes" every six months. These spikes may be due to inventory buildup around busy seasons (e.g., holidays). The star at the end of year 3 indicates the auditor's expectation based on the past trends. The auditor would investigate the cause of the large increase in ending inventory at the end of year 3. Note that the potentially problematic spikes would not have shown up at all if the auditor had just plotted year-end inventory balances rather than monthly balances! Again, using detailed data is critical in enhancing precision.

The foregoing discussion and examples have all related to the first step in the analytical procedures decision process (see Figure 5–3). The first step is the most important step in performing effective substantive analytical procedures.

Purposes of Analytical Procedures

Analytical procedures are used for three purposes:

1. to assist the auditor in *planning* the nature, timing, and extent of other audit procedures
2. as a *substantive test* to obtain evidential matter about particular assertions related to account balances or classes of transactions
3. as an *overall review* of the financial information in the final review stage of the audit

Analytical procedures are required for use in the planning and overall review stages of all audits of financial statements made in accordance with GAAS. However, auditors should consider applying analytical procedures for all three purposes because such procedures have been shown to effectively detect errors.[8] Analytical procedures are also relatively inexpensive tests to perform.

Analytical Procedures Used in Planning the Audit

The objectives of the use of analytical procedures in planning an engagement are (1) to enhance the auditor's understanding of the client's business and the transactions and events that have occurred since the last audit and (2) to identify areas that may represent risks relevant to the audit. More specifically, the auditor needs to identify the existence of unusual transactions and events, amounts, and ratios or trends that may indicate matters having financial statement and audit planning implications.

At the planning stage, analytical procedures usually involve the use of trend or ratio analysis applied to data aggregated at a high level. For example, analytical procedures may consist of reviewing changes in account balances from the prior year using the unadjusted working trial balance. Material accounts that appear to be inconsistent with expectations, based on the auditor's knowledge of the client's business and industry, are subjected to further investigation by the auditor. This usually involves discussing these accounts with relevant client personnel and, in some instances, planning additional substantive tests of the accounts.

Analytical Procedures as a Substantive Test

Figure 5–5 presents an overview of the auditor's decision process when conducting analytical procedures as a substantive test to collect audit evidence. Following is a discussion of each of the major decision points illustrated in Figure 5–5.

Develop an Expectation   The first step in the decision process is to develop an expectation for the amount or account balance. This is the most important step in performing analytical procedures. Auditing standards require the auditor to have an expectation whenever analytical

---

[8]For example, see A. Wright and R. H. Ashton, "Identifying Audit Adjustments with Attention-Directing Procedures," *The Accounting Review* (October 1989), pp. 710–28. More recently, A. Eilitsen and W. F. Messier, Jr., "Auditor Detection of Misstatements: A Review and Integration of Empirical Research," *Journal of Accounting Literature* 2000 (19), pp. 1–43 reviews the audit research on this issue.

FIGURE 5–5

Overview of the Auditor's
Decision Process for
Analytical Procedures as a
Substantative Test

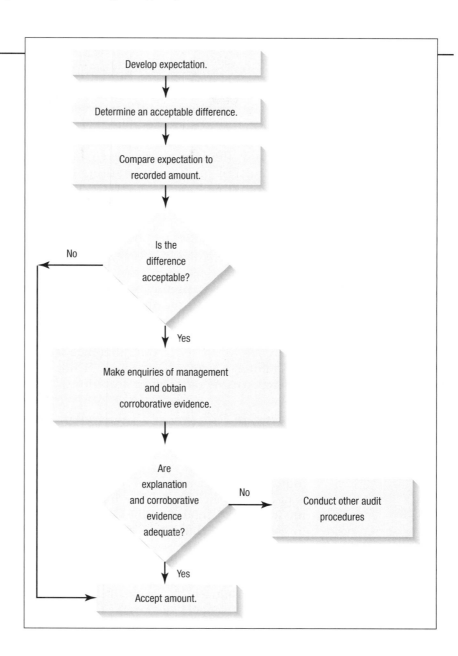

procedures are used. An expectation can be developed using any of the
types of analytical procedures discussed previously using information
available from a variety of sources, such as

- Financial and operating data
- Budgets and forecasts
- Industry publications
- Competitor information
- Management's analyses
- Analyst's reports

Define an Acceptable Difference   The second step in the analytical procedures decision process (see Figure 5–5) is to determine an acceptable or tolerable difference. Since the expectation developed by the auditor will rarely be identical to the client's recorded amount, the auditor must decide the amount of difference that would require further investigation. The size of the tolerable difference depends on the significance of the account, the desired degree of reliance on the substantive analytical procedure, the level of disaggregation in the amount being tested, and the precision of the expectation. The amount of difference that can be tolerated will always be lower than planning materiality, and when testing an entire account with a substantive analytical procedure, tolerable differences will usually be equal to the account's tolerable misstatement. Auditors often use rules of thumb such as, "tolerable difference is 10 percent of the predicted amount and/or a difference less than $75,000."

Compare the Expectation to the Recorded Amount   The next step in the analytical procedures decision process (Figure 5–5) is to determine if the amount of difference between the auditor's expectation and the recorded amount exceeds the auditor's predetermined "tolerable difference." If the observed difference is less than the tolerable difference, the auditor accepts the account. If not, the auditor must investigate the difference using other audit procedures.

Investigate Differences Greater than the Acceptable Difference   The fourth step in the analytical procedures decision process (Figure 5–5) is the investigation of significant differences and the formation of conclusions. Differences identified by substantive analytical procedures indicate an increased likelihood of misstatements. The more precise the expectation, the greater the likelihood that the difference is actually a misstatement. Enquiry of the client is frequently an important aspect of the investigation of differences. Nevertheless, client enquiry should not be the sole support for an explanation without quantification and corroboration (discussed below). There are four possible causes of significant differences—accounting changes, economic conditions or events, error, and fraud. In most instances, the cause of an identified difference involves a legitimate accounting change or an economic condition or event. However, even when a significant difference is due to error or fraud, the client may provide a plausible, yet ultimately untrue, business explanation. Thus, the effectiveness of substantive analytical procedures in identifying material misstatements is enhanced when auditors develop potential explanations *before* obtaining the client's explanation. By doing this, the auditor is better able to exercise appropriate professional scepticism and challenge the client's explanation, if necessary. The ultimate question is: Does management's explanation make sense in light of the auditor's understanding of the entity.

The development of potential explanations need not be time-consuming. Auditors typically re-examine and understand the various relationships in the financial and nonfinancial data. Then, based on their previous experience with the client, other audit work performed, and discussions with other members of the audit team, they develop potential explanations for the observed difference. The independent consideration of potential explanations is more important for more significant accounts and when a higher degree of assurance is desired from substantive analytical procedures.

Explanations for significant differences observed for substantive analytical procedures must be followed up and resolved through quantification, corroboration, and evaluation.

Quantification   It is usually not practicable to identify an explanation for the exact amount of a difference between an analytical procedure's expectation and the client's recorded amount. However, auditors should quantify the portion of the difference that can be explained. Quantification involves determining whether the explanation or error can explain the observed difference. This may require the recalculation of the expectation after considering the additional information. For example, a client may offer the explanation that the significant increase in inventory over the prior year is due to a 12 percent increase in raw materials prices. The auditor should compute the effects of the raw materials price increase and determine the extent to which the price increase explains (or does not explain) the increase in the overall inventory account.

Corroboration.   Auditors must corroborate explanations for unexpected differences by obtaining sufficient appropriate audit evidence linking the explanation to the difference and substantiating that the information supporting the explanation is reliable. This evidence should be of the same quality as the evidence obtained to support tests of details. Such evidence could vary from simply comparing the explanation to the auditor's knowledge from other areas, to employing other detailed tests to confirm or refute the explanation. Common corroborating procedures include examination of supporting evidence, enquiries of independent persons, and evaluating evidence obtained from other auditing procedures.

Evaluation.   The key mind-set behind effectively performing substantive analytical procedures is one of appropriate professional scepticism, combined with the desire to obtain sufficient appropriate audit evidence, similar to other auditing procedures. The auditor should evaluate the results of the substantive analytical procedures to conclude whether the desired level of assurance has been achieved. If the auditor obtains evidence that a misstatement exists and can be sufficiently quantified, the auditor makes note of his or her proposed adjustment to the client's financial statements. Toward the end of the audit, all such proposed adjustments are accumulated, summarized, and evaluated before being presented to the client (Chapter 15 provides further details).

If the auditor concludes that the substantive analytical procedure performed did not provide the desired level of assurance, additional substantive analytical procedures and/or tests of details should be performed to achieve the desired assurance.

Comprehensive EarthWear Example   Suppose we want to use substantive analytical procedures to test the reasonableness of interest expense reported by EarthWear Clothiers (i.e., a "reasonableness test"). Consider the following example:

EarthWear's 2006 income statement shows $983,000 of interest expense. To conduct a substantive analytical procedure on this account, the auditor could develop an expectation using reasonableness analysis by building a model in the following manner. Obtain the ending monthly balance for the short-term line of credit from the monthly bank loan statement and calculate the average monthly ending balance. Trace the monthly loan balances to the general ledger. Determine the average interest rate for the year for the short-term line of credit based on the bank's published rate in the monthly bank loan statement. Multiply the average monthly balance previously calculated by the average interest rate, and compare the result to the recorded interest expense. Suppose that the auditor obtained the following information from EarthWear's general ledger:

Month	Balance (in thousands)
January	$ 21,500
February	18,600
March	18,100
April	17,900
May	16,100
June	15,500
July	14,200
August	20,200
September	34,500
October	28,100
November	15,200
December	11,000
Total	$230,900
Average	$ 19,240

Further, assume that interest rates recorded on the loan statements have remained stable over the year, fluctuating between 5 and 5.5 percent. If the auditor uses 5.25 percent as the average interest rate, the expectation for interest expense is $1,010,000 ($19,240,000 × 0.525).

As shown in Figure 5–5, once an expectation is developed, the next step is to determine the tolerable difference. Because interest expense is a predictable account and because the information used to form the expectation is deemed reliable, the expectation is fairly precise. Accordingly, the acceptable difference is set at 5 percent of recorded interest expense or $49,150 (0.05% × $983,000). The next step is to compare the expectation of $1,010,000 to the recorded value of $983,000 to determine if the difference is greater than can be accepted. Because the difference between the auditor's expectation and the recorded amount, $27,000, is less than the acceptable difference, the auditor would accept the interest expense account as fairly stated. However, if the difference between the recorded amount and the expectation is greater than the acceptable difference, the auditor will need to investigate the difference. In the example above, the auditor would likely carefully examine loan activity within each month to determine if there was significant variation in the balance that was not accounted for by the month-end model used to form the expectation. If the difference could still not be explained, the auditor would enquire of management about the cause of the difference. If the client provides a plausible explanation (e.g., interest expense reported in the financial statements also includes interest paid for other short-term loans that were only outstanding for a few days at a time), auditing standards require the auditor to obtain corroborating evidence. If the client's explanation and the corroborating evidence are not adequate, or if no corroborative evidence is available, the auditor will need to conduct additional substantive audit procedures. If the explanation and evidence are adequate for resolving the difference, the auditor can accept the amount as being fairly presented.

When analytical procedures are used as direct substantive tests, the auditor is testing one or more assertions. For example, in the interest expense example, the auditor is testing primarily the completeness assertion. The effectiveness and efficiency of analytical procedures in identifying material misstatements depend on

- the nature of the assertion
- the plausibility and predictability of the relationship
- the availability and reliability of the data used
- the precision of the expectation

The Nature of the Assertion   Analytical procedures can be used to test all management assertions except ownership. However, they may be more effective at identifying certain types of misstatements than testing individual transactions. For example, they may be more effective at detecting omissions (completeness objective) than examining detailed documentary evidence. The key point is that the auditor needs to be sure that the analytical procedure performed is appropriate for the assertion being examined.

The Plausibility and Predictability of the Relationship   The main concern with plausibility is whether the relationship used to test the assertion or audit objective makes sense. In an earlier example, the auditor examined the change in accounts receivable by relating it to the change in sales. It is plausible to expect that an increase in sales should lead to an increase in accounts receivable. Many factors determine the predictability of the relationship. For example, income statement items tend to be more predictable than balance sheet items because income statement accounts involve only transactions from the current period. Similarly, if the client operates in a static environment, the relationships are likely to be more predictable than they are for a client that operates in a dynamic environment.

The Availability and Reliability of Data   The ability to develop expectations for certain audit objectives is a function of the reliability of the available data. The reliability of data for developing expectations depends on the three factors discussed in Chapter 4 under the competence of evidential matter: (1) the independence of the source of the evidence, (2) the effectiveness of internal controls, and (3) the auditor's direct personal knowledge. In addition, data for analytical procedures are more reliable if the data were subjected to audit in the current or prior periods and if the expectation was developed from multiple sources of data. For example, if the auditor is computing ratios based on *audited* data from prior periods, the data used in the computations would be considered reliable.

The Precision of the Expectation   The precision of the expectation is a function of the materiality and detection risk for the objective being tested. If the audit objective being tested requires a low level of detection risk, the precision of the expectation needs to be relatively small. However, as the precision gets smaller, the auditor will probably need to conduct more audit tests. Therefore, the auditor's decisions concerning materiality and detection risk for analytical procedures directly impact the amount of audit work to be performed.

An example will help to explain this further. Suppose the auditor decides to use an analytical procedure to assess the fair presentation of a client's amortization expense. Suppose further that the auditor expects amortization expense to be $3,500,000. Based on materiality and detection risk considerations, this expectation does not require tight precision, and a $200,000 difference would be acceptable. If the recorded amount equals $3,350,000, no further investigation would be necessary. Conversely, if the expectation requires a precision of $100,000, the auditor would need to enquire of management and obtain corroborating evidence because the difference between the expectation and the recorded amount is greater than $100,000. If there is no adequate explanation or corroborative evidence, the auditor would want to conduct additional audit procedures because the available evidence does not support management's assertions about amortization expense.

Documentation Requirements   When a substantive analytical procedure is used as a substantive procedure for a significant financial statement assertion, the auditor should document all of the following:

- The expectation and how it was developed.
- Results of the comparison of the expectation to the recorded amounts or ratios developed from recorded amounts.
- Any additional auditing procedures performed in response to significant unexpected differences arising from the analytical procedure and the results of such additional procedures.

Analytical Procedures in the Overall Review

The *CICA Handbook,* section 5301 discusses the use of analysis in the review phase of the audit. This is an important component of the quality control procedures that must be applied throughout the audit. The purpose at this point is to assist the auditor in forming an overall conclusion as to whether the financial statements as a whole are consistent with the auditor's understanding of the entity. This review is usually performed by a senior partner other than the engagement partner in the interests of bringing a fresh "set of eyes" to the process. Such a new perspective is free of the biases that may be present because of the engagement partner's close association with the financial information over the course of the audit. It can be thought of as an application of the "forest and trees" analogy.

If the reviewing partner's analytical procedures identify significant fluctuations or relationships that are inconsistent or unexplained, before concluding on the financial statements, the engagement audit team should investigate to obtain adequate explanations and appropriate corroborative audit evidence. If the application of analytical procedures identifies a previously unrecognized risk of material misstatement, the auditor may need to re-evaluate the audit procedures applied based on the revised consideration of assessed risks for all or some of the classes of transactions, account balances or disclosures and related assertions. It may be necessary to do additional audit work before an audit report can be issued.

The Audit Testing Hierarchy

LO 7> The risk-driven audit approach we have discussed so far in the text is often referred to as a "top-down" approach where the auditor obtains an understanding of the client's business objectives and strategies, identifies business and audit risks, documents an understanding of internal control, and then gathers sufficient, appropriate audit evidence using a combination of tests of controls, substantive analytical procedures, and tests of details to support the audit opinion.

Now that we have discussed evidence (Chapter 4) and introduced you to the types of audit tests (risk assessment procedures, tests of controls, substantive analytical procedures, and tests of details), you are ready to be introduced to the thought process auditors use in choosing audit tests and in what order. The overall decision approach used to gather evidence is depicted in Figure 5–6 and is referred to in later chapters as the *audit testing hierarchy*.

The audit testing hierarchy starts with tests of controls and substantive analytical procedures. Starting with controls and substantive analytical procedures is generally both more effective and more efficient than starting with tests of details.

- *Applying the audit testing hierarchy is more effective.* The auditor's understanding and testing of controls will influence the nature, timing, and extent of substantive testing and will enhance the auditor's ability to hone in on areas where misstatements are more likely to be found. If controls are highly effective, less extensive substantive procedures (i.e., substantive analytical procedures and tests of details) will need to be performed. Similarly, substantive analytical procedures can direct attention to higher-risk areas where the auditor can design and conduct focused tests of details.

- *Applying the audit testing hierarchy is more efficient.* Generally, tests of controls and substantive analytical procedures are less costly to perform than are tests of details. This is usually because tests of controls and substantive analytical procedures provide assurance on multiple transactions. In other words, by testing controls and related processes, the auditor generally gains a degree of assurance over thousands or even millions of transactions. Furthermore, substantive analytical procedures often provide evidence related to more than one assertion and often more than one balance or class of transactions. On the other hand, tests of details often only obtain assurance related to one or two specific assertions pertaining to the specific transaction(s) or balance tested.

Auditors perform substantive procedures for significant account balances and classes of transactions regardless of the assessed level of control risk. In other words, assurance obtained solely from testing controls is not sufficient for significant balances and classes of transactions. Substantive procedures include substantive analytical procedures and tests of details. For this reason, Figure 5–6 depicts that either substantive analytical procedures, tests of details, or both will always be conducted for significant accounts or classes of transactions. For high-risk areas or highly material accounts, the auditors will almost always perform some tests of details in addition to tests of controls and substantive analytical procedures.

The decision process depicted in Figure 5–6 recognizes that for some assertions, tests of details may be the only form of testing used, because in some cases it is more efficient and effective to move directly to tests of details. Examples of situations where the auditor might move directly to tests of details include a low volume of large transactions (e.g., two large notes payable issued) and poor controls resulting in client data that are unreliable for use in substantive analytical procedures.

| An "Assurance Bucket" Analogy | We have found that an analogy often helps students understand and visualize how an auditor decides on the proper mix of testing and evidence. Figure 5–7 illustrates what we call the "assurance bucket." The assurance bucket must be filled with sufficient evidence to obtain the level of assurance necessary to support the auditor's opinion. Following the top-down audit testing hierarchy means that auditors first begin to fill the bucket with evidence from the risk assessment procedures. In Figure 5–7, after completing risk assessment procedures, the auditor sees that the assurance bucket for a particular account and assertion is about 20 percent full. The auditor would next conduct control testing. In our example, control testing might add about another 30 percent to the bucket. How would the auditor know just how full the bucket is after testing controls? This is clearly a very subjective evaluation, and it is a matter of professional judgement.

The auditor next performs substantive analytical procedures and adds the assurance gained from these procedures to the bucket. |

FIGURE 5–6

Audit Testing Hierarchy: An Evidence Decision Process for Testing Significant Balances or Classes of Transactions

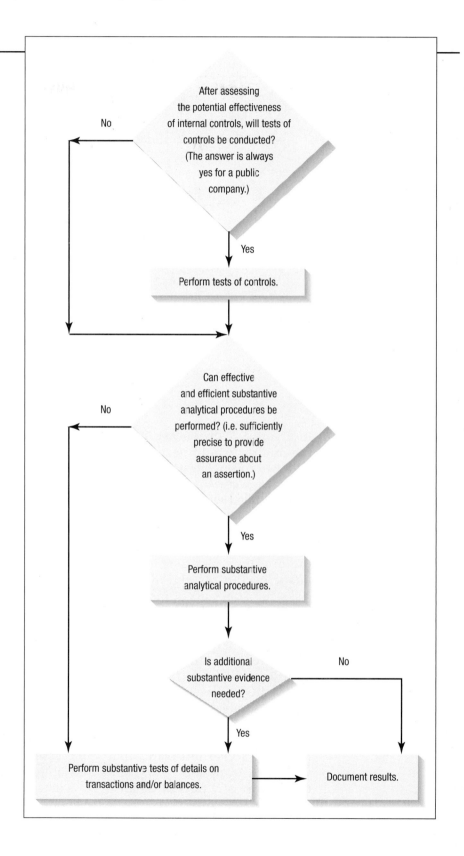

FIGURE 5–7

Filling the Assurance Bucket

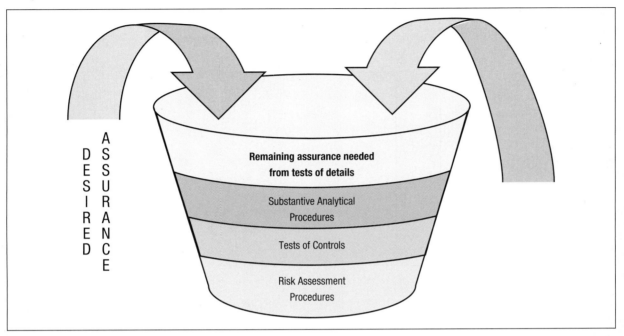

In Figure 5–7 the bucket is now about 70 percent full. In this illustration, the auditor would need to top off the assurance bucket with evidence obtained through tests of details.

For lower-risk, well-controlled accounts, the assurance bucket may be entirely filled with tests of controls and substantive analytical procedures. For other accounts or assertions, the bucket may be filled primarily with tests of details.

The size of the assurance bucket can vary, depending on the auditor's risk assessment and the assertion being tested. Obviously, certain assertions will be more important or present bigger risks for some accounts than for others. For instance, existence (or validity) is typically more important for accounts receivable than it is for accounts payable. After the auditor has determined the risks associated with the assertions for an account balance, she or he can determine the size of the assurance buckets (i.e., how much assurance is needed) and then begin filling the buckets by applying the audit testing hierarchy. Figure 5–8 illustrates these concepts for accounts payable. Note that the largest bucket is for the *completeness* assertion, because with liability accounts the auditor is primarily concerned with potential understatement errors. The example in Figure 5–8 also illustrates that some assertions may be filled entirely with tests of details (e.g., rights and obligations) and that others may not require any tests of details (e.g., existence). Again, these are subjective matters that require considerable professional judgement.

FIGURE 5–8

Accounts Payable Example of Filling the Assurance Buckets for Each Assertion

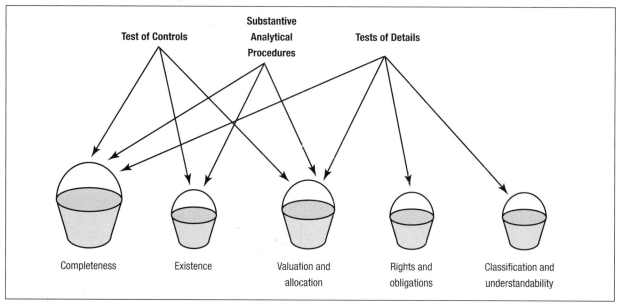

REVIEW QUESTIONS

LO 1 ⟩   **5-1**   What types of enquiries about a prospective client should an auditor make to third parties?

1 ⟩   **5-2**   Who is responsible for initiating the communication between the predecessor and successor auditors? What information should be requested from the predecessor auditor?

2 ⟩   **5-3**   In establishing the terms of the engagement, what topics should the auditor consider?

2 ⟩   **5-4**   What is the purpose of an engagement letter? List the important information that the engagement letter should contain.

3 ⟩   **5-5**   What factors should an external auditor use to assess the competence and objectivity of internal auditors?

3 ⟩   **5-6**   What is an audit committee, and what are its responsibilities?

4 ⟩   **5-7**   List the matters an auditor should consider when developing an overall audit plan.

4 ⟩   **5-8**   Discuss the knowledge an auditor must obtain about a client's business and industry and how that information can be gathered.

4 ⟩   **5-9**   Distinguish between errors and fraud. Give two examples of each.

4 ⟩   **5-10**   What is meant by the term *professional scepticism?*

4,5 ⟩   **5-11**   During the conduct of an audit, information that indicates that a material misstatement may be present may be uncovered. If an auditor discovers a larger-than-expected number of differences in accounts receivable confirmations, what types of errors or fraud might have led to such differences?

4 ⟩   **5-12**   List five circumstances that may indicate that an illegal act may have occurred.

T 3-10

4> **5-13** List three audit procedures that may be used to identify transactions with related parties.

5> **5-14** What are the two general types of audit tests? Define each type of audit test and give two examples.

6> **5-15** Define *analysis*.

6> **5-16** What are the objectives for using analytical procedures at the planning stage of an audit?

6> **5-17** List and discuss the four categories of financial ratios that are presented on the text website to the chapter at www.mcgrawhill.ca/olc/messier.

6> **5-18** When discussing the use of analytical procedures, what is meant by the "precision of the expectation"? In applying this notion to an analytical procedure, how might an auditor calculate an acceptable or tolerable difference?

6> **5-19** Significant differences between the auditor's expectation and the client's book value require explanation through quantification, corroboration, and evaluation. Explain each of these terms.

7> **5-20** Why does the "audit testing hierarchy" begin with tests of controls and substantive analytical procedures?

7> **5-21** Consider the "assurance bucket" analogy. Why are some of the buckets larger than others for particular assertions or accounts?

MULTIPLE-CHOICE QUESTIONS FROM PROFESSIONAL EXAMINATIONS

Unless otherwise indicated, these multiple-choice questions were adapted from the CPA examinations, courtesy of the American Institute of Certified Public Accountants.

1> **5-22** Before accepting an audit engagement, a successor auditor should make specific enquiries of the predecessor auditor regarding the predecessor's

a. Awareness of the consistency in the application of generally accepted accounting principles between periods.

b. Evaluation of all matters of continuing accounting significance.

c. Opinion of any subsequent events occurring since the predecessor auditor's report was issued.

d. Understanding as to the reasons for the change of auditors.

2,4> **5-23** An auditor who accepts an audit engagement and does *not* possess industry expertise pertaining to the business entity should

a. Engage specialists familiar with the nature of the business entity.

b. Obtain knowledge of matters that relate to the nature of the entity's business.

c. Refer a substantial portion of the audit to another professional accountant, who will act as the principal auditor.

d. First inform management that an unqualified opinion cannot be issued.

4> **5-24** Which of the following statements concerning illegal acts by clients is correct?

a. An auditor's responsibility to detect illegal acts that have a direct and material effect on the financial statements is the same as that for errors and fraud.

b. An audit in accordance with generally accepted auditing standards normally includes audit procedures specifically designed to detect illegal acts that have a material effect on the financial statements.

c. An auditor considers illegal acts from the perspective of the reliability of management's representations rather than their relation to audit objectives derived from financial statement assertions.

d. An auditor has *no* responsibility to detect illegal acts by clients that have an effect on the financial statements.

3> **5-25** In using the work of a specialist, an understanding should exist among the auditor, the client, and the specialist as to the nature of the work to be performed by the specialist. Preferably, the understanding should be documented and would include all of the following *except*

a. The objectives and scope of the specialist's work.

b. The specialist's representations as to his or her relationship, if any, to the client.

c. The specialist's understanding of the auditor's corroborative use of the specialist's findings in relation to the representations in the financial statements.

d. A statement that the methods or assumptions to be used are *not* inconsistent with those used by the client.

4> **5-26** Which of the following statements is correct concerning related-party transactions?

a. In the absence of evidence to the contrary, related-party transactions should be assumed to be outside the ordinary course of business.

b. An auditor should determine whether a particular transaction would have occurred if the parties had *not* been related.

c. An auditor should substantiate that related-party transactions were consummated on terms equivalent to those that prevail in arm's-length transactions.

d. The audit procedures directed toward identifying related-party transactions should include considering whether transactions are occurring but are *not* being given proper accounting recognition.

4> **5-27** When planning an examination, an auditor should

a. Consider whether the extent of substantive tests may be reduced based on the results of the internal control questionnaire.

b. Make preliminary judgements about materiality levels for audit purposes.

c. Conclude whether changes in compliance with prescribed internal controls justify reliance on them.

d. Prepare a preliminary draft of the management representation letter.

4> **5-28** A difference of opinion regarding the results of a sample cannot be resolved between the assistant who performed the auditing procedures and the in-charge auditor. The assistant should

a. Refuse to perform any further work on the engagement.

b. Accept the judgement of the more experienced in-charge auditor.

c. Document the disagreement and ask to be disassociated from the resolution of the matter.

d. Notify the client that a serious audit problem exists.

4> **5-29** Which of the following statements best describes an auditor's responsibility to detect errors and fraud?

a. The auditor should study and evaluate the client's internal control system and design the audit to provide reasonable assurance of detecting all errors and fraud.

b. The auditor should assess the risk that errors and fraud may cause the financial statements to contain material misstatements and determine whether the necessary internal controls are prescribed and are being followed satisfactorily.

c. The auditor should consider the types of errors and fraud that could occur and determine whether the necessary internal controls are prescribed and are being followed.

d. The auditor should assess the risk that errors and fraud may cause the financial statements to contain material misstatements and design the audit to provide reasonable assurance of detecting material errors and fraud.

4> **5-30** Morris suspects that a pervasive scheme of illegal bribes exists throughout the operations of Worldwide Import-Export, Inc., a new audit client of his firm. Morris has notified the audit committee and Worldwide's lawyers, but neither could assist Morris in determining whether the amounts involved were material to the financial statements or whether senior management is involved in the scheme. Under these circumstances, Morris should

a. Express an unqualified opinion with a separate explanatory paragraph.

b. Deny an opinion on the financial statements.

c. Express an adverse opinion on the financial statements.

d. Issue a special report regarding the illegal bribes.

3,4> **5-31** Miller Retailing, Inc., maintains a staff of three full-time internal auditors who report directly to the controller. In planning to use the internal auditors to help in performing the audit, the independent auditor most likely will

a. Place limited reliance on the work performed by the internal auditors.

b. Decrease the extent of the tests of controls needed to support the assessed level of detection risk.

c. Increase the extent of the procedures needed to reduce control risk to an acceptable level.

d. Avoid using the work performed by the internal auditors.

4,5,6> **5-32** An entity's financial statements were misstated over a period of years due to large amounts of revenue being recorded in journal entries that involved debits and credits to an illogical combination of accounts. The auditor could most likely have been alerted to this fraud by

a. Scanning the general journal for unusual entries.

b. Performing a revenue cutoff test at year-end.

c. Tracing a sample of journal entries to the general ledger.

d. Examining documentary evidence of sales returns and allowances recorded after year-end.

5,6> **5-33** The primary objective of analytical procedures used in the final review stage of an audit is to

a. Obtain evidence from details tested to corroborate particular assertions.

b. Identify areas that represent specific risks relevant to the audit.

c. Assist the auditor in assessing the validity of the conclusions reached.

d. Satisfy doubts when questions arise about a client's ability to continue in existence.

5,6,7> **5-34** To help plan the nature, timing, and extent of substantive auditing procedures, preliminary analytical procedures should focus on

a. Enhancing the auditor's understanding of the client's business and of events that have occurred since the last audit date.

b. Developing plausible relationships that corroborate anticipated results with a measurable amount of precision.

c. Applying ratio analysis to externally generated data such as published industry statistics or price indexes.

d. Comparing recorded financial information to the results of other tests of transactions and balances.

6> **5-35** Which of the following factors would *least* influence an auditor's consideration of the reliability of data for purposes of analytical procedures?

a. Whether the data were processed in a computerized system or in a manual accounting system.

b. Whether sources within the entity were independent of those who are responsible for the amount being audited.

c. Whether the data were subjected to audit testing in the current or prior year.

d. Whether the data were obtained from independent sources outside the entity or from sources within the entity.

5,6> **5-36** For all audits of financial statements made in accordance with generally accepted auditing standards, the use of analytical procedures is required to some extent

	In the Planning Stage	As a Substantive Test	In the Review Stage
a.	Yes	No	Yes
b.	No	Yes	No
c.	No	Yes	Yes
d.	Yes	No	No

6〉   **5-37**   Trend analysis is best described by

a. The comparison, across time or to a benchmark, of relationships between financial statement accounts or between an account and nonfinancial data.

b. Development of a model to form an expectation using financial data, nonfinancial data, or both to test account balances or changes in account balances between accounting periods.

c. The examination of changes in an account over time.

d. The examination of ratios over time.

7〉   **5-38**   The assurance bucket is filled with all of the following types of evidence except

a. Test of controls.

b. Business risks.

c. Substantive analytical procedures.

d. Tests of details.

PROBLEMS

1,2,3〉   **5-39**   Alicia Dodd audited Adams Company's financial statements for the year ended December 31, 2005. On November 1, 2006, Adams notified Dodd that it was changing auditors and that Dodd's services were being terminated. On November 5, 2006, Adams invited Hall & Co., LLP, to make a proposal for an engagement to audit its financial statements for the year ended December 31, 2006.

Required:

a. What procedures concerning Alicia Dodd should Hall & Co., LLP perform before accepting the engagement?

b. What additional procedures should Hall consider performing during the planning phase of this audit (after accepting the engagement) that would *not* be performed during the audit of a continuing client?

(AICPA, adapted)

2〉   **5-40**   For many years the financial and accounting community has recognized the importance of the use of audit committees and has endorsed their formation. By now the use of audit committees has become widespread. Independent auditors have become increasingly involved with audit committees and consequently have become familiar with their nature and function.

Required:

a. Describe what an audit committee is.

b. Identify the reasons why audit committees have been formed and are currently in operation.

c. Describe the functions of an audit committee.

(AICPA, adapted)

2,3,4 ▷ **5-41** The audit committee of the board of directors of Unicorn Corporation asked Tish & Field to audit Unicorn's financial statements for the year ended December 31, 2006. Tish & Field explained the need to make an enquiry of the predecessor auditor and requested permission to do so. Unicorn's management agreed and authorized the predecessor auditor to respond fully to Tish & Field's inquiries.

After a satisfactory communication with the predecessor auditor, Tish & Field drafted an engagement letter that was mailed to the audit committee of the board of directors of Unicorn Corporation. The engagement letter clearly set forth the arrangements concerning the involvement of the predecessor auditor and other matters.

Required:

a. What information should Tish & Field have obtained during their enquiry of the predecessor auditor prior to accepting the engagement?

b. What other matters would Tish & Field generally have included in the engagement letter?

(AICPA, adapted)

2 ▷ **5-42** A practitioner has been asked to audit the financial statements of a publicly held company for the first time. All preliminary verbal discussions and enquiries among the prospective auditor, the company, the predecessor auditor, and all other necessary parties have been completed. The practitioner is now preparing an engagement letter.

Required:

a. List the items that should be included in the typical engagement letter in these circumstances.

b. Describe the benefits derived from preparing an engagement letter.

(AICPA, adapted)

4,5,6 ▷ **5-43** Parker is the in-charge auditor with administrative responsibilities for the upcoming annual audit of FGH Company, a continuing audit client. Parker will supervise two assistants on the engagement and will visit the client before the field work begins.

Parker has started the planning process by listing procedures to be performed prior to the beginning of field work. The list includes

1. Reviewing correspondence and permanent files.

2. Reviewing prior years' audit working papers, financial statements, and auditor's reports.

3. Discussing matters that may affect the examination with the audit firm personnel responsible for providing audit and nonaudit services to the client.

4. Discussing with management current business developments affecting the client.

Required:

Complete Parker's list of procedures to be performed before the beginning of field work.

(AICPA, adapted)

2 >   **5-44**   Jane Strang was recently appointed auditor of Saltec Ltd., a public company. She had been approached by the audit committee of the company's board of directors and had communicated with the company's previous auditor before indicating that she would accept the appointment. She attended the shareholder's meeting at which she was appointed but has not yet visited the company's offices.

Required:

List the matters that Strang should attend to between now and the commencement of her detailed audit work in order to plan an effective audit of Saltec Ltd.

(CICA, adapted)

4,5,6 >   **5-45**   Analytical procedures consist of evaluations of financial information made by a study of plausible relationships among both financial and nonfinancial data. They range from simple comparisons to the use of complex models involving many relationships and elements of data. They compare recorded amounts, or ratios developed from recorded amounts, to expectations developed by the auditor.

Required:

a. Describe the broad purposes of analytical procedures.
b. Identify the sources of information from which an auditor develops expectations.
c. Describe the factors that influence an auditor's consideration of the reliability of data for the purpose of achieving audit objectives.

(AICPA, adapted)

EarthWear   5,6 >   **5-46**   At December 31, 2006, EarthWear had $5,890,000 in a liability account labelled "Reserve for returns." The footnotes to the financial statements contain the following policy: "At the time of sale, the company provides a reserve equal to the gross profit on projected merchandise returns, based on prior returns experience." The client has indicated that returns for sales that are six months old are negligible, and gross profit percentage for the year is 42.5 percent. The client has also provided the following information on sales for the last six months of the year:

Month	Monthly Sales (000s)	Historical Return Rate
July	$73,300	0.4%
August	82,800	0.6%
September	93,500	1.0%
October	110,200	1.5%
November	158,200	2.5%
December	202,500	3.2%

Required:

a. Using the information given, develop an expectation for the reserve for returns account.

b. What procedures should the auditor perform if the difference between the expectation and the book value is greater than tolerable misstatement?

4 > **5-47** Anita Lee accepted an engagement to audit the financial statements of General Company, a new client. General is a publicly held retailing entity that recently replaced its operating management. In the course of applying auditing procedures, Lee discovered that General's financial statements may be materially misstated due to the existence of fraud.

Required:

a. Describe Lee's responsibilities regarding the circumstance described.

b. Describe Lee's responsibilities to report on General's financial statements and other communications if Lee is precluded from applying necessary procedures in searching for fraud.

c. Describe Lee's responsibilities to report on General's financial statements and other communications if Lee concludes that General's financial statements are materially affected by fraud.

(AICPA, adapted)

5 > **5-48** Exhibit 5–3 contains a partial audit program for substantive tests of accounts receivable.

Required:

For audit procedures 1–4, identify the primary management asssertion(s) being tested.

6,7 > **5-49** The following independent situations represent misstatements that could occur in financial statements.

Required:

a. A company recorded fictitious sales by crediting sales revenue and debiting accounts receivable. Also, inventory was credited and Cost of Goods debited to correspond to the fictitious sales. Will this result in the current ratio being higher than, lower than, or the same as it would be in the absence of the misstatement?

b. At the end of its fiscal year, a company recorded the payment of some trade accounts payable but did not actually issue the cheques until the beginning of the next year. With reference to the current ratio, why would a company record a disbursement such as this before year-end?

c. A shipment of items for resale was received just before year-end and was properly included in inventory. However, the purchase transaction was not recorded until the following period. What would be the effect on the current ratio, the gross margin ratio, the cost of goods sold ratio, inventory turnover, and receivables turnover?

d. Although the amount provided in the allowance for bad debts is appropriate, even conservative, the controller is unwilling to write off individual customer accounts receivable. The gross receivables and the allowance both contain amounts that should have been written off. How would the failure to write off the receivables affect the current ratio, receivables turnover, days' sales in receivables, return on opening equity, and working capital/total assets?

5,6,7 **5-50** Rashed Balti is auditing the RCT Manufacturing Company as of February 28, 2007. As with all engagements, one of Balti's initial procedures is to make overall checks of the client's financial data by reviewing significant ratios and trends so that he better understands the business and can determine where to concentrate his audit efforts.

The financial statements prepared by the client with audited 2006 figures and preliminary 2007 figures are presented below in condensed form.

RCT MANUFACTURING COMPANY
Condensed Income Statements
Years Ended February 28, 2007 and 2006

	2007	2006
Net sales	$ 1,684,000	$ 1,250,000
Cost of goods sold	927,000	710,000
Gross margin on sales	$ 757,000	$ 540,000
Selling and administrative expenses	682,000	504,000
Income before federal income taxes	$ 75,000	$ 36,000
Income tax expense	30,000	14,400
Net income	$ 45,000	$ 21,600

RCT MANUFACTURING COMPANY
Condensed Balanced Sheets
February 28, 2007 and 2006

Assets	2007	2006
Cash	$ 12,000	$ 15,000
Accounts receivable, net	93,000	50,000
Inventory	72,000	67,000
Other current assets	5,000	6,000
Plant and equipment, net of amortization	60,000	80,000
	$242,000	$21,600

Equities	2007	2006
Accounts payable	$ 38,000	$ 41,000
Federal income taxes payable	30,000	15,000
Long-term liabilities	20,000	40,000
Common stock	70,000	70,000
Retained earnings	84,000	52,000
	$242,000	$218,000

Additional information:

- The company has only an insignificant amount of cash sales.
- The end-of-year figures are comparable to the average for each respective year.

Required:

For each year, compute the current ratio and a turnover ratio for accounts receivable. Based on these ratios, identify and discuss audit procedures that should be included in Arthur's audit of (1) accounts receivable and (2) accounts payable.

(AICPA, adapted)

DISCUSSION CASES

4,5 >   **5-51**   Forestcrest Woolen Mills is a closely held Quebec company that has existed since 1920. The company manufactures high-quality woolen cloth for men's and women's outerwear. Your firm has audited Forestcrest for 15 years.

Last year Forestcrest signed a consent decree with the Quebec Environmental Protection Agency. The company had been convicted of dumping pollutants (such as bleaching and dyeing chemicals) into the local river. The consent decree provided that Forestcrest construct a water treatment facility within eight years.

You are conducting the current-year audit, and you notice that there has been virtually no activity in the water treatment facility construction account. Your discussion with the controller produces the following comment: "Because of increased competition and lower sales volume, our cash flow has decreased below normal levels. You had better talk to the president about the treatment facility."

The president (and majority shareholder) tells you the following: "Given the current cash flow levels, we had two choices: lay off people or stop work on the facility. This is a poor rural area of Quebec with few other job opportunities for our people. I decided to stop work on the water treatment facility. I don't think that the province will fine us or close us down." When you ask the president if the company will be able to comply with the consent decree, he informs you that he is uncertain.

Required:

a. Discuss the implications of this situation for the audit and audit report.

b. Would your answer change if these events occurred in the seventh year after the signing of the consent decree?

5,6,7 >   **5-52**   The auditors for Weston University are conducting their audit for the fiscal year ended December 31, 2006. Specifically, the audit firm is now focusing on the audit of revenue from this season's home football games. While planning the audit of sales of football tickets, one of their newer staff people observed that, in prior years, many hours were spent auditing revenue. This staff associate pointed out that perhaps the firm could apply analytical procedures to evaluate whether it appears that the revenue account is properly stated.

The staff associate noted that information for a typical home game could be used to estimate revenues for the entire season. The home football season consisted of seven home games—one against a nationally ranked powerhouse, Bloomington University, and six games against conference opponents. One of these conference games is Weston's in-provincial archrival, Norwalk University. All of these games were day games except for the game against a conference opponent, Westport University.

The auditors will base their estimate on the game played against Kramer College, a conference opponent. This game is considered to be an average home game for Weston University. The following information concerning that game is available:

Total attendance   24,000 (stadium capacity is 40,000)

This attendance figure includes the 500 free seats described below, and the 24,000 figure should be used as a basis for all further calculations.

Ticket prices
Box seats	$12 per ticket
End-zone seats	$8 per ticket
Upper-deck seats	$5 per ticket

At the game against Kramer College, total attendance was allocated among the different seats as follows:

Box seats	70%
End-zone seats	20%
Upper-deck seats	10%

Based on information obtained in prior year audits, the following assumptions are made to assist in estimating revenue for the other games, all:

- Attendance for the Bloomington University game was expected to be 30 percent higher than total attendance for an average game, with the mix of seats purchased expected to be the same as for a regular game; however, tickets are priced 20 percent higher than for a normal game.

- The game against Norwalk University was expected to draw 20 percent more fans than a normal game, with 75 percent of these extra fans buying box seats and the other 25 percent purchasing upper-deck seats.

- To make up for extra costs associated with the night game, ticket prices were increased by 10 percent each; however, attendance was also expected to be 5 percent lower than for a normal game, with each type of seating suffering a 5 percent decline.

- 500 box seats at every game are given away free to players' family and friends. This number is expected to be the same for all home games.

Required:

1. Based on the information above, develop an expectation for ticket revenue for the seven home football games.

2. Reported ticket revenue was $2,200,000. Is the difference between your estimate and reported ticket revenue large enough to prompt further consideration? Why or why not? If further consideration is warranted, provide possible explanations for the difference between estimated and actual football ticket revenue. What evidence could you gather to verify each of your explanations?

3. Under what conditions are analytical procedures likely to be effective in a situation such as that described in this problem?

1,2,7 ⟩   **5-53**   As a result of a dispute between Alpha-Omega Technology Ltd. (AOT) and its incumbent auditors, your firm has been engaged to perform this year's audit. The dispute concerned the proper valuation of work-in-process inventory and the practice of "bill and hold"—the inclusion in sales of inventory that has not been shipped but that the company argues has been, for all practical purposes, completed and sold.

AOT has done very well in its field over the last two decades, primarily because of a number of successful mergers negotiated by Eric Tam, the president and chairman of the board of directors. AOT has continued to prosper, as evidenced by its constantly increasing earnings and growth. Only in the last two years have the company's profits turned downward. Tam has a reputation for having been able to hire an aggressive group of young executives by the use of relatively low salaries combined with an unusually generous profit-sharing plan.

A major difficulty you face in the new audit is the lack of sophisticated accounting records for a company the size of AOT. Tam believes that profits come mainly from intelligent and aggressive action based on forecasts, not by relying on historical data. Most of the forecast data are generated by the sales and production department rather than by the accounting department. The personnel in the accounting department do seem competent, but somewhat overworked and underpaid relative to other employees. One of the recent changes that will potentially improve the record-keeping is a changeover from the old computerized system to a new state-of-the-art IT system. All the accounting records are not converted yet, but such major areas as inventory and sales have been. Much of the new facility is being reserved for scientific purposes, specifically production and marketing on the grounds that these areas are more essential to operations than the recordkeeping function.

The first six months' financial statements include a profit of approximately only 10 percent less than for the first six months of the previous year, which is somewhat surprising considering the reduced sales volume of the company. The only major difficulty that AOT faces right now, according to financial analysts, is fairly severe underfinancing. There is an excessive amount of both current and long-term debt because of the depressed capital markets. Management is reluctant to obtain equity capital at this point because an increased number of shares would decrease the earnings per share even more than 10 percent. At the present time Tam is negotiating with several cash-rich companies in the hope of being able to merge with them as a means of overcoming the capital problems.

Required:

a. Identify the objectives and strategies, key business processes, and other business risks that you would need to be concerned with if you wished to adopt the strategic systems approach to the audit of AOT.

b. State the appropriate approach to investigating the significance of the items you identified in part (a).

4,5,6,7   5-54   Science World Entertainment Shops is a chain of science-based toy and novelty stores owned and operated by two brothers from a family of native Manitobans with a flamboyant lifestyle. Their business grew from one store in 1998 to 10 stores by the end of 2001. Their strategy is to offer the very latest in science (and science fiction) toys and novelties at low prices with aggressive sales tactics in their well-placed stores (all are in trendy shopping malls).

After a period of substantial growth, competition stiffened during 2005, and the brothers ceased their active expansion in order to tighten their controls over operations. They focused on inventory management and sought assistance from Alex, Louis & Co., (their auditor), in redesigning their system. Management feels that this redesign succeeded because inventory was lower at year-end, resulting in substantially increased inventory turnover (based on ending inventories). Furthermore, management is proud that it has continued to realize its target of 100 percent markup on the cost of its merchandise.

The 2005 and 2006 audited consolidated income statements for Science World are shown in Exhibit 1; a statement of store contributions to consolidated earnings is shown in Exhibit 2. The financial statements have been audited by Alex, Louis & Co., who gave them a standard three-paragraph audit report for both 2005 and 2006.

Your client, We're Easy Money, Inc. (WEMI), is considering acquiring Science World Entertainment Shops as of June 30, 2007. WEMI wants you to conduct a preacquisition review and inform it of any accounting or auditing problems. Due to the nature of the business, WEMI is especially concerned about the inventory. To facilitate negotiation of the sale, the brothers have given Alex, Louis & Co. permission to waive confidentiality and cooperate fully with you in answering questions about the company and their audit.

Your partner has met with the Alex, Louis & Co. partner in charge of the Science World audit. Her notes are attached as Exhibit 3. You are to finish her work by evaluating her review as well as conducting analytical procedures that you believe proper.

EXHIBIT 1

Audited Consolidated Earnings

SCIENCE WORLD ENTERTAINMENT SHOPS
Summary of Consolidated Earnings
Years Ended April 30, 2005 and 2006 (in thousands)

	2005		2006	
Sales		$106,893		$108,299
Cost of sales:				
Beginning inventory	$ 8,972		$ 9,953	
Purchases	54,727		52,986	
	$63,699		$62,939	
Ending inventory	9,953		8,445	
Cost of sales		53,746		54,494
Gross profit		$ 53,147		$ 53,805
Operating expenses (direct)		31,962		29,976
Net contribution of stores		$ 21,185		$ 23,829
Corporate expenses (total)		9,455		9,123
Net income		$ 11,730		$ 14,706

Note:

All inventories are valued at the lower of cost or market value. Cost is calculated using the first in, first-out method.

Required:

a. Prepare a list of misstatements that might have occurred in inventory and cost of sales and, if they had occurred, how they would affect the account values and ratios of account values.

b. Develop expectations about the likely audited value of inventory and cost of sales at each store based on your overall knowledge.

c. Does inventory appear to be "materially" overstated at any store or in the aggregate? What additional investigation, if any, would you recommend?

EXHIBIT 2

Unaudited Contribution to Earnings by Store

SCIENCE WORLD ENTERTAINMENT SHOPS
Net Contribution by Store
Year Ended April 30, 2006 (in thousands)

	Sales	Beginning Inventory	Purchases	Ending Inventory	Cost of Sales	Gross Profit	Operating Expenses	Net Contribution
Store 1	11,372	1,009	5,456	894	5,571	5,801	3,056	2,745
Store 2	10,990	982	5,370	688	5,664	5,326	2,996	2,330
Store 3	10,615	968	5,133	816	5,285	5,330	2,973	2,357
Store 4	12,052	979	5,938	966	5,951	6,101	3,126	2,975
Store 5	10,488	1,005	5,066	822	5,249	5,239	2,947	2,292
Store 6	11,653	980	5,806	918	5,868	5,785	3,092	2,693
Store 7	11,800	1,035	5,804	838	6,001	5,799	3,111	2,688
Store 8	10,995	1,016	5,468	901	5,583	5,412	3,007	2,405
Store 9	9,509	1,022	4,667	915	4,774	4,735	2,864	1,871
Store 10	8,825	957	4,278	687	4,548	4,277	2,804	1,473
Consolidated	$108,299	$9,953	$52,986	$8,445	$54,494	$53,805	$29,976	$23,829

EXHIBIT 3

Partner's Notes of Meeting with Alex, Louis & Co. and Her Review of Their Work Papers

Science World's Inventory Procedures:

Purchasing: Accounting for purchasing is conducted at the firm's home office in Winnipeg, Manitoba, but store managers are allowed great discretion in ordering unique items that they believe will sell in their own stores. Thus, there is no common chainwide product list, and inventory is established on a physical or periodic basis.

Inventory quantities: To strengthen control and to allow its store personnel to concentrate on operations, Science World relies on an independent inventory-counting firm to determine inventory quantities at each store. At fiscal year-end, the outside firm sends two count specialists to each store. Each specialist has a handheld computer designed for efficient recording of product codes and counts. Each specialist walks the aisles counting every product code item encountered. The count and item code are then entered into the handheld computer.

At the end of the counting process, the memory contents of each handheld computer are read into a PC program that matches the two sets of counts and identifies discrepancies. The two specialists locate the items in question, recount the stock, and enter a corrected amount. The PC then prepares a written inventory quantity summary for the store manager. It also prepares a diskette with the same information that is forwarded to the home office in Winnipeg, Manitoba.

Pricing and obsolescence: In Winnipeg, the inventory quantities on the diskettes are matched by computer against purchase records to price the inventory at first-in, first-out cost. Items without purchase records are noted for follow-up to complete the purchase/accounts payable records. The extended amounts are then summarized and entered as the general ledger amounts. A lower-of-cost-or-market (LCM) assessment is made by calculating inventory turnover by product groupings summarized across stores. All items with more than four months' supply are then reviewed by one of the brothers to assess whether an accounting adjustment is needed and whether the store manager should be contacted to discuss the overstock problem.

Alex, Louis & Co.'s Auditing Procedures:

Alex and Louis's auditors reviewed Science World's internal controls over inventory and were satisfied that they were well designed. The auditors arranged with Science World management to observe the outside count team procedures at stores 2 and 7. Also at both locations, Alex, Louis & Co. auditors randomly selected a substantial number of items, independently counted them, and noted the counts in their work papers. They observed no exceptions in procedure by the outside count personnel and only inconsequential quantity differences when their own counts were traced and compared with those in the final inventory summary that supported the Science World financial statements. During their store visit, Alex, Louis & Co.'s auditors also looked for out-of-the-way, musty, or dusty inventory and found none. This was followed by a testing of the "months' supply on hand" calculation that Science World personnel made at the home office. They were satisfied that the LCM adjustment was adequate.

Alex, Louis & Co. conducted overall analytical procedures by comparing the Science World balances and ratios with those for toy and novelty stores nationwide. Their comparison revealed that Science World has lower merchandise markup percentages than 80 percent of the industry but has been able to maintain its gross profit rate during 2006 while the industry average has fallen by about 1.5 percent. Also, median inventory turnover for the industry has risen from 4.5 to 4.8 over the same period.

(Adapted and used with permission of W. R. Kinney, Jr.)

INTERNET ASSIGNMENTS

3,4,5,6>   **5-55**   Using the information from the text, EarthWear Clothiers' website (www.mcgrawhill.ca/olc/messier/earthwear), and Willis & Adams's website (www.mcgrawhill.ca/olc/messier/willisandadams) prepare an audit planning memo. In preparing the memo, include information on each of the following items:

- Based on knowledge obtained about the client's business and industry, identify the key business processes of EarthWear.

- Establish audit risk and materiality (refer to Chapter 3), and assess inherent risk (cite all important factors and their possible effects on the audit).

- Assess a preliminary level of control risk (limit the assessment to the control environment and order entry).
- Assess the possibility of errors, fraud, and illegal acts.
- Conduct preliminary analytical procedures, including industry data.

4⟩   **5-56**   Visit the Institute of Internal Auditors' (IIA) website (www.theiia.org) and familiarize yourself with the information contained there. Search the site for information about the IIA's requirements for the objectivity and independence of internal auditors.

Chapter 6

Internal Control in a Financial Statement Audit

Learning Objectives

Upon completion of this chapter, you will be able to

1 Explain what internal control is, and its importance to management and auditors.

2 Identify the components of internal control.

3 Discuss the limitations on an entity's internal control.

4 Identify the tools available for documenting the understanding of internal control.

5 Describe how to plan an audit strategy based on a preliminary understanding of an entity's internal control.

6 Explain how to assess and document the level of control risk using tests of controls to support a reliance strategy.

7 Outline the considerations for the timing of audit procedures.

8 Outline the auditor's responsibilities when the client has accounting services performed by an outside service organisation.

9 Review the auditor's communication of internal control-related matters.

10 Briefly describe the effect of information technology on internal control.

RELEVANT ACCOUNTING AND ASSURANCE PRONOUNCEMENTS

CICA *Handbook*, section 5050, Using the work of internal audit

CICA *Handbook*, section 5141, Understanding the entity and its environment and assessing the risks of material misstatement

CICA *Handbook*, section 5143, The auditor's procedures in response to assessed risks

CICA *Handbook*, section 5220, Internal control in the context of an audit—Weaknesses in internal control

CICA *Handbook*, section 5310, Audit evidence consideration when an entity uses a service organization

CICA *Handbook*, section 5750, Communication of matters identified during the financial statement audit

CICA *Handbook*, section 5751, Communication with those having oversight responsibility for the financial reporting process

Risk Management and Governance Board, *Preface to Guidance of the Criteria of Control Board*

Risk Management and Governance Board, *Guidance on Control*

Risk Management and Governance Board, *Guidance on Assessing Control*

EARTHWEAR'S INTERNAL CONTROL—A KEY COMPONENT

EarthWear One of the most important components of EarthWear's financial reporting system is its system of *internal control*. EarthWear's system of internal control, created and maintained by management, often with oversight by the board of directors, particularly the audit committee, consists of policies, procedures, and practices designed to facilitate the achievement of EarthWear's objectives. Examples of such objectives are efficient and effective conduct of business, ensuring compliance with ethical standards, applicable laws and regulations, and timely, accurate generation, recording, and transmission of financial information. EarthWear makes use of such procedures as segregation of duties, review and authorization of purchase and sales transactions, reconciliation of subsidiary accounts to control accounts, and physical safeguards such as limited access requiring passcards, to achieve its objectives.

It is the controls over the generation, recording, and transmission of financial information that are of particular significance to Willis & Adams' audit of EarthWear. If after studying, understanding, and testing those controls, the auditors conclude that they provide reasonable assurance that the financial information of EarthWear, as reported in their financial statements, is materially correct, the evidence that the auditors have collected and documented about the internal control system becomes part of the sufficient appropriate audit evidence on which they will base their audit opinion.

The nature, timing, and extent of the audit procedures that Willis & Adams will employ are very much influenced by EarthWear's internal control.

Because EarthWear is listed on the TSX, senior management of EarthWear is required to provide, in its annual filings with the Ontario Securities Commission, specific certifications related to internal control over financial reporting. Willis and Adams will provide assistance with these required certifications by performing, in addition to the audit, a series of agreed-upon procedures examining specific components of EarthWear's internal control over financial reporting. This is not an assurance engagement, nor will it result in any expression of opinion by Willis and Adams. Willis and Adams will provide to the senior management of EarthWear a written report, for their internal use only, identifying the agreed-upon procedures they applied to the internal controls and the results of those procedures. The purpose of this report is to assist management in making the assessments necessary to issue the above-mentioned certifications.

This chapter focuses on the auditors' study of the internal control system and their assessment of control risk. It illustrates the importance of internal control and its components, and describes how the evaluation of internal control relates to substantive testing. It also discusses the timing of audit procedures and the communication of internal control-related matters.

Internal Control

Introduction

LO 1>

Internal control is designed and effected by the entity's board of directors, management, and other personnel to provide reasonable assurance about the achievement of the entity's objectives in relation to reliability of financial reporting, effectiveness and efficiency of operations, and compliance with applicable laws and regulations.

Internal control is important to both management and auditors. To management, internal control plays a key role in how it meets its stewardship and agency responsibilities; to auditors, internal control has a direct impact on the scope of the audit.

Management's Perspective

From management's perspective, the internal control system provides a way to meet its stewardship and agency responsibilities. For example, management can maintain controls that provide reasonable assurance that adequate control exists over the entity's assets and records by developing internal controls that require employees to follow corporate policies and procedures such as proper authorization for transactions. Such an internal control system not only ensures that assets and records are safeguarded but also creates an environment in which efficiency and effectiveness are encouraged and monitored. This is becoming more important as entities automate their information systems and operate more globally.

Management also needs a control system that generates reliable information for decision making. If the information system does not generate reliable information, management may be unable to make informed decisions about issues such as product pricing, cost of production, and profit information. In summary, management has numerous incentives for establishing and maintaining a strong system of internal controls. In 1995 the CICA created the Criteria of Control Board (CoCo), which has since been renamed the Risk Management and Governance Board. Its first publication was *Guidance on Control*, intended for management as well as owners, directors, investors, creditors, and auditors.[1]

The Auditor's Perspective

The importance of internal control to the auditor is rooted in the second examination standard which states

> The auditor should obtain an understanding of the entity and its environment, *including internal control* [emphasis added], sufficient to identify and assess the risks of material misstatement of the financial statements whether due to fraud or error, and sufficient to design and perform further audit procedures.

The controls that are relevant to the entity's ability to record, process, summarize, and report financial data consistent with management's assertions (e.g., existence, occurrence, completeness, rights and obligations, valuation, allocation, and presentation and disclosure) are the auditor's main concern. More specifically, the auditor needs assurance about the reliability of the data generated within the internal control system in terms of how it affects the fairness of the financial statements and how well the assets and records of the entity are safeguarded.

As we shall see in this chapter, the auditor's understanding of internal controls is a major factor in determining the overall audit strategy. The auditor's responsibilities for internal control are discussed under two major topics: (1) the components of internal control and (2) the auditor's consideration of internal control in planning and performing an audit.[2]

---

[1]Risk Management and Governance Board, *Guidance on Control* (Toronto: CICA, 1995).

[2]See also Risk Management and Governance Board, *Guidance on Assessing Control* (Toronto: CICA, 1999).

The Components of Internal Control

LO 2>   An entity's internal control consists of five interrelated components:

- control environment
- entity risk assessment process
- information system and related business processes relevant to financial reporting communication
- control procedures
- monitoring of controls

Table 6–1 defines each of the components and Figure 6–1 shows how the categories of objectives of internal control, including safeguarding of assets, relate to the five components. One can see that each of the five components impacts each of the objectives. The auditor is mainly concerned with how the five components affect the financial reporting objective. In summary, the controls relevant to the audit are those that are likely to prevent or detect material misstatements in the financial statement assertions. Each of the five components is discussed in more detail following.

Control Environment   The first and most important component of internal control is the control environment. The control environment sets the tone of an organization, influencing the control consciousness of its people. It is the foundation for all other components of internal control, providing discipline and structure.

The importance of the control environment to an entity is reflected in the overall attitude to, awareness of, and actions of the board of directors,

Table 6–1	**Components of Internal Control**

Control environment The control environment sets the tone of an organization, influencing the control consciousness of its people. It is the foundation for effective internal control, providing discipline and structure. The control environment includes the attitudes, awareness, policies, and actions of management and the board of directors concerning the entity's internal control and its importance in the entity.

The entity's risk assessment process The process for identifying and responding to business risks and the results thereof. For financial reporting purposes, the entity's risk assessment process includes how management identifies risks relevant to the preparation of financial statements that are fairly presented in conformity with generally accepted accounting principles, estimates their significance, assesses the likelihood of their occurrence, and decides upon actions to manage them.

The entity's information system and related business processes relevant to financial reporting, and communication The information system relevant to financial reporting objectives, which includes the accounting system, consists of the procedures, whether automated or manual, and records established to initiate, record, process, and report entity transactions and to maintain accountability for the related assets, liabilities, and equity. Communication involves providing an understanding of individual roles and responsibilities pertaining to internal control over financial reporting.

Control procedures Control procedures are the policies and procedures that help ensure that management directives are carried out, for example, that necessary actions are taken to address risks to achievement of the entity's objectives. Control procedures, whether automated or manual, have various objectives and are applied at various organizational and functional levels.

Monitoring of controls A process to assess the quality of internal control performance over time. It involves assessing the design and operation of controls on a timely basis and taking necessary corrective actions.

FIGURE 6–1

The Relationship of the Categories of Objectives of Internal Control to the Five Components of Internal Control

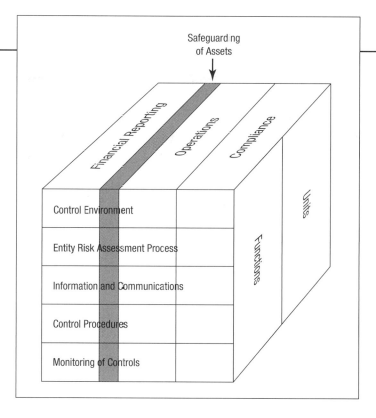

management, and owners regarding control. The control environment can be thought of as an umbrella that covers the entire entity and establishes the framework for implementing the entity's accounting systems and internal controls. The elements of the entity's internal control environment are discussed below.

Integrity and Ethical Values   The effectiveness of an entity's internal controls is a function of the integrity and ethical values of the individuals who create, administer, and monitor the controls. An entity needs to establish ethical and behavioural standards that are communicated to employees and are reinforced by day-to-day practice. For example, management should remove incentives or opportunities that might lead personnel to engage in dishonest, illegal, or unethical acts. Some examples of incentives that may lead to unethical behaviour are pressures to meet unrealistic performance targets and high performance-dependent rewards. Examples of opportunities include an ineffective board of directors, a weak internal audit function, and insignificant penalties for improper behaviour. Management can best communicate integrity and ethical behaviour within an entity through the use of policy statements and codes of conduct.

A Commitment to Competence   Competence consists of the knowledge and skills necessary to accomplish the tasks that define an individual's job. Conceptually, management must specify the competence level for a particular job and translate it into the required level of knowledge and skills. For example, an entity should have a formal or informal job description for each job. Management then must hire employees who have the appropriate competence for their jobs. Good human resource policies (discussed later in this section) help to attract and retain competent and trustworthy employees.

Participation of the Board of Directors or Audit Committee[3]   The board of directors and its audit committee significantly influence the control consciousness of the entity. As mentioned in Chapter 5, the audit committee is a subcommittee of the board of directors that is composed of directors who are not part of the management team. The board of directors and the audit committee must take their fiduciary responsibilities seriously and actively oversee the entity's internal control, accounting and reporting policies and procedures. Factors that affect the effectiveness of the board or audit committee include the following:

- its independence from management
- the experience and stature of its members
- the extent of its involvement with and scrutiny of the entity's activities
- the appropriateness of its actions
- the extent to which difficult questions are raised and pursued with management
- its interaction with the internal and external auditors

Management's Philosophy and Operating Style   Establishing, maintaining, and monitoring the entity's internal controls are management's responsibility. Management's philosophy and operating style may significantly affect the quality of internal control. Characteristics such as the following may signal important information to the auditor about management's philosophy and operating style:

- management's approach to taking and monitoring business risks
- management's attitudes and actions toward financial reporting (conservative or aggressive selection from available alternative accounting principles and the conscientiousness and conservatism with which accounting estimates are developed)
- management's attitudes toward information processing and accounting functions and personnel
- management's attitude to the importance of establishing and monitoring internal controls

Organizational Structure   The organizational structure defines how authority and responsibility are delegated and monitored. It provides the framework within which the entity's activities for achieving its objectives

---

[3]See Risk Management and Governance Board, *Guidance for Directors—Governance Processes for Control* (Toronto: CICA, 2000).

are planned, executed, controlled, and monitored. Each entity develops an organizational structure suited to its needs. Establishing a relevant organizational structure includes considering key areas of authority and responsibility and appropriate lines of reporting.

An entity develops an organizational structure that depends on its size and the nature of its business. Factors such as the level of technology in the entity's industry and external influences such as regulation play a major role in the type of organizational structure used. For example, an entity in a high-technology industry needs an organizational structure that can respond quickly to technological changes in the marketplace. Similarly, an entity that operates in a highly regulated industry, such as banking, needs to maintain a very tightly controlled organizational structure in order to comply with federal or provincial laws.

Assignment of Authority and Responsibility This control environment factor includes *how* authority and responsibility for operating activities are assigned and *how* reporting relationships and authorization hierarchies are established. It includes the policies regarding acceptable business practices, the knowledge and experience of key personnel, and the resources provided for carrying out duties. It also includes policies and communications directed at ensuring that all personnel understand the entity's objectives, know how their individual actions interrelate and contribute to those objectives, and recognize how and for what they will be held accountable.

An entity can use a number of controls to meet the requirements of this control environment factor. First, the entity can have a well-specified organizational chart that indicates the lines of authority and responsibility. Second, management and supervisory personnel should have job descriptions that include their control-related responsibilities.

Human Resource Policies and Procedures The quality of internal control is a direct function of the quality of the personnel operating the system. The entity should have sound personnel policies for hiring, training, evaluating, counselling, promoting, compensating, and taking remedial action. For example, in hiring employees, standards that emphasize seeking the most qualified individuals, with emphasis on educational background, prior work experience, and evidence of integrity and ethical behaviour, demonstrate an entity's commitment to employing competent and trustworthy people. Research into the causes of errors in accounting systems has shown personnel-related issues to be a major cause of error.[4]

The auditor should learn enough about the control environment to understand management's and the board of directors' attitude, awareness, and actions concerning the control environment, considering both the sub-

---

[4]For example, see A. Wright and R. H. Ashton, "Identifying Audit Adjustments with Attention-Directing Procedures," *The Accounting Review* (October 1989), pp. 710–28. This study indicates that approximately 55 percent of the errors detected by auditors resulted from personnel problems, insufficient accounting knowledge, and judgement errors.

stance of controls and their collective effect. Exhibit 6–1 presents a questionnaire that includes the type of information the auditor would document about EarthWear's control environment.[5] The auditor should concentrate on the substance of controls rather than on their form because controls may be established but not acted on. For example, management may establish formal conflict-of-interest policies but seldom follow up on whether employees are really complying with these policies.

The Entity's Risk Assessment Process

An entity's risk assessment process is its process for identifying and responding to business risks. This process includes how management identifies risks relevant to the preparation of financial statements, estimates their significance, assesses the likelihood of their occurrence, and decides upon actions to manage them. For example, the entity's risk assessment process may address how the entity identifies and analyzes significant estimates recorded in the financial statements.

This risk assessment process should consider external and internal events and circumstances that may arise and adversely affect the entity's ability to initiate, record, process, and report financial data consistent with the assertions of management in the financial statements. Once risks have been identified by management, it should consider their significance, the likelihood of their occurrence, and how they should be managed. Management should initiate plans, programs, or actions to address specific risks. In some instances, management may accept the consequences of a possible risk because of the costs to remediate or other considerations. Client business risks can arise or change due to the following circumstances:

- *Changes in the operating environment.* Changes in the regulatory or operating environment can alter competitive pressures and create significantly different risks.
- *New personnel.* New personnel may have a different focus on, or understanding of, internal control.
- *New or revamped information systems.* Significant and rapid changes in information systems can change the risk relating to internal control.
- *Rapid growth.* Significant and rapid expansion of operations can strain controls and increase the risk of a breakdown of controls.
- *New technology.* Incorporating new technologies into production processes or information systems may change the risk associated with internal control.
- *New business models, products, or activities.* Entering business areas or transactions with which an entity has little experience may introduce new risk associated with internal control.
- *Corporate restructuring.* Restructuring may be accompanied by staff reductions and changes in supervision and segregation of duties that may change the risk associated with internal control.

---

[5]Exhibit 6–1 shows how the understanding of internal control can be developed and documented using a separate internal control questionnaire. Some or all of the information on the components of the entity's internal control may be captured as part of the auditor's understanding the entity and its environment (see Chapter 3). In such cases, the information may be included in a questionnaire such as the one shown in Appendix 3A to Chapter 3.

EXHIBIT 6–1

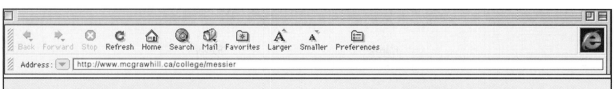

A Partial Questionnaire for Documenting the Auditor's Understanding of the Control Environment

CONTROL ENVIRONMENT QUESTIONNAIRE

Client: EarthWear Clothiers		**Balance Sheet Date:** 12/31/2006
Completed by: *SAA* **Date:** *9/30/06*		**Reviewed by:** *DRM* **Date:** 10/15/06

INTEGRITY AND ETHICAL VALUES

The effectiveness of controls cannot rise above the integrity and ethical values of the people who create, administer, and monitor them. Integrity and ethical values are essential elements of the control environment, affecting the design, administration, and monitoring of other components. Integrity and ethical behaviour are the product of the entity's ethical and behavioural standards, how they are communicated, and how they are reinforced in practice.

	Yes, No, N/A	**Comments**
Have appropriate entity policies regarding such matters as acceptable business practices, conflicts of interest, and codes of conduct been established, and are they adequately communicated?	*Yes*	*The permanent work papers contain a copy of EarthWear's conflict-of-interest policy.*
Does management demonstrate the appropriate "tone at the top," including explicit moral guidance about what is right or wrong?	*Yes*	*EarthWear's management maintains high moral and ethical standards and expects employees to act accordingly.*
Are everyday dealings with customers, suppliers, employees, and other parties based on honesty and fairness?	*Yes*	*EarthWear's management maintains a high degree of integrity in dealing with customers, suppliers, employees, and other parties; it requires employees and agents to act accordingly.*
Does management document or investigate deviations from established controls?	*Yes*	*To our knowledge, management has not attempted to override controls. Employees are encouraged to report attempts to bypass controls to appropriate individuals within the organization.*

COMMITMENT TO COMPETENCE

Competence is the knowledge and skills necessary to accomplish tasks that define the individual's job. Commitment to competence includes management's consideration of the competence levels for particular jobs and how those levels translate into requisite skills and knowledge.

Does the company maintain formal or informal job descriptions or other means of defining tasks that comprise particular jobs?	*Yes*	*EarthWear has formal written job descriptions for all supervisory personnel, and job duties for nonsupervisory personnel are clearly communicated.*
Does management determine to an adequate extent the knowledge and skills needed to perform particular jobs?	*Yes*	*The job descriptions specify the knowledge and skills needed. The Human Resources Department uses this information in hiring, training, and promotion decisions.*
Does evidence exist that employees have the requisite knowledge and skills to perform their job?	*Yes*	*Our prior experiences with EarthWear personnel indicate that they have the necessary knowledge and skills.*

- *International operations.* The expansion or acquisition of international operations carries new and often unique risks that may impact internal control.
- *Accounting pronouncements.* Adopting new accounting principles or changing accounting principles may affect the risk involved in preparing financial statements.

The auditor should obtain sufficient information about the entity's risk assessment process to understand how management considers risks relevant to financial reporting objectives and decides what to do to address those risks. Consider existing risks due to environmental sensitivity. For example, suppose a client operates in the oil industry, where there is always some risk of environmental damage. The auditor should obtain sufficient knowledge about how the client manages such environmental risk, because environmental accidents can result in costly litigation against the entity. Exhibit 6–2 presents a questionnaire that includes the type of information the auditor would document about EarthWear's risk assessment process.

EXHIBIT 6–2

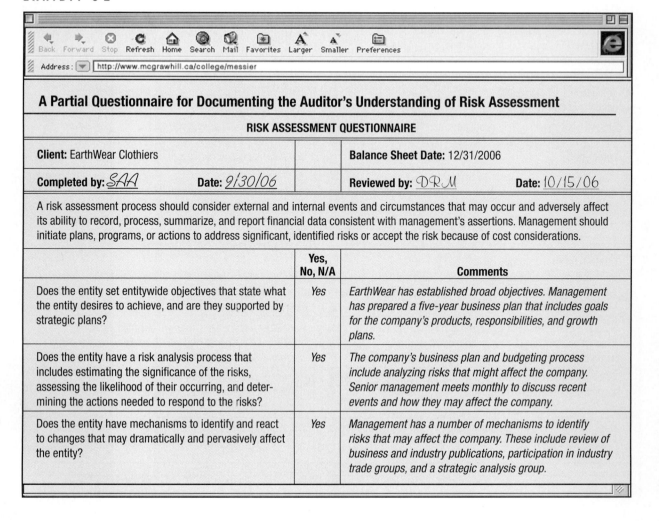

Address: http://www.mcgrawhill.ca/college/messier

A Partial Questionnaire for Documenting the Auditor's Understanding of Risk Assessment

RISK ASSESSMENT QUESTIONNAIRE

Client: EarthWear Clothiers		Balance Sheet Date: 12/31/2006
Completed by: *SAA* Date: *9/30/06*		Reviewed by: *DRM* Date: 10/15/06

A risk assessment process should consider external and internal events and circumstances that may occur and adversely affect its ability to record, process, summarize, and report financial data consistent with management's assertions. Management should initiate plans, programs, or actions to address significant, identified risks or accept the risk because of cost considerations.

	Yes, No, N/A	Comments
Does the entity set entitywide objectives that state what the entity desires to achieve, and are they supported by strategic plans?	Yes	*EarthWear has established broad objectives. Management has prepared a five-year business plan that includes goals for the company's products, responsibilities, and growth plans.*
Does the entity have a risk analysis process that includes estimating the significance of the risks, assessing the likelihood of their occurring, and determining the actions needed to respond to the risks?	Yes	*The company's business plan and budgeting process include analyzing risks that might affect the company. Senior management meets monthly to discuss recent events and how they may affect the company.*
Does the entity have mechanisms to identify and react to changes that may dramatically and pervasively affect the entity?	Yes	*Management has a number of mechanisms to identify risks that may affect the company. These include review of business and industry publications, participation in industry trade groups, and a strategic analysis group.*

Information and Communication

The information system relevant to the financial reporting objectives, which includes the accounting system, consists of methods and records established to record, process, summarize, and report an entity's transactions and to maintain accountability for the related assets and liabilities. An effective accounting system gives appropriate consideration to establishing methods and records that will

- identify and record all valid transactions
- describe the transactions on a timely basis in sufficient detail to permit proper classification of transactions for financial reporting
- measure the value of transactions in a manner that permits recording their proper monetary value in the financial statements
- determine the time period in which transactions occurred to permit their recording in the proper accounting period
- properly present the transactions and related disclosures in the financial statements

Communication involves providing an understanding of individual roles and responsibilities pertaining to internal control over financial reporting. It includes the extent to which personnel understand how their activities in the financial reporting information system relate to the work of others and the means of reporting exceptions to an appropriate higher level within the entity. Policy manuals, accounting and reporting manuals, and memoranda communicate policies and procedures to the entity's personnel. Communications can also be made orally or through the actions of management.

The auditor should obtain sufficient understanding of the information system relevant to financial reporting to understand the following:

- the classes of transactions in the entity's operations that are significant to the financial statements
- the procedures, both automated and manual, by which transactions are initiated, recorded, processed, and reported from their occurrence to their inclusion in the financial statements
- the related accounting records, whether electronic or manual, supporting information, computer media, and specific accounts in the financial statements that are involved in initiating, recording, processing, and reporting transactions
- how the information system captures other events and conditions that are significant to the financial statements
- the financial reporting process used to prepare the entity's financial statements, including significant accounting estimates and disclosures

A well-designed information system that is operating effectively can reduce the risk of material misstatement. The auditor must learn about each business process that affects significant account balances in the financial statements. This includes understanding how transactions are initiated, how documents and records are generated, and how the documents and records flow to the general ledger and financial statements. Understanding the information system also requires knowing how IT is used to process data.

The auditor should understand the automated and manual procedures used by the entity to prepare financial statements and related disclosures. Such procedures include

- the procedures used to enter transaction totals into the general ledger
- the procedures used to initiate, record, and process journal entries in the general ledger
- the procedures used to record all other recurring and nonrecurring adjustments to the financial statements

In addition, the auditor should obtain sufficient knowledge of how the entity communicates financial reporting roles and responsibilities and significant matters relating to financial reporting.

Control procedures

Control activities are the policies and procedures that help ensure that necessary actions are taken to address the risks involved in achieving the entity's objectives. Control activities relevant to the audit are discussed below.

Performance Reviews   A strong accounting system should have controls that independently check the performance of the individuals or processes in the system. Some examples include comparing actual performance with budgets, forecasts, and prior-period performance; investigating the relationship of operating and financial data followed by analysis, investigation of unexpected differences, and corrective actions; and reviewing functional or activity performance.

Information Processing Controls   There are two broad categories of information systems control procedures: general controls and application controls. *General controls* relate to the overall information processing environment and include controls over data centre and network operations; system software acquisition, development, and maintenance; access security; and application system acquisition, development, and maintenance. For example, an entity's controls for developing new programs for existing accounting systems should include adequate documentation and testing before implementation.

Application controls apply to the processing of individual applications and help to ensure the completeness, accuracy, authorization, and validity of transaction processing. Two examples are (1) the entity should have controls that ensure that each transaction that occurs in an entity's accounting system is properly authorized and (2) the entity should design documents and records so that all relevant information is captured in the accounting system.

General and application controls are covered in more detail in Appendix C available online at www.mcgrawhill.ca/college/messier.

Physical Controls   These controls include the physical security of assets. Physical controls include adequate safeguards, such as secured facilities, authorization for access to computer programs and data files, and periodic counting of assets such as inventory and comparison to control records.

Segregation of Duties It is important for an entity to segregate the authorization of transactions, recording of transactions, and custody of the related assets. Independent performance of each of these functions reduces the opportunity for any one person to be in a position to both perpetrate and conceal errors or fraud in the normal course of his or her duties. Two examples will help to demonstrate the importance of good segregation of duties. First, if an employee can authorize the sale of marketable securities and has access to the stock certificates, the assets can be misappropriated. Second, if an employee receives payment from customers on account and has access to the accounts receivable subsidiary ledger, it may be possible for that employee to misappropriate the cash and cover the shortage in the accounting records.

As the auditor learns about the other components (control environment, risk assessment, information and communication, and monitoring) he or she is also likely to obtain information about some control procedures. For example, in examining the information system that pertains to accounts receivable, the auditor is likely to see how the entity grants credit to customers. The auditor should consider the knowledge gained about the presence or absence of control procedures that has been obtained from learning about the other four components in determining whether it is necessary to investigate control procedures in order to plan the audit.

The audit strategy adopted is a function of the extent of the auditor's understanding and assessment of control procedures. As discussed previously, the auditor is required (by the second examination standard of GAAS) to obtain a preliminary understanding of the entity's internal control "sufficient to identify and assess the risks of material misstatement." Based on the preliminary review of the entity's internal control, in rare circumstances, the auditor may decide it is more efficient and effective to follow a substantive audit strategy rather than a combined or reliance strategy. However, where a combined strategy is chosen, the auditor must obtain a thorough understanding of the control procedures that relate to audit objectives for which a lower level of control risk is expected.

Exhibit 6–3 presents a questionnaire that includes the type of information the auditor would document on EarthWear's control procedures.

Monitoring of Controls

Monitoring of controls is a process that assesses the quality of internal control over time. To provide reasonable assurance that an entity's objectives will be achieved, management should monitor controls to determine whether they are operating as intended and that they are modified as appropriate for changes in conditions. It involves appropriate personnel assessing the design and operation of controls on a timely basis and taking necessary action.

Monitoring can be done through ongoing activities or separate evaluations. Ongoing monitoring procedures are built into the normal, recurring activities of the entity and include regular management and supervisory activities. For example, production managers at the corporate or divisional levels of an entity can monitor operations at lower levels by reviewing activity reports and questioning reported activity that differs significantly from their knowledge of the operations.

EXHIBIT 6-3

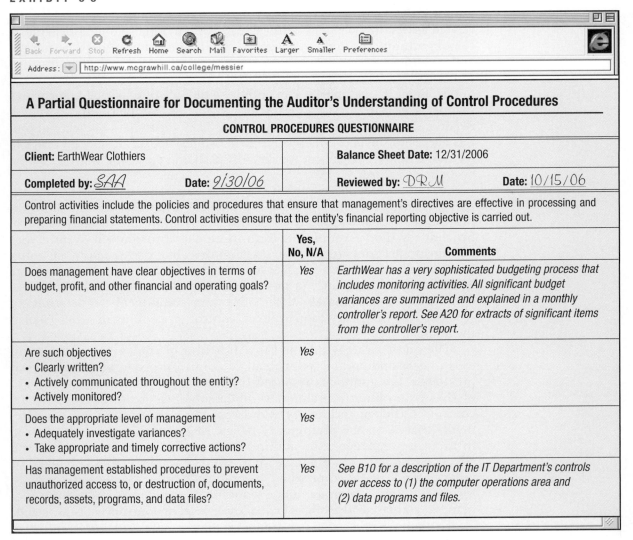

A Partial Questionnaire for Documenting the Auditor's Understanding of Control Procedures

CONTROL PROCEDURES QUESTIONNAIRE

Client: EarthWear Clothiers		Balance Sheet Date: 12/31/2006
Completed by: *SAA* Date: *9/30/06*		Reviewed by: *DRM* Date: 10/15/06

Control activities include the policies and procedures that ensure that management's directives are effective in processing and preparing financial statements. Control activities ensure that the entity's financial reporting objective is carried out.

	Yes, No, N/A	Comments
Does management have clear objectives in terms of budget, profit, and other financial and operating goals?	Yes	*EarthWear has a very sophisticated budgeting process that includes monitoring activities. All significant budget variances are summarized and explained in a monthly controller's report. See A20 for extracts of significant items from the controller's report.*
Are such objectives • Clearly written? • Actively communicated throughout the entity? • Actively monitored?	Yes	
Does the appropriate level of management • Adequately investigate variances? • Take appropriate and timely corrective actions?	Yes	
Has management established procedures to prevent unauthorized access to, or destruction of, documents, records, assets, programs, and data files?	Yes	*See B10 for a description of the IT Department's controls over access to (1) the computer operations area and (2) data programs and files.*

Management may use internal auditors or personnel performing similar functions to monitor the operating effectiveness and efficiency of internal controls. An effective internal audit function has clear lines of authority and reporting, qualified personnel, and adequate resources to enable these personnel to carry out their assigned duties. The presence of a strong internal audit function strengthens the control environment.

The auditor should know how the entity monitors the performance of internal control over financial reporting, including how corrective action is initiated. Exhibit 6–4 presents a questionnaire that includes the type of information the auditor would document about EarthWear's monitoring process.

EXHIBIT 6–4

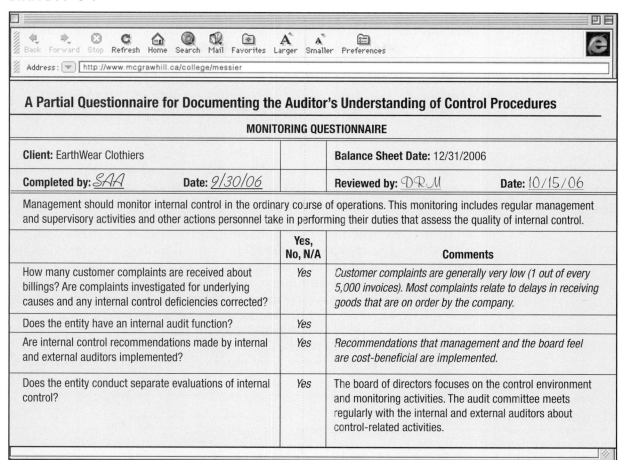

<table>
<tr><td colspan="3">A Partial Questionnaire for Documenting the Auditor's Understanding of Control Procedures</td></tr>
<tr><td colspan="3" align="center">MONITORING QUESTIONNAIRE</td></tr>
</table>

Client: EarthWear Clothiers		Balance Sheet Date: 12/31/2006
Completed by: *SAA* Date: *9/30/06*		Reviewed by: DRM Date: 10/15/06

Management should monitor internal control in the ordinary course of operations. This monitoring includes regular management and supervisory activities and other actions personnel take in performing their duties that assess the quality of internal control.

	Yes, No, N/A	Comments
How many customer complaints are received about billings? Are complaints investigated for underlying causes and any internal control deficiencies corrected?	Yes	*Customer complaints are generally very low (1 out of every 5,000 invoices). Most complaints relate to delays in receiving goods that are on order by the company.*
Does the entity have an internal audit function?	Yes	
Are internal control recommendations made by internal and external auditors implemented?	Yes	*Recommendations that management and the board feel are cost-beneficial are implemented.*
Does the entity conduct separate evaluations of internal control?	Yes	The board of directors focuses on the control environment and monitoring activities. The audit committee meets regularly with the internal and external auditors about control-related activities.

The Effect of Entity Size on Internal Control

The size of an entity may affect how the various components of internal control are implemented. While large entities may be able to implement the components in the fashion just described, small to midsize entities may use alternative approaches that may not adversely affect their internal control. One of the control environment factors that might differ between small and large entities is the use of a written code of conduct. While a large entity may have a written code of conduct, a small or midsize entity may not. However, a small entity may develop a culture that emphasizes integrity and ethical behaviour through oral communication and the example of the owner-manager.

While the basic concepts of the risk assessment, control procedures, and information and communication components should be present in all entities, they are likely to be less formal in a small or midsize entity than in a large entity. For example, in a small entity, the owner-manager's involvement in day-to-day activities can provide a highly effective control that identifies risks that may affect the entity and monitors activities.

A small entity can also have effective communication channels due to its size, the fact that there are fewer levels in the organizational hierarchy, and management's greater visibility. The monitoring component can also be effective in a small to midsize entity as a result of management's close involvement in operations. For example, the owner may review all daily cash disbursements to ensure that only authorized payments are made to vendors. By being involved in day-to-day operations, management may be better able to identify variances from expectations and inaccuracies in financial data.

The Limitations of an Entity's Internal Control

LO 3>

An internal control system should be designed and operated to provide reasonable assurance that an entity's objectives are being achieved. The concept of reasonable assurance recognizes that the cost of an entity's internal control system should not exceed the benefits that are expected to be derived. The necessity of balancing the cost of controls with the related benefits requires considerable estimation and judgement on the part of management. The effectiveness of any internal control system is subject to certain inherent limitations, including management override of internal control, personnel errors or mistakes, and collusion. For example, in a recent survey by KPMG (see Figure 6–2), management override and collusion are reasons why fraud occurs in many companies. Note that the most recent survey results show a substantial decline in "inadequate internal controls" as a reason why fraud occurred, perhaps partly due to

FIGURE 6–2

Factors Contributing to Fraud in the Organization (percentages)

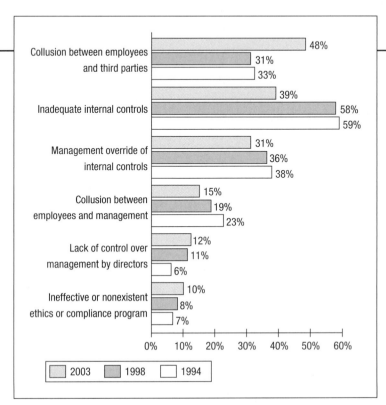

Source: KPMG, *2003 Fraud Survey* (New York: KPMG, 2003). Used with permission of KPMG.

the 2002 *Sarbanes-Oxley Act* in the United States. Also note the increase in "collusion between employees and third parties" as a cause. Because it involves individuals external to the entity, this type of collusion is one of the most difficult types of frauds for auditors to detect.

Management Override of Internal Control   An entity's controls may be overridden by management. For example, a senior-level manager can require a lower-level employee to record inappropriate entries in the accounting records that are not consistent with the substance of the transactions and violate the entity's controls. The lower-level employee may record the transaction, even though he or she knows that it violates the entity's controls, out of fear of losing his or her job.

The auditor is particularly concerned when senior management is involved in such activities because it raises serious questions about management's integrity. Violations of control procedures by senior management, however, may be difficult to detect with normal audit procedures.

Human Errors or Mistakes   The internal control system is only as effective as the personnel who implement and perform the controls. For example, employees may misunderstand instructions or make errors of judgement. Employees may also make mistakes because of personal carelessness, distraction, or fatigue. The auditor should carefully consider the quality of the entity's personnel when evaluating internal control.

Collusion   The effectiveness of segregation of duties lies in individuals' performing only their assigned tasks or in the performance of one person being checked by another. There is always a risk that collusion between individuals will destroy the effectiveness of segregation of duties. For example, an individual who receives cash receipts from customers can collude with the one who records those receipts in the customers' records in order to steal cash from the entity.

Relevance   One last aspect of internal control that may limit its use by the auditor is the relevance of the control. While an entity's internal controls address objectives in each category, not all of these objectives and their related internal controls are relevant to a financial statement audit. Generally, internal controls pertaining to the preparation of financial statements for external use are relevant to an audit. For example, controls that relate to the safeguarding of assets are relevant because omitting assets will result in misstated financial statements. Other controls may be relevant when they relate to data the auditor uses to apply auditing procedures. For example, the internal controls that relate to operating or production statistics may be utilized by the auditor as nonfinancial data for analytical procedures. On the other hand, some controls that relate to management's planning or operating decisions may not be relevant for audit purposes. For example, controls related to issues such as product design or production locations are not likely to be relevant to a financial statement audit.

Documenting the Understanding of Internal Control

LO 4 >   A number of methods are available to the auditor to document the understanding of internal control. These include

- copies of relevant extracts of the entity's procedures manuals and organizational charts
- narrative descriptions
- internal control questionnaires
- flowcharts

The auditor documents the understanding of the entity's internal control components using these tools. On many engagements, auditors combine these methods to document their understanding of the components of internal control. The combination depends on the complexity of the entity's internal control system and the extensiveness of the audit procedures to be performed. For example, in a complex entity, the auditor may document the control environment, assessment of risk, and monitoring activities using a memorandum and internal control questionnaire. Documentation of the information system and communications, as well as control activities, may be accomplished through the use of an internal control questionnaire and a flowchart. For a small entity, documentation using a memorandum may be sufficient.

An auditor should also document his or her understanding of an entity's internal control to provide evidence that the auditor conducted the audit in conformity with GAAS.

Procedures Manuals and Organizational Charts   Many organizations prepare procedures manuals that document the entity's policies and procedures. Portions of such manuals may include documentation of the accounting systems and related control procedures. The entity's organizational chart presents the designated lines of authority and responsibility. Copies of both of these documents can help the auditor document his or her understanding of the internal control system.

Narrative Description   The understanding of internal control may be documented in a memorandum. This documentation approach is most appropriate when the entity has a simple internal control system because a narrative description will be difficult to follow and analyze for a more complex entity, such as EarthWear Clothiers. Exhibit 6–5 presents an example of a partial memorandum for documenting the auditor's understanding of the control environment of a small client.

Internal Control Questionnaires   Exhibits 6–1 through 6–4 presented examples of the use of internal control questionnaires. Internal control questionnaires are one of many types of questionnaires used by auditors. Questionnaires serve as "memory joggers" in that they provide a systematic means for the auditor to investigate areas such as internal control. An internal control questionnaire is generally used for entities with more

EXHIBIT 6–5

An Example of a Partial Audit Memorandum for Documenting the Auditor's Understanding of an Entity's Control Environment

WORCESTER WOOLEN MILLS
Audit Memo—Control Environment and Procedures
December 31, 2007

The company manufactures high-quality woolen cloth for women's outerwear. There is one location in Toronto, Ontario. Jonathan Worcester is chairman of the board and chief executive officer. His son Wally is chief operating officer. The family controls 97 percent of the common stock. The board of directors is composed of family members, but Jonathan and Wally monitor the business and make most of the business decisions.

Jim Johansen, the controller, and Mary Margarita, the bookkeeper, handle most of the significant accounting functions. Wally reviews cash receipts and cash disbursements and signs the cheques. Jonathan and Wally have conservative attitudes toward accounting, and they consider lower taxes to be important. Our firm is consulted on the accounting for unusual transactions, and there are rarely any adjustments for errors from routine transaction processing.

The company uses a microcomputer and a standard accounting software package. Access to the computer and files is limited to Wally, Jim, and Mary. Jonathan and Wally review the computerized prepared financial statements and monitor revenues and expenses as compared to budget and prior-year results.

complex internal control. It contains questions about the important factors or characteristics of the five components discussed earlier in this chapter. As shown in those exhibits, the auditor's responses to the questions included in the internal control questionnaire provide the documentation for his or her understanding.

Flowcharts   Flowcharts provide a diagrammatic representation, or "picture," of the entity's accounting system. The flowchart outlines the configuration of the system in terms of functions, documents, processes, and reports. This documentation facilitates an auditor's analysis of the system's strengths and weaknesses. Figure 6–3 presents a simple example of a flowchart for the order entry portion of a revenue cycle. The text website provides more information about flowcharting techniques. Flowcharts are used extensively in this book to represent accounting systems.

Planning an Audit Strategy

LO 5〉   Figure 6–4 presents a flowchart of the auditor's decision process when considering internal control in planning an audit. Once the auditor has obtained a preliminary understanding of how the five components of internal control operate in the entity, for example, through the use of questionnaires as illustrated in Exhibits 6–1 to 6–4, he or she uses that knowledge to decide on an audit strategy. The following sections outline the various steps in this decision process.

F I G U R E 6–3

An Example of a Flowchart for the Order Entry Portion of the Revenue Cycle

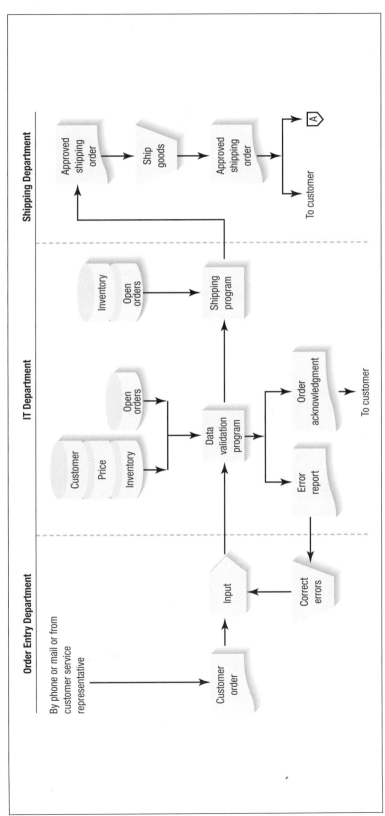

Flowchart of the Auditor's Consideration of Internal Control and Its Relation to Substantive Tests

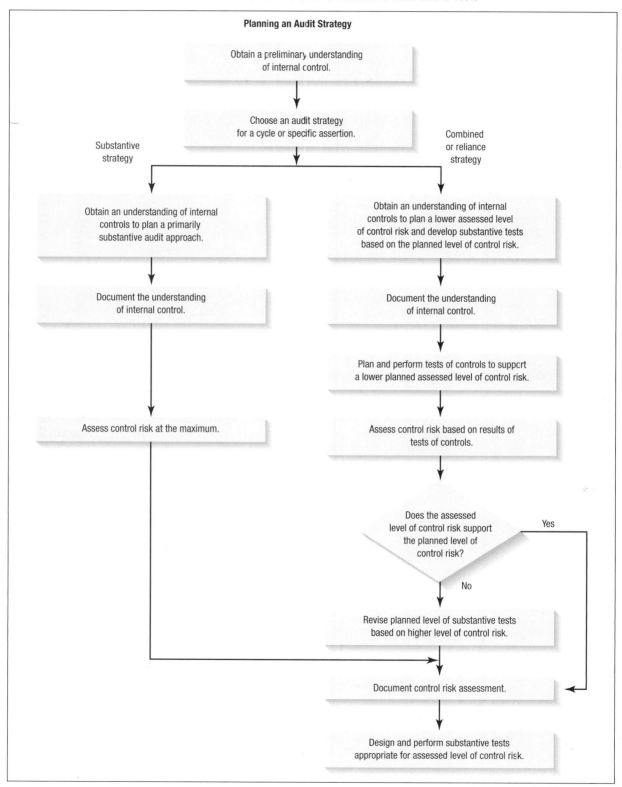

Introduction

In a recurring engagement, the auditor is likely to possess substantial knowledge about the client's internal control system. In that case, the auditor's choice of audit strategy may require only updating of the understanding of the entity's internal control system. For a new client, the auditor may delay making a judgement about an audit strategy until a more detailed understanding of internal control is obtained.

Based on the preliminary evaluation of internal control, the auditor can choose from two strategies. If the internal control system is judged to be ineffective, or the auditor decides it would be inefficient to test the controls, the auditor will choose a *substantive strategy*. If the internal control system is judged to be effective or somewhat effective (the normal case in most audits), the auditor will use a *combined* or *reliance strategy*. However, there is no one audit strategy for the entire audit; rather the auditor establishes a strategy for individual business processes (such as revenue or purchasing) or by specific assertion (validity, valuation, and so on) within a business process.

The auditor should consider the following factors when choosing between a substantive and combined or reliance strategies:

- the nature of the assertion
- the volume of transactions or data related to the assertion
- the nature and complexity of the systems, including the use of IT, by which the entity processes and controls information supporting the assertion
- the nature of the available evidential matter, including audit evidence that is available only in electronic form

The auditor may find that the entity electronically initiates, records, processes, or reports a significant amount of information that supports relevant financial statement assertions. In such cases, the auditor may be unable to design effective substantive tests because the audit evidence may be available only in electronic form. The appropriateness and sufficiency of this evidence usually depends on the effectiveness of controls over its accuracy and completeness. In such circumstances, the auditor may have to follow a combined or reliance strategy.

Situations where the auditor may find it necessary to follow such a strategy include the following:

- An entity that initiates orders using electronic data interchange (EDI) for goods based on predetermined decision rules and pays the related payables based on system-generated information regarding receipt of goods. No other documentation is produced or maintained.
- An entity that provides electronic services to customers, such as an Internet service provider or a telephone company, and uses IT to log services provided to users, initiate bills for the services, process the billing transactions, and automatically record such amounts in electronic accounting records.

Substantive Strategy

Following the left-hand side of Figure 6–4, the auditor first obtains an understanding of internal control sufficient to plan a substantive audit approach. A substantive audit approach means that the auditor has decided not to rely on the entity's controls and to directly audit the related financial statement amounts and disclosures.

The auditor may decide to follow a substantive strategy and set control risk at the maximum for some or all assertions because of one or all of the following factors:

- the controls do not pertain to an assertion
- the controls are assessed as ineffective
- evaluating the effectiveness of controls is inefficient

The auditor needs to be very certain that performing only substantive tests would be effective in restricting detection risk to an acceptable level. For example, the auditor may determine that performing only substantive tests would be effective and more efficient than performing tests of controls for an entity that has a limited number of long-term debt transactions because corroborating evidence can be obtained by examining the loan agreements and confirming relevant information. In circumstances where the auditor is performing only substantive tests and where the information used by the auditor to perform such substantive tests is produced by the entity's information system, the auditor should obtain evidence about the accuracy and completeness of the information.

Combined or Reliance Strategy

Following the right-hand side of Figure 6–4, the auditor first obtains an understanding of internal control as the basis for assessing a level of control risk below maximum. The combined or reliance strategy requires a more detailed understanding of internal control than the substantive strategy does because the auditor intends to rely on the controls. The auditor next documents his or her understanding of internal control and plans and performs tests of controls. Control risk is then assessed based on the results of the tests. If the assessed level of control risk does not support the planned level of control risk, the planned substantive tests are revised. If the planned level of control risk is supported, no revisions of the planned substantive tests are required. The assessed level of control risk is documented, and substantive tests are designed and performed. If the planned level of control risk is not supported, the auditor normally increases the planned substantive tests and documents the revised control risk assessment. The reader should remember that there may be different degrees of reliance for different business processes or audit objectives within a process.

As mentioned previously, control risk should be assessed for an accounting cycle or for relevant assertions or audit objectives related to a business process.

If the auditor plans to use a combined or reliance strategy for all or some parts of the audit, his or her next step is to obtain a more thorough understanding of the internal control system. This understanding includes knowledge about the design of relevant internal controls and whether they have been placed in operation by the entity.[6] Chapter 4 explained the management assertions relevant to revenue and expense transactions.

---

[6]See also Canadian Institute of Chartered Accountants, *Assessing the Effectiveness of Management Control: A System Perspective* (Toronto: CICA, 1991).

Table 6–2	**Examples of the Relationship between Management Assertions and Internal Control Procedures**

Management Assertion	*Basic Control Procedures*
Occurence	• Prenumbered documents that are accounted for.
	• Segregation of duties.
Completeness	• Procedures for prompt recording of transactions.
Cutoff and Disclosure	• Procedures to ensure transactions are recorded in proper period.
Presentation	• Internal verification of amounts and calculations.
	• Regular reconciliation of subsidiary accounts to control account by an independent person.
	• Internal review and verification.

Control risk is often assessed in terms of the control procedures that relate to the relevant assertions. Table 6–2 shows examples of basic control procedures that are normally in place for selected assertions to protect against material misstatement. For example, the use of prenumbered documents that are accounted for is a basic control procedure found in most business processes to ensure occurrence and completeness. In a revenue process, prenumbered shipping documents that are regularly accounted for provide reasonable assurance that all revenue is recorded. Another control procedure, reconciliation of the accounts receivable subledger accounts to the general ledger control account provides a control to ensure completeness and proper financial statement presentation and disclosure. These control procedures become the focus of the auditor's tests of controls. This knowledge is used to

- identify the types of potential misstatements
- consider factors that affect the risk of material misstatement
- design tests of controls

In deciding on the level of the understanding of internal control needed for the engagement, the auditor should also consider the following items:

- knowledge obtained from other sources about the types of misstatement that could occur
- information from previous audits
- an understanding of the entity's industry and markets
- the assessment of inherent risk
- judgements about materiality
- the complexity and sophistication of the entity's operations and systems, including the extent to which the entity relies on manual controls or automated controls

Each of these items needs to be considered explicitly when the auditor is examining a client's internal control. For example, the auditor will devote more attention to understanding internal control as the complexity and sophistication of the entity's operations and systems increase. The auditor may determine that the engagement team needs specialized skills to determine the effect of IT on the audit. An IT specialist may be either on the audit firm's staff or an outside professional. In determining whether such an IT specialist is needed on the engagement team, the following factors should be considered:

- the complexity of the entity's IT systems and controls and the manner in which they are used in conducting the entity's business
- the significance of changes made to existing systems, or the implementation of new systems
- the extent to which data is shared among systems
- the extent of the entity's participation in electronic commerce
- the entity's use of emerging technologies
- the significance of audit evidence that is available only in electronic form

The IT specialist can be used to enquire of the entity's IT personnel about how data and transactions are initiated, recorded, processed, and reported and how IT controls are designed; inspect systems documentation; observe the operation of IT controls; and plan and perform tests of IT controls. The auditor should have sufficient IT-related knowledge to communicate the audit objectives to the IT specialist, to evaluate whether the specified procedures meet the auditor's objectives, and to evaluate the results of the audit procedures completed by the IT specialist.

To properly understand a client's internal control, an auditor must understand the five components of internal control (control environment, risk assessment, control procedures, information systems and communication, and monitoring). The main difference between the combined or reliance and substantive audit strategies, in terms of the understanding of internal control, is the *extent* of required knowledge about each of the components; a greater understanding is normally required if a combined or reliance strategy is followed.

Assessing Control Risk to Support a Combined or Reliance Strategy

LO 6 Assessing control risk is the process of evaluating the effectiveness of an entity's internal control in preventing or detecting material misstatements in the financial statements. As discussed earlier, the auditor can assess control risk at the maximum (a substantive strategy) or at a lower level (a combined or reliance strategy). As shown in Figure 6–4, when the auditor assesses control risk at the maximum, the control risk assessment is documented and planned substantive tests are performed. The discussion in this section focuses on the situation where the auditor has decided to assess control risk below the maximum. Assessing control risk below the maximum involves three steps:

- identifying specific controls that will be relied upon
- performing tests of controls
- concluding on the assessed level of control risk

Identifying Specific Controls that Will be Relied Upon

The auditor's understanding of internal control is used to identify the controls that are likely to prevent or detect material misstatement in specific assertions. In identifying controls to be relied upon, the auditor should consider that the controls could have a pervasive effect on many assertions. For example, the conclusion that an entity's control environment is highly effective may influence the auditor's decision about the number of an entity's locations at which auditing procedures are to be performed. Alternatively, some controls only affect an individual assertion contained in a financial statement account, such as, for example, a credit check performed on a customer's order specifically related to the valuation assertion for the accounts receivable balance.

Appendix C on the OLC provides a detailed discussion of the types of general and application controls. General controls are pervasive to all information systems while application controls relate to a specific business process such as sales or purchasing. It is important to note that the reliability of application controls, especially those that are automated, are affected by the reliability of the general controls. For example, if there were ineffective general controls over program changes, it may be possible for a programmer to change the controls that exist in a specific information system.

Performing Tests of Controls

As discussed in Chapter 5, audit procedures directed toward evaluating the effectiveness of either the *design* or the *operation* of an internal control are referred to as *tests of controls*. Tests of controls are performed in order to provide evidence to support the lower level of control risk. Tests of controls directed toward the effectiveness of the design of a control are concerned with evaluating whether that control is suitably designed to prevent material misstatements. Tests of controls directed toward the operating effectiveness are concerned with assessing how the control was applied, the consistency with which it was applied during the audit period, and by whom it was applied. Procedures used to assess controls include

- enquiry of appropriate entity personnel (e.g., asking the purchasing supervisor what the process for approval of purchase order is, and what evidence there is that the process was performed)
- inspection of documents, reports, or electronic files indicating the performance of the control (e.g., examining purchase orders for the purchasing supervisor's signature or initials indicating approval)
- observation of the application of the control (e.g., observe the payroll supervisor's review and approval of the weekly payroll)
- walk-throughs, which involve tracing a transaction from its origination to its inclusion in the financial statements through a combination of audit procedures including enquiry, observation, and inspection (see previous items)
- reperformance of the application of the control (e.g., reextending and refooting the approved purchase order)

A combination of these procedures may be necessary to evaluate the effectiveness of the design or operation of a control. The operating effectiveness of the control can be affected by whether the control is performed manually or is automated. If the control is performed manually it may be subject to an individual's errors or mistakes. If properly designed, automated controls should operate more effectively. Because of the inherent consistency of IT processing, the auditor may be able to reduce the extent of testing of an automated control. For example, an automated application control should function consistently unless the program is changed. To test automated controls, the auditor may need to use techniques that are different from those used to test manual controls. For example, computer-assisted audit techniques may be used to test automated controls. Appendix C on the OLC discusses computer-assisted audit techniques.

Concluding on the Assessed Level of Control Risk

The conclusion that results from this step is referred to as the *assessed level of control risk*. The auditor uses the assessed level of control risk and the assessed level of inherent risk to determine the acceptable level of detection risk. The level of detection risk is used to determine the nature, extent, and timing of substantive tests (see following).

Figure 6–4 shows the decision process followed by the auditor upon completing the planned tests of controls. If the tests of controls are consistent with the auditor's planned assessment of control risk, no revision in the nature, extent, or timing of substantive tests is necessary. On the other hand, if the tests of controls indicate that the controls are not operating as preliminarily assessed, the level of control risk will have to be increased, and the nature, extent, and timing of planned substantive tests will have to be modified.

Documenting the Assessed Level of Control Risk

Auditing standards require the auditor to document the basis for his or her conclusions about the achieved level of control risk. For those assertions where the achieved level of control risk is set below the maximum level, the auditor should document the basis for his or her conclusion that the effectiveness of the design and operation of controls supports that assessed level. The auditor's assessment of control risk and the basis for the achieved level can be documented using a working paper, an internal control questionnaire, or a memorandum.

EarthWear   **An Example**   Table 6–3 presents two account balances from EarthWear Clothiers' financial statements that differ in terms of their nature, size, and complexity. The differences in these characteristics result in different levels of understanding of internal control and different control risk assessments.

In this example, inventory is a material account balance that is composed of numerous products. This account also contains significant inherent risk, and the data for this account are generated by a sophisticated computer system. For inventory, the auditor must understand the control environment factors, risk management factors, monitoring activities, significant classes of transactions, inventory pricing policies, the flow of transactions, and what control procedures will be relied upon. The auditor will likely use all of the audit procedures just discussed to obtain an understanding of internal control for inventory. In contrast, prepaid advertising is a significant account; however, it contains few transactions. Inherent risk is low and the accounting records are simple, so the knowledge needed about risk assessment, the information system and communications, and

Table 6–3 An Example of How Account Characteristics Affect the Auditor's Understanding of Internal Control, Control Risk Assessment, and Planned Substantive Procedures

EarthWear Account Balance	Account Characteristics	Extent of Understanding Needed to Plan the Audit	Control Risk Assessment	Planned Substantive Procedures
Inventory ($122,337,000)	• Material balance. • Numerous transactions from a large product base. • Significant inherent risk related to overstock and out-of-style products. • Complex computer processing.	• Entity control environment factors. • Risk assessment factors. • Monitoring activities. • Significant classes of transactions. • Inventory pricing policies. • Initiation, processing, and recording of transactions. • Control activities to be relied upon.	• Tests of controls conducted on relevant controls in the purchasing and inventory cycles were consistent with the planned assessment of control risk. • Control risk is assessed to be *low*.	*Substantive procedures will include* • Physical examination of inventory. • Information technology–assisted audit techniques to audit the inventory compilation.
Prepaid advertising ($11,458,000)	• Significant balance. • Few transactions. • Low inherent risk. • Simple accounting procedures.	• Entity control environment factors. • Nature of the account balance. • Monitoring activities.	• Because there are few transactions and the procedures for amortizing advertising expenditures are simple, a substantive strategy is selected. • Control risk is assessed at the *maximum*.	• Substantive procedures will recalculate the amortization of a sample of the advertising expenditures.

monitoring is minimal. In this instance, the auditor needs only to understand the control environment factors, the nature of the account balance, and the monitoring activities. No knowledge of control activities is necessary for this account. Audit procedures for the prepaid advertising account would likely be limited to vouching any major additions to the prepaid advertising account, and recalculation of amortization of advertising.

Substantive Tests

Even if the auditor has adopted a combined or reliance strategy, some detailed substantive testing will be performed in addition to substantive analytical procedures. The amount of substantive testing will depend on the detection risk, which in turn will vary with the overall level of audit risk that the auditor deems acceptable and will vary inversely with the assessed strength of the internal controls.

Table 6–4 presents two examples of how the nature, timing, and extent of substantive testing may vary as a function of the detection risk level for a purchasing cycle and inventory account. Assume that audit risk is set low for both clients but that client 1 has a high level of inherent risk and control risk while client 2 has a low level of inherent risk and control risk. The use of the audit risk model results in setting acceptable detection risk at low for client 1 and high for client 2. For client 1, the low acceptable detection risk requires that (1) more reliable types of evidence, such as confirmation and reperformance, be obtained, (2) most of the audit work be conducted at year-end, and (3) the tests be extensive. In contrast, client 2 has a higher acceptable detection risk, which means that (1) less reliable types of evidence, such as analytical procedures, can be obtained,

Table 6–4	**Audit Strategies for the Nature, Timing, and Extent of Substantive Testing Based on Different Levels of Detection Risk for Inventory**

Low Acceptable-Detection-Risk Strategy (high level of inherent/control risk)—Client 1

Nature	Audit tests for all significant audit objectives using the following types of audit procedures:
	• Physical examination (conducted at year-end).
	• Review of external documents.
	• Confirmation.
	• Reperformance.
Timing	All significant work completed at year-end.
Extent	Extensive testing of significant accounts or transactions.

High Acceptable-Detection-Risk Strategy (low level of inherent/control risk)—Client 2

Nature	Corroborative audit tests using the following types of audit tests:
	• Physical examination (conducted at an interim date).
	• Analytical procedures.
	• Substantive tests of transactions and balances.
Timing	Interim and year-end.
Extent	Limited testing of accounts or transactions.

(2) most of the audit work can be conducted at an interim date, and (3) tests of the inventory account can be limited. Another major difference between the two strategies involves the physical examination of the inventory on hand. For the low acceptable detection-risk strategy, physical inventory would be examined at year-end because the control risk was assessed to be high. For the high acceptable detection-risk strategy, the auditor can examine the physical inventory at an interim date because the control risk assessment indicates little risk of material misstatement.

Timing of Audit Procedures

LO 7〉   *EarthWear*   This section provides more information on the timing of the application of different types of audit procedures, a topic that was alluded to in the previous discussion of substantive testing. Audit procedures may be conducted at an interim date or at year-end. Figure 6–5 presents an example of a timeline for planning and performing a midsize to large audit for an entity such as EarthWear Clothiers with a December year-end. In this example, the audit is planned and preliminary analytical procedures are conducted around the end of July. The interim tests of controls are conducted sometime during the time frame August to mid-January of the following year. Substantive tests are planned for the time frame December to mid-February of the following year, when the audit report is to be issued. As shown in Figure 6–5 there may be overlap in the performance of interim and substantive procedures. The auditor's considerations of conducting tests of controls and substantive tests at an interim date are discussed in turn.

Interim Tests of Controls

If the audit is of a continuing client, or if, in the case of a new client, the auditor is appointed partway through the fiscal year to be audited, the auditor will usually begin to test controls at an interim date. There are several reasons for beginning the tests of controls at an interim date. One important reason is that if the controls are found not to be operating effectively, testing them at an interim date gives the auditor more time to reassess the control risk and modify the audit plan. It also gives the auditor time to inform management so that likely misstatements can be located and corrected before the rest of the audit is performed. An additional

FIGURE 6–5

A Timeline for Planning and Performing the Audit of EarthWear Clothiers

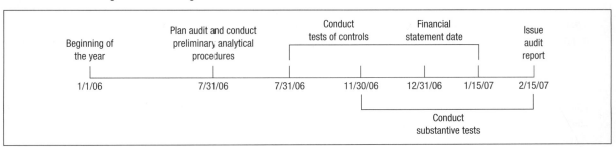

reason why it may be more efficient to conduct interim tests of controls is that staff accountants may be less busy at the time, and it may minimize the amount of overtime needed at year-end.

It should be noted that when the auditor returns after year-end to complete the audit, the auditor will normally extend the tests of controls begun at interim to cover the period to the end of the year. In order to rely on the internal controls, the *CICA Handbook* requires that the auditor must be satisfied as to the existence, effectiveness, and *continuity* of the controls. In other words in order to rely on the internal controls, the auditor must obtain evidence that they were functioning throughout the period of reliance. The usual way to obtain such evidence is by extending the tests of controls of those controls tested at interim, to the year-end, although the *Handbook* stresses the exercise of professional judgement in the auditor's decision as to how to obtain sufficient evidence about the internal control system.

Interim Substantive Tests

In some audits, such as an audit of a continuing client where the auditor knows internal control to be strong, it may be efficient to conduct some of the substantive tests at the interim date. This is sometimes known as a *hard close and roll-forward*. The auditor will audit the chosen interim balances "as if" they were the year-end balances and rely on the internal control system to ensure that the accounting system generates accurate information during the period remaining. A circumstance where this approach might be used is where a client's audited financial statements are required as soon as possible after year-end by its parent company for consolidation. However, this is a high-risk strategy—the auditor should know the client well and have strong evidence that the internal control system is reliable.

The auditor should consider the following factors when substantive tests are to be completed at an interim date:

- the level of control risk
- changing business conditions or circumstances that may cause management to misstate financial amounts in the remaining period
- control procedures for ensuring that the account is properly analyzed and adjusted, including proper cutoff procedures
- the auditor's ability to investigate the remaining period

If the entity's accounting system has control weaknesses that result in a high level of assessed control risk, it is unlikely that the auditor would conduct substantive tests at an interim date. In this instance, the auditor has little assurance that the accounting system will generate accurate information during the remaining period. Similarly, the auditor must consider the controls followed by the entity to ensure that the account is properly analyzed and adjusted, including cutoff procedures. The auditor must have some assurance that these controls are performed both at the interim date and at year-end.

When the auditor conducts substantive tests of an account at an interim date, some additional substantive tests are ordinarily conducted in the remaining period. Generally, this would include comparing the year-end account balance with the interim account balance. It might also involve conducting some analytical procedures or reviewing related journals and ledgers for large or unusual transactions. If misstatements are detected during interim testing, the auditor will have to revise the planned substantive tests for the remaining period or reperform some substantive tests at year-end.

Auditing Accounting Applications Processed by Outside Service Organizations

LO 8 > In some instances, a client may have some or all of its accounting transactions processed by an outside service organization. Examples of such service organizations include mortgage bankers that service mortgages for others and trust departments that invest or hold assets for employee benefit plans. More frequently, however, service organizations are IT service centres that process transactions such as payroll and the related accounting reports. *CICA Handbook,* sections 5310, "Audit evidence considerations when an enterprise uses a service organization," and 5900, "Opinions on control procedures at a service organization," provide guidance to the auditor when a client uses a service organization to process certain transactions.

When a client obtains services from a service organization, those services are part of an entity's information system if they affect any of the following:

- how the client's transactions are initiated
- the accounting records, supporting information, and specific accounts in the financial statements involved in the processing and reporting of the client's transactions
- the accounting processing involved from the initiation of the transactions to their inclusion in the financial statements, including electronic means (such as computers and electronic data interchange) used to transmit, process, maintain, and access information
- the financial reporting process used to prepare the client's financial statements, including significant accounting estimates and disclosures

The significance of the controls of the service organization to those of the client depends on the nature of the services provided by the service organization, primarily the nature and materiality of the transactions it processes for the user organization and the degree of interaction between its activities and those of the user organization. For example, if the client initiates transactions and the service organization executes and does the accounting processing of those transactions, there is a high degree of interaction.

Because the client's transactions are subjected to the controls of the service organization, one of the auditor's concerns is the internal control system in place at the service organization.

The auditor's understanding of the client's internal control components may include controls placed in operation by the client and the service organization whose services are part of the entity's information system.

After obtaining an understanding of internal control, the auditor identifies controls that are applied by the client or the service organization that will allow an assessment of reduced control risk. The auditor may obtain evidence to support the lower assessment of control risk by testing the client's controls over the activities performed by the service organization or by tests of controls at the service organization.

Because service organizations process data for many customers, it is not uncommon for them to have an auditor issue a report on their operations. Such reports can be distributed to the auditors of a service organization's customers. *CICA Handbook*, section 5900, provides for two types of reports by a service organization's auditor on its internal control. One type of report is a description of the service organization's controls and an assessment of whether they are suitably designed to achieve specified internal control objectives. The other type of report goes further by testing whether the controls provide reasonable assurance that the related control objectives were achieved during the period. An auditor may reduce control risk below the maximum only on the basis of a service auditor's report that includes tests of the controls.

Communication of Internal Control-Related Matters

LO 9> During the engagement, the auditor may identify certain matters related to the entity's internal control. *CICA Handbook*, sections 5220, "Internal control in the context of an audit—Weaknesses in internal control," 5750, "Communication of matters identified during the financial statement audit," and 5751, "Communication with those having oversight responsibility for the financial reporting process," all discuss the auditor's responsibility to communicate identified weaknesses in internal control to either the client's management, the audit committee (or equivalent) of the client's board of directors or both.

One of the ancillary services normally provided by the auditor at the end of the audit is to prepare a *management letter* for the client's senior management. An important purpose of the management letter is to inform management of weaknesses in internal control, such as those listed in Table 6–5, noted by the auditor during the course of the audit. These are often related to financial statement assertions and audit objectives, but they may also include suggestions for improving the efficiency and effectiveness of the conduct of the entity's business. Chapter 15 provides an example of a management letter.

During the course of the audit, the auditor may identify significant weaknesses in internal control, defined in paragraph 5220.04 of the *CICA Handbook* as weaknesses where "...the deficiency is such that a material misstatement is not likely to be prevented or detected in the financial statements being audited." In such circumstances the *CICA Handbook* states that the auditor should inform the audit committee (or equivalent) of the board of directors. The *Handbook* recommends that this should be done "in a timely manner," which is to say that it may be appropriate to do so before the end of the audit.

Table 6–5	**Examples of Internal Control Weaknesses**

Deficiencies in Internal Control Design:

- Inadequate overall internal control design.
- Absence of appropriate segregation of duties consistent with appropriate control objectives.
- Absence of appropriate reviews and approvals of transactions, accounting entries, or systems output.
- Inadequate procedures for appropriately assessing and applying accounting principles.
- Inadequate provisions for safeguarding assets.
- Absence of other control techniques considered appropriate for the type and level of transaction activity.
- Evidence that a system fails to provide complete and accurate output that is consistent with objectives and current needs because of design flaws.

Failures in the Operation of Internal Control:

- Evidence of failure of identified controls in preventing or detecting misstatements of accounting information.
- Evidence that a system fails to provide complete and accurate output consistent with the entity's control objectives because of the misapplication of control procedures.
- Evidence of failure to safeguard assets from loss, damage, or misappropriation.
- Evidence of intentional override of internal control by those in authority to the detriment of the overall objectives of the system.
- Evidence of failure to perform tasks that are part of internal control, such as reconciliations not prepared or not prepared in a timely fashion.
- Evidence of wilful wrongdoing by employees or management.
- Evidence of manipulation, falsification, or alteration of accounting records or supporting documents.
- Evidence of intentional misapplication of accounting principles.
- Evidence of misrepresentation by client personnel to the auditor.
- Evidence that employees or management lack the qualifications and training to fulfill their assigned functions.

Other:

- Absence of a sufficient level of control consciousness within the organization.
- Failure to follow up and correct previously identified internal control deficiencies.
- Evidence of significant, unusual, or extensive undisclosed related-party transactions.
- Evidence of undue bias or lack of objectivity by those responsible for accounting decisions.

The Effect of Information Technology on Internal Control

LO 10 > The extent of an entity's use of information technology (IT) can affect any of the five components of internal control. Information technology encompasses automated means of originating, processing, storing, and communicating information, and includes recording devices, communication systems, computer systems (including hardware and software components and data), and other electronic devices. Appendix C on the OLC provides more detailed discussion of the types of IT that may affect an entity's internal control.

The use of IT also affects the way that transactions are initiated, recorded, processed, and reported. In a manual system, an entity uses manual procedures, and information is generally recorded in a paper format. For example, individuals may manually prepare sales orders, shipping reports, and invoices on paper. Controls in such a system are manual and may include such procedures as approvals and reviews of activities, and reconciliations and follow-up of reconciling items.

On the other hand, an entity may have complex, highly integrated IT systems that share data and that are used to support all aspects of the entity's financial reporting, operations, and compliance objectives. Such information systems use automated procedures to initiate, record, process, and report transactions in electronic format. Controls in most IT systems consist of a combination of manual controls and automated controls. In such situation, manual controls may be independent of IT. Manual controls may also use information produced by IT, or they may be limited to monitoring the functioning of IT and automated controls and to handling exceptions. An entity's mix of manual and automated controls varies with the nature and complexity of the entity's use of IT.

Table 6–6 lists some benefits and risks of using IT for an entity's internal control. The risks to internal control vary depending on the nature and characteristics of the entity's information system. For example, where multiple users may access a common database, a lack of control at a single user entry point may compromise the security of the entire database. This may result in improper changes to or destruction of data. When IT personnel or users are given, or can gain, access privileges beyond those necessary to perform their assigned duties, a breakdown in segregation of

Table 6–6	**Potential Benefits and Risks to an Entity's Internal Control from IT**

Benefits

- Consistent application of predefined business rules and performance of complex calculations in processing large volumes of transactions or data.
- Enhancement of the timeliness, availability, and accuracy of information.
- Facilitation of additional analysis of information.
- Enhancement of the ability to monitor the performance of the entity's activities and its policies and procedures.
- Reduction in the risk that controls will be circumvented.
- Enhancement of the ability to achieve effective segregation of duties by implementing security controls in applications, databases, and operating systems.

Risks

- Reliance on systems or programs that inaccurately process data, process inaccurate data, or both.
- Unauthorized access to data that may result in destruction of data or improper changes to data, including the recording of unauthorized or nonexistent transactions or inaccurate recording of transactions.
- Unauthorized changes to data in master files.
- Unauthorized changes to systems or programs.
- Failure to make necessary changes to systems or programs.
- Inappropriate manual intervention.
- Potential loss of data.

duties can occur. This may result in unauthorized transactions or changes to programs or data.

Appendix C in the OLC, "The Effects of Information Technology on the Audit Function," provides more information about how a client's use of IT affects the auditor, particularly with respect to internal control evaluation, and also briefly discusses how the auditor can use computerized audit techniques to assist in the performance of the audit engagement.

REVIEW QUESTIONS

LO 1   **6-1**   What are management's incentives for establishing and maintaining strong internal control? Why must the auditor obtain an understanding of internal control?

2   **6-2**   Describe the five components of internal control.

2   **6-3**   What are the factors that affect the control environment?

2   **6-4**   Why is it important to maintain proper segregation of duties among the authorization of transactions, the recording of transactions, and the custody of assets?

2   **6-5**   How does the size of an entity affect internal control?

2   **6-6**   What is meant by the concept of reasonable assurance in terms of internal control? What are the inherent limitations of internal control?

5   **6-7**   What are the major differences between a substantive strategy and a reliance strategy when the auditor considers internal control in planning an audit?

6   **6-8**   List the audit objecti... ...rol risk. How do the interna... ...dit objectives for tests

2,3,4,5   **6-9**   ... of internal control?

2   **6-10**   ...nderstanding of the ...onent?

4   **6-11**   ...or can use to docu-

10   **6-12**   ...n entity's internal c...

6   **6-13**   D... ...g the design and th... ...rnal control.

6   **6-14**   W... ...ents under auditing standards for documenting the assessed level of the risk of material misstatement?

7   **6-15**   What factors should the auditor consider when substantive tests are to be completed at an interim date? If the auditor conducts tests at an interim date, what audit procedures would normally be completed for the remaining period?

9   **6-16**   Distinguish between a weakness in internal control and a significant weakness in internal control. List an example of each.

9   **6-17**   What is the auditor's responsibility for communicating weaknesses in internal control? What is the auditor's responsibility for communicating significant weaknesses in internal control?

MULTIPLE-CHOICE QUESTIONS FROM PROFESSIONAL EXAMINATIONS

Unless otherwise indicated, these multiple-choice questions were adapted from the CPA examinations, courtesy of the American Institute of Certified Public Accountants.

2>   6-18 Which of the following is not a component of an entity's internal control system?

a. Control risk.

b. Risk assessment.

c. Control activities.

d. Control environment.

5,6>   6-19 After obtaining an understanding of an entity's internal control system and assessing control risk, an auditor may

a. Perform tests of controls to verify management's assertions that are embodied in the financial statements.

b. Consider whether audit evidence is available to support a further reduction in the assessed level of control risk.

c. Apply analytical procedures as substantive tests to validate the assessed level of control risk.

d. Evaluate whether the internal controls detected material misstatements in the financial statements.

1,3>   6-20 Which of the following statements about internal control is correct?

a. A properly maintained internal control system reasonably ensures that collusion among employees cannot occur.

b. The establishment and maintenance of internal control is an important responsibility of the internal auditor.

c. An exceptionally strong internal control system is enough for the auditor to eliminate substantive tests on a significant account balance.

d. The cost–benefit relationship is a primary criterion that should be considered in designing an internal control system.

5,6>   6-21 After obtaining an understanding of an entity's internal control system, an auditor may assess control risk at the maximum level for some assertions because he or she

a. Believes the internal controls are unlikely to be effective.

b. Determines that the pertinent internal control components are *not* well documented.

c. Performs tests of controls to restrict detection risk to an acceptable level.

d. Identifies internal controls that are likely to prevent material misstatements.

5>   6-22 In which of the following situations would an auditor most likely use a combined or reliance strategy?

a. The client has been slow to update its IT system to reflect changes in billing practices.

b. The auditor hired an IT specialist whose report to the auditor reveals that the specialist did not perform sufficient procedures to allow the auditor to properly assess the effect of the IT system on control risk.

c. A client receives sales orders, bills customers, and receives payment based only on information generated from its IT system—no paper trail is generated.

d. The auditor has been unable to ascertain whether all changes to a client's IT system were properly authorized.

1,2> **6-23** An auditor's primary consideration regarding an entity's internal controls is whether they

a. Prevent management override.

b. Relate to the control environment.

c. Reflect management's philosophy and operating style.

d. Affect the financial statement assertions.

6> **6-24** Audit evidence concerning proper segregation of duties ordinarily is best obtained by

a. Inspection of third-party documents containing the initials of those who applied control procedures.

b. Direct personal observation of the employee who applies control procedures.

c. Preparation of a flowchart of duties performed and available personnel.

d. Making enquiries of co-workers about the employee who applies control procedures.

5> **6-25** In planning an audit of certain accounts, an auditor may conclude that specific procedures used to obtain an understanding of an entity's internal control system need not be included because of the auditor's judgements about materiality and assessments of

a. Control risk.

b. Detection risk.

c. Sampling risk.

d. Inherent risk.

6> **6-26** As the acceptable level of detection risk increases, an auditor may change the

a. Assessed level of control risk from below the maximum to the maximum level.

b. Assurance provided by tests of controls by using a larger sample size than planned.

c. Timing of substantive tests from year-end to an interim date.

d. Nature of substantive tests from a less effective to a more effective procedure.

6> **6-27** Regardless of the assessed level of control risk, an auditor would perform some

a. Tests of controls to determine the effectiveness of internal controls.

b. Analytical procedures to verify the design of internal controls.

c. Substantive tests to restrict detection risk for significant transaction classes.

d. Dual-purpose tests to evaluate both the risk of monetary misstatement and preliminary control risk.

6> **6-28** Which of the following audit techniques would most likely provide an auditor with the most assurance about the effectiveness of the operation of an internal control?

a. Enquiry of client personnel.

b. Recomputation of account balance amounts.

c. Observation of client personnel.

d. Confirmation with outside parties.

4,6> **6-29** When control risk is assessed at the maximum level for all financial statement assertions, an auditor should document the auditor's

	Understanding of the Entity's Internal Control Components	Conclusion That Control Risk Is at the Maximum Level	Basis for Concluding That Control Risk Is at the Maximum Level
a.	Yes	No	No
b.	Yes	Yes	No
c.	No	Yes	Yes
d.	Yes	Yes	Yes

8> **6-30** Payroll Data Co. (PDC) processes payroll transactions for a retailer. Cook is engaged to express an opinion on a description of PDC's internal controls placed in operation as of a specific date. These controls are relevant to the retailer's internal control, so Cook's report may be useful in providing the retailer's independent auditor with information necessary to plan a financial statement audit. Cook's report should

a. Contain a disclaimer of opinion on the operating effectiveness of PDC's controls.

b. State whether PDC's controls were suitably designed to achieve the retailer's objectives.

c. Identify PDC's controls relevant to specific financial statement assertions.

d. Disclose Cook's assessed level of control risk for PDC.

9> **6-31** When communicating internal control-related matters noted in an audit, an auditor's report issued on significant weaknesses in internal control should indicate that

a. Errors or fraud may occur and *not* be detected because there are inherent limitations in any internal control system.

b. The issuance of an unqualified opinion on the financial statements may depend on corrective follow-up action.

c. The deficiencies noted were *not* detected within a timely period by employees in the normal course of performing their assigned functions.

d. The purpose of the audit was to report on the financial statements and *not* to provide assurance on internal control.

4> **6-32** An advantage of using systems flowcharts to document information about internal control instead of using internal control questionnaires is that systems flowcharts

a. Identify internal control weaknesses more prominently.

b. Provide a visual depiction of clients' activities.

c. Indicate whether controls are operating effectively.

d. Reduce the need to observe clients' employees performing routine tasks.

4> **6-33** An auditor's flowchart of a client's accounting system is a diagrammatic representation that depicts the auditor's

a. Program for tests of controls.

b. Understanding of the system.

c. Understanding of the types of fraud that are probable, given the present system.

d. Documentation of the study and evaluation of the system.

PROBLEMS

1,2> **6-34** An understanding of the client's system of internal control is essential to the auditor in the performance of an audit.

Required:

a. What are the auditor's objectives in reviewing the client's system of internal control?

b. Explain the conditions that must be present for an auditor to be able to rely on the client's system of internal control?

c. Upon examining the system of internal control in an enterprise, the auditor may or may not find all aspects of that system to be usable for the purposes of the audit examination.

(i) Compare management's general concerns about the system of internal control with those of the auditor.

(ii) Identify two situations where a particular internal control may not have any "attest significance (i.e., have any value) to the auditor. Give an example of each.

(CGA-Canada, adapted)

2,4,5,6> **6-35** An auditor is required to obtain sufficient understanding of each component of an entity's internal control system to plan the audit of the entity's financial statements and to assess control risk for the assertions embodied in the account balance, transaction class, and disclosure components of the financial statements.

Required:

a. What are the components of an entity's internal control system?

b. For what purpose should an auditor's understanding of the internal control components be used in planning an audit?

c. Why may an auditor assess control risk at the maximum level for one or more assertions embodied in an account balance?

  d. What must an auditor do to support an assessment of control risk at less than the maximum level when he or she has determined that controls have been placed in operation?

  e. What should an auditor consider when seeking a further reduction in the planned assessed level of control risk?

  f. What are an auditor's documentation requirements concerning an entity's internal control system and the assessed level of control risk?

2,5   **6-36**   TameBird Industries produces meals for airlines and nursing homes. For the prior two audit engagements, your firm has written a management letter recommending that TameBird establish better segregation of duties in the accounts receivable and accounts payable functions. Tom Tuffnut, controller for TameBird, has received authorization to hire an additional clerk to work in the accounting area. Tom now has three accounting clerks available, and he has asked you to provide advice on how to best assign the following functions:

1. Responsibility for petty cash fund.
2. Opening of mail and listing of cash receipts.
3. Depositing cash receipts in bank.
4. Maintaining accounts receivable subsidiary records.
5. Determining which accounts receivable are uncollectible.
6. Maintaining cash disbursements journal.
7. Preparing cheques for signature.
8. Reconciling bank statements.

Required:

Prepare a recommendation to Tom Tuffnut on how best to distribute the various functions among the three accounting clerks.

5,6   **6-37**   Johnson, CPA, has been engaged to audit the financial statements of Rose, Inc., a publicly held retailing company. Before assessing control risk, Johnson is required to obtain an understanding of Rose's control environment.

Required:

a. Identify additional control environment factors (excluding the factor illustrated in the following example) that set the tone of an organization, influencing the control consciousness of its people.

b. For each control environment factor identified in part (a), describe the components and why each component would be of interest to the auditor.

Use the following format:

Integrity and Ethical Values

The effectiveness of controls cannot rise above the integrity and ethical values of the people who create, administer, and monitor them. Integrity and ethical values are essential elements of the control environment, affecting the design, administration, and monitoring of other components. Integrity and ethical behaviour are the product of the entity's ethical and behavioural standards, how they are communicated, and how they are reinforced in practice.

4,6>   6-38   Auditors use various tools to document their understanding of an entity's internal control system, including narrative descriptions, internal control questionnaires, and flowcharts.

Required:

a. Identify the relative strengths and weaknesses of each tool.

b. Briefly describe how the complexity of an entity's internal control system affects the use of the various tools.

9>   6-39   During an audit made in accordance with generally accepted auditing standards, an auditor may become aware of matters relating to the client's internal control that may interest the client's audit committee or individuals with an equivalent level of authority and responsibility, such as the board of directors, the board of trustees, or the owner in an owner-managed enterprise.

Required:

a. What is meant by the term *significant weaknesses in internal control*?

b. What are an auditor's responsibilities in identifying and reporting these matters?

9>   6-40   Ken Smith, the partner in charge of the audit of Houghton Enterprises, identified the following conditions during the audit of the December 31, 2007, financial statements:

1. Controls for granting credit to new customers were not adequate. In particular, the credit department did not adequately check the creditworthiness of customers with an outside credit agency.

2. There were not adequate physical safeguards over the company's inventory. No safeguards prevented employees from stealing high-value inventory parts.

Required:

Draft the required communications to the management of Houghton Enterprises.

1,2,5,6>   6-41   Alto Co. Ltd. is a manufacturer and seller, at the wholesale level, of fine furniture. One of its key business processes is the sales/accounts receivable/cash receipts cycle. The following scenarios below describe four different aspects of Alto Co.'s operations of this cycle.

1. The retail consumer market for furniture is quite volatile and companies in the retail consumer market can be "here today and gone tomorrow." For that reason Alto is very concerned about selling to bad credit risks. Poor credit control could result in large bad debts. Therefore the credit department manager has to approve every credit sale. She indicates approval by initialling the customer order, which is attached to a copy of the sales invoice and filed by date in the accounting department.

2. Billing clerks use a standardized price list to price the goods in the shipment. The amounts are entered on the three-part invoice. Copy one goes to the customer, copy two is the basis for recording the sales amount and is then filed in the accounts receivable department by date. Copy three is sent to the billing department where it is filed by date.

3. Alto's policy is to recognize a sale when the goods are shipped to the customer. There is a two-part prenumbered shipping document—one part goes, with the order, to the customer as a packing slip and the other is kept in the shipping department where it is filed in numerical order. The shipping clerk notes the date, quantity shipped, and shipping order number on copy three of the invoice. It is sent to the billing department where it is filed after the information is entered as a sale.

4. Sales to subsidiary companies are handled slightly differently. A billing supervisor reviews each invoice copy two to ensure that if the sale was to a subsidiary company, the invoice is stamped "Sale to subsidiary."

Required:

For each of the preceding descriptions:

a. Identify the account(s) where potential misstatement(s) could occur, and the nature of the misstatement(s).

b. State whether you think the control procedure(s) in place would prevent the potential misstatement identified in part (a).

c. If you believe the control procedure(s) are insufficient, state what additional procedure(s) you would put in place.

d. Identify one test of controls that you would use to see if the stated control procedure(s) are being performed. Make sure you identify the audit procedure you would apply and where you would obtain the document to test.

DISCUSSION CASES

3,4   **6-42**   Assume that you are an audit senior in charge of planning the audit of a client that your firm has audited for the previous four years. During the audit-planning meeting with the manager and partner in charge of the engagement, the partner noted that the client recently adopted an IT-based accounting system to replace its manual system. The manager and partner have limited experience with IT-based accounting systems and are relying on you to help them understand the audit implications of the client's change. Consequently, they have asked you to respond to a few concerns regarding automated accounting systems.

Required:

a. In previous years, the audit firm has relied heavily on substantive tests as a source of audit evidence for this client. Given that the client now has changed its accounting system, what are some of the factors that you should consider when deciding whether to move to a reliance strategy?

b. Under what conditions should the audit firm consider hiring an IT specialist to assist in the evaluation? If the firm hires an IT specialist, what information should the auditors ask the specialist to provide?

c. How are the five components of the client's internal control affected by the client's change to an IT-based accounting system?

1,2,10 ⟩   **6-43**   Smallco Limited, a Canadian private corporation, has specialized in the wholesaling of welding supplies since 1989. In 2001, the company was bought by Peter Mateus.

Mr. Mateus, a former internal auditor, is fully aware of the importance of good leadership and sound internal controls in business. Therefore, like the previous owner/manager, he participates actively in the daily affairs of the corporation. Although he approves most of the significant transactions, participates in the cheque-signing process, and reviews monthly financial statements, he does not sign or initial documents as evidence of his review.

The bank, which assisted Mr. Mateus in financing the purchase of Smallco Limited, requires that the company have an annual audit. Mr. Mateus has approached you about performing the company's audit.

He says to you, "Before deciding who will do the audit, I need to resolve two issues. First, I think that many auditors don't really know how to audit a small business. They think that the audit of a small business is the same as that of a large company, only smaller. They do not understand the characteristics that differentiate my size of company. Second, my experience with auditors has convinced me that in most situations a compliance-based audit is more efficient than a substantive-based audit. I firmly believe that an auditor can indeed rely on the controls that I as owner provide, regardless of whether or not I scrawl my initials on a document.

"Before you submit a formal audit proposal, I would like you to describe your position on internal control reliance and your audit strategy for a business like mine. These will be key considerations in deciding on who I will engage to perform this year's audit."

Required:

Draft a response to Mr. Mateus.

(CICA, adapted)

1,2,5 ⟩   **6-44**   You are an auditor with Lawson and Mawson, auditors of Chartrand Plastics Limited (CPL). At the August 2007 meeting of CPL's audit committee, the topic of derivatives came up. Derivatives are financial instruments that derive their value from some underlying asset or liability, such as a currency or a debt security. The committee members, aware that a number of organizations—including industrial corporations, banks, and municipalities—have been bankrupted by derivatives recently, grilled the treasurer on the company's use of such new instruments. Not satisfied with her answers regarding controls, the audit committee has requested that Lawson and Mawson be engaged to provide a report to the audit committee identifying weaknesses in, the management of, and internal controls over, derivative transactions. The report should also provide recommendations for improvements. You are responsible for the assignment and for drafting the report. You have met with the treasurer and her staff and have prepared the following notes:

1. The treasurer and vice president of finance each report to CPL's president. The financial reporting department reports to the vice president of finance. Derivatives operations are managed by the director of cash management and investments (the director), who has a staff of six people. The director is primarily responsible for derivatives strategy and reports to the treasurer. Two members of the director's staff are traders who execute money-market (fixed income) and derivative transactions. Two other members of the director's staff are involved in accounting for these transactions, and the remaining two are involved in banking/cash management. One of the traders has considerable derivatives experience from a large bank. The second trader is an accountant who recently received a promotion to the trader position and is learning on the job. The director's unit is operated as a profit centre for performance evaluation purposes.

2. CPL enters into derivative transactions with various financial institutions. Examples include the following:

   • Interest-rate swaps require that CPL exchange floating-rate interest payments for fixed-rate payments for a defined term. This turns the company's floating (variable) rate borrowing into fixed-rate borrowing. Typically an upfront percentage fee is charged by the financial institution based on the principal amount of the swap.

   • Foreign-currency forward contracts require that CPL buy or sell foreign currency at specified rates and dates. These contracts are no-cost agreements that are used to hedge specified foreign-currency exposures resulting from foreign purchases and sales of goods.

   • Loan-rate agreements (LRAs) require that CPL lend or borrow funds, at a specified interest rate and term, at a future date. CPL enters into LRAs without incurring out-of-pocket costs. CPL uses these strictly to try to earn profits, rather than to hedge. Normally, CPL will not actually borrow or lend the money. The director has been successful in predicting future market interest rates and closing out the LRAs at a profit, before maturity.

3. All the derivative instruments fluctuate in value continuously, based on market conditions. Market value information is easy to obtain. These derivative instruments can be closed out before maturity. For example, one of CPL's existing LRAs is in a profit position and could be closed out today by a payment

of $1.34 million from the financial institution to CPL. Three months ago, however, this LRA would have cost CPL $845,000 to close out. This change is due to fluctuations in interest rates. The director reviews the market value of all instruments monthly.

The director is looking into speculating in other new and "exotic" derivative instruments.

4. There are no existing company policies pertaining to derivatives. Therefore, the company applies three rules from its money market investment policy to derivative transactions:

   • fixed income instruments can be purchased from major Canadian or international banks only,

   • the traders are allowed to transact on behalf of CPL, and

   • the maximum term to maturity is five years.

5. All derivative transactions are entered into on the telephone and are legally binding based on the oral agreement between CPL's trader and the bank's trader. The director has instructed the traders to enter into transactions only on his instructions, usually communicated orally. After a transaction is entered into, the trader writes up a document called a "ticket." The financial institution faxes confirmation of the deal to the trader within a day or two. The trader then agrees the details to the ticket, staples the two documents together, and forwards them to one of the director's accountants. The accountant, who sits beside the traders, files the ticket by maturity date. Where CPL must pay for the instrument the same day, a copy of the ticket is immediately sent to the director who authorizes a wire transfer of funds to the financial institution. The cost of the instruments that CPL pays for is entered into the general ledger.

6. The notional principal of the 84 LRA's derivative instruments outstanding at the most recent month end was $654 million. To close out CPL's derivative position, a cash payment by CPL of $21.2 million would be required.

Required:

Prepare the draft report.

(CICA, adapted)

2⟩ **6-45** Preview Company, a diversified manufacturer, has five divisions that operate throughout Canada, the United States, and Mexico. Preview has historically allowed its divisions to operate autonomously. Corporate intervention occurred only when planned results were not obtained. Corporate management has high integrity, but the board of directors and audit committee are not very active. Preview has a policy of hiring competent people. The company has a code of conduct, but there is little monitoring of compliance by employees. Management is fairly conservative in terms of accounting principles and practices, but employee compensation packages depend highly on performance. Preview Company does not have an internal audit department, and it relies on your firm to review the controls in each division.

Chip Harris is the general manager of the Fabricator Division. The Fabricator Division produces a variety of standardized parts for small appliances. Harris has been the general manager for the last seven years, and each year he has been able to improve the profitability of the division. He is compensated based largely on the division's profitability. Much of the improvement in profitability has come through aggressive cost cutting, including a substantial reduction in control procedures over inventory.

During the last year a new competitor has entered Fabricator's markets and has offered substantial price reductions in order to grab market share. Harris has responded to the competitor's actions by matching the price cuts in the hope of maintaining market share. Harris is very concerned because he cannot see any other areas where costs can be reduced so that the division's growth and profitability can be maintained. If profitability is not maintained, his salary and bonus will be reduced.

Harris has decided that one way to make the division more profitable is to manipulate inventory because it represents a large amount of the division's balance sheet. He also knows that controls over inventory are weak. He views this inventory manipulation as a short-run solution to the profit decline due to the competitor's price cutting. Harris is certain that once the competitor stops cutting prices or goes bankrupt, the misstatements in inventory can be corrected with little impact on the bottom line.

Required

a. Identify the strengths and weaknesses of Preview Company's control environment and discuss the effect they would have on the company operations.

b. What factors in Preview Company's control environment have led to and facilitated Harris's manipulation of inventory?

(Used with permission of the PricewaterhouseCoopers LLP Foundation.)

2,5 **6-46** Western Canada Meat Processors buys BSE-free livestock at auction, processes it, and sells it to supermarkets. Following is a description of their procedures:

1. Each livestock buyer submits a daily report of his or her purchases to the plant supervisor. This report shows the dates of purchase and expected delivery, the vendor, and the number, total mass, and type of livestock purchased. As shipments are received, any available plant employee counts the number of each type received and places a check mark beside the quantity on the buyer's report. When all shipments listed on the report have been received, the report is returned to the buyer.

2. Vendors' invoices are checked for clerical accuracy and are then sent to the buyer for approval who forwards them to the accounting department. A disbursement voucher and a cheque for the approved amount are prepared in the accounting

department. Cheques are forwarded to the treasurer for her signature. The treasurer's office sends signed cheques directly to the buyer for delivery to the vendor.

3. Livestock carcasses are processed by lots. Each lot is assigned a number. At the end of each day a tally sheet reporting the lots processed, the number and type of animals in each lot, and the carcass mass is sent to the accounting department where a perpetual inventory record of processed carcasses and their mass is maintained.

4. Processed carcasses are stored in a refrigerated cooler located in a small building adjacent to the employee parking lot. The cooler is locked when the plant is not open, and a company guard is on duty when the employees report for work and leave at the end of their shifts. Supermarket truck drivers wishing to pick up their orders have been instructed to contact someone in the plant if no one is in the cooler.

5. Substantial quantities of by-products are produced and stored, either in the cooler or elsewhere in the plant. By-products are accounted for as they are sold. At this time, the sales manager prepares a two-part form—one copy serves as authorization to transfer the goods to the customer and the other becomes the basis for billing the customer.

Required:

For each of the parts 1 through 5, identify the weaknesses, if any, in the present inventory internal control procedures and your suggestions, if any, for improvements.

(AICPA, adapted)

2,5⟩   **6-47**   You have been asked by the treasurer of the board of trustees at the local church to review its accounting procedures. As part of this review, you have prepared the following comments relating to the collections made at weekly services and recordkeeping for members' pledges and contributions:

• The church's board of trustees has delegated responsibility for financial management and audit of the financial records to the finance committee. This group prepares the annual budget and approves major disbursements, but it is not involved in collections or recordkeeping. No audit has been considered necessary in recent years because the same trusted employee has kept church records and served as financial secretary for 15 years.

• A team of ushers takes the collection at the weekly service. The head usher counts the collection in the church office following each service. She then places the collection and a notation of the amount counted in the church safe. The next morning the financial secretary opens the safe and recounts the collection. The secretary withholds about $150 to meet petty cash expenditures the coming week and deposits the remainder of the collection intact. In order to facilitate the deposit, members who contribute by cheque are asked to draw their cheques to "cash."

- At their request, a few members are furnished with prenumbered, predated envelopes in which to insert their weekly contributions. The head usher removes the cash from the envelopes to be counted with the loose cash included in the collection and discards the envelopes. No record of the issuance or return of envelopes is maintained and the envelope system is not encouraged.

- Each member is asked to prepare a contribution pledge card annually. The pledge is regarded as a moral commitment by the member to contribute a stated weekly amount. Based on the amounts shown on the pledge cards, the financial secretary furnishes a letter to requesting members to support the tax deductibility of their contributions.

Required:

Describe the weaknesses and recommend improvements in procedures for

a. collections made at weekly services

b. recordkeeping for members' pledges and contributions

Organize your response under the headings: Weakness; Recommended Improvement.

(AICPA, adapted)

INTERNET ASSIGNMENT

 2,4,5 **6-48** Complete the following control environment questionnaire for each of the control environment factors shown for EarthWear Clothiers. Refer to the information in the text and EarthWear Clothiers website (www.mcgrawhill.ca/college/messier/earthwear) for the necessary information to answer each question. If the information needed to answer the question is not available, list how the missing information would be obtained by the auditor.

Part IV AUDIT TESTING

Audit Sampling: An Overview and Application to Tests of Controls and Substantive Tests of Account Balances

 Chapter 7

Learning Objectives

Upon completion of this chapter, you will be able to

1 ▶ Define audit sampling.

2 ▶ Determine the types of audit procedures that do not involve sampling.

3 ▶ Review basic sampling terminology.

4 ▶ Compare nonstatistical to statistical sampling.

5 ▶ Apply attribute sampling to tests of controls.

6 ▶ Apply statistical sampling for tests of controls.

7 ▶ Apply variables sampling for substantive tests of balances.

8 ▶ Apply statistical sampling for substantive tests of account balances.

RELEVANT ACCOUNTING AND ASSURANCE PRONOUNCEMENTS

CICA Handbook, **section 5135,** The auditor's responsibility to consider fraud

CICA Handbook, **section 5142,** Materiality

CICA Handbook, **section 5150,** Planning

HOW DOES THE AUDITOR KNOW WHAT TO EXAMINE?

EarthWear is a multimillion dollar company. In the course of a year it undertakes tens or even hundreds of thousands of transactions, such as sales and purchases; its asset and liability accounts are made of hundreds or thousands of individual items and amounts. Although EarthWear uses a sophisticated IT system to handle its transactions and Willis & Adams can use their own sophisticated audit technology in conjunction with that IT system in the audit examination, the sheer volume of EarthWear's activity makes it impossible to examine everything.

When the engagement team from Willis & Adams performs the audit of EarthWear, one of the most important aspects of the examination is to determine *what* to examine. The only practical way for Willis & Adams to carry out the examination is to use *sampling*. They will use audit sampling in their tests of controls to examine EarthWear's system of internal control. For example, they may test internal control over a sample of transactions in EarthWear's revenue process by selecting a sample of recorded sales transactions from throughout the year and tracing them through the accounting and recording system to ensure that the relevant management assertions such as occurrence, completeness, accuracy, and so on are valid. They will use audit sampling for substantive tests of balances in EarthWear's financial statements. For example, they may send confirmation requests to a sample of customers shown in EarthWear's records as having outstanding accounts receivable at December 31, 2006 to test the validity of the relevant management assertions such as existence, rights and obligations, valuation and allocation, and so on.

This chapter provides an overview of audit testing, discussing audit sampling in tests of controls and substantive tests of balances. The coverage is at a fundamental level and the concepts are equally applicable to non-statistical and statistical sampling. Detailed examples of statistical sampling techniques are presented on the accompanying text website at www.mcgrawhill.ca/olc/messier.

Introduction

In the early days of auditing, it was not unusual for the independent auditor to examine all of the records of the company being audited. However, as companies grew in size and complexity, it became uneconomical to examine all of the accounting records and supporting documents. Auditors found it necessary to draw conclusions about the fairness of a company's financial statements based on an examination of a subset of the records and transactions. Three questions arise if the auditor is going to examine a subset of the entity's records and transactions: (1) How many items should be examined? (2) Which specific items should be examined? and (3) What conclusions can the auditor draw about the population, based on the results of the sample? The introduction of statistical sampling was an attempt to answer these questions in a rigorous, scientific manner. Statistical sampling methodology was adopted by all of the major firms.

However, recent years have seen an apparent decline in the use of statistical sampling by auditors. Studies have reported that auditors use statistical sampling in only 10 percent of their sampling applications, while nonstatistical sampling is used in the remaining 90 percent.[1] A number of explanations have been proposed for the decline in use of statistical sampling. First, auditors have found that other types of evidence-gathering techniques, such as analytical procedures, can be nearly as effective as statistical sampling and not as costly to conduct. Second, companies have developed well-controlled accounting systems that process few routine transactions erroneously.[2] In such cases, auditors can test the systems' controls and focus their substantive testing on nonroutine transactions. Third, the advent of powerful PC audit software allows auditors to perform 100 percent testing rather than sampling. However, the authors believe that the study of audit sampling is important for auditing students. Concepts such as sampling risk that underlie sampling provide a sound basis for making audit judgements and reaching conclusions about the fair presentation of the financial statements. Also, given the recent spectacular audit failures (e.g., Enron and Global Crossings), there may be renewed interest in the more rigorous methodology and conclusions that statistical sampling can provide.

Sampling Defined

LO 1 >

Audit sampling can be defined as the application of an audit procedure to less than 100 percent of the items within an account balance or class of transactions for the purpose of evaluating some characteristic of the balance or class. The fact that an audit involves sampling is expressed to users of the financial statements by the phrase "An audit includes examining, on a test basis" contained in the scope paragraph of the auditor's report.

When sampling is used by an auditor, an element of uncertainty enters into the auditor's conclusions. This element of uncertainty, referred to as *sampling risk,* was discussed briefly under detection risk in Chapter 3. Sampling risk refers to the possibility that the sample drawn is not representative of the population and that, as a result, the auditor will reach an incorrect conclusion about the account balance or class of transactions based on the sample.

The auditor must also consider another type of risk, *nonsampling risk.* Nonsampling risk arises from the possibility that the auditor may use inappropriate audit procedures, fail to detect a misstatement when applying an audit procedure, or misinterpret an audit result. No sampling method allows the auditor to measure nonsampling risk but the uncertainty related to nonsampling risk can be controlled by adequate training, proper planning, and effective supervision.

---

[1]See W. F. Messier, Jr., S. J. Kachelmeier, and K. Jensen, "An Experimental Assessment of Recent Professional Developments in Nonstatistical Sampling Guidance," *Auditing: A Journal of Practice and Theory* (March 2001, pp. 81–96).

[2]See R. K. Elliott, "The Future of Audits," *Journal of Accountancy* (September 1994), pp. 74–82; R. K. Elliott, "Confronting the Future: Choices for the Attest Function," *Accounting Horizons* (September 1994) pp. 106–124.

Table 7–1	**Audit Evidence Choices That Do Not Involve Audit Sampling**

- Enquiry and observation.
- Analytical procedures.
- Procedures applied to every item in the population.
- Classes of transactions or account balances not tested.

Audit Evidence Choices That Do Not Involve Sampling

LO 2

In assessing inherent risk or control risk, or in auditing an account balance or a class of transactions, the auditor seldom relies on a single test. Generally, the auditor applies a number of audit procedures in order to reach a conclusion. Some audit tests involve sampling while others do not. Table 7–1 lists evidence choices that generally do not involve sampling.

Enquiry and Observation   Enquiry and observation are used extensively as a source of evidential matter. For example, auditors use enquiry and observation to understand the components of internal control. Enquiry of upper-level management is also used to evaluate many of the inherent risk factors discussed in Chapter 3. Finally, auditors use observation to establish the existence of inventories. Because of the nature of enquiry and observation, they do not involve sampling.

Analysis   Most simple analytical procedures utilized by auditors do not involve sampling. This includes the analytical procedures discussed in Chapter 5, such as simple comparison of last year's balances with the current year's balances and comparison of ratios across accounting periods. However, auditors use statistical techniques such as regression analysis as analytical procedures to predict account balances. Such statistical techniques are subject to both sampling and nonsampling risks.

Procedures Applied to Every Item in the Population   Sometimes the auditor examines all the items that constitute a class of transactions or an account balance. Because the entire class or balance is subjected to a 100 percent examination, such an audit procedure does not involve sampling. The population for audit sampling purposes, however, does not need to be the entire class of transactions or account balance. For example, the auditor may decide to audit all accounts receivable customer balances greater than a specified dollar amount, such as $10,000, and then use sampling for customer account balances less than $10,000. Alternatively, the auditor could decide to apply analytical procedures to the receivable accounts under $10,000 or to apply no audit procedures to them because an acceptably low risk of material misstatement exists in this group. In these instances, the auditor is not using sampling for either group of accounts receivable.

Classes of Transactions or Account Balances Not Tested   In some instances, the auditor may decide that a class of transactions or an account balance does not need to be examined, either because it is not material or because an acceptably low risk of material misstatement exists. Such untested transactions or account balances are not subject to audit sampling.

Terminology

LO 3⟩   The terminology used in this text is consistent with auditing practice. Three terms are discussed: *sampling risk, Type I* and *Type II errors,* and *precision.*

Sampling Risk

In auditing terms, sampling risk arises from the possibility that, when a test of controls or a substantive test is restricted to a sample, the auditor's conclusions may differ from the conclusions he or she would reach if the test were applied to all items in the population. Sampling risk is a function of sample size: the larger the sample, the lower the sampling risk. Auditors use the concept of risk instead of the statistical concepts of reliability or confidence level. (A *confidence level* in statistics measures the proportion of all such sample estimates that would contain the unknown population characteristic.) Risk is the *complement* of reliability or confidence level. For example, the auditor may set sampling risk for a particular sampling application at 5 percent. The reliability or confidence level is therefore specified as 95 percent.

Type I and Type II Errors

In auditing, Type I and Type II errors are the two types of decision errors an auditor can make when deciding that sample evidence supports or does not support a test of controls or a substantive test based on a sampling application. In relation to tests of controls, Type I and Type II errors can be defined as follows:

- *Risk of assessing control risk too high (Type I).* The risk that the assessed level of control risk based on the sample is greater than the true operating effectiveness of the control.
- *Risk of assessing control risk too low (Type II).* The risk that the assessed level of control risk based on the sample is less than the true operating effectiveness of the control.

In relation to substantive tests, these types of errors can be defined as

- *Risk of incorrect rejection (Type I).* The risk that the sample supports the conclusion that the recorded account balance is materially misstated when it is not materially misstated.
- *Risk of incorrect acceptance (Type II).* The risk that the sample supports the conclusion that the recorded account balance is not materially misstated when it is materially misstated.

The risk of assessing control risk too high and the risk of incorrect rejection relate to the *efficiency* of the audit. Both of these decision errors can result in the auditor conducting more audit work than necessary in order to reach the correct conclusion. The risk of assessing control risk too low and the risk of incorrect acceptance relate to the *effectiveness* of the audit. These decision errors can result in the auditor failing to detect a material misstatement in the financial statements. This can lead to litigation against the auditor by parties that rely on the financial statements.

Precision	The term *allowance for sampling risk* reflects the statistical concept of precision in a sampling application. In less technical terms it could be called the "margin for error." Thus, the allowance for sampling risk at the planning stage of a sampling application is the tolerable *difference* between the expected mean of the population and the misstatement. For example, if an auditor expected that a control would have a 2 percent error or failure rate (also called the deviation rate) and he or she was willing to tolerate a failure rate of 5 percent, the allowance for sampling risk would be 3 percent. At the evaluation stage, the allowance for sampling risk is the difference between the mean of the sample tested and the computed limit for the sample result. Following the previous example, if the auditor tested 100 items and found one deviation, the sample deviation rate is 1 percent. If the auditor determined the acceptable upper limit for the test to be 3.5 percent, the allowance for sampling risk is 2.5 (3.5 − 1.0) percent.

Types of Audit Sampling

Nonstatistical versus Statistical Sampling LO 4>	There are two general approaches to audit sampling: *nonstatistical* and *statistical*. In nonstatistical (or judgemental) sampling the auditor considers sampling risk when evaluating the results of an audit sample without using statistical theory to measure sampling risk. Statistical sampling, on the other hand, uses the laws of probability to select and evaluate the results of an audit sample, thereby permitting the auditor to quantify the sampling risk for the purpose of reaching a conclusion about the population. Both approaches require the use of the auditor's professional judgement to plan, perform, and evaluate the sample evidence. The major advantages of statistical sampling are that it helps the auditor (1) design an efficient sample, (2) measure the sufficiency of evidence obtained, and (3) quantify sampling risk. The disadvantages of statistical sampling include additional costs of (1) training auditors in the proper use of sampling techniques and (2) designing and conducting the sampling application. With a nonstatistical sampling application, the auditor must rely on his or her professional judgement rather than the laws of probability to reach a conclusion about the audit test. Therefore, the disadvantage of nonstatistical sampling is that it may not be as effective as statistical sampling. The remainder of the chapter outlines the phases and steps the auditor should follow in applying sampling in tests of controls and substantive tests of balances. You should keep in mind that the following concepts underlying the use of audit sampling are valid whether the application is nonstatistical (judgemental) or statistical. The use of statistical sampling adds a degree of rigour to some aspects of the process, but does not change the fundamentals.

Audit Sampling for Tests of Controls

Introduction

LO 5

Audit sampling in a test-of-controls context is known as *attribute sampling*. The term *attribute* refers to the fact that the sampled items either do or do not possess a certain attribute (i.e., characteristic). For example, if the test involves examining a sample of purchase orders for a signature indicating approval by the purchasing manager, the sampled items will either bear the signature ("Yes") or not ("No"). The results of the test will be in the form of a frequency or rate of errors (*deviation rate*). The deviation rate determines whether the control can be relied upon to support the auditor's assessed level of control risk for that business process.

The three phases of an attribute sampling application are planning, performance, and evaluation. The following section outlines the steps in the three phases of an attribute sampling application, using an example from the revenue process. Table 7–2 lists each of the steps in the phases of an audit sampling application. Remember that while the use of statistical sampling makes some of these steps more explicit, the process outlined by the steps is equally applicable to a judgemental or statistical sampling application.

Planning

The audit sampling application must be well planned and give adequate consideration to (1) the relationship of the sample to the objective(s) of the test; (2) the maximum deviation rate from a control that would support the planned level of control risk for a test of controls; and (3) the risk of assessing control risk too low.

Table 7–2   **Steps in an Attribute-Sampling Application**

Planning
1. Determine the objective(s) of the tests of controls.
2. Define the deviation from the control policy or procedure.
3. Define the population.
4. Define the sampling unit.
5. Determine the sample size.
    a. Determine the acceptable risk of assessing control risk too low.
    b. Determine the tolerable error or deviation rate.
    c. Determine the expected population deviation rate.
    d. Consider the effect of population size.
6. Randomly select the sample items.

Performance
7. Perform the audit procedures.

Evaluation
8. Calculate the sample results.
9. Perform error analysis.
10. Draw final conclusions.

Proper planning of an attribute-sampling application involves completing the following steps. Each of these steps, in turn, requires the use of professional judgement on the part of the auditor.

Step 1: Determine the Objective(s) of the Tests of Controls   The objective of attribute sampling when applied to tests of controls is to evaluate the operating effectiveness of the internal control that the auditor intends to rely upon to reduce control risk below the maximum. Thus, the auditor assesses the error or deviation rate that exists for each control selected for testing. Audit sampling for tests of controls is generally appropriate when the application of the control leaves documentary evidence. For example, in most revenue cycles, goods are billed after they are shipped. Therefore, no sales transaction should be recorded unless a properly authorized shipping document is present prior to recording in the sales journal. The auditor can test a sample of sales invoices for proper recording by examining the corresponding shipping documents.

Step 2: Define the Deviation from the Control Policy or Procedure   For tests of controls, a deviation is a departure from adequate performance of the internal control. It is important for the auditor to define carefully what is considered a deviation. For example, suppose the client has implemented a specified policy for granting credit to customers that is performed in the following manner. For *new* customers, the client has the credit department conduct a background credit check. Based on this credit check, the customer is either granted a line of credit or denied credit. For *existing* customers, when a new order is received, the amount of the current sales transaction is added to the customer's account receivable balance and compared to the customer's approved line of credit. If the total is less than the line of credit, the sale is made. If the total exceeds the credit limit, the sale is subjected to management review before it is completed. For this control policy, the auditor would have to define a deviation in terms of how the policy is applied to a new customer versus an existing customer. For a new customer, a deviation would involve the credit department's failing to complete a credit check properly or granting credit to an unworthy customer. For an existing customer, a deviation would involve a sale that exceeds the customer's credit limit at the time of sale without additional approval by management.

Step 3: Define the Population   The items that constitute the account balance or class of transactions make up the population. The auditor must determine that the population from which the sample is selected is appropriate for the specific financial statement assertion because sample results can be projected only to the population from which the sample was selected. For example, suppose the auditor is interested in testing whether all shipments to customers were billed. If the auditor uses the population of sales invoices, he or she is not likely to detect goods shipped but not billed. The population of sales invoices includes only recorded sales. In this example, the correct population for testing the completeness assertion would be the population of all shipped goods as documented by bills of lading.

Once the population has been defined, the auditor must determine that the physical representation (referred to as the *frame*) of the population is complete. Because the auditor selects the sample from the frame, any conclusions relate only to that physical representation of the population. If the frame and the population differ, the auditor might draw the wrong conclusion about the population. For example, in a revenue process, a typical control employed to fulfill the completeness objective is the use of prenumbered documents that are accounted for by client personnel. If the population for the sampling application is defined as all sales in the period, the auditor could review the numeric file that contains the copies of the sales invoices and reconcile those numbers to the numbers included in the sales journal. Alternatively, the auditor might be able to rely on the client's control for ensuring that the frame that represents the population is intact.

Another decision the auditor must make when defining the population is the period to be covered by the test. An application of attribute sampling for tests of controls can cover either the entire period under audit or some interim period. On some audits, it may not be efficient to define the population as all transactions executed throughout the audit period. In such cases, the auditor can define the population to be the period from the first day of the year to some interim date. The results of the sampling application in this case would apply only to the period tested. However, the auditor must also consider whether to conduct additional tests in the remaining period. Some of the factors the auditor might consider when deciding whether additional evidence needs to be obtained for the remaining period are shown in Table 7–3. For example, the auditor may decide that no additional detailed work is necessary on the basis of favourable results of the tests of controls for the interim period. However, at a minimum, the auditor should enquire whether any changes have been made to the accounting system or controls during the remaining period. In other situations, the auditor may decide to review journals or ledgers affected by the business process for unusual transactions or adjustments during the remaining period.

Table 7–3	**Factors Influencing the Decision to Gather Additional Evidence in the Remaining Period**

- The significance of the assertion being tested.
- Any changes in the internal controls that were tested during the interim period.
- Employee turnover.
- The results of the tests of controls performed during the interim period.
- The length of the remaining period.
- The audit evidence about the design or operation that may result from the substantive tests to be performed during the remaining period

Step 4: Define the Sampling Unit The individual members of the population are called the *sampling units*. A sampling unit may, for example, be a document, an entry, or a line item. Each sampling unit makes up one item in the population. The sampling unit should be defined in relation to the control being tested. In a previous example, the control for granting credit was presented. In this case the sampling unit can be defined as the sales invoice packet that contains the customer order, sales order, bill of lading, and sales invoice. The sales order would typically show some indication that the credit department had followed the client's credit-granting procedures.

Step 5: Determine the Sample Size The auditor should consider the following four factors when determining the sample size:

- The acceptable risk of assessing control risk too low.
- The tolerable error or deviation rate.
- The expected population error or deviation rate.
- The population size.

The first three factors affect the sample size significantly. The fourth factor, population size, typically has a limited effect except when the population is relatively small.

a. ***Determine the acceptable risk of assessing control risk too low.*** The risk of assessing control risk too low is the risk that the deviation rate in the sample will appear to support the auditor's planned degree of reliance on the control when the true deviation rate for the population does not justify such reliance (a Type II error). This risk influences the effectiveness of the audit. If the auditor assesses control risk too low and overrelies on the controls, the level of substantive tests may be too low to detect material misstatements that may be present in the financial statement account because detection risk was set too high. In setting the acceptable risk of assessing control risk too low, the auditor considers the importance of the assertion on which the control provides assurance and the degree of reliance to be placed on the control. However, the auditor must remember that there is an *inverse* relationship between the risk of assessing control risk too low and sample size: the smaller the risk of assessing control risk too low, the larger the sample size must be. Thus, the auditor must balance effectiveness concerns with efficiency concerns when setting the acceptable risk of assessing control risk too low. It is not uncommon for auditors to establish one level of acceptable risk for all tests of controls.

b. ***Determine the tolerable error or deviation rate.*** The tolerable error or deviation rate is the maximum error or deviation rate that the auditor is willing to accept and still rely on the control procedure. Table 7–4 provides some examples of the relationship between the planned level of control risk and the tolerable error or deviation rate.

Table 7–4	Suggested Tolerable Error or Deviation Rates for Assessed Levels of Control Risk

Planned Assessed Level of Control Risk	Tolerable Error or Deviation Rate
Low	2–5%
Moderate	6–9%
Slightly below maximum	10–12%
Maximum	Omit test

A low tolerable rate (such as 2–6%) would be used when the auditor plans to place substantial reliance on the control and thus plans to assess control risk low. A higher tolerable rate (7–10%) would be used when the auditor plans a moderate level of control risk.

The tolerable error or deviation rate is *inversely* related to the sample size. The lower the tolerable error or deviation rate, the larger the sample size.

c. ***Determine the expected population error or deviation rate.*** The expected population error or deviation rate is the rate the auditor expects to exist in the population. The auditor can develop this expectation based on prior years' results or on a pilot sample. If the auditor believes that the expected population error or deviation rate exceeds the tolerable error or deviation rate, he or she should conclude that reliance on the control is not warranted and substantive tests should be used. The expected population error or deviation rate has a *direct* relationship to sample size: the larger the expected population error or deviation rate, the larger the sample size must be.

d. ***Consider the effect of the population size.*** While it may seem surprising, population size generally has only a small effect on sample size. For example, if the population contains more than 5,000 units, increases beyond that number, even by a factor of 10 or 20, have a negligible effect on the appropriate sample size.

Table 7–5 summarizes the effect of the four factors on the size of the sample to be selected.

A number of public accounting firms establish guidelines for nonstatistical sample sizes for tests of controls. For example, a firm might establish guidelines as follows:

Planned Assessed Level of Control Risk	Sample Size
Slightly below the maximum	10–15
Moderate	20–35
Low	30–60

In using such guidelines, if one or more deviations are found in the sample, the auditor needs to expand the sample or increase the assessed level of control risk.

| Table 7–5 | The Effects of Sample Selection Factors on Sample Size |

		Examples	
Factor	Relationship to Sample Size	Change in Factor	Effect on Sample
Acceptable risk of assessing control risk too low	Inverse	Lower	Increase
		Higher	Decrease
Tolerable deviation rate	Inverse	Lower	Increase
		Higher	Decrease
Expected population deviation rate	Direct	Lower	Decrease
		Higher	Increase
Population size	Increases sample size only when population size is small (5,000 or fewer items). Therefore, population size generally has no effect on sample size.		

Step 6: Select the Sample Items It is important to remember that the auditor is concerned with the rate of errors or deviations in the population. Therefore, to continue the purchase order example, it does not matter if the particular purchase order was for $10,000 or $1,000,000; what matters is whether the supervisor approved the purchase order. Thus, all items, regardless of dollar value, must have an equal opportunity to be selected. The auditor's objective is to choose a sample that is representative of the population. Following is an overview of the sample selection methods that the auditor could use.

Random-Number Selection The auditor may select a random sample using a random-number table or random numbers generated by audit sampling computer software.[3] Whether the auditor determined the appropriate sample size by judgementally combining the four above factors or by statistical calculations based on the factors, using this method of selection results in a random sample because every sampling unit (such as a document or customer account) has the same probability of being selected as every other sampling unit in the population.

Systematic Selection When using a systematic selection approach to select a sample, the auditor determines a sampling interval by dividing the physical population by the sample size. A starting number is selected in the first interval, and then every *nth* item is selected. When a random starting point is used, systematic selection provides a sample where every sampling unit has an equal chance of being selected. For example, suppose the auditor wishes to select 100 items from a population of 15,000 items. The sampling interval in this case is 150 (15,000 ÷ 100). The auditor chooses a random number, say 125, and that item is selected for testing. The second item is 375 (125 + 150), the third item is 525, and so on.

[3]See H. Arkin, *Handbook of Sampling for Auditing and Accounting* (New York: McGraw-Hill, 1974), for an example of a random-number table.

To avoid any possible bias in the population, the auditor should use several random starting points. In our example, after selecting 10 items, the auditor could use a new random start to select the 11th item.

Haphazard Selection   When a haphazard selection approach is used, sampling units are selected without any conscious bias, that is, without a special reason for including or omitting items from the sample. This does not imply that the items are selected in a careless manner; rather, the sampling units are selected to represent the population. Haphazard selection is not appropriate for statistical sampling because the auditor cannot measure the probability of an item being selected.

Performance

Step 7: Perform the Audit Procedures   After the sample items have been selected, the auditor conducts the planned audit procedures. Using the control discussed earlier for testing the completeness of sales transactions, the auditor would examine the sales invoice packet for the presence of a shipping document to support each sales invoice. If the shipping document is present, the auditor considers the control properly applied. If the shipping document is not present, the sample item is considered a deviation from the control procedure.

In conducting the audit procedures for tests of controls, the auditor may encounter the following situations:

- *Voided documents.* The auditor may occasionally select a voided document in a sample. If the transaction has been properly voided, it does not represent a deviation. The item should be replaced with a new sample item.
- *Unused or inapplicable documents.* Sometimes a selected item is not appropriate for the definition of the control. For example, the auditor may define a deviation for a purchase transaction as a vendor's bill not supported by a receiving report. If the auditor selects a telephone or utility bill, there will not be a receiving report to examine. In such a case, the absence of the receiving report would not be a deviation. The auditor would simply replace the item with another purchase transaction.
- *Missing documents.* For most tests of controls, the auditor examines documents for evidence of the performance of the control. If the auditor is unable to examine a document or to use an alternative procedure to test whether the control was adequately performed, the sample item is a deviation for purposes of evaluating the sample results.
- *Stopping the test before completion.* If a large number of deviations are detected early in the tests of controls, the auditor should consider stopping the test, as the results of the test will not support the planned assessed level of control risk. In such a case, the auditor may rely on other internal controls or set control risk at the maximum for the audit objective affected, and revise the related substantive tests.

After the audit procedures have been completed, the auditor proceeds with his or her evaluation of the sample results.

Evaluation

The evaluation phase includes the following steps.

Step 8: Calculate the Sample Results After completing the audit procedures, the auditor should summarize the deviations by the controls tested and project the sample results to the population.

With a nonstatistical sample, the auditor can calculate the sample deviation rate but cannot quantify the computed upper deviation rate and the sampling risk associated with the test. Some guidelines for the auditor considering sampling risk in nonstatistically based tests of controls may be found in *Audit Sampling*, a publication of the AICPA.[4]

> [I]t is generally appropriate for the auditor to assume that the sample results do not support the planned assessed level of control risk if the rate of deviation identified in the sample exceeds the expected population deviation rate used in designing the sample. In that case there is likely to be an unacceptably high risk that the true deviation rate in the population exceeds the tolerable rate. If the auditor concludes that there is an unacceptably high risk that the true population deviation rate could exceed the tolerable rate, it might be practical to expand the test to sufficient additional items to reduce the risk to an acceptable level. Rather than testing additional items, however, it is generally more efficient to increase the auditor's assessed level of control risk to the level supported by the results of the original sample.

To illustrate the above quota, suppose an auditor planned a nonstatistical sampling application by assessing the expected population deviation rate at 2 percent, and setting the tolerable deviation rate at 6 percent. Assume the auditor judgementally chooses a sample size of 30 items. If the auditor detects no control deviations, the sample deviation rate is 0 percent. In this instance, the sample deviation rate (0 percent) is less than the expected population deviation rate (2 percent), and there is an acceptable risk that the true population deviation rate exceeds the tolerable deviation rate. If one control deviation is detected, the sample deviation rate is 3.3(1/35) percent. Because the sample deviation rate is greater than the expected population deviation rate (2 percent), there is an unacceptably high risk that the true population deviation rate exceeds the tolerable deviation rate.

Step 9: Perform Error Analysis The auditor should evaluate the qualitative aspects of the deviations identified. This involves two considerations. First, the nature of each deviation and its cause should be considered. For example, the auditor should determine if a deviation is an unintentional error or a fraud. Relatedly, the auditor should attempt to determine whether a deviation resulted from a cause such as misunderstanding of instructions or carelessness. Understanding the nature and cause of a deviation helps the auditor better assess control risk. Second, the auditor should consider how the deviations may impact the other phases of the audit. For example, suppose that most of the deviations found in a test of the revenue cycle resulted from improper granting of credit. As a result,

---

[4]American Institute of Certified Public Accountants, *Audit Sampling* (Audit Guide), (New York: AICPA, 2001), p. 28.

the auditor would expect that the valuation objective was not met for accounts receivable and would therefore increase the amount of audit work for the substantive tests of the allowance for uncollectible accounts.

Step 10: Draw Final Conclusions   In drawing a conclusion about the sampling application for tests of controls, the auditor compares the tolerable sample error or deviation rate to the projected upper sample error or deviation rate. If the projected upper deviation rate is less than the tolerable deviation rate, the auditor can conclude that the controls can be relied upon. If the projected upper deviation rate exceeds the tolerable deviation rate, the auditor must conclude that the controls are not operating at an acceptable level.

The final conclusion about control risk for the accounting system being tested is based on the auditor's professional judgement of the sample results and other relevant tests of controls such as enquiry and observation. If the auditor concludes that the evidence supports the planned level of control risk, no modifications of the planned substantive tests are necessary. On the other hand, if the planned level of control risk is not supported by the sample results and other tests of controls, the auditor should either (1) test other control procedures that could support the planned level of control risk or (2) increase the assessed level of control risk and modify the nature, extent, or timing of substantive tests.

Table 7–6 shows the auditor's risks when evaluating sample evidence on the planned level of control risk. If the evidence supports the planned level of control risk and the internal control is reliable, the auditor has made a correct decision. Similarly, if the evidence does not support the planned level of control risk and the internal control is not reliable, a correct decision has been made. The other two combinations result in decision errors by the auditor. If the evidence supports the planned level of control risk and the internal control is not reliable, the auditor will have set control risk too low and overrelied on internal control (Type II error). This results in the auditor establishing detection risk too high and leads to a lower level of evidence being gathered through substantive tests. Thus, the auditor's risk of not detecting material misstatement is increased. This can lead to a lawsuit against the auditor. If the evidence does not support the planned level of control risk and the internal control is reliable (Type I error), the auditor will

Table 7–6	**The Auditor's Risks When Evaluating Sample Evidence on the Planned Level of Control Risk**	
	True State of Internal Control	
Auditor's Decision Based on Sample Evidence	*Reliable*	*Not Reliable*
Supports the planned level control risk	Correct decision	Risk of assessing control risk too low
Does not support the planned level of control risk	Risk of assessing control risk too high	Correct decision

not have placed sufficient reliance on internal control and detection risk will have been set too low. Thus, a higher level of evidence will be gathered by substantive tests, leading to overauditing and an inefficient audit.

Statistical Sampling for Tests of Controls

LO 6⟩ When conducting a statistical sampling application for a test of controls, the auditor considers each of the steps in Table 7–2. The differences between statistical and nonstatistical sampling occur in the following steps:

- determining the sample size
- selecting the sample items
- projecting the sample results to the population

Determining the Sample Size

When using statistical methodology, the auditor can assess the four factors of: (1) acceptable risk of assessing control risk too low, (2) tolerable error (deviation) rate, (3) expected population deviation rate, and (4) population size, and compute a sample size that will allow the auditor to draw statistically valid inferences about the population, based on the sample. The effect of each of the four factors is shown in the following tables. The sample sizes are not absolute—they illustrate the changes in sample size resulting from a change in the factor, holding other factors constant.

Acceptable Risk of Assessing Control Risk Too Low	Sample Size
10%	77
5%	93

Tolerable Deviation Rate	Sample Size
2%	149
6%	49
10%	29

Expected Population Deviation Rate	Sample Size
1%	93
1.5%	124
2%	181
3%	Sample size is too large to be cost effective for most audit applications

Population Size	Sample Size
100	64
500	87
1000	90
5000	93
100,000	93

Selecting the Sample Items

In statistical sampling applications, the method of choosing sample items must be one that results in every population item having an equal chance of being selected into the sample. If random number selection is used to choose the sample items, with or without systematic selection, the auditor can use specialized computer software to generate the necessary random number or numbers.

Projecting the Sample Result

If the auditor has determined the sample size and chosen the sample items according to proper statistical procedures, valid inferences may be drawn regarding the population, based on the sample results. Projecting the sample results to the population for a statistical attribute sampling application can be done using a computer program or attribute-sampling table. This allows the auditor to compute the *upper deviation rate*, which is the sum of the sample deviation rate and the allowance for sampling risk. It represents the upper limit for the population deviation rate based on the sample size, number of deviations observed and the planned level of risk of assessing control risk too low. Attribute tests are typically one-sided because the auditor is generally concerned only with the maximum deviation rate in the population.

An example of an application of statistical testing to a test of controls can be found on the text website at www.mcgrawhill.ca/college/messier.

Audit Sampling for Substantive Tests of Account Balances

LO 7 Audit sampling for substantive tests of account balances may be referred to as *variables sampling*. The objective of substantive tests of account balances is to confirm or disconfirm a value or range of values rather than to estimate a frequency as with tests of controls. However, comparison of the sequence of steps for substantive tests of account balances in Table 7–7 with the sequence of steps for tests of controls in Table 7–2 shows the high degree of similarity between the two. The following sections outline the sequence of steps within the three phases in Table 7–7 in more detail.

Planning

Step 1: Determine the Objective(s) of the Test   Sampling may be used for substantive testing (1) to test the reasonableness of assertions about a financial statement amount or (2) to develop an estimate of some amount. The first use, which is the most frequent application of sampling as a substantive test on a financial statement audit, tests the hypothesis that a financial statement account is not materially misstated. The second use is less frequent but is occasionally used to develop an estimate of an amount as part of a consulting engagement or to review a client's application in an audit. The discussion in this chapter is limited to the use of audit sampling for hypothesis testing. Therefore, the objective or purpose of sampling for substantive testing is to test the hypothesis that no material misstatements exist in an account balance, a class of transactions, or a disclosure component of the financial statements.

Table 7–7	Steps in a Sampling Application for Substantive Testing

Planning
1. Determine the objective(s) of the test.
2. Define the population.
3. Define the sampling unit.
4. Choose an audit sampling technique.
5. Determine the sample size.
   a. Consider the variation within the population.
   b. Determine the acceptable risk of incorrect acceptance.
   c. Determine the tolerable misstatement.
   d. Determine the expected amount of misstatement.
   e. Consider the population size.
6. Determine the method of selecting the sample items.

Performance
7. Perform the audit procedures.

Evaluation
8. Calculate the sample results.
9. Perform error analysis.
10. Draw final conclusions.

Step 2: Define the Population   The auditor must define the population so that the selected sample is appropriate for the audit objective(s) being tested because sample results can be projected only to the population from which the sample was selected. If the auditor is concerned about understatements that result from omitted items (the completeness objective), the sample cannot be drawn from a population of *recorded* transactions. In order to detect such understatements, the auditor should select the items from a population that included the omitted items. For example, if the auditor is concerned about goods shipped but not billed, the population of shipping documents rather than sales invoices is the appropriate population for drawing the sample.

As in the discussion of sampling for tests of controls, once the population has been defined, the auditor must determine that the physical representation, or *frame*, of the population is complete. For example, if the auditor is testing the accounts receivable account, he or she might foot the accounts receivable subsidiary ledger and agree the total to the general ledger account to verify the completeness of the frame. Because the auditor selects the sample from the frame, any conclusions about the population relate only to that physical representation of the population. If the frame and the population differ, the auditor might draw the wrong conclusion about the population.

Step 3: Define the Sampling Unit   Items that make up the population can be used as the sampling unit. Therefore, a sampling unit might be a customer account, an individual transaction, a line item on a transaction, or an individual dollar in an account. For example, in a sampling application on an accounts receivable balance at year-end, the sampling unit might be the balance in a customer's account or an invoice that makes up the customer's balance. Similarly, if sampling is applied to ending inventory, the sampling unit might be a line item on the physical inventory listing or an item from the perpetual inventory records. As we shall see later in the chapter, when monetary-unit sampling is used, the sampling unit is an individual dollar (or other currency) contained in the population.

Step 4: Choose an Audit Sampling Technique   The auditor has to decide on the appropriate sampling method to use for the substantive test. The first decision is whether to use a statistical or a nonstatistical approach. The main difference between statistical and nonstatistical sampling is, as is the case in statistical sampling for tests of controls, the auditor's ability to quantify sampling risk using a statistical approach. Regardless of the choice of nonstatistical or statistical sampling, the auditor's decision process follows the same logical sequence.

Step 5: Determine the Sample Size   Considerable judgement is required in determining the sample size. The following five factors must be considered:

- the variation within the population
- the acceptable risk of incorrect acceptance
- the tolerable misstatement
- the expected misstatement
- the population size

a. ***Consider the variation within the population.*** In most accounting populations, the amounts of the individual items vary significantly. For example, a population may contain a small number of large dollar amounts and a large number of small dollar amounts. A measure of this variability is called the *standard deviation*. The auditor can estimate population variation by taking a pilot sample or using the results of prior years' tests. As the population variation increases, the sample size must also be increased. One way of reducing the effect of variability is to stratify the population into groups that are more homogeneous. Each group into which the population is divided is called a *stratum*. Separate samples are taken from each stratum, and the results are combined to form an overall conclusion about the population.

b. ***Determine the acceptable risk of incorrect acceptance.*** The risk of incorrect acceptance is the risk that the sample supports the conclusion that the recorded account balance is not materially misstated when in fact it is (a Type II error). This risk is the same as the risk of assessing control risk too low, as discussed in tests of controls, except that it relates to a decision about an account balance instead of a control procedure. This risk relates to the effectiveness of the audit. In determining an acceptable risk of incorrect acceptance, the auditor should consider the components of the audit risk model: the acceptable level of audit risk and the assessed levels of inherent and control risk. For practical purposes, the acceptable risk of incorrect acceptance is the same as detection risk (*DR*) after considering the assessed level of detection risk based on other substantive tests such as analytical procedures. If the auditor incorrectly accepts an account balance as being fairly presented when it is materially misstated, he or she will allow the issuance of financial statements that are not fairly presented. The users of those financial statements may then sue the auditor for damages that result from relying on those financial statements. There is an *inverse* relationship between the risk of incorrect acceptance and sample size: the lower the acceptable risk for incorrect acceptance, the larger the sample size must be.

c. ***Determine the tolerable misstatement.*** The tolerable misstatement is the amount of the preliminary judgement about materiality that is explicitly or implicitly allocated to an account. It represents the maximum amount by which the account can be misstated with the auditor still accepting the account as being fairly presented. In the terminology of the previous section, this is the precision of the estimate. (Review Chapter 3 for a more detailed explanation of tolerable materiality.) Tolerable misstatement is also *inversely* related to sample size: the lower the amount of tolerable misstatement, the larger the sample size must be.

d. ***Determine the expected misstatement.*** The expected misstatement is the amount of misstatement that the auditor believes exists in the population. The auditor can develop this expectation based on the assessment of inherent risk, prior years' results, a pilot sample, the results of related substantive tests, or the results of tests of controls. As the expected misstatement approaches the tolerable misstatement, the auditor needs more precise information from the sample. Therefore, there is a *direct* relationship to sample size: the larger the expected misstatement, the larger the sample size must be.

e. ***Consider the effect of population size.*** Population size has a *direct* effect on sample size. Other factors being constant, larger populations will require larger sample sizes.

In statistical sampling, the auditor explicitly considers these factors quantitatively and in judgemental sampling the auditor's consideration of the factors is more implicit. However, if the auditor wishes to inject a degree of quantitative rigour into the judgemental determination of the sample size, the following formula may be used:

$$\text{Sample size} = \left(\frac{\text{Population book value}}{\text{Tolerable misstatement}} \right) \times \text{Assurance}$$

where "Population book value" excludes the amount of items to be individually audited and "Tolerable misstatement" represents the amount of materiality allocated to the account being audited. The assurance factor is determined by assessing inherent and control risk and the risk that other relevant substantive auditing procedures will fail to detect material misstatements. Table 7–8 contains the assurance factors for various combinations of these two assessments.

Table 7–9 summarizes the effect of the five factors on sample size.

After planning the sampling application, the auditor performs each of the following steps.

Table 7–8	Assurance Factors for Nonstatistical Sampling

Combined Assessment of Inherent and Control Risk	**Risk That Other Substantive Procedures Will Fail to Detect Material Misstatements**			
	Maximum	*Slightly below Maximum*	*Moderate*	*Low*
Maximum	3.0	2.7	2.3	2.0
Slightly below maximum	2.7	2.4	2.1	1.6
Moderate	2.3	2.1	1.6	1.2
Low	2.0	1.9	1.2	1.0

Risk that other substantive procedures will fail to detect a material misstatement:
Maximum: No other substantive procedures are performed to test the same assertion(s).
Slightly below maximum: Other substantive procedures that are performed to test the assertion(s) are expected to be slightly effective in detecting material misstatements in those assertion(s).
Moderate: Other substantive procedures that are performed to test the assertion(s) are expected to be moderately effective in detecting material misstatements in those assertion(s).
Low: Other substantive procedures that are performed to test the assertion(s) are expected to be highly effective in detecting material misstatements in those assertion(s).

Table 7–9	The Effect of Sample Selection Factors on Sample Size

Factor	*Relationship to Sample Size*	**Examples**	
		Change in Factor	*Effect on Sample*
Population variability	With monetary-unit sampling, the population variability, or standard deviation has no effect on the sample size. With nonstatistical sampling and classical variables sampling, variability affects the sample size, but its effects can be controlled through stratification of the population.		
Acceptable risk of incorrect acceptance	Inverse	Lower	Increase
		Higher	Decrease
Tolerable misstatement	Inverse	Lower	Increase
		Higher	Decrease
Expected misstatement	Direct	Lower	Decrease
		Higher	Increase
Population size	Direct	Lower	Decrease
		Higher	Increase

Step 6: Determine the Method of Selecting the Sample Items The auditor may use nonstatistical (judgemental) sampling, statistical sampling, or a combination of the two. In many cases, specific items in the population will be selected according to predetermined criteria, and some form of random sampling will be applied to the remainder.

To ensure coverage of a sufficient portion of the value of an account and/or to ensure that those items that are high risk are selected, the auditor may first choose sample items according to one of the following two criteria:

High Value Item Selection   It is common for a large proportion of the value of a balance to be accounted for by a small proportion of the population. In fact, many of the items individually may exceed the tolerable misstatement. For example, an auditor may be examining a client's accounts receivable balance in which 20 customer accounts make up 60 percent of the account balance. The auditor may decide to examine the 20 large accounts and sample from the remaining customer accounts. In this case, the remaining 40 percent of the accounts receivable account is subjected to audit sampling.

Key Item Selection   The auditor may wish to select population items into the sample for other reasons than just size. For example, stale or overdue accounts receivable or accounts receivable that have proven troublesome in the past may be specifically selected.

Once the auditor has selected any sample items according to the above criteria he or she should randomly sample from the remaining population items.

Performance

Step 7: Perform the Audit Procedures   After the sample items have been selected, the auditor conducts the planned audit procedures. In some instances, the auditor may not be able to conduct the planned procedures on a sampling unit. This may occur, for example, because a supporting document is missing. Unless other evidence is available, such items should be considered in error. The auditor must also be careful to conduct the audit procedures so as to avoid nonsampling errors. After all audit procedures have been completed, the auditor evaluates the sample results.

Evaluation

The evaluation phase of the sampling application includes the following steps.

Step 8: Calculate the Sample Results   The auditor projects the amount of misstatement found in the sample to the population.

One method of projecting the amount of misstatement is to divide the amount of misstatement by the fraction of the dollars of the population included in the sample. For example, if the auditor finds misstatements in a sample totalling $1,500 and the sample items constitute 10 percent of the population, the projected misstatement will be $15,000 ($1,500 ÷ 10 percent).

The second method projects the average misstatement between the audited and recorded amounts of each item in the sample to all items in the population. For example, if the misstatements in a sample of 100 items total $300 and the population contains 10,000 items, the projected misstatement will be $30,000. This amount is determined by calculating the average misstatement in the sample of $3 ($300 ÷ 100 items) and multiplying it by the number of items in the population ($3 × 10,000 items).

These two methods of projecting misstatements give identical results if the sample includes the same proportion of items in the population as the proportion of the population's recorded amount included in the sample. If the proportions are different, the auditor chooses between the two methods on the basis of his or her understanding of the magnitude and distribution of misstatements in the population. If the auditor expects the amount of misstatement to relate closely to the size of the item, the first method should be used. If the auditor expects the misstatements to be relatively constant for all items in the population, the second method should be used.

In evaluating the results of a nonstatistical sample, the auditor uses professional judgement and experience to draw a conclusion. Because a nonstatistical sampling approach is used, the allowance for sampling risk cannot be quantified. However, if the projected misstatement is close to or exceeds the tolerable misstatement, the auditor should conclude that there is an unacceptably high risk that the account is misstated. If the projected misstatement is considerably less than the tolerable misstatement, the auditor should compare the projected misstatement to the expected misstatement. If the projected misstatement is less than the expected misstatement, the auditor can conclude that there is an acceptably low sampling risk that the projected misstatement exceeds the tolerable misstatement. Conversely, if the projected misstatement significantly exceeds the expected misstatement, the auditor would generally conclude that there is an unacceptably high risk that the true misstatement exceeds the tolerable misstatement.

Step 9: Perform Error Analysis   The auditor should evaluate the qualitative aspects of the misstatements identified. This involves two considerations. First, the nature of the misstatements and their causes should be considered. For example, the auditor should determine if the misstatements are unintentional errors or fraud. The auditor should also attempt to determine whether the misstatements resulted from causes such as misunderstanding of instructions or carelessness. Understanding the nature and causes of misstatements helps the auditor better assess detection risk. Second, the auditor should consider how these misstatements may impact the other phases of the audit. For example, the nature of the misstatements may provide additional evidence that certain controls are not operating as effectively as previously assessed. This may require the auditor to reassess control risk and expand substantive tests for the audit objectives that are affected by the control that is not operating effectively.

Step 10: Draw Final Conclusions   In drawing a conclusion about a sampling application, the auditor should calculate the total projected misstatement including a judgementally or statistically determined allowance for sampling risk, and assess whether there is a material misstatement. If the auditor has allocated total financial statement materiality to

Table 7–10   The Auditor's Risks When Evaluating a Financial Statement Account Based on Sample Evidence

Auditor's Decision Based on Sample Evidence	True State of Internal Control	
	Not Materially Misstated	*Materially Misstated*
Supports the fairness of the account balance	Correct decision	Risk of incorrect acceptance
Does not support the fairness of the account balance	Risk of incorrect rejection	Correct decision

individual accounts, groups of accounts, or transaction classes (called in such cases, "tolerable misstatement") a comparison can be made at that time at that level. Otherwise the amount of the projected misstatement will usually be added to the cumulative total in the proposed adjustment summary (PAS) for further consideration when the audit examination is completed. Subsequent discussions in this text will use the concept of tolerable error in individual accounts, groups of accounts, or transaction classes; although this is not mandated by the CICA, the concept is utilized in practice, either explicitly or implicitly, by most firms.

Table 7–10 shows the auditor's risks when evaluating an account balance based on sample evidence. If the evidence supports the fairness of the account balance based on the sample evidence and the account is not materially misstated, the auditor has made a correct decision. If the evidence does *not* support the fairness of the account based on the sample evidence and the account is materially misstated, a correct decision has also been made. The other two combinations result in decision errors by the auditor. If the evidence supports the account as fairly stated when it contains a material misstatement, the auditor will have incorrectly accepted the account (Type II error). This can lead to lawsuits against the auditor for issuing a report on misleading financial statements. If the evidence does not support the fairness of the account when it is not materially misstated (Type I error), the auditor will have incorrectly rejected the account. This can lead to overauditing and an inefficient audit.

An Example

The senior-in-charge of the audit of Calabro Digital Services, Don Jones, has decided to design a *nonstatistical* sampling application to examine the accounts receivable balance of Calabro at December 31, 2006. As of December 31, there were 11,800 accounts receivable accounts with a balance of $3,717,900 ($3,582,600 + $135,300 for the allowance for doubtful accounts), and the population is composed of the following strata:

Number and Size of Accounts	*Book Value of Stratum*
15 accounts > $25,000	$ 550,000
250 accounts > $3,000	850,500
11,535 accounts < $3,000	2,317,400

Jones has made the following decisions:

- Based on the results of the tests of controls, a low assessment is made for inherent and control risk.
- The tolerable misstatement allocated to accounts receivable is $40,000, and the expected misstatement is $15,000.
- There is a moderate risk that other auditing procedures will fail to detect material misstatements.
- All customer account balances greater than $25,000 are to be audited.

Based on these decisions, the sample size is determined as follows: First, individually significant items are deducted from the account balance, leaving a balance of $3,167,900 ($3,717,900 − $550,000) to be sampled. Second, the sample size for the remaining balance is determined using the sample size formula:

$$\text{Sample size} = \left(\frac{\$3,167,900}{\$40,000}\right) \times 1.2 = 95$$

The assurance factor of 1.2 is determined by using Table 7–8 and a low assessment for inherent and control risk and a moderate risk that other auditing procedures will fail to detect material misstatements. The 95 sample items are divided between the two strata based on the recorded amount for each stratum. Accordingly, 26 of the 95 [$850,500 ÷ ($3,167,900 ÷ 95)] are allocated to the stratum of accounts greater than $3,000 and 69 to the stratum of accounts less than $3,000. The total sample size for this test is 110, composed of 15 individually significant accounts and a sample of 95 items.

Jones mailed positive confirmations to each of the 110 accounts selected for testing. Either the confirmations were returned to Jones, or he was able to use alternative procedures to determine that the receivables were valid. Four customers indicated that their accounts were overstated, and Jones determined that the misstatements had resulted from unintentional errors by client personnel. The results of the sample are summarized as follows.

Stratum	Book Value of Stratum	Book Value of Sample	Audit Value of Sample	Amount of Overstatement
>$25,000	$ 550,000	$ 550,000	$ 549,500	$ 500
>$3,000	850,500	425,000	423,000	2,000
<$3,000	2,317,400	92,000	91,750	250

Based on analysis of the misstatements found, Jones concluded that the amount of misstatement in the population was likely to correlate to the total dollar amount of the items in the population and not to the number of items in the population. Thus, he decided to use the first method (misstatements divided by the fraction of dollars sampled) for projecting the results. His projection of the misstatements follows:

Stratum	Amount of Misstatement	Percentage of Stratum Sampled	Projected Misstatement
>$25,000	$ 500	100%	$ 500
>$3,000	2,000	$425,000 ÷ $850,500 = .50	4,000
<$3,000	250	$92,000 ÷ $2,317,400 = .04	6,250
Total projected misstatement			$10,750

The total projected misstatement is $10,750. Jones should conclude that there is an acceptably low risk that the true misstatement exceeds the tolerable misstatement because the projected misstatement of $10,750 is less than the expected misstatement of $15,000.

Before reaching a final conclusion on the fair presentation of Calabro's accounts receivable balance, Jones would consider the qualitative characteristics of the misstatements detected and the results of other auditing procedures. If these steps are successfully completed, Jones can conclude that the accounts receivable balance is fairly presented in conformity with GAAP.

Statistical Sampling for Substantive Tests of Account Balances

LO 8> When conducting a statistical application for substantive tests of account balances, the auditor considers each step in Table 7–6. The difference between statistical sampling and judgemental sampling occurs in the following steps:

- determining the sample size
- selecting the random sample items
- projecting the sample results to the population

The two most commonly used statistical sampling techniques are outlined following.

Determining the Sample Size

The auditor explicitly considers the five factors previously covered to determine the sample size.

Monetary Unit Sampling   For populations where the auditor expects a low error rate and where the objective is to test for overstatement errors, *monetary unit sampling* (*MUS*, sometimes called *probability-proportional-to-size sampling*) is often used. Following are some advantages and disadvantages of MUS.

Advantages:
- When the auditor expects no misstatements, monetary-unit sampling usually results in a smaller sample size than classical variables sampling.
- The calculation of the sample size and the evaluation of the sample results are *not* based on the variation (that is, the standard deviation) between items in the population. The standard deviation is required to compute the sample size for a classical variables sampling application because it relies on the central limit theorem.
- When applied using a probability-proportional-to-size sample selection procedure as outlined in this text, monetary-unit sampling automatically results in a stratified sample because sampled items are selected in proportion to their dollar amounts. Thus, larger dollar items have a higher probability of being selected. With classical variables sampling, the population must be stratified in order to get an efficient sample size.

Disadvantages:
- The selection of a zero or negative balances generally requires special design consideration. For example, if examining zero balances (for example, searching for unrecorded liabilities in accounts payable) is important, the auditor must test those items separately because such items will not be selected using a probability-proportional-to-size selection method. Alternatively, if an account such as accounts receivable contains credit balances, the auditor should segregate those items and test them separately.
- The general approach to monetary-unit sampling assumes that the audited amount of the sample item is not in error by more than 100 percent. If the auditor detects items that are in error by more than 100 percent, special adjustments will be necessary when calculating sample results. For example, suppose an accounts receivable account contains a book value of $1,500. If the auditor determines that the correct value for the account should be a credit balance of $3,000, the account will be in error by 300 percent. Such an item would require special consideration when the auditor projects the amount of misstatement.
- When more than one or two misstatements are detected using a monetary-unit sampling approach, the sample results calculations as shown in the text may overstate the allowance for sampling risk. This occurs because the methods used to determine the amount of misstatement are very conservative. Thus, an auditor is more likely to reject an acceptable recorded book value and overaudit.[5]

Classical Variables Sampling   Classical variables sampling (CVS) is based on normal distribution theory.

Classical variables sampling can easily handle both overstatement and understatement errors. It is most appropriate for populations that contain a moderate to high rate of misstatement. Some applications of this sampling approach include auditing accounts receivable in which unapplied credits exist or a large amount of misstatement is expected, and inventory in which significant audit differences are expected between test counts and pricing tests. Following are some of the advantages and disadvantages of classical variables sampling.

Advantages:
- When the auditor expects a large number of differences between book and audited values, classical variables sampling will normally result in a smaller sample size than monetary-unit sampling.
- Classical variables sampling techniques are effective for both overstatements and understatements. No special evaluation

---

[5]There are alternative methods that overcome this disadvantage. However, these methods are more complex. See D. A. Leslie, A. D. Teitlebaum, and R. J. Anderson, *Dollar Unit Sampling: A Practical Guide for Auditors* (Toronto: Copp, Clark and Pitman, 1979), and W. L. Felix, Jr., R. A. Grimlund, F. J. Koster, and R. S. Roussey, "Arthur Andersen's New Monetary-Unit Sampling Approach," *Auditing: A Journal of Practice & Theory* (Fall 1990), pp. 1–16, for a discussion of alternative approaches.

considerations are necessary if the sample data include both types of misstatements.

- The selection of zero balances generally does not require special sample design considerations because the sampling unit will not be an individual dollar but rather an account, a transaction, or a line item.

Disadvantages:
- In order to determine the sample size, the auditor must estimate the standard deviation of the audited value or differences. However, the auditor may be able to develop a reasonably good estimate of the standard deviation by measuring the standard deviation of the book values, calculating the standard deviation from a pilot sample, or basing the estimate on prior years' audit results.
- If few misstatements are detected in the sample data, the true variance tends to be underestimated, and the resulting projection of the misstatements to the population is likely not to be reliable.

The mathematical computations required for CVS are more complex and auditors typically use computer software to perform the computations.

Selecting the Random Sample Items

Monetary Unit Sampling   MUS samples from the dollars in the population. The determination of sample size simultaneously computes a sampling interval of every nth dollar. The auditor can select a sample for MUS by using a computer program for random number generation and systematic selection. A benefit of using probability-proportional-to-size sample selection is that since it gives each dollar in the population an equal chance of being selected, it automatically gives larger account balances a greater chance of being selected.

Classical Variables Sampling   Sample selection in CVS normally relies on random selection techniques. For example, in a CVS test of an accounts receivable balance, if the sampling unit is defined to be a customer account, the accounts to be examined can be selected from the aged trial balance of accounts receivable.

Projecting the Sample Results

Monetary Unit Sampling   The misstatements detected in the sample can be projected to the population, and since the identification and selection of the sample items was based on statistical principles, it is possible to quantify the allowance for sampling risk. The total of the projected misstatement and the allowance for sampling risk is the *upper limit of misstatements* (ULM), which may be compared to tolerable misstatement for the account balance or accumulated on the proposed adjustment schedule.

Classical Variables Sampling   The sample results generate a point estimate of the population value that can be used to construct a confidence limit for the true value of the population. Because the design of the sampling application was based on statistical principles, this confidence limit contains an allowance for sampling risk.

Detailed examples of MUS and CVS are provided on the text website as Appendices F and E at www.mcgrawhill.ca/college/messier.

REVIEW QUESTIONS

LO 1   **7-1**   Define *audit sampling*. Why do auditors sample instead of examining every transaction?

2   **7-2**   List audit evidence choices that do not involve sampling.

3   **7-3**   Distinguish between Type I and Type II errors. What terms are used to describe these errors when the auditor is conducting tests of controls and substantive tests? What costs are potentially incurred by auditors when such decision errors occur?

4   **7-4**   Distinguish between nonstatistical and statistical sampling. What are the advantages and disadvantages of using statistical sampling?

5   **7-5**   Define *attribute sampling*. Why is this sampling technique appropriate for tests of controls?

5   **7-6**   List the four factors that enter into the sample size decision. What is the relationship between sample size and each of these factors?

5   **7-7**   In performing certain audit procedures the auditor may encounter voided documents, inapplicable documents, or missing documents. How should each of these situations be handled within the attribute-sampling application?

5   **7-8**   If the planned level of control risk is not supported by the sampling results, what should the auditor do?

6   **7-9**   How are the risk of incorrect acceptance, the tolerable misstatement, and the expected misstatement related to sample size in variables sampling?

7,8   **7-10**   What items considered by an auditor differ when a nonstatistical sampling application is used rather than a statistical sampling application?

7   **7-11**   How do changes in the variation of items in the population, the risk of incorrect acceptance, and the tolerable and expected misstatements affect the sample size in a nonstatistical sampling application?

7   **7-12**   Describe the two methods suggested for projecting a nonstatistical sample result. How does an auditor determine which method should be used?

6,7,8   **7-13**   After defining the population, the auditor must make what additional decisions concerning the population?

5,7,   **7-14**   The auditor should perform error analysis when deviations are found in a sampling application. What are the purposes of performing error analysis?

7   **7-15**   How should the results of a nonstatistical sample be evaluated in terms of considering sampling risk?

MULTIPLE-CHOICE QUESTIONS FROM PROFESSIONAL EXAMINATIONS

Unless otherwise indicated, these multiple-choice questions were adapted from the CPA examinations, courtesy of the American Institute of Certified Public Accountants.

5   **7-16**   An auditor plans to examine a sample of 20 purchase orders for proper approval as prescribed by the client's internal accounting control procedures. One of the purchase orders in the chosen sample of 20 cannot be found, and the auditor is unable to use alternative procedures to test whether that purchase order was properly approved. The auditor should

a. Choose another purchase order to replace the missing purchase order in the sample.

b. Consider this compliance test invalid and proceed with substantive tests because internal control cannot be relied upon.

c. Treat the missing purchase order as a deviation for the purpose of evaluating the sample.

d. Select a completely new set of 20 purchase orders.

5⟩   **7-17**   Which of the following combinations results in a decrease in sample size in an attribute sample for a test of controls?

	Risk of Assessing Control Risk Too Low	*Tolerable Deviation Rate*	*Expected Population Deviation Rate*
a.	Increase	Decrease	Increase
b.	Decrease	Increase	Decrease
c.	Increase	Increase	Decrease
d.	Increase	Increase	Increase

3,6,7⟩   **7-18**   The likelihood of assessing control risk too high is the risk that the sample selected to test controls

a. Does *not* support the tolerable deviation rate for some or all of management's assertions.

b. Does *not* support the auditor's planned assessed level of control risk when the true operating effectiveness of the control justifies such an assessment.

c. Contains misstatements that could be material to the financial statements when aggregated with misstatements in other account balances or transaction classes.

d. Contains proportionately fewer monetary errors or deviations from prescribed internal controls than exist in the balance or class as a whole.

5,6⟩   **7-19**   Samples to test internal controls are intended to provide a basis for an auditor to conclude whether

a. The controls are operating effectively.

b. The financial statements are materially misstated.

c. The risk of incorrect acceptance is too high.

d. Materiality for planning purposes is at a sufficiently low level.

4,5,6⟩   **7-20**   An advantage of statistical sampling over nonstatistical sampling is that statistical sampling helps an auditor to

a. Eliminate the risk of nonsampling errors.

b. Reduce audit risk and materiality to a relatively low level.

c. Measure the sufficiency of the evidential matter obtained.

d. Minimize the failure to detect errors and fraud.

5,6>   **7-21**   To determine the sample size for a test of controls, an auditor should consider the tolerable deviation rate, the allowable risk of assessing control risk too low, and the

a. Expected population deviation rate.

b. Computed upper precision limit.

c. Risk of assessing control risk too high.

d. Risk of incorrect rejection.

3,5>   **7-22**   The following table depicts the auditor's estimated computed upper deviation rate compared with the tolerable deviation rate, and also depicts the true population deviation rate compared with the tolerable deviation rate.

	True State of Population	
Auditor's Estimate Based on Sample Results	**Deviation Rate Is Less Than Tolerable Deviation Rate**	**Deviation Rate Exceeds Tolerable Deviation Rate**
Computed upper deviation rate is less than tolerable deviation rate.	I	III
Computed upper deviation rate exceeds tolerable deviation rate.	II	IV

As a result of tests of controls, the auditor assesses control risk higher than necessary and thereby increases substantive testing. This is illustrated by situation

a. I.

b. II.

c. III.

d. IV.

3,5>   **7-23**   As a result of sampling procedures applied as tests of controls, an auditor incorrectly assesses control risk lower than appropriate. The most likely explanation for this situation is that

a. The deviation rates of both the auditor's sample and the population exceed the tolerable deviation rate.

b. The deviation rates of both the auditor's sample and the population are less than the tolerable deviation rate.

c. The deviation rate in the auditor's sample is less than the tolerable deviation rate, but the deviation rate in the population exceeds the tolerable deviation rate.

d. The deviation rate in the auditor's sample exceeds the tolerable deviation rate, but the deviation rate in the population is less than the tolerable deviation rate.

7,8>   **7-24**   An auditor may decide to increase the risk of incorrect rejection when

   a. Increased reliability based on the sample is desired.

   b. Many differences (audit value minus recorded value) are expected.

   c. The initial sample results do *not* support the planned level of control risk.

   d. The cost and effort of selecting additional sample items are low.

8>   **7-25**   Which of the following statements concerning monetary-unit sampling is correct?

   a. The sampling distribution should approximate the normal distribution.

   b. Overstated units have a lower probability of sample selection than units that are understated.

   c. The auditor controls the risk of incorrect acceptance by specifying the risk level for the sampling plan.

   d. The sampling interval is calculated by dividing the number of physical units in the population by the sample size.

5,7>   **7-26**   Which of the following sampling methods would be used to estimate a numeric measurement of a population, such as a dollar value?

   a. Random sampling.

   b. Numeric sampling.

   c. Attribute sampling.

   d. Variable sampling.

5,6>   **7-27**   The risk of incorrect acceptance and the likelihood of assessing the control risk too low relate to the

   a. Effectiveness of the audit.

   b. Efficiency of the audit.

   c. Preliminary estimates of materiality levels.

   d. Allowable risk of tolerable misstatement.

7>   **7-28**   When planning a sample for a substantive test of details, an auditor should consider the tolerable misstatement for the sample. This consideration should

   a. Be related to the auditor's business risk.

   b. Not be adjusted for qualitative factors.

   c. Be related to preliminary judgements about materiality levels.

   d. Not be changed during the audit process.

4,5,7>   **7-29**   In assessing the sampling risk, the risk of incorrect rejection and the risk of assessing control risk too high relate to the

   a. Efficiency of the audit.

   b. Effectiveness of the audit.

   c. Selection of the sample.

   d. Audit quality controls.

7> **7-30** In estimation sampling for variables, which of the following must be known in order to estimate the appropriate sample size required to meet the auditor's needs in a given situation?

    a. The qualitative aspects of misstatements.

    b. The total dollar amount of the population.

    c. The acceptable level of risk.

    d. The estimated rate of misstatement in the population.

7> **7-31** Which of the following sample planning factors would influence the sample size for a substantive test of details for a specific account?

	Expected Misstatement	Tolerable Misstatement
a.	No	No
b.	Yes	Yes
c.	No	Yes
d.	Yes	No

7> **7-32** A number of factors influence the sample size for a substantive test of details of an account balance. All other factors being equal, which of the following would lead to a larger sample size?

    a. Greater reliance on internal controls.

    b. Greater reliance on analytical procedures.

    c. Smaller expected frequency of misstatements.

    d. Smaller amount of tolerable misstatement.

PROBLEMS

1,2,4> **7-33** Sampling (statistical or nonstatistical) is a basic audit technique. A decision to apply sampling procedures involves both conceptual and practical considerations.

Required:

Identify and discuss these considerations.

(CICA, adapted)

2> **7-34** Following is a list of audit procedures used as tests of controls in the revenue process.

    1. Observing and evaluating segregation of duties.

    2. Testing of whether sales invoices are supported by authorized customer orders and shipping documents.

    3. Reviewing client's procedures for accounting for the numerical sequence of shipping documents.

    4. Examining sales orders for proper credit approval.

    5. Recomputing the information on copies of sales invoices.

    6. Comparing the average days outstanding in accounts receivable with industry averages.

Required:

Indicate those audit procedures that do not involve sampling.

5> **7-35** Calgari Clothing Company manufactures high-quality silk ties that are marketed under a number of copyrighted names. Winkle & Huss have been the company's auditors for five years. Lisa Austen, the senior-in-charge of the audit, has reviewed Calgari's control system over purchasing and inventory, and she determined that a number of controls can be relied upon to reduce control risk. Austen has decided to test two control procedures over purchases and inventory: (1) purchase orders are agreed to receiving reports and vendor's invoices for product, quantity, and price; and (2) inventory is transferred to raw material stores using an approved, prenumbered receiving report.

Austen decided to use a nonstatistical sampling approach based on the following judgements for each control procedure and has judgementally decided to use a sample size of 40 purchase orders for control 1 and 20 receiving reports for control 2.

	Control Procedure	
Parameters	*1*	*2*
Risk of assessing control risk too low	5%	10%
Tolerable deviation rate	6%	8%
Expected population deviation rate	3%	3%

After completing the examination of the sample items, Austen noted one deviation for each control procedure.

Required:

What conclusion should Austen reach about each control procedure? Justify your answer.

5> **7-36** Doug Iceberge, senior-in-charge of the audit of Fisher Industries, has decided to test the following two controls for Fisher's revenue cycle.

1. All sales invoices are supported by proper documentation, that is, a sales order and a shipping document.
2. All sales invoices are mathematically correct.

Iceberge has decided to use a nonstatistical sampling approach based on judgements for each control (see the table in Problem 7–31) and has judgementally decided to use a sample size of 50 sales invoice packets.

After completing the examination of the 50 sample items, Iceberge noted one deviation for control 1 and two deviations for control 2.

Required:

What should Iceberge conclude about each control? Justify your answer.

1> **7-37** Audit sampling is defined as applying an audit procedure to less than 100 percent of the population. The fact that an audit involves sampling is noted in the scope paragraph of the auditor's report, which contains the phrase "An audit includes examining, on a test basis." When an auditor uses sampling, an element of uncertainty enters into the auditor's conclusions.

Required:

a. Explain the auditor's justification for accepting the uncertainties that are inherent in the sampling process.

b. Discuss the uncertainties that collectively embody the concept of audit risk.

c. Discuss the nature of sampling risk and nonsampling risk. Include the effect of sampling risk on tests of controls.

DISCUSSION CASE

5,6>   7-38   Ray Baker was engaged to audit Mill Company's financial statements for the year ended September 30. After studying Mill's internal control, Baker decided to obtain audit evidence about the effectiveness of both the design and the operation of the controls that may support a low assessed level of control risk concerning Mill's shipping and billing functions.

Baker wanted to assess control risk at a low level, so a tolerable deviation rate of 20 percent was established. To estimate the population deviation rate and the computed upper deviation rate, Baker decided to apply a discovery sampling technique of attribute sampling that would use an expected population deviation rate of 3 percent for the 8,000 shipping documents and to defer consideration of the allowable risk of assessing control risk too low until the sample results were evaluated. Baker used the tolerable deviation rate, the population size, and the expected population deviation rate to determine that a sample size of 80 would be sufficient. When it was subsequently determined that the actual population was about 10,000 shipping documents, Baker increased the sample size to 100.

Baker's objective was to ascertain whether Mill's shipments had been properly billed. Baker took a sample of 100 invoices by selecting the first 25 invoices from the first month of each quarter. Baker then compared the invoices to the corresponding prenumbered shipping documents.

When Baker tested the sample, eight deviations were discovered. Additionally, one shipment that should have been billed at $10,443 was actually billed at $10,434. Baker considered this $9 to be immaterial and did not count it as an error.

In evaluating the sample results, Baker made the initial determination that a 5 percent risk of assessing control risk too low was desired and, using the appropriate statistical sampling table, determined that for eight observed deviations from a sample size of 100, the computed upper deviation rate was 14 percent. Baker then calculated the allowance for sampling risk to be 5 percent, the difference between the actual sample deviation rate (8 percent) and the expected error rate (3 percent). Baker reasoned that the actual sample deviation rate (8 percent) plus the allowance for sampling risk (5 percent) was less than the computed upper deviation rate (14 percent); therefore, the sample supported a low level of control risk.

Required:

Describe each incorrect assumption, statement, and inappropriate application of attribute sampling in Baker's procedures.

(AICPA, adapted)

7> **7-39** You are responsible for the audit of the accounts receivable of XLT, Inc., a company that supplies office equipment and supplies (such as printer ink cartridges), to a wide variety of customers, both resellers and commercial end users. Following is information about the accounts receivable:

Accounts receivable balance per client	$3,857,000
Number of individual accounts	8,125

You have selected a judgemental sample of all accounts over $15,000 (26 accounts worth a total of $535,000) and 84 accounts under $15,000 (worth $93,500) for a total of 110 accounts to be confirmed. Inherent risk is assessed as high. Control risk is assessed as moderate. Materiality has been set at $120,000. No other substantive procedures have been performed.

Fortunately, all confirmation requests were answered. Following are the results of the confirmation process:

Account	Client Value	Audit Value
Accounts over $15,000	$515,000	$488,000
Accounts under $15,000	93,500	89,750
Detail of Accounts Under $15,000:		
Able Ltd.	6,200	6,000
Baker, Inc.	4,680	4,430
Delta, Inc.	2,475	1,475
Evan Ltd.	1,670	0
Raston, Inc.	5,980	5,890
Garry Ltd.	1,495	1,385
Witten Ltd.	4,550	4,400
Cortan, Inc.	1,170	990
	$28,230	$24,570

Required:

Evaluate the results of this judgemental sample. Your evaluation should address conceptual issues related to using sampling, and the specific results of this sample.

(CICA, adapted)

7> **7-40** You have just completed the inventory observation of Able Pipefitters, a company that manufactures pipe fittings such as elbow bends and S-bends for pipes, primarily for plumbing applications. These fittings come in a large variety of combinations of shapes and diameters, totalling 1,595 unique types. The total value of the inventory, per the client's records, was $577,000. A random (nonstatistical) sample of 75 was selected for physical observation and price tests. The tolerable misstatement for the account is set at \$15,000. The client's value for the 75 items was \$85,000. You identified the following misstatements in the sample of 75 items:

Part #	Book Value	Audited Value
54E22	\$685.00	\$648.50
63S78	22.50	21.30
77S09	153.90	148.25
32E67	448.00	425.00
12E84	34.60	33.20
83S08	376.60	357.60
56E74	287.50	282.50
44S26	129.00	109.00

Required:

Calculate the projected likely misstatement using the pro rata projection method discussed in the text for projecting identified misstatements to the population.

7-41 Doug Stevens is interested in testing the fairness of the ending inventory balance at an audit client, Morris Co. Doug has relatively little experience using statistical sampling methods and, quite frankly, doesn't like to turn anything over to random chance—especially the selection of items to test. Ray used a judgemental method of selecting items for testing. The method involves testing the inventory-item balances that he deems most risky or most likely to be misstated. Ray identified items to test based on size of balance, findings from prior years, age of inventory, description, and professional judgement.

He selected 26 items with a total book value of \$720,000. In his "sample," he found a combined \$80,000 in overstatement errors. The book value of inventory on the client's records is \$1,090,000. Overall materiality for the engagement is \$500,000. Ray's policy is to use 50 percent or less of overall materiality as tolerable error for any one account.

Required:

a. What is your opinion of Ray's method of selecting his "sample"?

b. Evaluate Ray's results. Does he have sufficient evidence to conclude the balance is fairly stated?

Part V   AUDITING BUSINESS PROCESSES

Auditing the Revenue Process

Chapter **8**

Learning Objectives

Upon completion of this chapter, you will be able to

1 Recognize the relationship between an entity's revenue recognition policies and the way in which revenue is accounted for in the financial statements.

2 Describe the revenue process.

3 Identify the types of transactions in the revenue process and the financial statement accounts affected.

4 Explain the functions in the revenue process and the related documents and records used.

5 Demonstrate the appropriate segregation of duties for the revenue process.

6 Identify and evaluate inherent risks relevant to the revenue process.

7 Identify key controls for the revenue process and develop appropriate tests of controls for revenue, cash receipts, and sales return transactions.

8 Explain how the assessment of control risk relates to substantive testing.

9 Apply substantive testing procedures to the transactions and accounts in the revenue process.

10 Explain the confirmation process and how confirmations are used to obtain evidence about accounts receivable.

11 Evaluate the audit findings and reach a final conclusion on accounts receivable and revenue-related accounts.

RELEVANT ACCOUNTING AND ASSURANCE PRONOUNCEMENTS

CICA Handbook, **section 3400,** Revenue
CICA Handbook, **section 5095,** Reasonable assurance and audit risk

CICA Handbook, **section 5135,** The auditor's responsibility to consider fraud

CICA Handbook, **section 5141,** Understanding the entity and its environment and assessing the risks of material misstatement
CICA Handbook, **section 5142,** Materiality
CICA Handbook, **section 5143,** The auditor's procedures in response to assessed risks
CICA Handbook, **section 5300,** Audit evidence

CICA Handbook, **section 5301,** Analysis
CICA Handbook, **section 5303,** Confirmation
CICA Handbook, **section 5305,** Audit of accounting estimates
CICA Handbook, **section 6010,** Audit of related-party transactions

AUDITING EARTHWEAR'S REVENUE PROCESS

EarthWear Planning and performing the audit of EarthWear's revenue process is one of the most important components of Willis & Adams' audit of EarthWear's financial statements. The main type of activity in the revenue process is transactions between EarthWear and external parties, i.e., customers purchasing products from EarthWear. Customer orders may be received by telephone, on-line, or by mail using the forms enclosed in the catalogues. Willis & Adams needs to gain assurance that the information in EarthWear's financial statements correctly represents the economic reality of its sales and cash receipts transactions with its customers. Willis & Adams will collect audit evidence to confirm or disconfirm the explicit and implicit management assertions about those transactions, such as occurrence, completeness and so on.

Because EarthWear has hundreds of thousands of transactions in a year, in obtaining this assurance they will rely heavily on EarthWear's controls over the revenue process. Therefore they will spend a significant amount of audit effort understanding and testing those controls. They will also collect audit evidence to support or refute the explicit and implicit management assertions, such as existence, and rights and obligations, about the accounts and balances affected

by those transactions. The primary account affected is accounts receivable and as well as understanding and testing EarthWear's controls related to accounts receivable, Willis & Adams will also employ substantive procedures, particularly confirmations, in testing this account.

The chapter starts out by reviewing the basic concepts related to revenue recognition. It then presents an overview of EarthWear's revenue process and the documents and records created by that process, to aid in understanding and visualizing the revenue process. This is followed by a discussion of the factors that affect the assessment of inherent risk for the revenue process and the auditor's assessment of control risk in the revenue process. The chapter then discusses the procedures the auditor may use to test these controls and gain assurance about the management assertions relevant to EarthWear's sales transactions. This approach is then applied to the tests of controls over cash receipts transactions and over sales returns and allowances transactions. The chapter concludes with a discussion of the substantive procedures that may be applied to the tests of the associated account balances, particularly confirmation of accounts receivable.

Revenue Recognition

LO 1 Revenue recognition is briefly reviewed at the beginning of this chapter because knowledge of this underlying concept is fundamental to auditing the revenue cycle. Additionally, revenue must be recognized in conformity with GAAP in order for an auditor to issue an unqualified opinion. The *CICA Handbook*, paragraph 3400.03, defines revenue as

> The inflow of cash, receivables and other consideration arising in the course of the ordinary activities of the enterprise, normally from the sale of goods, the rendering of services and the use by others of enterprise resources yielding interest, royalties, and dividends.

Revenues are measured by the exchange value of the goods and services provided. In general, the entity receives cash or claims to cash for the goods or services provided. Claims to cash are usually referred to as trade accounts receivable. Before revenue is recognized (recorded), it must be *realized* and *earned.* Revenue is realized when a product or service is exchanged for cash, a promise to pay cash, or other assets that can be converted into cash. Revenue is earned when an entity has substantially completed the earning process, which generally means a product has been delivered or a service has been provided. Paragraphs 3400.06 and 3400.07 in the *CICA Handbook*, recommend that revenue should be recognized when the following conditions have been fulfilled:

a) the seller of the goods has transferred to the buyer the significant risks and rewards of ownership, in that all significant acts have been completed and the seller retains no continuing managerial involvement in, or effective control of, the goods transferred to a degree usually associated with ownership; and

b) reasonable assurance exists regarding the measurement of the consideration that will be derived from the sale of the goods, and the extent to which the goods may be returned.

c) collection is reasonably assured.

Revenue recognition continues to pose a significant audit risk to auditors and has resulted in questions about the integrity of the financial reporting process. In addition to the fraud risk factors mentioned in Chapter 3, the auditor should be alert for the following issues related to revenue recognition:

- Side agreements are arrangements that are used to alter the terms and conditions of recorded sales in order to entice customers to accept delivery of goods and services.
- Channel stuffing (also known as trade loading) is a marketing practice that suppliers sometimes use to boost sales by inducing distributors to buy substantially more inventory than they can promptly resell (see Exhibit 8–1).

For most entities, this revenue recognition process occurs over a short period of time, but in certain industries, such as construction or defence, the revenue recognition process may extend over a period of years.

An entity's revenue recognition policies affect how transactions are processed and how they are accounted for in the financial statements. Thus, an auditor must understand an entity's revenue recognition policies in order to audit the revenue process.

EXHIBIT 8–1

Revenue Recognition Leads to Restating Reported Earnings

Lucent Technologies, Inc., the once high-flying telecommunications equipment maker, restated its earnings downward for the 2000 fiscal year, which ended on September 30, by $679 million. The restatement included $199 million in credits offered to customers by sales teams, $28 million from the recognition of the sale of a system that had been incompletely shipped, and $452 million in equipment sales to distributors that were not utilized or passed on to customers. It appears that a strong push by the CEO, Richard McGinn, to meet revenue forecasts may have led Lucent sales personnel to promise customers credits and to "stuff" the distribution channel. Lucent's board of directors fired Mr. McGinn and numerous stockholder lawsuits have been filed against the company.

Lucent is not the only company that has restated earnings due to revenue recognition issues. A study by the Financial Executives International found that there were 464 restatements over the period 1998–2000. That's higher than the prior 10 years combined. The most frequent cause of the restatements was improper revenue recognition practices.

Sources: Lucent News Release, "Lucent Technologies Reports Results of Operational and Financial Review," December 21, 2000 (www. Lucent. Com); D.K. Berman, M. Schroeder, and S. Young, "SEC Probes Lucent Accounting Practices," *The Wall Street Journal* (February 9, 2001), pp. A3, A5; D.K. Berman and R. Blumenstein, "Behind Lucent's Woes: All-Out Revenue Goal and Pressure to Meet It," *The Wall Street Journal* (March 29, 2001), pp. A1, A8; J. Weil, "Restatement of Earnings Have Multiplied," *The Wall Street Journal* (June 7, 2001).

Overview of the Revenue Process

LO 2  In this section an overview of the revenue process for EarthWear Clothiers, Inc., is presented, beginning with an order from a customer, proceeding to the exchange of goods or services for a promise to pay, and ending with the receipt of cash. Exhibit 8–2 describes EarthWear's revenue process. Figure 8–1 presents the flowchart of EarthWear's revenue process, which will provide a framework for discussing controls and tests of controls in more detail. The discussion of the revenue process in this chapter can be applied equally well to manufacturing, wholesale, and service organizations. You should keep in mind, however, that an accounting system must be tailored to meet the specific needs of an entity. Therefore, you should concentrate on understanding the basic concepts presented so that they can be applied to specific revenue processes. Problem 8–36 presents an example of a document flowchart for a revenue process that is basically a manual system. If you have limited knowledge of information technology (IT), this flowchart provides a simpler example of a revenue process.

You should also notice that the revenue process shown in Figure 8–1 interacts with the inventory process. Many accounting systems integrate the revenue, purchasing, payroll , and inventory processes. The flowcharts used in this text to represent those processes show the points where the processes interact with one another. As entities use more advanced IT technology, it is becoming easier to integrate the information flow among the various accounting processes.

EXHIBIT 8–2

Description of EarthWear's Revenue Process

EarthWear provides 24-hour toll-free telephone numbers that may be called seven days a week (except Christmas Day) to place orders. Telephone calls are answered by the company's sales representatives, who use on-line computer terminals to enter customer orders and to retrieve information about product characteristics and availability. The company's sales representatives enter orders into an on-line order entry and inventory control system. Customers using the company's Internet site complete a computer screen that requests information on product code, size, colour, and so forth. When the customer finishes shopping for products, he or she enters delivery and credit card information into a computer-based form. EarthWear provides assurance through CA *WebTrust* that the website has been evaluated and tested to meet *WebTrust* Principles and Criteria.

Computer order processing is performed each night on a batch basis, at which time shipping tickets are printed with bar codes for optical scanning. Inventory is picked based on the location of individual products rather than orders, followed by computerized sorting and transporting of goods to multiple packing stations and shipping zones. The computerized inventory control system also handles items that customers return. Orders are generally shipped by Canada Post or United Parcel Service (UPS) at various tiered rates, depending upon the total dollar value of each customer's order. Other expedited delivery services are available for additional charges.

With the exception of sales to groups and companies for corporate incentive programs, customers pay in cash (in stores) or with credit cards. EarthWear's major bank is reimbursed directly by credit card companies, usually within three days. Group and corporate accounts are granted credit by the credit department. When group or corporate orders are received from new customers, the credit department performs a credit check following corporate policies. A credit authorization form is completed with the credit limit entered into the customer database. When a group or corporate order is received from an existing customer, the order is entered, and the data validation program performs a credit check by comparing the sum of the existing order and the customer's balance to the customer's credit limit.

We now discuss the following topics related to the revenue process:

- types of transactions and financial statement accounts affected
- types of documents and records
- the major functions
- segregation of duties

Types of Transactions and Financial Statement Accounts Affected

LO 3

Three types of transactions are typically processed through the revenue process:

- the sale of goods or rendering of a service for cash or credit
- the receipt of cash from the customer in payment for the goods or services
- the return of goods by the customer for credit or cash

The key controls involved in each of these transactions are discussed later in the chapter. For some entities, other types of transactions that may occur as part of the revenue cycle include scrap sales, intercompany sales, and related-party sales. Although such transactions are not covered specifically in this text, the auditor should be aware of how these transactions are

FIGURE 8–1

Flowchart of the Revenue Process—EarthWear Clothiers, Inc.

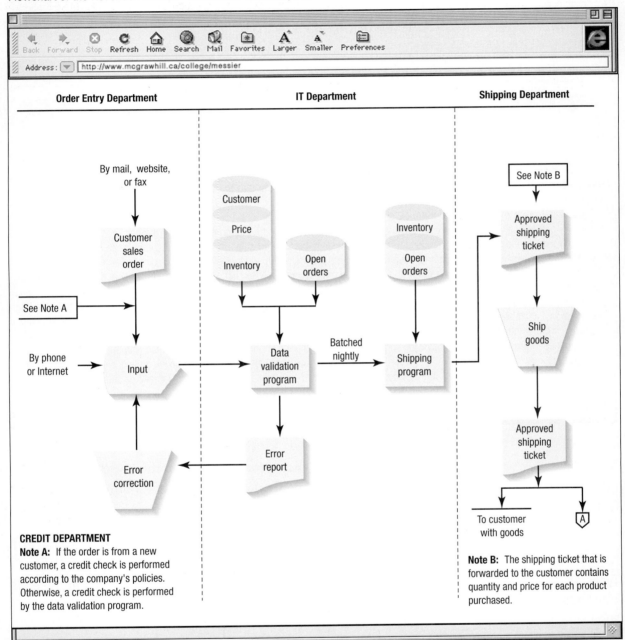

FIGURE 8–1 (*continued*)

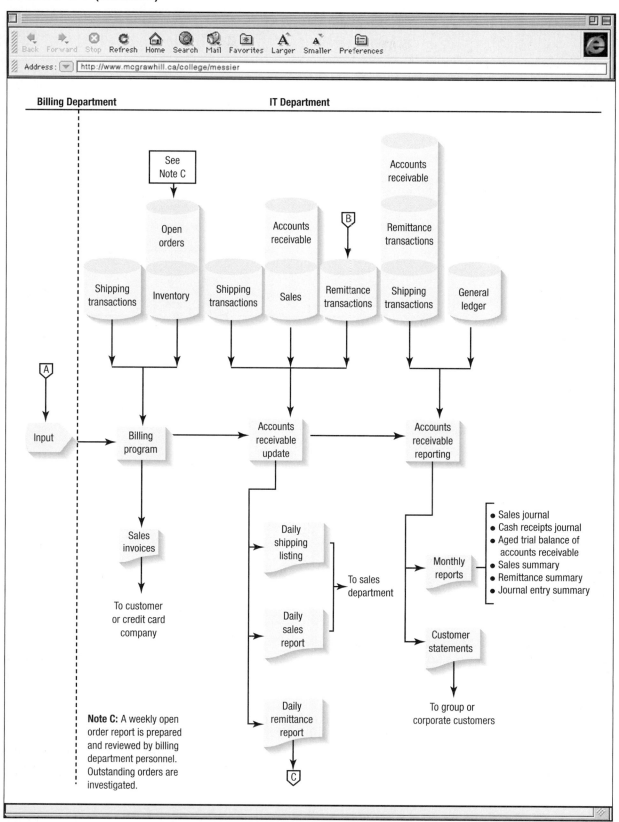

FIGURE 8–1 (concluded)

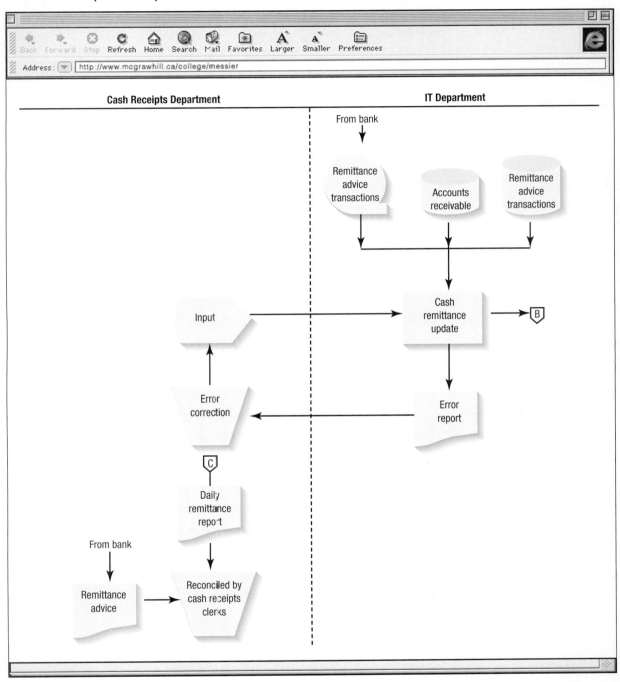

processed and their related controls when they represent material amounts in the financial statements.

The revenue process affects numerous accounts in the financial statements. The most significant accounts affected by each type of transaction are as follows:

Type of Transaction	Account Affected
Sales transactions	Trade accounts receivable
	Sales
	Allowance for uncollectible accounts
	Bad-debt expense
Cash receipts transactions	Cash
	Trade accounts receivable
	Cash discounts
Sales return and allowance transactions	Sales returns
	Sales allowances
	Trade accounts receivable

The Major Functions, Documents, and Records

LO 4⟩

The principal objective of the revenue process is selling the entity's goods or services at prices and terms that are consistent with management's policies. The revenue process consists of numerous steps, from the receipt of the customer order to the final disposition of the economic effect of the transaction on the financial statements. Many of the steps or functions involve the creation of documents. Each of the descriptions below briefly describes the function and, where applicable, the related document created by that function. Table 8–1 summarizes the functions that normally take place in a typical revenue process and Table 8–2 summarizes the documents and records in the revenue process. The reader should keep in mind that in advanced IT systems some of these documents and records may exist for only a short period of time or may be maintained only in machine-readable form.

Order Entry   The initial function in the revenue process is the entry of new sales orders into the system. It is important that sales or services be consistent with management's authorization criteria before entry into the revenue process. In most entities, there is a separate order entry department (see Figure 8–1).

Table 8–1   Functions in the Revenue Process

• Order entry	Acceptance of customer orders for goods and services into the system in accordance with management criteria.
• Credit authorization	Appropriate approval of customer orders for creditworthiness.
• Shipping	Shipping of goods that has been authorized.
• Billing	Issuance of sales invoices to customers for goods shipped or services provided; also, processing of billing adjustments for allowances, discounts, and returns.
• Cash receipts	Processing of the receipt of cash from customers.
• Accounts receivable	Recording of all sales invoices, collections, and credit memoranda in individual customer accounts.
• General ledger	Proper accumulation, classification, and summarization of revenues, collections, and receivables in the financial statement accounts.

Table 8–2	Documents and Records Included in the Revenue Process

- Customer sales order.
- Credit approval form.
- Open-order report.
- Shipping document.
- Sales invoice.
- Sales journal.
- Customer statement.
- Accounts receivable subledger.
- Aged trial balance of accounts receivable.
- Remittance advice.
- Cash receipts journal.
- Credit memorandum.
- Write-off authorization.

The document created by the order entry function is the *customer sales order*. This document contains the details of the type and quantity of products or services ordered by the customer. In EarthWear (Figure 8–1), order entry personnel enter the mailed or faxed information from customer sales orders into the revenue system. Phone or Internet sales orders are entered directly into the data validation program.

Customer orders that have been received but for which processing has not been completed are often listed on an *open-order report*. In the typical revenue process, after the goods have been shipped and billed, the order would be marked as filled. The open-order report should be reviewed daily or weekly, and old orders should be investigated to determine if any goods have been shipped but not billed or to determine why orders have not been filled. Testing for shipments for which the customer has not been billed provides evidence as to the completeness assertion. Figure 8–1 shows that EarthWear has an open-order file.

Credit Authorization   The credit authorization function must determine that the customer is able to pay for the goods or services. Failure to perform this function properly may result in bad-debt losses. In many entities, customers have preset credit limits. The credit authorization function must ensure that the credit limit is not exceeded without additional authorization. Where credit limits are programmed into the computer system, a sale that causes a customer's balance to exceed the authorized credit limit should not be processed. The system should also generate an exception report or review by the credit function prior to further processing. Periodically, each customer's credit limits should be reviewed to ensure that the amount is consistent with the customer's ability to pay.

The credit authorization function also has responsibility for monitoring customer payments. An aged trial balance of accounts receivable should be prepared and reviewed by the credit function. Payment should be requested from customers who are delinquent in paying for goods or services. The credit function is usually responsible for preparing a report of customer accounts that may require write-off as bad-debts. However, the final approval for writing off an account should come from an officer of the company who is not responsible for credit or collections. If the authorization for bad-debt write-off is part of the credit function, it is possible for credit personnel who have access to cash receipts to conceal misappropriation of cash by writing off customers' balances. In many large organizations, the treasurer approves the write-off of customer accounts because this individual is responsible for cash management activities and the treasurer's department is usually separate from the credit function. In some entities, the accounts written off are turned over to a collection agency for continuing collection efforts. By following this procedure, an entity discourages the use of fictitious bad-debt write-offs to conceal the misappropriation of cash. Most entities have a separate credit department.

The *credit approval form* is used to document the results of these procedures, including the amount of the credit limit for the customer. When credit limits are included in the client's computer files, the approval forms represent the source documents authorizing the amounts contained in the information system. EarthWear follows such a policy for its group and corporate customers (see Exhibit 8–2).

Shipping Goods should not be shipped, nor should services be provided, without proper authorization. The main control that authorizes shipment of goods or performance of services is payment or proper credit approval for the transaction. The shipping function must also ensure that customer orders are filled with the correct product and quantities. To ensure timely billing of customers, completed orders must be promptly forwarded to the billing function. The shipping function is normally completed within a separate shipping department.

When goods are shipped to the customer, a *shipping document* often called a "bill of lading" is prepared. The shipping document contains information on the type of product shipped, the quantity shipped, and other relevant information. A copy of the shipping document is sent to the customer while another copy of the shipping document is used to initiate the billing process. Figure 8–1 shows that EarthWear follows a similar process using what they term a "shipping ticket."

Billing The main responsibility of the billing function is to ensure that all goods shipped and all services provided are billed at authorized prices and terms. The entity's controls should prevent goods from being shipped to customers who are not being billed. In an IT system, an open-order report should be prepared and reviewed for orders that have not been filled on a timely basis. In other systems, all prenumbered shipping documents should be accounted for and matched to their related sales invoices. Any open or unmatched transactions should be investigated by billing department or sales department personnel.

The billing function is also responsible for handling goods returned for credit. The key control here is that a credit memorandum should not be issued unless the goods have been returned. A receiving document should first be issued by the receiving department to acknowledge receipt of the returned goods.

The document used to bill the customer is the *sales invoice*. The sales invoice contains information on the type of product or service, the quantity, the price, and the terms of trade. The original of the sales invoice, prepared from information on the shipping document, is usually sent to the customer, and copies are distributed to other departments with the organization. The sales invoice is typically the source document that signals the recognition of revenue. Once a sales invoice has been issued, the *sales journal* is used to record the necessary information for each sales transaction. The *customer statement* is the document that contains the details of all sales, cash receipts, and credit transactions processed through the customer's account for the period. It is usually prepared and sent to customers monthly.

Credit transactions such as for the return of goods or to record allowances that will be issued to the customer are recorded in a *credit memorandum*. Its form is generally similar to that of a sales invoice, and it may be processed through the system in the same way as a sales invoice. Exhibit 8–3 describes how EarthWear handles goods returned from customers.

Cash Receipts The collection function must ensure that all cash collections are properly identified and promptly deposited intact at the bank. Many companies use a lockbox system, in which customers' payments are sent directly to the entity's bank. The bank then forwards a file of cash receipts transactions and remittance advices to the entity. In situations where payments are sent directly to the entity, the cheques should

EXHIBIT 8–3

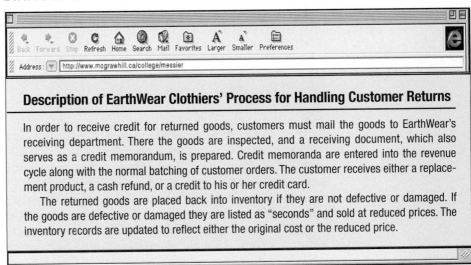

Address: http://www.mcgrawhill.ca/college/messier

Description of EarthWear Clothiers' Process for Handling Customer Returns

In order to receive credit for returned goods, customers must mail the goods to EarthWear's receiving department. There the goods are inspected, and a receiving document, which also serves as a credit memorandum, is prepared. Credit memoranda are entered into the revenue cycle along with the normal batching of customer orders. The customer receives either a replacement product, a cash refund, or a credit to his or her credit card.

The returned goods are placed back into inventory if they are not defective or damaged. If the goods are defective or damaged they are listed as "seconds" and sold at reduced prices. The inventory records are updated to reflect either the original cost or the reduced price.

be restrictively endorsed and a "prelisting" or control listing prepared. All cheques should be deposited daily. The entity's cash receipts are recorded in the *cash receipts journal*.

Accounts Receivable   The accounts receivable function is responsible for ensuring that all billings, adjustments, and cash collections are properly recorded in customers' accounts receivable records. Any entries in customers' accounts should be made from authorized source documents such as sales invoices, remittance advices, and credit memoranda. In an IT system, the entries to the customers' accounts receivable records may be made directly as part of the normal processing of these transactions. The use of control totals and daily activity reports provides the control for ensuring that all transactions are properly recorded. The accounts receivable function is normally performed within the billing department or a separate accounts receivable department.

The details of transactions with each customer are contained in the *accounts receivable subledger*. For computerized systems such as EarthWear's, this information is maintained in the accounts receivable file (see Figure 8–1).

Most companies prepare a monthly *aged trial balance of accounts receivable*. This report summarizes all the customer balances in the accounts receivable subsidiary ledger. Customer balances are reported in categories (such as, less than 30 days, 30–60 days, 60–90 days, more than 90 days old) based on the time expired since the date of the sales invoice. The aged trial balance of accounts receivable is used to monitor the collection of receivables and to ensure that the details of the accounts receivable subsidiary ledger agree with the general ledger control account. The auditor uses this report for conducting much of the substantive audit work in accounts receivable and in the assessment of the adequacy of the client's allowance for doubtful accounts. If the client determines that an account receivable is uncollectible, a *write-off authorization* document is normally used to remove that account from the accounts receivable. The write-off authorization is normally initiated in the credit department, with final approval for the write-off coming from the treasurer.

General Ledger   The main objective of the general ledger function in terms of a revenue process is to ensure that all revenues, collections, and receivables are properly accumulated, classified, and summarized in the accounts. In an IT system, the use of control or summary totals ensures that this function is performed correctly. One important function is the reconciliation of the accounts receivable subsidiary ledger to the general ledger control account. The general ledger function is also normally responsible for mailing the monthly customer account statements.

Segregation of Duties

LO 5〉

One of the most important controls in any accounting system is proper segregation of duties. This is particularly important in the revenue process because of the potential for theft and fraud. The general rule is to separate custody of assets, recordkeeping, and authorization of transactions. Therefore, individuals involved in the order entry, credit, shipping, or billing functions should not have access to the accounts receivable records, the general ledger, or any cash receipts activities. If IT is used extensively in the revenue application, there should be proper segregation of duties in the IT department. Table 8–3 contains some of the key segregation of duties for the revenue process, as well as examples of possible errors or fraud that can result from conflicts in duties.

Table 8–4 shows an effective segregation of duties for individual revenue functions across the various departments that process revenue transactions.

Table 8–3	Key Segregation of Duties in the Revenue Process and Possible Errors or Fraud
Segregation of Duties	*Possible Errors or Fraud Resulting from Conflicts of Duties*
The credit function should be segregated from the billing function.	If one individual has the ability to grant credit to a customer and also has responsibility for billing that customer, it is possible for sales to be made to customers who are not creditworthy. This can result in bad debts.
The shipping function should be segregated from the billing function.	If one individual who is responsible for shipping goods is also involved in the billing function, it is possible for unauthorized shipments to be made and for the usual billing procedures to be made and for the usual billing procedures to be circumvented. This can result in unrecorded sales transactions and theft of goods.
The accounts receivable function should be segregated from the general ledger function.	If one individual is responsible for the accounts receivable records and also for the general ledger, it is possible for that individual to conceal unauthorized shipments. This can result in unrecorded sales transactions and theft of goods.
The cash receipts function should be segregated from the accounts receivable function.	If one individual has access to both the cash receipts and the accounts receivable records, it is possible for cash to be diverted and the shortage of cash in the accounting records to be covered. This can result in theft of the entity's cash.

Table 8–4	Segregation of Duties for Revenue and Accounts Receivable Functions by Department

Revenue and Accounts Receivable Functions	Order Entry	Credit	Shipping	Accounts Receivable	Cash Receipts	IT
Receiving and preparing customer order	X					
Approving credit		X				
Shipping goods to customer and completing shipping document			X			
Preparing customer invoice				X		X
Updating accounts receivable records for sales				X		X
Receiving customer's remittance					X	
Updating accounts receivable for remittances				X		X
Preparing accounts receivable aged trial balance				X		X

Inherent Risk Assessment

LO 6 Section 5141 of the *CICA Handbook*, "Understanding the entity and its environment and assessing the risks of material misstatement," provides guidance for the auditor in assessing inherent risk. The guidance in the *CICA Handbook* is consistent with the strategic systems approach to auditing—the auditor must have a comprehensive understanding of the client's business operations and its key business processes. The auditor uses this comprehensive knowledge to develop expectations about key assertions in the financial statements. A major component of this is an understanding of the client's ability to create value, realize and recognize revenue, and generate future cash flows. With respect to the revenue process, such factors as the products the client produces and sells, the methods of revenue generation and recognition, and the conversion of accounts receivable into cash receipts are key business processes.

The auditor must understand the risks inherent in the client's key business processes and how those risks could impair those key business processes to the point of causing potential misstatements in the financial statements. Chapter 3 categorized risk factors that relate to possible misstatements into three groups: management's characteristics and influence over the control environment, industry conditions, and operating characteristics and financial stability. Management's characteristics and influence over the control environment are pervasive and are likely to affect all of the accounting cycles. Specific inherent risk factors that may affect the key business processes in the revenue cycle include the following:

- industry related factors
- the complexity and contentiousness of revenue recognition issues
- the difficulty of auditing transactions and account balances resulting from estimates
- misstatements detected in prior audits

Industry-Related Factors

Factors such as the profitability and health of the industry in which an entity operates, the level of competition within the industry, and the industry's rate of technological change affect the potential for misstatements in the revenue process. For example, if the industry is experiencing a lack of demand for its products, the entity may be faced with a declining sales volume, which can lead to operating losses and poor cash flow. Similarly, competition within the industry can affect the entity's pricing policies, credit terms, and product warranties. If such industry-related factors are present, management may engage in activities that can result in misstatements.

The level of governmental regulation within the industry may also affect sales activity. While all industries are regulated by legislation restricting unfair trade practices such as price fixing, a number of industries are more highly regulated. For example, banks and insurance companies are subject to both provincial and federal laws that may limit an entity's operations. The products developed and sold by pharmaceutical companies are regulated by Health Canada. Finally, most provinces have consumer protection legislation that may affect product warranties, returns, financing, and product liability. Industry-related factors directly impact the auditor's assessment of inherent risk for assertions such as valuation.

The Complexity and Contentiousness of Revenue Recognition Issues

For most entities the recognition of revenue is not a major problem because revenue is recognized when a product is shipped or a service is provided. However, for some entities the recognition of revenue may involve complex calculations. Examples include recognition of revenue on long-term construction contracts, long-term service contracts, lease contracts, and instalment sales. There may be disputes between the auditor and management over when revenue, expenses, and related profits should be recognized. For example, for software and high-technology industries, revenue recognition has been a contentious issue. The anticipatory revenue recognition policies of companies such as AOL and Enron resulted in what were subsequently determined to be significant overstatements of income, which since have been restated downwards.[1] In such circumstances, the auditor should assess the possibility of material misstatement to be high. Revenue recognition may also have a significant impact on the occurrence and cutoff assertions.

Section 5135 of the *CICA Handbook*, "The auditor's responsibility to consider fraud," stresses that material misstatements in the financial statements due to fraudulent financial reporting (i.e., on a broader scale) are often a result of manipulation of revenues through premature or delayed recognition. It directs the auditor to "ordinarily presume that there are risks of fraud in revenue recognition and consider which types of revenue, revenue transactions or assertions may give rise to such risks." Appendix B of section 5135 lists some specific audit procedures that the auditor may employ in assessing the risk of material misstatement due to fraudulent financial reporting resulting from revenue recognition. Some examples are:

- Performance of substantive analytical procedures relating to revenue using disaggregated data
- Confirmation with customers of certain relevant contract terms and the absence of side agreements
- Enquiries of sales and marketing personnel or in-house legal counsel regarding sales or shipments near the end of the period and their knowledge of any unusual terms associated with those transactions
- Physical attendance at one or more locations at period end to observe goods being shipped or being readied for shipping and performing other sales and inventory cutoff procedures.

If the auditor concludes that revenue recognition does not present any risk of material misstatement due to fraud, the auditor is required to document that conclusion and to provide reasons to support that conclusion.

---

[1]See American Institute of Certified Public Accountants, *Auditing Revenue in Certain Industries*, Audit Guide (New York: AICPA, 2001) for a discussion of the complexities of revenue recognition and, in particular, the software and high-technology industries.

| The Difficulty of Auditing Transactions and Account Balances Resulting from Estimates | Accounts that are difficult to audit can pose inherent risk problems for the auditor. For example, transaction and account amounts that are the result of accounting estimates may be particularly difficult to audit. Some of the above-mentioned anticipatory revenue recognition policies of companies such as Enron and AOL were based on inflated management estimates of revenues to be recognized in future; even for companies whose revenue is derived from sales of much more tangible physical products, estimates may be a significant factor. Consider a company that manufactures and sells major appliances. At least two major determinants of the company's revenue recognition, bad-debts expense and warranty expense, are the result of accounting estimates. Section 5305 of the *CICA Handbook*, "Audit of accounting estimates," suggests that to evaluate estimates such as those above, the auditor should look at whether the estimates are consistent with what he or she considers to be reasonable assumptions, and whether they are consistent with prior years after making allowances for current versus past economic conditions. In the final analysis, the auditor should also consider whether, when all the estimates are considered together, they seem to indicate a possible bias on the part of management, perhaps to smooth earnings over two or more accounting periods or to achieve a designated earnings level. |

| Misstatements Detected in Prior Audits | As previously discussed, the presence of misstatements in previous audits is a good indicator that misstatements are likely to be present during the current audit. With a continuing engagement, the auditor has the results of prior years' audits to help in assessing the potential for misstatements in the revenue process. |

Control Risk Assessment

LO 7> The concepts involved in control risk assessment were discussed in Chapter 6. The following sections apply the approach outlined in those chapters to the revenue process. For discussion purposes, it is assumed that the auditor has decided to follow a reliance strategy. Figure 8–2 summarizes the three steps for assessing control risk when a reliance strategy is being followed. Each of these steps is briefly reviewed within the context of the revenue process.

| Understanding and Documenting Internal Control | In order to assess the control risk for the revenue process, the auditor must understand the five components of internal control. In order to document the understanding of control risk, the auditor may use an internal control questionnaire, a narrative description, a flowchart, or some combination thereof, as discussed in Chapter 6. |

Control Environment   Because the control environment factors have a pervasive effect on all accounting applications, understanding the control environment is generally completed on an overall entity basis. The auditor should, however, consider how the various control environment factors may affect the individual accounting applications. In the remaining discussion of the revenue process, it is assumed that the control environment factors, including general IT controls, are reliable.

FIGURE 8–2

Major Steps in Assessing
Control Risk for the
Revenue Process

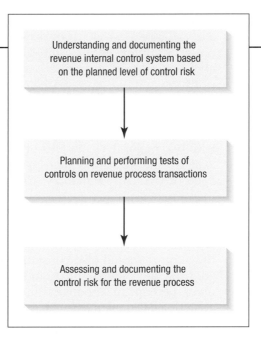

The Entity's Risk Assessment Process   The auditor must understand how management considers risks that are relevant to the revenue process, estimates their significance, assesses the likelihood of their occurrence, and decides what actions to take to address those risks. Some of these risks include a new or revamped information system, rapid growth, and new technology. Each of these factors can represent a serious risk to an entity's internal controls over the revenue process.

Information Systems and Communication   For each major class of transactions in the revenue process, the auditor needs to obtain the following knowledge:

- the process by which sales, cash receipts, and credit memoranda transactions are initiated
- the accounting records, supporting documents, and accounts that are involved in processing sales, cash receipts, and sales returns and allowances transactions
- the flow of each type of transaction from initiation to inclusion in the financial statements, including computer processing of the data
- the process used to prepare estimates for accounts such as the allowance for uncollectible accounts and sales returns

The auditor typically develops an understanding of an accounting (information) system such as the revenue process by conducting a transaction walk-through. This involves the auditor's "walking" a transaction through the accounting system and documenting the various functions that process it. In the case of a continuing audit, the auditor has the prior years' process documentation to assist in the walk-through, although the possibility of changes in the system must be considered. If the system has been changed substantially, or the audit is for a new client, the auditor should prepare new documentation of the system.

Control Procedures   When a reliance strategy is adopted for the revenue process, the auditor needs to understand the controls that exist to ensure that management's objectives are being met. More specifically, the auditor identifies what controls ensure that the internal control objectives are being met. The auditor's understanding of the revenue process can be documented using procedures manuals, narrative descriptions, internal control questionnaires, and flowcharts.

Monitoring of Controls   The auditor needs to understand the client's monitoring processes over the revenue process. This includes understanding how management assesses the design and operation of controls in the revenue process. It also involves understanding how supervisory personnel within the process review the personnel who perform the controls and evaluate the performance of the entity's data processing system.

Planning and Performing Tests of Controls	In performing this step, the auditor systematically examines the client's revenue process to identify relevant controls that help to prevent, or detect and correct, material misstatements. Because these controls are relied upon in order to assess a lower level of control risk, the auditor conducts tests of controls to ensure that the controls in the revenue process operate effectively. Audit procedures used to test controls in the revenue process include enquiry of client personnel, inspection of documents and records, observation of the operation of the control, and reperformance by the auditor of the control procedures.

Subsequent sections examine tests of controls for each major type of transaction in the revenue process more specifically. Chapter 7 discussed audit sampling in the context of tests of controls.

Assessing and Documenting the Control Risk	Once the tests of controls in the revenue process have been completed, the auditor judges the assessed level of control risk. If the results of the tests of controls support the planned level of control risk, the auditor conducts the planned level of substantive tests for the related account balances. If the results of the tests of controls do not support the planned level of control risk, the auditor should assess control risk at a level higher than planned. Additional substantive tests in the accounts affected by the revenue cycle must then be conducted.

The auditor should document both the *assessed level* of control risk and the *basis* for his or her conclusion. The level of control risk for the revenue process can be assessed using either quantitative amounts or qualitative terms such as "low," "medium," and "high." The documentation of the assessed level of control risk for the revenue process would include documentation of the accounting system such as the flowchart included in Figure 8–1, the results of the tests of controls, and a memorandum indicating the overall conclusions about control risk.

Control Procedures and Tests of Controls Revenue Transactions

EarthWear Table 8–5 presents the management assertions about transactions and events as they apply to the revenue process and Table 8–6 summarizes the management assertions, possible misstatements, control procedures, and selected tests of controls for revenue transactions. Most of these controls exist within EarthWear's revenue cycle (Figure 8–1).

The auditor's decision process on planning and performing tests of controls involves considering the possible misstatements that could occur if internal control does not operate effectively. The auditor evaluates the client's accounting system to determine the controls that will prevent or detect such misstatements. When controls are present and the auditor decides to rely on them, they must be tested to evaluate their effectiveness. For example, suppose the auditor's evaluation of the entity's revenue cycle indicates that monthly statements are mailed to customers by the accounts receivable department with complaints being handled by the billing department. This control is intended to prevent the recording of fictitious sales transactions. The auditor can review and test the client's procedures for mailing customer statements and handling complaints. If no exceptions or an immaterial number are noted, the auditor has evidence that the control is operating effectively.

Each of the management assertions shown in Table 8–6 for sales transactions is discussed mainly in terms of control procedures and tests of controls. The column for test of controls includes both manual tests and computer assisted audit techniques. The choice of which type of test of controls is appropriate for a particular internal control objective will be a function of the following:

- the volume of transactions or data
- the nature and complexity of the systems by which the entity processes and controls information
- the nature of the audit evidence, including audit evidence that is available only in electronic form

Table 8–5	Assertions about Classes of Transactions and Events for the Period under Audit

Occurrence. All revenue and cash receipt transactions and events that have been recorded have occurred and pertain to the entity.

Completeness. All revenue and cash receipt transactions and events that should have been recorded have been recorded.

Accuracy. Amounts and other data relating to recorded revenue and cash receipt transactions and events have been recorded appropriately.

Cutoff. All revenue and cash receipt transactions and events have been recorded in the correct accounting period.

Classification. All revenue and cash receipt transactions and events have been recorded in the proper accounts.

Table 8–6

Summary of Assertions, Possible Misstatements, Control Procedures, and Tests of Controls for Revenue Transactions

Assertion	Possible Misstatement	Control Procedure	Test of Controls
Occurrence	Fictitious sales Revenue recorded, goods not shipped, or service not performed	Segregation of duties	Observation and evaluation of proper segregation of duties.
		Sales recorded only with approved customer order and shipping document	Testing of a sample of sales invoices for the presence of authorized customer order and shipping document; if IT application, examination of application controls.
		Accounting for numerical sequences of sales invoices	Review and testing of client procedures for accounting for numerical sequence of sales invoices; if IT application, examination of application controls.
		Monthly customer statements; complaints handled independently	Review and testing of client procedures for mailing and handling complaints about monthly statements.
Completeness	Goods shipped or services performed, revenue not recorded	Accounting for numerical sequences of shipping documents and sales invoices	Review and testing of client's procedures for accounting for numerical sequence of shipping documents and sales invoices; if IT application, examination of application controls.
		Shipping documents matched to sales invoices	Tracing of a sample of shipping documents to their respective sales invoices and to the sales journal.
		Sales invoices reconciled to daily sales report	Testing of a sample of daily reconciliations.
		An open-order file that is maintained currently and reviewed periodically	Examination of the open-order file for unfilled orders.
Accuracy	Revenue transaction recorded at an Incorrect dollar amount	Authorized price list and specified terms of trade	Comparison of prices and terms on sales invoices to authorized price list and terms of trade; if IT application, examination of application controls for authorized prices and terms.
		Each sales invoice agreed to shipping document and customer order for product type and quantity; mathematical accuracy of sales Invoice verified	Examination of sales invoice for evidence that client personnel verified mathematical accuracy. Recomputation of the information on a sample of sales invoices; if IT application, examination of application controls and consideration of use of computer-assisted audit techniques.
	Revenue transactions not posted correctly to the sales journal or customers' accounts in accounts receivable subsidiary ledger	Sales Invoices reconciled to daily sales report	Examination of reconciliation of sales invoices to daily sales report.
		Daily postings to sales journal reconciled with posting to subsidiary ledger	Examination of reconciliation of entries to sales journal with entries to subsidiary ledger.

(*continued*)

Table 8–6	Summary of Assertions, Possible Misstatements, Control Procedures, and Tests of Controls for Revenue Transactions *(concluded)*

Assertion	Possible Misstatement	Control Procedure	Test of Controls
	Amounts form sales journal not posted correctly to general journal	Subsidiary ledger reconciled to general ledger control account	Review of reconciliation of subsidiary ledger to general ledger control account.
		Monthly customer statements with independent review of complaints	Review and testing of client procedures for mailing and handling complaints related to monthly statements.
		All shipping documents forwarded to the billing function daily	
Cutoff	Revenue transactions recorded in the wrong period	Daily billing of goods shipped	Comparison of the dates on sales invoices with the dates of the relevant shipping documents.
			Comparison of the dates on sales invoices with the dates they were recorded in the sales journal.
		Chart of accounts	Review of sales journal and general ledger for proper classification.
Classification	Revenue transaction not properly classified	Proper codes for different types of products or services	Examination of sales Invoices for proper classifications; if IT application, testing of application controls for proper codes.

The following sections present a discussion of control procedures and tests of controls that are relevant for EarthWear's revenue process.

Occurrence of Revenue Transactions

Auditors are concerned about the occurrence assertion for revenue transactions because clients are more likely to overstate sales than to understate them. The auditor is concerned about two major types of material misstatements: sales to fictitious customers and recording of revenue when goods have not been shipped or services have not been performed. The control procedures shown in Table 8–6 are designed to reduce the risk that revenue is recorded before goods are shipped or services are performed. The major control for preventing fictitious sales is proper segregation of duties between the shipping function and the order entry and billing functions. If these functions are not properly segregated, unauthorized shipments can be made to fictitious customers by circumvention of normal billing control procedures. Requiring an approved customer sales order and shipping document before revenue is recognized also minimizes the recording of fictitious sales in a client's records. Accounting for the numerical sequence of sales invoices can be accomplished manually or by computer. The use of monthly customer statements also reduces the risk of revenue being recorded before goods are shipped or services are performed because customers are unlikely to recognize an obligation to pay in such a circumstance. Figure 8–1 shows that EarthWear's revenue process includes these internal control procedures where applicable.

For each of the controls shown, a corresponding test of control is indicated. For example, the auditor can observe and evaluate the segregation of duties. The auditor can also examine a sample of sales invoices for the presence of an authorized customer order and shipping document for each one. In an IT environment, such as EarthWear's revenue process, the auditor can test the application controls to ensure that sales are recorded only after an approved customer order has been entered and the goods shipped.

Completeness of Revenue Transactions

The major misstatement that concerns both management and the auditor is that goods are shipped or services are performed and no revenue is recognized. Failure to recognize revenue means that the customer may not be billed for goods or services and the client does not receive payment. Control procedures that ensure that the completeness internal control objective is being met include accounting for the numerical sequence of shipping documents and sales invoices, matching shipping documents with sales invoices, reconciling the sales invoices to the daily sales report, and maintaining and reviewing the open-order file. For example, EarthWear (Figure 8–1) reconciles the batch totals of orders entered and provides a reconciliation of the daily shipping listing and the daily sales report. Additionally, the open-order file is reviewed periodically with follow-up on any order older than some predetermined date.

Tests of controls for these control procedures are listed in Table 8–6. For example, in a manual system, the auditor could select a sample of bills of lading and trace each one to its respective sales invoice and to the sales journal. If all bills of lading in the sample were matched to sales invoices and included in the sales journal, the auditor would have evidence that all goods shipped are being billed. The auditor could also use a generalized audit software package to print the items in the open-order file that are older than the client's predetermined time frame for completing a transaction. These transactions would then be investigated to determine why the sales were not completed.

Accuracy of Revenue Transactions

Accuracy is an important assertion because revenue transactions that are not processed accurately result in misstatements that directly affect the amounts reported in the financial statements. Again, the presence of an authorized price list and terms of trade reduces the risk of inaccuracies. There should also be controls that ensure proper verification of the information contained on the sales invoice, including type of goods and quantities shipped, prices, and terms. The sales invoice should also be verified for mathematical accuracy before being sent to the customer. In a manual system, the sales invoice may contain the initials of the client personnel who verified the mathematical accuracy. In an IT application such as EarthWear's, most of these controls would be programmed. For example, the price list is maintained in a master file. However, the client still needs controls to ensure that the authorized price list is updated promptly and that only authorized changes are made to the master file. The auditor can verify the application controls by using CAATs.

The accuracy assertion also includes the possibility that transactions are not properly summarized from source documents or posted properly from journals to the subsidiary and general ledgers. In the revenue process, control totals should be utilized to reconcile sales invoices to the daily sales report, and the daily recordings in the sales journal should be reconciled with the posting to the accounts receivable subsidiary ledger. The accounts receivable subsidiary ledger should periodically be reconciled to the general ledger control account. In a properly designed computerized revenue system, such controls are programmed and reconciled by the control groups in the IT Department and the user departments. The auditor can examine and test the application controls and various reconciliations. The use of monthly customer statements may also identify posting errors.

Cutoff of Revenue Transactions

If the client does not have adequate controls to ensure that revenue transactions are recorded on a timely basis, sales may be recorded in the wrong accounting period. The client should require that all shipping documents be forwarded to the billing function daily. The auditor can test this control by comparing the date on a bill of lading with the date on the respective sales invoice and the date the sales invoice was recorded in the sales journal. All billing should occur with only a minimum delay. In EarthWear's revenue process, the shipping department forwards the approved shipping order to the billing department for entry into the billing program. In such a system, sales should be billed and recorded within one or two days of shipment.

Classification of Revenue Transactions

The use of a chart of accounts and proper codes for recording transactions should provide adequate assurance about this objective. The auditor can review the sales journal and general ledger for proper classification, and can test sales invoices for proper classification by examining programmed controls to ensure that sales invoices are coded by type of product or service.

The accuracy assertion also includes the possibility that transactions are not properly summarized from source documents or posted properly from journals to the subsidiary and general ledgers. In the revenue process, control totals should be utilized to reconcile sales invoices to the daily sales report, and the daily recordings in the sales journal should be reconciled with the posting to the accounts receivable subsidiary ledger. The accounts receivable subsidiary ledger should periodically be reconciled to the general ledger control account. In a properly designed computerized revenue system, such controls are programmed and reconciled by the control groups in the IT Department and the user departments. The auditor can examine and test the application controls and various reconciliations. The use of monthly customer statements may also identify posting errors.

Cash Receipts Transactions

An important part of the overall revenue process is the cash receipts transactions arising from the payment by customers. Table 8–7 summarizes the management assertions, possible misstatements, control procedures, and selected tests of controls for cash receipts transactions. In assessing the control risk for cash receipts transactions, the auditor follows the same decision process as described for revenue transactions. Each of the management assertions shown in Table 8–7 is discussed with an emphasis on the control procedures and tests of controls.

Occurrence of Cash Receipts Transactions

The possible misstatement that concerns the auditor when considering the occurrence assertion is that cash receipts are recorded but not deposited in the client's bank account. In order to commit such a fraud, an employee needs access to both the cash receipts and the accounts receivable records; segregation of duties normally prevents this type of defalcation. Thus, proper segregation of duties between the cash receipts function and the

Table 8–7 — Summary of Assertions, Possible Misstatements, Control Procedures, and Tests of Controls for Cash Receipts Transactions

Assertion	Possible Misstatement	Control Procedure	Test of Controls
Occurrence	Cash receipts recorded but not received or deposited	Segregation of duties	Observation and evaluation of proper segregation of duties.
		Use of lockbox system	Enquiry of management about lockbox policy.
		Monthly bank reconciliations prepared and independently reviewed	Review of monthly bank reconciliation for indication of independent review.
Completeness	Cash receipts stolen or lost before recording	Same control procedures as above	Same tests of controls as above.
		Checks restrictively endorsed when received and daily cash list prepared	Observation of the endorsement of cheques.
		Daily cash receipts reconciled with posting to accounts receivable subsidiary ledger	Testing of the reconciliation of daily cash receipts with posting to accounts receivable subsidiary ledger.
		Customer statements prepared on a regular basis; complaints handled independently	Enquiry of client personnel about handling of monthly statements and examination of resolution of complaints.
Authorization	Cash discounts not properly taken	Procedures specifying policies for cash discounts	Testing of a sample of cash receipts transactions for proper cash discounts
Accuracy	Cash receipts recorded at incorrect amount	Daily remittance report reconciled to control listing of remittance advices	Review and testing of reconciliation.
		Monthly bank statement reconciled and independently reviewed	Examination of monthly bank reconciliation for independent review.
Cutoff	Cash receipts recorded in wrong period	Use of lockbox system or a control procedure to deposit cash receipts daily	Examination of cash receipts for daily deposit.
	Cash receipts posted to wrong customer account.	Daily remittance report reconciled daily with postings to cash receipts journal and accounts receivable subsidiary ledger	Review and testing of reconciliation; if IT application, testing of application controls for posting.
		Monthly customer statements with Independent review of complaints	Review and testing of client procedures for mailing statements and handling complaints from customers.
	Cash receipts not properly posted to general ledger accounts	Monthly cash receipts journal agreed to general ledger posting	Review of posting from cash receipts journal to the general ledger.
		Accounts receivable subsidiary ledger reconciled to general ledger control account	Examination of reconciliation of accounts receivable subsidiary ledger to general ledger control account.
Classification	Cash receipts recorded in wrong financial statement account	Chart of accounts	Tracing of cash receipts from listing to cash receipts journal for proper classification.
			Review of cash receipts journal for unusual Items.

accounts receivable function is one internal control procedure that can prevent such misstatements. Another very strong control that prevents such misstatements is the use of a lockbox system, such as the system used by EarthWear (Figure 8–1). With a lockbox system, the customers' cash receipts are mailed directly to the client's bank, thereby preventing the client's employees from having access to cash. The cash is deposited in the client's account, and the bank forwards the remittance advices and a file of the cash receipts transactions to the client for processing. Finally, preparation of monthly bank reconciliations that are independently reviewed reduces the possibility that cash receipts will be recorded but not deposited. Table 8–7 lists tests of controls the auditor could conduct to assess the effectiveness of the client's controls over the occurrences assertion.

Completeness of Cash Receipts Transactions

A major misstatement related to the completeness assertion is that cash or cheques are stolen or lost before being recorded in the cash receipts records. Proper segregation of duties and a lockbox system are strong controls for ensuring that this objective is met. When a lockbox system is not used, cheques should be restrictively endorsed when received, and a daily cash listing should be prepared. An additional control is reconciliation of the daily cash receipts with the amounts posted to customers' accounts in the accounts receivable subsidiary ledger. An example of this control is shown in EarthWear's system, where the total of the remittance advices is reconciled with the daily remittance report by the cash receipts department.

In terms of tests of controls, the tests conducted for the occurrence assertion also provide some evidence about completeness. In addition, the auditor can observe the client's personnel endorsing the cheques and preparing the cash listing. The reconciliation of the daily cash receipts with the postings to the accounts receivable subsidiary ledger can be tested by the auditor on a sample basis.

When the client does not have adequate segregation of duties or if collusion is suspected, the possibility of defalcation is increased. An employee who has access to both the cash receipts and the accounts receivable records has the ability to steal cash and manipulate the accounting records to hide the misstatement. This is sometimes referred to as *lapping*. When lapping is used, the perpetrator covers the cash shortage by applying cash from one customer's account against another customer's account. For example, suppose customer 1 has a balance of $5,000 and mails a cheque for $3,000 as payment on the account. A client's employee who has access to both the cash receipts and the accounts receivable records can convert the $3,000 payment to his or her personal use. The theft of the cash can be covered in the following way: The $3,000 payment is not reflected in the customer's account. When a payment is subsequently received from customer 2, the payment is deposited in the client's cash account but applied to customer 1's accounts receivable account. Now the shortage of cash is reflected in customer 2's accounts receivable account. The client employee who stole the cash keeps hiding the theft by shifting the $3,000 difference from one customer's accounts receivable account to another's. If cash is stolen *before* it is recorded as just described, the fraud is difficult and time-consuming for the auditor to detect. If the auditor suspects that this has occurred, the individual cash receipts have to be traced to the customers' accounts receivable accounts to ensure that each cash receipt has been posted to the correct account. If a cash receipt is posted to a different account, this may indicate that someone is applying cash to different accounts to cover a cash shortage. However, if duties are not properly segregated, that person may also be able to hide the theft through use of a credit memorandum, bad-debt write-off, or no recognition of the revenue transaction. For example, the employee could issue a credit memorandum for $3,000 against the customer's accounts receivable account to cover the $3,000 difference.

Accuracy of Cash Transactions

There are several reasons why cash receipts might be recorded at an incorrect amount. For example, the wrong amount could be recorded from the remittance advice, or the receipt could be incorrectly processed during data entry. The controls listed in Table 8–7 provide reasonable assurance that such errors would be detected and corrected. The corresponding tests of controls involve examining and testing the various reconciliations that take place in this part of the revenue process.

The other major misstatements that can occur for the accuracy assertion are cash receipts being posted to the wrong customer account or the wrong general ledger account. This last misstatement should not be confused with the misstatement discussed under the classification assertion. For the classification assertion, the misstatement results from the wrong financial statement accounts being credited in the cash receipts journal. The misstatement related to the accuracy assertion involves posting to the accounts receivable subsidiary ledger or from the totals in the cash receipts journal to the general ledger accounts.

The use of monthly customer statements provides a check on posting to the correct customer account because a customer who has made a payment and whose monthly statement does not reflect it will complain to the client. The other controls mainly involve the use of various reconciliations that ensure that cash receipts transactions are properly summarized and posted to the general ledger. Tests of controls that may be used by the auditor are presented for each control procedure shown in Table 8–7.

Cutoff of Cash Receipts Transactions

If the client uses a lockbox system or if cash is deposited daily in the client's bank, there is a small possibility of cash being recorded in the wrong period. Generally, the auditor has little concern with this type of misstatement because most entities use such internal control procedures.

Classification of Cash Receipts

The auditor seldom has major concerns about cash receipts being recorded in the wrong financial statement account. The major control for preventing cash from being recorded in the wrong account is a chart of accounts. The auditor's concern is with applying appropriate account codes to the individual cash receipts, especially cash receipts from unusual sources such as scrap sales, notes receivable, and proceeds from sales of equipment. The auditor can trace a sample of remittance advices to the cash receipts journal to ensure proper classification. The cash receipts journal can also be reviewed for unusual items.

Sales Returns and Allowances Transactions

For most entities, sales returns and allowances transactions are few and do not represent a material amount in the financial statements. As a result, this text does not cover them in as much detail as revenue or cash receipts

For example, a comparison of gross profit percentage to previous years' or industry data may provide valuable evidence on unrecorded revenue (an understatement) or fictitious revenue (an overstatement) and related accounts receivable when this ratio is significantly higher or lower than previous years' or industry data. This ratio may also provide information on changes in pricing policies.

The five ratios shown under the "Accounts Receivable" subheading in Table 8–8 provide evidence on whether accounts receivable properly reflect net realizable value. Each ratio aids the auditor in assessing the fairness of the allowance for uncollectible accounts, which in turn affects the fairness of accounts receivable and bad-debt expense. The days outstanding in accounts receivable ratio for EarthWear provides a good example of a substantive analytical procedure that provides strong evidential support for the accurate valuation of accounts receivable. The days outstanding in accounts receivable ratio is 4.91 and 4.94 days for 2006 and 2007, suggesting that EarthWear collects its accounts receivable quickly. This result is consistent with the majority of the company's sales being made with credit cards. EarthWear is reimbursed in three to five days by its credit card providers. Given this result, EarthWear's auditors may do no further audit work on accounts receivable.

Last, comparing the ratio of sales returns or sales discounts to revenue with previous years' and industry data provides the auditor with evidence on whether all sales returns or sales discounts have been recorded. The auditor can also estimate sales commission expense by multiplying the average commission rate by net sales and comparing that amount with recorded commission expense. In many situations, the auditor may be able to accept the sales returns, sales discounts, and sales commission expense as fairly presented without conducting any additional substantive tests if such substantive analytical procedures produce results that are consistent with the auditor's expectations.

Tests of Details of Classes of Transactions, Account Balances, and Disclosures

Table 8–9 presents the assertions for accounts receivable, allowance for uncollectible accounts, and bad-debt expense along with related tests of transactions, account balances, and disclosures.

Tests of details of transactions (substantive tests of transactions) are tests conducted to detect monetary misstatements in the individual transactions processed through all accounting applications. Often the auditor conducts substantive tests of transactions at the same time as tests of controls. Additionally, it is often difficult to distinguish a substantive test of transactions from a test of controls because the specific audit procedure may both test the operation of a control procedure and test for monetary misstatement. Table 8–9 presents a substantive test of transactions for each assertion for revenue transactions. Normally, most of these tests are conducted as tests of controls. However, if the controls are not operating effectively or if the auditor did not rely on those controls, substantive tests of transactions may be necessary for the auditor to reach an appropriate level of evidence. The cutoff assertion is the one that is most often conducted as a substantive procedure.

Table 8–9 also presents the assertions for account balances and disclosures. For each assertion, one or more tests of details are presented. In the following subsection, we discuss how the auditor approaches the audit of each important assertion for accounts receivable and related accounts. We begin with the completeness assertion for the accounts receivable balance

Table 8–9	**Summary of Assertions and Related Tests of Transactions, Account Balances and Disclosures—Accounts Receivable, Allowance for Uncollectible Accounts, and Bad-Debt Expense**

Assertions about Classes of Transactions	Substantive Tests of Transactions*
Occurrence	For a sample of sales transactions recorded in the sales journal, tracing of the sales invoices back to customer orders and shipping documents.
Completeness	Tracing of a sample of shipping documents to the details of the sales invoices and to the sales journal and customers' accounts receivable subsidiary ledger.
Accuracy	Comparison of prices and terms on a sample of sales invoices with authorized price list and terms of trade.
Cutoff	Comparison of the dates on a sample of sales invoices with the dates of shipment and with the dates they were recorded in the sales journal.
Classification	Examine a sample of sales invoices for proper classification into revenue accounts.

Assertions about Account Balances	Tests of Details of Account Balances
Existence	Confirmation of selected accounts receivable.
	Performance of alternative procedures for accounts receivable confirmation exceptions and nonresponses.
Rights and obligations	Review of bank confirmations for any liens on receivables.
	Enquiry of management, review of any loan agreements, and review of board of directors' minutes for any indication that the accounts receivable have been sold.
Completeness	Obtaining of aged trial balance of accounts receivable and agreeing total to general ledger control accounts.
	Review results of testing the completeness assertion for assessing control risk; tracing of shipping documents into sales journal and to accounts receivable subsidiary ledger if such testing was not performed as a test of controls.
Valuation and allocation	Examination of the results of confirmations of selected accounts receivable.
	Examination of the adequacy of the allowance for uncollectible accounts.

Assertions about Presentation and Disclosure	Tests of Details of Disclosures
Occurrence, and rights and obligations	Determine whether any receivables have been pledged, assigned, or discounted. Determine if such items require disclosure.
Completeness	Complete financial reporting checklist to ensure that all financial statement disclosures related to accounts receivable and related accounts have been disclosed.
Classification and understandability	Review of aged trial balance for material credits, long-term receivables, and nontrade receivables. Determine whether such items require separate disclosure on the balance sheet.
Accuracy and valuation	Read footnotes to ensure that required disclosures are understandable.
	Read footnotes and other information to ensure that the information is accurate and properly presented at the appropriate amounts.

*Each of these substantive tests of transactions could be conducted as a test of controls or a dual-purpose test. Of these five assertions, the test of the cutoff assertion is the one that is most likely to be conducted as a substantive procedure.

because the auditor must establish that the detailed records that support the account to be audited agree with the general ledger account.

Completeness

The auditor's concern with completeness is whether all accounts receivable have been included in the accounts receivable subsidiary ledger and the general ledger accounts receivable account. The reconciliation of the aged trial balance to the general ledger account should detect an omission of a receivable from *either* the accounts receivable subsidiary ledger or the general ledger account. If the client's accounting system contains proper control totals and reconciliations, such errors should be detected and corrected by the relevant control procedures for accuracy and completeness. For example, in EarthWear's revenue process (Figure 8–1), control totals exist for daily shipping and billing. Personnel in the billing department would be responsible for reconciling the two totals. If such control procedures do not exist in a client's accounting system, or if they are not operating effectively, the auditor will have to trace a sample of shipping documents to sales invoices, the sales journal, and the accounts receivable subsidiary ledger to ensure that the transactions were included in the accounting records.

This process followed by the auditor is to agree the accounts receivable subsidiary ledger of customer accounts to the general ledger accounts receivable (control) account. This is typically accomplished by obtaining a copy of the aged trial balance of accounts receivable and comparing the total balance with the general ledger accounts receivable account balance. Exhibit 8–4 presents an aged trial balance of accounts receivable working paper for Calabro Digital Services (see Problem 3–38). An aged trial

EXHIBIT 8–4

Example of an Aged Trial Balance of Accounts Receivable Working Paper

	CALABRO DIGITAL SERVICES Aged Trial Balance—Accounts Receivable 12/31/2006				E10 DLJ 2/15/2007
Customer Name	Total	<30 Days	30–60 Days	60–90 Days	>90 Days
Abbott Construction	$ 10,945¥	$ 9,542	$ 1,403		
ACTION Labs	$ 9,705		5,205	$ 4,500	
•	•	•	•	•	•
•	•	•	•	•	•
•	•	•	•	•	•
Wright industries	29,875¥	18,875	11,000		
Zorcon, inc.	4,340				$ 4,340
Total	$3,717,900	$ 2,044,895	$ 1,301,215	$ 260,253	$ 111,537
	F,T/B	F	F	F	F

F = Footed.
T/B = Agreed to trial balance.
   ¥ = Customer account traced to subsidiary ledger; agreed to total and proper aging tested.

balance of the subsidiary ledger is used because the auditor will need this type of data to examine the allowance for uncollectible accounts.

The auditor must also have assurance that the detail making up the aged trial balance is accurate. This can be accomplished in a number of ways. One approach involves mainly manual audit procedures. First, the aged trial balance is footed and crossfooted. *Footing* and *crossfooting* mean that each column of the trial balance is added, and the column totals are then added to ensure that they agree with the total balance for the account. Then a sample of customer accounts included in the aged trial balance is selected for testing. For each selected customer account, the auditor traces the customer's balance back to the subsidiary ledger detail and verifies the total amount and the amounts included in each column for proper aging. A second approach involves the use of computer-assisted audit techniques. If the general controls over IT are adequate, the auditor can use a generalized audit software package to examine the accuracy of the aged trial balance generated by the client's accounting system.

Cutoff

The cutoff assertion attempts to determine whether all revenue transactions and related accounts receivable are recorded in the proper period. In some instances, the auditor can obtain enough assurance about the cutoff assertion for sales by conducting tests of controls. However, in most cases, cutoff tests are conducted as substantive tests of transactions. Additionally, sales cutoff is coordinated with inventory cutoff because the shipment of goods normally indicates that the earnings process is complete. The auditor wants assurance that if goods have been shipped in the current-period, the resulting sale has been recorded, and also that if the sales have been recorded, the corresponding inventory has been removed from the accounting records. In addition, the auditor needs to determine if there is proper cutoff for sales returns.

If there is not a proper cutoff of revenue transactions, both revenue and accounts receivable will be misstated for the current and following years. In most instances, errors related to sales cutoff are unintentional and are due to delays in recognizing the shipment of goods or the recognition of the sale. In other instances, the client may intentionally fail to recognize revenue transactions in the current-period or may recognize sales from the next period in the current-period (see Exhibit 8–5 and Problem 8–45). The first situation can occur by the revenue transactions not being recorded in the sales journal until the next period. For example, sales that take place on the last two days of the current-year are recorded as sales in the next year by delaying entry until the current-year sales journal is closed. The second situation is generally accomplished by leaving the sales journal "open" and recognizing sales from the first few days of the next period as current-period sales.

The client's accounting system should have controls that ensure timely recording of revenue transactions. The results of tests of controls, if performed, should provide evidence of the cutoff assertion. Additionally, the client should have end-of-period control procedures for ensuring a proper sales cutoff between accounting periods.

The test of sales cutoff is straightforward. The auditor first identifies the number of the last shipping document issued in the current-period. Then a sample of sales invoices and their related shipping documents is selected for a few days just prior to, and subsequent to, the end of the period. Assuming that sales are recorded at the time of shipment

EXHIBIT 8–5

Sunbeam Corporation Restates Financial Results

Sunbeam Corporation restated its financial results for 1996, 1997, and the first quarter of 1998 based on an extensive audit by its audit committee and two public accounting firms. The special audit found that the previously issued financial statements overstated the loss for 1996, over stated profits for 1997, and understated the loss for the first quarter of 1998. Sunbeam reported that, for certain periods, revenue was incorrectly recognized in the wrong period, partly because of the company's "bill and hold" practice of billing customers in the current period for products that were delivered in a later period. The company also booked a significant amount of sales that were made to customers under such liberal terms that they did not constitute valid sales at all, but rather appeared to be consignments or guaranteed sales. In 1997 revenue was restated from $1,186 million to $1,073 million, and earnings were reduced from $123.1 million to $52.3 million. The reporting of these financial irregularities led to the resignation of Sunbeam's CEO, Al Dunlap.

In 2001, the SEC sued five ex-executives of Sunbeam and Andersen LLP agreed to pay $110 million to settle an accounting-fraud lawsuit over its audit work for Sunbeam.

Sources: J. R. Liang, "Dangerous Games: Did 'Chainsaw Al' Dunlap Manufacture Sunbeam's Earnings Last Year?" *Barron's* (June 8, 1998), pp. 17–19; M. Brannigan, "Sunbeam Audit to Repudiate '97 Turnaround," *The Wall Street Journal* (October 20, 1998), p. A3; "Sunbeam to Restate Financial Results; Discloses Adjustments for 1996, 1997, and First Quarter 1998," *The PointCast Network* (October 20, 1998); N. Harris, "Andersen to Pay $110 Million to Settle Sunbeam Account Fraud-Lawsuit," *The Wall Street Journal* (May 2, 2001), A3; and J. Weil, "Five Sunbeam Ex-Executives Sued by SEC," *The Wall Street Journal* (May 16, 2001), A3.

(FOB–shipping point), sales invoices representing goods shipped prior to year-end should be recorded in the current-period, and invoices for goods shipped subsequent to year-end should be recorded as sales in the next period. Any transaction recorded in the wrong period should be corrected by the client. For example, suppose the last shipping document issued in the current-period was numbered 10540. None of the recorded revenue transactions sampled from a few days prior to year-end should have related shipping document numbers higher than 10540, and none of the sampled revenue transactions recorded in the first few days of the subsequent period should have related shipping document numbers lower than 10540. In a computerized system such tests are still necessary because a delay in entering data may occur, or management may manipulate the recognition of the transactions.

The processing of sales returns may differ across entities. When sales returns are not material, or if they occur irregularly, the entity may recognize a sales return at the time the goods are returned. However, for entities like EarthWear, sales returns may represent a material amount or may occur regularly. In this instance, the client may estimate an allowance for sales returns. When sales returns represent a material amount, the auditor needs to test for proper cutoff.

Substantive analytical procedures may be used to test cutoff for sales returns. The ratio of sales returns to sales may indicate to the auditor that sales returns are consistent with expectations and therefore that the sales returns cutoff is adequate. If the auditor decides to conduct more detailed tests, the receiving documents used to acknowledge receipt of the returned goods must be examined. Using procedures similar to those for testing sales cutoff, the auditor selects a sample of receiving documents for a few days prior to and subsequent to the end of the period. The receiving documents are traced to the related credit memoranda. Sales returns recorded in the wrong period should be corrected, if material.

Existence

The existence of accounts receivable is one of the more important assertions because the auditor wants assurance that this account balance is not overstated through the inclusion of fictitious customer accounts or amounts. The major audit procedure for testing the existence assertion for accounts receivable is confirmation of customers' account balances. If a customer does not respond to the auditor's confirmation request, additional audit procedures may be necessary. The confirmation process is discussed later in this chapter.

Rights and Obligations

The auditor must determine whether the accounts receivable are owned by the entity because accounts receivable that have been sold should not be included in the entity's financial statements. For most audit engagements, this does not represent a problem because the client owns all the receivables. However, in some instances a client may sell its accounts receivable. The auditor can detect such an action by reviewing bank confirmations, cash receipts for payments from organizations that factor accounts receivable, or corporate minutes for authorization of the sale or assignment of receivables.

Valuation and Allocation

The major valuation issue related to accounts receivable is concerned with the net realizable value of accounts receivable. The auditor is concerned with determining that the allowance for uncollectible accounts, and thus bad-debt expense, is fairly stated. The allowance for uncollectible accounts is affected by internal factors such as the client's credit-granting and cash collection policies and external factors such as the state of the economy, conditions in the client's industry, and the financial strength of the client's customers.

In verifying the adequacy of the allowance for uncollectible accounts, the auditor starts by assessing the client's policies for granting credit and collecting cash. If the client establishes strict standards for granting credit, the likelihood of a large number of bad debts is reduced. Generally, the auditor assesses the adequacy of the allowance account by first examining the aged trial balance for amounts that have been outstanding for a long time. The probability of collecting these accounts can be assessed by discussing them with the credit manager, examining the customers' financial statements, obtaining credit reports (such as from Dun & Bradstreet), or reviewing the customers' communications with the client related to payment.

The second step in assessing the adequacy of the allowance account involves examining the client's prior experience with bad debts. The problem with examining only delinquent accounts is that no consideration is given to accounts that are current but that may result in bad debts. By maintaining good statistics on bad debts, the client can determine what percentage of each aging category will become uncollectible. The auditor can test these percentages for reasonableness. Following is an example of how this approach would work.

Table 8–11	**Management Assertions about Account Balances and Disclosures for Accounts Receivable and Related Accounts**

Assertions about account balances at the period end:

- Existence. Recorded accounts receivable and related accounts exist.

- Rights and obligations. The entity holds or controls the rights to accounts receivable and related accounts, and any liabilities related to those accounts are the obligations of the entity.

- Completeness. All accounts receivable and related accounts that should have been recorded have been recorded.

- Valuation and allocation. Accounts receivable and related accounts are included in the financial statements at appropriate amounts, and any resulting valuation or allocation adjustments are appropriately recorded.

Assertions about presentation and disclosure:

- Occurrence and rights and obligations. All disclosed events, transactions, and other matters relating to accounts receivable and related accounts have occurred and pertain to the entity.

- Completeness. All disclosures relating to accounts receivable and related accounts that should have been included in the financial statements have been included.

- Classification and understandability. Financial information relating to accounts receivable and related accounts is appropriately presented and described, and disclosures are clearly expressed.

- Accuracy and valuation. Financial and other information relating to accounts receivable and related accounts are disclosed fairly and at appropriate amounts.

for information about a particular item affecting financial statement assertions. Confirmation of accounts receivable is considered a generally accepted auditing procedure, and therefore auditors normally request confirmation of accounts receivable during an audit. However, auditing standards (*CICA Handbook*, paragraph 5303.28) allow the auditor to omit confirming accounts receivable in the following circumstances:

- The auditor has assessed the risk of material misstatement associated with the financial statement assertions being audited as low and other substantive audit procedures would provide sufficient appropriate evidence in these circumstances; or
- Confirmation would be ineffective in providing reliable audit evidence, based on information considered by the auditor in planning the audit.

Because of the importance of accounts receivable confirmations, the auditor should document completely the decision not to gather such evidence.

Confirmations can address more than one assertion. However, confirmations normally provide different levels of assurance for different assertions. Accounts receivable confirmations are generally a good source of evidence for testing the existence assertion. If the customer confirms the amount owed to the client, the auditor has competent evidence that the account receivable is valid.[3] Accounts receivable confirmations may also provide evidence on the completeness, valuation and allocation, and rights and obligation assertions. For example, a customer's confirmation

---

[3]Research has shown that accounts receivable confirmations are not always a reliable source of evidence. See P. Caster, "An Empirical Study of Accounts Receivable Confirmations as Audit Evidence," *Auditing: A Journal of Practice and Theory* (Fall 1990) pp. 75–91.

of the dollar amount owed provides some evidence on the valuation and allocation assertion.

A number of factors affect the reliability of accounts receivable confirmations. The auditor should consider each of the following factors when using confirmations to test accounts receivable:

- the type of confirmation request
- prior experience with the client or similar engagements
- the intended respondent

The types of confirmations are discussed in the next section. The auditor should consider prior experience with the client in terms of confirmation response rates, misstatements identified, and the accuracy of returned confirmations when assessing the reliability of accounts receivable confirmations. For example, if response rates were low in prior audits, the auditor might consider obtaining evidence using alternative procedures. The intended respondents to accounts receivable confirmations may vary from individuals with little accounting knowledge to large corporations with highly qualified accounting personnel. The auditor should consider each respondent's competence, knowledge, ability, and objectivity when assessing the reliability of confirmation requests. For example, if an auditor is confirming accounts receivable for a small retail organization, it is possible that the respondents may not have the knowledge or ability to respond appropriately to the confirmation request. On the other hand, if confirmations are sent to medium-size or large corporations with well-controlled accounts payable systems, the information received in response to such confirmation requests is likely to be reliable. However, some large organizations and government agencies do not respond to confirmations because it may be difficult to accumulate the necessary data since they are on a voucher system. Such nonresponses must be tested using procedures discussed later in the chapter.

Types of Confirmations

There are two types of confirmations: *positive* and *negative*. A positive accounts receivable confirmation requests that customers indicate whether they agree with the amount due to the client stated in the confirmation. Thus, a response is required regardless of whether the customer believes the amount is correct or incorrect. Sometimes an auditor will use a "blank" form of positive confirmation, in which the request requires the customer to provide the amount owed to the client. Positive confirmations are generally used when an account's individual balances are large or if errors are anticipated because the control risk has been judged to be high. Exhibit 8–7 presents an example of a positive confirmation request.

A negative confirmation requests that customers respond only when they disagree with the amount due to the client. An example of a negative confirmation request is shown in Exhibit 8–8. Negative confirmation requests are used when there are many accounts with small balances, control risk is assessed to be low, and the auditor believes that the customers will devote adequate attention to the confirmation. On many audit engagements, a combination of positive and negative confirmations is used to test accounts receivable because of materiality considerations and a mix of customers. For example, positive confirmations may be sent to selected large-dollar customer accounts and negative confirmations sent to a sample of small-dollar customer accounts.

EXHIBIT 8–7

Example of a Positive Confirmation Request

CDS   **CALABRO DIGITAL SERVICES**

Wright Industries
1060 Notre Dame St.
Winnipeg, MB R3R 3R3

Dear Customers:

Please examine the accompanying statement carefully and either confirm its correctness or report any differences to our auditors

              Abbott & Johnson, LLP
              P.O. Box 669
              Winnipeg, MB R3T 2N4

who are auditing our financial statements.
     Your prompt attention to this request will be appreciated. An envelope is enclosed for your reply. Please do not send your payments to the auditors.

Sincerely,
Jan Rodriguez
Controller, Calabro Digital Services

Confirmation:

The balance receivable from us for $29,875 as of December 31, 2006, is correct except as noted below:

_____
_____
_____

Wright Industries

Date_____By_____

Because positive accounts receivable confirmations require that customers respond to the auditor, any amounts for which responses are not received must be verified by the auditor using alternative procedures. Negative accounts receivable confirmations require a response only when the information about the customer's balance is incorrect. Therefore, a nonresponse to a negative confirmation request is generally assumed to represent a valid accounts receivable. This can be a major drawback to the use of negative confirmations.

The accuracy of the accounts receivable confirmation request can generally be improved if a copy of the customer's monthly statement is enclosed with the confirmation request.

EXHIBIT 8–8

Example of a Negative Confirmation Request

                              CALABRO DIGITAL SERVICES

Zorcon, Inc.
246 Airport Rd.
Winnipeg, MB R2N 1X5

Dear Customers:

Please examine the accompanying statement carefully. If it does NOT agree with your records, please report any differences directly to our auditors

Abbott & Johnson, LLP
P.O. Box 669
Winnipeg, MB R3T 2N4

who are auditing our financial statements.
    Your prompt attention to this request will be appreciated. An envelope is enclosed for your reply. Please do not send your payments to the auditors.

Sincerely,

Jan Rodriguez
Controller, Calabro Digital Services

Timing

Accounts receivable may be confirmed at an interim date or at year-end. Such considerations were discussed in Chapter 6. The confirmation request should be sent soon after the end of the accounting period in order to maximize the response rate. Sending the confirmations at the end of the accounting period reduces the chance of timing differences arising due to processing of purchases and cash disbursements by the customers.

Confirmation Procedures

The auditor must maintain control over the accounts receivable confirmations so as to minimize the possibility that direct communication between the customers and the auditor is biased by interception or alteration of the receivable confirmation by the client. For control purposes, the auditor should mail the confirmations outside the client's facilities. Direct mailing from the public accounting firm's office generally provides the best control. To ensure that any confirmations that are undeliverable by the post office are returned to the auditors and not the client, the confirmations should be mailed in envelopes with the public accounting firm's address listed as the return address. The envelope used by customers for returning the confirmation response should also be addressed to the public accounting firm.[4]

---

[4]R.H. Ashton and R.E. Hylas, "The Return of 'Problem' Confirmation Requests by the US Postal Service," *The Accounting Review* (October 1980), pp. 275–85, shows that the US Postal Service does an excellent job of returning undeliverable confirmations to the return address.

The fact that undeliverable confirmations are returned directly to the auditor also provides some assurance that fictitious customers are identified.

The auditor should maintain a record of the confirmations mailed and those returned. When positive confirmations are used, the auditor generally follows up with second, and possibly third, requests to customers who do not reply, in an attempt to increase the response rate to the confirmation requests. In some cases, a customer may respond using electronic media (such as e-mail or fax) or orally. In such situations the auditor should verify the source and contents of the communication. For example, a fax response may be verified by a telephone call to the respondent, and an oral response can be verified by requesting a written communication from the respondent.

Each confirmation exception (that is, difference between the recorded balance and the balance confirmed by the customer) should be carefully examined by the auditor to determine the reason for the difference. In many cases, exceptions result from what are referred to as *timing differences*. Such differences occur because of delays in recording transactions in either the client's or the customer's records. For example, the client may ship goods to a customer on the last day of the period and record it as a current-period sale. The customer will probably receive and record the goods as a purchase in the next period. Such situations are not errors and result only because of a delay in recording the transaction. Payment for goods by a customer at the end of the period can result in a timing difference if the customer prepares and records the check in the current-period but the client receives and records the check in the following period. Again, the difference in the confirmed amount results from a timing difference. Exhibit 8–9 presents a checklist by Willis and Adam's audit procedures for confirmation of EarthWears accounts receivable and Table 8–12 presents some examples of exceptions and their potential causes.

The need to maintain control over accounts receivable confirmations and responses does not preclude the use of internal auditors in the confirmation process. For example, internal auditors may confirm accounts receivable as part of their normal duties, or they may directly assist the auditor in performing accounts receivable confirmations as part of the annual audit. If internal auditors are used in this capacity, their work should be supervised, reviewed, evaluated, and tested by the independent auditor.

Alternative Procedures

When the auditor does not receive responses to positive confirmations, he or she must apply alternative procedures to determine the validity and valuation of the accounts receivable. Auditors normally send second and third requests; they also perform the following alternative audit procedures:

- examination of subsequent cash receipts
- examination of customer orders, shipping documents, and duplicate sales invoices
- examination of other client documentation

EXHIBIT 8–9

Revenue Process and Related accounts

EarthWear

EarthWear Clothiers
Accounts Receivable Confirmation Checklist
12/31/06

E15
SAA
1/17/07

Audit Procedures	Work done by (initials)	WP page no.
1. Obtain trial balance of accounts receivable as at selected confirmation date. Add and agree to general ledger.	RT	E 15.1
2. Select accounts for confirmation and note basis of selection of accounts for positive (and negative, if any) confirmation.	SAA	E 15.1
3. Agree individual subsidiary ledger account balances and particulars to confirmation requests.	RT	E 15.1
4. Mail confirmation requests in auditor's envelopes. Maintain control over requests at all times until actual mailing.	RT	E 15.1
5. Mail second request if a reply is not received to the first request.	RT	E 15.1
6. Forward copies of all confirmations indicating differences to client to clear. Obtain satisfactory explanations for these differences.	RT	E 15.2
7. Give a list of customers not replying to confirmations to a responsible client employee (not directly concerned with cash and accounts receivable) to ensure customers are bona fide.	RT	E 15.2
8. Report all differences to a responsible client employee.	RT	E 15.2
9. List all accounts not confirmed at client's request and state reason's for client's request. Investigation reason and determine its validity.	N/A	E 15.2
10. Perform alternative auditing procedures on confirmations not returned or those that are unsatisfactory (e.g., agree subsequent payments to the account and to duplicate deposit slips: agree shipping records and sales invoices to the account; examine other supporting documentation).	SAA	15.3
11. Agree names and addresses on confirmations on test basis to telephone directories or trade publications to ensure accounts are not fictitious.	RT	E 15.1
12. Complete confirmation statistics summary.	SAA	E 16
13. Ensure that auditing procedures in related areas (e.g., cash count, investment count) are coordinated where necessary.	SAA	___

Examination of subsequent cash receipts involves checking the accounts receivable subsidiary ledger for payments of the specific sales invoices included in the customers' accounts receivable balances that were outstanding at the date of the confirmation. If the client has strong controls for recording cash receipts, the auditor may stop at this point. If the client's controls are weak, the auditor may extend the testing by tracing the payment in the subsidiary ledger to the cash receipts journal and to the bank statement. If the customer has paid for the goods, the auditor has strong evidence concerning the validity and valuation of the accounts receivable.

If a customer has not paid the account receivable, the auditor can examine the underlying documentation that supports the sales

Table 8–12	**Examples of Exceptions to Confirmation Requests**

Type of Difference	Potential Cause
Goods not received by customer	Timing difference Goods delivered to wrong customer Invoice sent to wrong customer Fictitious sale
Payment not recorded in client's records	Timing difference Payment applied to wrong customer account Cash misappropriated
Goods returned for credit by customer	Timing difference
Processing error	Incorrect quantity or price Recording error
Amount in dispute	Price of goods in dispute Goods do not meet specifications Goods damaged in transit

transaction. This documentation includes the original customer order, shipping document, and duplicate sales invoice. If this documentation indicates that the customer ordered the goods and the goods were shipped, then the auditor would have evidence supporting the validity of the accounts receivable. Last, the auditor may need to examine other correspondence between the client and the customer to obtain adequate evidence on the validity and valuation of the accounts receivable.

Evaluating the Audit Findings—Accounts Receivable and Related Accounts

LO 11 When the auditor has completed the planned substantive tests, the likely misstatement (the projected misstatement plus an allowance for sampling risk) for accounts receivable is determined using either statistical or nonstatistical sampling techniques. The likely misstatement is then compared to the tolerable misstatement allocated to the account. If the likely misstatement is less than the tolerable misstatement, the auditor may accept the account as fairly presented. Conversely, if the likely misstatement exceeds the tolerable misstatement, the auditor may conclude that the account is not fairly presented. For example, suppose that a tolerable misstatement of $80,000 was allocated to a client's net accounts receivable balance of $3,933,000. Suppose that, after completing the substantive tests, the auditor determines that the likely misstatement is $40,000. In this case, the auditor may conclude that the client's accounts receivable are not materially misstated. However, if the likely misstatement is $95,000, the auditor's conclusion will be that the account is materially misstated.

The auditor should also analyze the misstatements discovered through substantive tests of transactions, analytical procedures, and tests of account balances. In some instances, these misstatements may provide additional evidence on control risk. By identifying the causes of the misstatements, the auditor may determine that the original assessment of control risk was too low. For example, the auditor may lower his or her evaluation of the effectiveness of the control for granting credit (that is, may increase control risk) based on a large number of misstatements detected during tests of the allowance for uncollectible accounts. This may impact the auditor's assessment of audit risk.

If the auditor concludes that audit risk is unacceptably high, additional audit procedures should be performed, the client should adjust the related financial statement accounts to an acceptable level, or a qualified report should be issued. In the previous example, if the auditor determined that the likely misstatement was $95,000, additional audit procedures might be required. Such audit procedures would typically be directed at the *systematic* errors detected by the substantive tests. For example, if the substantive tests of transactions indicated that sales invoices were priced incorrectly, the auditor's additional audit procedures would focus on determining the extent of pricing misstatements. Alternatively, the auditor could conclude that accounts receivable are fairly presented if the client's management adjusts the financial statements by $15,000 or more ($95,000–$80,000). This would result in the likely misstatement being equal to or less than the tolerable misstatement of $80,000.

In summary, the final decision about accounts receivable and the related accounts is based on whether sufficient appropriate audit evidence has been obtained from the substantive tests conducted.

REVIEW QUESTIONS

LO 1 >	**8-1**	Accounting standards require that revenue must be earned and realized before it can be recognized. Discuss what is meant by the terms *earned* and *realized*.
4,5,7 >	**8-2**	Describe the credit function's duties for monitoring customer payments and handling bad debts.
4,5,7 >	**8-3**	Describe how the collection function should be controlled when a lockbox system is not utilized.
7 >	**8-4**	In understanding the accounting system in the revenue process, the auditor typically performs a walk-through to gain knowledge of the system. What knowledge should the auditor try to obtain about the accounting system?
5,7 >	**8-5**	When a client does not adequately segregate duties, the possibility of cash being stolen before it is recorded is increased. If the auditor suspects that this type of defalcation is possible, what type of audit procedures can he or she use to test this possibility?
6 >	**8-6**	The auditor needs to understand how selected inherent risk factors affect the transactions processed by the revenue cycle. Discuss the potential effect that industry related factors and misstatements

detected in prior periods have on the inherent risk assessment of the revenue cycle.

7> **8-7** What are the two major controls for sales returns and allowances transactions?

9> **8-8** What are the three types of substantive tests? Define each type.

9> **8-9** List four analytical procedures that can be used to test revenue related accounts. What potential misstatements are indicated by each of these analytical procedures?

9> **8-10** Describe how the auditor verifies the accuracy of the aged trial balance.

9> **8-11** What are the two major issues related to the valuation of accounts receivable?

9> **8-12** Describe how the auditor tests the adequacy of the allowance for uncollectible accounts. Why is examination of only the delinquent accounts typically not adequate for assessing the adequacy of the allowance for uncollectible accounts?

9> **8-13** Describe how the auditor tests sales cutoff. Why would a test of sales cutoff typically be coordinated with the test of inventory cutoff?

10> **8-14** List and discuss the three factors mentioned in the chapter that may affect the reliability of confirmations of accounts receivable.

10> **8-15** Distinguish between positive and negative confirmations. Under what circumstances would positive confirmations be more appropriate than negative confirmations?

10> **8-16** What is meant by a timing difference when a confirmation exception is noted? Provide two examples.

10> **8-17** Identify three other types of receivables the auditor could examine. What audit procedures might be used to audit other receivables?

MULTIPLE-CHOICE QUESTIONS FROM PROFESSIONAL EXAMINATIONS

Unless otherwise indicated, these multiple choice questions were adapted from the CPA examinations, courtesy of the American Institute of Certified Public Accountants.

2,7> **8-18** When evaluating internal control of an entity that processes revenue transactions on the Internet, an auditor would be most concerned about the

a. Lack of sales invoice documents as an audit trail.

b. Potential for computer disruptions in recording sales.

c. Inability to establish an integrated test facility.

d. Frequency of archiving and data retention.

2,7> **8-19** The completeness of IT generated sales figures can be tested by comparing the number of items listed on the daily sales report with the number of items billed on the actual invoices. This process uses

a. Cheque digits.

b. Control totals.

c. Validity tests.

d. Process tracing data.

5,7,10 >   **8-20**   For the control procedures to be effective, employees maintaining the accounts receivable subsidiary ledger should not also approve

a. Employee overtime wages.

b. Credit granted to customers.

c. Write-offs of customer accounts.

d. Cash disbursements.

2,7 >   **8-21**   An auditor selects a sample from the file of shipping documents to determine whether invoices were prepared. This test is performed to satisfy the audit objective of

a. Accuracy.

b. Completeness.

c. Control.

d. Existence.

2,7 >   **8-22**   Which of the following controls is most likely to help ensure that all credit sales transactions of an entity are recorded?

a. The billing department supervisor sends a copy of each approved sales order to the credit department for comparison to the customer's authorized credit limit and current account balance.

b. The accounting department supervisor independently reconciles the accounts receivable subsidiary ledger to the accounts receivable control account each month.

c. The accounting department supervisor controls the mailing of monthly statements to customers and investigates any differences reported by customers.

d. The billing department supervisor matches prenumbered shipping documents with entries in the sales journal.

2,5,7,9 >   **8-23**   During a review of a small business client's internal control system, the auditor discovered that the accounts receivable clerk approves credit memos and has access to cash. Which of the following controls would be most effective in offsetting this weakness?

a. The owner reviews errors in billings to customers and postings to the subsidiary ledger.

b. The controller receives the monthly bank statement directly and reconciles the chequing accounts.

c. The owner reviews credit memos after they are recorded.

d. The controller reconciles the total of the detailed accounts receivable accounts to the amount shown in the ledger.

2,5,7 >   **8-24**   Cash receipts from sales on account have been misappropriated. Which of the following acts would conceal this defalcation and be least likely to be detected by an auditor?

a. Understating the sales journal.

b. Overstating the accounts receivable control account.

c. Overstating the accounts receivable subsidiary ledger.

d. Understating the cash receipts journal.

2,5,7>   **8-25**   An auditor would consider a cashier's job description to contain compatible duties if the cashier receives remittances from the mailroom and also prepares

a. The prelisting of individual cheques.

b. The monthly bank reconciliation.

c. The daily deposit slip.

d. Remittance advices.

2,5,7>   **8-26**   Which of the following internal controls would be most likely to deter the lapping of collections from customers?

a. Independent internal verification of dates of entry in the cash receipts journal with dates of daily cash summaries.

b. Authorization of write-offs of uncollectible accounts by a supervisor independent of the credit approval function.

c. Segregation of duties between receiving cash and posting the accounts receivable ledger.

d. Supervisory comparison of the daily cash summary with the sum of the cash receipts journal entries.

7>   **8-27**   Smith Corporation has numerous customers. Customer files are kept on disk. Each customer file contains a name, an address, a credit limit, and an account balance. The auditor wishes to test this file to determine whether credit limits are being exceeded. The best procedure for the auditor to follow would be to

a. Develop test data that would cause some account balances to exceed the credit limit and determine if the system properly detects such situations.

b. Develop a program to compare credit limits with account balances and print out the details of any account with a balance exceeding its credit limit.

c. Request a printout of all account balances so that they can be manually checked against the credit limits.

d. Request a printout of a sample of account balances so that they can be individually checked against the respective credit limits.

9>   **8-28**   Which of the following is most likely to be detected by an auditor's review of a client's sales cutoff?

a. Unrecorded sales for the year.

b. Lapping of year-end accounts receivable.

c. Excessive sales discounts.

d. Unauthorized goods returned for credit.

9,10>   **8-29**   The negative request form of accounts receivable confirmation is useful particularly when

	The Assessed Level of Control Risk Relating to Receivables Is	The Number of Small Balances Is	Consideration by the Recipient Is
a.	Low	High	Likely
b.	Low	Low	Unlikely
c.	High	Low	Likely
d.	High	High	Likely

9,10 ▷ **8-30** Negative confirmation of accounts receivable is less effective than positive confirmation of accounts receivable because

a. A majority of recipients usually lack the willingness to respond objectively.

b. Some recipients may report incorrect balances that require extensive follow up.

c. The auditor cannot infer that all nonrespondents have verified their account information.

d. Negative confirmations do not produce evidential matter that is statistically quantifiable.

9,10 ▷ **8-31** An auditor should perform alternative procedures to substantiate the existence of accounts receivable when

a. No reply to a positive confirmation request is received.

b. No reply to a negative confirmation request is received.

c. The collectibility of the receivables is in doubt.

d. Pledging of the receivables is probable.

9,11 ▷ **8-32** An auditor's purpose in reviewing credit ratings of customers with delinquent accounts receivable is most likely to obtain evidence concerning management's assertions about

a. Presentation and disclosure.

b. Existence or occurrence.

c. Rights and obligations.

d. Valuation or allocation

9,11 ▷ **8-33** In evaluating the adequacy of the allowance for doubtful accounts, an auditor most likely reviews the entity's aging of receivables to support management's financial statement assertion of

a. Existence or occurrence.

b. Valuation or allocation.

c. Completeness.

d. Rights and obligations.

PROBLEMS

1 ▷ **8-34** For each of the following situations indicate how and/or when the client should recognize the revenue. Justify your decision. You may wish to refer to *CICA Handbook* section 3400.

1. Your client, Thomson Telecom, maintains an inventory of telecommunications equipment. Bayone Telephone Company placed an order for 10 new transformers valued at $5 million and Thomson delivered them just prior to December 31. Thompson's normal business practice for this class of customer is to enter into a written sales agreement that requires the signatures of all the authorized representatives of Thomson and its customer before the contract is binding. However, Bayone has not signed the sales agreement because it is awaiting the requisite approval by the legal department. Bayone's purchasing department has orally agreed to the contract and the purchasing manager has assured you that the contract will be approved the first week of next year.

2. Best Products is a retailer of appliances that offers "layaway" sales to its customers twice a year. Best retains the merchandise, sets it aside in its inventory, and collects a cash deposit from the customer. The customer signs an installment note at the time the initial deposit is received, but no payments are due until 30 days after delivery.

3. Dave's Discount Stores is a discount retailer who generates revenue from the sale of membership fees it charges customers to shop at its stores. The membership arrangement requires the customer to pay the entire membership fee (usually $48) at the beginning of the arrangement. However, the customer can unilaterally cancel the membership arrangement and receive a refund of the unused portion. Dave's estimates that 35 percent of the customers will cancel their memberships before the end of the contract.

3,4,5,7,9⟩   **8-35**   Jim Boxer Ltd. (Boxer) is a private company, specializing in distributing high quality silk boxer shorts. You are the new senior on the Boxer audit. You are completing the interim audit and have made some system notes and observations (Exhibit 1).

You have come to know Boxer's staff very well over the past two weeks and the marketing assistant quietly mentions that you and your staff may want to attend the employee warehouse sale on Friday. The sale is on a cash only basis and the marketing assistant collects the cash in a cash box and prepares the deposit slip at the end of the sales that occur every month. The marketing assistant prepares the journal entry to record these sales. The controller does not review this entry.

You have scheduled a follow up meeting with the controller for Friday morning to discuss your notes and observations.

Required:

For each system weakness: describe the weakness identified, the corrective action(s) Boxer could take, and the specific year-end audit procedure(s) you would perform as a result of each weakness.

(ICABC, adapted)

EXHIBIT 1	**System Notes and Observations November 2006**

The receivables collection manager is very busy collecting accounts from many small boutiques. No procedures exist to evaluate and monitor credit risk. The collection manager writes off bad accounts. The collection manager approves the limits once a year. Due to staff turnover the collection manager also opens all mail and distributes it to the appropriate department. Cheques received in the mail are then given to the accounts receivable clerk.

Uncollectible accounts are higher this year. The collection manager indicates the higher write off is a result of the poor economy and slowing interest in boxer shorts. The accounts receivable clerk processes payments and in order to reduce the collection manager's workload, processes adjustments less than $100 to the general ledger. The accounts receivable clerk posts miscellaneous cash collections to the general ledger.

In order to reduce waste and paper flow, Boxer has an invoiceless system. The phone orders are recorded directly into the system based on the perpetual inventory levels. A numbered packing slip is produced and printed in the warehouse. The slip is used to select items from the shelves to fill the order. The only copy is given to the customer. The customer is not required to sign for the goods since they are the ones ordering the goods by phone. If customers return goods, they are returned to the warehouse where they are put aside for the employee warehouse sale. Adjustments to customer accounts are initiated by the customer through payment on accounts.

2,5,7 > **8-36** The flowchart below depicts activities relating to the sales, shipping, billing, and collection processes used by Newton Hardware, Inc.

Required:

Identify the weaknesses in internal control relating to the activities of (a) the warehouse clerk, (b) bookkeeper A, and (c) the collections clerk. Do not identify weaknesses relating to the sales clerk or

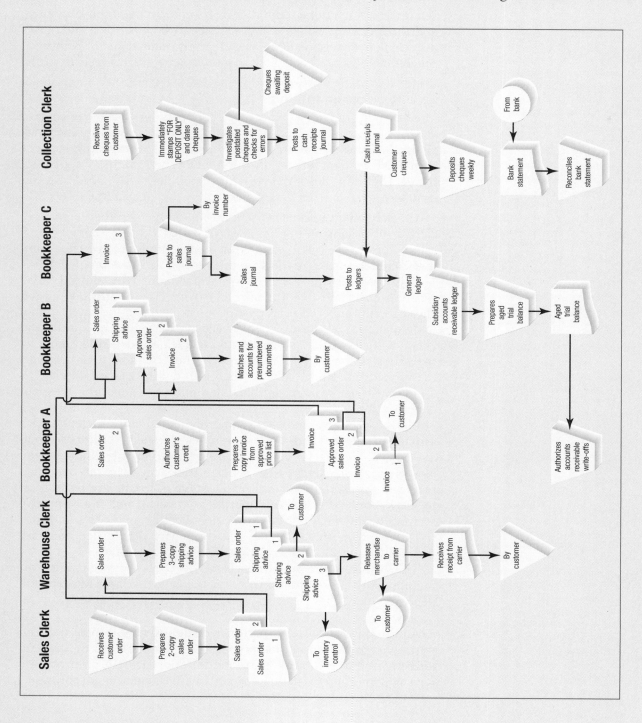

bookkeepers B and C. Do not discuss recommendations concerning the correction of these weaknesses.

(AICPA, adapted)

2,4,5,6,7,10 >   **8-37**   The audit working papers include the following narrative description of the cash receipts and billing portions of internal control of Parktown Veterinary Clinic Ltd. Parktown is a large veterinary clinic that is owned by a publicly held corporation. It employs seven salaried veterinarians, ten nurses, three support staff in a common laboratory, and three clerical workers. The clerical workers perform such tasks as reception, correspondence, cash receipts, billing, and appointment scheduling and are adequately bonded. They are referred to in the narrative as "office manager," "clerk 1," and "clerk 2."

Cash Receipts and Billing

Most owners pay for services for their pets by cash or cheque at the time services are rendered. Credit is not approved by the clerical staff. The veterinarian who is to perform the respective services approves credit based on an interview. When credit is approved, the veterinarian files a memo with the billing clerk (clerk 2) to set up the receivable from data generated by the veterinarian.

The servicing veterinarian prepares a charge slip that is given to clerk 1 for pricing and preparation of the client's bill. Clerk 1 transmits a copy of the bill to clerk 2 for preparation of the revenue summary and for posting in the accounts receivable subsidiary ledger.

The cash receipts functions are performed by clerk 1, who receives cash and cheques directly from clients and gives each client a prenumbered cash receipt. Clerk 1 opens the mail, immediately stamps all cheques "FOR DEPOSIT ONLY," and lists cash and cheques for deposit. The cash and cheques are deposited daily by the office manager. The list of cash and cheques, together with the related remittance advices, is forwarded by clerk 1 to clerk 2. Clerk 1 also serves as receptionist and performs general correspondence duties.

Clerk 2 prepares and sends monthly statements to clients with unpaid balances. Clerk 2 also prepares the cash receipts journal and is responsible for the accounts receivable subsidiary ledger. No other clerical employee is permitted access to the accounts receivable subsidiary ledger. Uncollectible accounts are written off by clerk 2 only after the veterinarian who performed the respective services believes the account to be uncollectible and communicates the write-off approval to the office manager. The office manager then issues a write-off memo that clerk 2 processes.

The office manager supervises the clerks, issues write-off memos, schedules appointments for the veterinarians, makes bank deposits, reconciles bank statements, and performs general correspondence duties.

Additional services are performed monthly by a local accountant, who posts summaries prepared by the clerks to the general ledger, prepares income statements, and files the appropriate payroll forms and tax returns directly with the parent corporation.

Required:

a. Prepare a flowchart of Parktown Veterinary Clinic's cash receipts and billing internal control system.

b. Based only on the information in the narrative, describe at least one resulting misstatement that could occur and not be prevented or detected by Parktown's internal control system concerning the cash receipts and billing function. Do *not* describe how to correct the potential misstatement.

(AICPA, adapted)

2,5,7,10 > **8-38** The Art Appreciation Society operates a museum for the benefit and enjoyment of the community. During the hours the museum is open to the public, two clerks who are positioned at the entrance collect a five dollar admission fee from each nonmember patron. Members of the Art Appreciation Society are permitted to enter free of charge upon presentation of their membership cards.

At the end of each day one of the clerks delivers the proceeds to the treasurer. The treasurer counts the cash in the presence of the clerk and places it in a safe. Each Friday afternoon the treasurer and one of the clerks deliver all cash held in the safe to the bank and receive an authenticated deposit slip, which provides the basis for the weekly entry in the cash receipts journal.

The board of directors of the Art Appreciation Society has identified a need to improve the internal control system over cash admission fees. The board has determined that the cost of installing turnstiles or sales booths or otherwise altering the physical layout of the museum would greatly exceed any benefits that might be derived. However, the board has agreed that the sale of admission tickets must be an integral part of its improvement efforts.

Smith has been asked by the board of directors of the Art Appreciation Society to review the internal control over cash admission fees and suggest improvements.

Required:

Indicate weaknesses in the existing internal control system over cash admission fees, which Smith should identify, and recommend one improvement for each of the weaknesses identified. Organize your answer as indicated in the following example:

Weakness	Recommendation
1. There is no basis for establishing the documentation of the number of paying patrons.	1. Prenumbered admission tickets should be issued upon payment of the admission fee.

(AICPA, adapted)

3,4,5,6,7,10 > **8-39** You have been approached by the president of the Helping Elderly Low Income People Foundation (HELP), a registered charity, to assist on a special project to set up their accounting system. HELP is a relatively new organization, established on January 1, 2007.

The government at both the federal and provincial levels regulates HELP. The foundation is required to maintain current financial records to withstand public scrutiny. HELP's records must be available to anyone who is interested in reviewing them. It must spend 75 percent of all revenues on charitable causes. It is now June 1, 2007 and HELP has come to you with a shoebox of receipts and bank statements. You notice that the bank statements are in the envelopes from the bank, and have not been opened.

Revenue primarily comes from donations. A van driver takes volunteers around the city. Volunteers canvas door to door, and must hand out a donation receipt for donations over $10. Since volunteering takes a considerable amount of time, the charity has had a lot of short-term volunteers. Anyone is welcome to be a volunteer.

Fortunately for HELP, two car companies generously donated mini vans to the organization. The van drivers are paid $10 a day, which they take from the donations. Drivers keep a summary of the total donations collected by the volunteers, and at the end of the day take the money to a bank drop box to deposit. Drivers also pay for their gas out of the donated funds.

HELP also held a fundraising dance last month. The president said he was disappointed with the project, as it did not bring in much money. However, it did raise public awareness. To keep costs down, the president made the dance tickets by photocopying tickets and cutting them up. He gave them out to volunteers to sell for $25 each. He figures he printed 500 tickets, but can only account for about $3,000 of revenues turned in by his volunteers.

When you asked what charitable work had been done to date, the president replied that so far they had purchased some food and clothing for needy families for about $5,000. The other expenses incurred related to administering the charity, including the $1,000 per month salary that he is currently drawing.

Required:

a. List the internal control weaknesses in the revenue/receivables/receipts transaction cycle, and describe the impact of each weakness. For each weakness, recommend an improvement to the systems and controls.

b. The president wants to know if there are any reasons you could not provide a letter to the government stating that they are meeting the 75 percent spending requirement. Discuss the president's request.

c. The partner has asked you to briefly summarize the audit risk associated with this job.

(ICABC, adapted)

9,10   **8-40**   Adam Tamura was auditing Defense Industries, Ltd. Tamura sent positive accounts receivable confirmations to a number of Defense's government customers. He received a number of returned confirmations marked "We do not confirm balances because we are on a voucher system."

Required:

List three audit procedures that Tamura might use to ensure the validity of these accounts.

9> **8-41**   You are the senior on the audit of Great Eastern Hotels (GEH). This two star hotel is located in a major coastal city and as such is prone to seasonal fluctuations. The 200 room hotel is open all year round with a standard room rate of $90 per night. The client charges $95 per room in the summer and $85 per room in the winter, the same as the prior year. The hotel includes a bar and restaurant as well as underground parking. From the audit work performed to date, you are satisfied that analytical procedures will give you sufficient audit coverage over the income statement accounts (Exhibit 1). You have also researched some industry information shown below GEH's income statement.

EXHIBIT 1

Great Eastern Hotels Statement of Income for the Year Ended December 31

	2007	2006
Revenue:		
Hotel Room Rental	$5,235,617	$5,165,176
Food and Beverage	1,497,612	1,488,619
Parking, Telephone, and Other	417,602	396,158
Interest	56,711	58,610
	$7,207,542	$7,108,563
Expenses:		
Direct Costs:		
Hotel Room Rental	3,165,992	3,105,644
Food and Beverage	1,388,691	1,452,107
Other	389,917	365,223
	$4,944,600	$4,922,974
Gross Margin	$2,262,942	$2,185,589
General and Administration	1,617,532	1,574,805
Advertising and Promotion	364,817	349,576
Other	216,911	166,978
	$2,199,260	$2,091,359
Net Income Before Tax	$ 63,682	$ 94,230
Income Tax Expense	26,754	40,519
Net Income	$ 36,928	$ 53,711

SUPPLEMENTARY INFORMATION

2007 Quarterly Revenue ($000s)

	Q1	Q2	Q3	Q4
Hotel Room Rental	1,193	1,245	1,471	1,327

Industry Statistics

2007 Hotel Occupancy Rates:

	Q1 Summer	Q2 Fall	Q3 Winter	Q4 Spring
First Class	77%	75%	86%	71%
Two Star	76%	70%	84%	71%
Third Rate	69%	74%	78%	60%

Required:

a. Identify analytical review procedures that could be performed on the income statement of Great Eastern.

b. Analyze and provide your conclusion on GEH's 2007 hotel room rental revenue.

(ICABC, adapted)

9,11 ▷   8-42   During the year Strang Corporation began to encounter cash flow difficulties, and a cursory review by management revealed receivable collection problems. Strang's management engaged Stanley Lee, to perform a special investigation. Lee studied the billing and collection process and noted the following:

- The accounting department employs one bookkeeper, who receives and opens all incoming mail. This bookkeeper is also responsible for depositing receipts, filing remittance advices on a daily basis, recording receipts in the cash receipts journal, and posting receipts in the individual customer accounts and the general ledger accounts. There are no cash sales. The bookkeeper prepares and controls the mailing of monthly statements to customers.

- The concentration of functions and the receivable collection problems caused Lee to suspect that a systematic defalcation of customers' payments through a delayed posting of remittances (lapping of accounts receivable) is present. Lee was surprised to find that no customers complained about receiving erroneous monthly statements.

Required:

Identify the procedures Lee should perform to determine whether lapping exists. *Do not discuss deficiencies in the internal control system.*

(AICPA, adapted)

11> **8-43** Friendly Furniture, Inc., a manufacturer of fine hardwood furniture, is a publicly held OSC registered company with a December 31 year-end. During May, Friendly had a flood due to heavy rains at its major manufacturing facility that damaged about $525,000 of furniture. Friendly is insured for the property loss at replacement value and carries business interruption insurance for lost production. The company anticipates that the total insurance proceeds will exceed the carrying value of the destroyed furniture and the cost of repairing the facility will be in the range of $700,000 to $1.75 million. The company believes that the insurance carrier will advance approximately 50 percent of the expected proceeds sometime during July. The company has resumed its operations to about one-half of normal capacity and expects to operate at full capacity by September. The company does not expect to file a formal insurance claim until then, because it expects that the entire cost of the business interruption will not be known until September. Friendly expects to receive the proceeds of the settlement from the insurance carrier during its fourth quarter.

The company is in the process of making a stock offering and will file a registration statement with the OSC at the end of July, in which it will present stub period financial statements covering the six-month period through June 30. Based on the minimum amount of the expected proceeds, Friendly would like to recognize a receivable for the insurance proceeds and to report a gain in its financial statements for the period ended June 30. The company would also like to allocate a portion of the expected proceeds to cost of products sold.

Required:

a. How much of the expected proceeds from insurance coverage, if any, should Friendly include in its June 30 financial statements?

b. Assuming that Friendly records a receivable from the insurance company at June 30 for the proceeds, what type of audit evidence would the auditor gather to support the amount recorded?

9,10> **8-44** Assertions are expressed or implied representations by management that are reflected in the financial statement components. The auditor performs audit procedures to gather evidence to test those assertions.

Required:

Your client is All's Fair Appliance Company, an appliance wholesaler. Select the most appropriate audit procedure from the following list and enter the number in the appropriate place on the grid on the next page. (An audit procedure may be selected once, more than once, or not at all.)

Audit Procedure:

1. Review of bank confirmations and loan agreements.
2. Review of drafts of the financial statements.

3. Selection of a sample of revenue transactions and determination that they have been included in the sales journal and accounts receivable subsidiary ledger.
4. Selection of a sample of shipping documents for a few days before and after year-end.
5. Confirmation of accounts receivable.
6. Review of aging of accounts receivable with the credit manager.

Specific Audit Objective	Audit procedure

a. Ensure that the entity has legal title to accounts receivable (rights and obligations).
b. Confirm that recorded accounts receivable include all amounts owed to the client (completeness).
c. Verify that all accounts receivable are recorded in the correct period (cutoff).
d. Confirm that the allowance for uncollectible accounts is properly stated (valuation and allocation).
e. Confirm that recorded accounts receivable are valid (existence).

9,11⟩   8-45   You are engaged to audit the Ferrick Corporation for the year-ended January 31, 2007. Only merchandise shipped by the Ferrick Corporation to customers up to and including January 30, 2007, has been eliminated from inventory. The inventory as determined by physical inventory count has been recorded on the books by the company's controller. No perpetual inventory records are maintained. All sales are made on an FOB–shipping point basis. You are to assume that all purchase invoices have been correctly recorded.

The following lists of sales invoices are entered in the sales journal for the months of January 2007 and February 2007, respectively.

	Sales Invoice Amount	Sales Invoice Date	Cost of Merchandise Sold	Date Shipped
			January 2007	
a.	$ 3,000	Jan. 21	$2,000	Jan. 31
b.	2,000	Jan. 31	800	Dec. 13
c.	1,000	Jan. 29	600	Jan. 30
d.	4,000	Jan. 31	2,400	Feb. 3
e.	10,000	Jan. 30	5,600	Jan. 29*
			February 2007	
f.	$ 6,000	Jan. 31	$4,000	Jan. 30
g.	4,000	Feb. 2	2,300	Feb. 2
h.	8,000	Feb. 3	5,500	Jan. 31

*Shipped to consignee

Required:

You are to ensure that there is proper cutoff of sales and inventory. If an item is not properly recorded, prepare the necessary adjusting entries.

DISCUSSION CASES

9,10〉 **8-46** In the past, the records to be evaluated in an audit have been printed reports, listings, documents, and written papers, all of which are visible output. However, in fully computerized systems that update transaction files daily, output and files are frequently in machine readable form such as cards, tapes, or disks. Thus, the auditor often has an opportunity to use the computer in performing an audit.

Required:

Discuss how the computer could aid the auditor in examining accounts receivable in such a fully computerized system.

(AICPA, adapted)

7〉 **8-47** Automotive Parts Incorporated (API) is a federally incorporated wholesaler and distributor of automotive parts. API has been in business since the early 1990s and believes that its "paperless" sales system, implemented at the beginning of its current fiscal year, will provide a competitive edge. The paperless sales system includes order entry, invoicing, receivables, and collection.

API operates its information system using microcomputer-based local area networks (LANs) at its head office and in each of its five branch offices across the country. Each branch office has its own warehouse. Exhibit 1 contains notes from an interview that you conducted in March 2006 with Jim Cook, the manager of the management information system (MIS), about the overview of the paperless sales system.

API's customers are able to connect directly with one of API's branch offices, look up product availability at any of API's warehouses, and place an order via the web.

EXHIBIT 1

API Corporation Overview of Paperless Sales System Environment
API's paperless system for order-entry/invoicing/receivables and collection functions as follows:
1. In API's organization, the manager of MIS reports to the manager of finance and administration. The manager of finance and administration as well as the managers of marketing and distribution and the general manager report directly to the president. There is one network supervisor at head office and one at each branch. They report to the manager of MIS. Each of these individuals has been with API since well before the decision to implement the paperless system. They are highly trained specialists in the operating system, communications and network software purchased and used by API. In addition, they have been thoroughly trained in the use of the application software packages purchased by API.

(continued)

EXHIBIT 1

API Corporation Overview of Paperless Sales System Environment
(continued)

2. A customer who wants to establish an account dials into the head office LAN (a toll-free number), using any microcomputer communications software package, and completes an on-screen credit application. Besides the standard information normally associated with a credit application, the applicant must provide a valid credit card number or bank account number that will be charged for all purchases, as well as the telephone number from which all electronic orders will be placed. The applicant's credit status is verified electronically with a credit rating agency, and the API credit manager approves the applicant as a customer within two business days. One of two credit clerks then telephones the customer at the number supplied and provides the customer with a branch specific user identification code (UID) and a password that the user must change when he or she first dials in. The diskette containing API's order-entry and communication software is subsequently sent to the customer, who is then able to place orders by dialling up the branch office to which he or she has been pre-assigned.

3. Using a microcomputer and API's order-entry software, a customer dials up the pre-assigned API branch office and identifies himself or herself using the assigned UID and the chosen password. The customer must then hang up and wait for API's system to call back. A reconnection is established within two minutes, and the customer looks up product availability at any of API's five warehouses and places an order. Orders are filled at the warehouse(s) specified by the customer. The warehouse ships the order to the customer's pre-assigned branch warehouse which arranges delivery to the customer. The orders are received by the customer within 72 hours, a guaranteed service level about which API boasts.

4. When a customer finishes placing an order, API's system dials up the previously identified bank or credit card network that will authorize the transfer of funds, to ensure that sufficient credit or cash on deposit is available. After the bank or credit card network has authorized the amount, the customer must enter his or her personal identification number (PIN) for the bank. Entry of the PIN signifies that the customer has approved the transaction. Next, the bank issues its own approval code and transmits the code to API. API records this code on an electronic order confirmation that has a unique order number, assigned sequentially by API's computer to every order placed within its system. The order confirmation and invoice are electronically transmitted to the customer. Funds are electronically transferred to API's bank account one week after an order has been placed, to allow customers to inspect goods before paying for them. The customers have the right to cancel the transfer of funds by informing the bank if the goods are not satisfactory.

5. Each branch has one microcomputer that is equipped with communications software and a modem. During the day, the microcomputer processes transactions in "memo mode" only. "Memo mode" means that the branch's own inventory data base is updated instantly but that the transactions are not yet processed or transferred to the master file. Branches can update the inventory levels at their location only. Orders placed at other branches are not updated until the next morning.

6. Each evening, the network supervisor at each branch performs an end-of-day routine that identifies every transaction processed that day. The routine writes these transactions to an overnight transfer file. The routine ends with activating the communications software, which waits for a phone call from the LAN at head office. The communications software at head office dials up each branch, and the overnight transfer files are retrieved over the communication lines. Head office performs the real processing overnight. After all branches have been successfully polled and the processing at head office is completed (i.e., all files are updated), the head office LAN again dials up each branch. The LAN then transfers a complete copy of all updated computerized data files so that each branch has current customer, item number, order information, and inventory levels at all branches.

7. Three types of packing slips are printed every morning from the updated file. For example, the three types of packing slips printed at branch A would be: sales to branch A's pre-assigned customers filled by branch A's warehouse; sales to other branches' pre-assigned customers

EXHIBIT 1

API Corporation Overview of Paperless Sales System Environment *(concluded)*

filled by branch A's warehouse; sales to branch A's pre-assigned customers filled by other warehouses. Using hand-held computers, the shipping clerks scan the bar-coded shelf labels and enter the quantity they ship using the numeric keys. Every day the hand-held units are placed in a cradle that electronically retrieves the shipping information and compares it to the order. A daily exception report file is created for follow-up that can be accessed by warehouse personnel. Customer accounts are credited for any shortages, and overages are charged if the dollar amount is material. Otherwise, overages are written off as part of API's policy to place the customer first.

8. Head office administers all master file updates (e.g., customer and inventory item additions, modifications and deletions). The software at each branch has the same internal control features built in as the head office software. Only the head office network supervisor has access to the master files. He serves as the security administrator for the LANs at all locations.

9. Each branch is equipped with a high-capacity tape system that backs up the files every night. The software allows an automatic backup to be performed at a pre-determined time.

You are responsible for the audit of API, which your firm has audited since its inception. The partner in charge warns you to prepare an audit planning memo for the paperless sales system. Your memo should include a description of both the controls on which you intend to rely and your approach to testing them. For any concerns noted with the system, prepare a draft report addressing recommendations for improvement to be presented to the client. Your firm has not been involved in the development of the paperless sales system.

Required:

Prepare the memo and the draft report.

(CICA, adapted)

10> **8-48** You are in charge of the Accounts Receivable Section of Harken Ltd. for this year's audit (fiscal year-ending December 31, 2006). You sent out accounts receivable confirmation requests early in 2007 to confirm the client's year-end balances in the accounts receivable subledger (total value of accounts receivable $1,121,000, total number of accounts—246). Eighty of these accounts, with a total value of $744,000, were selected for confirmation. It is now March 16, 2007 and you are reviewing the responses to the confirmation requests. Of the confirmation requests, 22 were not returned, 32 were returned signed without comment, 16 had minor differences that have been reconciled or otherwise cleared satisfactorily, and the remaining 10 were returned with various comments, shown below:

1. We are sorry but we cannot respond to your request for confirmation of our accounts payable balance at December 31, 2006 as we use an accounts payable voucher system.

2. The balance of $1,100 was paid on December 23, 2006.

3. The balance of $8,800 was paid on January 5, 2007.

4. We do not owe anything at December 31, 2006 as the goods identified in the invoice #34587 of December 30, 2006 in the amount of $12,480, were received on January 4, 2007 on FOB destination terms.

5. We made an advance payment of $3,000 on November 22, 2006, which should cover the two invoices totalling $1,500 each on the statement attached.

6. We have not received these goods.

7. We are contesting the propriety of this amount of $13,450; we believe the charge to be excessive.

8. The balance on the statement attached has been paid.

9. The amount is correct. Since the goods were shipped to us on consignment, we will remit payment upon sale of the goods.

10. Your credit of $560 dated December 15, 2005 cancels the above balance.

Required:

Explain the steps you would take in each case to satisfactorily clear each of the above 10 comments.

(AICPA, adapted)

INTERNET ASSIGNMENTS

8-49 Visit the website of a catalogue retailer similar to EarthWear Clothiers and determine how it processes sales transactions, recognizes revenue, and reserves for returns.

8-50 Visit the OSC or SEC website (www.osc.gov.on.ca or www.sec.gov respectively) and identify a company that has been recently cited for revenue recognition problems. Prepare a memo summarizing the revenue recognition issues for the company.

Auditing the Purchasing Process

Chapter **9**

Learning Objectives

Upon completion of this chapter, you will be able to

1 Explain the relationship between an entity's expense and liability recognition policies and the way in which they are accounted for in the financial statements.

2 Develop an understanding of the purchasing process.

3 Identify the types of transactions in the purchasing process and the financial statement accounts affected.

4 Describe the functions in the purchasing process and the related types of documents and records used.

5 Determine the appropriate segregation of duties for the purchasing process.

6 Identify and evaluate inherent risks relevant to the purchasing process and related accounts.

7 Identify key controls for the purchasing process, develop appropriate tests of controls, for purchasing, cash disbursements and purchase returns and allowances transactions.

8 Explain how the assessment of control risk relates to substantive testing.

9 Apply substantive testing procedures to the transactions and accounts in the purchasing process.

10 Describe how confirmations are used to obtain evidence about accounts payable.

11 Evaluate the audit findings and reach a final conclusion on accounts payable and accrued expenses.

RELEVANT ACCOUNTING AND ASSURANCE PRONOUNCEMENTS

CICA Handbook, **section 1000,** Financial statement concepts

CICA Handbook, **section 5095,** Reasonable assurance and audit risk

CICA Handbook, **section 5141,** Understanding the entity and its environment and assessing the risks of material misstatement

CICA Handbook, **section 5142,** Materiality

CICA Handbook, **section 5143,** The auditor's procedures in response to assessed risks
CICA Handbook, **section 5300,** Audit evidence
CICA Handbook, **section 5301,** Analysis

CICA Handbook, **section 5303,** Confirmation
CICA Handbook, **section 5305,** Audit of accounting estimates
CICA Handbook, **section 6010,** Audit of related party transactions

This chapter begins by reviewing expense and liability recognition concepts with particular emphasis on the categories of expenses. The framework developed in Chapter 8 on the revenue process is used to present the auditor's consideration of internal control. This framework starts with an overview of the purchasing process, including the types of transactions, the documents and records involved, and the functions included in the process. Inherent risk factors that relate directly to the purchasing process are covered next. Assessment of control risk is then presented, followed by a discussion of control procedures and tests of controls. The last sections of the chapter cover the audit of accounts payable and accrued expenses, the major liability accounts affected by the process. Auditing the expense accounts affected by the purchasing process is covered in Chapter 13.

AUDITING EARTHWEAR'S PURCHASING PROCESS

EarthWear's purchasing process is "the other side of the coin" from the revenue process. In order to support its revenue process, EarthWear must have merchandise to sell. As is the case with most of its competitors, EarthWear purchases almost all of its merchandise for resale. It has a large number of suppliers and a large number of transactions in this process. Willis & Adams needs to gain assurance that the information in EarthWear's financial statements correctly represents the economic reality of its purchases and cash disbursements transactions with its many suppliers.

Willis & Adams will collect audit evidence to confirm or refute the explicit and implicit management assertions about those transactions, such as occurrence, completeness, and so on. Because EarthWear has hundreds of thousands of transactions in a year, in obtaining this assurance they will rely heavily on EarthWear's controls over the purchasing process. Therefore they will spend a significant amount of audit effort understanding and testing those controls. The results of the tests of controls will affect the nature, timing, and extent of subsequent audit procedures.

Willis and Adams will also collect audit evidence to support or refute the explicit and implicit management assertions, such as existence, and rights and obligations, about the accounts and balances affected by those transactions. The primary account affected is accounts payable and as well as understanding and testing EarthWear's controls related to accounts payable, Willis & Adams will also employ substantive tests in testing this account. Because purchases is an expense (i.e., it becomes the cost of goods sold) and accounts payable is a liability, the auditors' concern is normally with possible understatement rather than with overstatement as was the case with revenues and accounts receivable.

Expense and Liability Recognition

LO 1> Many transactions processed through a typical purchasing process involve the recognition of an expense and its corresponding liability. As a result, the auditor should understand the basic underlying concepts of expense and liability recognition in order to audit the purchasing process. The *CICA Handbook* does not have a section for expenses analogous to section 3400 for revenues. However, *CICA Handbook*, section 1000, defines expenses and liabilities as follows:

> Expenses are decreases in economic resources, either by way of outflows or reductions of assets or incurrences of liabilities, resulting from an entity's ordinary revenue generating or service delivery activities.
>
> Liabilities are obligations of an entity arising from past transactions or events, the settlement of which may result in the transfer or use of assets, provision of services, or other yielding of economic benefits in the future.

An entity's expense recognition policies and the type of expenses involved affect how the transactions are recorded and accounted for in the financial statements. Expenses can be classified into three categories.

1. Certain expenses can be matched directly with specific transactions or events and are recognized upon recognition of revenue. These types of expenses are referred to as *product costs* and include expenses such as cost of goods sold.
2. Many expenses are recognized during the period in which cash is spent or liabilities incurred for goods and services that are used up at that time or shortly thereafter. Such expenses cannot be directly related to specific transactions and are assumed to provide no future benefit. These expenses are referred to as *period costs*. Examples of such expenses include administrative salaries and rent expense.
3. Some expenses are allocated by systematic and rational procedures to the periods during which the related assets are expected to provide benefits. Amortization of plant and equipment is an example of such an expense.

In general, the liabilities normally incurred as part of the purchasing cycle are trade accounts payable. Other incurred expenses are accrued as liabilities at the end of each accounting period. Most expenses recognized are product or period costs.

Overview of the Purchasing Process

LO 2> A purchase transaction usually begins with a purchase requisition being generated by a department or support function. The purchasing department prepares a purchase order for the purchase of goods or services from a vendor. When the goods are received or the services have been rendered, the entity records a liability to the vendor. Finally, the entity pays the vendor. Exhibit 9–1 describes EarthWear's purchasing system.

EarthWear Figure 9–1 presents the flowchart for EarthWear's purchasing system, which serves as a framework for discussing control procedures and tests of controls. As mentioned previously, accounting processes are tailored to meet the specific needs of the client.

EXHIBIT 9–1

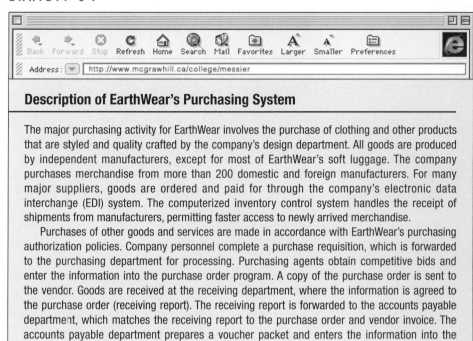

Address: http://www.mcgrawhill.ca/college/messier

Description of EarthWear's Purchasing System

The major purchasing activity for EarthWear involves the purchase of clothing and other products that are styled and quality crafted by the company's design department. All goods are produced by independent manufacturers, except for most of EarthWear's soft luggage. The company purchases merchandise from more than 200 domestic and foreign manufacturers. For many major suppliers, goods are ordered and paid for through the company's electronic data interchange (EDI) system. The computerized inventory control system handles the receipt of shipments from manufacturers, permitting faster access to newly arrived merchandise.

Purchases of other goods and services are made in accordance with EarthWear's purchasing authorization policies. Company personnel complete a purchase requisition, which is forwarded to the purchasing department for processing. Purchasing agents obtain competitive bids and enter the information into the purchase order program. A copy of the purchase order is sent to the vendor. Goods are received at the receiving department, where the information is agreed to the purchase order (receiving report). The receiving report is forwarded to the accounts payable department, which matches the receiving report to the purchase order and vendor invoice. The accounts payable department prepares a voucher packet and enters the information into the accounts payable program.

When payment is due on a vendor invoice, the accounts payable program generates a cash disbursement report that is reviewed by the accounts payable department. Items approved for payment are entered into the cash disbursement program, and a cheque is printed. The cheques are sent to the cashier's department for mailing. Final approval for electronic funds transfer for EDI transactions is made by the accounts payable department.

You should focus on the basic concepts to apply them to the specific purchasing processes encountered. The following topics related to the purchasing process are covered:

- types of transactions and financial statement accounts affected
- types of documents and records
- major functions
- segregation of duties

Types of Transactions and Financial Statement Accounts Affected

LO 3

Three types of transactions are processed through the purchasing process:

- purchase of goods and services for cash or credit
- payment of the liabilities arising from such purchases
- return of goods to suppliers for cash or credit

The first type is a purchase transaction that includes acquiring goods and services. The second type is a cash disbursement transaction that involves paying the liabilities that result from purchasing goods and services. The final type is a purchase return transaction, in which goods previously purchased are returned to a supplier for cash or credit.

FIGURE 9–1

Flowchart of the Purchasing Process—EarthWear Clothiers, Inc.

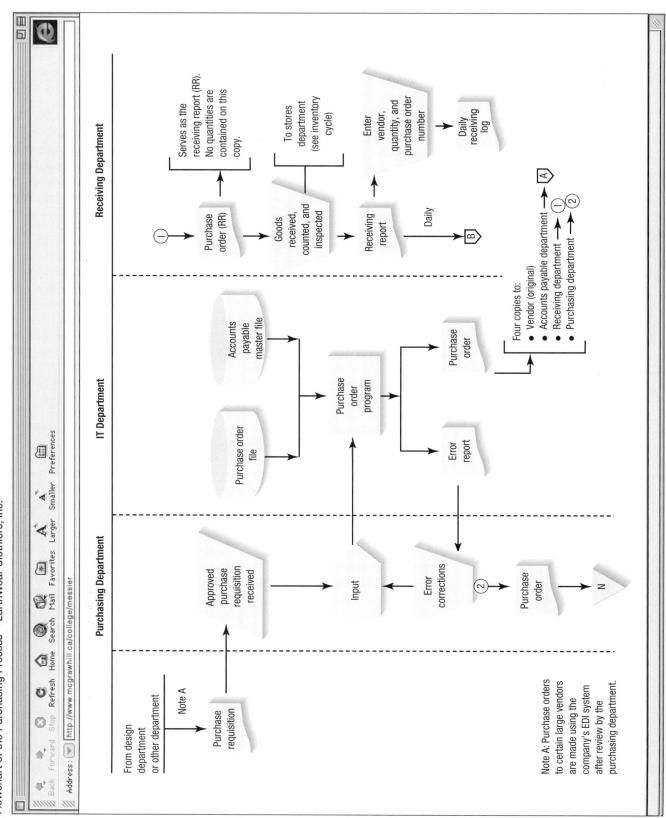

F I G U R E   9–1

Flowchart of the Purchasing Process—EarthWear Clothiers, Inc. (concluded)

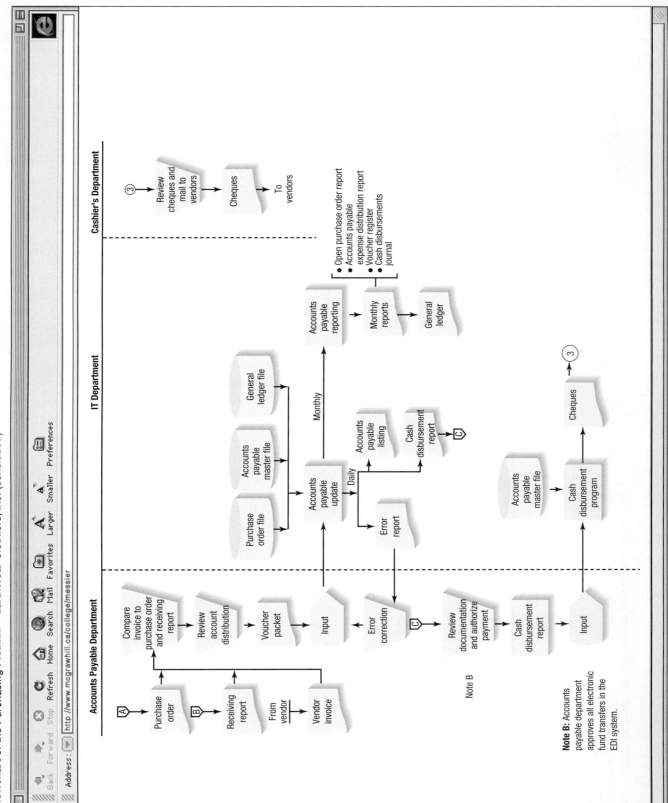

The purchasing process affects many accounts in the financial statements. The more common accounts affected by each type of transaction are

Type of Transaction	Account Affected
Purchase transaction	Accounts payable
	Inventory
	Purchases or cost of goods sold
	Various asset and expense accounts
Cash disbursement transaction	Cash
	Accounts payable
	Cash discounts
	Various asset and expense accounts
Purchase return transaction	Purchase returns
	Purchase allowances
	Accounts payable
	Various asset and expense accounts

The Major Functions, Documents, and Records

LO 4

The principal business objectives of the purchasing process are acquiring goods and services at the lowest cost consistent with quality and service requirements and effectively using cash resources to pay for those goods and services. The purchasing process consists of numerous steps, from the recognition of the need for the product to the final disposition of the economic effect of the transaction on the financial statements. Many of the steps or functions involve the creation of document. Each of the descriptions below briefly describes the function and, where applicable, the related document or documents created by that function. Table 9–1 lists the functions that are normally part of the purchasing process and Table 9–2 summarizes the documents and records in the purchasing process.

Requisitioning The initial function in the purchasing process is a request for goods or services by an authorized individual from any department or functional area within the entity (see Figure 9–1). The

Table 9–1	Functions of the Purchasing Process
• *Requisitioning*	Initiation and approval of requests for goods and services by authorized individuals consistent with management criteria.
• *Purchasing*	Approval of purchase orders and proper execution as to price, quantity, quality, and vendor.
• *Receiving*	Receipt of properly authorized goods or services.
• *Invoice processing*	Processing of vendor invoices for goods and services received; also, processing of adjustments for allowances, discounts, and returns.
• *Disbursements*	Processing of payment to vendors.
• *Accounts payable*	Recording of all vendor invoices, cash disbursements, and adjustments in individual vendor accounts.
• *General ledger*	Proper accumulation, classification, and summarization of purchases, cash disbursements, and payables in the general ledger.

Table 9–2	Documents and Records Involved in the Purchasing Process

- Purchase requisition.
- Purchase order.
- Receiving report.
- Vendor invoice.
- Voucher.
- Voucher register/purchases journal.
- Accounts payable subsidiary ledger.
- Vendor statement.
- Cheque.
- Cash disbursements journal/cheque register.

important issue is that the request meets the authorization procedures implemented by the entity. One frequent organizational control is the establishment of authorization dollar limits for different levels of employees and executives. For example, department supervisors may be authorized to acquire goods or services up to $1,000, department managers up to $5,000, and divisional heads up to $25,000, while any expenditure greater than $100,000 requires approval by the board of directors.

The document created by the requisition function is the *purchase requisition*. This document requests goods or services for an authorized individual or department within the entity. Examples of such requests include an order for supplies from an office supervisor and an order for newspaper advertising space from a marketing manager. In EarthWear's purchasing system, the design department would generate purchase requisitions to acquire goods for sale.

Purchasing   The purchasing function, triggered by the purchase requisition executes properly authorized purchase orders. This function is normally performed by a purchasing department (see Figure 9–1), which is headed by a purchasing manager (or agent) and has one or more buyers responsible for specific goods or services. The purchasing function ensures that goods and services are acquired in appropriate quantities and at the lowest price consistent with quality standards and delivery schedules. Using multiple vendors and requiring competitive bidding are two ways the purchasing function can achieve its objectives.

The *purchase order* includes the description, quality, and quantity of, and other information on, the goods or services being purchased. The purchase order also indicates who approved the acquisition and represents the authorization to purchase the goods or services. The purchase order may be mailed, faxed, or placed by telephone with the supplier or vendor. At EarthWear some purchase orders may be generated by the design department, reviewed by a purchasing agent, and then sent to a vendor using the company's EDI system.

Receiving   The receiving function is responsible for receiving, counting, and inspecting goods received from vendors. The personnel in the receiving department complete a receiving report that is forwarded to the accounts payable function.

The receipt of goods is recorded on the *receiving report*. Normally, the receiving report is a copy of the purchase order with the quantities omitted. This procedure requires receiving department personnel to make an independent count of the goods received. Receiving department personnel record the date, description, quantity, and other information on this document. In some instances, the quality of the goods is determined by receiving department personnel. In other cases, an inspection department determines whether the goods meet the required specifications. The receiving report is important because receiving goods is generally the event that leads to recognition of the liability by the entity.

Invoice Processing   The accounts payable department (see Figure 9–1) processes invoices from suppliers to ensure that all goods and services received are recorded as assets or expenses and that the corresponding liability is recognized. This function involves matching purchase orders to receiving reports and vendor invoices as to terms, quantities, prices, and extensions. The invoice-processing function also compares the account distributions with established account classifications.

The invoice-processing function is also responsible for purchased goods returned to vendors. Appropriate records and control procedures must document the return of the goods and initiate any charges back to the vendor.

The bill from the vendor is the *vendor invoice*. The vendor invoice includes the description and quantity of the goods shipped or services provided, the price including freight, the terms of trade including cash discounts, and the date billed.

Disbursements   The disbursement function is responsible for preparing and signing cheques for paying vendors. Adequate supporting documentation must verify that the disbursement is for a legitimate business purpose, that the transaction was properly authorized, and that the account distribution is appropriate. To reduce the possibility that the invoice will be paid twice, all documentation (such as, purchase order, receiving report, and vendor invoice) should be marked "CANCELLED" or "PAID" by the cashier's department. Finally, the cheques should be mailed to the vendor by the cashier's department or treasurer.

If IT is used to prepare cheques, adequate user controls must ensure that only authorized transactions are submitted for payment. Adequate control totals should also be used to agree the amount of payables submitted with the amount of cash disbursed. Cheques over a specified limit should be reviewed. For example, in EarthWear's system (see Figure 9–1), the accounts payable department matches the purchase order to the receiving report and the vendor's invoice. The voucher is then input into the accounts payable program. When the vouchers are due for payment, they are printed out on a cash disbursement report. Accounts payable personnel review the items to be paid and input them into the cash disbursement program. The cheques are forwarded to the cashier's department for review and mailing to vendors. If a signature plate is used for signing cheques, it must be properly controlled within the cashier's department or by the treasurer.

The document frequently used by entities to control payment for acquired goods and services is the *voucher*. This document serves as the basis for recording a vendor's invoice in the voucher register or purchases journal. In many purchasing systems, such as EarthWear's, the voucher is attached to the purchase requisition, purchase order, receiving report, and vendor invoice to create a *voucher packet*. The voucher packet thus contains all the relevant documentation supporting a purchase transaction.

A *voucher register* is used to record the vouchers for goods and services. The voucher register contains numerous columns for recording the account classifications for the goods or services, including a column for recording credits to accounts payable, and columns for recording debits to asset accounts such as inventory and expense accounts such as repairs and maintenance. The voucher register also contains columns for miscellaneous debits and credits. Some entities use a purchases journal instead of a voucher register. With a purchases journal, either vouchers or vendors' invoices may be used to record the liability. The major difference between a voucher register and a purchases journal is in the way individual vouchers or vendor invoices are summarized. When a voucher register is used, the details of accounts payable are normally represented by a list of unpaid vouchers. With a purchases journal, subsidiary records are normally maintained by the vendor in an *accounts payable subsidiary ledger* in much the same manner as an accounts receivable subsidiary ledger. However, with computerization of accounts payable records, such distinctions are disappearing. By assigning a vendor number to each voucher, the voucher register can be sorted by vendor to produce a subsidiary ledger for accounts payable.

The cheque, signed by an authorized individual, pays for goods or services. Again, in some advanced IT systems, goods and services may be paid for through electronic transfer of funds.

Disbursements made by cheque are recorded in the cash disbursements journal, sometimes referred to as a *cheque register*. The cash disbursements journal contains columns for recording credits to cash and debits to accounts payable and cash discounts. Columns may also record miscellaneous debits and credits. Payments recorded in the cash disbursements journal are also recorded in the voucher register or in the accounts payable subsidiary ledger, depending on which system is used by the entity.

Accounts Payable The accounts payable department (see Figure 9–1) is also responsible for ensuring that all vendor invoices, cash disbursements, and adjustments are recorded in the accounts payable records. In IT systems, these entries may be made directly as part of the normal processing of purchase, cash disbursement, or returns and allowances transactions. Proper use of control totals and daily activity reports provides controls for proper recording.

General Ledger   The main objective of the general ledger function for the purchasing process is to ensure that all purchases, cash disbursements, and payables are properly accumulated, classified, and summarized in the accounts. In an IT system, such as at EarthWear, the use of control or summary totals ensures that this function is performed correctly. The accounting department is normally responsible for this function.

A Vendor Statement is often sent monthly by the vendor to indicate the beginning balance, current-period purchases and payments, and the ending balance. The vendor's statement represents the purchase activity recorded on the vendor's records. It may differ from the client's records because of errors or, more often, timing differences due to delays in shipping goods or recording cash receipts. The client verifies the accuracy of its records by comparing vendor statements with the accounts payable records.

Segregation of Duties

LO 5⟩

As discussed in previous chapters, proper segregation of duties is one of the most important control procedures in any accounting system. Duties should be assigned so that no one individual can control all phases of processing a transaction in a way that permits errors or fraud to go undetected. The general rule is to separate custody of assets, recordkeeping, and authorization of transactions. Because of the potential for theft and fraud in the purchasing cycle, individuals responsible for requisitioning, purchasing, and receiving should be segregated from the invoice-processing, accounts payable, and general ledger functions. If IT is used extensively in the purchasing application, there should be proper segregation of duties in the IT department. Table 9–3 shows the key segregation of duties for the purchasing process and examples of possible errors or fraud that can result from conflicts in duties.

Table 9–4 shows the proper segregation of duties for purchasing and accounts payable functions across the various departments that process purchase transactions.

Inherent Risk Assessment

LO 6⟩

The previous section has outlined the key business processes involved in an entity's acquisition of goods and services, recognition of obligations and expenses, and extinguishments of accounts payable. As is the case in the revenue process, the auditor should gain a comprehensive understanding of these key business processes and use this comprehensive knowledge to develop expectations about assertions in the financial statements. As well, the auditor must understand how inherent risks may impact the client's key business processes and how these inherent risks could cause potential misstatements in the financial statements. The following factors taken from Chapter 3 should be considered by the auditor in assessing the inherent risk for the purchasing process.

Industry-Related Factors

When auditing the purchasing process, the auditor must consider two important industry-related factors in assessing inherent risk: whether the supply of raw materials is adequate and the volatility of raw material prices.

Table 9–3	Key Segregation of Duties in the Purchasing Process and Possible Errors or Fraud

Segregation of Duties	*Possible Errors or Fraud Resulting from Conflicts of Duties*
The purchasing function should be segregated from the requisitioning and receiving functions.	If one individual is responsible for the requisition, purchasing, and receiving functions, fictitious or unauthorized purchases can be made. This can result in the theft of goods and possibly payment for unauthorized purchases.
The invoice-processing function should be segregated from the accounts payable function.	If one individual is responsible for the invoice-processing and the accounts payable functions, purchase transactions can be processed at the wrong price or terms, or a cash disbursement can be processed for goods or services not received. This can result in overpayment for goods and services or the theft of cash.
The disbursement function should be segregated from the accounts payable function.	If one individual is responsible for the disbursement function and also has access to the accounts payable records, unauthorized cheques supported by fictitious documents can be issued, and unauthorized transactions can be recorded. This can result in theft of the entity's cash.
The accounts payable function should be segregated from the general ledger function.	If one individual is responsible for the accounts payable records and also for the general ledger, that individual can conceal any defalcation that would normally be detected by reconciling subsidiary records with the general ledger control account.

Table 9–4	Segregation of Duties for Purchasing and Accounts Payable Functions by Department

Purchasing and Accounts Payable Function	Department				
	Purchasing	*Receiving*	*Accounts Payable*	*Cashier's*	*IT*
Preparation and approval of purchase order	X				
Receipt, counting, and inspection of purchased materials		X			
Receipt of vendor invoices and matching them with supporting documents			X		
Coding (or checking) of account distributions			X		
Updating of accounts payable records			X		X
Preparation of vendor cheques					X
Signing and mailing of vendor cheques				X	
Preparation of voucher register					X
Reconciliation of voucher register to general ledger			X		

If the entity deals with many vendors and prices tend to be relatively stable, there is less risk that the entity's operations will be affected by raw material shortages or that production costs will be difficult to control.

Some industries, however, are subject to industry-related factors. For example, in the high-technology sector, there have been situations in which an entity has depended on a single vendor to supply a critical component, such as a specialized computer chip or disk drive. When the vendor has been unable to provide the component, the entity has suffered production shortages and shipping delays that have significantly affected financial performance. Other industries that produce basic commodities such as oil, coal, and precious metals can find their financial results significantly affected by swings in the prices of their products. Additionally, industries that use commodities such as oil as raw materials may be subject to both shortages and price instability. The auditor needs to assess the effects of such industry-related inherent risk factors in terms of audit objectives such as valuation.

Misstatements Detected in Prior Audits

Generally, the purchasing process and its related accounts are not difficult to audit and do not result in contentious accounting issues. However, auditing research has shown that the purchasing process and its related accounts are more likely than other accounts to contain material misstatements.[1] The auditor's previous experience with the entity's purchasing process should be reviewed as a starting point for determining the inherent risk.

Control Risk Assessment

LO 7> The discussion of control risk assessment follows the framework outlined in Chapter 6 on internal control and Chapter 8 on the revenue process. Again it is assumed that the auditor has decided to follow a reliance strategy. Figure 9–2 summarizes the major steps involved in assessing the control risk for the purchasing process.

Understanding and Documenting Internal Control

In order to assess the control risk for the purchasing process, the auditor must understand the five components of internal control.

Control Environment Chapter 6 discussed the factors that affect the control environment. Two factors are particularly important when the auditor considers the control environment and the purchasing process: the entity's organizational structure and its methods of assigning authority and responsibility. The entity's organizational structure for purchasing may impact the auditor's assessment of control risk because control procedures are implemented within an organizational structure. Authority and

[1]For example, see A. Eilifsen and W. F. Messier Jr., "Auditor Detection of Misstatement: A Review and Integration of Empirical Research," *Journal of Accounting Literature* 2000 (19), pp. 1–43.

FIGURE 9–2

Major Steps in Assessing
Control Risk for the
Purchasing Process

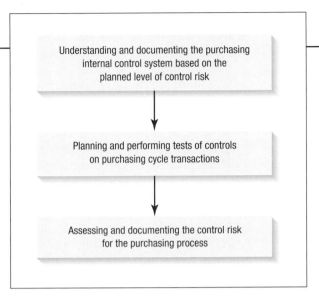

responsibility for purchasing are usually granted via procedures that limit the amount of purchases that can be made by various levels of authority within the entity. The remaining discussions of the purchasing process assume that the control environment factors are reliable.

The Entity's Risk Assessment Process   The auditor must understand how management weighs the risks that are relevant to the purchasing process, estimates their significance, assesses the likelihood of their occurrence, and decides what actions to take to address those risks. Some of these risks include a new or revamped information system, rapid growth, and new technology. Each of these factors can represent a serious risk to an entity's internal control system over purchases.

Information Systems and Communication   For each major class of transactions in the purchasing process, the auditor again needs to obtain the following information:

- how purchase, cash disbursements, and purchase return transactions are initiated
- the accounting records, supporting documents, and accounts that are involved in processing purchases, cash disbursements, and purchase return transactions
- the flow of each type of transaction from initiation to inclusion in the financial statements, including computer processing of the data
- the process used to estimate accrued liabilities

The auditor develops an understanding of the purchasing process by conducting a transaction walk-through. In the case of a continuing audit, the auditor has the prior years' documentation of the process to assist in the walk-through, although the possibility of changes in the system must be considered. If the system has been changed substantially or the audit is for a new client, the auditor should prepare new documentation of the system.

Control Procedures When a reliance strategy is adopted for the purchasing process, the auditor needs to understand the controls that exist to ensure that management's objectives are being met. More specifically, the auditor identifies the controls that assure the auditor that the internal control audit objectives are being met.

Monitoring of Controls The auditor needs to understand the client's monitoring processes over the purchasing process, including how management assesses the design and operation of controls. It also involves understanding how supervisory personnel within the process review the personnel who perform the controls and evaluating the performance of the entity's IT system.

The auditor can document the purchasing process using procedures manuals, narrative descriptions, internal control questionnaires, and flowcharts.

Planning and Performing Tests of Controls

The auditor systematically analyzes the purchasing process in order to identify controls that ensure that material misstatements are either prevented or detected and corrected. The controls can be relied upon by the auditor to reduce the control risk. For example, the client may have formal procedures for authorizing the acquisition of goods and services. The auditor may decide to rely on these controls to reduce the control risk for the authorization objective. Tests of controls would then be necessary to verify that this control is operating effectively. The auditor would examine a sample of purchase transactions to determine if the acquisition of the goods or services is consistent with the entity's authorization policy.

Assessing and Documenting Control Risk

After the controls are tested, the auditor assesses the level of control risk. When tests of controls results support the planned level of control risk, no modifications are normally necessary to the planned level of detection risk, and the auditor may proceed with the planned substantive tests. When the tests of controls do not support the planned level of control risk, the auditor must assess a higher level of control risk. This results in a lower level of detection risk and leads to more substantive tests than originally planned.

As discussed earlier, the auditor should establish and document the assessed level of control risk using either quantitative amounts or qualitative terms. Documentation of the control risk for the purchasing process might include a flowchart, the results of tests of controls, and a memorandum indicating the auditor's overall conclusion about the control risk.

Table 9–5 presents the assertions about transactions and events, while Table 9–6 summarizes the assertions and possible misstatements for purchase transactions. The table also includes key control procedures designed to prevent the possible misstatements and examples of tests of controls that can test the effectiveness of the control procedures.

Table 9–5	**Assertions about Classes of Transactions and Events for the Period under Audit**

- **Occurrence.** All purchase and cash disbursement transactions and events that have been recorded have occurred and pertain to the entity.
- **Completeness.** All purchase and cash disbursement transactions and events that should have been recorded have been recorded.
- **Accuracy.** Amounts and other data relating to recorded purchase and cash disbursement transactions and events have been recorded appropriately.
- **Cutoff.** Purchase and cash disbursement transactions and events have been recorded in the correct accounting period.
- **Classification.** Purchase and cash disbursement transactions and events have been recorded in the proper accounts.

Table 9–6	**Summary of Assertions, Possible Misstatements, Control Procedures, and Tests of Controls for Purchase Transactions**

Assertion	Possible Misstatement	Control Procedure	Test of Controls
Occurrence	Purchase recorded, goods or services not ordered or received	Segregation of duties	Observe and evaluate proper segregation of duties.
		Purchase not recorded without approved purchase order and receiving report	Test a sample of vouchers for the presence of an authorized purchase order and receiving report; if IT application, examine application controls.
		Accounting for numerical sequence of receiving reports and vouchers	Review and test client procedures for accounting for numerical sequence of receiving reports and vouchers; if IT application, examine application controls.
		Cancellation of documents	Examine paid vouchers and supporting documents for indication of cancellation.
Completeness	Purchases made but not recorded	Accounting for numerical sequence of purchase orders, receiving reports, and vouchers	Review client's procedures for accounting for numerical sequence of purchase orders, receiving reports, and vouchers; if IT application, examine application controls.
		Receiving reports matched to vendor invoices and entered in the purchases journal	Trace a sample of receiving reports to their respective vendor invoices and vouchers. Trace a sample of vouchers to the purchases journal.

(continued)

Table 9–6	Summary of Assertions, Possible Misstatements, Control Procedures, and Tests of Controls for Purchase Transactions (*concluded*)

Assertion	Possible Misstatement	Control Procedure	Test of Controls
Accuracy	Vendor invoice improperly priced or incorrectly calculated	Mathematical accuracy of vendor invoice verified	Recompute the mathematical accuracy of vendor invoice.
		Purchase order agreed to receiving report and vendor's invoice for product, quantity, and price	Agree the information on a sample of voucher packets for product, quantity, and price.
	Purchase transactions not posted to the purchases journal or the accounts payable subsidiary records	Vouchers reconciled to daily accounts payable listing	Examine reconciliation of vouchers to daily accounts payable report; if IT application, examine application controls.
	Amounts from purchases journal not posted correctly to the general ledger	Daily postings to purchases journal reconciled with postings to accounts payable subsidiary records	Examine reconciliation of entries in purchases journal with entries to accounts payable subsidiary records; if IT application, examine application controls.
		Voucher register or accounts payable subsidiary records reconciled to general ledger control account	Review reconciliation of subsidiary records to general ledger control account; if IT application, examine application controls.
		Vouchers reconciled to daily accounts payable listing	Test a sample of daily reconciliations.
Cutoff	Purchase transactions recorded in the wrong period	All receiving reports forwarded to the accounts payable department daily	Compare the dates on receiving reports with the dates on the relevant vouchers.
		Existence of procedures that require recording the purchases as soon as possible after goods or services are received	Compare the dates on vouchers with the dates they were recorded in the purchases journal.
Classification	Purchase transaction not properly classified	Chart of accounts	Review purchases journal and general ledger for reasonableness.
		Independent approval and review of accounts charged for acquisitions	Examine a sample of vouchers for proper classification.

Note: Receiving reports are used to acknowledge the receipt of tangible goods such as raw materials, office supplies, and equipment. For services such as utilities and advertising, receiving reports are not used.

Most of these controls exist within EarthWear's purchasing process (see Figure 9–1). The following sections also discuss control procedures and tests of controls that are relevant for EarthWear's purchasing process.

Occurrence of Purchase Transactions

The auditor's concern in testing the occurrence of purchase transactions is that fictitious or nonexistent purchases may have been recorded in the client's records. If fraudulent transactions are recorded, assets or expenses will be overstated. A liability will also be recorded and a resulting payment made, usually to the individual who initiated the fictitious purchase transactions. Proper segregation of duties is the major control for preventing fictitious purchases. The critical segregation of duties is the separation of the requisitioning and purchasing functions from the accounts payable and disbursement functions. If one individual can both process a purchase order and access the accounting records, there is an increased risk that fictitious purchase transactions will be recorded.

The other control procedures shown in Table 9–6 also reduce the risk of purchase transactions being recorded without the goods or services being received. Even with proper segregation of duties, no purchase transaction should be recorded without an approved purchase order and a receiving report. The presence of an approved purchase order ensures that the purchase was authorized, and the presence of a receiving report indicates that the goods were received. In an IT environment, such as EarthWear's, the auditor can test the application controls to ensure that purchases are recorded only after an approved purchase order has been entered and the goods received. Accounting for the numerical sequence of receiving reports and vouchers can be accomplished either manually or by the computer. This control prevents the recording of fictitious purchase transactions through the use of receiving documents or vouchers that are numbered outside the sequence of properly authorized documents. Cancellation of all supporting documents ensures that a purchase transaction is not recorded and paid for a second time.

Completeness of Purchase Transactions

If the client fails to record a purchase that has been made, assets or expenses will be understated, and the corresponding accounts payable will also be understated. Controls that ensure that the completeness assertion is being met include accounting for the numerical sequences of purchase orders, receiving reports, and vouchers; matching receiving reports with vendor invoices; and reconciling vouchers to the daily accounts payable report. For example, EarthWear uses control totals to reconcile the daily number of vouchers processed with the daily accounts payable listing.

Tests of controls for these control procedures are listed in Table 9–6. For example, the auditor can trace a sample of receiving reports to their corresponding vendor invoices and vouchers. The vouchers can then be traced to the voucher register to ensure that each voucher was recorded. Again, these tests can be performed either manually or with CAATs. If each receiving report is matched to a vendor invoice and voucher and the voucher was included in the voucher register, the auditor has a high level of assurance as to the completeness assertion.

The auditor's concern with the completeness assertion also arises when the accounts payable and accrued expenses accounts are audited at year-end. If the client has strong controls for the completeness assertion, the auditor can reduce the scope of the search for unrecorded liabilities at year-end. This issue is discussed in more detail later in this chapter.

Accuracy of Purchase Transactions

A possible misstatement for the accuracy assertion is that purchase transactions may be recorded at incorrect amounts due to improper pricing or erroneous calculations. The purchase order should contain the expected price for the goods or services being purchased, based on price quotes obtained by the purchasing agents or prices contained in catalogues or published price lists. If the goods or services are purchased under a contract, the price should be stipulated in the contract. For example, an accounts payable clerk should compare the purchase order with the receiving report and vendor invoice (see Figure 9–1) and investigate significant differences in quantities, prices, and freight charges. The accounts payable clerk also checks the mathematical accuracy of the vendor invoice. The auditor's test of controls for this assertion involves reperforming the accounts payable clerk's duties on a sample of voucher packets.

The accuracy assertion is also concerned with proper posting of information to the purchases journal, accounts payable subsidiary records, and general ledger. Control totals should be used to reconcile vouchers to the daily accounts payable listing, or else the daily postings to the purchases journal should be reconciled to the accounts payable subsidiary records. In addition, the voucher register or accounts payable subsidiary ledger should be reconciled to the general ledger control account. If these control procedures are performed manually, the auditor can review and examine the reconciliations prepared by the client's personnel. In an IT application, such controls would be programmed and reconciled by the control groups in the IT and accounts payable departments. The auditor can examine the programmed controls and review the reconciliations.

Cutoff of Purchase Transactions

The client should have controls to ensure that purchase transactions are recorded promptly and in the proper period. For example, the client's procedures should require that all receiving reports be forwarded to the accounts payable department daily. There should also be a requirement in the accounts payable department that receiving reports be matched on a timely basis with the original purchase order and the related vendor invoice. In EarthWear's system, the receiving department forwards the receiving report to the accounts payable department daily. Within the accounts payable department, the vendor invoices are matched immediately with the original purchase orders and the receiving reports. The auditor can test these control procedures by comparing the date on the receiving report with the date on the voucher. There should seldom be a long period between the two dates. The auditor also wants to ensure that the vouchers are recorded in the accounting records in the correct period. This can be tested by comparing the dates on vouchers with the dates the vouchers were recorded in the voucher register.

Classification of Purchase Transactions

Proper classification of purchase transactions is an important assertion for the purchasing process. If purchase transactions are not properly classified, asset and expense accounts will be misstated. Two main controls are used for ensuring that purchase transactions are properly classified. First, the client should use a chart of accounts. Second, there should be independent approval and review of the general ledger accounts charged for the acquisition. A typical procedure is for the department or function that orders the goods or services to indicate which general ledger account to charge. Accounts payable department personnel then review the account distribution for reasonableness (see Figure 9–1). A test of controls for this assertion involves examining a sample of voucher packets for proper classification.

Control Procedures and Tests of Controls—Cash Disbursement Transactions

Table 9–7 summarizes the assertions and possible misstatements for cash disbursement transactions. The table also includes key internal controls related to each assertion and examples of tests of controls that can assess control risk.

Occurrence of Cash Disbursement Transactions

For the occurrence assertion, the auditor is concerned with a misstatement caused by a cash disbursement being recorded in the client's records when no payment has actually been made. A number of possibilities exist for the cause of this misstatement. For example, a cheque may be lost or stolen before it is mailed. The primary control procedures used to prevent such misstatements include proper segregation of duties, independent reconciliation and review of vendor statements, and monthly bank reconciliations. In the purchasing system shown in Figure 9–1, cheques are distributed by the cashier's department, which is independent of the accounts payable department (the department authorizing the payment).

Table 9–7 lists tests of controls that the auditor can use to verify the effectiveness of the client's controls. For example, the auditor can observe and evaluate the client's segregation of duties and review the client's procedures for reconciling vendor statements and monthly bank statements.

Completeness of Cash Disbursement Transactions

The major misstatement related to the completeness assertion is that a cash disbursement is made but not recorded in the client's records. In addition to the control procedures used for the occurrence assertion, accounting for the numerical sequence of cheques and reconciliation of the daily cash disbursements with postings to the accounts payable subsidiary records (see Figure 9–1) helps to ensure that all issued cheques are recorded. The auditor's tests of controls may include reviewing and testing the client's procedures for accounting for the sequence of cheques and reviewing the client's reconciliation procedures.

Accuracy of Cash Disbursement Transactions

The potential misstatement related to the accuracy assertion is that the payment amount is recorded incorrectly. To detect such errors, the client's personnel should reconcile the total of the cheques issued on a particular day with the daily cash disbursements report. The client's control procedures should require monthly reconciliation of vendor statements to

Table 9–7	**Summary of Assertions, Possible Misstatements, Control Procedures, and Tests of Controls for Cash Disbursement Transactions**		
Assertion	*Possible Misstatement*	*Control Procedure*	*Test of Controls*
Occurrence	Cash disbursement recorded but not made	Segregation of duties	Observe and evaluate proper segregation of duties.
		Vendor statements independently reviewed and reconciled to accounts payable records	Review client's procedures for reconciling vendor statements.
		Monthly bank reconciliations prepared and reviewed	Review monthly bank reconciliations for indication of independent review.
Completeness	Cash disbursement made but not recorded	Same as above	Same as above
		Accounting for the numerical sequence of cheques	Review and test client's procedures for numerical sequence of cheques; if IT application, test application controls.
		Daily cash disbursements reconciled to postings to accounts payable subsidiary records	Review procedures for reconciling daily cash disbursements with postings to accounts payable subsidiary records; if IT application, test application controls.
Accuracy	Cash disbursement recorded at incorrect amount	Daily cash disbursements report reconciled to cheques issued	Review reconciliation.
		Vendor statements reconciled to accounts payable records and independently reviewed	Review reconciliation.
		Monthly bank statements reconciled and independently reviewed	Review monthly bank reconciliations.
	Cash disbursement posted to the wrong vendor account	Vendor statemets reconciled and independently reviewed	Review reconciliation.
	Cash disbursements journal not summarized properly or not properly posted to general ledger accounts	Monthly cash disbursements journal agreed to general ledger postings	Review postings from cash disbursements journal to the general ledger.
		Accounts payable subsidiary records reconciled to general ledger control account	Review reconciliation.
Cutoff	Cash disbursement recorded in wrong period	Daily reconciliation of cheques issued with postings to the cash disbursements journal and accounts payable subsidiary records	Review daily reconciliations.
Classification	Cash disbursement charged to wrong account	Chart of accounts	Review cash disbursements journal for reasonableness of account distribution.
		Independent approval and review of general ledger account on voucher packet	Review general ledger account code on voucher packet for reasonableness.

the accounts payable records. Monthly bank reconciliations also provide controls for detecting misstatements caused by cash disbursements being made in incorrect amounts. Each of these reconciliations should be independently reviewed by the client's personnel. The auditor's test of controls involves reviewing the various reconciliations.

Two other possible misstatements are of concern with the accuracy assertion: (1) cash disbursements are posted to the wrong vendor accounts and (2) the cash disbursements journal is not summarized properly or the wrong general ledger account is posted. The reconciliation of vendors' monthly statements is an effective control procedure for detecting payments posted to the wrong vendor accounts. Agreement of the monthly cash disbursements journal to general ledger postings and reconciliation of the accounts payable subsidiary records to the general ledger control account are effective control procedures for preventing summarization and posting errors (see Figure 9–1). The auditor's tests of controls would include checking postings to the general ledger and reviewing the various reconciliations.

Cutoff of Cash Disbursement Transactions	The client should establish procedures to ensure that when a cheque is prepared, it is recorded on a timely basis in the cash disbursements journal and the accounts payable subsidiary records. As shown in Figure 9–1, when a cheque is prepared, it is simultaneously recorded in the accounting records by the application programs that control transaction processing. The auditor's tests of controls include reviewing the reconciliation of cheques with postings to the cash disbursements journal and accounts payable subsidiary records. The auditor also tests cash disbursements before and after year-end to ensure transactions are recorded in the proper period.
Classification of Cash Disbursement Transactions	The auditor's concern with proper classification is that a cash disbursement may be charged to the wrong general ledger account. In most purchasing systems, purchases are usually recorded through the voucher register or purchases journal. Thus, the only entries to the cash disbursements journal are debits to accounts payable and credits to cash. If these procedures are followed, proper classification of cash disbursements is not a major concern. Sometimes a client pays for goods and services directly from the cash disbursements journal without recording the purchase transaction in the purchases journal. If a client does pay for goods and services directly from the cash disbursements journal, controls must be present to ensure proper classification. The use of a chart of accounts, as well as independent approval and review of the account code on the voucher packet, should provide an adequate control. The auditor can review the cash disbursements journal for reasonableness of account distribution as well as the account codes on a sample of voucher packets.
Control Procedures and Tests of Controls—Purchase Return Transactions	The number and magnitude of purchase return transactions are not material for most entities. However, because of the possibility of manipulation the auditor should, at a minimum, enquire about how the client controls purchase return transactions. When goods are returned to a vendor, the

client usually prepares a document (sometimes called a debit memo) that reduces the amount of the vendor's accounts payable. This document is processed through the purchasing process in a manner similar to the processing of a vendor invoice.

Because purchase returns are often few in number and not material, the auditor normally does not test controls of these transactions. Substantive analytical procedures are usually performed to test the reasonableness of purchase returns. For example, comparison of purchase returns as a percentage of revenue to prior years' and industry data may disclose any material misstatement in this account.

Relating the Assessed Level of Control Risk to Substantive Testing

LO 8> The decision process followed by the auditor is similar to that discussed in Chapter 8 for the revenue cycle. If the results of the tests of controls support the assessed level of control risk, the auditor conducts substantive tests at the assessed level. If the results indicate that the control risk can be reduced further, the auditor can increase the detection risk, which will reduce the nature, extent, and timing of substantive tests needed. However, if the results of the tests of controls do not support the assessed level of control risk, the detection risk has to be set lower and the substantive testing increased.

The main accounts affected by the auditor's assessment of control risk for the purchasing process include accounts payable, accrued expenses, and most of the expense accounts in the income statement. Additionally, the tests of controls over purchase transactions affect the assessment of detection risk for other processes. For example, purchase transactions for the acquisition of inventory and property, plant, and equipment are subject to the controls included in the purchasing process. If those controls are reliable, the auditor may be able to increase the detection risk for the affected financial statement accounts and therefore reduce the number of substantive tests needed.

Substantive Testing

Auditing Accounts Payable and Accrued Expenses

LO 9>

The assessments of inherent risk and control risk for the purchasing process are used to determine the level of detection risk for conducting substantive procedures for accounts payable and accrued expenses. Accounts payable generally represent normal recurring trade obligations. Accrued expenses represent expenses that have been incurred during the period but that have not been billed or paid for as of the end of the period; these include accruals for taxes, interest, royalties, and professional fees. A number of accrued expenses are also related to payroll. Because there is little difference between accounts payable and accrued expenses, they are covered together in this section.

Substantive analytical procedures and tests of details of classes of transactions, account balances, and disclosures are used to test accounts payable and accrued expenses. Substantive analytical procedures are

Table 9–8	**Management Assertions about Account Balances, and Disclosures for Accounts Payable and Accrued Expenses**

Assertions about Account Balances at the Period End:

- **Existence.** Accounts payable and accrued expenses are valid liabilities.

- **Rights and obligations.** Accounts payable and accrued expenses are the obligations of the entity.

- **Completeness.** All accounts payable and accrued expenses have been recorded.

- **Valuation and allocation.** Accounts payable and accrued expenses are included in the financial statements at appropriate amounts, and any resulting valuation or allocation adjustments are appropriately recorded.

Assertions about Presentation and Disclosure:

- **Occurrence and rights and obligations.** All disclosed events, transactions, and other matters relating to accounts payable and accrued expenses have occurred and pertain to the entity.

- **Completeness.** All disclosures relating to accounts payable and accrued expenses that should have been included in the financial statements have been included.

- **Classification and understandability.** Financial information relating to accounts payable and accrued expenses is appropriately presented and described, and disclosures are clearly expressed.

- **Accuracy and valuation.** Financial and other information relating to accounts payable and accrued expenses are disclosed fairly and at appropriate amounts.

used to examine plausible relationships among accounts payable and accrued expenses. Tests of details focus on transactions, account balances, or disclosures. In the purchasing process, tests of details of transactions (also called *substantive tests of transactions*) focus mainly on the purchases and cash disbursement transactions. Tests of details of account balances concentrate on the detailed amounts or estimates that make up the ending balance for accounts payable and accrued expenses. Tests of details of disclosures are concerned with the presentation and disclosures related to accounts payable and accrued expenses.

Table 9–7 presented the assertions for purchases and cash disbursement transactions and events; Table 9–8 lists the assertions for account balances and disclosures as they apply to accounts payable and accrued expenses. The reader should note that the auditor may test assertions related to transactions (substantive tests of transactions) in conjunction with testing internal controls. If the tests of controls indicate that the controls are not operating effectively, the auditor may need to test transactions at the date the account balance is tested.

Substantive Analytical Procedures

Substantive analytical procedures can be useful substantive procedures for examining the reasonableness of accounts payable and accrued expenses. Substantive analytical procedures can effectively identify accounts payable and accrual accounts that are misstated, as well as provide evidence regarding the fairness of the recorded accounts. Table 9–9 contains some examples of substantive analytical procedures that can be used in the auditing of accounts payable and accrued expenses.

EXHIBIT 9–2

Example of an Accounts Payable Listing Working Paper

EarthWear

N10
DLJ
2/14/2007

EARTHWEAR CLOTHIERS
Accounts Payable Listing
12/31/06

Vendor Name	Amount Due
Aarhus Industries	$ 52,758†V
Anderson Clothes, Inc.	237,344V
.	
.	
.	
.	
Washington Mfg., Inc.	122,465†V
Zantec Bros.	7,750
Total	$62,509,740
	F T/B

F = Footed.
† = Traced to accounts payable subsidiary records.
V = Voucher packets examined for transaction validity. No exceptions
T/B = Agreed to trial balance.

EXHIBIT 9–3

Account Analysis for the Accrued Real Estate Taxes Account Working Paper

EarthWear

N21
DLJ
2/5/2007

EARTHWEAR CLOTHIERS
Analysis of Accrued Real Estate Taxes
12/31/06

		Beginning balance	$ 22,333‡
Cash disbursements for real		12 monthly accruals for	
estate tax payments	233,911Γ	real estate taxes	235,245
		Ending balance	$ 23,667L✔
			F

F = Footed.
‡ = Agreed to prior year's working papers.
✔ = Amount of real estate taxes accrued appears reasonable.
Γ = Payments traced to real estate tax bills and cash disbursements journal.
L = Agreed to general ledger.

payments. This schedule is footed and agreed to the accrued real estate taxes account in the general ledger.

The second major test of the completeness assertion is for accounts payable and accruals concerned with unrecorded liabilities. Therefore, auditors frequently conduct extensive tests to ensure that all liabilities are recorded. Such tests are commonly referred to as a *search for unrecorded liabilities*. The following audit procedures may be used as part of the search for unrecorded liabilities:

1. Ask management about control procedures used to identify unrecorded liabilities and accruals at the end of an accounting period.
2. Obtain copies of vendors' monthly statements and reconcile the amounts to the client's accounts payable records.
3. Confirm vendor accounts, including accounts with small or zero balances.
4. Vouch large-dollar items from the purchases journal and cash disbursements journal for a limited time after year-end; examine the date on each receiving report or vendor invoice to determine if the liability relates to the current audit period.
5. Examine the files of unmatched purchase orders, receiving reports, and vendor invoices for any unrecorded liabilities.

Existence

The auditor's major concern with the existence assertion is whether the recorded liabilities are valid obligations of the entity. To verify the validity of liabilities, the auditor can vouch a sample of the items included on the listing of accounts payable, or the accrued account analysis, to voucher packets or other supporting documents. If adequate source documents are present, the auditor has evidence that the amounts represent valid liabilities (see Exhibit 9–2). In some circumstances, the auditor may obtain copies of the monthly vendor statements or send confirmation requests to vendors to test the validity of the liabilities. Confirmation of accounts payable is discussed later in this chapter.

Cutoff

The cutoff assertion attempts to determine whether all purchase transactions and related accounts payable are recorded in the proper period. On most audits, purchase cutoff is coordinated with the client's physical inventory count. Proper cutoff should also be determined for purchase return transactions.

The client should have control procedures to ensure that a proper purchase cutoff takes place. The auditor can test purchase cutoff by first obtaining the number of the last receiving report issued in the current period. A sample of voucher packets is selected for a few days before and after year-end. The receiving reports contained in the voucher packets are examined to determine if the receipt of the goods is consistent with the recording of the liability. For example, suppose that the last receiving report issued by EarthWear in 2006 was number 15,755. A voucher packet recorded in the voucher register or accounts payable in 2006 should have a receiving report numbered 15,755 or less. If the auditor finds a voucher packet recorded in 2006 with a receiving report number higher than 15,755, the liability has been recorded in the wrong period. Accounts payable for 2006 should be adjusted and the amount included as a liability in the next period. For voucher packets recorded in 2007, the receiving reports should be numbered 15,756 or higher. If the auditor finds a voucher packet with a receiving report with a number less than 15,756, the liability belongs in the 2006 accounts payable.

Purchase returns seldom represent a material amount in the financial statements. If the client has adequate control procedures for processing purchase return transactions, the auditor can use substantive analytical procedures to satisfy the cutoff assertion for purchase returns. For example, the prior-year and current-year amounts for purchase returns as a percentage of revenue or cost of sales can be compared. If the results of the substantive analytical procedures are consistent with the auditor's expectation, no further audit work may be necessary.

Rights and Obligations

Generally, there is little risk related to this assertion because clients seldom have an incentive to record liabilities that are not obligations of the entity. Review of the voucher packets for adequate supporting documents relating liabilities to the client provides sufficient evidence to support this assertion.

Valuation

The valuation of individual accounts payable is generally not a difficult assertion to test. Accounts payable are recorded at either the gross amount of the invoice or the net of the cash discount if the entity normally takes a cash discount. The tests of details of account balances noted in Table 9–10 normally provide sufficient evidence as to the proper valuation of accounts payable.

The valuation of accruals depends on the type and nature of the accrued expenses. Most accruals are relatively easy to value, and proper valuation can be tested by examining the underlying source documents. Real estate taxes and interest are examples of accruals that are generally easy to value. In the first case, real estate appraisals or bills usually serve as the basis for the accrual amount (see Exhibit 9–3). In the second case, the amount of interest accrued relates directly to the amount of debt and the interest rate stipulated in the loan agreement. Other accruals, however, may require the auditor to verify the client's estimates. Auditing standards provide the auditor with guidance in auditing client's estimates. Examples of such estimates include accruals for vacation pay, pension expense, warranty expense, and income taxes.

Classification and Understandability

The major issues related to the presentation and disclosure assertion about classification are (1) identifying and reclassifying any material debits contained in accounts payable, (2) segregating short-term and long-term payables, and (3) ensuring that different types of payables are properly classified. Proper classification can usually be verified by reviewing the accounts payable listing and the general ledger accounts payable account. If material debits are present, they should be reclassified as receivables or as deposits if the amount will be used for future purchases. Any long-term

Table 9–11	Examples of Disclosure Items for Purchasing Process and Related Accounts

Payables by type (trade, officers, employees, affiliates, and so on).
Short- and long-term payables.
Long-term purchase contracts, including any unusual or adverse purchase commitments.
Purchases from and payables to related parties.
Dependence on a single vendor or a small number of vendors.
Costs by reportable segment of the business.

EXHIBIT 9–4

A Sample Disclosure for Purchase Commitments

The company has various agreements that provide for the purchase, at market prices, of wood chips, bark, and other residual fiber from trees.

The company also has an agreement to purchase at market prices through 2007 the entire production of an unbleached kraft paper–making machine at Johnson Forest Products Company. The capacity of this machine is estimated to be 30,000 tons a year.

payables should be identified and reclassified to the long-term liability section of the balance sheet. Also, payables to officers, employees, or related parties should not be included with the trade accounts payable. The auditor should also ensure that accrued expenses are properly classified.

Other Presentation Disclosure Assertions

Even though management is responsible for the financial statements, the auditor must ensure that all necessary financial statement disclosures are made for accounts payable and accrued expenses. Again, a reporting checklist is a useful tool. Table 9–11 presents examples of items that should be disclosed for accounts payable and accrued expenses.

Two disclosures are particularly important. The auditor must ensure that all related-party purchase transactions have been identified. If material, such purchase transactions should be disclosed. The other major disclosure issue is purchase commitments. When the client has entered into a formal long-term purchase contract, adequate disclosure of the terms of the contract should be provided in a footnote. Exhibit 9–4 provides a sample disclosure for a purchase commitment.

Accounts Payable Confirmations

LO 10 >   Chapter 8 discussed the confirmation process in general and accounts receivable confirmations specifically. This section expands that discussion to include confirmation of accounts payable. Accounts payable confirmations are used less frequently by auditors than accounts receivable confirmations because the auditor can test accounts payable by examining vendor invoices and monthly vendor statements. These documents originate from sources external to the client, so this evidence is viewed as reliable. However, if the client has weak internal control, vendor statements may not be available to examine. In such a case, confirmations may be used as a main source of evidence.

While accounts payable confirmations provide evidence on a number of assertions, they primarily test the completeness assertion. If the client has strong control procedures for ensuring that liabilities are recorded, the auditor focuses on confirmation of large-dollar accounts. However, if the auditor has concerns about liabilities not being recorded, regular vendors with small or zero balances and a sample of other accounts may be confirmed in addition to large-dollar accounts. Small- and zero-balance accounts are confirmed because the client may owe such vendors for purchases but the amounts may not be recorded in the client's accounting records.

When confirming accounts payable, auditors generally use a form of positive confirmation referred to as a *blank* or *zero-balance* confirmation. This type of positive confirmation does not state the balance owed. Instead, the confirmation requests that the recipient fill in the amount or furnish other information. Exhibit 9–5 presents an example of an accounts

EXHIBIT 9–5

Example of an Accounts Payable Confirmation Request

 EARTHWEAR CLOTHIERS

January 7, 2007

Zantec Bros.
P.O. Box 1469
Vancouver, BC V5B 1S1

Gentlemen:

Our auditors, Willis & Adams, are conducting an audit of our financial statements as of December 31, 2006. Please confirm to them the amount of our accounts payable. Additionally, please provide the following information as of that date:

1. An itemized statement of our account.
2. A list of any notes payable to you including any discounted notes. Please include the original dates and amounts, due dates, and amounts still outstanding.
3. A list of any consigned inventory held by us.

Sincerely,

Sally Jones
Controller, EarthWear Clothiers

Willis & Adams
P. O. Box 4080
Calgary, Alberta T1T 2B2

    We confirm that EarthWear Clothiers' accounts payable balance at

December 31, 2006, is _____.

Signature _____   Position _____

8 >   **9-14**   Identify four possible disclosure issues related to the purchasing cycle and related accounts.

9 >   **9-15**   What are the differences between accounts receivable and accounts payable confirmations?

MULTIPLE-CHOICE QUESTIONS FROM PROFESSIONAL EXAMINATIONS

Unless otherwise indicated, these multiple-choice questions were adapted from the CPA examinations, courtesy of the American Institute of Certified Public Accountants.

7 >   **9-16**   When goods are received, the receiving clerk should match the goods with

a. The purchase order and the requisition form.

b. The vendor invoice and the receiving report.

c. The vendor shipping document and the purchase order.

d. The receiving report and the vendor shipping document.

7 >   **9-17**   In a properly designed accounts payable system, a voucher is prepared after the invoice, purchase order, requisition, and receiving report are verified. The next step in the system is

a. Cancellation of the supporting documents.

b. Entry of the cheque amount in the cheque register.

c. Entering of the voucher into the voucher register.

d. Approval of the voucher for payment.

7 >   **9-18**   An internal control questionnaire indicates that an approved receiving report is required to accompany every cheque request for payment of merchandise. Which of the following procedures provides the greatest assurance that this control is operating effectively?

a. Selection and examination of cancelled cheques and ascertainment that the related receiving reports are dated *no later* than the cheques.

b. Selection and examination of cancelled cheques and ascertainment that the related receiving reports are dated *no earlier* than the cheques.

c. Selection and examination of receiving reports and ascertainment that the related cancelled cheques are dated *no earlier* than the receiving reports.

d. Selection and examination of receiving reports and ascertainment that the related cancelled cheques are dated *no later* than the receiving reports.

7 >   **9-19**   Internal control is strengthened when the quantity of merchandise ordered is omitted from the copy of the purchase order sent to the

a. Department that initiated the requisition.

b. Receiving department.

c. Purchasing agent.

d. Accounts payable department.

5,7>   **9-20**   Which of the following internal control procedures is *not* usually performed in the accounts payable department?

    a. Matching the vendor's invoice with the related receiving report.

    b. Approving vouchers for payment by having an authorized employee sign the vouchers.

    c. Indicating the asset and expense accounts to be debited.

    d. Accounting for unused prenumbered purchase orders and receiving reports.

7>   **9-21**   Which of the following is the most effective control procedure to detect vouchers prepared for the payment of goods that were *not* received?

    a. Counting of goods upon receipt in storeroom.

    b. Matching of purchase order, receiving report, and vendor invoice for each voucher in the accounts payable department.

    c. Comparison of goods received with goods requisitioned in receiving department.

    d. Verification of vouchers for accuracy and approval in internal audit department.

5,7>   **9-22**   In a properly designed purchasing process, the same employee most likely would match vendors' invoices with receiving reports and also

    a. Post the detailed accounts payable records.

    b. Recompute the calculations on vendors' invoices.

    c. Reconcile the accounts payroll ledger.

    d. Cancel vendors' invoices after payment.

5,7>   **9-23**   For effective internal control purposes, which of the following individuals should be responsible for mailing signed cheques?

    a. Receptionist.

    b. Treasurer.

    c. Accounts payable clerk.

    d. Payroll clerk.

5,7>   **9-24**   Budd, the purchasing agent of Lake Hardware Wholesalers, has a relative who owns a retail hardware store. Budd arranged for hardware to be delivered by manufacturers to the retail store on a C.O.D. basis, thereby enabling his relative to buy at Lake's wholesale prices. Budd was probably able to accomplish this because of Lake's poor internal control over

    a. Purchase requisitions.

    b. Cash receipts.

    c. Perpetual inventory records.

    d. Purchase orders.

4,7,9>   **9-25**   To determine whether accounts payable are complete, an auditor performs a test to verify that all merchandise received is recorded. The population of documents for this test consists of all

    a. Vendor invoices

    b. Purchase orders.

c. Receiving reports.

d. Cancelled cheques.

7>   **9-26**   Which of the following controls would most effectively ensure that recorded purchases are free of material errors?

a. The receiving department compares the quantity ordered on purchase orders with the quantity received on receiving reports.

b. Vendor invoices are compared with purchase orders by an employee who is independent of the receiving department.

c. Receiving reports require the signature of the individual who authorized the purchase.

d. Purchase orders, receiving reports, and vendor invoices are independently matched in preparing vouchers.

9>   **9-27**   Which of the following procedures is *least* likely to be performed before the balance sheet date?

a. Test of internal control over cash.

b. Confirmation of receivables.

c. Search for unrecorded liabilities.

d. Observation of inventory.

10>   **9-28**   When using confirmations to provide evidence about the completeness assertion for accounts payable, the appropriate population most likely would be

a. Vendors with whom the entity has previously done business.

b. Amounts recorded in the accounts payable subsidiary ledger.

c. Payees of cheques drawn in the month after year-end.

d. Invoices filed in the entity's open invoice file.

7,9>   **9-29**   Purchase cutoff procedures should be designed to test whether all inventory

a. Purchased and received before the end of the year was paid for.

b. Ordered before the end of the year was received.

c. Purchased and received before the end of the year was recorded.

d. Owned by the company is in the possession of the company at the end of the year.

7,9>   **9-30**   Which of the following audit procedures is best for identifying unrecorded trade accounts payable?

a. Examination of unusual relationships between monthly accounts payable balances and recorded cash payments.

b. Reconciliation of vendors' statements to the file of receiving reports to identify items received just prior to the balance sheet date.

c. Investigation of payables recorded just prior to and just subsequent to the balance sheet date to determine whether they are supported by receiving reports.

d. Review of cash disbursements recorded subsequent to the balance sheet date to determine whether the related payables apply to the prior period.

PROBLEMS

9,10> **9-31** John Coltrane is auditing Jang Wholesaling Company's financial statements and is about to perform substantive audit procedures on Jang's trade accounts payable balances. After obtaining an understanding of Jang's internal control for accounts payable, Coltrane assessed control risk below the maximum. Coltrane requested and received from Jang a schedule of the trade accounts payable prepared using the trade accounts payable subsidiary ledger (voucher register).

Required:

Describe the substantive audit procedures Coltrane should apply to Jang's trade accounts payable balances. Do *not* include procedures that would be applied only in the audit of related-party payables, amounts withheld from employees, and accrued expenses such as pensions and interest.

(AICPA, adapted)

4,5,7> **9-32** In 2006 Kida Company purchased more than $10 million worth of office equipment under its "special" ordering system, with individual orders ranging from $5,000 to $30,000. "Special" orders entail low-volume items that have been included in an authorized user's budget. Department heads include in their annual budget requests the types of equipment and their estimated cost. The budget, which limits the types and dollar amounts of office equipment a department head can requisition, is approved at the beginning of the year by the board of directors. Department heads prepare purchase requisition forms for equipment and forward them to the purchasing department. Kida's "special" ordering system functions as follows:

- *Purchasing:* Upon receiving a purchase requisition, one of five buyers verifies that the person requesting the equipment is a department head. The buyer selects the appropriate vendor by searching the various vendor catalogues on file. The buyer then phones the vendor, requests a price quotation, and gives the vendor a verbal order. A prenumbered purchase order is processed with the original sent to the vendor, a copy to the department head, a copy to receiving, a copy to accounts payable, and a copy filed in the open requisition file. When the buyer is orally informed by the receiving department that the item has been received, the buyer transfers the purchase order from the unfilled file to the filled file. Once a month the buyer reviews the unfilled file to follow up on and expedite open orders.

- *Receiving:* The receiving department receives a copy of the purchase order. When equipment is received, the receiving clerk stamps the purchase order with the date received and, if applicable, in red pen prints any differences between the quantity shown on the purchase order and the quantity received. The receiving clerk forwards the stamped purchase order and equipment to the requisitioning department head and orally notifies the purchasing department.

- *Accounts payable:* Upon receiving a purchase order, the accounts payable clerk files it in the open purchase order file. When a vendor invoice is received, the invoice is matched with the applicable purchase order, and a payable is set up by debiting the equipment account of the department requesting the items. Unpaid invoices are filed by due date, and at the due date a cheque is prepared. The invoice and purchase order are filed by purchase order number in a paid invoice file, and the cheque is then forwarded to the treasurer for signature.
- *Treasurer:* Cheques received daily from the accounts payable department are sorted into two groups: those over $10,000 and those $10,000 and less. Cheques for $10,000 and less are machine-signed. The cashier keeps the key and signature plate to the cheque-signing machine and records all use of the cheque-signing machine. All cheques over $10,000 are signed by the treasurer or the controller.

Required:

a. Prepare a flowchart of Kida Company's purchasing and cash disbursements internal control system.

b. Describe the internal control weaknesses relating to purchases of and payments for "special" orders of Kida Company for the purchasing, receiving, accounts payable, and treasurer functions.

(AICPA, adapted)

2,3,5,7   **9-33**   See-Well Partners (SP) is a firm of optometrists that operates four clinics in a large Canadian city. The partnership was formed in 1995 and, as of August 31, 2006, had four partners and 15 support staff. Three of the four clinics are located in suburban shopping malls. The downtown clinic and head office are located in a 19th century mansion that is owned by SP.

On September 8, 2006, SP dismissed its controller, Jason Gilbert, for incompetence and hired John Sullivan, a professional accountant, to replace him. Jason had been working for SP since September 1994. When reconciling the August 2006 bank statement, Sullivan discovered two cheques on which the payee had been altered to "Jason Gilbert," but which were recorded in the cash disbursements journal as payable to Universal Optical, a supplier. In addition, Sullivan was unable to agree the daily billing summaries to the actual deposits made, and he noticed that bad-debt write-offs seemed unusually high. He brought these irregularities to the attention of the other partners.

SP has lost confidence in its present firm of auditors who, it believes, should have discovered the fraud. SP contacted the police and your firm, Mason & Co. to assist in an investigation of its accounts. Specifically, SP would like you to explain why its system of internal controls did not alert it to the fraud and to suggest changes to prevent a recurrence.

EXHIBIT 1

| **Information Obtained from SP** |

1. SP's year-end is March 31, and a review engagement has always been performed. The partners receive monthly financial statements but perform no detailed analysis as long as the net income and bank balance seem reasonable.
2. The controller does not have signing authority. Cheques must be signed by one of the four partners. A copy of each invoice to be paid is presented to a partner for review prior to his signing the cheque. Cheques and invoices are then returned to the controller for mailing and filing respectively.
3. Billings (for patient visits and sales of contact lenses, eyeglasses, etc.) are of two kinds: those covered by provincial health care and private insurers, and those paid by the patient. All billings are recorded when the service is rendered. Accounts receivable are material, and collection periods have lengthened due to changes in provincial health-care coverage. The controller is responsible for assessing the collectibility of accounts receivable.
4. The receptionist at each clinic prepares the daily deposit, and agrees it to the daily billing summary. All documents and cash/cheques are then forwarded to the controller.
5. SP carries a large inventory of frames and lenses. Demand for frames is heavily dependent upon short-lived fashion trends. The cost of lenses has decreased sharply in recent months. Inventory is counted only at year-end. Book to physical adjustments are not investigated.
6. The controller's responsibilities include:
   - preparing monthly bank reconciliations,
   - preparing all accounting entries,
   - preparing monthly financial statements and explanations of significant variations from month to month, and
   - since February, 1995, taking deposits for all clinics to the bank.
7. John Sullivan estimates that 25 to 30 altered cheques made payable to Gilbert were cleared on SP's bank account over the past year. All were coded to the inventory account. He is unable to estimate the amount of any other losses.

William Mason, the partner assigned to this engagement, met with the partners of SP last week and obtained the information outlined in Exhibit 1. He has asked you to prepare a draft report to the client dealing with its internal control system.

Required:

Prepare the draft report and planning memo.

(CICA, adapted)

4,5,7 >   **9-34**   The flowchart on the following page depicts the activities relating to the purchasing, receiving, and accounts payable departments of Model Company, Ltd.

Required:

Based only on the flowchart, describe the internal control procedures (strengths) that most likely would provide reasonable assurance that specific internal control objectives for the financial statement assertions regarding purchases and accounts payable will be achieved. Do *not* describe weaknesses in internal control.

(AICPA, adapted)

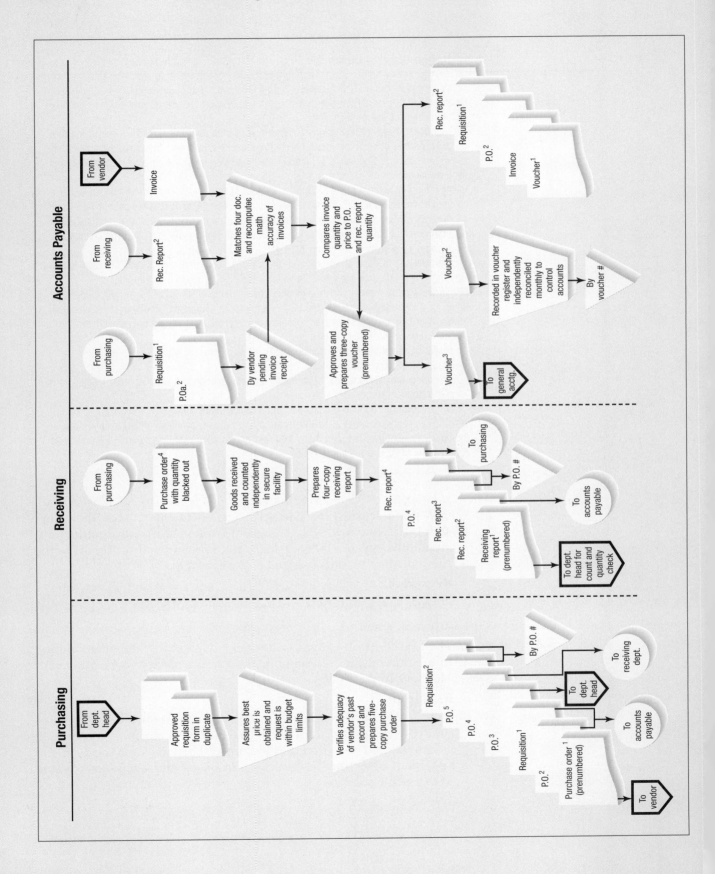

7> **9-35** Lacey's Furniture Ltd. (Lacey's) is owned and operated by Stan Lacey. He started the business 30 years ago by opening a small store in Richmond, Ontario. The business has expanded over the years and Lacey's is now one of the largest furniture retail businesses in the metropolitan area.

In the past, Lacey's has been a review engagement for your firm, Burke & Co. As Stan Lacey plans to retire from the business in the next five years, he has been gradually removing himself from the daily operations. Consequently, he wants Burke & Co. to perform an audit of Lacey's for the year ended December 31, 2006 as he understands this will provide him with additional assurance on the financial statements.

Stan hopes that his daughter will eventually take over the daily operations of Lacey's. To aid in this transition, Stan has made her responsible for signing all the cheques. He believes this will enable her to better understand the costs of doing business. She is presently the accounts payable clerk.

You are the senior in charge of the Lacey audit and have just completed the documentation of the purchasing system (see Figure 1 on page 402).

Required:

a. List the control weaknesses in Lacey's purchases system. For each control weakness identified, list the potential impacts of the weakness.

b. List the existing effective controls in Lacey's purchases system and the related reason for having each control.

(ICABC, adapted)

9,10> **9-36** In obtaining audit evidence in support of financial statement assertions, the auditor develops specific audit objectives in light of those assertions. Audit procedures are then selected to accomplish the audit objectives.

Required:

Your client is All's Fair Appliance Company, an appliance wholesaler. Select the most appropriate audit procedure from the list below and enter the number in the appropriate place on the grid on page 403. (An audit procedure may be selected once, more than once, or not at all.)

Audit Procedure:

1. Compare selected amounts from the accounts payable listing with the voucher and supporting documents.
2. Review drafts of the financial statements.
3. Search for unrecorded liabilities.
4. Select a sample of receiving documents for a few days before and after year-end.
5. Confirm accounts payable.
6. Obtain a listing of the accounts payable and agree total to general ledger control account.

FIGURE 1

Lacey's Furniture Ltd. Purchasing System

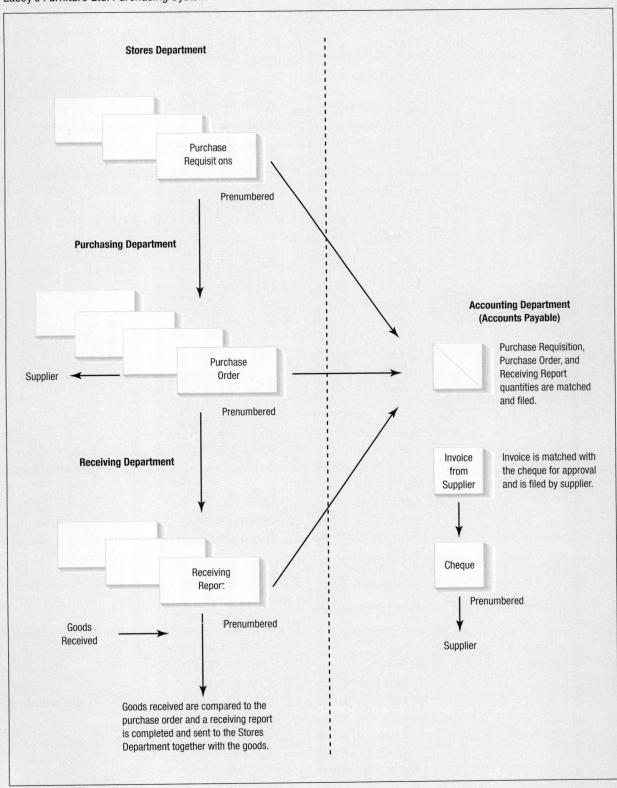

Stores Department

Purchase
Requisit ons

Prenumbered

Purchasing Department

Supplier ←

Purchase
Order

Prenumbered

Receiving Department

Goods
Received →

Receiving
Repor:

Prenumbered

Goods received are compared to the
purchase order and a receiving report
is completed and sent to the Stores
Department together with the goods.

**Accounting Department
(Accounts Payable)**

Purchase Requisition,
Purchase Order, and
Receiving Report
quantities are matched
and filed.

Invoice
from
Supplier

Invoice is matched with
the cheque for approval
and is filed by supplier.

Cheque

Prenumbered

Supplier

Specific Audit Objective	Audit Procedure
a. Determine whether all accounts payable are properly valued.	5
b. Verify that recorded accounts payable include all amounts owed to vendors.	3
c. Verify that all accounts payable are recorded in the correct period.	4
d. Determine whether accounts payable have been properly accumulated from the journal to the general ledger.	6
e. Determine whether recorded accounts payable are valid.	1

5,7   **9-37**   Dunbar Camera Manufacturing, Inc., manufacturers high-priced precision motion picture cameras in which the specifications of component parts are vital to the manufacturing process. Dunbar buys valuable camera lenses and large quantities of sheet metal and screws. Screws and lenses are ordered by Dunbar and are billed by the vendors on a unit basis. Sheet metal is ordered by Dunbar and is billed by the vendors on the basis of weight. The receiving clerk is responsible for documenting the quality and quantity of merchandise received.

A preliminary review of internal control indicates that these procedures are being followed:

Receiving Report

Properly approved purchase orders, which are prenumbered, are filed numerically. The copy sent to the receiving clerk is an exact duplicate of the copy sent to the vendor. Receipts of merchandise are recorded on the duplicate copy by the receiving clerk.

Sheet Metal

The company receives sheet metal by railroad. The railroad independently weighs the sheet metal and reports the weight and date of receipt on a bill of lading (waybill), which accompanies all deliveries. The receiving clerk checks only the weight on the waybill against the purchase order.

Screws

The receiving clerk opens cartons containing screws, then inspects and weighs the contents. The weight is converted to the number of units by means of conversion charts. The receiving clerk then checks the computed quantity against the amount shown on the purchase order.

Camera Lenses

Each camera lens is delivered in a separate corrugated carton. The receiving clerk counts the cartons and checks the number of cartons against the amounts shown on the purchase orders.

Required:

a. Explain why the internal control procedures as they apply individually to receiving reports and the receipt of sheet metal, screws, and camera lenses are adequate or inadequate. Do *not* discuss recommendations for improvements.

b. What financial statement distortions may arise because of the inadequacies in Dunbar's system of internal control, and how may they occur?

(AICPA, adapted)

9,10 >   **9-38**   Miles Taylor is auditing Rex Wholesaling for the year ended December 31, 2006. Taylor has reviewed internal control relating to the purchasing, receiving, trade accounts payable, and cash disbursement cycles and has decided not to test controls. Based on analytical review procedures, Taylor believes that the trade accounts payable balance on the balance sheet as of December 31, 2006, may be understated.

Taylor has requested and obtained a client-prepared trade accounts payable schedule listing the total amount owed to each vendor.

Required:

What additional substantive audit procedures should Taylor apply in examining the trade accounts payable?

(AICPA, adapted)

2,4,5,7,10 >   **9-39**   Chris Leung has been engaged to audit the financial statements of Sommer Manufacturing, Inc. Sommer is a medium-size entity that produces a wide variety of household goods. All acquisitions of materials are processed through the purchasing, receiving, accounts payable, and treasurer functions.

Required:

Prepare the "Purchases" segment of the internal control questionnaire to be used in evaluating Sommer's internal control system. Each question should elicit either a yes or no response. Do *not* prepare the receiving, accounts payable, or treasurer segments of the internal control questionnaire. Do *not* discuss the internal controls over purchases. Use the following format:

Questions	Yes	No

DISCUSSION CASES

10,11 >   **9-40**   Robert Mincin is the auditor of the Raleigh Corporation. Mincin is considering the audit work to be performed in the accounts payable area for the current year's engagement. The prior year's working papers show that confirmation requests were mailed to 100 of Raleigh's 1,000 suppliers. The selected suppliers were based on Mincin's sample, which was designed to select accounts with large-dollar balances. A substantial number of hours was spent by Raleigh and Mincin in resolving relatively minor differences between the confirmation replies and Raleigh's accounting records. Alternative audit procedures were used for suppliers who did not respond to the confirmation requests.

Required:

a. Discuss the accounts payable assertions that Mincin must consider in determining the audit procedures to be followed.

b. Discuss situations in which Mincin should use accounts payable confirmations, and discuss whether Mincin is required to use them.

c. Discuss why the use of large-dollar balances as the basis for selecting accounts payable for confirmation might not be the most efficient approach, and indicate what more efficient procedures could select accounts payable for confirmation.

(AICPA, adapted)

9-41 It is March 15, 2006 and you are very excited, as you have just been promoted to manager at a public accounting firm in Nanaimo, BC. You and the senior partner, Chip, are meeting with your first client, Marvelous Mocha Inc. (Mocha), a local coffee outlet. Mocha has been a client of the firm for many years and has purchased a bakery in Nanaimo, The Delectable Sweets Ltd. (Sweets). The deal closes on April 30, 2006. Chip and the president of Mocha, Jim Bean, have a very good business relationship and the audit of Mocha has always gone extremely well. Jim relies heavily on Chip for both accounting and business assistance.

Sweets was incorporated in 2000 and has been reviewed by another accounting firm since incorporation. It has always received an unqualified review report and Jim is hoping the acquisition will proceed smoothly.

Jim: *This bakery will be great for us. Then we can build a big coffee and dessert café. Going "out for coffee" seems to be the big event these days. I figure we'll make a mint.*

Chip: *What does Sweets' financial position look like? Any problems?*

Jim: *Everything looks good to me, although there is one situation I think you should know about. The bookkeeper, Tina, left Sweets on December 22, 2005. Apparently only vendors who phone have been getting paid as no one can figure out the payables situation. Apparently Tina did all the purchasing, receiving, and paying of the bills. She had signing authority on the bank account, as the owners are not interested in the paper work part of the business. It is clear that Tina was not very good.*

Chip: *Sounds like a bit of a nightmare situation. We'll look into it and let you know what we find out.*

You and Chip return to the office to plan the work on Sweets and Mocha. Chip asks you to look into the problem with the payables. The notes from your review of the prior year working papers and your visit to Sweets are in Exhibit 1 on page 406.

Required:

a. Prepare a memo on the internal control situation regarding accounts payable that discusses any weaknesses, audit implications, and suggested improvements.

EXHIBIT 1

Additional Information Regarding The Delectable Sweets Ltd.
March 15, 2006

1. From reviewing the working paper files of the review procedures, internal controls were not reviewed; however, Sweets does have written operating procedures as follows:
   - All purchase requests for cooking ingredients are to be supported by a purchase order with the head baker's signature.
   - The office manager may order all purchases for office supplies under $500. Any purchases greater than $500 must have the president's approval.
   - The accounts payable clerk prepares and signs the cheques for all amounts less than $1,000. All amounts over $1,000 must have two signatures (president—secretary treasurer and accounts payable clerk).
   - All purchases are to be recorded in the purchase journal.
   - All purchase discounts are to be taken.
   - All disbursements are recorded in the cash disbursement journal.
   - Cheques are numerically sequenced and all cancelled or voided cheques are to be retained.
   - Bank reconciliations are to be performed each month.
2. The bank account has not been reconciled since December 31, 2005
3. The receptionist made all deposits since December 31, 2005.
4. Upon scanning cheques written since December 31, 2005, I did not notice any individual cheques greater than $500; however, there were many cheques written to the same suppliers each month and I did not review all cheques at this time.
5. There were many unrecorded purchase invoices in a pile on Tina's desk.
6. The head baker was complaining to the president, as he was getting very low on a variety of ingredients he had issued purchase orders for.
7. The cash disbursement journal was missing certain cheque numbers.
8. The head baker was concerned that ingredient prices were rising even though price quotes from suppliers did not indicate any changes in the prices. It appears that many invoices were being paid late and therefore discounts were being missed.
9. All the accounts receivable that were recorded at December 31, 2005 were collected subsequent to year-end.
10. There are 10 leases for machinery and equipment. Four of these leases are for a variety of office equipment (photocopiers, fax machines, etc.). The equipment is replaced every four years and it appears from an initial review of the lease agreements that these are properly classified as operating leases. However, the other six leases are for baking equipment and appear to meet the classification of a capital lease, primarily because of either the life of the lease or the present value of the payments. None of the lease agreements have any indication of an automatic title transfer or bargain purchase option, so they are operating leases for tax purposes, but not for accounting. My initial review of the leases indicates that the capital assets should increase by $150,000, the accumulated amortization by $42,000, and the capital lease liability by $125,000 as of December 31, 2005. The income statement impact will be primarily one of classification as the combined unrecorded interest and amortization expense was approximately equal to the rental expense recorded.
11. There are 20 employees of Sweets; one head baker, eight bakers, three prep cooks, four sales staff, accounts payable clerk, secretary, maintenance person, and receptionist. In addition, the two owners are involved in the baking of products. They have limited involvement in the financial side of the business. The accounts payable clerk essentially ran the accounting operations because she wrote all the cheques, including payroll, and made all the deposits. The accounting system is a simple accounting package that she updated whenever she had the time, which generally occurred at the end of each month. The previous accountants determined all accruals and adjusting entries during the year-end review procedures.
12. Accounts receivable were not confirmed at December 31, 2005.
13. Inventory was counted on December 31, 2005. The accountants attended the count, no material discrepancies were found and all adjustments were recorded. Even though the accountants were not auditing Sweets, they did perform all procedures related to inventory that would have been necessary in an audit engagement.
14. Materiality was 6 percent of pre-tax earnings.

b. Draft an audit work program, without assertions, for accounts payable and the accounts payable confirmation procedures.

c. Because this is a first-time audit, document the first-time audit considerations to ensure that all procedures are carefully followed. (Do not spend any time addressing fraud or potential fraud in your responses.)

(ICABC, adapted)

2,4,5,6,7 ⟩   **9-42**   Your firm is the auditor of Supertel Inc., a Canadian company that manufactures and distributes cellular telephones. Supertel Inc. has branches in Vancouver, Toronto, Montreal, and Halifax, and its head office is located in Ottawa. The company's year-end is December 31.

Patrick Grant, vice president of information systems, has called the partner in charge of the audit of Supertel Inc., Jeanne Roy, to a meeting in his office.

Patrick: *To take advantage of new technologies and to be more effective, we are planning to install a new accounts payable system. The proposed system will enable us to better utilize our staff and improve controls. Our rapid expansion has generated more than $525 million in purchases this year. It is high time that we changed systems. Also, we expect to open new branches in the United States within the next two years.*

Jeanne: *Have you already selected the new system?*

Patrick: *Yes, we have. Last week, we signed an agreement with Infotech to lease hardware and to purchase software. You must surely have heard about this company; it's one of the most reputable information system development firms, and it offers the latest technology.*

Jeanne: *Yes, I have heard about Infotech. I believe you have made a good decision to install a new accounts payable system. However, you have to be very careful when implementing a new system and converting from one system to another.*

Patrick: *That's precisely why I wanted to see you today. I'm a little nervous about the implementation of the proposed system. And, as you are aware, we have not yet had a chance to start up an internal audit department; it's one of our next projects. Since you understand our systems so well, I would like you to evaluate the proposed accounts payable system and the way Infotech intends to proceed with the implementation. I would also like to have any other recommendations you can provide to ensure an orderly conversion of the system.*

It is now September 30. Upon returning to her office, Jeanne asks you to prepare a draft report to Mr. Grant. You have been provided with some background information on the accounts payable system (Exhibit 1 on page 408) and with the system implementation plan (Exhibit 2 on page 409).

EXHIBIT 1

Background Information

Current System:
Each branch is responsible for its own accounts payable. The head office receives accounts payable reports from the branches once a week only, and the reports vary from one branch to the next. Cash flow management by the head office is therefore not optimal. Each branch has its own system and supplier data base.

Proposed System:
Accounts payable will be centralized at the head office. Centralization should enable Supertel Inc. to save money, to maintain better control over its accounts payable, and to improve reporting.

Operational Overview of the Proposed System:
The branches will continue to receive invoices from suppliers. A clerk will match the invoices to receiving reports and code the invoices (i.e., specify which asset or expense account will be affected).

The branch supervisor will then sign the invoice to be paid and give it to a clerk who will "scan" the invoice, thereby transferring the image into a computer file. At the end of the day, files containing all the scanned invoices will be sent by modem to the head office in Ottawa. The invoices will be kept in the branches for one year and subsequently destroyed to save on storage costs.

Head office will receive the files containing the scanned invoices daily. To ensure proper authorization, a clerk will compare the branch supervisor's signature on the invoice as it appears on the monitor with a sample signature stored in a computer file. The sample signature file will also contain information on the limits of approval (maximum amount) and types of goods/services that the branch supervisor can approve. The clerk will then enter the following information into the accounts payable system: the name of the supplier (the name and address will be automatically compared with the master accounts payable file), the amount to be paid, and the financial coding (i.e., which asset or expense account will be affected).

Next, the accounts payable file will be updated for the company as a whole. The head office supervisor will check the accounts payable file for unusual amounts and will enter a code that allows cheques to be printed using information contained in the file.

All files will be stored on a hard disk at the head office. At the end of each month, the information will be copied onto laser disk for future reference.

Required:
Prepare the draft report.

(CICA, adapted)

INTERNET ASSIGNMENTS

9-43 Visit the website of a catalogue retailer similar to EarthWear Clothiers and determine how they process purchase transactions and recognize expenses. Note that you may have to examine the entity's annual report.

9-44 Visit the OSC or SEC website (www.osc.gov.on.ca or www.sec.gov respectively) and identify a company that has been recently cited for financial reporting problems related to the recognition of expenses. Prepare a memo summarizing the expense issues for the company.

EXHIBIT 2

System Implementation Plan

Current System:

Phase 1: Determination of needs and specifications

Members of Infotech, Patrick Grant, and members of the finance department will meet to identify the needs and objectives of Supertel Inc. with regard to the accounts payable system, e.g., type of reports that the system will have to generate, size of the system.

They will then specify, among other things:
- the information to be entered into the proposed system,
- the computer files (master files and transactions files) to be created,
- the data processing required (a proven software program that already operates in several other large companies will be modified slightly to meet the needs of Supertel Inc.), and
- the information that the system will produce, in either file or report form.

Phase 2: Phase-in of the new system

A terminal and scanner will be placed in each branch in the same location as the old computers. The main computer will be located at the head office in Ottawa, on the fifth floor, in a locked room near the employee cafeteria.

A backup computer will be available in case of disaster or in an emergency. This computer will be located on the second floor of the head office.

Phase 3: Testing of the new system

A programmer from Infotech will perform tests to ensure that the program logic and the various hardware components work well.

Another Infotech representative will perform tests on one of the branches selected at random. This branch will operate its existing system and the new system concurrently for one month. The results of the two systems will then be compared.

Phase 4: Staff training and documentation

Infotech will provide one day of training to clerks in the branches.

Infotech will distribute one video to each branch explaining how the software works. Patrick Grant will receive documentation on the design and operation of the new system and on the software program.

The standard Infotech user guide will be provided for clerks and supervisors.

Phase 5: Security measures

The system will be protected against unauthorized electronic access. Each user will have a password that will be changed every month.

The system will be physically protected. Each terminal and scanner in the branches will be located in a locked room. At the head office, the computer (on the fifth floor) containing the programs and the data base will be located in a locked room, with an alarm system designed to limit access.

Phase 6: Conversion

In early December, each branch will send its accounts payable file to the head office. Since the files are incompatible with the new system, a person will be in charge of entering all the information into the new system. A master file will thus be created (name of supplier, address, quantity discounts, term of payment, etc.) as well as a transactions file (details of purchases and balance payable to each supplier). A few tests will be performed for each branch comparing the information in the files received with the information entered into the new system.

Cutoff procedures will be performed to ensure that no transaction has been omitted or processed twice. All transactions carried out three days before conversion and two days after conversion will be re-examined.

Phase 7: Maintenance

Infotech offers a five-year warranty on the proposed system. In addition, if a problem occurs, Infotech guarantees that it will be resolved within five working days.

Every six months, Infotech will inspect the system to ensure that everything is working well and to do the maintenance.

Auditing the Human Resource Management Payroll Process

Learning Objectives

Upon completion of this chapter, you will be able to

1 Develop an understanding of the human resource management payroll process.

2 Identify the types of transactions in the HRM payroll process and the financial statement accounts affected.

3 Describe the functions in the HRM payroll process and the related document and records.

4 Identify the appropriate segregation of duties for the HRM payroll process.

5 Identify and evaluate inherent risks relevant to the HRM payroll process and related accounts.

6 Assess control risk for the HRM payroll process, apply appropriate tests of controls, and relate the assessment of control risk to substantive testing.

7 Apply substantive testing procedures to the transactions and accounts in the HRM payroll process.

8 Evaluate the audit findings and reach a final conclusion on payroll expense and payroll-related accrued expenses.

9 Explain the auditor's responsibilities when an entity's HRM payroll process is provided by an outside service organization.

RELEVANT ACCOUNTING AND ASSURANCE PRONOUNCEMENTS

CICA Handbook, **section 3461,** Employee future benefits

CICA Handbook, **section 5095,** Reasonable assurance and audit risk

CICA Handbook, **section 5141,** Understanding the entity and its environment and assessing the risks of material misstatement

CICA Handbook, **section 5142,** Materiality

CICA Handbook, **section 5143,** The auditor's procedures in response to assessed risks

CICA Handbook, **section 5300,** Audit evidence

CICA Handbook, **section 5301,** Analysis

CICA Handbook, **section 5310,** Audit evidence considerations when an enterprise uses a service organization

This chapter starts with an overview of the human resource management payroll process and then discusses the three components of the audit risk model. Then the inherent risks that affect the human resource management payroll process are addressed. This is followed by a discussion of the auditor's control risk assessment. Last, the chapter covers substantive tests for detection risk for payroll and related accounts.

AUDITING EARTHWEAR'S HUMAN RESOURCE PAYROLL PROCESS

EarthWear EarthWear has a labour force which ranges from approximately 3,500 to 5,300. The labour force increases 2,700 or 77 percent, due to the needs of the peak winter sales season. From an audit perspective, EarthWear can be viewed as having two different sets of employees. Auditing the "core" employees is a relatively straightforward process for Willis & Adams; EarthWear's human resource management payroll process is stable and well controlled. Employee relations are good. For the seasonal, temporary employees, Willis & Adams will need to focus on the system whereby these employees are added to the payroll process when hired and removed from the payroll process when terminated at the end of the peak season. It is also important to make sure that EarthWear's systems properly handle government information requirements and the additional costs to the company for deductions such as Canada Pension and Employment Insurance. Because many individuals are involved in the payroll process, the risks in the human resource management payroll process are likely to be risks associated with material misstatements at the individual transaction or account level. Fraud at the individual transaction or account level, as opposed to fraudulent reporting at the financial statement level, may be a concern. Good controls, such as segregation of duties, are important in this process and Willis & Adams will want to assure themselves that there are strong controls in place over this process.

Overview of the Human Resource Management Payroll Process

LO 1 The human resources process starts with the establishment of sound policies for hiring, training, evaluating, counselling, promoting, compensating, and taking remedial actions for employees. Once an individual has been hired as an employee, the main transaction that affects the financial statement accounts is a payroll (payment) transaction. A payroll transaction usually begins with an employee performing some job and recording the time spent on a time card. The time card is approved by a supervisor before being forwarded to the payroll department. The data are then reviewed and sent to the IT department for processing. Finally, payment is made directly to the employee or deposited in the employee's bank account.

EarthWear Figure 10–1 presents a flowchart of EarthWear's payroll system that serves as a framework for discussing control procedures and tests of controls. Although the description of EarthWear's payroll system is fairly typical, the reader should focus on the basic

FIGURE 10–1

Flowchart of the Payroll Process—EarthWear Clothiers

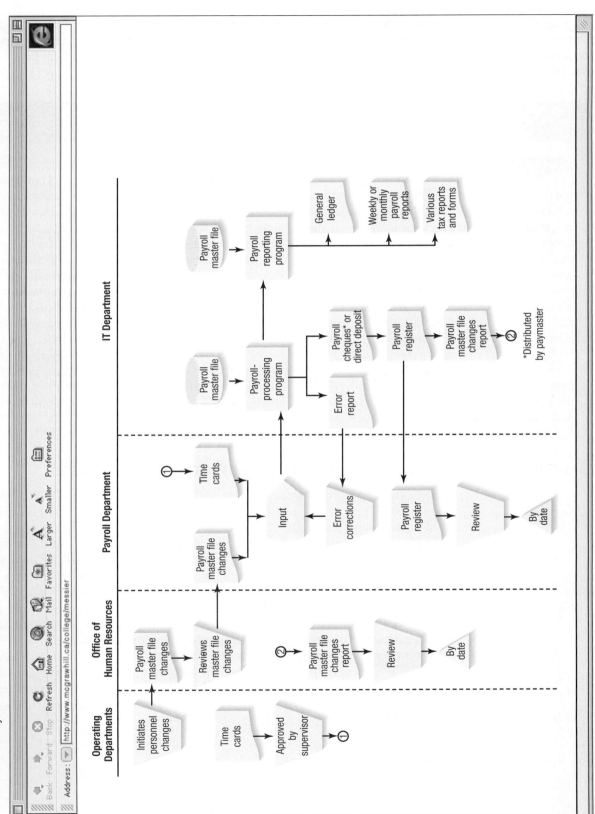

concepts so that they can be applied to the specific payroll cycles encountered. The following topics related to the payroll application[1] are covered:

- types of transactions and financial statement accounts affected
- the major functions
- types of documents and records
- the key segregation of duties

Types of Transactions and Financial Statement Accounts Affected

LO 2>

Two main types of transactions are processed through the payroll application:

- payments to employees for services rendered
- accrual and payment of payroll-related liabilities arising from employees' services, including liabilities for Canada Pension Plan (CPP) contributions and Employment Insurance (EI) premiums

The discussion of internal control focuses on payments to employees, including a description of how such transactions are processed and the key control procedures that should be present to ensure that no material misstatements occur. The audit of payroll-related accruals is discussed later in the chapter.

The financial statement accounts that are generally affected by the two types of payroll-related transactions are

Type of Transaction	*Account Affected*
Payroll transactions	Cash.
	Inventory.
	Direct and indirect labour expense acccunts.
	Various payroll-related liability and expense accounts.
Accrued payroll liability transactions	Cash.
	Various accruals (such as payroll taxes and pension costs).

The Major Functions and Reports and Documents

LO 3>

The next section describes the major activities of the payroll function and the associated documents and records typically created by those functions. The principal objectives of the payroll application are to (1) record production and other types of payroll costs in the accounts, (2) ensure that payroll costs are for legitimate entity activities, and (3) accrue liabilities for salaries and wages, payroll taxes, and various employee benefit programs. Table 10–1 lists the functions that are normally part of the payroll application and Table 10-2 lists the documents and records.

Personnel   The personnel function is responsible for managing the human resource needs of the organization. This includes hiring and terminating employees, setting wage rates and salaries, and establishing and monitoring employee benefit programs. Most large organizations centralize these activities in an office of human resources or personnel department. However, in a small organization, these activities may be combined with the duties of selected operating and administrative person-

---

[1]The terms "payroll process" and "payroll application" are used interchangeably to refer to the payroll function within the human resource management process.

Table 10–1	Functions in the Payroll Application

• *Personnel*	Authorization of hiring, firing, wage-rate and salary adjustments, salaries, and payroll deductions.
• *Supervision*	Review and approval of employees' attendance and time information; monitoring of employee scheduling, productivity, and payroll cost variances.
• *Timekeeping*	Processing of employees' attendance and time information and coding of account distribution.
• *Payroll processing*	Computation of gross pay, deductions, and net pay; recording and summarization of payments and verification of account distribution.
• *Disbursement*	Payment of employees' compensation and benefits.
• *General ledger*	Proper accumulation, classification, and summarization of payroll in the general ledger.

Table 10–2	Documents and Records Involved in the Payroll Association

Personnel records, including wage-rate or salary authorizations.

TD-1 and other deduction authorization forms.

Time card.

Payroll cheque/direct deposit records.

Payroll register.

Payroll master file.

Payroll master file changes report.

Periodic payroll reports.

Various tax reports and forms.

nel. In such organizations, control over human resource activities may not be as strong as when such activities are centralized. The office of human resources maintains employees' personnel records. The office of human resources may also be responsible for defining job requirements and descriptions, administering union contracts, and developing performance criteria and employee evaluation procedures.

Personnel records, including wage rate or salary authorizations, contain information on each employee's work history including hiring date, wage rate or salary, payroll deduction authorization forms, wage-rate and salary adjustment authorizations, performance evaluations, and termination notice, if applicable. Personnel records are normally maintained in the human resources department.

The employee must complete a *TD-1 form* to authorize deductions from his or her pay. The organization should therefore use authorization forms to document such deductions. For example, the employee must complete a TD-1 form to authorize the withholding of provincial and federal income tax. Similar forms should be used for deductions for medical insurance, retirement contributions, and other benefits.

Supervision   Supervisors within operating and supporting departments are responsible for reviewing and approving employees' attendance and time information. When time cards or other documents are used to record an employee's time worked and job classification, the supervisor approves this information before processing by the payroll function. Additionally, supervisors should monitor labour productivity and labour cost variances. Standardized labour performance measures, such as standard productivity and wage rates, improve the monitoring of payroll costs. Labour cost variances should be investigated by supervisory personnel and communicated to upper-level management. When employees are not required to complete time cards or job classification documents, the entity needs to have control procedures to notify the timekeeping or payroll-processing function about employees' absences and changes in employees' job classifications. This might be accomplished by having the supervisor submit a periodic attendance and job classification report.

A *time card* is used to record the hours worked by the employee, including the time the employee has started and stopped work. In some cases the employee fills in the time worked; in other cases a time clock records the time. In more current applications, the process may be computerized.

Timekeeping   The timekeeping function prepares employees' time information for payroll processing. When payroll cost distribution is determined at the operating department level, the timekeeping function reviews this information before processing. Otherwise, the timekeeping function should be responsible for coding the payroll costs to appropriate accounts. In some organizations, a separate timekeeping department handles these functions. At EarthWear (see Figure 10–1), the operating and supporting departments are responsible for the timekeeping function.

Payroll Processing   The payroll-processing function is responsible for computing gross pay, deductions, and net pay. This function is also responsible for recording and summarizing payments and verifying account distribution. When IT is used to process payroll, as at EarthWear, the entity must have strong application controls to ensure proper payroll processing.

The payroll processing function is supported by a number of different types of documentation. The *payroll register*, which is also referred to as the *payroll journal*, summarizes all payroll payments issued to employees. A payroll register normally indicates employee's gross pay, deductions, and net pay. In a computerized environment, the details for this document are maintained in the *payroll master file*, which also includes information on each employee such as name, social insurance number, pay rate, and authorized deductions.

The *payroll master file changes report* contains a record of the changes made to the payroll master file. The human resource department reviews this report to ensure that all authorized changes have been properly made. At the end of the each week or month, a number of summary *periodic payroll reports* may be prepared. The type of reports prepared depends on the type of organization. A manufacturing entity might have a payroll expense report that showed the allocation of direct labour to various products. EarthWear Clothiers reports a summary of payroll by various job classifications and departments. Department heads use this report to monitor payroll expense variances.

Disbursement The disbursement function is responsible for paying employees for services and benefits. In particular, this function oversees the preparation and distribution of payroll cheques. Again, cheque preparation normally occurs in the IT department. Therefore, it is necessary to have control procedures over access to blank cheques and cheque signature plates. Cheques are normally distributed by a paymaster, who is typically a member of the treasurer's department. When payments are directly deposited in employees' bank accounts, strong IT application controls are necessary.

The *payroll cheque* or *direct deposit records* indicate the amount paid to the employee for services rendered. The amount paid is the gross pay less any deductions. In many cases, the employee's pay is directly deposited into the individual's bank account and the company produces a listing of employees' payments that were sent to their bank accounts.

General Ledger The general ledger function for the payroll cycle is responsible for properly accumulating, classifying, and summarizing payroll and benefit transactions in the general ledger. When IT is used to process payroll transactions, control totals can help ensure that this function is performed properly. This function is normally performed by the general accounting department.

Finally, most companies are required to prepare various payroll tax and information reports for both the federal and provincial governments. Employment insurance forms may also need to be completed periodically Additionally, an entity must provide each employee with a T-4 form at the end of the year.

The Key Segregation of Duties

LO 4>

As discussed in prior chapters, proper segregation of duties is one of the most important control procedures in any accounting system. Duties should be assigned to individuals in such a way that no one individual can control all phases of processing a transaction, thus permitting misstatements to go undetected. Individuals responsible for supervision and timekeeping should be segregated from the personnel, payroll-processing, and general ledger functions. If IT is used extensively in the payroll application, duties should be properly segregated in the IT department. Table 10–3 contains some of the key segregation of duties for the payroll application and examples of possible errors or fraud that can result from conflicts in duties.

Table 10–4 shows more detailed segregation of duties for individual payroll functions across the various departments that are involved in processing payroll transactions.

Inherent Risk Assessment

LO 5>

As mentioned in the introduction to this chapter, the recruitment and retention of qualified personnel are extremely important in an enterprise's achievement of its strategic objectives. Accordingly, the payroll application and remuneration-related activities represent key business processes. However, generally speaking, few inherent risk factors directly affect the

Table 10–3	Key Segregation of Duties in the Payroll Application and Possible Errors or Fraud

Segregation of Duties	*Possible Errors or Fraud Resulting from Conflicts of Duties*
The supervision function should be segregated from the personnel records and payroll-processing functions.	If one individual is responsible for the supervision, personnel records, and payroll-processing functions, fictitious employees can appear on the payroll records or unauthorized payments can be made. This can result in unauthorized payments to existing employees or payments to fictitious employees.
The disbursement function should be segregated from the personnel records, supervision, and payroll-processing functions.	If one individual is responsible for the disbursement function and also has the authority to hire and fire employees, approve time reports, or prepare payroll cheques, unauthorized payroll cheques can be issued.
The payroll-processing function should be segregated from the general ledger function.	If one individual is responsible for processing payroll transactions and also for the general ledger, that individual can conceal any defalcation that would normally be detected by independent review of accounting entries made to the general ledger.

Table 10–4	Segregation of Duties for Payroll Functions by Department

Payroll Function	*Department*					
	Operating or Supporting	*Personnel*	*Timekeeping*	*Payroll*	*IT*	*Treasurer*
Initiation of wage or salary changes	X					
Initiation of employee hiring and firing	X					
Approval of wage or salary changes		X				
Updating of personnel records		X				
Updating of payroll records		X				
Approval of time cards and job classification	X					
Review of time data and payroll distribution			X			
Preparation of payroll				X	X	
Preparation and signing of payroll cheques					X	
Distribution of payroll cheques						X
Updating of general ledger of payroll activity					X	
Comparison of montly departmental payroll expense to budget	X					
Calculation and recording of payroll taxes				X		

payroll application and its related accounts. Some factors the auditor might consider are the effect of economic conditions on payroll costs, the supply of skilled workers, and the frequency of employee turnover. Additionally, the presence of labour contracts and legislation such as the provincial Workers' Compensation Board regulations may also affect the auditor's assessment of inherent risk. However, because the payroll application and its related accounts generally contain few inherent risks, the auditor is normally able to assess the inherent risk as low. However, it may not be appropriate to set inherent risk associated with officer compensation as low because, as illustrated in Exhibit 10-1, officers may have motive and opportunity to take advantage of their position in the form of excessive compensation.

Control Risk Assessment

LO 6 ❯   The discussion of control risk assessment follows the framework outlined in previous chapters. However, the discussion is not as thorough as the discussion of the revenue or purchasing processes because it is assumed that

---

EXHIBIT 10–1

Executive Compensation Abuses at Tyco

Tyco International Ltd.'s Dennis Kozlowski looms large as a rogue CEO for the ages. His $6,000 shower curtain and vodka-spewing, full-size ice replica of Michelangelo's David will not be soon forgotten. In essence, prosecutors accused Kozlowski and former Chief Financial Officer Mark Swartz of running a criminal enterprise within Tyco's executive suite. The two were hit with 38 felony counts for pilfering $170 million directly from the company and for pocketing an additional $430 million through tainted sales of stock. Ironically, both Kozlowski and Swartz were former auditors; Kozlowski has become the personification of the widespread irrational exuberance of the late 1990s. Kozlowski handpicked some of the members of the compensation committee, and the changes worked to his benefit as his total compensation rose from $8.8 million in 1997 to $67 million in 1998 to $170 million in 1999. But it appears that Kozlowski believed that he deserved more money than he was making. The more he was paid as a reward for Tyco's soaring stock price, the more he spent on luxuries—and the more he allegedly stole. During these years, Kozlowski was secretly selling lots of stock—$280 million worth, according to the Manhattan DA's indictment of Kozlowski.

Kozlowski also ran up a $242 million tab at Tyco under a loan program designed to finance the purchase of company stock. Rather than use the money to buy Tyco stock, he used it to purchase fine art and antiques, a yacht, and a Nantucket estate. The loans were forms of compensation, but characterizing the compensation as a loan provided significant tax and accounting benefits to the executive and the corporation. Tyco's board approved some, but not all, of the forms of compensation Kozlowski had tapped into.

When Congress learned of the level of abuse in corporate loans, it was shocked. In the *Sarbanes-Oxley Act* of 2002, Congress forbid public companies to make or even arrange new loans to executives or to modify or renew old ones. The penalties for a violation are up to 20 years in jail and fines reaching $5 million for executives and $25 million for companies.

Sources: Ashlea Ebeling, "The Lending Game," *Forbes* (May 10, 2004), and Anthony Bianco, William Symonds, Nanette Byrnes, and David Polek, "The Rise and Fall of Dennis Kozlowski," *Business Week* (December 12, 2002)

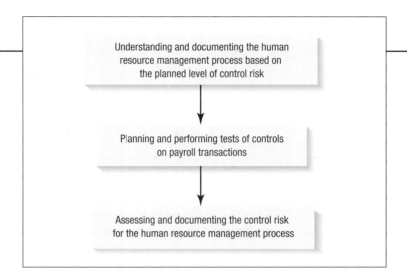

FIGURE 10–2

Major Steps in Assessing Control Risk for the Human Resource Management Application

the reader has now developed a reasonable understanding of the decision process followed by the auditor when assessing control risk. Figure 10–2 summarizes the three major steps involved in assessing control risk for the human resource management payroll application.

Understanding and Documenting Internal Control

The level of understanding of the five internal control components should be similar to that obtained for the other processes. The auditor's understanding of the payroll system is normally gained by conducting a walk-through of the system to gather evidence about the various functions that are involved in processing the transactions through the system. For an ongoing audit, this process merely involves updating prior years' documentation of the payroll system by noting any changes that have occurred. For a new engagement, or if the system has undergone major changes, more time and effort are needed to document the understanding of internal control. The auditor's understanding of internal control for the payroll system should be documented in the working papers using flowcharts, internal control questionnaires, and memoranda.

Because the control environment pervasively affects all accounting applications, including the payroll system, two factors shown in Table 6–1 in Chapter 6 should be considered. First, the entity's organizational structure, its personnel practices, and its methods of assigning authority and responsibility must be examined. The proper organizational structure for processing payroll transactions was discussed in the previous section. Second, the entity should have sound policies for hiring, training, promoting, and compensating employees. These policies should include specific authority and responsibility for hiring and firing employees, for setting wage rates and making salary changes, and for establishing benefits.

Planning and Performing Tests of Controls

When a reliance strategy is followed, the auditor must identify the control procedures that ensure that material misstatements are either prevented or detected and corrected. For example, the client may have formal procedures for classifying payroll costs in appropriate accounts. The auditor may decide to rely on this control procedure to reduce the control risk for the classification objective. In this case, the client's procedures for classifying payroll transactions by types of payroll costs should be examined by the auditor.

Assessing and Documenting the Control Risk

After the tests of controls are completed, the auditor assesses the level of control risk and documents that assessment. The documentation supporting the assessed level of control risk for the payroll application might include a flowchart, the results of tests of controls, and a memorandum indicating the overall conclusion about control risk.

Control Procedures and Tests of Controls—Payroll Transactions

Table 10–5 summarizes the assertions and possible misstatements for payroll transactions. The table also includes key control procedures for each assertion and examples of tests of controls that can test the effectiveness of the control procedures. The discussion that follows focuses only on the most important assertions for the payroll system. EarthWear's payroll system contains all of the relevant control procedures.

Table 10–5	**Summary of Assertions, Possible Misstatements Control Procedures, and Tests of Controls for Payroll Transactions**

Assertion	Possible Misstatement	Control Procedure	Test of Controls
Occurrence	Payments made to fictitious employees	Segregation of duties	Observe and evaluate proper segregation of duties.
	Payments made to terminated employees	Adequate personnel files	Review and test personnel files.
	Payments made to valid employees who have not worked	Initiation of changes in employment status, wages or salaries, and benefits made by operating departments reported to the office of human resources	Review and test client's procedures for changing employees's records; if IT application, examine application controls.
		Time clocks used to record time	Observe employees' use of the time clock.
		Time cards approved by supervisors	Inspect time cards presented for approval by supervisor.
		Only employees with valid employee numbers paid	Review and test client's procedures for entering and removing employee numbers from payroll master file; if IT application, examine application controls.
		Use of payroll budgets with review by departments supervisors	Review client's budgeting procedures.

(continued)

Table 10–5	**Summary of Assertions, Possible Misstatements Control Procedures, and Tests of Controls for Payroll Transactions (concluded)**		
Assertion	*Possible Misstatement*	*Control Procedure*	*Test of Controls*
Completeness	Employee services provided but not recorded	Prenumbered time cards accounted for by client personnel	Check numerical sequence of time cards; if IT application, examine application controls.
Accuracy	Employee compensation and payroll deductions computed incorrectly	Verification of payroll amounts and benefit calculation	Review and test client's verification procedures; if IT application, examine application controls.
		Review of payroll register for unusual amounts	If IT-prepared, use computer-assisted audit techniques to test computer program logic for calculating amounts.
		Use of payroll budgets with review by department supervisors	Review client's budgeting procedures.
	Payroll transactions not posted correctly to the payroll journal	Changes to master payroll file verified through "before and after" reports	Examine reconciliation of "before and after" reports to payroll master file if IT application, examine application controls.
	Amounts from payroll journal not posted correctly to general ledger	Payroll master file (payroll register) reconciled to general ledger payroll accounts	Review reconciliation of payroll master file to general ledger payroll accounts; if IT application, examine application controls.
Cutoff	Payroll transactions recorded in the wrong period	Notices of additions, terminations, and changes to salaries, wages, and deductions reported promptly to the payroll processing function, after which the changes are updated promptly on the master payroll file	Review and test client's procedures for changes to master payroll file; if IT application, examine application controls.
		All time cards forwarded to the payroll department weekly	Review and test procedure for processing time cards.
		Procedures that require recording payroll liabilities as soon as possible after they are incurred	Review and test procedures for recording payroll liabilities.
Classification	Payroll transactions not properly classified	Chart of accounts	Review chart accounts
		Independent approval and review of accounts charged for payroll	Review and test procedures for classifying payroll costs.
		Use of payroll budgets with review by department supervisors	Review client's budgeting procedures.

Occurrence of Payroll Transactions

The auditor wants assurance that payments for payroll-related services are being made to valid employees for time actually worked. Thus, the client needs control procedures that prevent payments to fictitious employees and to valid employees who have not worked. Controls must also ensure that payroll payments stop once an employee is terminated. Proper segregation of duties provides the main control against payments to fictitious employees. As noted in Table 10–4, proper segregation of duties among operating and supporting departments, the human resources department, and the payroll department minimizes the possibility of fictitious employees existing within the system. The maintenance of adequate personnel files should also prevent such misstatements.

The human resources department approves the termination of an employee and ensures that he or she is removed from the master payroll file. Required completion and approval of a time card also prevent payments to terminated employees. Proper review and approval of time cards by supervisors should prevent valid employees from being paid for work not performed.

Finally, when payroll transactions are processed by an IT system, a payroll cheque should not be prepared unless the employee transaction has a valid employee number. Review and observation are the main tests of controls the auditor uses to examine the control procedures shown in Table 10–5.

Accuracy of Payroll Transactions

The main concern related to the accuracy assertion is that an employee's gross pay and payroll deductions may be incorrectly computed. For example, an employee may be paid at a higher rate than authorized or payroll deductions may be incorrectly computed. The client should maintain verification procedures to ensure correct payroll and benefit calculations. The auditor can review the client's verification procedures as a test of control. When IT is used to prepare the payroll, the auditor can use computer-assisted audit techniques (CAATs) to test the program logic for proper calculations. In a manual system, or if a service bureau is used, the auditor can recompute the payroll calculations for a sample of payroll transactions.

Classification of Payroll Transactions

Because classification is an important assertion for payroll transactions, control procedures must ensure that the appropriate payroll accounts are charged. If payroll expense is charged to the wrong accounts, the financial statements may be misstated. For example, if payroll expense is not properly classified between direct and indirect labour, inventory and cost of goods sold may not be valued properly. The use of an adequate chart of accounts is one control procedure that helps to prevent misclassification. Additionally, the timekeeping function should review the payroll categories assigned by the operating departments. Budgets that compare actual payroll costs to budgeted payroll costs by each category of labour also provide a control over proper classification of payroll. The auditor can review and test the client's control procedures for classifying payroll costs.

Relating the Assessed Level of Control Risk to Substantive Procedures

If the results of the tests of controls for the payroll cycle support the assessed level of control risk, the auditor conducts substantive tests of payroll-related accounts at the assessed level. EarthWear, for example, has a strong set of internal control procedures for processing payroll transactions. If the auditor's tests of EarthWear's controls indicate that the controls are operating effectively, then no adjustment of detection risk is necessary. However, if the results of the control tests do not support the assessed level of control risk for EarthWear's payroll cycle, the detection risk will have to be set lower. This would require that the nature and extent of substantive testing of payroll-related accounts be increased.

Auditing Payroll-Related Accounts

LO 7> Two categories of substantive procedures for auditing payroll expense and payroll-related liabilities are discussed here: (1) substantive analytical procedures and (2) tests of details of classes of transactions, account balances, and disclosures. Table 10–6 presents the assertions for classes

| Table 10–6 | **Assertions about Classes of Transactions, Events, Account Balances, and Disclosures for Payroll Expense and Payroll-Related Accruals** |

Assertions about Classes of Transactions and Events:

- **Occurrence.** Payroll transactions and events are valid.

- **Completeness.** All payroll transactions and events have been recorded.

- **Accuracy.** Payroll transactions have been properly computed, and payroll expense has been properly accumulated from journals and ledgers.

- **Cutoff.** Payroll expense and related accruals are recorded in the correct accounting period.

- **Classification.** Payroll expense and related accruals have been recorded in the proper accounts.

Assertions about Account Balances at the Period End:

- **Existence.** Payroll expense is a valid expense and related accruals are valid liabilities.

- **Rights and obligations.** The payroll-related accruals are the obligations of the entity.

- **Completeness.** All payroll expense and related accruals have been recorded.

- **Valuation and allocation.** Payroll expense and related accruals are included in the financial statements at appropriate amounts, and any resulting valuation or allocation adjustments are appropriately recorded.

Assertions about Presentation and Disclosure:

- **Occurrence and rights and obligations.** All disclosed events, transactions, and other matters relating to payroll expense and related accruals have occurred and pertain to the entity.

- **Completeness.** All disclosures relating to payroll expense and related accruals that should have been included in the financial statements have been included.

- **Classification and understandability.** Financial information relating to payroll expense and related accruals is appropriately presented and described, and disclosures are clearly expressed.

- **Accuracy and valuation.** Financial and other information relating to payroll expense and related accruals are disclosed fairly and at appropriate amounts.

of transactions, events, account balances, and disclosures as they apply to payroll expense and payroll-related liabilities, which are often called *accrued payroll expenses*. The term accrued payroll expenses or liabilities mainly refers to the cost of employment benefits that are paid by the company on behalf of the full-time employees. This includes such things as the employer's share of EI contributions, the employer's share of CPP (or QPP) contributions, and pension plan contributions if the company contributes to a pension plan for its employees. The company must also periodically remit to the government the source deductions it has withheld from employees. You should note that the auditor may test assertions related to transactions (substantive tests of transactions) in conjunction with testing the internal controls. If the tests of controls indicate that the controls are not operating effectively, the auditor may need to test transactions at the date the account balance is tested.

Substantive Analytical Procedures

Substantive analytical procedures can be useful substantive tests for examining the reasonableness of payroll expenses and payroll-related accrual accounts. When utilized as part of planning, preliminary analytical procedures can effectively identify payroll expense accounts and accrual accounts that may be misstated. Table 10–7 shows examples of substantive analytical procedures that can be used for auditing payroll. Two examples will help demonstrate their application in practice. First, the auditor can compare budgeted payroll costs with actual payroll costs. Variances due to quantity and wage differences should show up in the client's cost-accounting

Table 10–7	Substantive Analytical Procedures for Auditing Payroll Accounts and Payroll-Related Accruals
Substantive Analytical Procedure	*Possible Misstatement Detected*
Payroll Expense Accounts	
Compare current-year balances in the various payroll expense accounts with prior years' balances after adjustment for pay changes and number of employees	Over- or understatement of payroll expense.
Compare payroll costs as a percentage of sales with prior years' and industry data.	Over- or understatement of payroll expense.
Compare labour utilization rates and statistics with industry data.	Over- or understatement of payroll expense.
Compare budgeted payroll expenses with actual payroll expenses.	Over- or understatement of payroll expense.
Estimate sales commissions by applying commission formulas to recorded sales totals.	Over- or understatement of sales commissions.
Payroll-Related Accrual Accounts	
Compare current-year balances in payroll-related accrual accounts with prior years' balances after adjusting for changes in conditions	Over- or understatement of accrued liabilities.
Test reasonableness of accrual balances	Over- or understatement of accrued liabilities.

system (on weekly or monthly reports). If the variances are immaterial, the auditor has some evidence that payroll costs are reasonable. If the variances are material, the auditor should investigate the potential causes of the differences. Analytical procedures can be very effective here because the relationship between the amount of the company's obligations for benefits such as EI, CPP, etc., and the amount of payroll is very stable (the amounts are determined by applying a percentage to the amount of the payroll). As a result, variances from expectation are quite easily identified.

Substantive analytical procedures also help the auditor to determine the proper valuation of inventory when standard costs are used to value inventory. The auditor can use analytical procedures to test the reasonableness of the balances in accrued wages payable. For example, if accrued wages represent payroll for two days, the auditor can multiply the total weekly payroll by 40 percent (2 days ÷ 5 days). If the auditor's calculation is close to the accrued amount, no further audit work may be required on the accrued wages account.

Tests of Details of Classes of Transactions, Account Balances, and Disclosures

Table 10–6 presented the assertions for payroll expense and payroll-related liabilities. The intended purpose of tests of details of transactions is to detect monetary misstatements in the individual transactions processed through the payroll application. As previously mentioned, tests of details of transactions are often conducted in conjunction with tests of controls. Table 10–8 presents examples of tests of details of transactions, account balances, and disclosures for assertions related to payroll. The discussion that follows focuses on tests of details of account balances of payroll expense and accrued payroll liabilities.

Payroll Expense Accounts

Payroll transactions affect many expense accounts, including direct and indirect manufacturing expense, general and administrative salaries, sales salaries, commissions, and payroll tax expenses. Some companies account for such expenses by product line or division. In addition, fringe benefits such as medical and life insurance are usually paid for at least partly by the organization. If the entity's internal control is reliable, the auditor generally does not need to conduct detailed tests of these payroll expense accounts. On such audits, sufficient evidence can be gathered through an understanding of internal control, tests of controls, substantive tests of transactions, and analytical procedures. Additional testing is necessary only when control weaknesses exist or when the other types of audit tests indicate that material misstatements may be present.

Several payroll expense accounts may still be examined even when control risk is low. For example, it is common to verify the compensation paid to officers of the company because information on executive salaries and bonuses is needed for proxy statements and the corporate tax returns. Limits may also be placed on officers' salaries and bonuses as part of lending agreements. If such limits are exceeded, the entity may be in default on the debt. Officers' compensation is also examined because officers are in a

Table 10–8	Examples of Payroll Tests of Transactions, Account Balances, and Disclosures

Assertions about Classes of Transactions	Substantive Tests of Transaction
Occurrence	Trace a sample of payroll cheques to the master employee list to verify validity.*
Completeness	Tracing of a sample of time cards to the payroll register.*
Accuracy	Recompute the mathematical accuracy of a sample of payroll cheques: CAATS may be used to test the logic of the computer programs for proper calculation of gross pay, deductions, and net pay.
Cutoff	Trace a sample of time cards before and after period end to the appropriate weekly payroll report, and trace the weekly payroll report to the general ledger to verify payroll transactions are recorded in the proper period.*
Classification	Examine a sample of payroll cheques for proper classification into expense accounts.*

Assertions about Account Balances at Period End	Tests of Details of Account Balances
Existence	Vouch selected amounts from the account analysis schedules for the accruals to supporting documentation (payroll tax returns, corporate benefit policies, etc.).
Rights and obligations	Review supporting documentation to determine that the entity is legally obligated to pay the liability Test a sample of bank reconciliations for the payroll bank account (see Chapter 14).
Completeness	Search for unrecorded liabilities (see Chapter 9). Use CAATs to foot weekly payroll reports and reconcile the total to the general ledger (payroll expense and related accruals).
Valuation and allocation	Obtain an account analysis schedule for accrued payroll liabilities; foot schedules and agree total to general ledger. Compare amounts accrued to supporting documentation, such as payroll tax returns.

Assertions about Presentation and Disclosure	Tests of Details of Disclosures
Occurrence, and rights and obligations	Enquire about accruals to ensure that they are properly disclosed.
Completeness	Complete financial reporting checklist to ensure that all financial statement disclosures related to payroll expense and related accruals have been made.
Classification and understandability	Review accrued payroll liabilities for proper classification between short-term and long-term liabilities Read footnotes to ensure that required disclosures are understandable.
Accuracy and valuation	Review benefit contracts for proper disclosure of pension and postretirement benefits. Read footnotes and other information to ensure that the information is accurate and properly presented at the appropriate amounts.

* These tests of details of transactions are commonly conducted as dual-purpose tests (i.e., in conjunction with tests of controls).

EXHIBIT 10–2

Questionable Salary Payments at Lincoln Savings and Loan

One of the most notorious cases noted during the savings-and-loan debacle in the US was Lincoln Savings and Loan. In 1978 Charles Keating, Jr., founded American Continental Corporation (ACC), which acquired Lincoln six years later. In 1989 the Federal Home Loan Bank Board seized control of Lincoln Savings and Loan. The closing of Lincoln cost US taxpayers approximately $2 billion. Exercising his ownership powers over Lincoln, Keating installed his son, Charles Keating III, as chairman of the board at an annual salary of $1 million. An examination report on ACC indicated that "funds sent by Lincoln to ACC were being used by ACC to fund treasury stock transactions [and] pay debt service, consulting fees, and exorbitant management salaries." The report estimated that $34 million had been expended on "Keating family benefits."

Source: The People, Plaintiff and Respondent, v. Charles H. Keating, Jr., Defendant and Appellant (31 Cal., App. 4th 1688, 1993).

position to override the control procedures and pay themselves more than they are authorized to receive (see Exhibit 10–2). Officers' compensation expense can be verified by comparing the amounts shown in the payroll records with the amounts authorized in either board of directors' minutes or employment contracts and by using CAATS to search for other cash payments made to the officer, his or her family members, or related parties.

Accrued Payroll Liabilities

An entity incurs a number of payroll-related liabilities. In addition to these accrued expenses, the entity also withholds various amounts from an employee's pay. These withholdings include payroll taxes (federal and provincial income taxes), medical and life insurance premiums, pension, and other miscellaneous deductions. Some examples of accrued payroll liabilities include

- accrued wages and salaries
- accrued payroll taxes
- accrued commissions
- accrued bonuses
- accrued benefits such as vacation and sick pay

In auditing accrued payroll liabilities, the auditor is concerned with the assertion of *existence, completeness, valuation, cutoff,* and *presentation and disclosure.* When control risk is low or the amounts in the accounts are relatively small, the auditor can verify accrued payroll liabilities using analytical procedures. For example, the auditor can compare the prior year's balance in each accrual with the current year's balance after considering changing conditions.

For accrued payroll liability accounts for which the control risk is high or whose amounts are material, the auditor can obtain a detailed account analysis schedule. For example, Exhibit 10–3 shows an account analysis schedule for EarthWear's accrued payroll taxes. The credits to the account represent the recognition of payroll tax expense at the end of each pay period. These amounts can be traced to the various payroll tax returns or other documentation filed by the entity and should agree with the amount

EXHIBIT 10–3

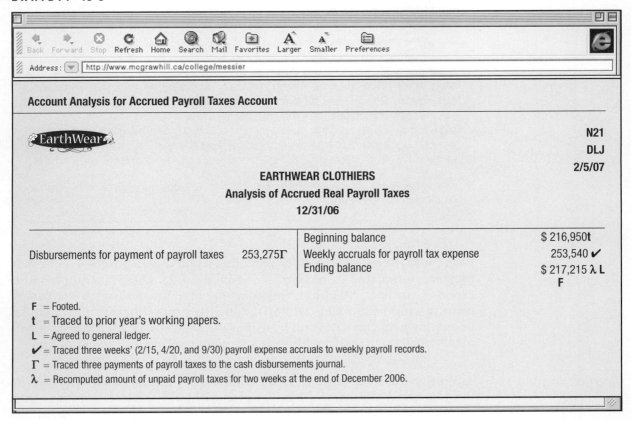

Account Analysis for Accrued Payroll Taxes Account

<EarthWear>

N21
DLJ
2/5/07

EARTHWEAR CLOTHIERS
Analysis of Accrued Real Payroll Taxes
12/31/06

Disbursements for payment of payroll taxes	253,275Γ	Beginning balance	$ 216,950t
		Weekly accruals for payroll tax expense	253,540 ✔
		Ending balance	$ 217,215 λ L
			F

F = Footed.
t = Traced to prior year's working papers.
L = Agreed to general ledger.
✔ = Traced three weeks' (2/15, 4/20, and 9/30) payroll expense accruals to weekly payroll records.
Γ = Traced three payments of payroll taxes to the cash disbursements journal.
λ = Recomputed amount of unpaid payroll taxes for two weeks at the end of December 2006.

of payroll tax expense included in the income statement. The debits to the account represent payments made to relevant government agencies. These payments can be verified by tracing the amounts to the cash disbursements journal.

Existence and Valuation   The existence and valuation assertions can generally be tested at the same time. The auditor's concerns are whether the recorded liabilities are valid obligations of the entity and whether they are included in the financial statements at the appropriate amount. To verify the existence and valuation of an accrued payroll liability, the auditor can generally trace the amounts included on the account analysis working paper to supporting documentation such as payroll tax reports. If adequate documentation is present, the auditor has evidence that the amount represents a valid liability. The auditor can usually verify the accuracy of the amounts by recalculating the figures.

Completeness   The auditor wants to make sure that all payroll-related liabilities are recorded. The auditor should be aware of the normal payroll amounts that are paid by the entity and therefore should be able to determine if accruals have been made for payroll-related liabilities such as Canada Pension Plan and Employment Insurance. In some instances, the auditor's search for unrecorded liabilities, which was explained in Chapter 9, may provide evidence that all payroll-related liabilities are recorded.

Cutoff   The auditor also wants to determine whether all payroll-related liabilities are recorded in the proper period. An examination of supporting documentation for the accruals provides evidence on the proper period for recording the expense or liability.

Presentation and Disclosure   The auditor must ensure that all necessary financial statement disclosures for the payroll cycle and related accounts are made. Table 10–9 presents examples of items that should be disclosed for payroll-related accounts.

 CICA Handbook section 3461, "Employee future benefits," requires detailed disclosures of postretirement benefits. Although discussion of the audit of these items is beyond the scope of this text, the reader should be aware that such disclosures are important to the fairness of the financial statements. Profit-sharing plans and deferred compensation arrangements also require disclosure in the footnotes.

Evaluating the Audit Findings—Payroll-Related Accounts

LO 8   When the auditor has completed the planned substantive tests of the payroll-related accounts, all of the identified misstatements should be aggregated. The likely misstatement is compared to the tolerable misstatement allocated to the payroll-related accounts. If the likely misstatement is less than the tolerable misstatement, the auditor may accept the accounts as fairly presented. Conversely, if the likely misstatement exceeds the tolerable misstatement, the auditor should conclude that the accounts are not fairly presented.

 For example, suppose that a tolerable misstatement of $60,000 was allocated to EarthWear's accrued liabilities and that Willis & Adams detected a misstatement in recording payroll expense and bonuses that amounted to a $36,200 understatement of accrued liabilities. Because this misstatement ($36,200) is less than the tolerable misstatement of $60,000, Willis & Adams can conclude that the audit evidence supports fair presentation. However, if the misstatement was greater than the tolerable

Table 10–9	Sample Disclosure Items for the Payroll Cycle and Related Accounts

- Pension disclosures.
- Postretirement benefit disclosures.
- Profit-sharing plans.
- Deferred compensation arrangements

misstatement, the evidence would not support fair presentation. In either case the auditor would bring the error forward to the Proposed Adjustments Schedule (PAS) and follow one of several different courses of action. The most preferable course of action would be to have the client adjust the accounts to correct the error. If the client was unwilling to do so, the auditor would have to use his or her professional judgement to decide on the appropriate course of action. The amount of the misstatement is clearly less than overall materiality, but if the size of the misstatement compared to the value of the account is significant, it may be considered a qualitative factor (see AuG-41) to be taken into account. It is unlikely that the auditor would consider it appropriate to qualify the audit report for this misstatement, but given its size, would stress to the client the importance of adjusting the account.

The auditor should again analyze the misstatements discovered through the application of substantive tests of transactions, analytical procedures, and tests of account balances because these misstatements may provide additional evidence on the control risk for the payroll system. If the auditor concludes that the audit risk is unacceptably high, additional audit procedures should be performed, or the auditor must be satisfied that the client has adjusted the payroll-related financial statement accounts to an acceptable level. For example, suppose the auditor's analytical procedures indicate that commissions expense is overstated. The auditor might perform detailed computations of commissions expense or request that the client adjust the account by the amount of the estimated misstatement.

The Auditor's Responsibilities When the Payroll Process Is Performed by an Outside Service Organization

LO 9> The auditor's responsibilities when a client has its payroll process performed by an outside service organization were discussed in Chapter 6 in the context of internal control. It is briefly reviewed below. For a more complete review, the student should review the material in Chapter 6.

It is not uncommon for entities, even quite large ones, to have their payroll function performed by an outside organization that specializes in providing such services. *CICA Handbook*, section 5310, "Audit evidence considerations when an enterprise uses a service organization," discusses the auditor's responsibilities in such circumstances.

The auditor is still required by generally accepted auditing standards to obtain sufficient appropriate audit evidence. In some cases, the auditor may examine the systems and records of the service organization to obtain such evidence. However, for reasons of client confidentiality, and the business disruption that would result, service organizations generally do not grant the auditors of their clients access to their records. Instead they will engage an auditor of their own (a "service auditor") to provide an opinion on their operations to be used by their clients' auditors as evidence. (The responsibilities and report of the service auditors, covered in *CICA Handbook*, section 5900, are discussed in more detail in Chapter 19.)

In such circumstances the client's auditor is responsible for determining the reliability and relevance of the service auditor's report. Section 5310 suggests that the client's auditor may do so by obtaining the service auditor's acknowledgement that the service auditor is aware of the client auditor's intention to use the report as audit evidence, or by reviewing the service auditor's working papers. If the client auditor issues an unqualified audit opinion, there is no reference to the service auditor's work.

REVIEW QUESTIONS

LO 1 **10-1** Why is the payroll cycle of most entities computerized?

2 **10-2** What are the major types of transactions that occur in the payroll system? What financial statement accounts are affected by each of these types of transactions?

3 **10-3** Briefly describe each of the following documents or records: payroll register, payroll master file, and payroll master file changes report.

3 **10-4** What duties are performed within the personnel, timekeeping, and payroll-processing functions?

4 **10-5** List the key segregation of duties in the payroll application. What errors or fraud can occur if such duties are not segregated?

5,6 **10-6** Discuss the two control environment factors that an auditor should consider when examining the payroll application.

6 **10-7** What are the key authorization points in a payroll system?

6 **10-8** Why is it important for the client to establish control procedures over the classification of payroll transactions?

5 **10-9** List the inherent risk factors that affect the payroll application.

6,7 **10-10** Identify two tests of controls or substantive tests of transactions that can be performed using CAATs for payroll transactions.

7 **10-11** List two analytical procedures that can be used to test payroll expense accounts and payroll-related liabilities.

7 **10-12** Discuss how an auditor would audit the accrued payroll taxes account.

7 **10-13** Identify three possible disclosure items for payroll expense and payroll-related liabilities.

MULTIPLE-CHOICE QUESTIONS FROM PROFESSIONAL EXAMINATIONS

Unless otherwise indicated, these multiple-choice questions were adapted from the CPA examinations, courtesy of the American Institute of Certified Public Accountants.

6 **10-14** Which of the following control procedures could best prevent direct labour from being charged to manufacturing overhead?

   a. Comparison of daily journal entries with factory labour summary.

   b. Examination of routing tickets from finished goods on delivery.

   c. Reconciliation of work-in-process inventory with cost records.

   d. Recomputation of direct labour based on inspection of time cards.

4 **10-15** For an appropriate segregation of duties, journalizing and posting summary payroll transactions should be assigned to

a. The treasurer's department.

b. General accounting.

c. Payroll accounting.

d. The timekeeping department.

4,6 >   **10-16**   The purpose of segregating the duties of hiring personnel and distributing payroll cheques is to separate the

a. Human resources function from the controllership function.

b. Administrative controls from the internal accounting controls.

c. Authorization of transactions from the custody-related assets.

d. Operational responsibility from the recordkeeping responsibility.

6 >   **10-17**   Matthews Corporation has changed from a system of recording time worked on clock cards to a computerized payroll system in which employees record time in and out with magnetic cards. The IT system automatically updates all payroll records. Because of this change,

a. A generalized computer audit program must be used.

b. Part of the audit trail is altered.

c. The potential for payroll-related fraud is diminished.

d. Transactions must be processed in batches.

6 >   **10-18**   The auditor may observe the distribution of paycheques to ascertain whether

a. Pay-rate authorization is properly separated from the operating function.

b. Deductions from gross pay are calculated correctly and are properly authorized.

c. Employees of record actually exist and are employed by the client.

d. Paycheques agree with the payroll register and the time cards.

4,6 >   **10-19**   Which of the following departments should have the responsibility for authorizing payroll rate changes?

a. Personnel.

b. Payroll.

c. Treasurer.

d. Timekeeping.

6 >   **10-20**   An auditor who is testing IT controls in a payroll system would most likely use test data that contain conditions such as

a. Deductions *not* authorized by employees.

b. Overtime *not* approved by supervisors.

c. Time cards with invalid job numbers.

d. Payroll cheques with unauthorized signatures.

6,7> **10-21** Tracing selected items from the payroll register to employee time cards that have been approved by supervisory personnel provides evidence that

a. Internal controls relating to payroll disbursements were operating effectively.

b. Payroll cheques were signed by an appropriate officer independent of the payroll preparation process.

c. Only bona fide employees worked and their pay was properly computed.

d. Employees worked the number of hours for which their pay was computed.

6> **10-22** Effective control procedures over the payroll function may include

a. Reconciliation of totals on job time cards with job reports by employees responsible for those specific jobs.

b. Verification of agreement of job time cards with employee clock card hours by a payroll department employee.

c. Preparation of payroll transaction journal entries by an employee who reports to the supervisor of the personnel department.

d. Custody of rate authorization records by the supervisor of the payroll department.

6> **10-23** In a computerized payroll system environment, an auditor would be *least* likely to use test data to test controls related to

a. Missing employee numbers.

b. Proper approval of overtime by supervisors.

c. Time cards with invalid job numbers.

d. Agreement of hours per clock cards with hours on time cards.

3,6> **10-24** In meeting the control objective of safeguarding of assets, which department should be responsible for the following?

	Distribution of Paycheques	Custody of Unclaimed Paycheques
a.	Treasurer	Treasurer
b.	Payroll	Treasurer
c.	Treasurer	Payroll
d.	Payroll	Payroll

6> **10-25** If a control total was computed on each of the following data items, which would best be identified as a hash total for a payroll IT application?

a. Total debits and total credits.

b. Net pay.

c. Department numbers.

d. Hours worked.

6 >   **10-26** Which of the following procedures would most likely be considered a weakness in an entity's internal controls over payroll?

a. A voucher for the amount of the payroll is prepared in the general accounting department based on the payroll department's payroll summary.

b. Payroll cheques are prepared by the payroll department and signed by the treasurer.

c. The employee who distributes payroll cheques returns unclaimed payroll cheques to the payroll department.

d. The personnel department sends employees' termination notices to the payroll department.

6,7 >   **10-27** An auditor is most likely to perform substantive tests of details on payroll transactions and balances when

a. Cutoff tests indicate a substantial amount of accrued payroll expense.

b. The assessed level of control risk relative to payroll transactions is low.

c. Analytical procedures indicate unusual fluctuations in recurring payroll entries.

d. Accrued payroll expense consists primarily of unpaid commissions.

PROBLEMS

4,6 >   **10-28** The audit working papers contain a narrative description of a *segment* of the Croyden Factory, Ltd., payroll system and an accompanying flowchart as follows.

Narrative

The internal control system with respect to the personnel department functions well and is *not* included in the accompanying flowchart.

At the beginning of each workweek, payroll clerk 1 reviews the payroll department files to determine the employment status of factory employees and then prepares time cards and distributes them as each individual arrives at work. This payroll clerk, who is also responsible for custody of the signature stamp machine, verifies the identity of each payee before delivering signed cheques to the foreman.

At the end of each workweek, the foreman distributes the payroll cheques for the preceding workweek. Concurrent with this activity, the foreman reviews the current week's employee time cards, notes the regular and overtime hours worked on a summary form, and initials the time cards. The foreman then delivers all time cards and unclaimed payroll cheques to payroll clerk 2.

Croyden, Ltd., Factory Payroll System

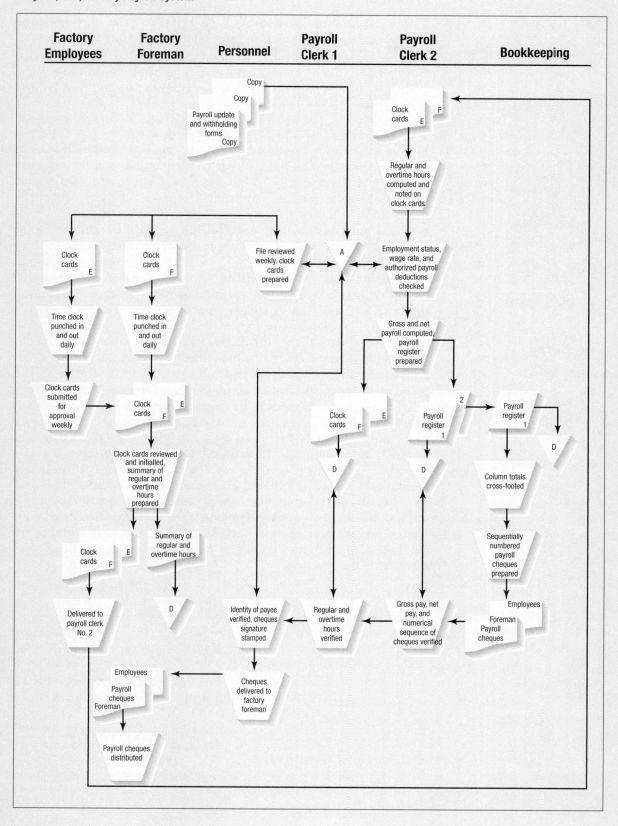

Required:

a. Based on the narrative and the flowchart on the previous page, what are the weaknesses in internal control?

b. Based on the narrative and the accompanying flowchart, what enquiries should be made to clarify possible additional weaknesses in internal control? Do *not* discuss the internal control system of the personnel department.

(AICPA, adapted)

1,2,3,6 ⟩   **10-29**   Your client, Fiesta Hotels Ltd. (Fiesta), has four hotels in various cities in Quebec. The hotel chain has expanded significantly during the past few years and has been very successful. During its expansion years, Fiesta's management has had the payroll coordinated through a payroll service organization. The manager at each separate hotel is responsible for all hiring, termination, and wage amounts, although they do rely on the department managers for most of the process.

Each hotel has at least 50 full-time employees and 25 to 100 part-time employees. The hotel management team, consisting of the manager, assistant manager, head chief, reservations supervisor, controller, maintenance manager, and room attendant supervisor are all paid a salary with yearly evaluations, salary adjustments, and bonuses based on their department's performance. The other employees, consisting of reservation clerks, administrative clerks, room attendants, restaurant employees, and maintenance workers, are all paid hourly wages with reviews every six months for their first two years and then once every year after that.

Fiesta is privately held and only has a review done each year rather than a full audit. In addition, each year, management asks your firm to perform specific audit procedures in certain areas, similar to the way an internal audit team would operate. This year you and the audit manager (Barb) were asked to attend Fiesta's annual meeting of the management team in early May. After playing a round of golf in sunny Shawinigan, you, the VP Finance for Fiesta (Shae), and the VP Human Resources for Fiesta (Ray), were discussing the meeting.

Ray: *Well, what did you think about the meeting? I thought it went well except for the discussions regarding payroll.*

Shae: *I agree. We have to simplify the coordination of payroll and human resources in each hotel. It is just too much work for the managers, as we heard during the meeting today. What did you think, Kim?*

You: *I think you are right. I heard that message loud and clear. I guess that's the reason you wanted Barb and I to attend the meeting.*

Ray: *That's right. We are designing a new payroll system that will simplify the payroll process and allow us to do our own payroll, preferably through head office. We want your input to ensure that we include all internal controls related to payroll that are necessary for you to be able to rely on the system during the audit. We are completely open to your suggestions with only two conditions. First, Shae will have the final say on all aspects of the design and second, we want the system to be as simple as possible.*

Shae: *As you both know, my experience is primarily in the human resources side of the business and not in the payroll preparation or controls. We are willing to increase our staff at head office or at the hotels if necessary. However, we will be using a direct deposit for all payroll and manual cheques will only be prepared in an emergency. All manual cheques will require two signatures and my approval. Right now the accounting records related to payroll are so bad that we don't even have people being charged to the correct departments. This upsets the managers as their bonus calculations are based on a comparison of budget to actual results.*

You: *It sounds like an interesting project. We might have to travel to each of the hotels to get a thorough understanding of the situation.*

Shae: *I am open to any internal controls that you both feel are necessary, but I would like you to indicate why the controls are required.*

Required:

Prepare a response to Shae's request regarding the internal controls for Fiesta Hotel Ltd.'s payroll system.

(ICABC, adapted)

7> **10-30** JoeMcCarthy was engaged to audit the financial statements of Kent Company, a continuing audit client. McCarthy is about to audit Kent's payroll transactions. Kent uses an in-house payroll department to process payroll data and to prepare and distribute payroll cheques.

During the planning process, McCarthy determined that the inherent risk of overstatement of payroll expense is high. In addition, McCarthy obtained an understanding of internal control and assessed the control risk for payroll-related assertions at the maximum level.

Required:

Describe the audit procedures McCarthy should consider performing in the audit of Kent's payroll transactions to address the risk of overstatement. Do *not* discuss Kent's internal control.

(AICPA, adapted)

7> **10-31** Collen James, who was engaged to examine the financial statements of Talbert Corporation, is about to audit payroll. Talbert uses a computer service centre to process weekly payroll as follows.

Each Monday Talbert's payroll clerk inserts data in appropriate spaces on the preprinted service centre–prepared input form and sends it to the service centre via messenger. The service centre extracts new permanent data from the input form and updates its master files. The weekly payroll data are then processed. The weekly payroll register and payroll cheques are printed and delivered by messenger to Talbert on Thursday.

Part of the sample selected for audit by James includes the following input form and payroll register on page 439:

TALBERT CORPORATION
Payroll Input
Week Ending Friday, November 26, 2006

| | Employee Data—Permanent File | | Current Week's Payroll Data | | | | | |
| | | | | Hours | | Special Deductions | | |
Name	Social Insurance Number	TD1 Information	Hourly Rate	Regular	Overtime	Stock Purchase Plan	Union Dues	Other
A. Bell	212 808 471	M-1	$12.00	35	5	$18.75		
B. Carioso	212 808 472	M-2	12.00	35	4			
C. Deng	212 808 473	S-1	12.00	35	6	18.75	$4.00	
D. Ellis	212 808 474	S-1	12.00	35	2		4.00	$50.00
E. Flaherty	212 808 475	M-4	12.00	35	1		4.00	
F. Gillis	212 808 476	M-4	12.00	35			4.00	
G. Hua	212 808 477	M-1	9.00	35	2	18.75	4.00	
H. Jones	212 808 478	M-2	9.00	35			4.00	25.00
I. King	212 808 479	S-1	9.00	35	4		4.00	
New Employee:								
J. Smith	212 808 470	M-3	9.00	35				

Required:

a. Describe how James should verify the information in the payroll input form shown.

b. Describe (but do not perform) the procedures that James should follow in examining the November 26, 2006, payroll register as shown.

(AICPA, adapted)

3,4,6,7,8 ▷   **10-32**   Better BC Trust Company was formed in 1982 and opened five branches in Greater Vancouver. By offering innovative and attractive financing alternatives to individuals and small businesses, Better BC grew rapidly and is widely considered a Canadian success story. Better BC now operates 95 branches across Western Canada and employs almost 1,400 staff. Preliminary financial statements for the year ended June 30, 2006 show salaries of $47.2 million, up 12 percent from the 2005 level.

You are member of the audit team of the public accounting firm that is auditing Better BC and are scheduled to review the internal controls of the company's payroll system. You have gathered the following initial information with respect to the payment of branch employees.

TALBERT CORPORATION
Payroll Register
November 26, 2004

Employee	Social Insurance Number	Hours Regular	Hours Overtime	Payroll Regular	Payroll Overtime	Gross Payroll	Tax deductions	Withholdings CPP Contributions	Withholdings EI premiums	Other Withheld	Net Pay	Cheque Number
A. Bell	212-808-471	35	5	$ 420.00	$ 90.00	$ 510.00	$ 76.00	$ 26.05	$ 27.40	$ 18.75	$ 361.80	1499
B. Carioso	212-808-472	35	4	420.00	72.00	492.00	65.00	25.13	23.60		378.27	1500
C. Deng	212-808-473	35	6	420.00	108.00	528.00	100.90	26.97	28.60	22.75	348.78	1501
D. Ellis	212-808-474	35	2	420.00	36.00	456.00	80.50	23.29	21.70	54.00	276.51	1502
E. Flaherty	212-808 475	35	1	420.00	18.00	438.00	43.50	22.37	15.90	4.00	352.23	1503
F. Gillis	212-808-476	35		420.00		420.00	41.40	21.46	15.00	4.00	338.14	1504
G. Hua	212-808-477	35	2	315.00	27.00	342.00	34.80	16.31	10.90	22.75	257.24	1505
H. Jones	212-808-478	35		315.00		315.00	26.40	15.02	8.70	29.00	235.88	1506
I. King	212-808-479	35	4	315.00	54.00	369.00	49.40	17.59	12.20	4.00	285.81	1507
J. Smith	212-808-470	35		315.00		315.00	23.00	15.02	7.80		269.18	1508
Total		350	24	$3,780.00	$405.00	$4,185.00	$540.90	$209.21	$171.80	$159.25	$3,103.84	

The executive committee reports directly to the board of directors. The committee sets pay scales, pay rates, and determines policy with respect to payroll administration. Branch managers must adhere to stated policy in regards to hiring and personnel functions. Better BC is an equal opportunity employer.

Within specific guidelines, the branch manager is responsible for hiring and terminating within the branch. With respect to hiring, the branch manager completes an employee application in electronic format. Electronic "forms" are accessed by user password and are downloaded to the main branch for appropriate processing. The method of sending these "forms" to appropriate user departments operates effectively.

The new employee application form is sent electronically from the branch manager to the corporate manager, payroll, at the main branch. This individual is responsible for approving the application and ensuring all guidelines are followed. Once approved, the corporate manager, payroll, sends approval to the branch manager and another copy of the approved application to the branch payroll administrator who is responsible for the processing and payment of payroll at the branch. The branch payroll administrator reports to the corporate manager, payroll, and the branch manager reports to the director of branch management. At many of Better BC's smaller branches, the branch payroll administrator and the branch manager are the same person.

Employees are paid semi-monthly via direct deposit to the employee's account. Better BC requires all employees to maintain an account with the trust company for this purpose. All employees complete an authorization for Better BC to make direct deposits to his/her account. Better BC does not apply service charges of any kind on employee's accounts as an incentive to increase their business within the organization.

Three working days before the payroll payment date, the branch payroll administrator electronically prepares the payroll authorization form approving the payment of payroll for each individual at that branch and any changes that may have occurred, e.g., hires, terminations, pay scale changes, address or direct-deposit bank account changes. Certain branch employees submit a time summary form from which the branch payroll administrator prepares the payroll authorization form (the transfer of detailed time summary data to the computer system is not checked for accuracy). The payroll authorization form is sent to the branch manager for approval, then forwarded to the payroll processing department at the main branch for final processing. Internal system checks recompute employee deductions and the manager of payroll processing uses a variety of analytical tools to compare the payroll to the previous period and to check the reasonability of the payroll amounts. All discrepancies or unusual payroll entries are documented and investigated. Once payroll processing is complete, a summary of the payroll is forwarded to accounting.

Required:

a. Based on information provided, list possible errors that could occur and describe the controls in place to help prevent or detect each error identified.

b. Identify weaknesses in Better BC's system for which no controls exist.

(ICABC, adapted)

DISCUSSION CASES

6 > **10-33** Service Corporation hired an independent computer programmer to develop a simplified payroll application for its newly purchased computer. The programmer developed an online database system that minimized the level of knowledge required of the operator. It was based on typing answers to input cues that appeared on the terminal's viewing screen, examples of which follow:

A. Access routine:
   1. Operator access number to payroll file?
   2. Are there new employees?

B. New employee routine:
   1. Employee name?
   2. Employee number?
   3. Social Insurance number?
   4. Rate per hour?
   5. Single or married?
   6. Number of dependants?
   7. Account distribution?

C. Current payroll routine:
   1. Employee number?
   2. Regular hours worked?
   3. Overtime hours worked?
   4. Total employees this payroll period?

The auditor is attempting to verify that certain input validation (edit) checks exist to ensure that errors resulting from omissions, invalid entries, or other inaccuracies are detected during the typing of answers to the input cues.

Required:

a. Discuss the various types of input validation (edit) controls that the auditor would expect to find in the IT system.

b. Describe the assurances provided by each identified validation check.

(AICPA, adapted)

2,3>   **10-34**   Your client, Mr. Fix-it, performs minor home repairs and maintenance. Mr. Fix-it has experienced tremendous growth due to its high-quality work force and flexible scheduling policy. Jan Datel saw a need for a home repair service due to the increase in two-income families and founded Mr. Fix-it in 1997. Mr. Fix-it's 2006 sales were $2 million and it now operates from four locations.

Jan has processed Mr. Fix-it's payroll manually for the past five years. She uses manual payroll tables and calculates payroll deductions for an increasing number of employees. Recently Jan hired a part-time bookkeeper to help her with the payroll. Due to the increasing time required to process payroll, she is considering purchasing a computer payroll system. Your CA firm, Hays, Wheat & Rye, perform all monthly bookkeeping.

Before purchasing the system Jan would like to know the specific tasks that a computer payroll system could perform that would increase the efficiency and effectiveness of the processing. You have taken notes on Mr. Fix-it's existing payroll system (Exhibit 1). In addition, Jan would like you to list the benefits of a computer payroll system.

Required:

Respond to Jan.

(ICABC, adapted)

6,7>   **10-35**   Executive compensation ballooned in the 1990s, and as highlighted in Exhibit 10–1, there were notable compensation abuses. The most popular form of executive compensation in the 1990s was company stock (or options to purchase stock). Designers of these compensation plans argue that by compensating officers with stock, the officers will take actions in the best interest of the shareholders. Critics claim executive compensation is often too high in proportion to average salaries at companies and that the compensation levels motivate officers to take selfish actions.

EXHIBIT 1

Mr. Fix-it Payroll System

Workers prepare time sheets. Work crew supervisors approve time sheets and submit them to Jan. Jan checks the hours and the work performed, records the rate of pay, calculates the tax withholding from the payroll tables, and costs the time sheet (calculates gross pay, net pay, deductions). She then batches all the time sheets and calculates the total wage costs. She types paycheques, reconciles the cheque run to the total wage cost, and prepares the journal entry for the general ledger. Paycheques are then distributed to workers. At month end she reconciles the payroll bank account to the general ledger and calculates and prepares the remittance to the Receiver General.

Required:

a. Research executive compensation of some well-known companies. (You can find executive compensation in SEC filings on EDGAR at www.sec.gov or on SEDAR at www.osc.com, or on a variety of Internet sites, such as eComp www.ecomponline.com). Use your best judgement to compute the proportion of executive compensation to average salary (i.e., are executives earning 5 times, or 10 times, or 100 times the average employee). In your opinion, are the executives worth it?

b. In your opinion, what are the costs and benefits associated with compensating executives with stock or options to purchase stock?

c. What do you believe are the most effective audit procedures to use to test for executive compensation abuse or fraud? Please explain why.

INTERNET ASSIGNMENT

7> **10-36**   Using an Internet browser, search for information on labour costs in the retail catalogue industry (for example, labour costs as a percentage of sales). A survey of industry practice could help the auditor form expectations against which to compare EarthWear's labour costs in analytical review.

Auditing the Inventory Management Process

Learning Objectives

Upon completion of this chapter, you will be able to

1 Explain the inventory management process.

2 Outline the functions in the inventory management process and describe the types of documents and records used.

3 Identify the appropriate segregation of duties for the inventory management process.

4 Identify and evaluate inherent risks relevant to the inventory management process and related accounts.

5 Assess control risk for the inventory management process, apply appropriate tests of controls, and relate the assessment of control risk to substantive testing.

6 Apply substantive testing procedures to the transactions and accounts in the inventory management process.

7 Observe physical inventory.

8 Evaluate the audit findings and reach a final conclusion on inventory and related accounts.

9 Audit standard costs.

RELEVANT ACCOUNTING AND ASSURANCE PRONOUNCEMENTS

CICA Handbook, **section 3030**, Inventories

CICA Handbook, **section 5049**, Use of specialists in assurance engagements

CICA Handbook, **section 5095**, Reasonable assurance and audit risk

CICA Handbook, **section 5141**, Understanding the entity and its environment and assessing the risks of material misstatement

CICA Handbook, **section 5142**, Materiality

CICA Handbook, **section 5143**, The auditor's procedures in response to assessed risks

CICA Handbook, **section 5300**, Audit evidence

CICA Handbook, **section 5301**, Analysis

CICA Handbook, **section 5303**, Confirmation

CICA Handbook, **section 5305**, Audit of accounting estimates

CICA Handbook, **section 6030**, Inventories

AUDITING EARTHWEAR'S INVENTORY MANAGEMENT PROCESS

EarthWear   Because EarthWear is a merchandising business, the inventory management process is key to the successful attainment of its strategic goals. Inventory is material to the financial statements; EarthWear's balance sheet for 2006 shows that inventory accounts for more than 35 percent of the total assets of the company. The company purchases its inventory items from over 200 different manufacturers. EarthWear's inventory management process is highly complex and utilizes very advanced technology. Both the receipt of goods and the processing of inventory once received are handled by a computerized inventory control system in order to keep track of the large number of different goods coming in from the many suppliers. Both the ordering of inventory and payment of suppliers is handled by Electronic Data Interchange (EDI). Auditing the inventory process poses a number of challenges for Willis & Adams. The volume of transactions, both into and out of inventory, is very high. Willis & Adams must place reliance on EarthWear's inventory management system and the controls over that system. In order to do so they must test the internal control system thoroughly. Since EarthWear uses EDI in dealing with its suppliers there is a very limited audit trail and the integrity of, and controls over, the IT system are paramount. Another major concern with regard to EarthWear's inventory is valuation. Since the customers of EarthWear are individual consumers, and the business is highly seasonal, the possibility of inventory obsolescence is always present.

The chapter coverage of the audit of the inventory management process also follows the three components of the risk model. An overview of the inventory management process is presented, followed by discussion of inherent risk factors and control risk assessment. This is then linked to the auditor's substantive testing decisions, including observing physical inventory and auditing standard costs.

Overview of the Inventory Management Process

LO 1   The inventory management process is affected by the internal control procedures previously discussed for the revenue, purchasing, and payroll processes. Figure 11–1 shows how each of these processes interacts with the inventory management process. The acquisition of and payment for inventory are controlled via the purchasing process. The cost of both direct and indirect labour assigned to inventory is controlled through the payroll process. Last, finished goods are sold and accounted for as part of the revenue process. Thus, the "cradle-to-grave" cycle for inventory begins when goods are purchased and stored and ends when the finished goods are shipped to customers.

EarthWear   Exhibit 11–1 describes EarthWear's inventory system, while Figure 11–2 flowcharts the system. This description and flowchart provide a framework for discussing the internal control procedures and tests of controls for the inventory management process in more detail. However, because of differences in products and their subsequent processing, the inventory system usually differs from one entity to the next. The reader should concentrate on understanding the basic concepts of internal control.

FIGURE 11–1

The Relationship of the Inventory Management Process to Other Accounting Processes

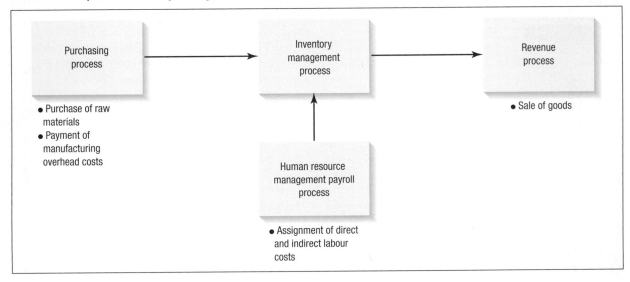

EXHIBIT 11–1

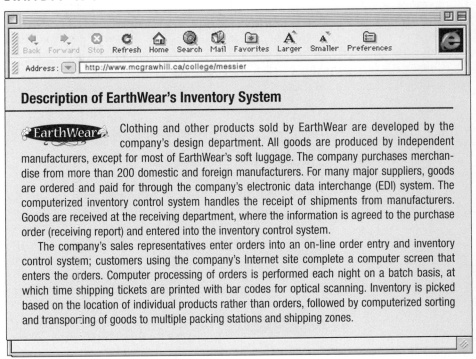

Description of EarthWear's Inventory System

EarthWear   Clothing and other products sold by EarthWear are developed by the company's design department. All goods are produced by independent manufacturers, except for most of EarthWear's soft luggage. The company purchases merchandise from more than 200 domestic and foreign manufacturers. For many major suppliers, goods are ordered and paid for through the company's electronic data interchange (EDI) system. The computerized inventory control system handles the receipt of shipments from manufacturers. Goods are received at the receiving department, where the information is agreed to the purchase order (receiving report) and entered into the inventory control system.

The company's sales representatives enter orders into an on-line order entry and inventory control system; customers using the company's Internet site complete a computer screen that enters the orders. Computer processing of orders is performed each night on a batch basis, at which time shipping tickets are printed with bar codes for optical scanning. Inventory is picked based on the location of individual products rather than orders, followed by computerized sorting and transporting of goods to multiple packing stations and shipping zones.

The Major Functions   Table 11–1 summarizes the functions that normally take place in a typical inventory management process and Table 11–2 lists the associated documents and records. These tables follow on page 448.

FIGURE 11–2

Flowchart of the Inventory Management Process—EarthWear Clothiers

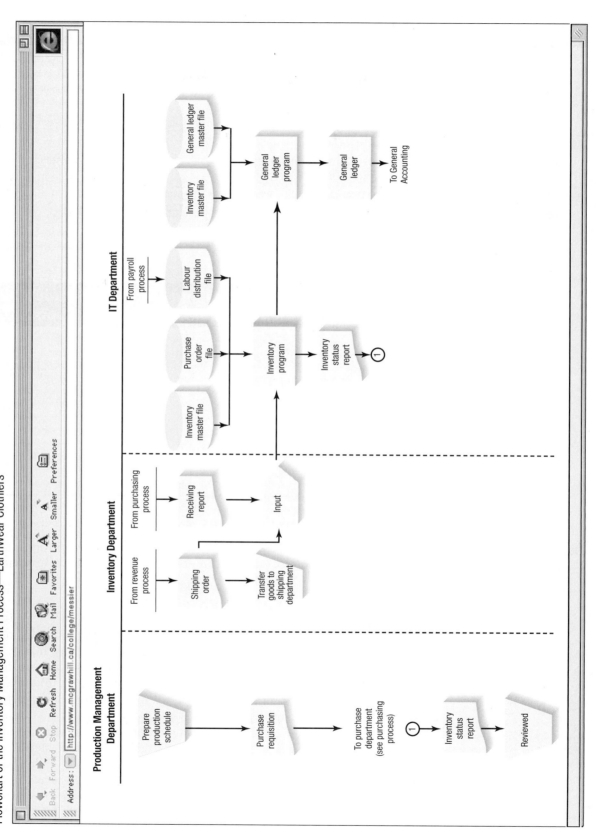

Table 11–1	**Functions in the Inventory Management Process**

• *Inventory management*	Authorization of production activity and maintenance of inventory at appropriate levels; issuance of purchase requisitions to the purchasing department (see Chapter 10 on the purchasing process).
• *Raw materials stores*	Custody of raw materials and issuance of raw materials to manufacturing departments.
• *Manufacturing*	Production of goods.
• *Finished goods stores*	Custody of finished goods and issuance of goods to the shipping department (see Chapter 9 on the revenue process).
• *Cost accounting*	Maintenance of the costs of manufacturing and inventory in cost records.
• *General ledger*	Proper accumulation, classification, and summarization of inventory and related costs in the general ledger.

Table 11–2	**Documents and Records Included in the Inventory Management Process**

Production schedule.
Receiving report.
Materials requisition.
Inventory master file.
Production data information.
Cost accumulation and variance report.
Inventory status report.
Shipping order.

Documents and Records

LO 2>

The next section describes the major activities of the inventory management process and the associated documents and records typically created by those functions.

EarthWear   Inventory Management   At EarthWear, the inventory management function is performed by the design department. This department is responsible for maintaining inventory at appropriate levels. It issues purchase requisitions to the purchasing department and thus represents the point at which the inventory management process integrates with the purchasing process. In a manufacturing company, a production management department would be responsible for managing inventory through planning and scheduling manufacturing activities.

A *production schedule* is normally prepared periodically based on the expected demand for the entity's products. The expected demand may be based on the current backlogue of orders or on sales forecasts from the sales or marketing department. In EarthWear's system, this schedule is prepared by the design department. Production schedules determine the quantity of goods needed and the time at which they must be ready in order to meet the production scheduling. Many organizations use material requirements planning or just-in-time inventory programs to assist with production planning. Production schedules give the auditor information on the planned level of operating activity.

Raw Materials Stores   In a manufacturing company, this function is responsible for the receipt, custody, and issuance of raw materials. When goods are received from vendors, they are transferred from the receiving department to the raw materials stores department. Once goods arrive in the raw materials storage area, they must be safeguarded against pilferage or unauthorized use. Finally, when goods are requested for production through the issuance of a materials requisition, this function issues the goods to the appropriate manufacturing department.

The *receiving report* records the receipt of goods from vendors. This document was discussed as part of the purchasing process. It is reconsidered in the inventory management process because a copy of this document accompanies the goods to the inventory department and is used to update the client's perpetual inventory records. Note in Figure 11–2 that the data from the receiving report are input into the inventory program to update the inventory master file, which contains the information on the client's perpetual records.

Materials requisitions are normally used by manufacturing companies to track materials during the production process. Materials requisitions are normally prepared by department personnel as needed for production purposes. For example, the materials requisition is the document that authorizes the release of raw materials from the raw materials department. A copy of the materials requisition may be maintained in the raw materials department, and another copy may accompany the goods to the production departments.

Manufacturing   The manufacturing function is responsible for producing the product. From an auditing perspective, there must be adequate control over the physical flow of the goods and proper accumulation of the costs attached to inventory. The manner in which costs are accumulated varies substantially from one entity to another. Entities may produce goods using a job order cost system, a process cost system, or some combination of both.

In a manufacturing company, *production data information* about the transfer of goods and related cost accumulation at each stage of production should be reported. This information updates the entity's perpetual inventory system. It is also used as input to generate the cost accumulation and variance reports that are produced by the inventory system.

Finished Goods Stores   This function is responsible for the storage of and control over finished goods. When goods are completed by the manufacturing function, they are transferred to finished goods stores. Again, there must be adequate safeguards against pilferage or unauthorized use. When goods are ordered by a customer, a shipping order is produced by the revenue process and forwarded to the finished goods stores department. The goods are then transferred to the shipping department for shipment to the customer. Because EarthWear is a merchandising company, it maintains only finished goods (see Figure 11–2).

The finished goods stores or inventory is supported by the *inventory master file* and the *inventory status report*. The *inventory master file* contains all the important information related to the entity's inventory, including the perpetual inventory records. In sophisticated inventory systems such as EarthWear's, the inventory master file also contains information on the costs used to value inventory. In a manufacturing company, it would not be unusual for the inventory master file to contain the standard costs used to value the inventory at various stages of production.

The *inventory status report* shows the type and amount of products on hand. Such a report is basically a summary of the perpetual inventory records. This report can also be used to determine the status of goods in process. In sophisticated inventory systems, this type of information can be accessed directly through computer terminals or PCs.

The shipping order was discussed as part of the revenue process. It is reconsidered here because a copy of this document is used to remove goods from the client's perpetual inventory records. Note in Figure 11–2 that the inventory master file is updated when open orders are processed and a shipping order is generated.

Cost Accounting   This function is responsible for ensuring that costs are properly attached to inventory as goods are processed through the manufacturing function. Cost accounting reviews the cost accumulation and variance reports after such data are processed into the accounting records.

Most inventory control systems in a manufacturing setting produce reports similar to a *cost accumulation and variance report*. Material, labour, and overhead costs are charged to inventory as part of the manufacturing process. The cost accumulation report summarizes the various costs charged to departments and products. The variance reports present the results of inventory processing in terms of actual costs versus standard or budgeted costs. The cost accounting and manufacturing departments review these reports for appropriate charges.

General Ledger   The main objective of the general ledger function is to ensure that all inventory and costs of production are properly accumulated, classified, and summarized in the general ledger accounts. In an IT system, control or summary totals ensure that this function is performed correctly. One important control performed by the general ledger function is the reconciliation of the perpetual inventory records to the general ledger inventory accounts.

The Key Segregation of Duties

LO 3

Segregation of duties is a particularly important control in the inventory management process because of the potential for theft and fraud. Therefore, individuals involved in the inventory management and inventory

Table 11–3	**Key Segregation of Duties and Possible Errors or Fraud**

Segregation of Duties	*Possible Errors or Fraud Resulting from Conflicts of Duties*
The inventory management function should be segregated from the cost-accounting function.	If the individual responsible for inventory management also has access to the cost-accounting records, production and inventory costs can be manipulated. This may lead to an over- or understatement of inventory and net income.
The inventory stores function should be segregated from the cost-accounting function.	If one individual is responsible for both controlling and accounting for inventory, unauthorized shipments can be made or theft of goods can be covered up.
The cost-accounting function should be segregated from the general ledger function.	If one individual is responsible for the inventory records and also for the general ledger, it is possible for that individual to conceal unauthorized shipments. This can result in the theft of goods, leading to an overstatement of inventory.
The responsibility for supervising physical inventory should be separated from the inventory management and inventory stores functions.	If the individual responsible for production management or inventory stores functions is also responsible for the physical inventory, it is possible that inventory shortages can be covered up through the adjustment of the inventory records to the physical inventory, resulting in an overstatement of inventory.

Table 11–4	**Segregation of Duties for Inventory Functions by Department**

| *Inventory Function* | **Department** | | | | |
	Inventory Management	*Raw Materials Stores*	*Finished Goods Stores*	*Cost Accounting*	*IT*
Preparation of production schedules	X				
Issuance of materials requisitions that accompany goods to the manufacturing department		X			
Updating of cost records with materials, labour, and overhead usage				X	X
Updating of inventory records				X	X
Release of goods to the shipping department			X		
Approval and issuance of purchase requisitions	X				

stores functions should not have access to the inventory records, the cost-accounting records, or the general ledger. When the inventory system is highly computerized, there should be proper segregation of duties within the IT department. Table 11–3 shows the key segregation of duties for the inventory management process and examples of possible errors or fraud that can result from conflicts in duties.

Table 11–4 shows the proper segregation of duties for individual inventory functions across the various departments that control inventory processing.

Inherent Risk Assessment

LO 4 For entities whose business is the provision of physical goods, as opposed to services, business processes related to the management of inventory are key processes in the attainment of the organization's strategic goals. Inventory interacts with both sales and accounts receivable, on one side, and with purchases and accounts payable on the other. As a result, some of the strategic considerations have been discussed in the preceding chapters. The auditor must consider whether and how current economic conditions will affect the entity's competitive advantages, suppliers, and customers. For instance do poor economic conditions result in a significant risk of reduced payment of accounts receivable due to bankrupt or financially distressed customers and could that affect the allowance for bad debts and bad debts expense?

However, in addition to such considerations, the auditor needs to consider how risk factors that relate more specifically to inventory affect business processes and the risk of material misstatement. These can be grouped into industry-related factors and operating and engagement characteristics (see Chapter 3).

Industry-Related Factors

A number of industry factors may indicate the presence of material misstatements in inventory. For example, if industry competition is intense, there may be problems with the proper valuation of inventory in terms of lower-of-cost-or-market values. Rapid technology changes in certain industries may also promote material misstatement due to obsolescence (see Exhibit 11–2).

Engagement and Operating Characteristics

A number of engagement and operating characteristics are important to the assessment of inherent risk for inventory. First, the type of product sold by the client can increase the potential for defalcation. For example, products that are small and of high value, such as jewellery, are more susceptible to theft than large products are. Second, inventory is often difficult to audit, and its valuation may result in disagreements with the

EXHIBIT 11–2

> ### Digital Cameras Sink Polaroid
>
> Polaroid, the once high-flying company, filed for Chapter 11 bankruptcy in October 2001 after it was unable to meet payments on its heavy debt load. In August, the company's auditors, KPMG LLP, raised issue with the company's ability to continue as a going-concern. The company, founded by Edward H. Land, was once one of the world's leading photography companies. Its main product was instant colour film that developed when exposed to light. However, since 1995, Polaroid had faced stiff competition from one-hour photo shops and, more recently, from digital cameras. Polaroid was unable to restructure its debt or find a buyer for the company prior to seeking bankruptcy protection.
>
> *Sources:* J. Bandler, "Polaroid Sustains Latest Setback as Auditor Questions Its Future," *The Wall Street Journal*, August 10, 2001, and J. Bandler and M. Pacelle, "Polaroid is Using Chapter 11 to Seek Buyer," *The Wall Street Journal*, October 15, 2001.

client. Finally, the auditor must be alert to possible related-party transactions for acquiring raw materials and selling finished product. For example, the client may purchase raw materials from a company controlled by the chief executive officer at prices in excess of market value. In such a case, the value of inventory will be overstated, and cash will have been misappropriated from the entity.

Audit research has also shown that inventory is likely to contain material misstatements.[1] Therefore, the auditor should consider whether material misstatements were found in prior years' audits. If so, the auditor should consider whether such misstatements may be present in the current inventory and plan the audit accordingly. Exhibit 11–3 describes a series of inventory frauds at Centennial Technologies, inc.

Control Risk Assessment

LO 5 > The auditor may follow a substantive strategy when auditing inventory and cost of goods sold. When this is done, the auditor places no reliance on the control procedures in the inventory management process and sets the level of control risk at the maximum. The auditor then relies on substantive tests to determine the fairness of inventory. Such a strategy may be appropriate when internal control is not adequate.

In many cases, however, the auditor can rely on internal control for inventory. This normally occurs when the client has an integrated cost-accounting/inventory management system. For discussion purposes, it is assumed that the auditor has decided to follow a reliance strategy. Figure 11–3 summarizes the three steps for assessing the control risk following this strategy. Each of these steps is only briefly reviewed within the context of the inventory management process because you should by now have a thorough understanding of the control risk assessment process followed by auditors.

Understanding and Documenting Internal Control	In order to assess the control risk for the inventory management process, the auditor must understand the five internal control components. Two points should be mentioned. First, if the client uses sophisticated IT techniques for monitoring the flow of goods and accumulating costs, the auditor will need to evaluate both the general IT controls and the inventory application controls. Second, the auditor will need a thorough understanding of the process used by the client to value inventory.
Planning and Performing Tests of Controls	In performing this step, the auditor again must identify the relevant control procedures within the client's inventory management process that ensure that material misstatements are either prevented or detected and corrected. Audit procedures used to test the client's control procedures in the inventory management process are discussed in subsequent sections.
Assessing and Documenting the Control Risk	Once the controls in the inventory process have been tested, the auditor assesses the level of control risk. The auditor should document the assessed level of control risk using either quantitative amounts or

[1]A. Eilifsen and W. F. Messier, Jr., "Auditor Detection of Misstatements: A Review and Integration of Empirical Research," *Journal of Accounting Literature* 2000 (19), pp. 1–43.

EXHIBIT 11–3

Inventory Scams at Centennial Technologies

Background

Centennial Technologies designed, manufactured, and marketed an extensive line of PC cards: rugged, lightweight, credit card–sized devices inserted into a dedicated slot in a broad range of electronic equipment that contain microprocessors, such as portable computers, telecommunications equipment, and manufacturing equipment. The company's customer list included companies such as Digital Equipment Corporation, Philips Electronics, Sharp Electronics Corporation, and Xerox Corporation.

Emanuel Pinez was the CEO of technology highflier Centennial Technologies, Inc., in the mid-1990s. In 1996, Centennial's surging stock graduated to the New York Stock Exchange just two years after going public. It finished 1996 as the best-performing stock on the big board, up a stunning 451 percent. Just before the fraud was uncovered, analysts still had "strong buy" recommendations outstanding.

Pinez had an impressive résumé, but it turns out much of it was false. After the scandal broke, investors and the auditors learned what Pinez's wife knew, that he was a "pathological liar." For example, as a young man he claimed to set a world record in an international swimming competition across the English Channel. The reports were published, and Pinez was hailed briefly as a national hero—until the truth came out that there was no such competition or record. Pinez constantly made aggressive estimates regarding Centennial's growth, and in 1996 he began telling investors that Centennial was negotiating an order worth more than $300 million with AT&T (no such deal ever took place or apparently even existed). At about the same time as Pinez was touting the pending sale to AT&T, he was boosting inventory and profits with a variety of accounting scams.

PCMCIA Card Scam

Centennial's growth attracted several sophisticated institutional investors, such as Oppenheimer Funds Inc. and Fidelity Investments. Some investors started to crave a firsthand look at Centennial's operations. One investor sent an analyst to meet with Pinez and tour the headquarters in Billerica, Massachusetts. Although the analyst noticed some computer equipment in the administrative offices, he was somewhat surprised that there was none in Pinez's office. During a tour of Centennial's manufacturing facilities, he saw "a room full of people banging on cards with rubber mallets. I had a bad feeling." He returned to his firm and "dumped the Centennial shares immediately."

In truth, Pinez had enlisted a handful of employees in the company's Billerica manufacturing plant to assemble fake memory cards by simply welding the casings together and leaving out a critical silicon computer chip. These fake cards made their way into inventory and sales. Most of the sales of these cards are alleged to have gone to other companies controlled by Pinez.

Flash 98 Scam

In the fourth quarter of 1996 Centennial began shipping a new product called "Flash 1998." It was a miniature memory card for notebook computers. Sales for fiscal year 1996 amounted to about $2 million. The company told the auditors that it wanted to keep the details of the card relatively quiet for a few more months for competitive reasons. Pinez indicated that due to design advances developed by Centennial's research and development team, these new cards had an extremely low production cost, about 10 cents, with a sales price of a whopping $500. It turns out there was no such product. All sales were to one company, BBC. The company was run by a close personal friend of Pinez. To fool the auditors into thinking an actual sale took place, Pinez wired $1 million of his own personal funds to a third company, St. Jude Management Corp., which then paid Centennial on behalf of BBC for its Flash 98 purchases. The explanation provided for this rather unconventional form of payment was a "financial agreement" between St. Jude and BBC. Even though the check was from St. Jude Management, the $1 million payment was considered reasonable evidence supporting the sale. After the fraud was uncovered, the auditors, Coopers & Lybrand, claimed that the Flash 98 scam was a "unique" fraud because it appeared that a product was going out and cash was coming in.

Aftermath

From his prison cell, Pinez denied any wrongdoing and indicated that his actions were undertaken to benefit the company. Pinez attributed his problems to the scrutiny that inevitably comes with success: "You get lightning when you're very high."

Sources: M. Beasley, F. Buckless, S. Glover, and D. Prawitt, *Auditing Cases: An Interactive Learning Approach*, 2nd ed. Prentice Hall, 2003, and J. Auerbach, "How Centennial Technologies, a Hot Stock, Cooled," *The Wall Street Journal* (April 11, 1997).

FIGURE 11–3

Major Steps in Assessing the
Control Risk in the Inventory
Management Process

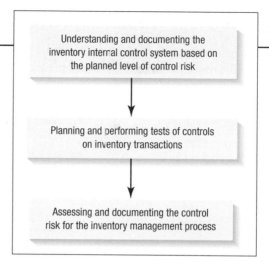

Understanding and documenting the
inventory internal control system based on
the planned level of control risk

Planning and performing tests of controls
on inventory transactions

Assessing and documenting the control
risk for the inventory management process

qualitative terms. The documentation supporting the assessed level of control risk for the inventory management process might include a flowchart such as the one shown in Figure 11–2, the results of the tests of controls, and a memorandum indicating the overall conclusions about control risk.

Planning and Performing Tests of Controls

In performing this step, the auditor again must identify the relevant control procedures within the client's inventory system that ensure that material misstatements are either prevented or detected and corrected. Audit procedures used to test the client's control procedures in the inventory management process are discussed in subsequent sections.

Setting and Documenting the Control Risk

Once the controls in the inventory system have been tested, the auditor sets the level of control risk. The auditor should document the achieved level of control risk using either quantitative amounts or qualitative terms. The documentation supporting the achieved level of control risk for the inventory management process might include a flowchart such as the one shown in Figure 11–2, the results of the tests of controls, and a memorandum indicating the overall conclusions about control risk.

Table 11–5 provides a summary of the possible misstatements, control procedures, and selected tests of controls for inventory transactions. The discussion includes control procedures that are present in a manufacturing setting. Because EarthWear is a retailer, the controls over the production process are not relevant. A number of control procedures in the revenue and purchasing processes provide assurance for selected assertions for inventory. The discussion that follows is limited to the more important assertions.

Occurrence of Inventory Transactions

The auditor's main concern is that all recorded inventory exists. The major control procedure for preventing fictitious inventory transactions from being recorded is proper segregation of duties, in which the inventory management and inventory stores functions are separated from the departments responsible for inventory and cost-accounting records. This control prevents operating personnel from having access to both inventory and the perpetual inventory records. Additionally, prenumbered documents

Table 11–5	Summary of Assertions, Possible Misstatements, Control Procedures, and Tests of Controls for Inventory Transactions		
Assertion	**Possible Misstatement**	**Control Procedure**	**Test of Controls**
Occurrence	Fictitious inventory	Segregation of duties	Observe and evaluate proper segregation of duties.
		Inventory transferred to inventory department using an approved, prenumbered receiving report	Review and test procedures for the transfer of inventory.
		Inventory transferred to manufacturing using prenumbered materials requisitions	Review and test procedures for issuing materials to manufacturing departments
		Accounting for numerical sequence of materials requisitions	Review and test client procedures for accounting for numerical sequence of materials requisitions.
	Inventory recorded but not on hand due to theft	Physical safeguards over inventory	Observe the physical safeguards over inventory.
Completeness	Inventory received but not recorded	The same as the control procedures for completeness in the purchasing process (see Table 9–6)	The same as the tests of controls performed on the control procedures in the purchasing process (see Table 9–6).
	Consigned goods not properly accounted for	Procedures to include goods out on consignment and exclude goods held on consignment	Review and test client's procedures for consignment goods.
Accuracy	Inventory quantities recorded incorrectly	Periodic or annual comparison of goods on hand with amounts shown in perpetual inventory records	Review and test procedures for taking physical inventory.
	Inventory and cost of goods sold not properly costed	Standard costs that are reviewed by management	Review and test procedures used to develop standard costs.
		Review of cost accumulation and variance reports	Review and test cost accumulation and variance reports.
	Inventory obsolescence	Inventory management personnel review inventory for obsolete, slow-moving, or excess quantities	Review and test procedures for identifying obsolete, slow-moving, or excess quantities.
	Inventory transactions not posted to the perpetual inventory records	Perpetual inventory records reconciled to general ledger control account monthly	Review the reconciliation of perpetual inventory to general ledger control account.
	Amounts for inventory from purchases journal not posted correctly to the general ledger inventory account		

(continued)

Table 11–5	Summary of Assertions, Possible Misstatements, Control Procedures, and Tests of Controls for Inventory Transactions *(concluded)*		
Assertion	*Possible Misstatement*	*Control Procedure*	*Test of Controls*
Cutoff	Inventory transactions recorded in the wrong period	All receiving reports processed daily by the IT department to record the receipt of inventory	Review and test procedures for processing inventory included on receiving reports into the perpetual records.
		All shipping documents processed daily to record the shipment of finished goods	Review and test procedures for removing inventory from perpetual records based on shipment of goods.
Classification	Inventory transactions not properly classified among raw materials, work in process, and finished goods	Materials requisitions and production data forms used to process goods through manufacturing	Review the procedures and forms used to classify inventory.

to handle the receipt, transfer, and withdrawal of inventory may prevent the recording of fictitious inventory in the accounting records.

The auditor should also be concerned that goods may be stolen. The auditor's concern about theft of goods varies depending upon the type of product sold or manufactured by the client. Products that are large or cumbersome may be difficult to steal. However, some products that are small and of high value, such as jewellery or computer memory chips, may be susceptible to theft. The client should maintain physical safeguards over inventory that are consistent with the susceptibility and value of the goods.

Review and observation are the main tests of controls used by the auditor to test the control procedures shown in Table 11–5. For example, the auditor can observe and evaluate the employees' segregation of duties. The auditor can also review and test the client's procedures for the transfer of raw materials from the receiving department and their issuance to the manufacturing departments.

Completeness of Inventory Transactions

The control procedures for the completeness assertion relate to recording inventory that has been received. Typically, the control procedures for this assertion are contained within the purchasing process. These control procedures and the related tests of controls were presented in Table 9–6 in Chapter 9. For example, in some instances, additional control procedures may be used in the raw materials stores department to ensure that the goods are recorded in the perpetual inventory records. This might include comparing a summary of the receiving reports to the inventory status report.

If goods are consigned, the client must have control procedures to ensure that goods held on consignment by other parties are included in inventory and goods held on consignment for others are excluded from inventory. The auditor can review the client's procedures for including or excluding consigned goods.

Accuracy of Inventory Transactions

Accuracy is an important assertion because inventory transactions that are not properly recorded result in misstatements that directly affect the amounts reported in the financial statements for cost of goods sold and inventory. The accurate processing of inventory purchase transactions involves applying the correct price to the actual quantity received. Similarly, when inventory is shipped, accurate processing requires that the actual number of items shipped be removed from inventory and that the proper cost be recorded to cost of goods sold. The use of a perpetual inventory system in conjunction with a periodic or annual physical inventory count should result in the proper quantities of inventory being shown in the client's perpetual inventory records. EarthWear maintains the purchase cost of its products in its master inventory file. Many manufacturing companies use standard costing systems to value their inventory. Standard costs should approximate actual costs, and the presence of large variances is one signal that the inventory may not be costed at an appropriate value. Auditing the client's physical inventory and standard costs is discussed in more detail later in the chapter.

Accurate valuation also considers inventory obsolescence. Inventory management personnel should periodically review inventory on hand for obsolete, slow-moving, or excess inventory. Such inventory should be written down to its fair market value. The auditor can review the client's procedures for identifying obsolete, slow-moving, or excess inventory. EarthWear's design department closely monitors its products to identify any end-of-season merchandise or overstocks, which are then sold at liquidation prices through special catalogue inserts.

Classification of Inventory Transactions

Classification is not an important assertion for EarthWear because all goods are finished and ready for sale. However, in a manufacturing company, the client must have control procedures to ensure that inventory is properly classified as raw materials, work in process, or finished goods. This can usually be accomplished by determining which departments in the manufacturing process are included in raw materials, work in process, and finished goods inventory. Thus, by knowing which manufacturing department holds the inventory, the client is able to classify it by type.

Relating the Assessed Level of Control Risk to Substantive Testing

The same judgement process is followed in assessing control risk in the inventory process that was used with other processes. For example, EarthWear has strong controls over the processing of inventory transactions. The auditor can rely on those controls if tests of controls indicate that the controls are operating effectively. If the results of the tests of controls for the inventory system do not support the planned level of control risk, the auditor would judge control risk to be higher and set detection risk lower. This would lead to increased substantive procedures.

Auditing Inventory

LO 6 ⟩ The discussion of the audit of inventory follows the process outlined in prior chapters. Two categories of substantive procedures are discussed: substantive analytical procedures and tests of details of classes of transactions, account balances, and disclosures. Table 11–6 presents the assertions

Table 11–6	Assertions about Classes of Transactions, Events, Account Balances, and Disclosures for Inventory

Assertions about Classes of Transactions and Events:

- **Occurrence.** Inventory transactions and events are valid.
- **Completeness.** All inventory transactions and events have been recorded.
- **Accuracy.** Inventory transactions have been properly computed, and ending inventory and related revenue and cost of good sold have been properly accumulated from journals and ledgers.
- **Cutoff.** Inventory receipts and shipments are recorded in the correct accounting period.
- **Classification.** Inventory is recorded in the proper accounts (e.g., raw materials, work in process, or finished goods).

Assertions about Account Balances at the Period End:

- **Existence.** Inventory recorded on the books and records actually exists.
- **Rights and obligations.** The entity has the legal right (i.e., ownership) to the recorded inventory.
- **Completeness.** All inventory is recorded.
- **Valuation and allocation.** Inventory is properly recorded in accordance with GAAP (e.g., lower of cost or market).

Assertions about Presentation and Disclosure:

- **Occurrence and rights and obligations.** All disclosed events, transactions, and other matters relating to inventory have occurred and pertain to the entity.
- **Completeness.** All disclosures relating to inventory that should have been included in the financial statements have been included.
- **Classification and understandability.** Financial information relating to inventory is appropriately presented and described, and disclosures are clearly expressed.
- **Accuracy and valuation.** Financial and other information relating to inventory are disclosed fairly and at appropriate amounts.

for classes of transactions, events, account balances, and disclosures as they apply to inventory. You should note that the auditor may test assertions related to transactions (substantive tests of transactions) in conjunction with testing the internal controls. If the tests of controls indicate that the controls are not operating effectively, the auditor may need to test transactions at the date the account balance is tested.

Substantive Analytical Procedures

Substantive analytical procedures are useful audit tests for examining the reasonableness of inventory and cost of goods sold. When performed as part of audit planning, preliminary analytical procedures can effectively identify whether the inventory and cost of goods sold accounts contain material misstatements. Final analytical procedures are useful as an overall review for inventory and related accounts to identify obsolete, slow-moving, and excess inventory. Substantive analytical procedures are useful for testing the valuation assertion for inventory. Such tests can also identify problems with improper inclusion or exclusion of costs in overhead. Table 11–7 lists substantive analytical procedures that are useful in auditing inventory and related accounts at either the planning stage or as an overall review.

For example, the inventory turnover ratio (cost of goods sold ÷ inventory) can be compared over time or to an industry average. A high inventory turnover ratio normally indicates efficient inventory policies, while a

Table 11–7	**Substantive Analytical Procedures for Inventory and Related Accounts**

Substantive Analytical Procedure	*Possible Misstatement Detected*
Compare raw material, finished goods, and total inventory turnover to previous years' and industry averages.	Obsolete, slow-moving, or excess inventory
Compare days outstanding in inventory to previous years' and industry average.	Obsolete, slow-moving, or excess inventory
Compare gross profit percentage by product line with previous years' and industry data.	Unrecorded or fictitious inventory
Compare actual cost of goods sold to budgeted amounts.	Over- or understated inventory
Compare current-year standard costs with prior years' after considering current conditions.	Over- or understated inventory
Compare actual manufacturing overhead costs with budgeted or standard manufacturing overhead costs.	Inclusion or exclusion of overhead costs

low ratio may indicate the presence of slow-moving or obsolete inventory. The gross profit percentage can also be compared to previous years' or industry data and may provide valuable evidence on unrecorded inventory (an understatement) or fictitious inventory (an overstatement). This ratio may also provide information on the proper valuation of inventory. For example, a small or negative gross profit margin may indicate issues related to the lower-of-cost-or-market valuation of inventory. It is important that the auditor use sufficiently disaggregated analytical procedures in order to identify unusual patterns like the one illustrated in Figure 5–4, in Chapter 5.

Tests of Details of Classes of Transactions, Account Balances, and Disclosures

Table 11–6 presented the assertions for inventory. The intended purpose of tests of details of transactions is to detect monetary misstatements in the inventory account. The auditor may conduct tests of details of transactions specifically for inventory. However, because the inventory management process interacts with the revenue, purchasing, and human resource management processes, transactions involving the receipt of goods, shipment of goods, and assignment of labour costs are normally tested as part of those processes. For example, receiving department personnel prepare a receiving report that includes the quantity and type of goods received. The receiving report and vendor invoice are then used to record the accounts payable. If the auditor intends to obtain substantive evidence on the perpetual inventory records, the tests of receipt and shipment of goods can be extended by tracing the transactions into the perpetual inventory records. For example, the receiving report is generally used by the client to record the goods in the perpetual inventory records or inventory master file (see Figure 11–2). The auditor can perform a test of detail of transactions by tracing a sample of receiving reports into the perpetual inventory records. Labour costs can also be traced to individual inventory transactions and into the cost-accounting records.

As previously mentioned, tests of details of transactions are often conducted in conjunction with tests of controls. Table 11–8 presents examples of tests of details of transactions, account balances, and disclosures for assertions related to inventory. The discussion that follows focuses primarily on tests of details of account balances of inventory.

Table 11–8 summarizes the tests of the inventory account balance for each assertion. Accuracy is discussed first because the auditor must establish that the detailed records that support the inventory account agree with the general ledger account.

Accuracy

Testing the accuracy of inventory requires obtaining a copy of the compilation of the physical inventory that shows inventory quantities and prices. The inventory compilation is footed, and the mathematical extensions of quantity multiplied by price are tested. Additionally, test counts made by the auditor during the physical inventory and tag control information are traced into the compilation.

Many times the client will have adjusted the general ledger inventory balance to agree to the physical inventory amounts (referred to as *book-to-physical adjustment*) before the auditor begins the substantive tests of account balances. If the client has made the book-to-physical adjustment, the totals from the compilation for inventory should agree with the general ledger.

When the client maintains a perpetual inventory system, the totals from the inventory compilation should also be agreed to these records. The auditor can use computer-assisted audit techniques to accomplish these audit steps. For example, the auditor can use a generalized or custom audit software package to trace costs used to price goods in the inventory compilation to standard cost files. The extensions and footing can also be tested at the same time.

Cutoff

In testing the cutoff assertion for inventory, the auditor attempts to determine whether all sales of finished goods and purchases of raw materials are recorded in the proper period. For sales cutoff, the auditor can examine a sample of shipping documents for a few days before and after year-end for recording of inventory shipments in the proper period. For purchases cutoff, the auditor can examine a sample of receiving documents for a few days before and after year-end for recording of inventory purchases in the proper period. Chapters 8 and 9 discuss sales and purchases cutoff.

Existence

Existence is one of the more important assertions for the inventory account. The observation of the physical inventory is the primary audit step used to verify this assertion. If the auditor is satisfied with the client's physical inventory count, the auditor has sufficient, competent evidence on the existence of recorded inventory.

Completeness

The auditor must determine whether all inventory has been included in the inventory compilation and the general ledger inventory account. The tests related to the observation of the physical inventory count provide assurance that all goods on hand are included in inventory. Tracing test counts and tag control information into the inventory compilation provide assurance that the inventory counted during the physical inventory observation is included in the compilation. In some cases, inventory is held

Table 11–8	Examples of Inventory Tests of Transactions, Account Balances, and Disclosures

Assertions about Classes of Transactions	Substantive Tests of Transaction*
Occurrence	Vouch a sample of inventory additions (i.e., purchases) to receiving reports and purchase requisitions.
Completeness	Trace a sample of receiving reports to the inventory records (i.e., master file, status report).
Accuracy	Recompute the mathematical accuracy of a sample of inventory transactions (i.e., price X quantity).
	Audit standard costs or other methods used to price inventory (see discussion in the chapter for the audit procedures used to audit standard costs).
	Trace costs used to price goods in the inventory compilation to standard costs or vendors' invoices.
Cutoff	Trace a sample of time cards before and after period end to the appropriate weekly inventory report, and trace the weekly inventory report to the general ledger to verify inventory transactions are recorded in the proper period.
Classification	Examine a sample of inventory checks for proper classification into expense accounts.

Assertions about Account Balances at Period End	Tests of Details of Account Balances
Existence	Observe count of physical inventory (see discussion in chapter for proper inventory observation procedures)
Rights and obligations	Verify that inventory held on consignment for others is not included in inventory.
	Verify that "bill-and-hold" goods are not included in inventory.
Completeness	Trace test counts and tag control information to the inventory compilation
Valuation and allocation	Obtain a copy of the inventory compilation and agree totals to general ledger.
	Trace test counts and tag control information to the inventory compilation.
	Test mathematical accuracy of extensions and foot the inventory compilation.
	Enquire of management concerning obsolete, slow-moving, or excess inventory.
	Review book-to-physical adjustment for possible misstatements (see Table 11–9).

Assertions about Presentation and Disclosure	Tests of Details of Disclosures
Occurrence, and rights and obligations	Enquire of management and review any loan agreements and board of directors' minutes for any indication that inventory has been pledged or assigned.
	Enquire of management about issues related to warranty obligations.
Completeness	Complete financial reporting checklist to ensure that all financial statement disclosures related to inventory are made.

(continued)

Table 11–8	Examples of Inventory Tests of Transactions, Account Balances, and Disclosures *(concluded)*
Assertions about Presentation and Disclosure	**Tests of Details of Disclosures**
Classification and understandability	Review inventory compilation for proper classification among raw materials, work in process, and finished goods.
	Read footnotes to ensure that required disclosures are understandable.
Accuracy and valuation	Determine if the cost method is accurately disclosed (e.g., LIFO).
	Enquire of management about issues related to LIFO liquidations.
	Read footnotes and other information to ensure that the information is accurate and properly presented at the appropriate amounts.

*Many of these tests of details of transactions are commonly conducted as dual-purpose tests (i.e., in conjunction with tests of controls).

on consignment by others or is stored in public warehouses. The auditor normally confirms or physically observes such inventory.

Rights and Obligations

The auditor must determine whether the recorded inventory is actually owned by the entity. Two issues related to ownership can arise. First, the auditor must be sure that the inventory on hand belongs to the client. If the client holds inventory on consignment, such inventory should not be included in the physical inventory. Second, in some industries, goods are sold on a "bill-and-hold" basis. In such cases, the goods are treated as a sale but the client holds the goods until the customer needs them. Again, the auditor must be certain that such goods are segregated and not counted at the time of the physical inventory.

Valuation and Allocation

A number of important valuation issues are related to inventory. The first issue relates to the costs used to value the inventory items included in the compilation. When the client, such as EarthWear, purchases inventory, valuation of the inventory can normally be accomplished by vouching the costs to vendors' invoices. When the client uses standard costs, the auditor audits the standard costs as discussed previously. The second valuation issue relates to the lower-of-cost-or-market tests for inventory. The auditor normally performs such tests on large-dollar items or on the client's various product lines. At EarthWear, the auditors would likely perform the lower-of-cost-or-market test on merchandise noted by management for liquidation. A third valuation issue relates to obsolete, slow-moving, or excess inventory. The auditor should ask management about such issues. When these issues exist, the inventory should be written down to its current market value. Finally, the auditor should investigate any large adjustments between the amount of inventory shown in the general ledger account and the amount determined from the physical inventory count (book-to-physical adjustments) for possible misstatements. Table 11–9 presents a list of items that may lead to book-to-physical differences.

Table 11–9	Possible Causes of Book-to-Physical Differences

Inventory cutoff errors.

Unreported scrap or spoilage.

Pilferage or theft.

Classification and Understandability

The presentation and disclosure assertion of classification of inventory for EarthWear is not an issue because the company sells only finished products. However, in a manufacturing company, the auditor must determine that inventory is properly classified as raw materials, work in process, or finished goods. In most manufacturing companies, proper classification can be achieved by determining which manufacturing processing department has control of the inventory on the date of the physical count. For example, if inventory tags are used to count inventory and they are assigned numerically to departments, classification can be verified at the physical inventory. The auditor can ensure that each department is using the assigned tags. The tag control information by department can be compared to the information on the inventory compilation to ensure that it is properly classified among raw materials, work in process, and finished goods.

Other Presentation and Disclosure Assertions

Several important disclosure issues are related to inventory. Table 11–10 presents some examples of disclosure items for inventory and related accounts. For example, management must disclose the cost method, such as weighted average or FIFO, used to value inventory. Management must also disclose the components (raw materials, work in process, and finished goods) of inventory either on the face of the balance sheet or in the footnotes. *EarthWear* Exhibit 11–4 presents EarthWear's financial statement disclosure for inventory. Note that the company uses weighted average to value inventory, and it discloses the approximate inventory value if FIFO had been used.

Table 11–10	Examples of Disclosure Items for Inventory and Related Accounts

Cost method (FIFO, weighted average, retail method).

Components of inventory.

Long-term purchase contracts.

Consigned inventory.

Purchases from related parties.

Pledged or assigned inventory.

Disclosure of unusual losses from write-downs of inventory or losses on long-term purchase commitments.

Warranty obligations.

EXHIBIT 11–4	**EarthWear's Financial Statement Disclosure for Inventory**
	Inventory is stated weighted average cost, which is lower than market. If the first-in, first-out method of accounting for inventory had been used, inventory would have been approximately $10.8 million and $13.6 million higher than reported at December 31, 2006 and 2005, respectively.

Observing Physical Inventory

LO 7〉 Technological advances such as the widespread use of UPC codes has greatly enhanced companies' ability to maintain perpetual inventory records. Since physically counting inventory may require a temporary stoppage in production or an interruption in the flow of incoming or outgoing shipments, many companies have adopted such advanced technology. However, even companies that have a sophisticated perpetual inventory system should, if they produce or sell tangible products, physically count inventory periodically, at least at year-end if not more frequently, mainly to determine if any adjustments are necessary to the perpetual records, e.g., inventory shrinkage or theft.

The auditor's observation of inventory is a generally accepted auditing procedure (*CICA Handbook,* section 6030). However, the auditor is not required to observe all inventory, but only inventory that is material. Internal auditors may also observe physical inventory. The primary reason for observing the client's physical inventory is to establish the *validity* or *existence* of the inventory. The observation of the physical inventory also provides some evidence on the *ownership* and *valuation* audit objectives. Based on the physical inventory count, the client compiles the physical inventory. While the form of compilation may differ among entities, it normally contains a list of the items by type and quantity, the assigned cost for each item, the inventory value for each item, and a total for the inventory.

Prior to the physical count of inventory, the auditor should be familiar with the inventory locations (Exhibit 11–5), the major items in inventory, and the client's instructions for counting inventory.

EXHIBIT 11–5	**The Challenges of Counting Inventory**
	The logistics of counting inventory can be challenging. This is especially true in the Canadian natural resource industry, particularly if there are geographic impediments to a count. For example, one of the authors is familiar with inventory counts using helicopters over the interior of British Columbia to estimate timber reserves for a forestry company, and using miniature tugboats in inlets of the Pacific Ocean to count logs in 500-metre-long log booms for a pulp-and-paper company. For some types of specialized natural resources, for example, oil and gas reserves for an oil exploration and development company, the auditor should consider employing the services of an independent expert. *CICA Handbook,* section 5049, "Use of specialists in assurance engagements," discusses the auditor's responsibilities in such circumstances.

During the observation of the physical inventory count, the auditor should do the following:

- Ensure that no production is scheduled. Or, if production is scheduled, ensure that proper controls are established for movement between departments in order to prevent double counting.
- Ensure that there is no movement of goods during the inventory count. If movement is necessary, the auditor and client personnel must ensure that the goods are not double counted and that all goods are counted.
- Make sure that the client's count teams are following the inventory count instructions. If the count teams are not following the instructions, the auditor should notify the client representative in charge of the area.
- Ensure that inventory tags are issued sequentially to individual departments. For many inventory counts, the goods are marked with multicopy inventory tags. The count teams record the type and quantity of inventory on each tag, and one copy of each tag is then used to compile the inventory. If the client uses another method of counting inventory, such as detailed inventory listings, the auditor should obtain copies of the listings prior to the start of the inventory count.
- Perform test counts and record a sample of counts in the working papers. This information will be used to test the accuracy and completeness of the client's inventory compilation.
- Obtain tag control information for testing the client's inventory compilation. Tag control information includes documentation of the numerical sequence of all inventory tags and accounting for all used and unused inventory tags. If inventory listings are used by the client, copies of the listings will accomplish the objective of documenting the entire inventory count.
- Obtain cutoff information, including the number of the last shipping and receiving documents issued on the date of the physical inventory count.
- Observe the condition of the inventory for items that may be obsolete, slow-moving, or carried in excess quantities.
- Enquire about goods held on consignment for others or held on a "bill-and-hold" basis. Such items should not be included in the client's inventory. The auditor must also enquire about goods held on consignment for the client. These goods should be included in the inventory count.

If these audit procedures are followed, the auditor has reasonable assurance that a proper inventory count has been taken.

Evaluating the Audit Findings—Inventory

LO 8 When the auditor has completed the planned substantive tests of the inventory account, all of the identified misstatements should be aggregated. The likely misstatement is compared to the tolerable misstatement allocated to the inventory account. If the likely misstatement is less than the tolerable misstatement, the auditor may accept the inventory account as fairly presented. Conversely, if the likely misstatement exceeds the tolerable misstatement, the auditor should conclude that the inventory account is not fairly presented.

For example, suppose that a tolerable misstatement of $250,000 was allocated to EarthWear's inventory and that Willis & Adams detected an overstatement of inventory of potentially $120,000 based on a projection of the test sample. Because this misstatement is less than the tolerable misstatement of $250,000, Willis & Adams can conclude that the audit evidence supports fair presentation. However, if the misstatement had been greater than the tolerable misstatement, the evidence would not support fair presentation. In this case the auditor would have two choices: adjust the accounts to reduce the misstatement to an amount less than the tolerable misstatement or qualify the audit report.

In either case the auditor would bring the error forward to the SUM and follow one of several different courses of action. The most preferable course of action would be to have the client adjust the accounts to correct the error. If the client was unwilling to do so, the auditor would have to use his or her professional judgement to decide on the appropriate course of action. The amount of the misstatement is clearly less than overall materiality, but if the size of the misstatement compared to the value of the account is significant, it may be considered a qualitative factor (see AuG-41) to be taken into account. It is unlikely that the auditor would consider it appropriate to qualify the audit report for this misstatement, but given its size, would stress to the client the importance of adjusting the account.

The auditor should again analyze the misstatements discovered through the application of substantive tests of transactions, analytical procedures, and tests of account balances, because these misstatements may provide additional evidence on the control risk for the inventory management process. If the auditor concludes that the audit risk is unacceptably high, additional audit procedures should be performed, or the auditor must be satisfied that the client has adjusted the related financial statement accounts to an acceptable level.

Appendix: 11A   Auditing Standard Costs

LO 9 > Many manufacturing entities use a standard cost system to measure performance and to value inventory. If a standard cost system is integrated with the general accounting records, cost accumulation and variance reports are direct outputs of the client's inventory-accounting system. It should be noted that, according to *CICA Handbook*, section 3031, standard costs must be consistent with actual costs; otherwise, actual costs must be used to value inventory for external financial statements.

For proper valuation, standard costs should approximate actual costs. To test the standard costs, the auditor should first review the client's policies and procedures for constructing standard costs. Once the policies and procedures are understood, the auditor normally tests the component cost buildup for a representative sample of standard product costs.

Three components make up the cost of producing a product: materials, labour, and overhead. For discussion purposes, suppose that Calabro Digital Services (see Problem 3-38) assembles five types of pagers. Assume further that all parts used in the pagers are purchased from outside vendors. The process followed in auditing the three components that make up the standard costs for a type of pager follows.

Materials

Determining the materials costs requires testing the quantity and type of materials included in the product and the price of the materials. The quantity and type of materials are tested by reviewing the engineering specifications for the product. For example, in the case of pagers, the auditor can obtain a set of engineering specifications that includes a blueprint and a list of materials needed to manufacture a particular pager. The auditor can compare the list of materials with the standard cost card or other documentation used to support the cost accumulation. The prices used on the standard cost card can be traced to vendors' invoices as a test of actual costs.

Labour

The determination of labour costs requires evidence about the type and amount of labour needed for production and the labour rate. Following our example, the amount of labour necessary to assemble a pager can be tested by reviewing engineering estimates, which may be based on time-and-motion studies or on historical information. The labour rates for each type of labour necessary to assemble a pager can be tested by examining a schedule of authorized wages.

Overhead

The auditor tests overhead costs by reviewing the client's method of overhead allocation for reasonableness, compliance with GAAP, and consistency. The auditor can examine the costs included in overhead to be sure that such costs can appropriately be assigned to the product. The inclusion or exclusion of such costs should be consistent from one period to the next. Using the pager example, the auditor would obtain a listing of expense accounts used to make up the overhead pool of costs. The auditor can compare the actual costs for the period to the budgeted costs. The auditor can also compare the costs included in the current year's listing with those in the prior year's listing.

REVIEW QUESTIONS

LO 1 > **11-1** Why does inventory represent one of the more complex parts of the audit?

1 > **11-2** How does the inventory management process relate to the revenue, purchasing, and payroll processes?

3 > **11-3** Briefly describe each of the following documents or records: production schedule, materials requisition, inventory master file, production data information, and cost accumulation and variance reports.

2 > **11-4** What duties are performed within the inventory management, stores, and cost-accounting functions?

3> **11-5** List the key segregation of duties in the inventory management process. What errors or fraud can occur if such segregation of duties is not present?

4> **11-6** List the inherent risk factors that affect the inventory management process.

5> **11-7** List the major steps in assessing control risk in the inventory management process.

5> **11-8** What control procedures can a client use to prevent unauthorized inventory production?

6> **11-9** List three analytical procedures that can test the fairness of inventory and related accounts.

9> **11-10** Describe how an auditor audits standard costs.

7> **11-11** List the procedures the auditor should perform during the count of the client's physical inventory.

6> **11-12** What are some possible causes of book-to-physical inventory differences?

6> **11-13** List five items for inventory and related accounts that may require disclosure.

MULTIPLE-CHOICE QUESTIONS FROM PROFESSIONAL EXAMINATIONS

Unless otherwise indicated, these multiple-choice questions were adapted from the CPA examinations, courtesy of the American Institute of Certified Public Accountants.

2,5> **11-14** The objectives of internal control for an inventory management process are to provide assurance that transactions are properly executed and recorded and that

a. Independent internal verification of activity reports is established.

b. Transfers to the finished goods department are documented by a completed production report and a quality control report.

c. Production orders are prenumbered and signed by a supervisor.

d. Custody of work in process and finished goods is properly maintained.

3,5> **11-15** Which of the following would most likely be an internal control procedure designed to detect errors and fraud concerning the custody of inventory?

a. Periodic reconciliation of work in process with job cost sheets.

b. Segregation of functions between general accounting and cost accounting.

c. Independent comparisons of finished goods records with counts of goods on hand.

d. Approval of inventory journal entries by the storekeeper.

5> **11-16** Which of the following control procedures would be most likely to assist in reducing the control risk related to the existence or occurrence of manufacturing transactions?

a. Perpetual inventory records are independently compared with goods on hand.

b. Forms used for direct materials requisitions are prenumbered and accounted for.

c. Finished goods are stored in locked limited-access warehouses.

d. Subsidiary ledgers are periodically reconciled with inventory control accounts.

3,5 >   **11-17**   Independent internal verification of inventory occurs when employees who

a. Issue raw materials obtain materials requisitions for each issue and prepare daily totals of materials issued.

b. Compare records of goods on hand with physical quantities do *not* maintain the records or have custody of the inventory.

c. Obtain receipts for the transfer of completed work to finished goods prepare a completed production report.

d. Are independent of issuing production orders update records from completed job cost sheets and production cost reports on a timely basis.

5 >   **11-18**   An auditor's tests of controls over the issuance of raw materials to production would most likely include

a. Reconciliation of raw materials and work-in-process perpetual inventory records to general ledger balances.

b. Enquiry of the custodian about the procedures followed when defective materials are received from vendors.

c. Observation that raw materials are stored in secure areas and that storeroom security is supervised by a responsible individual.

d. Examination of materials requisitions and reperformance of client controls designed to process and record issuances.

5 >   **11-19**   Which of the following internal control procedures is most likely to address the completeness assertion for inventory?

a. The work-in-process account is periodically reconciled with subsidiary records.

b. Employees responsible for custody of finished goods do *not* perform the receiving function.

c. Receiving reports are prenumbered and periodically reconciled.

d. There is a separation of duties between payroll department and inventory accounting personnel.

5,6 >   **11-20**   A client maintains perpetual inventory records in both quantities and dollars. If the assessed level of control risk were high, an auditor would probably

a. Insist that the client perform physical counts of inventory items several times during the year.

b. Apply gross profit tests to ascertain the reasonableness of the physical counts.

c. Increase the extent of tests of controls of the inventory cycle.

d. Request that the client schedule the physical inventory count at the end of the year.

6> **11-21** When auditing merchandise inventory at year-end, the auditor performs a purchase cutoff test to obtain evidence that

a. All goods purchased before year-end are received before the physical inventory count.

b. No goods held on consignment for customers are included in the inventory balance.

c. No goods observed during the physical count are pledged or sold.

d. All goods owned at year-end are included in the inventory balance.

6> **11-22** An auditor using audit software would probably be *least* interested in which of the following fields in a computerized perpetual inventory file?

a. Economic order quantity.

b. Warehouse location.

c. Date of last purchase.

d. Quantity sold.

6,7> **11-23** Enquiries of warehouse personnel concerning possibly obsolete or slow-moving inventory items provide assurance about management's assertion of

a. Completeness.

b. Existence.

c. Presentation.

d. Valuation.

6> **11-24** Which of the following audit procedures would probably provide the most reliable evidence concerning the entity's assertion of rights and obligations related to inventory?

a. Tracing of test counts noted during the entity's physical count to the entity's summarization of quantities.

b. Inspection of agreements to determine whether any inventory is pledged as collateral or subject to any liens.

c. Selection of the last few shipping advices used before the physical count and determination of whether the shipments were recorded as sales.

d. Inspection of the open-purchase-order file for significant commitments that should be considered for disclosure.

6,7> **11-25** Periodic or cycle counts of selected inventory items are made at various times during the year rather than via a single inventory count at year-end. Which of the following is necessary if the auditor plans to observe inventory at interim dates?

a. Complete recounts are performed by independent teams.

b. Perpetual inventory records are maintained.

c. Unit cost records are integrated with production-accounting records.

d. Inventory balances are rarely at low levels.

6> **11-26** After accounting for a sequence of inventory tags, an auditor traces a sample of tags to the physical inventory listing to obtain evidence that all items

a. Included in the listing have been counted.
b. Represented by inventory tags are included in the listing.
c. Included in the listing are represented by inventory tags.
d. Represented by inventory tags are bona fide.

PROBLEMS

2,5> **11-27** Simone Yardley prepared the flowchart on the following page, which portrays the raw materials purchasing function of one of Yardley's clients, a medium-size manufacturing company, from the preparation of initial documents through the vouching of invoices for payment. The flowchart represents a portion of the work performed on the audit engagement to evaluate internal control.

Required:

Identify and explain the systems and control weaknesses evident from the flowchart. Include the internal control weaknesses resulting from activities performed or not performed. All documents are prenumbered.

(AICPA, adapted)

9> **11-28** Three Buoys Boatbuilders Ltd. (TBB) is a manufacturer of runabouts and pleasurecraft ranging from 5 to 7 metres in length. They are a volume manufacturer and have developed a comprehensive standard costing system.

Required:

List the audit procedures that you could apply to satisfy yourself that TBB's cost standards and related variance amounts have not distorted the value of inventory.

5,6,7> **11-29** James Rasch is the partner-in-charge of the audit of Bonner Distributing Corporation, a wholesaler that owns one warehouse containing 80 percent of its inventory. Rasch is reviewing the working papers that were prepared to support the firm's opinion on Bonner's financial statements, and Rasch wants to be certain that essential audit tests are well documented.

Required:

a. What evidence should Rasch find in the working papers to support the fact that the audit was adequately planned and the assistants were properly supervised?
b. What substantive tests should Rasch expect to find in the working papers to document management's assertion about completeness as it relates to the inventory quantities at the end of the year?

(AICPA, adapted)

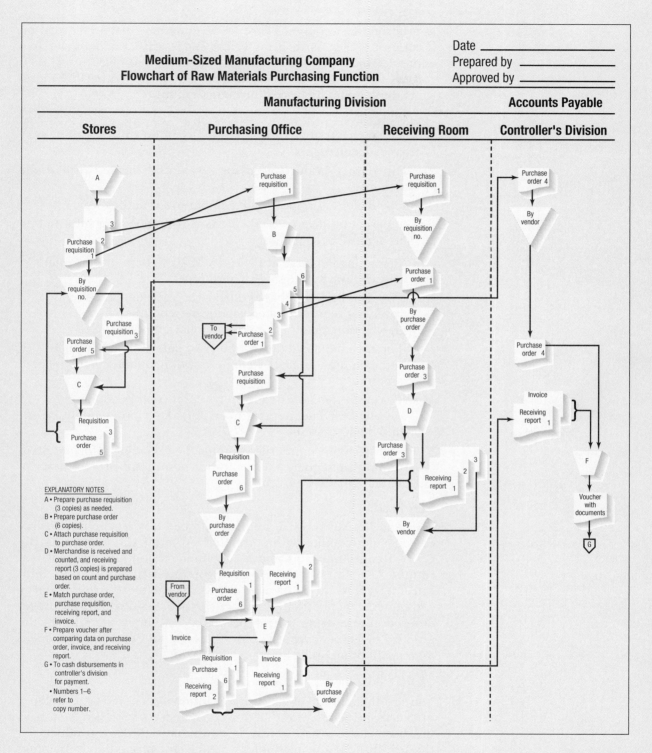

Medium-Sized Manufacturing Company
Flowchart of Raw Materials Purchasing Function

Date _____
Prepared by _____
Approved by _____

Manufacturing Division   **Accounts Payable**

Stores   **Purchasing Office**   **Receiving Room**   **Controller's Division**

EXPLANATORY NOTES
A • Prepare purchase requisition (3 copies) as needed.
B • Prepare purchase order (6 copies).
C • Attach purchase requisition to purchase order.
D • Merchandise is received and counted, and receiving report (3 copies) is prepared based on count and purchase order.
E • Match purchase order, purchase requisition, receiving report, and invoice.
F • Prepare voucher after comparing data on purchase order, invoice, and receiving report.
G • To cash disbursements in controller's division for payment.
• Numbers 1–6 refer to copy number.

6,7 ⟩   **11-30**   Alex Kachelmeier is auditing the financial statements of Big Z Wholesaling, Ltd., a continuing audit client, for the year ended January 31, 2006. On January 5, 2006, Kachelmeier observed the tagging and counting of Big Z's physical inventory and made appropriate test counts. These test counts have been recorded on a computer file. As in prior years, Big Z gave Kachelmeier two computer files. One file represents the perpetual inventory (FIFO) records for the year ended January 31, 2006. The other file represents the January 5 physical inventory count.

Assume that:

1. Kachelmeier issued an unqualified opinion on the prior year's financial statements.
2. All inventory is purchased for resale and located in a single warehouse.
3. Kachelmeier has appropriate computerized audit software.
4. The perpetual inventory file contains the following information in item number sequence:
    - Beginning balances at February 1, 2005: item number, item description, total quantity, and price.
    - For each item purchased during the year: date received, receiving report number, vendor item number, item description, quantity, and total dollar amount.
    - For each item sold during the year: date shipped, invoice number, item number, item description, quantity, and dollar amount.
    - For each item adjusted for physical inventory count differences: date, item number, item description, quantity, and dollar amount.
5. The physical inventory file contains the following information in item number sequence: tag number, item number, item description, and quantity.

Required:

Describe the substantive auditing procedures Kachelmeier may consider performing with computerized audit software using Big Z's two computer files and Kachelmeier's computer file of test counts. The substantive auditing procedures described may indicate the reports to be printed out for Kachelmeier's follow-up by subsequent application of manual procedures. Group the procedures by those using (a) the perpetual inventory file and (b) the physical inventory and test count files. Do *not* describe subsequent manual auditing procedures.

(AICPA, adapted)

6,7 ▷   **11-31**   You are the auditor of Software Solutions Corp. (SSC), developer of successful firms in the high-tech industry sector. SSC's success has been due to their ability to continually develop products on the leading edge of technology which are immediately in great demand. However, in a tour of their warehouse, you noted numerous stacks of cartons on palettes and shelves that appeared not to have been accessed for a long time. You are concerned about this. Because of the speed with which "new" products become "old" and "obsolete" in this sector, a problem that may arise in inventory verification is that slow-moving and obsolete items may be included at full values and not written down to their appropriate scrap or recoverable amount.

Required:

List the procedures that you could employ to determine whether slow-moving or obsolete items are appropriately valued in SSC's inventory.

7⟩ 11-32 Abbott Corporation does not conduct a complete annual physical count of purchased parts and supplies in its principal warehouse but instead uses statistical sampling to estimate the year-end inventory. Abbott maintains a perpetual inventory record of parts and supplies and believes that statistical sampling is highly effective in determining inventory values and is sufficiently reliable to make a physical count of each item of inventory unnecessary.

Required:

a. Identify the audit procedures that should be used by the auditor that change, or are in addition to, normal required audit procedures when a client utilizes statistical sampling to determine inventory value and does not conduct a 100 percent annual physical count of inventory items.

b. List at least 10 normal audit procedures that should be performed to verify physical quantities whenever a client conducts a periodic physical count of all, or part, of its inventory.

(AICPA, adapted)

7⟩ 11-33 You have acquired a reputation in your firm as someone who is very good at devising effective ways of confirming clients' inventory valuations in non-traditional circumstances. You are consulting on three new audit clients:

1. Foothills Cattle Co. runs 20,000 head of cattle on a 250,000 hectare ranch, mostly unfenced, in Alberta.
2. Carruthers Manufacturing has raw materials inventories consisting mostly of pig iron loaded on freight cars on a siding at the company's plant.
3. Melton Processing Ltd. is running at capacity on three full shifts around the clock and cannot shut down production operations during the physical inventory.

Required:

Describe the problems the auditor would encounter in the verification of inventory in these situations and suggest audit procedures to deal with the problems.

6,7⟩ 11-34 An auditor is examining the financial statements of a wholesale cosmetics distributor with an inventory consisting of thousands of individual items. The distributor keeps its inventory in its own distribution centre and in two public warehouses. An inventory computer file is maintained on a computer disk, and at the end of each business day the file is updated. Each record of the inventory file contains the following data:

- item number
- location of item
- description of item
- quantity on hand
- cost per item
- date of last purchase
- date of last sale
- quantity sold during year

The auditor plans to observe the distributor's physical count of inventory as of a given date. The auditor will have available a computer disk of the data on the inventory file on the date of the physical count and a general-purpose computer software package.

Required:

The auditor is planning to perform basic inventory-auditing procedures. Identify the basic inventory-auditing procedures and describe how the use of the general-purpose software package and the tape of the inventory file data might help the auditor perform such auditing procedures. Organize your answer as follows:

Basic Inventory-Auditing Procedure	How a General-Purpose Computer Software Package and Tape of the Inventory File Data Might Be Helpful
1. Observation of the physical count, making and recording test counts where applicable	1. By determining which items are to be test counted by selecting a random sample of a representative number of items from the inventory file as of the date of the physical count

(AICPA, adapted)

6,7 ⟩ **11-35** Joan Dunne is examining the financial statements of Doo-Right Wholesale Sales, Ltd., for the year ended December 31, 2006. Doo-Right has been in business for many years and has never had its financial statements audited. Dunne has gained satisfaction with respect to the ending inventory and is considering alternative audit procedures to verify management's representations concerning the beginning inventory, which was not observed.

Doo-Right sells only one product (bottled Brand X beer) and maintains perpetual inventory records. In addition, Doo-Right takes physical inventory counts monthly. Dunne has already confirmed purchases with the manufacturer and has decided to concentrate on evaluating the reliability of perpetual inventory records and performing analytical procedures to the extent that prior years' unaudited records will allow.

Required:

What audit tests, including analytical procedures, should Dunne apply in evaluating the reliability of perpetual inventory records and verifying the January 1, 2006, inventory?

(AICPA, adapted)

6⟩   11-36   In obtaining audit evidence in support of financial statement assertions, the auditor develops specific audit objectives in light of those assertions. Audit procedures are then selected to accomplish audit objectives.

Required:

Your client is Hillmart, a retail department store that purchases all goods directly from wholesalers or manufacturers. Select the most appropriate audit procedure from the list below and enter the number in the appropriate place on the grid. (An audit procedure may be selected once, more than once, or not at all.)

Audit Procedure:

1. Examine current vendor price lists.
2. Review drafts of the financial statements.
3. Select a sample of items during the physical inventory count and determine that they have been included on count sheets.
4. Select a sample of recorded items and examine supporting vendor invoices and contracts.
5. Select a sample of recorded items on count sheets during the physical inventory count and determine that items are on hand.
6. Review loan agreements and minutes of board of directors' meetings.

Specific Audit Objective	Audit Procedure
a. Ensure that the entity has legal title to inventory.	
b. Ensure that recorded inventory quantities include all products on hand.	
c. Verify that inventory has been reduced, when appropriate, to replacement cost or net realizable value.	
d. Verify that the cost of inventory has been properly determined.	
e. Verify that the major categories of inventory and their bases of valuation are adequately reported in the financial statements.	

DISCUSSION CASE

6,7,8⟩   11-37   Harris decided that the easiest way to make the Fabricator Division appear more profitable was through manipulating the inventory, which was the largest asset on the books. Harris found that by increasing inventory by 2 percent, income could be increased by 5 percent. With the weakness in inventory control, he felt it would be easy to overstate inventory. Employees count the goods using count sheets, and Harris was able to add two fictitious sheets during the physical inventory, even though the auditors were present and were observing the inventory. A significant amount of inventory was stored in racks that filled the warehouse. Because of their height and the difficulty of test counting them, Harris was able to cover an overstatement of inventory in the upper racks.

After the count was completed, Harris added four additional count sheets that added $350,000, or 8.6 percent, to the stated inventory. Harris notified the auditors of the "omission" of the sheets and convinced them that they represented overlooked legitimate inventory.

The auditors traced the items on these additional sheets to purchase invoices to verify their existence and approved the addition of the $350,000 to the inventory. They did not notify management about the added sheets. In addition, Harris altered other count sheets before sending them to the auditors by changing unit designations (for example, six engine blocks became six "motors"), raising counts, and adding fictitious line items to completed count sheets. These other fictitious changes added an additional $175,000 to the inflated inventory. None of them was detected by the auditors.

Required:

a. What audit procedures did the auditors apparently not follow that should have detected Harris's fraudulent increase of inventory?

b. What implications would there be to an auditor of failure to detect material fraud as described here?

c. What responsibility did the auditors have to discuss their concerns with the client's audit committee?

(Used with the permission of PricewaterhouseCoopers LLP Foundation.)

INTERNET ASSIGNMENTS

6〉 **11-38** Using an Internet browser, search for information on inventory turnover and merchandise liquidations in the retail catalogue industry.

5,6,8〉 **11-39** Visit the OSC or SEC website (www.osc.gov.on.ca or www.sec.gov respectively) and identify a company that has recently been cited for financial reporting problems related to inventory management. Prepare a memo summarizing the inventory issues in the company.

Auditing the Property Management Process and Selected Asset Accounts: Deferred Charges; Intangible Assets; and Property, Plant, and Equipment

Learning Objectives

Upon completion of this chapter, you will be able to

1 Explain the property management process.

2 Identify the types of transactions in the property management process.

3 Identify and evaluate inherent risks for property, plant, and equipment.

4 Assess control risk for property, plant, and equipment.

5 Know the appropriate segregation of duties for property, plant, and equipment.

6 Identify analytical procedures used to audit property, plant, and equipment.

7 Identify tests of account balances used to audit property, plant, and equipment.

8 Evaluate the audit findings and reach a final conclusion on property, plant, and equipment.

9 Identify the various types of deferred charges and intangible assets, and the major audit issues involved.

RELEVANT ACCOUNTING AND ASSURANCE PRONOUNCEMENTS

CICA Handbook, **section 3062,** Goodwill and other intangible assets

CICA Handbook, **section 5095,** Reasonable assurance and audit risk

CICA Handbook, **section 5141,** Understanding the entity and assessing the risks of material misstatement

CICA Handbook, **section 5142,** Materiality

CICA Handbook, **section 5143,** The auditor's procedures in response to assessed risks

CICA Handbook, **section 5300,** Audit evidence

CICA Handbook, **section 5301,** Analysis

CICA Handbook, **section 5303,** Confirmation

CICA Handbook, **section 5305,** Audit of accounting estimates

AUDITING EARTHWEAR'S PROPERTY MANAGEMENT PROCESS

EarthWear On EarthWear's Consolidated Balance Sheet for 2006, the net value of property, plant, and equipment and intangibles is close to $121 million, approximately 37 percent of the value of total assets. Comparison with 2005 indicates that the value of each of the subgroups of property, plant, and equipment has increased in 2006, particularly computer hardware and software. This is clearly an important area for Willis & Adams to audit. There are aspects of EarthWear's property management process upon which Willis & Adams will be able to place reliance. For example, a substantial portion of the transactions that affect the property, plant, and equipment accounts are entered via the purchasing process. Willis & Adams will have examined and assessed EarthWear's internal controls over this process already. However, those transactions that do not go through the standard purchasing process, such as large one-time capital additions, will need to be examined. For the most part, additions to property, plant, and equipment are purchased from outside vendors, which means that there will be source documents to support the assertions.

EarthWear leases its store and office space and accounts for the leases as operating leases. Willis & Adams will need to ensure that any leases meeting the criteria for capital leases are being accounted for as such. The proper treatment of expenses such as routine repairs and maintenance should be examined. Improper capitalization of expenses is an earnings management technique that is not uncommon (see Exhibit 12–1). The integrity and stability of EarthWear's management may make this seem like a somewhat unlikely event, but Willis & Adams would be remiss in not obtaining sufficient appropriate audit evidence to support the treatment of these transactions.

Auditing the Property Management Process

LO 1 ⟩ For most entities, property, plant, and equipment represent a material amount in the financial statements. When the audit is an ongoing engagement, the auditor is able to focus his or her efforts on the current year's activity because the assets acquired in earlier years were subjected to audit tests at the time of acquisition. On the other hand, for a new engagement, the auditor has to audit the appropriateness of the stated amounts of the assets that make up the beginning balances in the client's property, plant, and equipment accounts.

The size of the entity may also affect the auditor's approach. If the client is relatively small with few asset acquisitions during the period, it is generally more cost-effective for the auditor to follow a substantive strategy. Following this strategy, the auditor conducts analytical procedures and direct tests of the account balances. Large entities, on the other hand, are likely to have formal procedures for budgeting for and purchasing capital assets. While routine purchases might be processed through the purchasing cycle, as described in Chapter 9, acquisition or construction of specialized assets may be subject to different requisition and authorization procedures. When the entity has a formal control system over capital assets, the auditor may use a combined approach and test the internal control.

EXHIBIT 12–1

WorldCom Overstates PP&E and Net Income

WorldCom started as a mom-and-pop long-distance company in 1983. But in the 1990s, it matured into a powerhouse. In 1997 it shocked the industry with an unsolicited bid to take over MCI, a company more than three times its size. In 1998 *CFO Magazine* named WorldCom's CFO, Scott Sullivan, one of the country's best CFOs. At age 37 he was earning $19.3 million a year. In 1999 WorldCom founder Bernie Ebbers moved the company to Clinton, Mississippi, his old college town, and everything changed. The stock price went through the roof. However, by early 2001, overexuberance for the telecom market had created a glut of companies like WorldCom, and earnings started to fall.

In March 2002, Cynthia Cooper, a WorldCom vice president and head of internal audit was informed by a worried executive in the wireless division that corporate accounting had taken $400 million out of his reserve account and used it to boost WorldCom's income. When Cooper went to the auditors Arthur Andersen to inquire about the maneuver, she was told matter-of-factly that it was not a problem. When she didn't relent, Sullivan angrily told Cooper that everything was fine and she should back off. He was furious at her, according to a person involved in the matter. Says Cooper, "When someone is hostile, my instinct is to find out why."

As the weeks went on, Cooper directed her team members to widen their net. Having watched the Enron implosion and Andersen's role in it, she was worried they could not necessarily rely on the accounting firm's audits. So the internal auditors decided to reaudit some areas. She and her team began working late into the night, keeping their project secret. In late May, Cooper and her group discovered a gaping hole in the books. In public reports, the company had classified billions of dollars as property, plant, and equipment in 2001, meaning the costs could be stretched out over a number of years into the future. However, these expenditures were for regular fees WorldCom paid to local telephone companies to complete calls and therefore were operating costs, which should be expensed in full each year. It was as if an ordinary person had paid his or her phone bills but written down the payments as if he or she were building a phone tower in his or her backyard. The trick allowed WorldCom to turn a $662 million loss into a $2.4 billion profit in 2001.

Internal audit began looking for ways to somehow justify what it had found in the books. Finally, the internal auditors confronted WorldCom's controller, David Myers, who admitted the accounting could not be justified. Cooper told the audit committee that the company accountants had understated expenses and overstated income. Sullivan was provided the opportunity to present his side of the story, but he could not convince them regarding the propriety of the accounting. Within days, the company fired its famed chief financial officer, Scott Sullivan, and told the world that it had inflated its profits by $3.8 billion—the number has since grown to over $9 billion.

Source: Amanda Ripley, "The Night Detective (Persons of the Year)," *Time* (December 30, 2002–January 6, 2003), p. 36.

Types of Transactions

LO 2>

Four types of property, plant, and equipment transactions may occur:

- acquisition of capital assets for cash or other nonmonetary considerations
- disposition of capital assets through sale, exchange, retirement, or abandonment
- depreciation of capital assets over their useful economic life
- leasing of capital assets

Overview of the Property Management Process

EarthWear Larger entities generally use some type of computer-based system to process property, plant, and equipment transactions, maintain subsidiary records, and produce required reports. Figure 12–1 presents a flowchart of EarthWear's accounting system for

FIGURE 12–1

Flowchart of the Property Management Process (PP&E) Cycle—EarthWear Clothiers

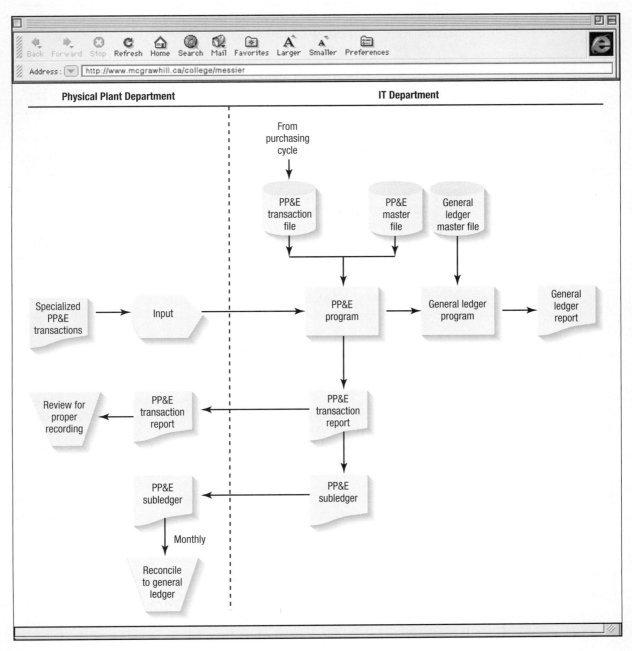

property, plant, and equipment. Transactions are periodically entered both from the purchasing process and through direct input into the system. The property, plant, and equipment master file is then updated, and a number of reports are produced. The periodic report for property, plant, and equipment transactions is reviewed for proper recording by the physical plant department. The property, plant, and equipment subsidiary ledger is a record of all capital assets owned by the entity. It contains information on the cost of the asset, the date acquired, the method of depreciation, and accumulated depreciation. The subsidiary ledger also includes the calculation of depreciation expense for both financial statement and income tax purposes. The general ledger is posted to reflect the new property, plant, and equipment transactions and depreciation expense. The subsidiary ledger should be reconciled to the general ledger control account monthly.

Inherent Risk Assessment—The Property Management Process

LO 3 The optimum employment of property, plant, and equipment, or fixed assets, is often crucial to the entity's attainment of its strategic goals. For that reason the auditor should be certain that he or she has a thorough understanding of the fixed asset section. The assessment of inherent risk for the purchasing process provides a starting point for assessing inherent risk for property, plant, and equipment. In addition, the following three inherent risk factors classified as operating characteristics require consideration by the auditor:

- complex accounting issues
- difficult-to-audit transactions
- misstatements detected in prior audits

Complex Accounting Issues

A number of different types of property, plant, and equipment transactions involve complex accounting issues. Lease accounting, self-constructed assets, and capitalized interest are examples of such issues. For example, in the case of a lease transaction the auditor must evaluate the client's decision either to capitalize the lease or to treat it as an operating lease. Because of the complexity of the capitalization decision and the subjectivity involved in assessing the capitalization criteria, it is not uncommon for such transactions to be accounted for incorrectly by the client. For example, EarthWear leases store and office space that is accounted for as operating leases. Willis & Adams should determine that these leases do not qualify as capital leases.

Difficult-to-Audit Transactions

The vast majority of property, plant, and equipment transactions are relatively easy to audit. When assets are purchased directly from vendors, most audit objectives can be tested by examining the source documents. However, transactions involving donated assets, nonmonetary exchanges, and self-constructed assets are more difficult to audit. For example, it may be difficult to verify the trade-in value of an asset exchanged or to properly audit the cost accumulation of self-constructed assets. The presence of these types of transactions should lead to a higher inherent risk assessment.

One of the largest accounting frauds in history, WorldCom, involved the overstatement of income by the improper capitalization of operating expenses as property, plant and equipment. Exhibit 12–1 gives a detailed description of the company, the fraud, and how the fraud was uncovered.

Misstatements Detected in Prior Audits	If the auditor has detected misstatements in prior audits, the assessment of inherent risk should be set higher than if few or no misstatements have been found in the past.[1] For example, in prior years the auditor may have found numerous client misstatements in accumulating costs for valuing capital assets. Unless the client has established new control procedures over cost accumulation, the auditor should also expect to find misstatements during the current year's audit and therefore set inherent risk as high.

Control Risk Assessment—The Property Management Process

LO 4>   Although the auditor generally follows a substantive strategy when auditing the property management process, an understanding of internal control is still required. The presentation that follows focuses on the major internal control objectives, key control procedures, and tests of controls that relate directly to the property management process. Other control procedures related to the property management process were discussed as part of the purchasing cycle. Important examples of segregation of duties are also presented.

Occurrence	The internal control procedures for the occurrence assertions is normally part of the purchasing process. Purchase requisitions are initiated in relevant departments and authorized at the appropriate level within the entity. However, large capital asset transactions may be subject to control procedures outside the purchasing process. For example, highly specialized technical equipment is likely to be purchased only after passing through a specific capital-budgeting process, which might require that purchase of equipment meet predefined internal rate-of-return criteria. The purchase of equipment may also require that highly skilled engineers approve the technical specifications for the equipment. For such transactions, the auditor may need to examine more than the vendor's invoice to test validity. A review of additional documentation, such as capital-budgeting documents and engineering specifications, may be needed.

Most entities have some type of authorization table for approving capital asset transactions. The client should have internal control procedures to ensure that the authorization to purchase capital assets is consistent with the authorization table. For example, the control procedures should specify dollar limits at each managerial level to ensure that larger projects are brought to the attention of higher levels of management for approval before commitments are made. Lease transactions should be subject to similar control procedures. The entity also needs to have control procedures for authorizing the sale or other disposition of capital assets. This should include a level of authorization above the department initiating the disposition. Control procedures should also identify assets

---

[1]Research has shown that property, plant, and equipment accounts frequently contain misstatements. See A. Eilifsen and W.F. Messier, Jr., "Audit Detection of Misstatements: A Review and Integration of Empirical Research," *Journal of Accounting Literature* 2000 (19), pp. 1–43, for a review of the audit research studies that have indicated that property, plant, and equipment accounts are likely to contain misstatements.

that are no longer used in operations because they may require different accounting treatment. Finally, all major maintenance or improvement transactions should be properly authorized by an appropriate level of management.

Completeness

Most entities use some type of software package to maintain detailed property records (see Figure 12–1). The detailed property, plant, and equipment subsidiary ledger usually includes the following information for each capital asset:

- description, location, and ID number
- date of acquisition and installed cost
- amortization methods for book and tax purposes, salvage value, and estimated useful life

The control procedures used in the purchasing process for ensuring completeness provide some assurance that all capital asset transactions are recorded in the property, plant, and equipment subsidiary ledger and general ledger. One procedure that helps to ensure that this objective is met is monthly reconciliation of the property, plant, and equipment subsidiary ledger to the general ledger control accounts.

Another control procedure that an entity may use to ensure that all capital assets are recorded is periodic comparison of the detailed records in the subsidiary ledger with the existing capital assets. This may be done in a number of ways. The client may take a complete physical examination of property, plant, and equipment on a periodic or rotating basis and compare the physical assets to the property, plant, and equipment subsidiary ledger. Alternatively, the physical examination may be limited to major capital assets or assets that are subject to loss. In both instances the entity's internal auditors may test the reliability of the subsidiary ledger. Larger entities sometimes employ outside specialists to physically examine property, plant, and equipment.

Segregation of Duties

LO 5

The existence of adequate segregation of duties for the property management process within an entity depends on the volume and significance of the transactions processed. For example, if an entity purchases large quantities of machinery and equipment, or if it has large capital projects under construction, it will likely have a formal internal control system. On the other hand, if an entity has few capital asset purchases, it will generally not have a formal control system over such transactions. Table 12–1 shows the key segregation of duties for property, plant, and equipment transactions and examples of possible errors or fraud that can result from conflicts in duties.

Substantive Testing—Property, Plant, and Equipment

As mentioned previously, when the number of transactions is limited or efficiency is a consideration, auditors often follow a substantive strategy when auditing property, plant, and equipment. Therefore, a detailed

Table 12–1	Key Segregation of Duties and Possible Errors or Fraud—Property Management Process

Segregation of Duties	*Possible Errors or Fraud Resulting from Conflicts of Duties*
The initiation function should be segregated from the final approval function.	If one individual is responsible for initiating a capital asset transaction and also has final approval, fictitious or unauthorized purchases of assets can occur. This can result in purchases of unnecessary assets, assets that do not meet the company's quality control standards, or illegal payments to suppliers or contractors.
The property, plant, and equipment records function should be segregated from the general ledger function.	If one individual is responsible for the property, plant, and equipment records and also for the general ledger functions, that individual can conceal any defalcation that would normally be detected by reconciling subsidiary records with the general ledger control account.
The property, plant, and equipment records function should be segregated from the custodial function.	If one individual is responsible for the property, plant, and equipment records and also has custodial responsibility for the related assets, tools and equipment can be stolen, and the theft can be concealed by adjustment of the accounting records.
If a periodic physical inventory of property, plant, and equipment is taken, the individual responsible for the inventory should be independent of the custodial and recordkeeping functions.	If the individual who is responsible for the periodic physical inventory of property, plant, and equipment is also responsible for the custodial and recordkeeping functions, theft of the entity's capital assets can be concealed.

discussion of the substantive tests for property, plant, and equipment is provided next. The discussion focuses on analytical procedures and substantive tests of transactions, account balances, and disclosures.

Analysis—Property, Plant, and Equipment

LO 6 The following analytical procedures can be used in the audit of property, plant, and equipment:

- compare prior-year balances in property, plant, and equipment and amortization expense with current-year balances after consideration of any changes in conditions or asset composition due to additions and disposals
- compute the ratio of amortization expense to the related property, plant, and equipment accounts and comparison to prior years' ratios
- compute the ratio of repairs and maintenance expense to the related property, plant, and equipment accounts and comparison to prior years' ratios
- compute the ratio of insurance expense to the related property, plant, and equipment accounts and comparison to prior years' ratios
- review capital budgets and comparison of the amounts spent with amounts budgeted

For example, the auditor can calculate the ratio of depreciation expense to the related property, plant, and equipment accounts and compare it to prior years' ratios. If the ratio is less than prior years' and few assets have been disposed of, the auditor might conclude that depreciation has not been taken on some assets included in the account.

Tests of Details of Transactions, Account Balances, and Disclosures—Property, Plant, and Equipment

LO 7 Table 12–2 summarizes the substantive tests of balances for the property, plant, and equipment accounts for each assertion. The discussion that follows focuses on the major audit procedures conducted by the auditor. Accuracy is discussed first because the auditor must establish that the detailed property, plant, and equipment records agree with the general ledger account.

Accuracy

The auditor verifies the accuracy of property, plant, and equipment by obtaining a lead schedule and detailed schedules for additions and dispositions of assets. This lead schedule is footed, and the individual accounts are agreed to the general ledger. The detailed schedules are also tested for accuracy. Exhibit 12–2 presents a lead schedule for EarthWear's property, plant, and equipment.

Completeness

The auditor has some assurance about the completeness assertion from the control procedures in the purchasing process and, if present, the additional control procedures discussed previously in this chapter. If the auditor still has concerns about the completeness assertion, he or she can physically examine a sample of assets and trace them into the property, plant, and equipment subsidiary ledger. If the assets are included in the subsidiary ledger, the auditor has sufficient evidence supporting the completeness assertion.

Cutoff

On most engagements, cutoff is tested as part of the audit work in accounts payable and accrued expenses. By examining a sample of vendor invoices from a few days before and after year-end, the auditor can determine if capital asset transactions are recorded in the proper period. Enquiry of client personnel and a review of lease transactions for the same period can provide evidence on proper cutoff for leases.

Classification

First, the classification of a transaction into the correct property, plant, and equipment account is normally examined as part of the testing of the purchasing process. The auditor's tests of controls and substantive tests of transactions provide evidence as to the effectiveness of the control procedures for this assertion.

Second, the auditor should examine selected expense accounts such as repairs and maintenance to determine if any capital assets have been incorrectly recorded in these accounts. An account analysis of transactions included in the repairs and maintenance account is obtained, and selected

Table 12–2	**Examples of Tests of Transactions and Account Balances for Property, Plant, and Equipment (PP&E)**

Assertions about Classes of Transactions	Substantive Tests of Transaction*
Occurrence	Vouch significant additions and dispositions to vendor invoices or other supporting documentation.
	Review lease agreements to ensure that lease transactions are accounted for properly.
Completeness	Trace a sample of purchase requisitions to loading dock reports and to the PP&E records (i.e., transaction and master file).
Accuracy	For assets written off, test amounts charged against income and accumulated amortization.
Cutoff	Examine the purchases and sales of capital assets for a few days before and after year-end.
Classification	Vouch transactions included in repairs and maintenance for items that should be capitalized.
	Review lease transactions for proper classification between operating and capital leases.

Assertions about Account Balances at Period End	Tests of Details of Account Balances
Existence	Verify the existence of major additions by physically examining the capital asset.
Rights and obligations	Examine or confirm deeds or title documents for proof of ownership.
Completeness	Obtain a lead schedule of property, plant, and equipment; foot schedule and agree totals to the general ledger.
	Obtain detailed schedules for additions and dispositions of property, plant, and equipment; foot schedule; agree amounts to totals shown on lead schedule.
	Physically examine a sample of capital assets and trace them into the property, plant, and equipment subsidiary ledger.
Valuation and allocation	Evaluate capital assets for significant write-offs or impairments by performing procedures such as
	• Identify the event or change in circumstance indicating that the carrying value of the asset may not be recoverable.
	• Verify impairment loss by determining the sum of expected future cash flows and comparing that sum to the carrying value.
	• Examine client documentation supporting impairment of write-off.
	Test amortization calculations for a sample of capital assets.

* These tests of details of transactions are commonly conducted as dual-purpose tests (i.e., in conjunction with tests of controls).

transactions are vouched to supporting documents. In examining the supporting documents, the auditor must determine if the transactions are truly expense items or whether it would be more appropriate to capitalize the costs. For example, the auditor may examine an invoice from a plumbing contractor that shows that the water pipe system for a building has been replaced during the current period. If the amount of this transaction was material and improved the building, it should not be expensed as a repair but rather should be capitalized as a building improvement.

An Example of a Lead Schedule for Property, Plant, and Equipment

EXHIBIT 12–2

EarthWear

EARTHWEAR CLOTHIERS
Lead Sheet—Property, Plant, and Equipment
12/31/06

K Lead
JLJ
1/15/07

Account	W/P Ref.	Cost				Accumulated Depreciation			
		Beginning Balance	Additions	Deletions	Ending Balance	Beginning Balance	Additions	Deletions	Ending Balance
Land	K10	$ 6,593,000**L**	$2,112,852	$ 1,786,852	$ 6,919,000				
Buildings	K20	60,211,250**L**	6,112,600	2,324,950	63,998,900	$23,638,300**L**	$ 3,411,493	$ 653,788	$26,396,005
Fixtures, Computers, and Equipment	K30	114,342,050**L**	19,791,763	1,634,988	132,498,825	51,162,450**L**	8,285,360	1,533,398	57,914,462
Leasehold Improvements	K40	2,894,100**L**	780,115	664,595	3,009,620	1,455,500**L**	413,952	194,019	1,675,433
Totals		$184,040,400**F**	$28,797,330**F**	$ 6,411,385**F**	$206,426,345**F**	$76,266,250**F**	$12,110,805**F**	$2,381,155**F**	$85,985,900**F**
		F	**F**	**F**	**F**	**F**	**F**	**F**	**F**

F = Footed and crossfooted.
L = Agreed to general ledger.
¶ = Agreed to prior year's working papers.

Last, the auditor should examine each material lease agreement to verify that the lease is properly classified as an operating or capital lease.

Existence

To test existence, the auditor obtains a listing of all major additions and vouches them to supporting documents such as vendors' invoices. If the purchase was properly authorized and the asset has been received and placed in service, the transaction is valid. In addition, the auditor may want to verify that assets recorded as capital assets actually exist. For major acquisitions, the auditor may physically examine the capital asset.

Similarly, disposition of assets must be properly authorized, and the supporting documentation such as sales receipts should indicate how the disposal took place. Generally, the auditor obtains a schedule of all major dispositions and verifies that the asset was removed from the property, plant, and equipment records. If the disposition is the result of a sale or exchange, the auditor would verify the cash receipt for the sale of the asset or documentation that another asset was received in exchange.

The auditor must also ascertain the validity of lease transactions by examining the lease agreements entered into by the entity. If the lease agreement is properly authorized and the asset is placed in service, the evidence supports the validity of the recorded asset.

Rights and Obligations

The auditor can test for rights or ownership by examining the vendor's invoices or other supporting documents. In some instances, the auditor may examine or confirm property deeds or title documents for proof of ownership by performing a "title search," checking the titles with the provincial registry office.

Valuation and Allocation

Capital assets are valued at acquisition cost plus any costs necessary to make the asset operational. The auditor tests the recorded cost of new assets by examining the vendor invoices and other supporting documents used by the client to establish the recorded value of the assets. If the client has material self-constructed assets, the auditor conducts detailed audit work on the construction-in-process account. This includes ensuring that interest is properly capitalized as a cost of the asset.

Valuation of capital assets in remote locations may be difficult, particularly if the location is not only remote, but in a foreign jurisdiction. Consider again the example of a mining company. Numerous Canadian mining companies have operations in foreign countries such as South America or South East Asia. In addition to the difficulties of verifying existence, the auditor may need to consider impairment to value arising from such things as political unrest (the possibility of expropriation without compensation) or currency instability in the foreign country.

An interesting example of a slightly different kind is the valuation of Canada's military hardware in the remote locations of its peacekeeping activities. There is substantial question that the hardware (which may be electronics or vehicles such as tanks) will last the duration of the peacekeeping assignment, or be repatriated when it is concluded. Nevertheless, it is the auditor's responsibility to obtain such evidence as is available to support the valuation of such assets. These examples are presented to illustrate the fact that this is not always a straightforward task.

The other valuation issue the auditor must address is the recognition of amortization expense. If the client uses a computer to process and account for capital assets, the auditor may be able to use computer-assisted audit techniques to verify the calculation of amortization for various assets. Alternatively, the auditor may recompute the amortization expense for a sample of capital assets. In making this calculation, the auditor considers the reasonableness of the estimated life of the asset, the amortization methods used for book and tax purposes, and any expected salvage value.

Section 3063 of the *CICA Handbook* requires that the fixed assets of an entity be valued at their fair value. For example, if a company stops using an asset in its originally-intended productive capacity, the appropriate treatment under generally accepted accounting principles is to revalue the asset downwards to its net realizable disposal value, if that is less than the net book value and clarified as held for sale. In cases where assets are not in production, the auditor should ensure that the treatment by the client is according to GAAP, and that the valuation is reasonable.

Disclosure

Table 12–3 shows a number of important items that may require disclosure as part of the audit of property, plant, and equipment. Some of these disclosures are made in the "summary of significant accounting policies" footnote, while other items may be disclosed in separate footnotes. Exhibit 12–3 is a sample disclosure for an entity's decision to discontinue operations at one of its operating facilities.

Evaluating the Audit Findings—Property, Plant, and Equipment

LO 8 The process for evaluating the audit findings for property, plant, and equipment is the same as was discussed in previous chapters. The auditor aggregates the likely misstatements and compares this amount

Table 12–3	**Examples of Disclosure Items— Property, Plant, and Equipment**

- Classes of capital assets and valuation bases.
- Amortization methods and useful lives for financial reporting and tax purposes.
- Nonoperating assets.
- Construction or purchase commitments.
- Liens and mortgages.
- Capital assets having been pledged as security – e.g., for a loan
- Acquisition or disposal of major operating facilities.
- Capitalized and other lease arrangements.

EXHIBIT 12–3

Sample Disclosure of Nonoperating Property

In March 2006 the company decided to temporarily suspend operations at the Southern Ontario Mill. The decision was made in response to adverse industry conditions, mainly reduced selling prices and increased raw material costs. In September 2006 it was further determined that because of continued deterioration of selling prices and the level of expenditures required to meet environmental restrictions, the Southern Ontario Mill would not resume operations. The assets of the mill cannot be sold for their historical cost, and in the third quarter the company wrote down the value of the mill to net realizable value, resulting in a $15.6 million loss.

to the tolerable misstatement. If the likely misstatement is less than the tolerable misstatement, the evidence indicates that the property, plant, and equipment accounts are not materially misstated. However, if the likely misstatement was greater than the tolerable misstatement, the auditor would either require adjustment of the accounts or issue a qualified audit report.

Deferred Charges and Intangible Assets

LO 9 The classification of deferred charges as assets arises primarily because of the objective of matching expenses with revenues. Payments for prepaid items such as rent or insurance create assets that are amortized to expenses as the services are consumed. The auditor can verify the amounts of prepaid rent or insurance by reference to the invoices or contracts, and can review the client's calculation of the amounts charged to expense in the period.

Intangible assets may be such items as trademarks, patents, and copyrights that must be amortized over, at most, their legal life. Regardless of the length of the legal life, a company should amortize the value of such an asset over its useful life. The auditor's responsibility with respect to these types of intangibles is primarily to ensure that the client's valuation in the financial statements is economically supported and that the intangible asset will continue to provide economic benefit.

Goodwill is defined by section 3062 of the *CICA Handbook* as "...the excess of the cost of an acquired enterprise over the net of the amounts assigned to assets acquired and liabilities assumed." Included in "assets acquired" in the definition are intangible assets such as those discussed above. Another characteristic of goodwill that distinguishes it from most other intangible assets is that it has an indefinite life—there is no legal limit as is the case with patents, trademarks, and copyrights.

The standards require that the management of the company reassess the amount of purchased goodwill anew every year and confirm its continuing value. Essentially the amount is to be re-established each year as if it was newly obtained. Consequently the auditor also must assess the appropriateness of management's assessment "afresh" each year. This is a much more conservative approach and has resulted in some firms taking large write-downs to their purchased goodwill accounts. Exhibit 12–4 presents an example of such a goodwill write-down.

EXHIBIT 12–4

Example of a Goodwill Write-down

At the end of January 2003, AOL Time Warner, the world's largest media and Internet company, announced that it was taking a $45.5 billion non-cash charge to goodwill to recognize the declining value of its America Online unit. The America Online unit had dragged the company's results down and had fallen far short of revenue projections. There was also concern that the digital revolution could make America Online's dialup services obsolete, thus severely limiting future revenue potential. Due in part to the goodwill write-down, the company reported a net loss for the year of more than $100 billion.

Sources: www.cbsnews.com/stories/2003/01/29/national/main538478.shtml; www.siliconvalley.com/mld/siliconvalley/2932648.htm

REVIEW QUESTIONS

LO 1 > **12-1** How does the purchasing process affect property, plant, and equipment transactions?

2 > **12-2** List four types of property, plant, and equipment transactions.

3 > **12-3** Describe three factors that the auditor should consider in assessing the inherent risk for property, plant, and equipment.

4 > **12-4** What is a typical control over authorization of capital asset transactions?

4 > **12-5** What type of information is maintained in the property, plant, and equipment subsidiary ledger?

5 > **12-6** What is the key segregation of duties for property, plant, and equipment transactions? What errors or fraud can occur if such segregation of duties is not present?

6 > **12-7** Identify three analytical procedures that can be used to audit property, plant, and equipment.

7 > **12-8** What procedures would an auditor use to verify the completeness, ownership, and valuation audit objectives for property, plant, and equipment?

9 > **12-9** Distinguish between deferred charges and intangible assets. Give examples of each of these "other assets."

9 > **12-10** Why would intangible assets present serious inherent risk consideration?

MULTIPLE-CHOICE QUESTIONS FROM PROFESSIONAL EXAMINATIONS

Unless otherwise indicated, these multiple-choice questions were adapted from the CPA examinations, courtesy of the American Institute of Certified Public Accountants.

4 > **12-11** To strengthen internal control over the custody of heavy mobile equipment, the client would most likely institute a policy requiring a periodic

a. Increase in insurance coverage.

b. Inspection of equipment and reconciliation with accounting records.

c. Verification of liens, pledges, and collateralizations.

d. Accounting for work orders.

4> **12-12** A weakness in internal control over recording retirement of equipment may cause an auditor to

a. Trace additions to the "other assets" account to search for equipment that is still on hand but no longer being used.

b. Select certain items of equipment from the accounting records and locate them in the plant.

c. Inspect certain items of equipment in the plant and trace those items to the accounting records.

d. Review the subsidiary ledger to ascertain whether depreciation was taken on each item of equipment during the year.

4> **12-13** When there are few property and equipment transactions during the year, the continuing auditor usually

a. Completely reviews the related control procedures and tests the control procedures being relied upon.

b. Completely reviews the related control procedures and performs analytical procedures to verify current-year additions to property and equipment.

c. Develops a preliminary understanding of internal control and performs a thorough examination of the balances at the beginning of the year.

d. Develops a preliminary understanding of internal control and performs extensive tests of current-year property and equipment transactions.

4,7> **12-14** Which of the following control procedures would most likely allow for a reduction in the scope of the auditor's tests of amortization expense?

a. Review and approval of the periodic equipment amortization entry by a supervisor who does not actively participate in its preparation.

b. Comparison of equipment account balances for the current year with the current-year budget and prior-year actual balances.

c. Review of the miscellaneous income account for salvage credits and scrap sales of partially depreciated equipment.

d. Authorization of payment of vendor's invoices by a designated employee who is independent of the equipment-receiving function.

4> **12-15** Property acquisitions that are misclassified as maintenance expense would most likely be detected by an internal control system that provides for

a. Investigation of variances within a formal budgeting system.

b. Review and approval of the monthly depreciation entry by the plant supervisor.

c. Segregation of duties of employees in the accounts payable department.

d. Examination by the internal auditor of vendor invoices and cancelled cheques for property acquisitions.

4,5,6⟩   **12-16**   Which of the following procedures is most likely to prevent the improper disposition of equipment?

a. Separation of duties between those authorized to dispose of equipment and those authorized to approve removal work orders.

b. The use of serial numbers to identify equipment that could be sold.

c. Periodic comparison of removal work orders to authorizing documentation.

d. Periodic analysis of the scrap sales and the repairs and maintenance accounts.

7⟩   **12-17**   An auditor analyzes repairs and maintenance accounts primarily to obtain evidence in support of the audit assertion that all

a. Noncapitalizable expenditures for repairs and maintenance have been properly charged to expense.

b. Expenditures for property and equipment have not been charged to expense.

c. Noncapitalizable expenditures for repairs and maintenance have been recorded in the proper period.

d. Expenditures for property and equipment have been recorded in the proper period.

6,7⟩   **12-18**   When there are numerous property and equipment transactions during the year, an auditor who plans to assess the control risk at a low level usually performs

a. Analytical procedures for property and equipment balances at the end of the year.

b. Tests of controls and extensive tests of property and equipment balances at the end of the year.

c. Analytical procedures for current-year property and equipment transactions.

d. Tests of controls and limited tests of current-year property and equipment transactions.

7⟩   **12-19**   Which of the following combinations of procedures would an auditor be most likely to perform to obtain evidence about fixed-asset additions?

a. Inspecting documents and physically examining assets.

b. Recomputing calculations and obtaining written management representations.

c. Observing operating activities and comparing balances to prior-period balances.

d. Confirming ownership and corroborating transactions through enquiries of client personnel.

4⟩   **12-20**   Which of the following internal controls is most likely to justify a reduced assessed level of control risk concerning plant and equipment acquisitions?

a. Periodic physical inspection of plant and equipment by the internal audit staff.

b. Comparison of current-year plant and equipment account balances with prior-year actual balances.

c. Review of prenumbered purchase orders to detect unrecorded trade-ins.

d. Approval of periodic amortization entries by a supervisor independent of the accounting department.

PROBLEMS

1,9⟩ **12-21** Jill Taylor has been engaged to audit the financial statements of Palmer Company, a continuing audit client. Taylor is about to perform substantive audit procedures on Palmer's goodwill (excess of cost over fair value of net assets purchased) that was acquired in prior years' business combinations. An industry slowdown has occurred recently, and the operations purchased have not met profit expectations.

During the planning process, Taylor determined that there was a high risk that material misstatements in the assertions related to goodwill could occur. Taylor obtained an understanding of internal control and assessed the control risk at the maximum level for the assertions related to goodwill.

Required:

a. Identify substantive audit procedures Taylor should consider performing in auditing Palmer's goodwill. Do *not* discuss Palmer's internal control system.

b. Describe the two significant assertions that Taylor would be most concerned with relative to Palmer's goodwill. Do *not* describe more than two.

(AICPA, adapted)

4,5⟩ **12-22** I. Nakamura has accepted an engagement to audit the financial statements of Grant Manufacturing Company, a new client. Grant has an adequate control environment and a reasonable segregation of duties. Nakamura is about to assess the control risk for the assertions related to Grant's property and equipment.

Required:

Describe the key internal controls related to Grant's property, equipment, and related transactions (additions, transfers, major maintenance and repairs, retirements, and dispositions) that Nakamura may consider in assessing the control risk.

(AICPA, adapted)

4,7,8⟩ **12-23** You are the senior on the audit of Calton Constuction Ltd. (CCL). In past years the property, plant, and equipment section of the audit has been somewhat of a problem. Listed below are some of the discrepancies and exceptions that have been noted in prior audits:

1. Acquisitions were not recorded at the proper amounts.

2. The acquisition cost of assets that should be capitalized has frequently been expensed.

3. The company amortized some items of its construction equipment over less than their useful lives.

4. Some of the amortization expense for major assets was charged to administrative expense.

5. Obsolete equipment and even equipment that has been disposed of was still being carried on the books.

6. There were problems with employee thefts of small tools (such as circular saws) and tools to be used to maintain the larger equipment.

7. A piece of major equipment was pledged as security against a loan but not disclosed. The company did not record the proceeds of the loan as a receipt because they were used for a downpayment on another item of operating equipment. That piece of equipment is not recorded in the records.

Required:

For each item:

a. Draft a memo to the controller of CCL, identifying an internal control that could be implemented to prevent such a misstatement from occurring.

b. Prepare a memo to the junior who will do this year's examination of property, plant, and equipment, informing her of a substantive audit procedure she could employ to discover such a misstatement, if it exists.

6,7,8>   **12-24**   To support financial statement assertions, an auditor develops specific audit objectives. The auditor then designs substantive tests to satisfy or accomplish each objective.

Required:

Items (a) through (c) on page 498 represent audit objectives for the property and equipment accounts. Select the most appropriate audit procedure from the following list and enter the number in the appropriate place on the grid. (An audit procedure may be selected once or not at all.)

Audit Procedure

1. Trace opening balances in the summary schedules to the prior year's audit working papers.

2. Review the provision for amortization expense and determine that useful lives and methods used in the current year are consistent with those used in the prior year.

3. Determine that the responsibility for maintaining the property and equipment records is segregated from the responsibility for custody of property and equipment.

4. Examine deeds and title insurance certificates.

5. Perform cutoff tests to verify that property and equipment additions are recorded in the proper period.

6. Determine that property and equipment are adequately insured.

7. Physically examine all major property and equipment additions.

Specific Audit Objective	Audit Procedure

a. Verify that the entity has the legal right to property and equipment acquired during the year.

b. Verify that recorded property and equipment represent assets that actually exist at the balance sheet date.

c. Verify that net property and equipment are properly valued at the balance sheet date.

(AICPA, adapted)

6,7,8 **12-25**   Brian Pierce was engaged to examine the financial statements of Wong Construction, Inc., for the year ended December 31, 2006. Wong's financial statements reflect a substantial amount of mobile construction equipment, used in the firm's operations. The equipment is accounted for in a subsidiary ledger. Pierce developed an understanding of internal control and assessed the control risk as moderate.

Required:

Identify the substantive audit procedures Pierce should utilize in examining mobile construction equipment and related amortization in Wong's financial statements.

(AICPA, adapted)

6,7 **12-26**   In connection with the annual examination of Sandhu Corporation, a manufacturer of janitorial supplies, you have been assigned to audit property, plant, and equipment. The company maintains a detailed property ledger for all property, plant, and equipment. You prepared an audit program for the balances of property, plant, and equipment but have yet to prepare one for accumulated amortization and amortization expense.

Required:

Prepare a separate comprehensive audit program for the accumulated amortization and amortization expense accounts.

(AICPA, adapted)

DISCUSSION CASES

2,4,7,8 **12-27**   Raul Gonzales, is the auditor for a manufacturing company with a balance sheet that includes the account "property, plant, and equipment." Gonzales has been asked by the company's management if audit adjustments or reclassifications are required for the following material items that have been included in or excluded from property, plant, and equipment:

1. A tract of land was acquired during the year. The land is to be the future site of the client's new headquarters, which will be constructed next year. Commissions were paid to the real estate agent used to acquire the land, and expenditures were made to relocate the previous owner's equipment. These commissions and expenditures were expensed and are excluded from property, plant, and equipment.

2. Clearing costs were incurred to ready the land for construction. These costs were included in property, plant, and equipment.

3. During the land-clearing process, timber and gravel were recovered and sold. The proceeds from the sale were recorded as other income and are excluded from property, plant, and equipment.

4. A group of machines was purchased under a royalty agreement that provides royalty payments based on units of production from the machines. The costs of the machines, freight costs, unloading charges, and royalty payments were capitalized and are included in property, plant, and equipment.

Required:

a. Describe the general characteristics of assets, such as land, buildings, improvements, machinery, equipment, fixtures, and so on, that should normally be classified as property, plant, and equipment, and identify assertions in connection with the examination of property, plant, and equipment. Do not discuss specific audit procedures.

b. Indicate whether each of the items numbered 1 to 4 requires one or more audit adjustments or reclassifications, and explain why such adjustments or reclassifications are required or not required. Organize your answer as follows:

Item Number	Is Auditing Adjustment or Reclassification Required? (Yes or No)	Reasons Why Audit Adjustments or Reclassifications Are Required or Not Required

(AICPA, adapted)

7,8 **12-28** On January 15, 2006, Leno, Inc., which has a March 31 year-end, entered into a transaction to sell the land and building that contained its manufacturing operations for a total selling price of $19,750,000. The book value of the land and the building was $3,420,000. The final closing was not expected to occur until sometime between July 2007 and March 2008.

On March 15, 2006, Leno, Inc., received an irrevocable letter of credit, issued by a major bank, for $5,000,000, which represented more than 25 percent of the sales price. Leno, Inc., would collect the $5,000,000 and would keep the money even if the buyer decided not to complete the transaction. The letter of credit had an option for an extension for up to one year for a total period of two years. At closing, the entire selling price was to be paid in cash.

Leno, Inc., was going to continue its manufacturing operations in the building and would continue to be responsible for all normal occupancy costs until final closing, when it would move to another location. After the sale, the building would be torn down and replaced by a large office building complex.

Required:

a. Based on relevant accounting pronouncements, how should Leno, Inc., account for the transaction at March 31, 2006?

b. What additional types of evidence should the auditor examine prior to recognizing any gain on the transaction?

7,8,9> **12-29** Towers Associates was formed as a joint venture on August 16, 2006, between Lynx, Ltd., and Francisco, Corp. Lynx contributed a parcel of land with an existing building, tower 1, and an attached annex located on the site. Francisco contributed $125 million in cash. Some floors in tower 1 have been vacated so that it can be renovated floor by floor. The remainder of the building will continue in use, and the remaining tenants will move to vacant floors during the renovation. Tower 2 and a plaza, which will serve both buildings, are under construction on the site on which the annex had been located. Because the parties are joint-venture partners, the assets contributed by Lynx were also valued at $125 million. That amount was allocated between the land and the building.

The value of the total parcel of land was appraised at $98 million, based on its highest and best use if vacant. To determine the fair value of the land in its current state, the value of the land at its highest and best use was reduced by the costs of removing the annex so that the land will be available for another use. The following two types of costs are related to removing the annex:

1. Approximately $4.5 million to demolish the annex.
2. Approximately $60 million for the relocation of tenants whose leases extended beyond 2006.

Relocation costs include the net rent costs of relocating tenants from the annex to buildings not owned by the venture, the costs of moving those tenants, and the costs of improving their new space.

The total cost of $64.5 million to get the land ready for another use has been discounted to $52.5 million at the joint venture's cost of funds and has been subtracted from the value of the land at its highest and best use. The resulting amount, $45.5 million, is the amount recorded as the contributed value of the land, which has been allocated between tower 1 and tower 2 (including the adjacent plaza) based on the relative square footage of the associated land. The contributed value of tower 1 was recorded as $79.5 million. The costs of developing the plaza will be allocated between tower 1 and tower 2 based on square footage.

Your client, Towers Associates, has been accumulating tenant relocation costs as part of construction in progress and would like to charge them to tower 2 and depreciate them over the life of the building. Your client would also like to defer amortizing the costs of renovating tower 1 and the costs of constructing the plaza until the first phase of the project (the renovation of tower 1 and the construction of the plaza) has been completed.

Additional Information

- The value of land was estimated by using the *development method,* where the ultimate sales value of the land as fully developed was estimated at its highest and best use and reduced by the costs of getting the land ready for its future use.
- The term *highest and best use* is defined as "that reasonable and probable use that supports the highest present value, as defined as of the effective date of the appraisal."

Required:

a. How should Towers Associates account for the cost of relocating tenants from the annex? Do the costs of relocating tenants have a future benefit to the entity?

b. Indicate how you would audit (1) the $4.5 million in demolition costs and (2) the $60 million in tenant relocation costs.

INTERNET ASSIGNMENTS

1,2,7,8⟩   12-30   Visit the website of another catalogue retailer similar to Earth-Wear Clothiers and determine what useful lives and amortization methods are used for property, plant, and equipment. Compare those methods to EarthWear's and, if different, consider the implications for using competitor data for analytical procedures. Note that you may have to examine the entity's annual report.

1,3,7,8,9,10⟩   12-31   Visit the OSC or SEC website (www.osc.gov.on.ca or www.sec.gov respectively) and identify a company that has been recently cited for problems related to property, plant, and equipment or lease accounting (e.g., Xerox Corporation). Prepare a memo summarizing the property, plant, and equipment accounting issues for the company.

Auditing Long-Term Liabilities, Shareholders' Equity, and Income Statement Accounts

 Chapter **13**

Learning Objectives

Upon completion of this chapter, you will be able to

1 Describe the types and features of long-term debt.

2 Assess control risk for long-term debt.

3 Identify key internal control procedures for long-term debt.

4 Conduct substantive audit procedures for long-term debt.

5 Explain the types of shareholders' equity transactions.

6 Assess control risk for shareholders' equity.

7 Identify key internal control procedures for shareholders' equity.

8 Outline the appropriate segregation of duties for shareholders' equity.

9 Conduct substantive audit procedures for share capital.

10 Conduct substantive audit procedures for dividends.

11 Conduct substantive audit procedures for retained earnings.

12 Conduct substantive audit procedures for income statement accounts.

RELEVANT ACCOUNTING AND ASSURANCE PRONOUNCEMENTS

CICA Handbook, **section 1520,** Income statement

CICA Handbook, **section 3210,** Long-term debt

CICA Handbook, **section 3240,** Share capital

CICA Handbook, **section 3251,** Equity

CICA Handbook, **section 3500,** Earnings per share

CICA Handbook, **section 3610,** Capital transactions

CICA Handbook, **section 3855,** Financial instruments—Recognition and Measurement

CICA Handbook, **section 3861,** Financial instruments—Disclosure and Presentation

CICA Handbook, **section 3862,** Financial instruments—Disclosures

CICA Handbook, **section 3863,** Financial instruments—Presentation

CICA Handbook, **section 5095,** Reasonable assurance and audit risk

CICA Handbook, **section 5141,** Understanding the entity and its environment and assessing the risks of material misstatement

CICA Handbook, **section 5142,** Materiality

CICA Handbook, **section 5143,** The auditor's procedures in response to assessed risks

CICA Handbook, **section 5300,** Audit evidence
CICA Handbook, **section 5301,** Analysis

CICA Handbook, **section 5303,** Confirmation
CICA Handbook, **section 5305,** Audit of accounting estimates

AUDITING EARTHWEAR'S LIABILITY, EQUITY, AND INCOME STATEMENT ACCOUNTS

EarthWear As a result of auditing EarthWear's major business processes such as the revenue process and the purchasing process, Willis & Adams has also examined many of EarthWear's major asset, liability, revenue, and expense accounts. However, Willis & Adams still needs to audit liability accounts and income statement accounts that were not examined as part of the major business processes, and shareholders' equity accounts. For many companies the most material liability account still to be examined will be long-term debt, although EarthWear does not use long-term debt to finance its operations. However, EarthWear does make use of lines of credit and Willis & Adams will need to satisfy themselves with respect to the recorded amount of the amount owing on those lines of credit and the associated interest expense. Applying analytical procedures to evaluate whether the amount of recorded interest expense for the year is appro-

priate given the amount of debt outstanding throughout the course of the year provides a check on both the liability balance and the expense. Willis & Adams will most likely follow a substantive audit strategy in the audit of the remaining liability and equity accounts because the number of transactions is few, and each transaction is usually very material.

To audit EarthWear's income statement Willis & Adams will place reliance on EarthWear's system of internal control and the indirect evidence it provides about the income statement items as well as the evidence about income statement amounts that was obtained in conjunction with the audit of the related balance sheet accounts—for example, evidence regarding bad debts expense obtained in conjunction with the audit of the allowance for uncollectible accounts or evidence regarding insurance expense obtained in conjunction with the audit of prepaid insurance.

Auditing Long-Term Debt

LO 1 Common types of long-term debt financing include notes, bonds, and mortgages. More sophisticated types of debt financing include collateralized mortgage obligations, repurchase and reverse repurchase agreements, interest-rate swaps, financial futures, derivatives (see Exhibit 13–1), and myriad other financial instruments. Accounting for such sophisticated debt instruments can be complex and, except for a brief discussion at the end of the "Substantive Tests of Long-Term Debt" section later in this chapter, is beyond the scope of this text. Capitalized lease obligations also represent a form of long-term debt. To simplify the presentation of the audit of long-term debt, the discussion focuses on notes and bonds, including the audit of interest payable and interest expense.

Long-term debt may have a number of features that can affect the audit procedures used. For example, debt may be convertible into shares, or it may be combined with warrants, options, or rights that can be exchanged for equity. Debt may be callable under certain conditions, or it may require

EXHIBIT 13–1

Derivatives Lead to Losses at Orange County and Major Corporations

Derivatives are contracts that are written between two parties and have a value that is derived from the value of an underlying asset, such as currencies, equities, commodities, or interest rates, or from stock market or other indicators. While derivatives can be used wisely by management to manage risk, in some instances derivatives have actually increased risk.

In 1994 highly leveraged interest-rate derivatives caused a $1.7 billion loss in the Orange County Investment Pool—money managed for the county and its cities, school districts, and other agencies. The loss occurred because the county's treasurer, Robert L. Citron, leveraged the pool's $7.6 billion to almost $20 billion and "bet" that interest rates would decline or remain steady. When the Federal Reserve Bank raised interest rates, Orange County's derivatives unraveled.

Losses on derivatives have also occurred for Procter & Gamble and Gibson Greeting Cards. Both companies entered into derivatives with Bankers Trust. Procter & Gamble announced losses in excess of $150 million and sued Bankers Trust over the transactions. Gibson had an estimated loss of $20 million but settled with Bankers Trust for $6.2 million.

Sources: Carol J. Loomis, "Untangling the Derivatives Mess," *Fortune* (March 20, 1995), pp. 50–68; and R. H. D. Molvar and J. F. Green, "The Question of Derivatives," *Journal of Accountancy* (March 1995), pp. 55–61.

the establishment of a sinking fund to ensure that the debt can be repaid. Last, debt may be either unsecured or secured by assets of the entity.

The auditor's consideration of long-term debt, however, is no different than for any other financial statement account. The auditor must be assured that the amounts shown on the balance sheet for the various types of long-term debt are not materially misstated. This assurance extends to the proper recognition of interest expense in the financial statements.

The approach to the audit of long-term debt varies depending on the frequency of the entity's financing activities. For entities that engage in frequent financing activities, the auditor may follow a reliance strategy under which internal control is formally evaluated and tests of controls are performed in order to assess the control risk. However, for the vast majority of entities, it is more efficient for the auditor to follow a substantive strategy and perform a detailed audit of long-term debt and the related interest accounts.

Control Risk Assessment—Long-Term Debt

LO 2>   When a substantive strategy is followed, the auditor needs a sufficient understanding of the entity's internal control system over debt to be able to anticipate the types of misstatements that may occur and thus plan the substantive tests. The following discussion of control risk assessment for long-term debt focuses on the general types of control procedures that should be present to minimize the likelihood of material misstatement. The internal control objectives that are of primary concern to the auditor are validity, authorization, completeness, valuation, and classification. Proper segregation of duties is important for ensuring the propriety of long-term debt.

In making a control risk assessment with respect to long-term debt, the auditor should pay attention to the existence of any debt covenants.

If a company is subject to debt covenants it might be in danger of breaching, there might be a potential bias for the company to include or exclude items or to misclassify items so as not to violate such covenants. The Emerging Issues Committee of the CICA has indicated in its *Abstract of Discussion* EIC-59 that if there is a violation of a covenant entitling the lender to call in the debt, it should be reclassified as a current liability on the company's financial statements. It is up to the auditor to ensure compliance with these provisions.

Assertions and Related Control Procedures

Following are some of the more common internal control procedures that should be present for each of the important control objectives for long-term debt.

LO 3> **Occurrence** The entity should have internal control procedures to ensure that any long-term borrowing is properly initiated by authorized individuals. First, adequate documentation must verify that a note or bond was properly authorized. The presence of adequate documentation, such as a properly signed lending agreement, allows the auditor to determine if the transaction was properly executed. Second, any significant debt commitments should be approved by the board of directors or by executives who have been delegated this authority. Entities that engage in recurring borrowing activities should have both general and specific controls. The board of directors should establish general controls to guide the entity's financing activities. The specific controls for borrowing and repayment may be delegated to an executive, such as the chief financial officer. When the chief financial officer or similar executive is responsible for both executing and accounting for long-term debt transactions, another executive body, such as the finance committee of the board of directors, should provide overall review and approval in the minutes. If the client has proper control procedures for issuing debt transactions, it is generally easy for the auditor to test those transactions at the end of the period.

Completeness The client should maintain adequate detailed records of long-term debt transactions to ensure that all borrowings and repayments of principal and interest are recorded. One approach to handling detailed debt transactions is to maintain a subsidiary ledger that contains information about all the long-term debt owed by the client. The debt amount recorded in the subsidiary ledger should be reconciled to the general ledger control account regularly.

Valuation Note and bond transactions are recorded in the accounting records at their face value plus or minus any premium or discount. Premium or discount should be amortized using the effective interest method to calculate interest expense. Sometimes an entity incurs issuing costs such as underwriter's fees, legal fees, and accounting fees. Such costs may be recorded as deferred charges and amortized over the life of the debt or simply added to the amount of the discount or premium. Valuation issues for sophisticated financing investments are far more complex. Although the client should have control procedures to ensure that long-term debt is properly valued, the client may ask the auditor to assist with recording the debt properly.

Disclosure-Classification   Control procedures should ensure that notes and bonds are properly classified. The major issue is to properly classify as a short-term liability the portion of long-term debt that is due in the next year.

One final issue related to the control risk for long-term debt is that the client should have adequate custodial procedures for any unissued notes or bonds to safeguard against loss from theft. Procedures should provide for periodic inspections by an individual independent of both the custodial and accounting responsibilities for long-term debt.

Substantive Tests of Long-Term Debt

LO 4>   A substantive strategy for auditing long-term debt involves examining any new debt agreements, determining the status of prior debt agreements, and confirming balances and other relevant information with outside parties.

Verification of recorded interest expense on long-term debt such as bonds payable may be accomplished using the results of the procedures outlined above. The client's recorded interest expense can be agreed to the amount of the outstanding debt times the stated interest rate on the bonds. If the bonds were originally sold at greater than or less than the face value, the recorded interest expense will be adjusted for the amortization of the premium or discount, in which case the auditor should verify the client's adjustment calculation.

Analytical procedures are useful in auditing interest expense because of the direct relationship between the stated interest rate and the amount of long-term debt. For example, the auditor could estimate interest expense by multiplying the 12 monthly balances for long-term debt by the average interest rate. The reasonableness of interest expense could then be assessed by comparing this estimate to the interest expense amount recorded in the general ledger. If the two amounts are not materially different, the auditor can conclude that interest expense is fairly stated. If the estimated amount of interest expense is materially higher than the recorded amount, the auditor might conclude that the client has failed to record a portion of interest expense. On the other hand, if the recorded amount of interest expense is materially higher than the estimated amount, the client may have failed to record debt. Refer to the example in Chapter 5 for an example of the use of an analytical procedure to test the relationship between EarthWear's short-term line of credit and related interest expense.

Table 13–1 summarizes the main tests of account balances for long-term debt. The following discussion delineates the general approach to auditing long-term debt.

The auditor generally begins the audit of long-term debt by obtaining an analysis schedule for notes payable, bonds payable, and accrued interest payable. Exhibit 13–2 presents an example of such a schedule. Because EarthWear does not have long-term debt, the example in Exhibit 13–2 is based on Calabro Digital Services (see Problem 3-38). If there are numerous transactions during the year, this schedule may include only the debt outstanding at the end of the period. Note that this schedule includes a considerable amount of information on each debt transaction, including the payee, date due, interest rate, original amount, collateral, and paid and accrued interest.

Table 13–1	**Examples of Tests of Transactions and Account Balances for Long-Term Debt**

Assertions about Classes of Transactions	**Substantive Tests of Transaction***
Occurrence	Examine copies of new note or bond agreements.
	Examine board of directors' minutes for approval of new lending agreements.
Completeness	Trace large cash receipts and payments to source documents and general ledger.
	Review interest expense for payments to debt holders not listed on the debt analysis schedule.
	Review notes paid or renewed after the balance sheet date to determine if there are unrecorded liabilities at year-end.
	Evaluate lease contracts to determine if leases are properly accounted for as an operating or capital leases.
Accuracy	Test a sample of receipts and payments.
Cutoff	Review debt activity for a few days before and after year-end to determine if the transactions are included in the proper period.
Classification	Examine the due dates on notes or bonds for proper classification between current and long-term debt.

Assertions about Account Balances at Period End	**Tests of Details of Account Balances**
Existence	Confirm notes or bonds directly with creditors (in many instances, creditors are banks or insurance companies) or trustees representing the creditors.
Rights and obligations	Examine copies of note and bond agreements.
Completeness	Obtain an analysis of notes payable, bonds payable, and accrued interest payable; foot schedule and agree totals to the general ledger.
	Obtain a standard bank confirmation that requests specific information on notes from banks.
	Confirm notes or bonds payable with creditors.
	Enquire of management regarding the existence of "off-balance sheet" activities.
	Review board meeting minutes for debt-related activity.
Valuation and allocation	Examine new debt agreements to ensure that they were recorded at the proper value.
	Confirm the outstanding balance for notes or bonds payable and the last date on which interest has been paid.
	Recompute accrued interest payable.
	Verify computation of the amortization of premium or discount.
Disclosure	Examine bond agreement for any restrictions that should be disclosed in the footnotes.

* These tests of details of transactions are commonly conducted as dual-purpose tests (i.e., in conjunction with tests of controls).

Exhibit 13–2 also indicates the audit procedures performed on the details of the debt schedule. The most important audit objectives are tested as follows: Each debt instrument is confirmed with the debtholders and includes a request to verify the amount owed and last date on which interest has been paid. Confirmation of the debt and accrued interest provides evidence on the validity, completeness, and valuation objectives. If the client's debt is guaranteed by another party, a confirmation should be sent to the guarantor to confirm the guarantee.

EXHIBIT 13–2

Analysis Schedule for Auditing Long-Term Debt and Accrued Interest Payable

CDS

P10
DLJ
2/27/07

CALABRO DIGITAL SERVICES

Schedule of Long-Term Debt and Accrued Interest Payable

12/31/06

Payee	Due Date	Face Amount	Security	Long-Term Debt Beginning Balance	Additions	Payments	Ending Balance	Accrued Interest Payable Beginning Balance	Expenses	Paid	Ending Balance
National Bank—Line of credit	11/1/07	$ 7,000,000	All assets**C**	$ 200,000	$900,000	$300,000Γ	$ 800,000	$ 1,875	$ 22,500λ	$ 22,815	$ 1,560
8.75% lease obligation—Patriot Insurance Co.	12/15/06	$ 2,000,000	Communications equipment**C**	238,637		48,230Γ	190,407	5,470	37,541λ	38,461	4,550
7% bonds payable—All Canadian Insurance Co.	6/30/09	$10,000,000	Land and buildings**C**	3,100,000		200,000Γ	2,900,000	36,850	224,602λ	219,820	41,632
Total				$3,538,637 **F**	$900,000 **F**	$548,230 **F**	$3,890,407**L** **F**	$44,195 **F**	$284,643**L** **F**	$281,096 **F**	$47,742**L** **F**

Less current portion of long-term debt   424,061 ✔

$3,466,346

L = Agreed to general ledger.
γ = Traced payments to cash disbursements journal
Γ = Recomputed interest expense
C = Agreed all information to confirmation.
F = Footed.
✔ = Tested amount of current portion of long-term debt.

EXHIBIT 13–3

Sample Disclosure of Restrictive Loan Covenants
The 7 percent bond agreement contains provisions (1) limiting funded debt, security interests, and other indebtedness, (2) requiring the maintenance of defined working capital and tangible net worth, and (3) imposing restrictions on the payment of cash dividends. The company was in compliance with, or received a waiver regarding, each of the agreements during the year ended 2006. Under the terms of these agreements, $825,000 of retained earnings was available for payment of cash dividends at December 31, 2006.

The requirements of section 3210 of the *CICA Handbook*, "Long-term debt," for classification and note disclosure of the entity's long-term debt are extensive. For example, with respect to statement presentation, the portion of long-term debt payable within one year should be shown as a current liability and if any long-term liabilities are secured, they should be shown separately. With respect to note disclosure, details such as restrictive covenants, due dates, interest rates, maturity dates, and redemption provisions should be provided, as should the details of any sinking fund or retirement provisions. The auditor should examine the debt agreements and their terms to ensure that the entity's statement presentation and disclosure satisfy the requirements of section 3210. Exhibit 13–3 is an example of the disclosure of restrictive covenants.

Financial Instruments

Related to the audit of long-term debt, an audit issue that should be mentioned is the difficulty of auditing the variety of complex financial (debt) instruments that exist. *CICA Handbook* section 3855, "Financial instruments—recognition and measurement," requires that accounting for such financial instruments follows that principle of substance over form. Issues such as the valuation of such financial instruments can be very complex (indeed, the difficulty of auditing financial instruments was a contributing factor to the audit failure in the case of Enron), but a relatively simple example will provide the flavour of the CICA's recommendations in this area. An entity may issue preferred shares with terms attached to them such that, according to the recommendations set out in section 3855, they should properly be accounted for as debt, and the payment of the related dividends shown on the income statement as an expense. It is the auditor's responsibility to ensure that all financial instruments are accounted for and disclosed in the financial statements in accordance with *CICA Handbook* section 3855, "Financial instruments—Recognition and measurement."

Auditing Shareholders' Equity

LO 5 ⟩   For most entities, shareholders' equity includes common shares, preferred shares, contributed surplus, and retained earnings. In recent years, numerous financial instruments have been developed that contain both debt and equity characteristics and affect the audit of shareholders' equity. Myriad share options and compensation plans also impact the audit of shareholders' equity. A discussion of these complex equity instruments and share option plans is beyond the scope of this text.

Following are the three major types of transactions that occur in share-holders' equity:

- *Issuance of shares.* This includes transactions such as sale of shares for cash; the exchange of shares for assets, services, or convertible debt; and issuance of shares for stock splits.
- *Repurchase of shares.* This includes the reacquisition of shares (referred to as *treasury shares*) and the retirement of shares.
- *Payment of dividends.* This includes the payment of cash dividends or issuance of share dividends.

Control Risk Assessment—Shareholders' Equity

LO 6> A substantive strategy is most often used to audit shareholders' equity because the number of transactions is usually small. Although control risk can then be assessed at the maximum, the auditor must still understand the types of control procedures that are in place to prevent the misstatement of equity transactions.

Many large entities, such as publicly traded companies, use an independent *registrar, transfer agent,* and *dividend-disbursing agent* to process and record equity transactions. The registrar is responsible for ensuring that all shares issued comply with the corporate charter and for maintaining the control totals for total shares outstanding. The transfer agent is responsible for preparing share certificates and maintaining adequate shareholders' records. The dividend-disbursing agent prepares and mails dividend cheques to the shareholders of record. When an entity uses an independent registrar, transfer agent, and dividend-disbursing agent, the auditor may be able to obtain sufficient evidence by confirming the relevant information with those parties.

If an entity uses its own employees to perform the share transfer and dividend disbursement functions, the auditor needs to perform more detailed testing of the share-related records and transactions that occurred during the period. The following internal control objectives, internal control procedures, and segregation of duties are relevant when client personnel transfer shares and disburse dividends.

Assertions and Related Control Procedures **LO 7**>	Following are the major internal control objectives for shareholders' equity: - verify that share and dividend transactions comply with the corporate charter (occurence) - verify that all share and dividend transactions have been properly posted and summarized in the accounting records (accuracy) - verify that share and dividend transactions have been properly valued (valuation)

Occurrence   One of the entity's officers, such as the corporate secretary or legal counsel, should ensure that every share or dividend transaction complies with the corporate charter or any regulatory requirement that affects the entity. This individual should also maintain the shareholders' ledger, which contains the name of each shareholder and the number of shares held by that shareholder.

Accuracy   The control procedures for this objective include reconciliation of the shareholders' records with the number of shares outstanding and reconciliation of dividends paid with the total shares outstanding on the dividend record date.

Valuation   Share issuances, share repurchases, and dividends should be recorded by the treasurer's department at an amount that conforms to GAAP. The auditor can recompute the recording of the share and dividend transactions.

Segregation of Duties

LO 8>

If the entity has enough personnel, the following segregation of duties should be maintained:

- The individual responsible for issuing, transferring, and cancelling share certificates should not have any accounting responsibilities.
- The individual responsible for maintaining the detailed shareholders' records should be independent of the maintenance of the general ledger control accounts.
- The individual responsible for maintaining the detailed shareholders' records should not also process cash receipts or disbursements.
- Appropriate segregation of duties should be established among the preparation, recording, signing, and mailing of dividend cheques.

Auditing Share Capital Accounts

LO 9>   The share capital accounts include common shares, preferred shares, and contributed surplus.[1] When auditing the share capital accounts, the auditor is normally concerned with the validity, completeness, valuation, and disclosure objectives. The auditor begins the audit of share capital by obtaining a schedule of all activity in the accounts for the current period. The beginning balance is agreed to the prior year's working papers, and the ending balance is agreed to the general ledger. The majority of the auditor's work then focuses on the current-period activity in each account.

Occurrence and Completeness

Share capital transactions are approved by the board of directors. Therefore, the auditor can test the occurrence of share capital transactions by tracing the transactions recorded in the current year to the board of directors' minutes. When an independent registrar and transfer agent are used by the entity, the auditor confirms the total number of shares outstanding at the end of the period. If the amount of shares listed as outstanding on

---

[1]Federally incorporated companies are now prohibited from issuing par or stated value shares. However, federally incorporated companies that issued stock prior to 1976 could do so, and companies incorporated in some provincial jurisdictions may still issue shares with a par or stated value.

the confirmation reconciles to the general ledger share capital accounts, the auditor has evidence that the total number of shares outstanding at the end of the year is correct.

If the entity does not use outside agents, it will maintain a share register and/or a share certificate book. The auditor may perform the following tests:

- trace the transfers of shares between shareholders to the share register and/or share certificate book (valuation and completeness)
- foot the shares outstanding in the share register and/or share certificate book and agree them to total shares outstanding in the general ledger share capital accounts (completeness)
- examine any cancelled share certificates (validity)
- account for and inspect any unissued share certificates in the share certificate book (completeness)

Valuation

When share capital is issued for cash, the assessment of proper valuation is straightforward. The proceeds from the shares issued is assigned to the share capital account. In jurisdictions where par or stated value shares are allowed to be issued, the difference between the price and par, or stated value is allocated to contributed surplus. The auditor can recompute the values assigned to each transaction. The proceeds from the sale of shares are normally traced to the cash receipts records.

The valuation issue is more complex when share capital is issued in exchange for assets or services, for a merger or acquisition, for convertible securities, or for a share dividend. For example, when a share dividend is declared, normally the dividend is recorded at fair market value. The fair market value of the share dividend is charged to retained earnings and credited to common shares. To test valuation, the auditor can recompute the share dividend and trace the entries into the general ledger.

Disclosure

The disclosure requirements under GAAP for components of the shareholders' equity section of the balance sheet are likewise extensive. Table 13–2 contains examples of shareholders' equity disclosures. The normal sources of this information include the corporate charter, minutes of the board of directors' meetings, and contractual agreements.

Table 13–2	Sample Disclosure Items for Shareholders' Equity

- Number of shares authorized, issued, and outstanding for each class of shares.
- Call privileges, prices, and dates for preferred shares.
- Preferred-share sinking funds.
- Stock option or purchase plans.
- Restrictions on retained earnings and dividends.
- Any completed or pending transactions (such as share dividends or splits) that may affect shareholders' equity.

One of the most important requirements for disclosure in the shareholders' equity section concerns the provision of earnings per share (EPS) information. *CICA Handbook*, section 3500, "Earning per share," discusses the requirements under GAAP and provides detailed examples of disclosure of EPS information. The auditor must ensure that the entity's calculations and disclosure of EPS information, particularly *diluted* EPS, are in accordance with GAAP.

Auditing Dividends

LO 10> Generally, all dividends that are declared and paid will be audited because of concerns with violations of corporate bylaws or debt covenants. When the entity uses an independent dividend-disbursing agent, the auditor can confirm the amount disbursed to the agent by the entity. This amount is agreed with the amount authorized by the board of directors. The auditor can recompute the dividend amount by multiplying the number of shares outstanding on the record date by the amount of the per share dividend approved by the board of directors. This amount should agree to the amount disbursed to shareholders and accrued at year-end. If the auditor is concerned about the client's controls over dividend disbursements, he or she may test the payee names and amounts on the individual cancelled cheques with the share register or share certificate book. The auditor also reviews the entity's compliance with any agreements that restrict the payments of dividends.

Auditing Retained Earnings

LO 11> Under normal circumstances, retained earnings are affected by the current year's income or loss, as well as dividends paid. However, certain accounting standards require that some transactions be included in retained earnings. Prior-period adjustments, correction of errors, and changes in appropriations of retained earnings are examples of such transactions.

The auditor begins the audit of retained earnings by obtaining a schedule of the account activity for the period. The beginning balance is agreed to the prior year's working papers and financial statements. Net income or loss can be traced to the income statement. The amounts for any cash or stock dividends can be verified as described earlier. If there are any prior-period adjustments, the auditor must be certain that the transactions satisfy the requirements of the relevant accounting standards. Any new appropriations or changes in existing appropriations should be traced to the contractual agreements that required the appropriations. Last, the auditor must make sure that all necessary disclosures related to retained earnings are made in the footnotes. For example, many debt agreements restrict the amount of retained earnings that is available for payment as dividends (see Exhibit 13–3).

One last audit step deserves specific mention. It is a substantive audit procedure, although of a slightly different kind, that is particularly relevant to the audit of liabilities and equity accounts. It is standard audit procedure to have a member of the audit team read and summarize the minutes of the board of directors' meetings. The existence of major liabilities and commitments are often the results of decisions of the board of directors, as are events affecting shareholders' equity such as decisions to issue more shares, to repurchase shares, or to declare dividends. The results of decisions documented in the minutes of the board of directors' meetings should be reflected in the financial statements, or in the case of future commitments, in the notes thereto.

Auditing Other Income Statement Accounts

LO 12⟩ The two largest income statement accounts, (sales) revenue and cost of goods sold (i.e., purchases) were discussed in Chapters 8 and 9 respectively. This section briefly discusses the audit of other selected income statement amounts.

In auditing income statement accounts, the auditor must be satisfied that the revenue and expense accounts are not materially misstated and that they are accounted for in accordance with GAAP. The income statement is viewed as an important source of information by various users of the financial statements. For example, creditors or potential creditors look to an entity's profitability as one indicator of the entity's ability to repay debt. Potential investors look to the income statement when deciding whether to purchase the entity's shares. Finally, vendors may examine the entity's earnings potential in order to assess whether the entity will be able to pay for goods or services purchased on credit.

The audit of the other revenue and expense accounts depends on their materiality and on the extent of work conducted by the auditor on the entity's internal control system and balance sheet accounts. For example, the likelihood of material misstatement in the various revenue and expense accounts is a function of the entity's internal control system. The level of control risk used to assess the different business processes directly affects the extent of testing that the auditor requires to audit the income statement accounts.

Auditing the income statement includes consideration of the results of audit work conducted in other parts of the audit and completion of additional substantive testing on selected income statement accounts, including the following:

- assessment of the results of testing controls for the various business processes
- assessment of the results of the direct tests of balance sheet accounts and the related income statement accounts
- performance of analytical procedures on income statement accounts
- tests of selected income statement accounts

Assessing Control Risk for Business Processes

In previous chapters, the auditor's approach to assessing the control risk for various business processes was discussed. If the control risk is set at the maximum, the auditor does not rely on controls but conducts extensive substantive tests of account balances. When a reliance strategy is followed, the auditor conducts tests of controls and substantive tests of transactions to determine if the client's control procedures are operating effectively. If the control procedures operate effectively, the auditor may reduce the control risk below the maximum.

To better understand the effect of a reduced control risk assessment on the audit of the revenue and expense accounts, consider the income statement accounts affected by the revenue and purchasing business processes. For example, a reduced control risk assessment for the revenue process provides evidence that the sales, accounts receivable, allowance for uncollectible accounts, and sales returns and allowances accounts are not materially misstated. Similarly, a reduced control risk assessment for the purchasing process provides evidence that financial statement accounts such as inventory; property, plant, and equipment; accounts payable; and most expense accounts are not materially misstated. The important point here is that the auditor already has reliable evidence on the accounts included in the income statement. The findings for the purchasing process are particularly relevant, since proper control procedures provide evidence on most of the expense accounts. This allows the auditor to do considerably less substantive testing for these income statement accounts.

Tests of Balance Sheet Accounts

Just as the major income statement revenue and purchase expense accounts are audited in conjunction with the audit of the balance sheet accounts, accounts receivable, and accounts payable, some of the other income statement accounts can be audited in conjunction with the audit of the related balance sheet accounts. Table 13–3 shows some of the related income statement accounts that can be verified directly or indirectly with balance sheet accounts. For example, when the allowance for uncollectible accounts is audited, bad-debt expense is also tested. Similarly, when auditing notes receivable, the auditor can test interest income.

Analysis

Analytical procedures can be used extensively to test the revenue and expense accounts. One type of analytical procedure involves comparing the current year's dollar amount for each revenue and expense account with the prior year's balances. Any account that deviates from the prior year's by more than a predetermined amount should be investigated. An alternative to this type of analytical procedure involves calculating the ratio of

Table 13–3	Examples of Income Statement Accounts Audited in Conjunction with the Balance Sheet Account

Balance Sheet Account Audited	*Related Income Statement Account Audited*
Accounts receivable/allowance for uncollectible accounts	Bad-debt expense
Notes receivable/investments/accrued interest receivable	Interest income
Property, plant, and equipment/accumulated amortization	Amortization expense, gain/losses on sales or retirements of assets
Long-term debt/accrued interest payable	Interest expense
Prepaid insurance	Insurance expense

individual expense accounts to net sales and comparing these percentages across years. The auditor can also compare these percentages to industry averages. Individual expense accounts that are judged by the auditor to be out of line are investigated further.

Analytical procedures can also be used to conduct direct substantive tests of *specific* revenue or expense accounts. For example, the auditor can test sales commissions by using the client's commission schedule and multiplying commission rates by eligible sales. This estimate can be compared to the recorded commission expense. Other examples might include overall reasonableness tests for interest and amortization expense. Exhibit 13–4 shows an example of a working paper analyzing EarthWear's legal and audit expenses for 2006.

Tests of Selected Account Balances

Even though the auditor has gathered considerable evidence about revenue and expense accounts based on the audit procedures just discussed, the auditor may want to examine some accounts further. For these accounts,

E X H I B I T   13–4

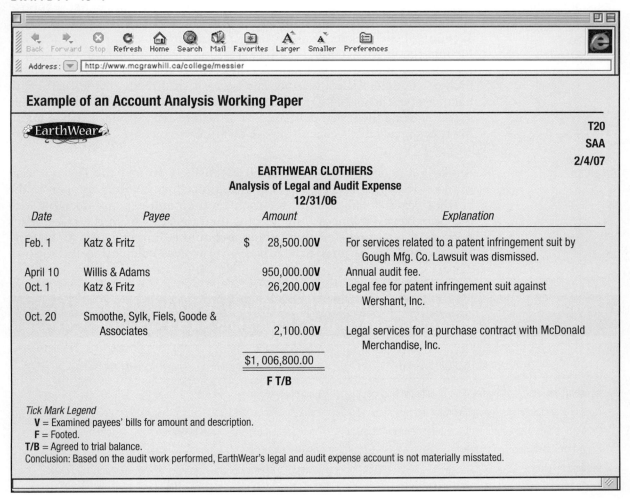

Example of an Account Analysis Working Paper

EarthWear

T20
SAA
2/4/07

EARTHWEAR CLOTHIERS
Analysis of Legal and Audit Expense
12/31/06

Date	Payee	Amount	Explanation
Feb. 1	Katz & Fritz	$ 28,500.00**V**	For services related to a patent infringement suit by Gough Mfg. Co. Lawsuit was dismissed.
April 10	Willis & Adams	950,000.00**V**	Annual audit fee.
Oct. 1	Katz & Fritz	26,200.00**V**	Legal fee for patent infringement suit against Wershant, Inc.
Oct. 20	Smoothe, Sylk, Fiels, Goode & Associates	2,100.00**V**	Legal services for a purchase contract with McDonald Merchandise, Inc.
		$1,006,800.00	
		F T/B	

Tick Mark Legend
  V = Examined payees' bills for amount and description.
  F = Footed.
T/B = Agreed to trial balance.
Conclusion: Based on the audit work performed, EarthWear's legal and audit expense account is not materially misstated.

the auditor typically analyzes in detail the transactions included in each account. The auditor verifies the transactions by examining (vouching) the supporting documentation. Accounts examined in this manner are generally accounts that are not directly affected by an accounting cycle, accounts that may contain sensitive information or unusual transactions, or accounts for which detailed information is needed for the tax return or other schedules included with the financial statements. Some examples of such accounts include legal expense, travel and entertainment, charity expense, other income and expenses, and any account containing related-party transactions. Exhibit 13–4 presents an account analysis for Earth-Wear's legal and audit expense. The auditor will vouch the transactions to the respective invoices. The auditor should examine the lawyers' invoices not only for the amounts but also for information on potential uncertainties, such as lawsuits against the client.

REVIEW QUESTIONS

LO 1,4,5,9 >	**13-1**	Why does the auditor generally follow a substantive strategy when auditing long-term debt and capital accounts?
2,3 >	**13-2**	What are the most important assertions for long-term debt? What documents would normally contain the authorization to issue long-term debt?
3 >	**13-3**	What are the key control procedures when the chief financial officer initiates, approves, and executes debt transactions?
4 >	**13-4**	Describe how analytical procedures may be used to test interest expense.
4 >	**13-5**	Confirmations of long-term debt provide evidence about which audit objectives?
4 >	**13-6**	List three disclosures that may be required for long-term debt.
5 >	**13-7**	Describe the three major types of transactions that occur in shareholders' equity.
5 >	**13-8**	What are the functions of the registrar, the transfer agent, and the dividend-disbursing agent?
8 >	**13-9**	What is the major segregation of duties that should be maintained when the client does not use a registrar or transfer agent and sufficient personnel are available to perform the stock transactions?
9 >	**13-10**	List two common disclosures for shareholders' equity and why such disclosures are necessary.
10,11 >	**13-11**	What approach would the auditor follow to audit dividends and retained earnings?
12 >	**13-12**	Describe the steps followed by the auditor when auditing the income statement.
12 >	**13-13**	List three analytical procedures that the auditor might use in auditing the income statement.
12 >	**13-14**	Why would the auditor do an account analysis and vouch selected transactions in income statement accounts such as legal expense, travel and entertainment, and other income/expenses?

MULTIPLE-CHOICE QUESTIONS FROM PROFESSIONAL EXAMINATIONS

Unless otherwise indicated, these multiple-choice questions were adapted from the CPA examinations, courtesy of the American Institute of Certified Public Accountants.

4> **13-15** The auditor can best verify a client's bond sinking fund transactions and year-end balance sheet by
a. Confirmation of retired bonds with individual holders.
b. Confirmation with the bond trustee.
c. Recomputation of interest expense, interest payable, and amortization of bond discount or premium.
d. Examination and count of the bonds retired during the year.

3,4> **13-16** Two months before year-end, the bookkeeper erroneously recorded the receipt of a long-term bank loan by a debit to cash and a credit to sales. Which of the following is the most effective procedure for detecting this type of error?
a. Analysis of the notes payable journal.
b. Analysis of bank confirmation information.
c. Preparation of a year-end bank reconciliation.
d. Preparation of a year-end bank transfer schedule.

3> **13-17** Which of the following questions would an auditor most likely include on an internal control questionnaire for notes payable?
a. Are assets that collateralize notes payable critically needed for the entity's continued existence?
b. Are two or more authorized signatures required on cheques that repay notes payable?
c. Are the proceeds from notes payable used to purchase noncurrent assets?
d. Are direct borrowings on notes payable authorized by the board of directors?

4> **13-18** An auditor's program to examine long-term debt would most likely include steps that require
a. Comparing the carrying amount of the debt to its year-end market value.
b. Correlating the interest expense recorded for the period with the outstanding debt.
c. Verifying the existence of the holders of the debt by direct confirmation.
d. Inspecting the accounts payable subsidiary ledger for unrecorded long-term debt.

4> **13-19** An auditor's purpose in reviewing the renewal of a note payable shortly after the balance sheet date is most likely to obtain evidence concerning management's assertions about
a. Existence or occurrence.
b. Presentation and disclosure.
c. Completeness.
d. Valuation or allocation.

7,8,9>   13-20   When a client company does *not* maintain its own share records, the auditor should obtain written confirmation from the transfer agent and registrar concerning

a. Restrictions on the payment of dividends.

b. The number of shares issued and outstanding.

c. Guarantees of preferred share liquidation value.

d. The number of shares subject to agreements to repurchase.

9>   13-21   An auditor should trace corporate share issuances and treasury share transactions to the

a. Numbered share certificates.

b. Articles of incorporation.

c. Transfer agent's records.

d. Minutes of the board of directors.

7,8>   13-22   The primary responsibility of a bank acting as a registrar of common shares is to

a. Ascertain that dividends declared do *not* exceed the statutory amount allowable in the jurisdiction of incorporation.

b. Account for share certificates by comparing the total shares outstanding to the total in the shareholders' subsidiary ledger.

c. Act as an independent third party between the board of directors and outside investors concerning mergers, acquisitions, and the sale of treasury shares.

d. Verify that shares have been issued in accordance with the authorization of the board of directors and the articles of incorporation.

12>   13-23   An auditor compares 2006 revenues and expenses with those of the prior year and investigates all changes exceeding 10 percent. By this procedure the auditor would be most likely to learn that

a. Fourth-quarter payroll taxes were *not* paid.

b. The client changed its capitalization policy for small tools in 2006.

c. An increase in property tax rates has *not* been recognized in the client's accrual.

d. The 2006 provision for uncollectible accounts is inadequate because of worsening economic conditions.

12>   13-24   Which of the following comparisons would be most useful to an auditor in evaluating the results of an entity's operations?

a. Prior-year accounts payable to current-year accounts payable.

b. Prior-year payroll expense to budgeted current-year payroll expense.

c. Current-year revenue to budgeted current-year revenue.

d. Current-year warranty expense to current-year contingent liabilities.

9>   13-25   Although the quantity and content of audit working papers varies with each particular engagement, an auditor's permanent files most likely include

a. Schedules that support the current year's adjusting entries.

b. Prior years' accounts receivable confirmations that were classified as exceptions.

c. Documentation indicating that the audit work was adequately planned and supervised.

d. Analyses of share capital and other owners' equity accounts.

PROBLEMS

1,4 ⟩   **13-26**   Yuri Maslovskaya has been engaged to examine the financial statements of Broadwall Corporation for the year ended December 31, 2006. During the year, Broadwall obtained a long-term loan from a local bank pursuant to a financing agreement that provided that

1. The loan was to be secured by the company's inventory and accounts receivable.

2. The company was not to pay dividends without permission from the bank.

3. Monthly instalment payments were to commence July 1, 2006.

In addition, during the year the company borrowed various short-term amounts from the president of the company, including substantial amounts just prior to year-end.

Required:

a. For purposes of the audit of the financial statements of Broadwall Corporation, what procedures should Maslovskaya employ in examining the described loans?

b. What financial statement disclosures should Maslovskaya expect to find with respect to the loans from the president?

(AICPA, adapted)

1,2,3,4 ⟩   **13-27**   Due to increased competition in the airline industry, Mexican Airlines International (MAI) has implemented a frequent flier program for its passengers. Management anticipates that this program will last for approximately two years. After the passenger signs up for the program, one free air mile is awarded for each air mile flown. Once the passenger has accumulated 10,000 air miles, they can be converted into free travel on MAI, or exchanged for free hotel accommodation at the world-class resort, Siesta Americana. Management has incorporated the frequent flier program into its computerized revenue system.

You are the audit senior for MAI. MAI's year-end is December 31. As at September 30, MAI had accrued a $2.3 million liability in its third quarter interim financial statements. You determined, during a meeting with the client, that in October passengers had redeemed 250,000 air miles worth approximately $100,000 in travel and accommodation.

Required:

Prepare a memo for the planning file indicating the approach to auditing MAI's frequent flier program. Ignore any accounting considerations.

(ICABC, adapted)

8,9> **13-28** John Lee, the continuing auditor of Wu, Ltd., is beginning to audit the common stock and treasury stock accounts. Lee has decided to design substantive tests without relying on the company's internal control system.

Wu has no par value common stock, and it acts as its own registrar and transfer agent. During the past year Wu both issued and reacquired shares of its own common stock, some of which the company still owned at year-end. Additional common shares transactions occurred among the shareholders during the year.

Common shares transactions can be traced to individual shareholders' accounts in a subsidiary ledger and to a stock certificate book. The company has not paid any cash or share dividends. There are no other classes of stock, stock rights, warrants, or option plans.

Required:

What substantive audit procedures should Lee apply in examining the common stock and treasury stock accounts?

(AICPA, adapted)

4> **13-29** Erik Rekdahl, senior-in-charge, is auditing Koonce Katfood, Inc.'s, long-term debt for the year ended July 31, 2006. Long-term debt is composed of two bond issues, which are due in 10 and 15 years, respectively. The debt is held by two insurance companies. Rekdahl has examined the bond indentures for each issue. The indentures provide that if Koonce fails to comply with the covenants of the indentures, the debt becomes payable immediately. Rekdahl identified the following covenants when reviewing the bond indentures:

1. "The debtor company shall endeavour to maintain a working capital ratio of 2 to 1 at all times, and in any fiscal year following a failure to maintain said ratio, the company shall restrict compensation of officers to a total of $650,000. Officers include the chairperson of the board and the president."

2. "The debtor company shall keep all property that is security for these debt agreements insured against loss by fire to the extent of 100 percent of its actual value. Policies of insurance comprising this protection shall be filed with the trustee."

3. "The company is required to restrict 40 percent of retained earnings from availability for paying dividends."

4. "A sinking fund shall be established with the First Canadian Bank, and semiannual payments of $500,000 shall be deposited in the fund. The bank may, at its discretion, purchase bonds from either issue."

Required:

a. Provide any audit steps that Rekdahl should conduct to determine if the company is in compliance with the bond indentures.

b. List any reporting requirements that the financial statements or footnotes should recognize.

(AICPA, adapted)

5,9 ▷   **13-30**   Airline Transport Ltd. (ATL) is an emerging national airline listed on a Canadian stock exchange. To finance expansion and acquisition, ATL issued from treasury two classes of non-voting preferred shares. These are titled class A and B preferred. Common shares (voting) were also issued from treasury and sold through private placements. ATL uses the services of Regal Trust Co., a well-recognized transfer agent. Regal maintains the share registers for all classes of share capital of ATL.

The common shares of ATL are listed on a Canadian stock exchange. In April 2006, the company went through a restructuring to ward off creditors and delay or change ATL's financial obligations. Regal has handled and continues to handle all the registers and certificates for all classes of shares of ATL. Regal controls the security of the bond and share certificates cancelled, redeemed and issued along with unissued share certificates. You are a manager with ATL's auditors, Wolf & Bear. The partner, Anne Wolf, is confident that Regal is independent and reliable, and has informed you that you need not test controls at the transfer agent.

In early January 2006, the holders of the corporate bonds approved the restructuring plan. Bondholders were to receive common shares or 40 percent of their obligations may be settled by the issuance of convertible subordinated notes, which are non-interest bearing for the first five years, with the remainder settled by the issuance of common shares. This option had to be elected upon on or before March 31, 2006 with Regal. The restructuring plan provides for a standard conversion rate of 2,000 common shares per $1,000 of bonds outstanding at December 31, 2005. No dividends were declared on common shares in 2006. All unpaid dividends at December 31, 2005 were converted into common shares on a three shares for every dollar of unpaid dividends basis.

A private placement for $250,000 was made for common shares to a related party.

Required:

a. Summarize by audit assertion the substantive audit procedures you will utilize in the audit of capital stock of ATL for the fiscal year ended December 31, 2006.

b. List the items to be confirmed by Regal (the transfer agent).

c. What is the effect of the share transactions and the private placement on the inherent risk of the audit.

(ICABC, adapted)

4> **13-31** The long-term debt working paper on the page 524 was prepared by client personnel and audited by Andy Fogelman, an audit assistant, during the calendar year 2006 audit of Canadian Widgets, Ltd., a continuing audit client. The engagement supervisor is reviewing the working paper thoroughly.

Required:

Identify the deficiencies in the working paper that the engagement supervisor should discover.

(AICPA, adapted)

DISCUSSION CASES

4> **13-32** On September 10, Melinda Johnson was auditing the financial statements of a new audit client, Mother Earth Foods, a health-food chain that has a June 30 year-end. The company is privately held and has just gone through a leveraged buyout with long-term financing that includes various restrictive covenants.

In order to obtain debt financing, companies often have to agree to certain conditions, some of which may restrict the way in which they conduct their business. If the borrower fails to comply with the stated conditions, it may be considered in default, which would give the lender the right to accelerate the due date of the debt, add other restrictions, waive the default for a stated period, or revise the covenants. Usually there is a grace period during which the borrower can cure the default.

Johnson believes that it is possible that at August 31 Mother Earth was in violation of the debt covenant restrictions, which became effective on that date. The debt covenants require the company to maintain a certain receivable turnover rate. Johnson is not certain, however, because the accounting records, including period-end cutoffs for sales and purchases, have not been well maintained. Nevertheless, Mother Earth's executives assure Johnson that if they were in violation, the company will be able to obtain a waiver or modification of the covenant.

Required:

a. Discuss the audit procedures that Johnson would conduct to determine if Mother Earth violated the debt covenants. How would Johnson determine whether Mother Earth would be able to obtain a waiver, assuming that the company was in violation of the debt covenants?

b. Based on the case scenario, should Mother Earth continue to classify this debt as noncurrent? Justify your answer.

5,9> **13-33** Your client, Rosenberg Corp. (the "Company"), bought certain assets of Howarth, Ltd., and accounted for them as a purchase in accordance with *CICA Handbook*, section 1581, "Business combinations." The letter of intent was executed on July 31, 2006, and the transaction closed on October 31, 2006. The purchase price was

CANADIAN WIDGETS, LTD.
Working Paper
December 31, 2006

	Initials	Date
Prepared By	AF	3/22/07
Approved By		

Lender	Interest Rate	Payment Terms	Collateral	Balance 12/31/05	2006 Borrowings	2006 Reductions	Balance 12/31/06	Interest Paid to	Accrued Interest Payable 12/31/06	Comments
City Commercial Bank φ	12%	Interest only on 25th of month, principal due in full 1/1/10; no prepayment penalty	Inventories	$ 50,000✔	$300,000A 1/31/02	$100,000✪ 6/30/02	$250,000CX	12/25/06	$2,500NR	Dividend of $80,000 paid 9/2/06 (W/P N-3) violates a provision of the debt agreement, which thereby permits lender to demand immediate payment; lender has refused to waive this covenant.
Lender's Capital Corporation φ	Prime plus 1%	Interest only on last day of month, principal due in full 3/5/15	2nd mortgage on Park Street Building	100,000✔	50,000A 2/29/06	—	200,000C	12/31/06	—	Prime rate was 8% to 9% during the year.
Gigantic Building & Loan Association φ	12%	$5,000 principal plus interest due on 5th of month, due in full 12/31/20	1st mortgage on Park Street Building	720,000✔	—	60,000θ	660,000C	12/5/06	5,642R	Reclassification entry for current portion proposed (see RJE-3).
J. Lott, majority shareholder φ	0%	Due in full 12/31/12	Unsecured	300,000✔	—	100,000N 12/31/06	200,000C	—	—	Borrowed additional $100,000 from J. Lott on 1/7/06.
				$1,170,000✔ F	$350,000 F	$260,000 F	$1,310,000T/B F		$8,142T/B F	

Interest costs from long-term debt
Interest expense for year $ 281,333T/B
Average loan balance outstanding $1,406,667R

Five-year maturities (for disclosure purposes)

Year-end	12/31/07	$ 60,000
	12/31/08	260,000
	12/31/09	260,000
	12/31/10	310,000
	12/31/11	60,000
	Thereafter	360,000
		$1,310,000 F

Tick Mark Legend
C = Confirmed without exception, W/P K-2.
F = Readded, foots correctly.
CX = Confirmed with exception, W/P K-3.
NR = Does not recompute correctly.
A = Agreed to loan agreement, validated bank deposit ticket, and board of directors' authorization, W/P W-7.
θ = Agreed to cancelled cheques and lender's monthly statements.
N = Agreed to cash disbursements journal and cancelled cheque dated 12/31/06, clearing 1/8/07.
T/B = Traced to working trial balance.
✔ = Agreed to 12/31/05 working papers.
φ = Agreed interest rate, term, and collateral to copy of note and loan agreement.
✪ = Agreed to cancelled cheque and board of directors' authorization, W/P W-7.

Conclusions: Long-term debt, accrued interest payable, and interest expense are correct and complete at 12/31/06.

$8,600,000, payable as $5,100,000 in cash ($2,700,000 of which was borrowed pursuant to a term loan) and 175,000 shares of the company's common stock, which account for approximately 10 percent of the shares issued. It was agreed by the parties that the common stock would be assigned a value of $20 per share.

Rosenberg is a privately held company that plans to go public within two years. Its common shares are thinly traded on the unlisted securities market in Canada. There have been no independent valuations of the company's shares.

In addition to the payment in cash and securities, Rosenberg executed a repurchase agreement with Howarth. The agreement requires Rosenberg to repurchase the shares issued to Howarth on the first anniversary date (October 31, 2007) for $20 per share. In substance, the agreement represents a mandatory "put" on the Rosenberg stock, which was issued to Howarth. The repurchase can be delayed for up to two succeeding anniversary dates if the company pays Howarth an amount equal to $1.80 per share ($315,000) on each anniversary date.

The put can be accelerated if any one of the following occurs: (1) substantially all of the company's assets are sold, (2) Rosenberg merges with another entity and does not survive as the controlling entity, or (3) substantially all of the company's common shares are sold to others.

The put is voided if any one of the following occurs: (1) the stock is sold in connection with a public offering of the company, (2) Howarth declines its right to put the shares, or (3) Howarth sells the shares to a third party. In addition, the company can void the option by redeeming the shares at the guaranteed price of $20 per share.

The repurchase agreement also contains an exchange clause whereby the common shares may be exchanged for a demand promissory note. The exchange right becomes operable if any one of the following occurs: (1) Rosenberg borrows in excess of $15 million, (2) Rosenberg issues equity securities with rights and preferences and limitations senior to the shares given to Howarth, or (3) Rosenberg fails to perform under the repurchase agreement.

The company's controller tells you that she plans to show the common shares issued to Howarth in the shareholders' equity section of the balance sheet. She also tells you that the company's president believes that the fair value of the shares is $20 per share and insists that it be recorded at that amount at inception.

Required:

a. What business reasons may have motivated Rosenberg to structure the transaction in this manner? Should the mandatorily redeemable common shares issued to Howarth be classified in the shareholders' equity section of the balance sheet?

b. At what amount should the common shares be valued? What audit procedures would you use to verify the common share valuation?

INTERNET ASSIGNMENT

6,7,8,11   **13-34**   Nortel Networks Corp., Canada's largest supplier of telecommunications equipment, has had to restate its earnings for 2001–2005 to the tune of approximately $1.5 billion.

Required:

Use the Internet to obtain information about Nortel's earnings restatement. Sources of information on this issue can be found at websites for Nortel, the SEC, and various news providers (*The Wall Street Journal, The Financial Post*). Prepare a memo summarizing the issues related to Nortel's accounting. Consider why Nortel's auditors (Andersen) might have allowed the company to account for those transactions in that manner.

Auditing Cash and Investments

Learning Objectives

Upon completion of this chapter, you will be able to

1 Describe the relationship of the various business processes to cash.

2 List the different types of bank accounts.

3 Identify substantive tests of transactions used to audit cash.

4 Identify tests of account balances used to audit cash.

5 Audit a bank reconciliation.

6 Explain fraud-related audit procedures for cash.

7 Identify key internal controls for investments.

8 Determine the appropriate segregation of duties for investments.

9 Identify tests of account balances used to audit investments.

RELEVANT ACCOUNTING AND ASSURANCE PRONOUNCEMENTS

CICA Handbook, **section 3000,** Cash

CICA Handbook, **section 3855,** *Financial Instruments—Recognition and Measurement*

CICA Handbook, **section 3861,** *Financial instruments—Disclosure and Presentation*

CICA Handbook, **section 3862,** *Financial instruments—Disclosures*

CICA Handbook, **section 3863,** *Financial instruments—Presentation*

CICA Handbook, **section 5095,** Reasonable assurance and audit risk

CICA Handbook, **section 5141,** Understanding the entity and its environment and assessing the risks of material misstatement

CICA Handbook, **section 5142,** The auditor's procedures in response to assessed risks

CICA Handbook, **section 5300,** Audit evidence

CICA Handbook, **section 5301,** Analysis

CICA Handbook, **section 5303,** Confirmation

CICA Handbook, **section 5306,** Auditing fair value measurements and disclosures

AUDITING EARTHWEAR'S CASH AND INVESTMENTS

EarthWear This chapter discusses the audit procedures that Willis & Adams will employ to audit EarthWear's Cash and Cash Equivalents balance sheet account. EarthWear's other business processes, such as revenue, purchasing, human resource management, and so on, all interact with cash. The audit evidence that Willis & Adams has collected in the course of auditing these processes affects the type and amount of evidence required to audit cash. For example, as a result of auditing the revenue and purchasing processes, Willis & Adams will know a great deal about the controls over cash receipts and disbursements. However, because cash, and to a slightly lesser extent, investments, are so liquid, they normally represent critical audit areas and therefore merit additional audit procedures. The caption on EarthWear's balance sheet refers to Cash and Cash Equivalents. Typically that one amount is made up of a number of different bank accounts and investments. For instance, EarthWear will have a general bank account, a bank account for payroll, a petty cash fund, etc. At year-end, Willis & Adams will obtain audit evidence to ensure that the assertions relevant to the components of the balance sheet account Cash and Cash Equivalents (e.g., existence) are supported. It will be efficient for Willis & Adams to use primarily substantive procedures to obtain this audit evidence, such as bank confirmation requests for the bank accounts and requests for confirmation of security ownership of any securities held on deposit by an agent such as a financial institution. Willis & Adams will also substantively test EarthWear's short-term investments to make sure they are properly classified, valued and disclosed, including any commitments or encumbrances, such as pledges or guarantees that affect this account.

Cash and the Effect of Other Business Processes

LO 1 The line item "cash" reported in the financial statements represents currency on hand and cash on deposit in bank accounts, including certificates of deposit, time deposits, and savings accounts. Frequently, certain "cash equivalents" are combined with cash for presentation in the financial statements. *CICA Handbook,* section 3000, defines *cash equivalents* as short-term, highly liquid investments that are readily convertible to cash or so near their maturity that there is little risk of change in their value. Examples of such financial instruments include Treasury bills, commercial paper, and money market funds.

Because virtually all accounting transactions pass through the cash account as part of their "cradle-to-grave" process, cash is affected in one way or another by all of the entity's business processes. Figure 14–1 shows the effect each major business process has on the cash account. Although the main source of cash receipts is the revenue process, other sources of cash include (1) the sale of property, plant, and equipment and (2) the proceeds from issuing long-term debt or capital stock. The main sources of disbursements from cash are the purchasing and payroll processes. Generally, large payments from the purchasing process are for acquisitions of inventory and property, plant, and equipment. Payments on long-term debt and repurchase of stock are other types of cash disbursements.

FIGURE 14–1

The Effects of Major Accounting Transactions/Processes on Cash

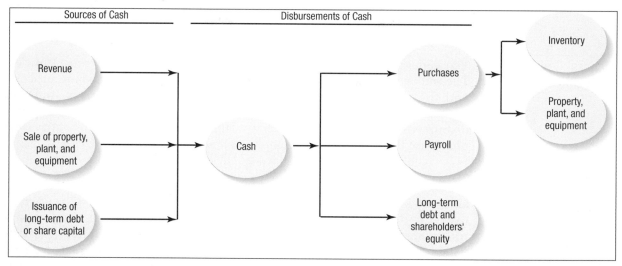

Because of the close relationship of cash to the revenue and purchasing processes, internal control system issues were discussed in Chapters 8 and 9, respectively. Table 8–6 summarized the assertions, possible misstatements, control procedures, and tests of controls for cash receipt transactions. A similar summary was provided for cash disbursement transactions in Table 9–6. A discussion of the control risk for cash receipt and disbursement transactions will not be repeated in this chapter. However, the auditor's assessment of the control risk for transactions processed through the revenue and purchasing processes strongly affects the nature and extent of testing for the ending cash balance. For example, if the control risk is below the maximum for both of these processes, the auditor can reduce the substantive testing of the cash balances. You should review the assessment of control risk for cash receipt and cash disbursement transactions.

Types of Bank Accounts

LO 2>

As mentioned, cash management is an important function in all organizations. In order to maximize its cash position, an entity implements procedures for accelerating the collection of cash receipts and properly delaying the payment of cash disbursements. Such procedures allow the entity to earn interest on excess cash or to reduce the cost of cash borrowings.

In spite of the sophisticated nature of cash management, the entity's management must still be concerned with the control and safekeeping of cash. Using different types of bank accounts aids in controlling the entity's cash. The following types of bank accounts are typically used:

- general cash accounts
- imprest cash accounts
- branch accounts

It is important to understand each of the different types of bank accounts used. While the audit approach to each type of account is similar, the extent of testing varies from one account to the next. Each type of bank account is briefly discussed.

General Cash Accounts

The general cash account is the principal cash account for most entities. The major source of cash receipts for this account is the revenue process, and the major sources of cash disbursements are the purchasing and payroll processes. This cash account may also be used for receipts and disbursements from other bank accounts maintained by the entity. For many small entities, this is the only cash account maintained.

Imprest Cash Accounts

An imprest cash account contains a stipulated amount of money, and the account is used for limited purposes. Imprest accounts are frequently used for disbursing payroll and dividend cheques. In the case of payroll, a separate bank account containing a minimum balance is established for disbursing payroll. Disbursement may be by cheque or direct deposit. Prior to the disbursement of payroll cheques, a cheque is drawn or a cash transfer is made from the general cash account to the payroll account for the amount of the net payroll. The payroll is then drawn on this imprest account. Thus, the payroll account serves as a clearing account for the payroll payments and facilitates the disbursement of cash while also maintaining adequate control over cash. Use of imprest accounts also minimizes the time required to reconcile the general cash account.

Branch Accounts

Companies that operate branches in multiple locations may maintain separate accounts at local banks. This allows each branch to pay local expenses and to maintain a banking relationship in the local community. Branch cash accounts can be operated in a number of ways. In some cases, the branch accounts are nothing more than imprest accounts for branch payments in which a minimum balance is maintained. The branch submits periodic cash reports to headquarters, and the branch account receives a cheque or transfer from the general cash account. In other cases, the branch account functions as a general cash account by recording both cash receipts and cash disbursements.

For proper control, the branch should be required to submit periodic cash reports to headquarters, and the entity's management should carefully monitor the cash balances in the branch accounts.

Analysis—Cash

Because of its residual nature, cash does not have a predictable relationship with other financial statement accounts. As a result, the auditor's use of analytical procedures for auditing cash is limited to comparisons with prior years' cash balances and to budgeted amounts. This limited use of analytical procedures is normally offset by (1) extensive tests of controls and/or substantive tests of transactions for cash receipts and cash disbursements or (2) extensive tests of the entity's bank reconciliations.

Substantive Tests of Details of Transactions and Balances

LO 3,4⟩   Table 14–1 contains examples of substantive tests of transactions for both cash receipts and cash disbursements. By testing both cash receipts and disbursements, the auditor obtains important evidence about the relevant assertions for the cash account. On most audits, the substantive tests of transactions for cash receipts and cash disbursements are conducted together with the tests of controls for the revenue and purchasing processes, respectively.

The Effects of Controls

The reliability of the client's controls over cash receipts and cash disbursements affects the nature and extent of the auditor's tests of details. The preceding chapters discussed a number of important controls for both cash receipts and disbursements. For example, incoming cheques are to be restrictively endorsed (stamped "For deposit only" to the company's bank account), and daily cash receipts are to be reconciled with postings to the accounts receivable subsidiary ledger. The effective operation of these controls provides strong evidence that the completeness assertion is being met. Similarly, outgoing cheques are to be signed only when all docu-

Table 14–1	**Examples of Tests of Details of Transactions for Cash Receipts and Disbursements**	
	Substantive Tests of Transactions*	
Assertions about Classes of Transactions	*Cash Receipts*	*Cash Disbursements*
Occurrence	Trace a sample of entries in the cash receipts journal to remittance advices, daily deposit slips, and bank statement.	Trace a sample of entries from the cash disbursements journal to cancelled cheques, voucher packet, and bank statement.
Completeness	Trace a sample of remittance advices to cash receipts journal and, if necessary, to deposit slips.	Trace a sample of cancelled cheques to the cash disbursements journal.
Accuracy	For a sample of daily deposits, foot the remittance advices and entries on the deposit slip and agree to the cash receipts journal and bank statement. For a sample of weeks, foot the cash receipts journal and agree posting to the general ledger.	For a sample of voucher packets, agree amounts in purchase order, receiving report, invoice, cancelled cheque, and disbursement journal. For a sample of weeks, foot the cash disbursements journal and agree posting to the general ledger.
Cutoff	Compare the dates for recording a sample of cash receipts transactions in the cash receipts journal with the dates the cash was deposited in the bank (note any significant delays). Observe cash on hand for the last day of the year, and trace deposits to cash receipts journal and cutoff bank statement	Compare the dates for a sample of cheques with the dates the cheques cleared the bank (note any significant delays). Record the last cheque issued on the last day of the year, and trace to cash disbursements journal.
Classification	Examine a sample of remittance advices for proper account classification	Examine a sample of cancelled cheques for proper account classification.

* These tests of details of transactions are commonly conducted as dual-purpose tests (i.e., in conjunction with tests of controls).

ments included in the voucher packet have been independently approved. The effective operation of this control procedure provides the auditor with evidence on the authorization assertion.

A major control that directly affects the audit of cash is the completion of a monthly bank reconciliation by client personnel who are independent of the handling and recording of cash receipts and cash disbursements. Such bank reconciliations ensure that the client's books reflect the same balance as the bank's after reconciling items have been considered. Control can be improved further if an independent party such as the internal auditor reviews the bank reconciliation.

If the client has good bank reconciliation procedures that are promptly performed, the auditor may be able to reduce the audit work on the ending cash balance.

Balance-Related Assertions

Table 14–2 summarizes the assertions and tests of details of account balances for cash accounts. The rights and obligations assertion is not included in Table 14–2 because it is seldom important to the audit of the cash balance. The major audit procedures for each cash account involve tests of the bank reconciliation. The approach to auditing a bank reconciliation is basically the same regardless of the type of bank account being examined. However, the type and extent of the audit work are more detailed for the general cash account because it normally represents a material amount and because of the large amount of activity in the account.

Auditing the General Cash Account

LO 5>

Table 14–2 shows that the main source of evidence for the existence, completeness, and valuation objectives is the audit work completed on the bank reconciliation. To audit a cash account, the auditor should obtain the following documents:

- a copy of the bank reconciliation
- a standard form to confirm account balance information with financial institutions (referred to as a *standard bank confirmation*)
- a cutoff bank statement

Table 14–2	**Examples of Tests of Details of Balance for Cash**
Assertions about Account Balances at Period End	*Tests of Details Account Balances*
Existence Completeness Valuation and Allocation	Test bank reconciliation for each account: • Foot the reconciliation and the outstanding cheque listing. • Trace balances per book to the general ledger. • Obtain standard bank confirmation and trace balance per bank to the bank reconciliation. • Obtain cutoff bank statement. • Trace deposits in transit, outstanding cheques, and other reconciling items to cutoff bank statement. If control risk is high or if fraud is suspected: • Perform extended bank reconciliation procedures. • Perform a proof of cash. • Test for kiting.

Bank Reconciliation Working Paper   Exhibit 14–1 provides an example of a bank reconciliation working paper for Earth-Wear's general cash account. Note that the difference between the cash balance showed in Exhibit 14–1 and the balance in cash on the financial statements is represented by cash equivalents (Treasury bills and commercial paper). On most audits, the auditor obtains a copy of the bank reconciliation prepared by the client's personnel. The working paper reconciles the balance per the bank with the balance per the books. The major reconciling items are deposits in transit, outstanding cheques, and other adjustments, such as bank service charges and any cheque returned because the customer did not have sufficient cash (NSF cheque) in its account to cover payment of the cheque. Many companies now use online banking. In such cases the auditor may request that the client provide printouts of daily banking transactions for a period after the year-end to assist with the reconciliation process.

Standard Bank Confirmation Form   Although information of bank balances is not a required audit procedure in every audit, the auditor generally confirms the account balance information with every bank or financial institution that maintains an account for the client. CICA and CGA-Canada have each jointly developed with the Canadian Bankers' Association, a standard form for use by the auditor in confirming such information. Exhibit 14–2 contains a completed copy of the bank confirmation form, which is also used to obtain information about any loans the client may have with the bank.

Note that the confirmation form does not require bank personnel to conduct a comprehensive, detailed search of the bank's records beyond the account information requested on the confirmation. However, it does request that bank personnel indicate any other deposits or loans that come to their attention while completing the confirmation. As a result, this confirmation request cannot be relied upon to identify *all* information about a client's bank deposits or loans. If the auditor believes that additional information is needed about a client's arrangements with a financial institution, a separate confirmation letter signed by the client should be sent to the official at the financial institution who is responsible for the client's accounts. Details regarding lines of credit and compensating balances are examples of information that might be confirmed in this manner. This issue is discussed later in this chapter.

Cutoff Bank Statement   A major step in auditing a bank reconciliation is verifying the propriety of the reconciling items such as deposits in transit and outstanding cheques. The auditor obtains a cutoff bank statement to test the reconciling items included in the bank reconciliation. A cutoff bank statement normally covers the 7- to 10-day period after the date on which the bank account is reconciled. Any reconciling item should have cleared the client's bank account during the 7- to 10-day period. The auditor obtains this cutoff bank statement by having the client request that the bank send the statement, including cancelled cheques, directly to the auditor.

EXHIBIT 14–1

Example of a Bank Reconcilliation Working Paper

EarthWear

C10
DLJ
2/14/07

EARTHWEAR CLOTHIERS
Bank Reconciliation
12/31/06

General Cash Account

Balance per bank: **C11**		$1,854,890**C**
Add:		
Deposits in transit:		
12/30/06	$156,940✓	
12/31/06	340,875✓	497,815
Deduct:		
Outstanding cheques:		
#1243	$121,843ϕ	
#1244	232,784ϕ	
#1247	30,431ϕ	
#1250	64,407ϕ	
#1251	123,250ϕ	(572,715)
Balance per books, unadjusted		1,779,990
Adjustments to books:		
Bank service charges	$ 250✓	
NSF cheque	7,400✓	(7,650)
Balance per books, adjusted		$1,772,340**L**
		F

F = Footed.
C = Traced balance to bank confirmation.
L = Agreed to cash lead schedule and general ledger.
✓ = Traced amount to cutoff bank statement.
ϕ = Examined cancelled cheque for proper payee, amount, and endorsement.

Note: The controller has signed for the return of the cutoff bank statement.

EXHIBIT 14–2

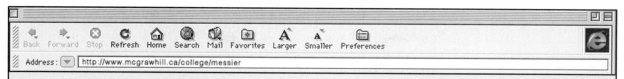

Address: http://www.mcgrawhill.ca/college/messier

Example of a Completed Standard Bank Confirmation Form

Bank Confirmation

C11
DIJ
2/14/07

Areas to be completed by client are marked §, while those to be completed by the financial institution are marked †

FINANCIAL INSTITUTION §
(Name, branch and full mailing address)

CIBC
P.O. Box 1947
Calgary, Alberta T2T 3Q1

CONFIRMATION DATE § December 31, 2006
(All information to be provided as of this date)
(See Bank Confirmation Completion Instructions)

CLIENT (Legal name) §

EarthWear Clothiers, Inc.

The financial institution is authorized to provide the details requested herein to the below-noted firm of accounts

§ *Sally Jones*

Client's authorized signature
Please supply copy of the most recent credit facility
agreement (initial if required) § _____

LOANS AND OTHER DIRECT AND CONTINGENT LIABILITIES (If balances are nil, please state)

NATURE OF LIABILITY/ CONTINGENT LIABILITY †	INTEREST (Note rate per contract)		DUE DATE †	DATE OF CREDIT FACILITY AGREEMENT †	DATE OF CREDIT FACILITY AGREEMENT †
	RATE †	DATE PAID TO †			

ADDITIONAL CREDIT FACILITY AGREEMENT(S) _____
Note the date(s) of any credit facility agreement(s) not drawn upon and not referenced above. † _____

DEPOSITS/OVERDRAFTS

TYPE OF ACCOUNT §	ACCOUNT NUMBER §	INTEREST RATE §	ISSUE DATE (If applicable) §	MATURITY DATE (If applicable) §	AMOUNT AND CURRENCY (Brackets if Overdraft)§
General Account	04-78925	None			$1,854,890.00 to C10
Payroll Account	01-04354	None			$ 5,000.00 to C20

EXCEPTIONS AND COMMENTS (See Bank Confirmation Completion Instructions) †

STATEMENT OF PROCEDURES PERFORMED BY FINANCIAL INSTITUTION †
The above information was completed in accordance with the Bank Confirmation Completion Instructions.

J J Hammer
Authorized signature of financial institution

BRANCH CONTACT _____
Name and telephone number

Please mail this form directly to our chartered accountant in the enclosed addressed envelope.

Name: Willis & Adams
Address: P.O. Box 4080, Calgary, Alberta, T1T 2R2
Telephone:
Fax:

Developed by the Canadian Bankers Association and the Canadian Institute of Chartered Accountants

Tests of the Bank Reconciliation   The auditor uses the following audit procedures to test the bank reconciliation:

1. *Test the mathematical accuracy of the bank reconciliation working paper and agree the balance per the books to the general ledger.* In Exhibit 14–1, the working paper has been footed and the balance per the books as shown on the reconciliation has been agreed to the general ledger.

2. *Agree the bank balance on the bank reconciliation with the balance shown on the standard bank confirmation.* The bank confirmation shown in Exhibit 14–2 has been prepared so that it corresponds to the bank reconciliation in Exhibit 14–1. The $1,854,890 shown on the bank reconciliation has been agreed to the $1,854,890 balance shown on the bank confirmation in Exhibit 14–2.

3. *Trace the deposits in transit on the bank reconciliation to the cutoff bank statement.* Following up on any outstanding deposit is an important audit procedure. Any deposit in transit shown on the bank reconciliation should be listed as a deposit shortly after the end of the period. The tick mark next to the deposits in transit shown in Exhibit 14–1 indicates that the deposits were traced by the auditor to the cutoff bank statement.

4. *Compare the outstanding cheques on the bank reconciliation working paper with the cancelled cheques contained in the cutoff bank statement for proper payee, amount, and endorsement.* The auditor should also ensure that no cheques dated prior to December 31 are included with the cutoff bank statement that are not included as outstanding cheques on the bank reconciliation. The tick mark next to the outstanding cheques shown in Exhibit 14–1 indicates that the cheques were traced by the auditor to the cutoff bank statement and that the cancelled cheques were examined for propriety.

5. *Agree any charges included on the bank statement to the bank reconciliation.* In some cases, these charges may result in an adjustment to the client's books. For example, the bank service charges of $250 and the NSF cheque for $7,400 shown in Exhibit 14–1 require adjustment of the client's records.

6. *Agree the adjusted book balance to the cash account lead schedule.* The adjusted book balance would be part of the amount included in the financial statements for cash.

Fraud-Related Audit Procedures for Cash

LO 6>

If the client does not have adequate control procedures over cash or the auditor suspects that some type of fraud or defalcation involving cash has occurred, it may be necessary to extend the normal cash audit procedures. Although many types of fraud, such as forgery or collusion, are difficult to detect, the auditor has a responsibility to plan and perform the audit to obtain reasonable assurance about whether the financial statements are free of material misstatement, whether caused by error or fraud.

Three audit procedures that auditors typically use to detect fraudulent activities in the cash accounts are

- extended bank reconciliation procedures
- proof of cash
- tests for kiting

Extended Bank Reconciliation Procedures In some instances, the year-end bank reconciliation can be used to cover cash defalcations. This is usually accomplished by manipulating the reconciling items in the bank reconciliation. For example, suppose a client employee was able to steal $5,000 from the client. The client's cash balance at the bank would then be $5,000 less than reported on the client's books. The employee could "hide" the $5,000 shortage in the bank reconciliation by including a fictitious deposit in transit. Thus, the typical approach to searching for possible fraud is to extend the bank reconciliation procedures to examine the disposition of the reconciling items included on the prior months' reconciliations and the reconciling items included in the current bank reconciliation.

For example, assume that the auditor suspected that some type of fraud had been committed. The auditor would examine the November and December bank reconciliations by ensuring that all reconciling items had been properly handled. For deposits in transit on the November bank reconciliation, the auditor would trace the deposits to the November cash receipts journal to verify that they were recorded. The deposits would also be traced to the December bank statement to verify that they were deposited in the bank. Cheques listed as outstanding on the November bank reconciliation would be traced to the November cash disbursements journal, and the cancelled cheques returned with the December bank statement would be examined for propriety. Other reconciling items such as bank charges, NSF cheques, and collections of notes by the bank would be similarly traced to the accounting records for proper treatment. The auditor would examine the reconciling items included on the December bank reconciliation in a similar fashion to ensure that such items were not being used to cover a cash defalcation. Further investigation would be required for any reconciling items not properly accounted for. The client's management should be informed if the auditor detects any fraudulent transactions.

A *proof of cash* is used to reconcile the cash receipts and disbursements recorded on the client's books with the cash deposited into and disbursed from the client's bank account for a specific time period. Exhibit 14–3 presents an example of a proof of cash for Calabro Digital Services (Problem 3-38) for one month, although on some audits a proof of cash is performed for the entire period under audit. Because the proof contains four columns, a proof of cash is commonly referred to as a *four-column proof of cash*. The four columns include

- a bank reconciliation for the beginning of the period
- a reconciliation of the cash deposited in the bank with the cash receipts recorded in the cash receipts journal

EXHIBIT 14–3

Example of a Proof of Cash

GDS

CALABRO DIGITAL SERVICES
Proof of Cash—General Cash Account
12/31/06

	11/30/06	December Receipts	December Disbursements	12/31/06
Balance per bank	$513,324	$457,822φ	$453,387φ	$517,759**F**
Deposits in transit:				
11/30/06	114,240	(114,240)		
12/31/06		116,437		116,437
Outstanding cheques:				
11/30/06	(117,385)		(117,385)	
12/31/06			115,312	(115,312)
Collection of note receivableν	(7,500)	7,500		
Balance per books, unadjusted	502,679	467,519γ	451,314μ	518,884**F**
Adjustments to books:				
Bank charges			125	(125)∈
NSF cheques		(5,250)		(5,250)∈
Balance per books, adjusted	$502,679	$462,269	$451,439	$513,509**FL**
	F	**F**	**F**	**F**

F = Footed and crossfooted.
L = Agreed to general ledger.
φ = Traced to December bank statement.
γ = Agreed to December cash receipts journal.
μ = Agreed to December cash disbursements journal.
ν = Traced to November bank statement and December cash receipts journal.
∈ = Traced to cutoff bank statement.

- a reconciliation of the cash disbursed through the bank account with the cash disbursements recorded in the cash disbursements journal
- a bank reconciliation for the end of the period

The primary purposes of the proof of cash are (1) to ensure that all cash receipts recorded in the client's cash receipts journal were deposited in the client's bank account, (2) to ensure that all cash disbursements recorded in the client's cash disbursements journal have cleared the client's bank account, and (3) to ensure that no bank transactions have been omitted from the client's accounting records. You should understand that a proof of cash will *not* detect a theft of cash when the cash was stolen *before* being recorded in the client's books. If the auditor suspects that cash was stolen before being recorded in the client's books, the audit procedures discussed under the completeness objective for cash receipt transactions in Chapter 8 should be performed. Recall also this discussion in Chapter 8 regarding possible concerns about *lapping*.

Tests for Kiting   When cash has been stolen by an employee, it is possible to cover the cash shortage by following a practice known as *kiting*. This involves an employee covering the cash shortage by transferring money from one bank account to another and recording the transactions improperly on the client's books. Concealing the cash shortage can be accomplished by preparing a cheque on one account before year-end but not recording it as a cash disbursement in the account until the next period. The cheque is deposited in a second account before year-end and recorded as a cash receipt in the current period. The deposit must occur close enough to year-end that it will not clear the first bank account before the end of the year.

One approach that auditors commonly use to test for kiting is the preparation of an *interbank transfer schedule* such as the one shown in Exhibit 14–4. This exhibit provides six examples of the types of cash transfers an auditor might encounter. For example, transfer 2 is an example of

EXHIBIT 14–4

Example of an Interbank Transfer Schedule

Transfer Number*	Amount	Account 1 Disbursement Dates		Account 2 Receipt and Deposit Dates	
		Per Client Books	Per Bank Statement	Per Client Books	Per Bank Statement
1	$15,000	12/28	12/30	12/28	12/29
2	7,500	12/30	1/2	12/30	12/31
3	8,400	12/31	1/2	12/31	1/2
4	10,000	1/2	1/2	12/30	12/31
5	3,000	1/3	1/3	1/3	12/30
6	17,300	1/2	1/4	1/2	1/2

*Explanation for each transfer in determining proper cash cutoff at 12/31/04:
1. The transfer was made on December 28 and recorded on the books as both a receipt and a disbursement on the same date. The cheque written was deposited on December 28 in the receiving bank account and credited on the bank statement the next day. The cheque cleared account 1 on December 30. All dates are in the same accounting period, so there are no questions as to the propriety of the cutoff.
2. This transfer is proper. However, the transfer cheque should appear as an *outstanding cheque* on the reconciliation of account 1.
3. Transfer 3 is also proper. In this example, the transfer should appear as a *deposit in transit* on the reconciliation of account 2 and as an outstanding cheque on the reconciliation of account 1.
4. This transfer could represent kiting because the receipt was recorded on the books in the period prior to that in which the corresponding disbursement was recorded. Cash is overstated by $10,000.
5. Transfer 5 is improper. In this case a deposit was made in the receiving bank in one period without the receipt being made in the books until the subsequent period. Unless this matter is explained on the reconciliation for the receiving bank, the transfer could have been made to temporarily cover a shortage in that account. While the shortage will become apparent in the accounts as soon as the transfer is recorded in the following period, it will be covered by an unrecorded deposit on the balance sheet date.
6. This transfer is proper.

a proper cash transfer. A cheque was drawn on account 1 and recorded as a cash disbursement on December 30. It was recorded as a cash receipt in account 2 on December 30 and deposited in that account on December 31. The cheque cleared account 1 on January 2. The auditor would examine this transfer by tracing the cheque to the cash disbursements journal, the cash receipts journal, and the December 31 bank reconciliation. Because the cheque cleared the bank on January 2, it should be listed as an outstanding cheque on the December 31 bank reconciliation for account 1. You will also notice that transfers 1, 3, and 6 are proper transfers.

Transfer 4 could represent an example of kiting. A cheque was written on account 1 before year-end, but the disbursement was not recorded in the disbursements journal until after year-end (January 2). The cheque was deposited in account 2 and recorded as a cash receipt before year-end. Thus, the cash shortage in account 2 is covered by a cash deposit from account 1, and cash is overstated by $10,000. In this case the appropriate audit adjusting entry would be to credit cash for $10,000 and debit payable for $10,000. If the auditor found what appeared to be evidence of kiting, such as that above, he or she would scrutinize more carefully the propriety of cash transactions. Transfer 5 could represent a different type of impropriety that would also require additional work on the part of the auditor to determine where the unreceipted $3,000 went to (see 5 on Exhibit 14–4).

In some instances an interbank transfer schedule is used even though control procedures are adequate and no fraud is suspected. When a client maintains many cash accounts, cash transfers may be inadvertently mishandled. The use of an interbank transfer schedule provides the auditor with evidence on the proper cutoff for cash transactions.

Auditing a Payroll or Branch Imprest Account

The audit of any imprest cash account such as payroll or a branch account follows the same basic audit steps discussed under the audit of the general cash account. The auditor obtains a bank reconciliation, along with a standard bank confirmation and a cutoff bank statement. However, the audit testing is less extensive for two reasons. First, the imprest balance in the account is generally not material. An imprest payroll or branch account may contain a balance of only $1,000. Second, the types of disbursements from the account are homogeneous. The cheques are for similar types of transactions and for relatively small amounts. For example, there may be a limit on the size of an individual payroll cheque.

Auditing a Petty Cash Fund

Most entities maintain a petty cash fund for paying certain types of expenses or transactions. Although the size of the fund is usually not material, there is a potential for defalcation because a client's employee may be able to process numerous fraudulent transactions through the fund over the course of a year. The auditor will document the internal control procedures over the petty cash fund in order to ensure proper control over petty cash transactions. Auditors seldom perform detailed substantive testing of the petty cash fund, except when fraud is suspected.

Control Procedures   A petty cash fund should be maintained on an imprest basis by an *independent* custodian. While it is preferable for the custodian not to be involved in any cash functions, this is not possible for many clients. When the petty cash custodian does have other cash-related functions to perform, another supervisory person such as the controller should review the petty cash activity.

Prenumbered petty cash vouchers should be used for withdrawing cash from the fund, and a limit should be placed on the size of reimbursements made from petty cash. Periodically, the petty cash fund is reimbursed from the general cash account for the amount of the vouchers in the fund. Accounts payable clerks should review the vouchers for propriety before replenishing the petty cash fund. Finally, someone independent of the cash functions should conduct surprise counts of the petty cash fund.

Audit Tests   The first step is for the auditor to gain an understanding of the client's control procedures over petty cash. The adequacy of the client's control procedures determines the nature and extent of the auditor's work. The audit of petty cash focuses on both the transactions processed through the fund during the period and the balance in the fund. The auditor may select a sample of petty cash reimbursements and examine the propriety of the items paid for by the fund. This may be done as part of the auditor's tests of controls or substantive tests of transactions for the cash disbursement functions. The auditor tests the balance in the petty cash fund by counting it. When the count is conducted, the total of cash in the fund plus the vouchers should equal the imprest balance. This count may be done at an interim date or at year-end.

Disclosure Issues for Cash

The auditor must consider a number of important financial statement disclosures when auditing cash. Some of the more common disclosure issues are shown in Table 14–3. Table 14–3 identifies restriction on cash such as sinking fund requirements as a disclosure item—a special case of restriction on cash balances may exist in not-for-profit or charitable organizations where certain funds have restrictions placed upon their use. The auditor's review of the minutes of board of directors' meetings, line-of-credit arrangements, loan agreements, and similar documents is the primary source of the information for the financial statement disclosures. In addition, the auditor typically confirms items such as compensating balances required under a bank line of credit.

Table 14–3	Sample Disclosure Items for Cash

- Accounting policy for defining cash and cash equivalents.
- Any restrictions on cash such as a sinking fund requirement for funds allocated by the entity's board of directors for special purposes.
- Contractual obligations to maintain compensating balances.
- Cash balances restricted by foreign exchange controls.
- Letters of credit.
- Restriction on the use of specific funds of cash in not-for-profit organizations.

Exhibit 14–5 illustrates a letter for confirmation of compensating balances, while Exhibit 14–6 presents an example of footnote disclosures for compensating balances.

Investments

The *CICA Handbook* contains a number of sections that provide guidance on how to account for investments in certain debt and equity securities. Such investments might include equity securities such as common and preferred stock, debt securities such as notes and bonds, and hybrid securities such as convertible bonds and shares.

EXHIBIT 14–5

Illustrative Letter for Confirmation of Compensating Balances

CALABRO DIGITAL SERVICES

December 31, 2006

Mr. Frank Lorchian
National Bank
Winnipeg, Manitoba R3T 2T2

Dear Mr. Lorchian:

In connection with an audit of the financial statements of Calabro Digital Services as of December 31, 2006, and for the year then ended, we have advised our independent auditors that as of the close of business on December 31, 2006, there were compensating balance arrangements as described in our agreement dated June 30, 2001. Withdrawal by Calabro Digital Services of the compensating balance was not legally restricted as of December 31, 2006. The terms of the compensating balance arrangements at December 31, 2006, were:

The company has been expected to maintain a compensating balance, as determined from your bank's ledger records without adjustment for estimated average uncollected funds, of 15 percent of its outstanding loans plus 10 percent of its unused line of credit.

The company was in compliance with, and there have been no changes in, the compensating balance arrangements during the year ended December 31, 2006, and subsequently through the date of this letter.

During the year ended December 31, 2006, and subsequently through the date of this letter, no compensating balances were maintained by the company at your bank on behalf of an affiliate, director, officer, or any other third party, and no third party maintained compensating balances at the bank on behalf of the company.

Please confirm whether the information about compensating balances presented above is correct by signing below and returning this letter directly to our independent auditors, Abbott & Johnson, LLP. P.O. Box 125, Winnipeg, Manitoba R5R 1S7.

Sincerely,

Calabro Digital Services

BY: _____
          Jan Rodriguez, Controller

Dear Abbott & Johnson, LLP:

The above information regarding the compensating balance arrangement with this bank agrees with the records of this bank.

BY: _____ Vice President   Date: _____

EXHIBIT 14–6

> **Sample Disclosure of Compensating Balances**
>
> *Lines of Credit:*
> On December 31, 2001, the company established a line of credit with a bank that provides for unsecured borrowings of $7,000,000 at the bank's prime rate (7 percent at December 31, 2006). At December 31, 2006 and 2005, $200,000 and $800,000, respectively, had been borrowed under this arrangement. Under the credit arrangement, the company is expected to maintain compensating balances equal to 5 percent of the borrowings in excess of $500,000. This requirement is generally met through normal operating cash balances, which are not restricted as to withdrawal.

Additional details are provided below as they relate to relevant assertion but in general terms, the auditor's consideration of investments is no different than for any other financial statement account. That is, the auditor must be assured that the amounts shown on the balance sheet for the various types of investments are not materially misstated. This includes the proper recognition of interest income, dividends, and changes in value that must be included in the financial statements.

The auditor's approach to the audit of investments varies depending on the size of the investment and the amount of investment activity. For an entity that has a large investment portfolio, the auditor is likely to follow a reliance strategy in which internal control is formally evaluated and tests of controls are performed in order to assess the control risk below the maximum. However, for the vast majority of entities, it is more efficient for the auditor to follow a substantive strategy and perform a detailed audit of the investment securities at year-end.

Control Risk Assessment—Investments

LO 7⟩ The discussion of investments that follows focuses on the general types of control procedures that should be present to minimize the likelihood of a material misstatement. Even when a substantive strategy is followed, the auditor must reasonably understand internal control over investments in order to anticipate the types of misstatements that may occur and plan the substantive tests. The main internal control objectives that concern the auditor are validity, authorization, completeness, valuation, and classification. Proper segregation of duties is important in ensuring the propriety of investments and will be discussed briefly.

Assertions and
Related Control
Procedures

Following are some of the more common controls that should be present for each of the important control objectives for investments.

Occurrence   Controls must ensure that the purchase or sale of any investment is properly initiated by authorized individuals. First, the client should have adequate documents to verify that a particular purchase or sale of a security was properly initiated and approved. The presence of adequate documentation allows the auditor to determine the validity of the transaction. Second, the commitment of resources to investment activities should be approved by the board of directors or by an executive who has been delegated this authority. An entity engaging in recurring investment activities should have both general and specific control procedures. The board of directors should establish general policies to guide the entity's investment activities, while the specific procedures for the purchase and sale of securities may be delegated to an individual executive, investment committee, or outside investment advisers. If the client has proper control procedures for initiating and authorizing securities transactions, it is generally easy for the auditor to verify security transactions at the end of the period.

Completeness   The client should maintain adequate controls to ensure that all securities transactions are recorded. One control procedure for handling the detailed securities transactions is maintenance of a securities ledger that records all securities owned by the client. This subsidiary ledger should be reconciled to the general ledger control account regularly. Personnel responsible for investment activities should periodically review the securities owned to ensure that all dividends and interest have been received and recorded in the entity's records.

Accuracy and Classification   Companies are becoming involved in more and more sophisticated forms of financial transactions and instruments. Two sections of the *CICA Handbook*, sections 3855 and 3862, address the measurement and valuation issues surrounding these transactions and instruments. For the most part, this material involves issues beyond the scope of this text. However, the sections address valuation and classification issues related to investment securities that have readily determinable fair values. *CICA Handbook*, section 3855, identifies three types of investments in financial instruments. The standard requires that these investments be accounted for as follows:

- Debt securities that the entity has the positive intent and ability to hold to maturity are classified as *held-to-maturity securities* and reported at amortized cost.
- Debt and equity securities that are bought and held principally for the purpose of selling them in the near term are classified as *held-for-trading* or *trading securities* and reported at fair value, with unrealized gains and losses included in earnings.
- Debt or equity securities not classified as either held-to-maturity or trading securities are classified as *available-for-sale securities* and are reported at fair value, with unrealized gains and losses excluded from earnings and reported in a separate component of shareholders' equity called "other comprehensive income."

The client's controls should ensure that securities are properly classified and that appropriate prices are used to accurately value investments for financial statement.

One final issue related to the control risk for investments is that the client should have adequate custodial procedures to safeguard against theft. When securities are held by the client, they should be stored in a safe or safe-deposit box. Procedures should provide for periodic inspections by an individual independent of both the custodial and accounting responsibilities for securities. If an independent custodian such as a broker maintains securities, the client needs to establish procedures for authorizing the transfer of securities. One approach would require dual authorization by appropriate management personnel.

Segregation of Duties

LO 8>

Only entities that engage in a significant number of investment activities are likely to have adequate segregation of duties. Table 14–4 contains some key segregation of duties for investments and examples of possible errors or fraud that can result from conflicts in duties.

Substantive Tests of Investments

LO 9>

As discussed earlier, it is generally more efficient to follow a substantive strategy for auditing investments. When the control risk is set at the maximum, the auditor conducts extensive substantive tests to reach the planned level of detection risk. Additionally, because of the nature of the audit work, substantive tests of transactions are seldom used as a source of evidence.

Table 14–4	Key Segregation of Duties and Possible Errors or Fraud—Investments

Segregation of Duties	Possible Errors or Fraud Resulting from Conflicts of Duties
The initiation function should be segregated from the final approval function.	If one individual is responsible for both the initiating and approving of securities transactions, fictitious transactions can be made or securities can be stolen.
The valuation-monitoring function should be segregated from the acquisition function.	If one individual is responsible for both acquiring and monitoring the valuation of securities, securities values can be improperly recorded or not reported to management.
Responsibility for maintaining the securities ledger should be separate from that of making entries in the general ledger.	If one individual is responsible for both the securities ledger and the general ledger entries, that individual can conceal any defalcation that would normally be detected by reconciliation of subsidiary records with general ledger control accounts.
Responsibility for custody of the securities should be separate from that of accounting for the securities.	If one individual has access both to securities and to the supporting accounting records, a theft of the securities can be concealed.

Analytical procedures such as the following can test the overall reasonableness of investments:

- comparison of the balances in the current year's investment accounts with prior years' balances after consideration of the effects of current-year operating and financing activities on cash and investments
- comparison of current-year interest and dividend income with the reported income for prior years and with the expected return on investments

Table 14–5 summarizes the tests of investment account balances for the relevant assertions. The discussion of the investment account tests focuses on the more important assertions. The procedures shown for the other audit objectives should be familiar to you.

Existence

The auditor may perform one or more of the following audit procedures when gathering evidence for validity:

- physical examination
- confirmation with the issuer
- confirmation with the custodian
- confirmation of unsettled transactions with the broker-dealer
- confirmation with the counterparty
- reading executed partnership or similar agreements

If the client maintains custody of the securities, the auditor normally examines the securities. During the physical count, the auditor should note the name of the client, interest rates or dividend payment rates, and other relevant information about the various securities. When the securities are held by an issuer or a custodian such as a broker or investment adviser, the auditor gathers sufficient, appropriate evidence for the validity objective by confirming the existence of the securities. The information contained in the confirmation needs to be reconciled with the client's investment records.

Valuation and Allocation

When securities are initially purchased, they are recorded at their acquisition cost. The auditor can verify the purchase price of a security by examining a broker's advice or similar document. Debt securities that are to be held to maturity should be valued at their amortized cost. The auditor should have verified the purchase price of the debt at the time of purchase, and the effective interest rate should be used to recognize the interest income, which the auditor can recompute. The fair value of most equity securities is available from securities exchanges registered with the appropriate Securities Commission or on the over-the-counter market. The auditor can verify these values by tracing them to sources such as brokers, *The Financial Post*, *The Wall Street Journal*, or other reliable financial literature.

The auditor must also determine if there has been any permanent decline in the value of an investment security. *CICA Handbook,*

Table 14–5	**Examples of Tests of Transactions and Account Balances and Disclosures-Investments**

Assertions about Account Balances at Period End	Test of Details of Account Balances
Existence	Inspect securities if maintained by client or obtain confirmation from independent custodian.
Rights and obligations	Examine brokers' advices for a sample of securities purchased during the year.
Completeness	Search for purchases of securities by examining transactions for a few days after year-end.
	Confirm securities held by independent custodian.
	Review and test securities information to determine if all interest and dividend income has been recorded.
Valuation and allocation	Review brokers' invoices for cost basis of securities purchased.
	Determine basis for valuing investments by tracing values to published quotations or marketable securities.
	Determine whether there has been any permanent impairment in the value of the cost basis of an individual security.
	Examine sales of securities to ensure proper recognition of realized gains or losses.
	Obtain a listing of investments by category (held-to-maturity, trading, and available-for-sale); foot listing and agree totals to securities register and general ledger.

Assertions about Presentation and Disclosure	Tests of Details of Disclosures
Occurrence, and rights and obligations	Determine whether any securities have been pledged as collateral by (1) asking management and (2) reviewing board of directors' minutes, loan agreements, and other documents.
Completeness	Determine that all required disclosures have been made for investments (both debt and equity securities).
	Complete financial reporting checklist to ensure all financial statement disclosures related to investments are made.
Classification and understandability	Review and enquire of management of proper classification of investments.
	Read footnotes to ensure that required disclosures are understandable.
Accuracy and valuation	Read footnotes and other information to ensure that the information is accurate and properly presented at the appropriate amounts.

paragraph 3051.20 and the appendix to section 3855, provide guidance for determining whether a decline in value is other than temporary. The following factors are cited as indicating other-than-temporary impairment of the investment:

- Fair value is significantly below cost.
- The decline in fair value is attributable to specific adverse conditions affecting a particular investment.
- The decline in fair value is attributable to specific conditions, such as conditions in an industry or in a geographic area.
- Management does not possess both the intent and the ability to hold the investment long enough to allow for any anticipated recovery in fair value.

- The decline in fair value has existed for an extended period.
- A debt security has been downgraded by a rating agency.
- The financial condition of the issuer has deteriorated.
- Dividends have been reduced or eliminated, or scheduled interest payments on debt securities have not been made.

If the investment value is determined to be permanently impaired, the security should be written down and a new carrying amount established. The auditor should review the client's determination and calculation of the appropriate carrying value of investments. Last, the auditor should examine the sale of any security to ensure that proper values were used to record the sale and any realized gain or loss.

Classification

Marketable securities need to be properly classified as held for trading or available-for-sale because both the balance sheet and income statement are affected by misclassification. Held for trading securities are reported as current assets. Individual available-for-sale securities should be classified as current or noncurrent assets based on whether management expects to convert them to cash within the next 12 months. If the security is expected to be converted to cash within 12 months, it should be classified as a current asset. The auditor should ask management about its plans for disposing of securities.

With respect to debt expected to be held to maturity, the auditor should evaluate management's intent and the entity's ability to hold the debt security to maturity. In evaluating management's intent, the auditor should consider whether investment activities corroborate or conflict with management's stated intent. The auditor should examine evidence such as written and approved records of investment strategies, records of investment activities, instructions to portfolio managers, and minutes of meetings of the board of directors or the investment committee. In evaluating an entity's ability to hold a debt security to maturity, the auditor should consider factors such as the entity's financial position, working capital needs, operating results, debt agreements, guarantees, and other relevant contractual obligations, as well as laws and regulations. The auditor should also consider operating and cash flow projections or forecasts when considering the entity's ability to hold the debt security to maturity.

The proper classification of investments as held-for-trading versus available-for-sale is important because of the different treatment of gains and losses on these two types of investments. Unrealized gains and losses on held-for-trading securities are included in the determination of net income and unrealized gains and losses on available-for-sale securities are part of comprehensive income but not net income. Thus there is potential for earnings management by classifying investments as a particular type. The auditor should review management's classifications to ensure that they are consistent with the facts and the nature of the investments.

REVIEW QUESTIONS

LO 1> **14-1** What types of items are included under the caption "cash and cash equivalents" in the financial statements?

2> **14-2** Briefly describe each type of bank account. How does an imprest account help to improve control over cash?

3> **14-3** Why are analytical procedures of limited use in the audit of the cash balance?

1> **14-4** How do the client's control procedures over cash receipts and disbursements affect the nature and extent of the auditor's substantive tests of cash balances?

4,5> **14-5** A bank reconciliation provides the auditor with evidence on which audit objectives?

4,5> **14-6** Explain why the standard bank confirmation form may *not* identify all information about a client's bank accounts or loans.

4,5> **14-7** Why does an auditor obtain a cutoff bank statement when auditing a bank account? What information is examined on the cancelled cheques returned with the cutoff bank statement?

5> **14-8** Briefly describe how a bank reconciliation is audited.

6> **14-9** List three fraud-related audit procedures for cash.

6> **14-10** What are the primary purposes of a proof of cash?

6> **14-11** What approach is used by the auditor to test for kiting?

4> **14-12** Identify the control procedures that should be present for petty cash. What audit procedures are normally conducted on petty cash?

7,8> **14-13** What are the main transaction-related assertions for investments? Identify the key segregation of investment-related duties and possible errors or fraud that can occur if this segregation is not present.

9> **14-14** Briefly describe the valuation issues related to investments in debt and equity securities.

9> **14-15** What two classification issues are important for the audit of investments?

MULTIPLE-CHOICE QUESTIONS FROM PROFESSIONAL EXAMINATIONS

Unless otherwise indicated, these multiple-choice questions were adapted from the CPA examinations, courtesy of the American Institute of Certified Public Accountants.

5> **14-16** An auditor ordinarily sends a standard confirmation request to all banks with which the client has done business during the year under audit, regardless of the year-end balance. A purpose of this procedure is to

a. Provide the data necessary to prepare a proof of cash.

b. Request that a cutoff bank statement and related cheques be sent to the auditor.

c. Detect kiting activities that may otherwise *not* be discovered.

d. Seek information about loans from the banks.

4> **14-17** When counting cash on hand, the auditor must exercise control over all cash and other negotiable assets to prevent

a. Theft.

b. Irregular endorsement.

c. Substitution.

d. Deposits in transit.

Questions 14–18 and 14–19 relate to the following bank transfer schedule.

MILES COMPANY
Bank Transfer Schedule
December 31, 2006

| Cheque Number | Bank Account | | Amount | Date Disbursed per | | Date Deposited per | |
	From	To		Books	Bank	Books	Bank
2020	First National	Suburban	$32,000	12/31	1/5◆	12/31	1/3▲
2021	First National	Capital	21,000	12/31	1/4◆	12/31	1/3▲
3217	Second State	Suburban	6,700	1/3	1/5	1/3	1/6
0659	Midtown	Suburban	5,500	12/30	1/5◆	12/30	1/3▲

4,6> **14-18** The tick mark ◆ most likely indicates that the amount was traced to the

a. December cash disbursements journal.

b. Outstanding cheque list of the applicable bank reconciliation.

c. January cash disbursements journal.

d. Year-end bank confirmations.

4,6> **14-19** The tick mark ▲ most likely indicates that the amount was traced to the

a. Deposits in transit of the applicable bank reconciliation.

b. December cash receipts journal.

c. January cash receipts journal.

d. Year-end bank confirmations.

5> **14-20** The primary evidence regarding year-end bank balances is documented in the

a. Standard bank confirmations.

b. Outstanding cheque listing.

c. Interbank transfer schedule.

d. Bank deposit lead schedule.

5> **14-21** On receiving the cutoff bank statement, the auditor should trace

a. Deposits in transit on the year-end bank reconciliation to deposits in the cash receipts journal.

b. Cheques dated before year-end to outstanding cheques listed on the year-end bank reconciliation.

c. Deposits listed on the cutoff statement to deposits in the cash receipts journal.

d. Cheques dated after year-end to outstanding cheques listed on the year-end bank reconciliation.

7,8> **14-22** Which of the following controls would most effectively ensure that the proper custody of assets in the investing process is maintained?

a. Direct access to securities in the safe-deposit box is limited to one corporate officer.

b. Personnel who post investment transactions to the general ledger are *not* permitted to update the investment subsidiary ledger.

c. Purchase and sale of investments are executed on the specific authorization of the board of directors.

d. The recorded balances in the investment subsidiary ledger are periodically compared with the contents of the safe-deposit box by independent personnel.

9> **14-23** To establish the existence and rights of an investment in the common shares of a publicly traded company, an auditor ordinarily performs a security count or

a. Relies on the client's internal controls if the auditor has reasonable assurance that the control procedures are being applied as prescribed.

b. Confirms the number of shares owned that are held by an independent custodian.

c. Determines the market price per share at the balance sheet date from published quotations.

d. Confirms the number of shares owned with the issuing company.

9> **14-24** An auditor testing investments would ordinarily use analytical procedures to ascertain the reasonableness of the

a. Existence of unrealized gains or losses in the portfolio.

b. Completeness of recorded investment income.

c. Classification between current and noncurrent portfolios.

d. Valuation of marketable equity securities.

4,6> **14-25** Which of the following cash transfers results in a misstatement of cash at December 31, 2006?

Bank Transfer Schedule

| | Disbursement | | Receipt | |
| | Recorded in Books | Paid by Bank | Recorded in Books | Received by Bank |
Transfer				
a.	12/31/06	1/4/07	12/31/06	12/31/06
b.	1/4/07	1/5/07	12/31/06	1/4/07
c.	12/31/06	1/5/07	12/31/06	1/4/07
d.	1/4/07	1/11/07	1/4/07	1/4/07

9> **14-26** An auditor would most likely verify the interest earned on bond investments by

a. Vouching the receipt and deposit of interest cheques.

b. Confirming the bond interest rate with the issuer of the bonds.

c. Recomputing the interest earned on the basis of face amount, interest rate, and period held.

d. Testing the internal controls over cash receipts.

9> **14-27** Which of the following is the most effective audit procedure for verifying dividends earned on investments in equity securities?

a. Trace deposits of dividend cheques to the cash receipts book.

b. Reconcile amounts received with published dividend records.

c. Compare the amounts received with prior-year dividends received.

d. Recompute selected extensions and footings of dividend schedules and compare totals to the general ledger.

PROBLEMS

4,6> **14-28** Sevcik Company's auditor received, directly from the banks, confirmations and cutoff statements with related cheques and deposit tickets for Sevcik's three general-purpose bank accounts. The auditor determined that the internal controls over cash are satisfactory and can be relied upon. The proper cutoff of external cash receipts and disbursements was established. No bank accounts were opened or closed during the year.

Required:

Prepare the audit program of substantive procedures to verify Sevcik's bank balances. Ignore any other cash accounts.

(AICPA, adapted)

7,8> **14-29** Cassandra Corporation, a manufacturing company, periodically invests large sums in investment (debt and equity) securities. The investment policy is established by the investment committee of the board of directors, and the treasurer is responsible for carrying out the investment committee's directives. All securities are stored in a bank safe-deposit vault.

The auditor's internal control questionnaire with respect to Cassandra's investments in debt and equity securities contains the following three questions:

- Is investment policy established by the investment committee of the board of directors?

- Is the treasurer solely responsible for carrying out the investment committee's directives?

- Are all securities stored in a bank safe-deposit vault?

Required:

In addition to these three questions, what questions should the auditor's internal control questionnaire include with respect to the company's investments in debt and equity securities?

(AICPA, adapted)

9> **14-30**   Rosalee Phung has been engaged to audit the financial statements of Vernon Distributors, a continuing audit client, for the year ended September 30. After obtaining an understanding of Vernon's internal control system, Phung assessed control risk at the maximum level for all financial statement assertions concerning investments. Phung determined that Vernon is unable to exercise significant influence over any investee and none are related parties. Phung obtained from Vernon detailed analyses of its investments in domestic securities showing

- A description of each security, including the interest rate and maturity date of bonds and the par value and dividend rate of stocks.

- A notation of the location of each security, either in the treasurer's safe or held by an independent custodian.

- The number of shares of stock or face value of bonds held at the beginning and end of the year.

- The beginning and ending balances at cost and at market, and the unamortized premium or discount on bonds.

- Additions to and sales from the portfolios for the year, including date, number of shares, face value of bonds, cost, proceeds, and realized gain or loss.

- Valuation allowances at the beginning and end of the year and changes therein.

- Accrued investment income for each investment at the beginning and end of the year, and income earned and collected during the year.

Phung then prepared the following partial audit program of substantive audit procedures:

1. Foot and crossfoot the analyses.
2. Trace the September 30 balances to the general ledger and financial statements.
3. Trace the beginning balances to the prior year's working papers.
4. Obtain positive confirmation of the investments held by any independent custodian as of the balance sheet date.
5. Determine that income from investments has been properly recorded as accrued or collected by reference to published sources, by computation, and by tracing to recorded amounts.

6. For investments in nonpublic entities, compare carrying value to information in the most recently available audited financial statements.

7. Determine that any other-than-temporary decline in the price of an investment has been properly recorded.

Required:

a. For procedures 4 to 7, identify the primary financial statement assertion relative to investments that would be addressed by each procedure and describe the primary audit objective of performing that procedure. Use the following format:

Primary Assertion	Objective

b. Describe three additional substantive auditing procedures Phung should consider in auditing Vernon's investments.

(AICPA, adapted)

5> **14-31** The client-prepared bank reconciliation on the following page is being examined by Zachary Kallick during the examination of the financial statements of Simmons Company.

Required:

Items (a) through (f) represent items an auditor would ordinarily find on a client-prepared bank reconciliation. The following list of audit procedures shows substantive auditing procedures. For each item, select one or more procedures, as indicated, that the auditor most likely would perform to gather evidence in support of that item. (The procedures on the list may be selected once, more than once, or not at all.)

Assume that

- The client prepared the bank reconciliation on 10/2/06.
- The bank reconciliation is mathematically accurate.
- The auditor received a cutoff bank statement dated 10/7/06 directly from the bank on 10/11/06.
- The 9/30/06 deposit in transit, outstanding cheques 1281, 1285, 1289, and 1292, and the correction of the error regarding cheque 1282 appear on the cutoff bank statement.
- The auditor assessed control risk concerning the financial statement assertions related to cash at the maximum.

Audit Procedure

1. Trace to cash receipts journal.
2. Trace to cash disbursements journal.
3. Compare to 9/30/06 general ledger.

SIMMONS COMPANY
Bank Reconciliation
Bank of Montreal Bank Account
September 30, 2006

Procedure(s)

a. Select 2 procedures	Balance per bank		$28,375	4,9
b. Select 5 procedures	Deposits in transit:			
	9/29/06	$4,500		⑨ 10,1,7,8+
	9/30/06	1,525	6,025	2,8
			$34,400	✓ ✓ ✓ ✓ ✓
				7,8,9,10,2
c. Select 5 procedures	Outstanding cheques:			
	988 8/31/06	2,200		
	1281 9/26/06	675		
	1285 9/27/06	850		
	1289 9/29/06	2,500		
	1292 9/30/06	7,225	(13,450)	
			$20,950	5
d. Select 1 procedure	Customer note collected by bank		(3,000)	5,9
e. Select 2 procedures	Error:			
	Cheque 1282, written on 9/26/06 for			
	$270, was erroneously charged by bank			
	as $720; bank was notified on 10/2/06.		450	
f. Select 1 procedure	Balance per books		$18,400	3

4. Directly confirm with bank.
5. Inspect bank credit memo.
6. Inspect bank debit memo.
7. Ascertain reason for unusual delay.
8. Inspect supporting documents for reconciling item not appearing on cutoff statement.
9. Trace items on bank reconciliation to cutoff statement.
10. Trace items on the cutoff statement to bank reconciliation.

(AICPA, adapted)

9 ▷ **14-32** To support financial statement assertions, the auditor designs substantive tests to obtain evidence to support or repute each assertion.

Required:

Items (a) through (c) in the table below represent assertions for investments. Select the most appropriate audit procedure from the following list and enter the number in the appropriate place on the grid. (An audit procedure may be selected once or not at all.)

Audit Procedure

1. Trace opening balances in the subsidiary ledgers to the prior year's audit working papers.
2. Determine that employees who are authorized to sell investments do not have access to cash.
3. Examine supporting documents for a sample of investment transactions to verify that prenumbered documents are used.
4. Determine that any impairments in the price of investments have been properly recorded.
5. Verify that transfers from the current to the investment portfolio have been properly recorded.
6. Obtain positive confirmations as of the balance sheet date of investments held by independent custodians.
7. Trace investment transactions to minutes of board of directors' meetings to determine that transactions were properly authorized.

(AICPA, adapted)

Assertion	Audit Procedure
a. Verify that investments are properly described and classified in the financial statements.	
b. Verify that recorded investments represent investments actually owned at the balance sheet date.	
c. Verify that investments are properly valued at the lower of cost or market at the balance sheet date.	

9> **14-33** Ron Geller who is auditing the financial statements of Bass Corporation for the year ended December 31 is about to commence an audit of the company's investment securities. Bass's records indicate that the company owns various bearer bonds that will be held to maturity, as well as 25 percent of the outstanding common stock of Commercial Industrial, Corp. Geller is satisfied with evidence that supports the presumption of significant influence over Commercial Industrial, Corp. The various securities are at two locations, as follows:

- Recently acquired securities are in the company's safe in the custody of the treasurer.
- All other securities are in a safe-deposit box in the company's bank.

All of the securities in Bass's portfolio are actively traded in a broad market.

Required:

a. Assuming that the internal control system over securities is satisfactory and may be relied upon, what are the objectives of examining these investment securities?

b. What audit procedures should Geller undertake with respect to examining Bass's noncurrent investment securities?

(AICPA, adapted)

5,6   **14-34**   You are the senior staff member on the audit of Roe Co. Ltd. (RCL). The accounting supervisor at RCL is concerned about the lack of control over cash transactions and is worried that the cashier has embezzled funds. She has provided you with the following information about the company's cash position as at October 31, 2006:

Cash balance per books	$18,901.62
	(including undeposited receipts)
Cash balance per bank	$15,550.00

Reconciling items:

Outstanding cheques:	
No. 162	$116.25
No. 183	150.00
No. 284	253.25
No. 8621	190.71
No. 8623	206.80
No. 8632	145.28
Unrecorded bank credit	100.00

In fact, the cashier had diverted all undeposited receipts in excess of $3,794.41 and prepared the following reconciliation:

Balance per books, October 31, 2006		$18,901.62
Add: Outstanding cheques		
No. 8621	$190.71	
No. 8623	206.80	
No. 8632	145.28	442.79
		19,344.41
Less: Undeposited receipts		3,794.41
Balance per bank, October 31, 2006		$15,550.00
Less: Unrecorded bank credit		100.00
True cash balance, October 31, 2006		$15,450.00

Required:

a. Prepare a schedule showing how much the cashier embezzled.

b. How did the cashier attempt to conceal his theft?

c. Based on the above description, identify two internal control features that were apparently missing.

(AICPA, adapted)

6   **14-35**   You are a junior staff member on the audit of Arcan Ltd. for the year ended December 31, 2006, and you have been assigned to audit the client's year-end bank reconciliation, as shown:

Bank Reconciliation

December 31, 2006

Balance per books, December 31, 2006		$17,174.86
Reconciling items		
Add:		
Cash collections received and recorded		
December 31 but not deposited		2,662.25
Debit memo for returned customer		
unpaid cheque (cheque is on hand but		
not entered into books)		5.50
		$20,142.61
Deduct:		
Outstanding cheques		
(see listing below)	$2,267.75	
Credit memo for proceeds of a note		
receivable left at the bank for		
collection but not recorded as collected	400.00	
Cheque No. 688 recorded on books		
as $240.90 but issued and paid by		
bank as $419.00	178.10	2,945.85
Computed balance		$17,196.76
Unreconciled difference		200.00
Balance per bank (agreed to bank confirmation)		$16,996.76

Outstanding Cheques

As at December 31, 2006

No.	Amount
573	$ 67.27
724	9.90
903	456.67
907	305.50
911	482.75
913	550.00
914	366.76
916	10.00
917	218.90
	$2,267.75

Required:

Prepare a corrected reconciliation and show the appropriate journal entries to correct items that should be adjusted prior to closing the books.

DISCUSSION CASE

7,8>   **14-36**   Derivatives are financial instruments that derive their value from some underlying asset or liability, such as a currency or a debt security. Chambord Plastics Limited (CPL) has recently been active in the derivatives market—both as speculative investments and as a way of hedging some of their exposure due to foreign currency business transactions.

CPL's audit committee has engaged your firm, Lawson, Mawson & Co., to provide a report to the audit committee identifying weaknesses in, the management of, and internal controls over, derivative transactions. The report should also provide recommendations for improvements.

You have met with the treasurer and her staff and have prepared the following notes.

1. The treasurer and vice president of finance each report to CPL's president. The financial reporting department reports to the vice president of finance. The director of cash management and investments, with a staff of six people, manages derivatives operations. The director is primarily responsible for strategy and reports to the treasurer. Two members of the director's staff are traders who execute money-market (fixed income) and derivative transactions. Two other members of the director's staff are involved in accounting for these transactions, and the remaining two are involved in banking/cash management. One of the traders has considerable derivatives experience from a large bank. The second trader is an accountant who recently received a promotion to the trader position and is learning on the job. The director's unit is operated as a profit centre for performance-evaluation purposes.

2. CPL enters into derivative transactions with various financial institutions. Examples include the following:
   - Interest-rate swaps require that CPL exchange floating-rate interest payments for fixed-rate payments for a defined term. This turns the company's floating (variable) rate borrowing into fixed-rate borrowing. Typically a $\frac{1}{2}$ percent upfront fee is charged by the financial institution based on the principal amount of the swap.
   - Foreign-currency forward contracts require that CPL buy or sell foreign currency at specified rates and dates. These contracts are no-cost agreements that are used to hedge specified foreign-currency exposures resulting from foreign purchases and sales of goods.

- Loan-rate agreements (LRAs) commit CPL to lend or borrow funds, at a specified interest rate and term, at a future date. CPL enters into LRAs without incurring out-of-pocket costs. CPL uses these strictly to try to earn profits, rather than to hedge. Normally, CPL will not actually borrow or lend the money—the director has successfully predicted future market interest rates and closed out the LRAs at a profit, before maturity.

3. All the derivative instruments fluctuate in value continuously, based on market conditions. Market value information is easy to obtain. These derivative instruments can be closed out before maturity. For example, one of CPL's existing LRAs is in a profit position and could be closed out today by a payment of $1.34 million from the financial institution to CPL. Three months ago, however, this LRA would have cost CPL $845,000 to close out. This change is due to fluctuations in interest rates. The director reviews the market value of all instruments monthly. The director is looking into speculating in other new and "exotic" derivative instruments.

4. There are no existing company policies pertaining to derivatives. Therefore, the company applies three rules from its money-market investment policy to derivative transactions:

   - fixed-income instruments can be purchased only from major Canadian or international banks,
   - only the traders are allowed to transact on behalf of CPL, and
   - the maximum term to maturity is five years.

5. All derivative transactions are entered into on the telephone and are legally binding based on the oral agreement between CPL's trader and the bank's trader. The director has instructed the traders to enter into transactions only on his instructions, usually communicated orally. After a transaction is entered into, the trader writes up a document called a "ticket." The financial institution faxes confirmation of the deal to the trader within a day or two. The trader then agrees the details to the ticket, staples the two documents together, and forwards them to one of the director's accountants. The accountant, who sits beside the traders, files the ticket by maturity date. Where CPL must pay for the instrument the same day, a copy of the ticket is immediately sent to the director who authorizes a wire transfer of funds to the financial institution. The cost of the instruments that CPL pays for is entered into the general ledger.

6. The notional principal of the 84 LRA's derivative instruments outstanding at the most recent month end was $654 million. To close out CPL's derivative position, a cash payment by CPL of $21.2 million would be required.

Required:

Prepare the draft report.

(CICA, adapted)

INTERNET ASSIGNMENT

9> **14-37** Both Intel (www.intel.com) and Microsoft (www.microsoft.com) have large amounts of investment securities. Visit their websites and review their financial statements for information on how they account for investment securities and the amounts of those securities.

a. Provide the data necessary to prepare a proof of cash.

b. Request that a cutoff bank statement and related cheques be sent to the auditor.

c. Detect kiting activities that may otherwise *not* be discovered.

d. Seek information about loans from the banks.

Part VI   COMPLETING THE AUDIT AND REPORTING RESPONSIBILITIES

Completing the Engagement   < Chapter 15

Learning Objectives

Upon completion of this chapter, you will be able to

1 Identify the audit issues related to contingent liabilities.

2 Determine the audit procedures used to identify contingent liabilities.

3 Describe the audit issues related to an enquiry letter to the client's lawyers.

4 Explain why the auditor must be concerned with commitments.

5 List the types of subsequent events.

6 List the audit procedures used to identify subsequent events.

7 Describe the effect of subsequent events on the dating of the audit report.

8 Take the necessary audit steps for finalizing the audit.

9 Identify and assess entities with going-concern problems.

10 Describe the auditor's communication with the audit committee and management and the matters that should be addressed.

11 Explain the auditor's responsibility for subsequent discovery of facts existing at the date of the auditor's report.

RELEVANT ACCOUNTING AND ASSURANCE PRONOUNCEMENTS

***CICA Handbook*, section 1300,** Differential reporting

***CICA Handbook*, section 3290,** Contingencies

***CICA Handbook*, section 3820,** Subsequent events

***CICA Handbook*, section 5135,** Auditor's responsibility to consider fraud

***CICA Handbook*, section 5136,** Misstatements—Illegal acts

***CICA Handbook*, section 5143,** The auditor's procedures in response to assessed risks

***CICA Handbook*, section 5370,** Management representations

***CICA Handbook*, section 5400,** The auditor's standard report

***CICA Handbook*, section 5405,** Date of the auditor's report

***CICA Handbook*, section 5510,** Reservations in the auditor's report

***CICA Handbook*, section 5750,** Communication of matters identified during the financial statement audit

CICA Handbook, **section 5751,** Communications with those having oversight responsibility for the financial reporting process

CICA Handbook, **section 6550,** Subsequent events

CICA Handbook, **section 6560,** Communication with law firms regarding claims and possible claims

COMPLETING THE AUDIT OF EARTHWEAR

EarthWear As the audit of EarthWear's 2006 financial statements draws to a close, there are a number of audit steps that Willis & Adams must perform in completing the audit. One of the most important of those steps is the search for contingent liabilities. It is not uncommon for companies such as EarthWear to become involved in disputes with suppliers over things such as the quality or condition of the goods provided by those suppliers. Willis & Adams must ensure that adequate disclosure of any outstanding or pending litigation is made, according to the standards set out in the *CICA Handbook*. In order to do so, they will need to make enquiries of EarthWear's lawyers. Similarly, Willis & Adams must ensure that EarthWear discloses any future commitments. In EarthWear's case, dealing internationally as they do, this might be a commitment to purchase a particular line of products from a supplier at specified times and prices in the future. Although EarthWear's fiscal year-end is December 31, Willis & Adams must be aware of any events that occur subsequent to the fiscal year-end but before they issue their audit report. Such subsequent events may require actual adjustment of the financial statements for the year under audit, or, at the least, disclosure in the notes to the financial statements.

This chapter discusses the auditor's responsibilities and required audit procedures for the above-mentioned items and discusses the other steps the auditor should take as part of the finalization process, such as the search for unrecorded liabilities, the final evidence evaluation process, formal and informal communications with management, and communications with the audit committee of the board of directors of EarthWear.

Review for Contingent Liabilities

LO 1 A *contingent liability* is defined as an existing condition, situation, or set of circumstances involving uncertainty as to possible *loss* to an entity that will ultimately be resolved when some future event occurs or fails to occur. *CICA Handbook,* section 3290, "Contingencies," states that when a contingent liability exists, the likelihood that the future event will result in a loss or impairment of an asset or the incurrence of a liability can be classified into three categories:

1. *Likely.* The chance of occurrence (or non-occurrence) of the future event(s) is high;
2. *Unlikely.* The chance of occurrence (or non-occurrence) of the future event(s) is slight;
3. *Not determinable.* The chance of occurrence (or non-occurrence) of the future event(s) cannot be determined.

EXHIBIT 15–1

Example of Disclosure Note for a Contingency

On October 31, 2003, a class action complaint was filed by a shareholder against the company and certain of its officers and directors in the Supreme Court of British Columbia ("the court"). Shortly thereafter, other shareholders filed similar class action complaints. On February 1, 2004, a consolidated amended class action complaint against the company and certain of its officers and directors was filed in the court. In their consolidated complaint, the plaintiffs seek to represent a class consisting generally of persons who purchased or otherwise acquired the company's common stock in the period from March 5, 2003, through August 14, 2003. These actions claim damages related to alleged material misstatements and omissions of fact and manipulative and deceptive acts in violation of federal and provincial securities laws and common-law fraud. In December 2004 a motion filed by the plaintiffs to certify a class of purchasers of the company's common stock was approved with limited exceptions, and a class period for certain claims was established from March 5, 2003, to August 14, 2003. Also in December 2004, in response to a motion by the company and individual defendants, claims of common-law fraud, deceit, and negligence, misrepresentation, and certain of the violations of the federal and provincial securities laws against certain of the individual defendants were dismissed. At this time, it is not possible to predict the outcome of the pending lawsuit or the potential financial impact on the company of an adverse decision.

If the event is likely and the amount of the loss can be reasonably estimated, the loss is accrued by a charge to income. When the outcome of the event is judged to be likely but the amount cannot be estimated, a disclosure of the contingency is made in the notes to the financial statements. Exhibit 15–1 presents an example of such disclosure. Contingent losses whose likelihood of occurrence is not determinable should be disclosed in the financial statements.

Examples of contingent liabilities include

- pending or threatened litigation
- actual or possible claims and assessments
- income tax disputes
- product warranties or defects (over and above normal provisions)
- guarantees of obligations to others
- agreements to repurchase receivables that have been sold

Audit Procedures for Identifying Contingent Liabilities
LO 2 >

The auditor may identify contingent liabilities while conducting audit procedures directed at audit objectives related to specific accounting cycles or financial statement accounts. Examples of such audit procedures include

1. reading the minutes of meetings of the board of directors, committees of the board, and shareholders
2. reviewing contracts, loan agreements, leases, and correspondence from government agencies
3. reviewing income tax liability, tax returns, and other tax-related material
4. confirming or otherwise documenting guarantees and letters of credit obtained from financial institutions or other lending agencies
5. inspecting other documents for possible guarantees

For example, the auditor normally reads the minutes of the board of directors' meetings for identification and approval of major transactions. Normally, the board of directors would discuss any material uncertainty that might exist for the entity. Similarly, the auditor examines the entity's income tax expense and accrued liability. The audit procedures for this account include determining if the CRA has audited the entity's prior year's tax returns. If so, the auditor should examine the CRA agents' report for any additional taxes assessed and determine whether the entity will contest the additional assessment.

In addition, near the completion of the engagement the auditor conducts specific audit procedures to identify contingent liabilities. Such procedures include

1. Enquiry of and discussion with management about its policies and procedures for identifying, evaluating, and accounting for contingent liabilities. Management has the responsibility for establishing policies and procedures to identify, evaluate, and account for contingencies. Large entities may implement such policies and procedures within their internal control systems. The management of smaller entities, however, may rely on legal counsel and auditors to identify and account for contingencies.

2. Examining documents in the entity's records such as correspondence and invoices from lawyers for pending or threatened lawsuits. Chapter 13 presented an account analysis of legal expense. Even though the amount of the legal expense account may be immaterial, the auditor normally examines the transactions in the account. The purpose of this examination is to identify actual or potential litigation against the client. The account analysis can also be used to develop a list of lawyers who have been consulted by the entity.

3. Obtaining a legal letter that describes and evaluates any litigation, claims, or assessments. Legal letters are discussed in the next section.

4. Obtaining written representation from management that all claims and possible claims have been disclosed. This information is obtained in a representation letter furnished by the client.

Enquiry Letters

LO 3>

CICA Handbook section 6560 "Communication with law firms regarding claims and possible claims" states that a letter of audit enquiry (referred to as an *enquiry letter*) sent to the client's lawyers is the primary means of obtaining or corroborating information about litigation, claims, and estimates. Auditors typically analyze legal expense for the entire period and send an enquiry letter to each lawyer who has been consulted by management. Auditors should be particularly careful with letters sent to the entity's general counsel and lawyers specializing in patent law or securities laws because the general counsel should be aware of major litigation, and patent infringement and securities laws are major sources of litigation. Additionally, an enquiry letter should be obtained from the entity's in-house counsel if such a position exists. Table 15–1 provides examples of types of litigation that the auditor may encounter.

Table 15–1	**Examples of Types of Litigation**

- Breach of contract.
- Patent infringement.
- Product liability.
- Violations of government legislation, including
  - Securities laws.
  - Antidiscrimination statutes based on race, sex, age, and other characteristics.
  - Antitrust laws.
  - Income tax regulations.
  - Environmental protection laws.

The auditor should request the client management to send an enquiry letter to the lawyers. The letter would normally:

a. list all entities to which the enquiry related

b. request that the law firm respond as of a specific date

c. list outstanding claims and possible claims on which the law firm has represented or advised the client

d. describe the nature and current status of each claim and possible claim

e. indicate the client's evaluation of the likelihood of loss (or gain) and the estimated amount thereof for each claim and possible claim

And request that the law firm address a reply to the client with a signed copy to be sent directly to the auditor, stating:

a. whether the claims and possible claims are properly described

b. whether the client's evaluations are reasonable

c. the names of the parties and the amount claimed in respect of any claim which is omitted from the enquiry letter

🌐EarthWear   Exhibit 15–2 presents an example of an enquiry letter following the format identified in Appendix A of *CICA Handbook* section 6560, "Communication with law firms regarding claims and possible claims." The timing of the auditor's sending the letter of enquiry should be approximately coincident with the completion of field work on the audit. Lawyers are generally willing to provide evidence on actual or pending claims. However, they are sometimes reluctant to provide information on possible claims. A possible claim is one where the entity is aware of the potential for a claim to be made against it but the injured party or potential claimant has not yet indicated to the entity intent to do so. The following situation is an example of a possible claim. Suppose that one of the entity's manufacturing facilities is destroyed by fire and a number of people are killed. Suppose further that a subsequent investigation shows that the client had failed to install proper fire safety equipment. The entity's fiscal year may end and the financial statements for

EXHIBIT 15–2

Example of an Enquiry Letter

 **EARTHWEAR CLOTHIERS, INC.**

January 15, 2007

Leon, Leon & Dalton
958 – 77th Avenue S.W.
Calgary, Alberta T6N 1Q7

Dear Sirs:

In connection with the preparation and audit of our financial statements for the fiscal period ended December 31, 2006, we have made the following evaluations of claims and possible claims with respect to which your firm's advice or representation has been sought:

Description	Evaluation
United Garments vs. EarthWear Clothiers, nonpayment of debt in the amount of $26,000, trial date not set.	EarthWear Clothiers disputes this billing on the grounds that the quality of the shipment (waterproof jackets) was substandard, and expects to successfully defend this action.
Consolidated Knitting Co. vs. EarthWear Clothiers, damages for breach of contract arising from a decision not to purchase fleece vests from Consolidated Knitting Co.	It is probable that this action will be successfully defended.
Wilderness Outfitters Ltd. has a possible claim in connection with a shipment of backpacks sold to EarthWear Clothiers. EarthWear has not paid the invoice on the grounds that the dimensions of the backpacks are not to the specifications stated in the contract with Wilderness Outfitters.	No claim has yet been made, and we are unable to estimate possible ultimate loss.

Would you please advise us, as of February 15, 2007, on the following points:

    Are the claims and possible claims properly described?
    Do you consider that our evaluations are reasonable?
    Are you aware of any claims not listed above which are outstanding?

If so, please include in your response letter the names of the parties and the amount claimed.

    This enquiry is made in accordance with the Joint Policy Statement of January 1978 approved by the Canadian Bar Association and the Auditing Standards Committee of the Canadian Institute of Chartered Accountants.
    Please address your reply, marked "Privileged and Confidential," to this company and send a signed copy of the reply directly to our auditors, Willis & Adams, P.O. Box 4080, Calgary, Alberta T1T 2R2.

Yours truly,

Calvin J. Rogers
Chief Executive Officer
EarthWear Clothiers

cc. Willis & Adams

the period that includes the fire may be released. Although the families of the employees have not yet initiated or threatened litigation, a possible claim may exist at the financial statement date.

The Joint Policy Statement of the CICA and CBA does not require the lawyers, in their response, to identify any claims or possible claims not already identified in the enquiry letter to them. Section 6560 directs the auditor to obtain written representation from management that it has disclosed to the auditor all claims and possible claims. As a result, it is important for the auditor to be diligent in identifying all possible claims that should be included in the letter.

Lawyers may also be unable to respond to the outcome of a matter because, in their opinion, the factors in the case do not allow them to reasonably estimate the likelihood of the outcome or to estimate the possible loss. Finally, refusal to furnish information in an enquiry letter is a limitation on the scope of the audit sufficient to preclude an unqualified opinion.

Commitments

LO 4 Companies often enter long-term commitments to purchase raw materials or to sell their products at a fixed price. The main purpose of entering into such a purchase or sales contract is to obtain a favourable pricing arrangement or to secure the availability of raw materials. The auditor may identify or confirm the existence of long-term commitments through enquiry of client personnel during the audit of the revenue and purchasing processes. Such commitments are required to be disclosed in a footnote to the financial statements.

Review for Subsequent Events

LO 5 Sometimes events or transactions that occur after the balance sheet date but before the issuance of the financial statements and auditor's report materially affect the financial statements. These events or transactions are referred to as *subsequent events* and require adjustment or disclosure in the financial statements.

Two types of subsequent events require consideration by management and evaluation by the auditor:

1. Events that provide additional evidence about conditions that existed at the date of the balance sheet and affect the estimates that are part of the financial statement preparation process. Such events require adjustment of the financial statements

2. Events that provide evidence about conditions that did not exist at the date of the balance sheet but arose subsequent to that date. Such events may require financial statement disclosure. In some instances, where the effect of the event or transaction is so significant, pro forma financial statements may be required in order to prevent the financial statements from being misleading.

Examples of the first type of events or conditions are (1) an uncollectible account receivable resulting from continued deterioration of a customer's financial condition leading to bankruptcy after the balance sheet date or (2) the settlement of a lawsuit after the balance sheet date for an amount different from the amount recorded in the year-end financial statements. Note that in both of these examples, additional evidence became available before the financial statements were issued that shed light on estimates previously made in the financial statements. Subsequent events affecting the realization of assets or the settlement of estimated liabilities normally require adjustment of the financial statements.

Examples of the second type of events that result in disclosure include

- purchase or disposal of a business by the entity
- sale of share capital or a bond issue by the entity
- loss of the entity's manufacturing facility or assets resulting from a casualty such as a fire or flood
- losses on receivables caused by conditions such as a casualty arising subsequent to the balance sheet date

Figure 15–1 presents a diagram of the subsequent-events period for EarthWear. *CICA Handbook*, section 6550, "Subsequent events," indicates that the auditor's responsibility to actively search for subsequent events normally extends to the audit report date, which is usually the date of completion of the important auditing procedures at the client's premises. During this time frame, the auditor actively conducts audit procedures related to the current-year audit. The period from the date of the auditor's report to the actual issuance of the financial statements is also part of the subsequent-events period, but the auditor is not responsible for making any enquiries or conducting any audit procedures after the date of the audit report. However, subsequent

FIGURE 15–1

The Subsequent-Events Period for EarthWear Clothiers

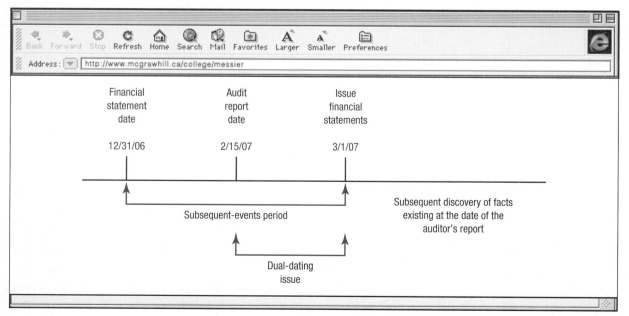

events may come to the auditor's attention during this period. If the subsequent event is of the first type, the financial statements should be adjusted. Depending on the event and its circumstances, additional disclosure may be made in the footnotes. When the subsequent event is of the second type, a footnote describing the event should be included with the financial statements.

Audit Procedures for Subsequent Events

LO 6

Some audit procedures for business processes and their related financial statement accounts are conducted before year-end, while others may be conducted during the subsequent-events period. Some of these audit procedures, such as testing proper sales and purchases cutoff, are applied to transactions after the balance sheet date. Such audit procedures may detect subsequent events. In addition, the auditor should conduct specific audit procedures for the period from the balance sheet date to the audit report date. Examples of audit procedures suggested in section 6550 include:

1. Reading any interim financial statements that are available for the period after year-end; they should be compared to the prior-period statements, and any unusual fluctuations should be investigated.
2. Examining the books of original entry (such as sales journal, purchases journal, cash receipts and cash disbursements journals, and general ledger) for the subsequent-events period and investigating any unusual transactions.
3. Asking management about the following matters: (a) whether there were or are any substantial contingent liabilities or commitments existing at the balance sheet date or at the date of enquiry; (b) whether there have been any significant changes in share capital, long-term debt, or working capital; (c) the current status of any items in the financial statements that were accounted for based on preliminary or inconclusive data; and (d) whether any unusual adjustments have been made during the subsequent-events period.
4. Reading the available minutes of meetings of shareholders, directors, or other committees for the subsequent-events period.
5. Enquiry of the client's lawyers regarding any claim or possible claims against the company.
6. Obtaining a representation letter from management.

Dual Dating

LO 7

When a subsequent event is recorded or disclosed in the financial statements after completion of the field work but before the issuance of the financial statements, the auditor must consider the dating of the auditor's report. For example, suppose that EarthWear notified Willis & Adams that the company had entered an agreement to purchase another catalogue retailer company on March 1, 2007. Such an event is not indicative of conditions that existed at the balance sheet date and therefore would require only disclosure in the footnotes to the December 31, 2006, financial statements. Two methods are available for dating the audit report: Willis & Adams may (1) "dual date" the report, using wording such as

"February 15, 2007, except for Note 10, as to which the date is March 1, 2007," or (2) use the date of the subsequent event. Dual dating is intended to limit the auditor's responsibility for events occurring subsequent to the completion of field work to the specific subsequent event referred to in the footnote. If the audit report is dated using only the March 1, 2007, date, the auditor's responsibility extends to that date. In this example, Willis & Adams's report would most likely be dual dated.

Figure 15–1 also includes the time period after the financial statements have been issued. This time period is discussed later in the chapter.

Finalizing the Audit

LO 8> In addition to the review for contingencies, the review for subsequent events, and the consideration of going-concern issues, the auditor conducts a number of audit steps before deciding on the appropriate audit report to issue for the entity. These include the following:

- performance of final analytical procedures
- obtaining a representation letter
- review of working papers
- final assessment of audit results
- evaluation of financial statement presentation and disclosure
- obtaining an independent review of the engagement

Analysis

CICA Handbook, section 5301, "Analysis," recommends that the auditor perform analytical procedures at the final review stage of the audit. The objective of conducting analytical procedures near the end of the engagement is to help the auditor assess the conclusions reached on the financial statement components and evaluate the overall financial statement presentation. These final analytical procedures may include recalculating some of the ratios discussed in Chapter 5 for planning the audit. However, more frequently, they involve reviewing the adequacy of the evidence gathered in response to unexpected fluctuations in the account balances identified during the planning of the audit and identifying any unusual or unexpected balances not previously considered. These final analytical procedures may indicate that more evidence is needed for certain account balances.

When the auditor performs analytical procedures at the final stage, it is a good time to consider the overall reasonableness of the financial statement amounts. In doing this analysis, the auditor should consider the critical issues and significant industry business risks and whether such risks might impact the financial statements. The auditor should also assess the structure and profitability of the industry and how the client fits within the industry in terms of its profitability and solvency. In other words, the auditor should consider whether the financial statement amounts make sense given the auditor's knowledge of the client's business risks.

Representation Letter

During the course of the audit, management makes a number of representations to the auditor as part of the enquiries made to obtain sufficient competent evidence. *CICA Handbook*, section 5730, "Management

Representations," requires the auditor to obtain written representations from management. As well, such written representation is recommended in other sections of the *Handbook* (e.g., section 5136, "Misstatements—illegal acts" and section 6010, "Audit of related party transactions"). In practice, most audit firms request written representations from management on an extensive list of topics. The purpose of this letter is to corroborate oral representations made to the auditor and to document the continued appropriateness of such representations. The representation letter also reduces the possibility of misunderstanding concerning the responses provided by management to the auditor's enquiries.

Exhibit 15–3 presents an example of a representation letter. Note the important types of information that management is asked to represent. The representation letter should be addressed to the auditor and generally given the same date as the auditor's report. Normally, the chief executive officer and chief financial officer sign the representation letter. Management's refusal to provide a representation letter results in a scope limitation that is sufficient to preclude an unqualified opinion and is ordinarily sufficient to cause an auditor to disclaim an opinion or withdraw from the engagement. In such cases, the auditor should also consider management's refusal when assessing whether he or she can rely on other management representations.

Working Paper Review

All audit work should be reviewed by an audit team member senior to the person preparing the working papers.[1] Thus, the senior-in-charge should conduct a detailed review of the working papers prepared by the staff and follow up on any unresolved problems or issues. In turn, the manager should review all working papers, although the extent of the manager's review may vary with how much the manager relies on the senior-in-charge. The engagement partner normally reviews working papers related to critical audit areas as well as working papers prepared by the manager. In reviewing the working papers, the reviewers must ensure that the working papers document that the audit was properly planned and supervised, that the evidence supports the audit objectives tested, and that the evidence is sufficient for the type of audit report issued.

Evaluating Audit Results

In conjunction with the review of the working papers, the auditor must evaluate the results of the audit tests. This evaluation is concerned with two issues: (1) the sufficiency of the audit evidence and (2) the effects of detected misstatements in the financial statements. In evaluating the audit evidence, the auditor determines whether there is sufficient evidence to support each relevant audit objective. This evaluation considers evidence obtained to support the assessment of inherent and control risk, as well as the evidence gathered to reach the planned level of detection risk (substantive tests of transactions, analytical procedures, and tests of account balances). If this evaluation indicates that the evidence is not sufficient to meet the planned level of audit risk, the auditor may need to gather additional evidence. For example, if the final analytical procedures

---

[1]See J. S. Rich, I. Solomon, and K. T. Trotman, "Multi-Auditor Judgment/Decision Making Research; A Decade Later," *Journal of Accounting Literature* Vol. 14 (1997), pp. 86–126, for a discussion of practice and research on the audit review process.

EXHIBIT 15–3

Example of a Representation Letter

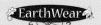 **EARTHWEAR CLOTHIERS, INC.**

March 5, 2007

Willis & Adams
P.O. Box 4080
Calgary, Alberta T1T 2R2

Gentlemen:

We are providing this letter in connection with your audit(s) of the consolidated balance sheets of EarthWear Clothiers as of December 31, 2006 and 2005, and the related consolidated statements of operations, shareholders' equity, and cash flows for the years then ended for the purpose of expressing an opinion as to whether the consolidated financial statements present fairly, in all material respects, the financial position, results of operations, and cash flows of EarthWear Clothiers in conformity with generally accepted accounting principles. We confirm that we are responsible for the fair presentation in the consolidated financial statements of financial position, results of operations, and cash flows in conformity with generally accepted accounting principles.

Certain representations in this letter are described as being limited to matters that are material. Items are considered material, regardless of size, if they involve an omission or misstatement of accounting information that, in the light of surrounding circumstances, makes it probable that the judgement of a reasonable person relying on the information would be changed or influenced by the omission or misstatement.

We confirm, to the best of our knowledge and belief, as of February 15, 2007, the following representations made to you during your audit(s).

1. The financial statements referred to above are fairly presented in conformity with generally accepted accounting principles.
2. We have made available to you all
    a. Financial records and related data.
    b. Minutes of the meetings of shareholders, directors, and committees of directors, or summaries of actions of recent meetings for which minutes have not yet been prepared.
3. There have been no communications from regulatory agencies concerning noncompliance with or deficiencies in financial reporting practices.
4. There are no material transactions that have not been properly recorded in the accounting records underlying the financial statements.
5. There has been no
    a. Fraud involving management or employees who have significant roles in internal control.
    b. Fraud involving others that could have a material effect on the financial statements.
6. The company has no plans or intentions that may materially affect the carrying value or classification of assets and liabilities.
7. The following have been properly recorded or disclosed in the financial statements:
    a. Related-party transactions, including sales, purchases, loans, transfers, leasing arrangements, and guarantees, and amounts receivable from or payable to related parties.
    b. Guarantees, whether written or oral, under which the company is contingently liable.
8. There are no
    a. Violations or possible violations of laws or regulations whose effects should be considered for disclosure in the financial statements or as a basis for recording a loss contingency.
    b. Possible claims that our lawyer has advised us may be brought against us and should be disclosed according to generally accepted accounting principles.
    c. Other liabilities or gain or loss contingencies that should be accrued or disclosed.

(*continued*)

EXHIBIT   15–3 (concluded)

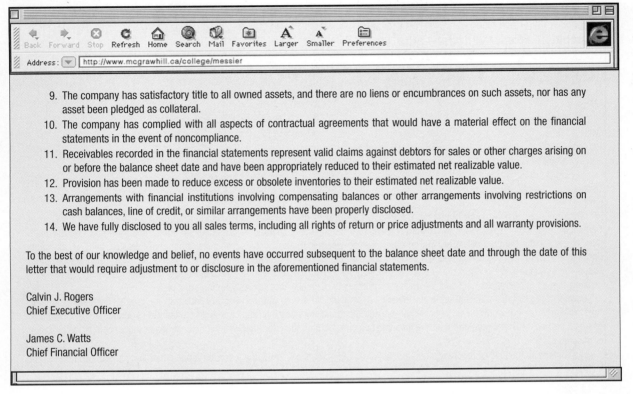

9. The company has satisfactory title to all owned assets, and there are no liens or encumbrances on such assets, nor has any asset been pledged as collateral.

10. The company has complied with all aspects of contractual agreements that would have a material effect on the financial statements in the event of noncompliance.

11. Receivables recorded in the financial statements represent valid claims against debtors for sales or other charges arising on or before the balance sheet date and have been appropriately reduced to their estimated net realizable value.

12. Provision has been made to reduce excess or obsolete inventories to their estimated net realizable value.

13. Arrangements with financial institutions involving compensating balances or other arrangements involving restrictions on cash balances, line of credit, or similar arrangements have been properly disclosed.

14. We have fully disclosed to you all sales terms, including all rights of return or price adjustments and all warranty provisions.

To the best of our knowledge and belief, no events have occurred subsequent to the balance sheet date and through the date of this letter that would require adjustment to or disclosure in the aforementioned financial statements.

Calvin J. Rogers
Chief Executive Officer

James C. Watts
Chief Financial Officer

indicate that inventory may still contain material misstatements, the auditor should further test the inventory account balance.

Any misstatements detected during the audit process must be considered in terms of their effects on the financial statements. In particular, the auditor must estimate the likely misstatements compared to materiality. (*Likely misstatements* include both known and projected misstatements.) The auditor should also consider the effects of unadjusted misstatements on aggregated components of the financial statements such as assets, liabilities, equity, revenues, and expenses.

Even if the misstatements are not material, either individually or in aggregate, it is common practice for the auditor to give those adjustments to the client in order to correct the books. However, the auditor would not require those adjustments to be booked.

When assessing the materiality of this year's misstatements, it is important for the auditor to consider the effect of any unadjusted misstatements from prior years' audits. The cumulative effect may be to push the misstatements over the materiality limit. Similarly, it is important for the auditor to remember to carry any unadjusted misstatements from this year forward to the ensuing years.

Evaluating Financial Statement Presentation and Disclosure

The auditor reviews the final draft of the financial statements, including footnotes, to ensure compliance with GAAP, proper presentation of accounts, and inclusion of all necessary disclosures. Most public accounting firms use some type of financial statement checklist to assist the auditor in this process.

Final disposition of any adjustments to the financial statements that the auditor feels are necessary, and the final form of the auditor's report, are discussed at a finalization meeting between the auditor and the entity's senior management. If the auditor has identified that no adjustments are required to the financial statements and that note disclosure is adequate, finalization can be quite expedient. However, if the auditor has identified adjustments, management of the entity may not wish to make some or all of the adjustments that the auditor wishes the entity to book, nor make the additional disclosures that the auditor feels are necessary. In that case, the finalization meeting may involve intense negotiations between the entity's management and the auditor to resolve the issues. The negotiation may ultimately be resolved with an outcome somewhere between the two positions, as long as that resolution satisfies the auditor's requirement that the resulting financial statements present fairly according to generally accepted accounting principles, the financial position, and the results of operations of the entity for the year under audit.

Independent Partner Review

A standard component of public accounting firms' quality control policies (quality control is discussed in more detail in the next chapter) is the requirement for a review by a second partner who is independent of the engagement.[2] The second partner, who is not associated with the details of the engagement, will review and assess the audit approach, findings, and conclusions for critical audit areas and should review the audit report, financial statements, and footnotes for consistency.

Going-Concern Considerations

LO 9> The auditor has a responsibility to evaluate whether there is substantial doubt about an entity's ability to continue as a going-concern for the foreseeable future, usually considered to be one year beyond the date of the financial statements being audited. While this assessment is made during the planning of the engagement, the auditor should also consider this issue near the end of the engagement.

Steps in the Going-Concern Evaluation

The auditor should follow three overall steps in making the going-concern evaluation:

1. Consider whether the results of audit procedures performed during the planning, performance, and completion of the audit indicate whether there is substantial doubt about the entity's ability to continue as a going concern for a reasonable period of time (one year).
2. If there is substantial doubt, the auditor should obtain information about management's plans to mitigate the going-concern problem and assess the likelihood that such plans can be implemented.

---

[2]See K. Epps and W. F. Messier, Jr., "Concurring Partner Review: An Examination of Audit Firm Practices," Working Paper, Georgia State University, 2002.

Table 15–2	**Normal Audit Procedures That May Identify Conditions Indicating Going-Concern Problems**

- Analysis.
- Review of subsequent events.
- Tests of compliance with debt agreements.
- Reading of board of directors and other committee minutes.
- Enquiry of the entity's lawyers.
- Confirmations with parties on arrangements to provide or maintain financial support.

3. If the auditor concludes, after evaluating management's plans, that there is substantial doubt about the ability of the entity to continue as a going concern, he or she should consider the adequacy of the disclosures about the entity's ability to continue and include an explanatory paragraph in the audit report.

CICA Handbook, section 5510, "Reservations in the auditor's report," identifies conditions, which, singly or in combination, could cast doubt on the entity's ability to continue as a going-concern. They include:

a. recurring operating losses
b. serious deficiencies in working capital
c. inability to obtain financing sufficient for continued operations
d. inability to comply with terms of existing loan agreements
e. the possibility of an adverse outcome of one or more contingencies
f. insufficient funds to meet liabilities
g. a plan to significantly curtail or liquidate operations
h. external factors which could force an otherwise solvent enterprise to cease operations

The auditor should evaluate the existence of any of these conditions and assess the implication of their existence for the ability of the entity to continue as a going-concern. Table 15–2 identifies some of the procedures that the auditor may use. As well as the audit procedures identified in Table 15–2, an additional approach for the auditor to employ in assessing the likelihood of bankruptcy is to use Altman's Z-Score Bankruptcy Model. This is a statistical model that uses a weighted combination of a number of financial statement ratios such as return on total assets, sales to total assets, debt to equity, working capital to total assets, and retained earnings to total assets.[3]

In light of the assessment, the auditor's responsibility is to review and evaluate the accounting treatment, disclosure, and statement presentation by the entity. The auditor should be satisfied that the information

---

[3]For further explanation of this model, see E. I. Altman, *The Z-Score Bankruptcy Model: Past, Present, and Future* (New York: John Wiley & Sons, 1977); and E.I. Altman, *Corporate Financial Distress and Bankruptcy* (New York: John Wiley & Sons, 1993).

EXHIBIT 15–4

Example of Note Disclosure for Going-Concern

Furthermore, if the company is not successful in its efforts to restructure, it is uncertain whether the company will be able to address its principal payments, which are presently scheduled in November 2003 and in February 2004. If the company is unsuccessful in restructuring its senior unsecured debt with its bankers and medium-term notes holders, there may be uncertainty as to the appropriateness of the going-concern assumption.

If the going-concern assumption was not appropriate for these financial statements, then adjustments would be necessary in the carrying value of assets and liabilities, the reported net loss, and the balance sheet classifications used.

Source: 2002 Annual Report of the Saskatchewan Wheat Pool.

explicitly draws the reader's attention to the possibility that the entity may not be able to continue as a going-concern. As an example of note disclosure in such circumstances, Exhibit 15–4 reproduces an excerpt from Note 2, "Accounting Policies and Basis of Presentation," from the 2002 financial statements of the Saskatchewan Wheat Pool.

Communications with the Audit Committee and Management

LO 10> The *CICA Handbook* discusses in several sections the auditor's responsibility to communicate certain matters related to the conduct of the audit to those individuals responsible for oversight of the financial reporting process. In particular, section 5135, "The auditor's responsibility to consider fraud," indicates that the auditor should inform the appropriate level of management, usually senior executive management and the audit committee of the board of directors, of any identified fraud or any evidence that indicates fraud may exist, whether or not it results in a material misstatement of the financial statements. Additionally, the audit committee of the board of directors should be informed of misstatements identified by the auditor that were determined by management to be not material to the financial statements, either individually, or in the aggregate.

Section 5136, "Misstatements—illegal acts," requires the auditor to communicate information about any disclosed illegal acts to the audit committee, or equivalent, on a timely basis. It may be appropriate to communicate with management, depending on the origin and nature of the illegal acts.

CICA Handbook, section 5750, "Communication with management of matters identified during the financial statement audit," establishes the requirement for formal communication between the auditor and management of the entity. Such communication may take place during, or after, the audit examination. It is characterized as a "derivative" of the audit process and is not intended for use by a third party. Section 5750 is intended to provide a framework for the communication of matters identified in other *Handbook* sections such as sections 5135, 5136, and 5210, "The auditor's procedures in response to assessed risks." Two specific examples of matters identified by section 5750 that may be contained in such a communication are:

a. Significant weakness in internal control that facilitated an ongoing employee fraud. Early communication of this weakness provides management with the opportunity to address the control deficiency immediately.

b. An illegal act, early communication of which may provide management with the opportunity to address the issue and avoid a penalty.

CICA Handbook, section 5751, "Communications with those having oversight responsibility for the financial reporting process," deals with communications between the auditor and the members of the audit committee of the board of directors, or equivalent individuals, depending on the organizational structure of the entity. As is the case with section 5750, some of the matters identified in section 5751 arise from other assurance standards concerning communication with the audit committee both during, and after, completion of the audit. Section 5751 also recommends that the auditor should communicate, prior to the completion of the audit, such things as:

- the audit and non-audit services that the auditor is providing to the entity and its related entities
- the level of responsibility assumed by the auditor under generally accepted auditing standards
- a summary of the audit approach.

In addition, section 5751 directs the auditor to communicate with the responsible individuals, at the conclusion of the audit, a number of other matters of importance, including:

- disagreements with management about matters that could be significant to the financial statements or auditor's report
- serious difficulties encountered while performing the audit, including significant delays in management providing required information
- any matters that have a significant effect on the qualitative aspects of the accounting principles used in the entity's financial statements
- any other matters arising from the audit that, in the judgement of the auditor, are important and relevant to the audit committee, including matters previously agreed with the audit committee to be communicated.

Consistent with the emphasis on independence, the auditor is also required by section 5751 to communicate at least annually with the audit committee. The communication should include:

- confirmation of the auditor's independence
- disclosure of all direct and indirect relationships between the auditor and the entity
- if the entity is publicly accountable, disclosure of the total fees charged for audit and non-audit services provided by the auditor to the entity during the last year.

This communication should be in writing and a copy of the communication should be included in the working papers. The report should indicate that it is intended solely for the use of the audit committee, the board of directors, and, if applicable, management.

Additionally, the auditor normally prepares a *management letter*. The general intent of a management letter is to make recommendations to the client based on observations during the audit; the letter may include areas such as organizational structure and efficiency issues. During the audit, the audit team members should be alert for opportunities to assist the client. Any areas recommended for improvement should be documented in the working papers. Generally, the management letter is addressed to the chief executive officer or chief financial officer. During the audit of the financial statements of EarthWear Clothiers, the auditors noticed two problems, one with the recordkeeping for defective merchandise that EarthWear returned to suppliers for repair or replacement, and another with the procedures in place for updating the allowance for doubtful accounts. An example of a management letter bringing these observations to the attention of the senior management of EarthWear is shown in Exhibit 15–5.

Subsequent Discovery of Facts Existing at the Date of the Auditor's Report

LO 11 ⟩ An auditor does not have any obligation to make any enquiries or conduct any audit procedures after the financial statements and audit report have been issued. However, facts may come to the auditor's attention after the issuance of the financial statements that might have affected the report had he or she known about them. In Figure 15–1, this would be events occurring after March 1, 2007. *CICA Handbook,* section 5405, "Date of the auditor's report," provides guidance for the auditor in those circumstances. While a number of situations may apply, the most common situation is where the previously issued financial statements contain material misstatements due to either unintentional or intentional actions by management. For example, the auditor may find out that a material amount of inventory was not included in the financial statements because of a computer error. Alternatively, the auditor may learn that management inflated inventory quantities and prices in an effort to increase reported profits. A number of such situations have arisen in recent years (see Exhibit 15–6). Events that occur after the issuance of the auditor's report, such as final settlements of litigation or additional information on accounting estimates becoming available, do not apply to this auditing standard.

When facts are encountered that may affect the auditor's previously issued report, the auditor should determine whether the facts are reliable and whether they existed at the date of the audit report. The auditor should discuss the matter with an appropriate level of management and request cooperation in investigating the potential misstatement.

If the auditor determines that the previously issued financial statements are in error and the audit report is affected, he or she should request that the client issue an immediate revision to the financial statements and auditor's report. The reasons for the revisions should be described in the footnotes to the revised financial statements. If the effect on the financial statements cannot immediately be determined, the client should notify persons known to be relying on the financial statements and auditor's report. If the shares are publicly traded or subject to regulatory jurisdiction, the client should contact the appropriate regulatory agencies.

EXHIBIT 15–5

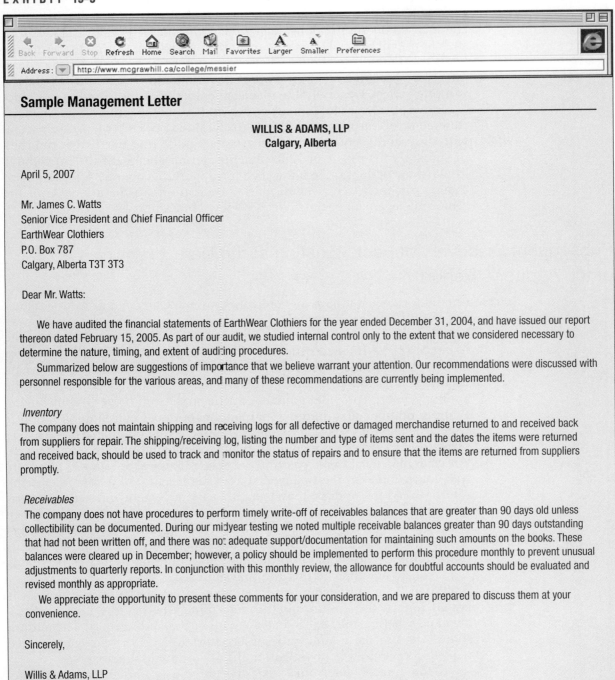

Sample Management Letter

WILLIS & ADAMS, LLP
Calgary, Alberta

April 5, 2007

Mr. James C. Watts
Senior Vice President and Chief Financial Officer
EarthWear Clothiers
P.O. Box 787
Calgary, Alberta T3T 3T3

Dear Mr. Watts:

We have audited the financial statements of EarthWear Clothiers for the year ended December 31, 2004, and have issued our report thereon dated February 15, 2005. As part of our audit, we studied internal control only to the extent that we considered necessary to determine the nature, timing, and extent of auditing procedures.

Summarized below are suggestions of importance that we believe warrant your attention. Our recommendations were discussed with personnel responsible for the various areas, and many of these recommendations are currently being implemented.

Inventory
The company does not maintain shipping and receiving logs for all defective or damaged merchandise returned to and received back from suppliers for repair. The shipping/receiving log, listing the number and type of items sent and the dates the items were returned and received back, should be used to track and monitor the status of repairs and to ensure that the items are returned from suppliers promptly.

Receivables
The company does not have procedures to perform timely write-off of receivables balances that are greater than 90 days old unless collectibility can be documented. During our midyear testing we noted multiple receivable balances greater than 90 days outstanding that had not been written off, and there was not adequate support/documentation for maintaining such amounts on the books. These balances were cleared up in December; however, a policy should be implemented to perform this procedure monthly to prevent unusual adjustments to quarterly reports. In conjunction with this monthly review, the allowance for doubtful accounts should be evaluated and revised monthly as appropriate.

We appreciate the opportunity to present these comments for your consideration, and we are prepared to discuss them at your convenience.

Sincerely,

Willis & Adams, LLP

If the client refuses to cooperate and make the necessary disclosures, the auditor should notify the board of directors and take the following steps, if possible:

EXHIBIT 15–6

> ## Rite Aid Restates Earnings after Seven-Month Investigation
>
> Rite Aid Corporation is the No. 3 drugstore chain, with approximately 77,000 full- and part-time associates serving customers in 30 states and the District of Columbia. Rite Aid currently operates more than 3,600 stores with reported total sales of $14.491 billion at the end of its 2001 fiscal year. In 2000, after a seven-month investigation that involved the assistance of two accounting firms and cost $50 million, the company restated its profit for the prior two years by $1.1 billion. It reduced its 1999 net income by $566.2 million and its 1998 net income by $492.1 million. The restatement was the result of management actions ranging from manipulating costs to hiding depreciation expenses. The company reached a settlement with shareholders for $200 million.
>
> *Sources:* D. Spurgeon and M. Maremont, "Rite Aid Posts Fiscal '00 Loss of $1.1 Billion," *The Wall Street Journal* (July 12, 2000), pp. A3, A6; M. Maremont, "Lawsuit Details Rite Aid's Accounting Woes," *The Wall Street Journal* (February 8, 2001), pp. C1, C14.

1. Notify the client that the auditor's report must no longer be associated with the financial statements.
2. Notify any regulatory agencies having jurisdiction over the client that the auditor's report can no longer be relied upon.
3. Seek legal advice regarding what actions are necessary to discharge his or her legal obligations to the client, and consider resigning from the engagement.

The practical outcome of these procedures is that the auditor has withdrawn his or her report on the previously issued financial statements. In notifying the client, regulatory agencies, and other persons relying on the auditor's report, the auditor should disclose the effect the information would have had on the auditor's report had it been known to the auditor.

REVIEW QUESTIONS

LO 1   **15-1**   Define what is meant by *contingent liability*. What three categories are used to classify a contingent liability? Give four examples of a contingent liability.

3   **15-2**   What information does the auditor ask the lawyer to provide on pending or threatened litigation? What is meant by a possible claim, and why are lawyers reluctant to provide information on possible claims in the enquiry letter?

4   **15-3**   Provide two examples of commitments. What is the appropriate treatment of a commitment in the financial statements?

5   **15-4**   What are the two types of subsequent events, and how is each type accounted for in the financial statements? Give two examples of each type.

5,7 >   **15-5**   Under what circumstances would the auditor dual date an audit report?

8 >   **15-6**   Are any analytical procedures required as part of the final overall review of the financial statements? What is the purpose of such analytical procedures?

8 >   **15-7**   Why does the auditor obtain a representation letter from management?

8 >   **15-8**   Describe the purposes of the independent partner review.

10 >   **15-9**   What items should be included in the auditor's communication with an audit committee or similar group?

11 >   **15-10**   What types of events would generally require revision of the issued financial statements? What procedures should the auditor follow when the client refuses to cooperate and make the necessary disclosures?

MULTIPLE-CHOICE QUESTIONS FROM PROFESSIONAL EXAMINATIONS

Unless otherwise indicated, these multiple-choice questions were adapted from the CPA examinations, courtesy of the American Institute of Certified Public Accountants.

3 >   **15-11**   An auditor should request that an audit client send a letter of enquiry to those lawyers who have been consulted concerning litigation, claims, or possible claims. The primary reason for this request is to provide

a. The opinion of a specialist as to whether loss contingencies are likely, unlikely, or not determinable.

b. A description of litigation, claims, and possible claims that have a reasonable possibility of unfavourable outcome.

c. An objective appraisal of management's policies and procedures adopted for identifying and evaluating legal matters.

d. Corroboration of the information furnished by management concerning litigation, claims, and possible claims.

1,2 >   **15-12**   An auditor would be most likely to identify a contingent liability by obtaining a(n)

a. Accounts payable confirmation.

b. Transfer agent confirmation.

c. Standard bank confirmation.

d. Related-party transaction confirmation.

6 >   **15-13**   Which of the following procedures would an auditor most likely perform to obtain evidence about the occurrence of subsequent events?

a. Recompute a sample of large-dollar transactions occurring after year-end for arithmetic accuracy.

b. Investigate changes in shareholders' equity occurring after year-end.

c. Enquire of the entity's lawyer concerning litigation, claims, and possible claims arising after year-end.

d. Confirm bank accounts established after year-end.

7> **15-14** An auditor issued an audit report that was dual dated for a subsequent event occurring after the completion of field work but before issuance of the auditor's report. The auditor's responsibility for events occurring subsequent to the completion of field work was

   a. Extended to subsequent events occurring through the date of issuance of the report.

   b. Extended to include all events occurring since the completion of field work.

   c. Limited to the specific event referenced.

   d. Limited to events occurring up to the date of the last subsequent event referenced.

9> **15-15** Analytical procedures used in the overall review stage of an audit generally include

   a. Considering unusual or unexpected amount balances that were *not* previously identified.

   b. Testing transactions to corroborate management's financial statement assertions.

   c. Gathering evidence concerning account balances that have *not* changed from the prior year.

   d. Retesting control procedures that appeared to be ineffective during the assessment of control risk.

11> **15-16** After issuing a report, an auditor has *no* obligation to make continuing enquiries or perform other procedures concerning the audited financial statements, unless

   a. Information that existed at the report date and may affect the report comes to the auditor's attention.

   b. The management of the entity requests the auditor to reissue the auditor's report.

   c. Information about an event that occurred after the end of field work comes to the auditor's attention.

   d. Final determinations or resolutions are made of contingencies that were disclosed in the financial statements.

8> **15-17** To which of the following matters would an auditor *not* apply materiality limits when obtaining specific written client representations?

   a. Disclosure of compensating balance arrangements involving restrictions on cash balances.

   b. Information concerning related-party transactions and related amounts receivable or payable.

   c. The absence of errors and unrecorded transactions in the financial statements.

   d. Fraud involving employees with significant roles in the internal control system.

8> **15-18** Which of the following matters is an auditor required to communicate to an entity's audit committee?

	Significant Audit Adjustments	Changes in Significant Accounting Policies
a.	Yes	Yes
b.	Yes	No
c.	No	Yes
d.	No	No

9>   **15-19**   Which of the following audit procedures is most likely to assist an auditor in identifying conditions and events that may indicate substantial doubt about an entity's ability to continue as a going-concern?

a. Review compliance with the terms of debt agreements.

b. Confirm accounts receivable from principal customers.

c. Reconcile interest expense with outstanding debt.

d. Confirm bank balances.

11>   **15-20**   Which of the following events occurring after the issuance of an auditor's report would be most likely to cause the auditor to make further enquiries about the previously issued financial statements?

a. A technological development that could affect the entity's future ability to continue as a going-concern.

b. The discovery of information regarding a contingency that existed before the financial statements were issued.

c. The entity's sale of a subsidiary that accounts for 30 percent of the entity's consolidated sales.

d. The final resolution of a lawsuit explained in a separate paragraph of the auditor's report.

PROBLEMS

1,2,3>   **15-21**   During an audit engagement, Ben Harper has satisfactorily completed an examination of accounts payable and other liabilities and now plans to determine whether there are any loss contingencies arising from litigation, claims, or possible claims.

Required:

What audit procedures should Harper follow with respect to the existence of loss contingencies arising from litigation, claims, and possible claims? Do *not* discuss reporting requirements.

(AICPA, adapted)

3>   **15-22**   Disposal Company (Disposal) is a privately owned company that collects garbage and disposes it at land fill sites. Peterson & Co. have been their auditors for several years and you are the senior in charge of the 2006 audit. Disposal's year-end is October 31, 2006.

While planning the audit you discover that Disposal has decided to diversify its operations and has developed a waste gasification system that uses chemicals and heat to gasify garbage. Through discussions with the controller you learn that Waste Company (Waste) has recently commenced a $1 million lawsuit against Disposal for using the gasification process Waste has patented.

The controller assures you that their claim is without merit as the processes used by the two companies are somewhat different.

Due to the complication of the legal action, the controller asks you to draft the legal enquiry letter to Disposal's lawyer, Smith & Co.

Subsequent to December 7, 2006, the final day of the audit fieldwork, you are discussing the finalization of the financial statements with the controller and he informs you that the legal action with Waste is not going as planned and there will likely be a material contingent loss. You have not yet received the legal response letter from Smith & Co.

Required:

a. Prepare the legal enquiry letter as requested by the controller.

b. What procedures should you perform given that the evaluation of the lawsuit has changed? What effect, if any, will this have on your audit report?

(ICABC, adapted)

3> **15-23** As senior in charge of the audit of Brett Building Supplies Ltd., you have just completed your review of the audit files for the year ended December 31, 2006. You are just about to follow up on the status of the legal letter when you receive a telephone call from your client.

"John Brady, our lawyer, won't release his response to our legal letter. It seems we may have a few problems in our evaluations of the claims, and we might have missed listing a few claims. I hope this doesn't affect your work at all, as we'd still like our statements by Friday."

Required:

a. List your actions in response to the comments made by Brett Building Supplies Ltd.

b. List the auditing procedures that might have brought this situation to light.

(ICABC, adapted)

3> **15-24** You have been supervising the field work on the audit of Tick-Vend, Ticket Brokers (the Company). In completing the contingencies and commitments section of the file, your staff became aware of rumours among the Company's staff of a lawsuit against the Company. You informed your partner and the client. The client stated that this matter would not result in any legal obligations on the Company's part and would likely "go away." The partner has instructed you to assist the client in preparing an enquiry letter to the Company's lawyer.

Required:

a. List the items that the client should include in the letter of enquiry to the Company's lawyer.

b. What would you expect to occur if the lawyer initially disagrees with the client's evaluation?

(CICA, adapted)

5,6> **15-25**   Richard Namiki is auditing the financial statements of Taylor Corporation for the year ended December 31, 2006. Namiki plans to complete the field work and sign the auditor's report about March 10, 2007. Namiki is concerned about events and transactions occurring after December 31, 2006, that may affect the 2006 financial statements.

Required:

a. What general types of subsequent events require Namiki's consideration and evaluation?

b. What auditing procedures should Namiki consider performing to gather evidence concerning subsequent events?

(AICPA, adapted)

5,6,7> **15-26**   For each of the following items, assume that Josh Feldstein is expressing an opinion on Scornick Company's financial statements for the year ended December 31, 2006; that he completed field work on January 21, 2007; and that he now is preparing his opinion to accompany the financial statements. In each item a subsequent event is described. This event was disclosed either in connection with the review of subsequent events or after the completion of field work. Indicate for each item the required accounting of the event. Each of the five items is independent of the other four and is to be considered separately.

1. A large account receivable from Agronowitz Company (material to financial statement presentation) was considered fully collectible at December 31, 2006. Agronowitz suffered a plant explosion on January 25, 2007. Because Agronowitz was uninsured, it is unlikely that the account will be paid.

2. The tax court ruled in favour of the company on January 25, 2007. Litigation involved deductions claimed on the 2002 and 2003 tax returns. In accrued taxes payable Scornick had provided for the full amount of the potential disallowances. CRA will not appeal the tax court's ruling.

3. Scornick's Manufacturing Division, whose assets constituted 45 percent of Scornick's total assets at December 31, 2006, was sold on February 1, 2007. The new owner assumed the bonded indebtedness associated with this property.

4. On January 15, 2007, R. E. Fogler, a major investment adviser, issued a negative report on Scornick's long-term prospects. The market price of Scornick's common stock subsequently declined by 40 percent.

5. At its January 5, 2007, meeting, Scornick's board of directors voted to increase substantially the advertising budget for the coming year and authorized a change in advertising agencies.

(AICPA, adapted)

8> **15-27**   Paul Arenas, an assistant accountant with the firm of Better & Best, is auditing the financial statements of Tech Consolidated

Industries, Ltd. The firm's audit program calls for the preparation of a written management representation letter.

Required:

a. In an audit of financial statements, in what circumstances is the auditor required to obtain a management representation letter? What are the purposes of obtaining the letter?

b. To whom should the representation letter be addressed, and when should it be dated? Who should sign the letter, and what would be the effect of his or her refusal to sign the letter?

c. In what respects may an auditor's other responsibilities be relieved by obtaining a management representation letter?

(AICPA, adapted)

8> **15-28** During the examination of the annual financial statements of Amis Manufacturing, Corp., the company's president, R. Heinrich, and Gordon Luddy, the auditor, reviewed the matters that were to be included in a written representation letter. Upon receipt of the following client representation letter, Luddy contacted Heinrich to state that it was incomplete.

> To: E. K. Luddy
>
> In connection with your examination of the balance sheet of Amis Manufacturing, Inc., as of December 31, 2006, and the related statements of income, retained earnings, and cash flows for the year then ended, for the purpose of expressing an opinion as to whether the financial statements present fairly the financial position, results of operations, and cash flows of Amis Manufacturing, Inc., in conformity with generally accepted accounting principles, we confirm, to the best of our knowledge and belief, the following representations made to you during your examination. There were no
>
> - Plans or intentions that may materially affect the carrying value or classification of assets and liabilities.
> - Communications from regulatory agencies concerning noncompliance with, or deficiencies in, financial reporting practices.
> - Agreements to repurchase assets previously sold.
> - Violations or possible violations of laws or regulations whose effects should be considered for disclosure in the financial statements or as a basis for recording a loss contingency.
> - Share capital repurchase options or agreements or share capital reserved for options, warrants, conversions, or other requirements.
> - Compensating balance or other arrangements involving restrictions on cash balances.
>
> R. Heinrich, President
>
> Amis Manufacturing, Inc.
>
> March 14, 2007

Required:

Identify the other matters that Heinrich's representation letter should specifically confirm.

(AICPA, adapted)

10⟩   **15-29**   It has been said that the most fundamental role of an audit committee is to enhance the auditor's independence. To ensure this role is fulfilled it is important for the auditor to communicate relevant information to the audit committee.

Required:

a. How does the audit committee enhance the auditor's independence?

b. List the matters that the auditor would normally communicate to the audit committee.

(ICABC, adapted)

6,11⟩   **15-30**   Real Estate Assets Limited (REAL) is a real estate investment company with investments in commercial real estate throughout the lower mainland. Most of their building assets were acquired in the mid to late 1980s, when real estate was booming. REAL leases out 12,000 square metres of commercial space. Most of the leases were signed for 10-year terms, at an average rate of $25 per square metre. Due to the large number of new properties on the market in recent years, vacancy rates have increased, and as a result rental rates are down. Last year REAL renewed two of its leases for $15 per square metre, which reflects the current market rents. This has caused a cash strain, since the mortgages are at a fixed rate. A majority of the remaining leases will also be up for renewal in the next three years.

REAL has mortgages on their properties totalling $20,000,000. The average interest rate on the mortgages is 8 percent. The company has $500,000 per year of general and administrative expenses. The bank requires that the company maintain an interest coverage ratio of 1.5 to 1. Historically, they have been close to, but within, this requirement.

REAL defaulted on its October and November monthly mortgage payments. However they obtained some private financing and paid these missed payments with a lump sum payment on December 20, 2006.

REAL's year-end is May 31. It is now June 28, 2007. Last Friday, the bank threatened to foreclose on a property in Hamilton, which has a vacancy rate of 80 percent. REAL had defaulted again on its last three payments. The mortgage balance owing on that property alone is $5,000,000.

Required:

a. You are the senior on the audit, and your manager has asked you to prepare the audit program for the audit of REAL's mortgages payable.

b. Describe the impact of last Friday's events on your audit procedures and audit report. Comment on what additional audit issues have arisen as a result of this event, and any concerns you have over meeting the bank's requirements.

(ICABC, adapted)

2,3,6,8,11 >   **15-31**   Items 1 through 19 represent a series of unrelated statements, questions, excerpts, and comments taken from various parts of an auditor's working paper file. Below is a list of the likely sources of the statements, questions, excerpts, and comments. Select, as the best answer for each item, the most likely source. Select only one source for each item. A source may be selected once, more than once, or not at all.

1. During our audit we discovered evidence of the company's failure to safeguard inventory from loss, damage, and misappropriation.

2. The company considers the decline in value of equity securities classified as available-for-sale to be temporary.

3. Was the difference of opinion on the accrued pension liabilities that existed between the engagement personnel and the actuarial specialist resolved in accordance with firm policy and appropriately documented?

4. Our audit is designed to provide reasonable assurance of detecting misstatements that, in our judgement, could have a material effect on the financial statements taken as a whole. Consequently, our audit will not necessarily detect all misstatements that exist due to error, fraudulent financial reporting, or misappropriation of assets.

5. There have been no communications from regulatory agencies concerning noncompliance with or deficiencies in financial reporting practices.

6. Nothing came to our attention that caused us to believe that at October 31, 2006, there was any change in the capital stock, increase in long-term debt, or decrease in consolidated net current assets or shareholders' equity as compared with the amounts shown in the September 30, 2006, unaudited condensed consolidated balance sheet.

7. It is our opinion that the possible liability to the company in this proceeding is nominal in amount.

8. As discussed in Note 4 to the financial statements, the company experienced a net loss for the year ended July 31, 2006, and is currently in default under substantially all of its debt agreements. In addition, on September 25, 2006, the company filed a prenegotiated voluntary petition for relief under Canadian bankruptcy law. These matters raise substantial doubt about the company's ability to continue as a going-concern.

9. During the year under audit, we were advised that management consulted with Better & Best. The purpose of this consultation was to obtain another firm's opinion concerning the company's recognition of certain revenue that we believe should be deferred to future periods. Better & Best's opinion was consistent with our opinion, so management did not recognize the revenue in the current year.

10. The company believes that all material expenditures that have been deferred to future periods will be recoverable.

11. Our use of professional judgement and the assessment of audit risk and materiality for the purpose of our audit mean that matters may have existed that would have been assessed differently by you. We make no representation as to the sufficiency or appropriateness of the information in our working papers for your purposes.

12. Indicate in the space provided below whether this information agrees with your records. If there are exceptions, please provide any information that will assist the auditor in reconciling the difference.

13. Blank cheques are maintained in an unlocked cabinet along with the cheque-signing machine. Blank cheques and the cheque-signing machine should be locked in separate locations to prevent the embezzlement of funds.

14. Our audit cannot be relied upon to disclose significant deficiencies in the design or operation of internal control. Nevertheless, we will communicate to you all reportable conditions and potential areas for improvement that we become aware of during the course of our audit.

15. The timetable set by management to complete our audit was unreasonable considering the failure of the company's personnel to complete schedules on a timely basis and delays in providing necessary information.

16. Several employees have disabled the antivirus detection software on their PCs because the software slows the processing of data and occasionally rings false alarms. The company should obtain antivirus software that runs continuously at all system entry points and that cannot be disabled by unauthorized personnel.

17. In connection with an audit of our financial statements, management has prepared, and furnished to our auditors, a description and evaluation of certain contingencies.

18. The company has no plans or intentions that may materially affect the carrying value or classification of assets and liabilities.

19. In planning the sampling application, was appropriate consideration given to the relationship of the sample to the audit objective and to preliminary judgements about materiality levels?

List of Sources

A. Practitioner's report on management's assertion about an entity's compliance with specified requirements.

B. Auditor's communications to management regarding a significant weaknesses in internal control.

C. Audit enquiry letter to lawyers.

D. Lawyer's response to audit enquiry letter.

E. Audit committee's communication to the auditor.

F. Auditor's communication to the audit committee.

G. Report on the application of accounting principles.

H. Auditor's engagement letter.

I. Letter for underwriters.

J. Accounts receivable confirmation request.

K. Request for bank cutoff statement.

L. Explanatory paragraph of an auditor's report on financial statements.

M. Partner's engagement review notes.

N. Management representation letter.

O. Successor auditor's communication with predecessor auditor.

P. Predecessor auditor's communication with successor auditor.

DISCUSSION CASES

8> **15-32** Medical Products, Inc. (MPI), was created in 2004 and entered the optical equipment industry. Their made-to-order optical equipment requires large investments in research and development. To fund these needs, MPI made a public stock offering, which was completed in 2005. Although the offering was moderately successful, MPI's ambitious management is convinced that they must report a good profit this year (2006) to maintain the current market price of the stock. MPI's president recently stressed this point when he told his controller, Pam Adams, "If we don't make $1.25 million pretax this year, our stock will fall significantly."

Adams was pleased that even after adjustments for accrued vacation pay, 2006 pretax profit was $1.35 million. However, MPI's auditors, Hammer & Bammer (HB), proposed an additional adjustment for inventory valuation that would reduce this profit to $900,000. HB's proposed adjustment had been discussed during the 2005 audit.

An additional issue discussed in 2005 was MPI's failure to accrue executive vacation pay. At that time HB did not insist on the adjustment because the amount ($20,000) was not material to the 2005 results and because MPI agreed to begin accruing vacation pay in future years. The cumulative accrued executive vacation pay amounts to $300,000 and has been accrued at the end of 2006.

The inventory issue arose in 2004 when MPI purchased $450,000 of specialized computer components to be used with their optical scanners for a special order. The order was subsequently cancelled, and HB proposed to write down this inventory in 2004. MPI explained, however, that the components could easily be sold without a loss during 2006, and no adjustment was made. However, the equipment was not sold by the end of 2006, and prospects for future sales were considered nonexistent. HB proposed a write-off of the entire $450,000 in 2006.

The audit partner, Johanna Schmidt, insisted that Adams make the inventory adjustment. Adams tried to convince her that there were other alternatives, but Schmidt was adamant. Adams knew the inventory was worthless, but she reminded Schmidt of the importance of this year's reported income. Adams continued her argument, "You can't take both the write-down and the vacation accrual in one year; it doesn't fairly present our performance this year. If you insist on taking that write-down, I'm taking back the accrual. Actually, that's a good idea because the executives are such workaholics, they don't take their vacations anyway."

As Adams calmed down, she said, "Johanna, let's be reasonable; we like you—and we want to continue our good working relationship with your firm into the future. But we won't have a future unless we put off this accrual for another year."

Required:

a. Should the inventory adjustment be taken in 2006?

b. Irrespective of your decision regarding the inventory adjustment, should the auditor insist on accrual of the executives' vacation pay?

c. Consider the conflict between Adams and Schmidt. Assuming that Schmidt believes the inventory adjustment and vacation pay accrual must be made and that she does not want to lose MPI as a client, what should she do?

1,2,3 ›   **15-33**   In February 2006, Ceramic Crucibles of Canada was notified by the province of Saskatchewan that the province was investigating the company's Lloydminster facility to determine if there were any violations of federal or provincial environmental laws. In formulating your opinion on the 2006 financial statements, you determined that, based primarily on management's representations, the investigation did not pose a serious threat to the company's financial well-being.

The company subsequently retained a local law firm to represent it in dealing with the provincial authority. At the end of 2006, you concluded that the action did not represent a severe threat. However, you have just received the lawyer's letter, which is a little unsettling. It states:

> On January 31, 2007, the Canada Environmental Assessment Agency (CEAA) listed the Lloydminster site on the National Priorities List under the *Comprehensive Environmental Response, Compensation, and Liability Act*. The site includes property adjoining the western boundary of Ceramic Crucibles' plant in Lloydminster and includes parts of Ceramic Crucibles' property. The CEAA has listed Ceramic Crucibles as one of the three "potentially responsible parties" ("PRPs") that may be liable for the costs of investigating and cleaning up the site. CEAA has authorized $400,000 for a "Remedial Investigation and Feasibility Study" of the site, but that study will not begin until sometime later in 2007. Thus, we do not deem it possible or appropriate at this time to evaluate this matter with regard to potential liability or cost to the company.

You immediately set up a meeting with Dave Buff, Ceramic Crucibles' vice president, Ron Bonner, the company's lawyer, and Margaret Osmond, a lawyer who specializes in CEAA-related issues. At the meeting you ascertain that

- Ceramic Crucibles bought the Lloydminster facility from TW Industries in 1990.

- TW Industries had operated the facility as a manufacturer of ceramic tiles, and they had used lead extensively in incorporating colour into the tile.

- The site has been placed on the National Priorities List ("the List") apparently because each province must have at least one site on the list. All sites on the list are rated on a composite score that reflects the relative extent of pollution. The Lloydminster site has a rating of 8.3 compared to a rating of no less than 25 for the other sites on the list.

- The most severe lead pollution (based on toxicity) is in an area located on the other side of a levee behind Ceramic Crucibles' facilities. Although the area close to the building contains traces of lead pollution, the toxicity in this area is about 50 parts per million (ppm), compared to 19,000 ppm beyond the levee.

- Although Ceramic Crucibles used lead in colouring its crucibles until about 1992, the lead was locked into a ceramic glaze that met Canadian Food Inspection Agency (CFIA) requirements for appliances used in the preparation of food. Apparently, the acids used in determining the leaching properties of lead for CEAA tests are stronger than that used by the CFIA. Since 1992, Ceramic Crucibles has used leadfree mud in its crucibles.

- Affidavits taken from present and former employees of Ceramic Crucibles indicate that no wastewater has been discharged though the levee since Ceramic Crucibles acquired the property in 1990.

- The other PRPs and TW Industries are viable companies that should be in a position to meet their responsibilities resulting from any possible CEAA action.

Materiality for purposes of evaluating a potential loss is $10 million to $13 million. This is based on the assumption that the loss would be deductible for income tax purposes. In that case, the loss would represent a reduction in shareholders' equity of 4.5 percent to 7.0 percent. Your best guess is that the company's exposure does not exceed that amount. Further, based on the financial strength of the company and its available lines of credit, you believe such an assessment would not result in financial distress to the company.

The creation of the Canadian Environmental Assessment Agency (CEAA) and that of the *Comprehensive Environmental Response, Compensation, and Liability Act* are a result of the increasing concern of Canadians about pollution. An amendment to the act permits the CEAA to perform the cleanup. As of the end of 2006, the CEAA had a national priorities list of 2,700 sites thought to be severely damaged. The average cost of conducting remedial investigation and feasibility studies ranges from $750,000 to $1 million, and such studies may take as long as three years. Cleanup costs are usually another $10 million to $12 million. It is said that the current estimates that $10 billion will be spent to clean up nonfederal hazardous waste sites may be conservative. The law requires the CEAA to identify toxic waste sites and request records from PRPs. The PRPs are responsible for the cost of cleanup, but if they lack the funds, the CEAA uses its funds for the cleanup. The CEAA has spent $350 million from its trust fund and collected only $6.5 million from polluters since the passage of the legislation.

Required:

a. How would this type of contingency be classified in the accounting literature, and how should it be accounted for?
b. Would the amount be material to the financial statements?
c. What additional evidence would you gather, and what kinds of representations should you require from the client?
d. Should the investigation affect your opinion on those financial statements?

INTERNET ASSIGNMENTS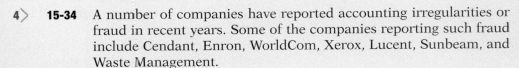

4>   15-34 A number of companies have reported accounting irregularities or fraud in recent years. Some of the companies reporting such fraud include Cendant, Enron, WorldCom, Xerox, Lucent, Sunbeam, and Waste Management.

Required:

a. Use an Internet search engine to find information on two of the companies listed. Prepare a memorandum describing the accounting irregularity or fraud.
b. Extend your search to identify two additional companies who have recently reported an accounting irregularity or fraud. Prepare a memorandum describing the accounting irregularity or fraud.

5>   15-35 It is unusual for an accounting firm to withdraw its opinion on a set of previously issued financial statements. Use an Internet search engine to find a recent example of a company whose public accounting firm has withdrawn its opinion.

Reports on Audited Financial Statements and Special Audit Reporting Issues

Learning Objectives

Upon completion of this chapter, you will be able to

1 Explain the auditor's standard unqualified audit report.

2 Identify situations that result in modification to the standard unqualified audit report.

3 Explain reservations in the audit report.

4 Explain the auditor's responsibility for issuing reservations of opinion.

5 Describe the auditor's responsibility for other information in the annual report.

6 Outline the auditor's responsibility for special reports.

7 Describe the public accountant's responsibility where performing agreed upon procedures regarding internal control over financial reporting and describe the report resulting from such an engagement.

RELEVANT ACCOUNTING AND ASSURANCE PRONOUNCEMENTS

CICA Handbook, **section 1300,** Differential reporting

CICA Handbook, **section 5020,** Association

CICA Handbook, **section 5100,** Generally accepted auditing standards

CICA Handbook, **section 5400,** The auditor's standard report

CICA Handbook, **section 5405,** Date of the auditor's report

CICA Handbook, **section 5510,** Reservations in the auditor's report

CICA Handbook, **section 5600,** Auditor's report on financial statements prepared using a basis of accounting other than generally accepted accounting principles

CICA Handbook, **section 5701,** Other reporting matters

CICA Handbook, **section 5805,** Audit reports on financial information other than financial statements

CICA Handbook, **section 5815,** Audit reports on compliance with agreements, statutes and regulations

CICA Handbook, **section 5970,** Auditor's report on controls at a service organization

CICA Handbook, **section 6930,** Reliance on another auditor

CICA Handbook, **section 7500,** The auditor's involvement with annual reports, interim reports, and other public documents

AuG-8, Auditor's report on comparative financial statements

AuG-41, Applying materiality and audit risk concepts in conducting an audit

EARTHWEAR'S AUDIT REPORT

EarthWear When all the audit evidence is collected and evaluated, including quality control procedures such as independent partner review, the final decision that Willis & Adams must make is the appropriate form of audit report to issue on EarthWear's financial statements. As a publicly traded entity, it is extremely important for EarthWear that it receive what is called the auditor's standard unqualified audit report, sometimes referred to as a "clean opinion." The consequences of receiving a reservation of opinion would be dire. Ontario Securities Commission regulations would require that trading in EarthWear's shares be suspended and investment analysts might revise their recommendations to clients regarding whether or not to purchase or even hold EarthWear's shares.

This chapter discusses the auditor's reporting framework in detail, including the possibility that the auditor's report is amended to reflect the fact that some aspect or aspects of the auditors' examination are unsatisfactory, either because they identify one or more material misstatements in the client's financial statements, or because they are unable to obtain sufficient appropriate audit evidence regarding one or more components of the financial statements. Such circumstances are very infrequent in practice. However, a *reservation of opinion* is possible, and examining the different types of possible reservations in the audit report brings into focus more clearly the message conveyed by the standard audit report.

This chapter also briefly discusses some of the other specialized reports that could be prepared by auditors.

The Auditor's Standard Unqualified Audit Report

LO 1 Chapter 2 presented the auditor's standard unqualified audit report. This report is issued when the auditor has gathered sufficient evidence, the audit was performed in accordance with GAAS, and the financial statements conform to GAAP. Exhibit 16–1 contains the auditor's standard unqualified audit report, which was presented in Exhibit 2–1. This report contains seven elements: (1) the report title, (2) the addressee, (3) the introductory paragraph, (4) the scope paragraph, (5) the opinion paragraph, (6) the name of the auditor, and (7) the audit report date. You may wish to return to Chapter 2 to review the discussion of the auditor's standard unqualified audit report.

Explanatory Language Added to the Standard Unqualified Audit Report

LO 2 Before discussing the different circumstances in which an auditor may have to issue a *reservation* and in some way *qualify* the auditor's report, it should be mentioned that there are a number of circumstances where the auditor may include additional explanatory language in the auditor's report, either in one of the paragraphs of the standard form of report or in a paragraph after the opinion paragraph. This section briefly describes those circumstances. It should be stressed that these explanations are included simply to provide the reader with additional information. They are not intended to be a qualification of the auditor's opinion that the financial statements present fairly.

EXHIBIT 16–1

The Auditor's Standard Unqualified Audit Report

Title:	Auditors' Report
Addressee:	To the Shareholders of Royal Bank of Canada.
Introductory paragraph:	We have audited the consolidated balance sheets of Royal Bank of Cananda as at October 31, 2005 and 2004, and the consolidated statements of income, changes in shareholders' equity and cash flows for each of the years in the three-year period ended October 31, 2005. These consolidated financial statements are the responsibility of the bank's management. Our responsibility is to express an opinion on these consolidated financial statements based on our audits.
Scope paragraph:	We conducted our audits in accordance with Canadian generally accepted auditing standards. Those standards require that we plan and perform an audit to obtain reasonable assurance whether the consolidated financial statements are free of material misstatement. An audit includes examining, on a test basis, evidence supporting the amounts and disclosures in the consolidated financial statements. An audit also includes assessing the accounting principles used and significant estimates made by management, as well as evaluating the overall consolidated financial statements presentation.
Opinion paragraph:	In our opinion, these consolidated financial statements present fairly, in all material respects, the financial position of the bank as at October 31, 2005 and 2004, and the results of its operation and its cash flows for each of the years in the three-year period ended October 31, 2005, in accordance with the Canadian generally accepted accounting principles.
Name of the auditor:	Deloitte & Touche LLP Chartered Accountants
Date of report:	Toronto, November 30, 2005

Source: Royal Bank of Canada.

[handwritten note: -reporting on both yr's b/c comparative. → 2005 done in 2005 → 2004 done in 2004]

Auditor's Report on Consolidated Financial Statements

A simple change occurs when the auditor is reporting on the financial statements of a company having one or more subsidiaries. Generally accepted accounting principles require that the statements be consolidated. In such cases the description in the auditor's report should include the word "consolidated." For example, in the introductory paragraph, the wording would be "I have examined the consolidated balance sheet... and consolidated statements of income... ."

Auditor's Report on Non-Consolidated Financial Statements

Where the auditor is reporting on non-consolidated financial statements that have been prepared in addition to audited consolidated financial statements of a company with subsidiaries, the description of the financial statements will include the word "non-consolidated" ("I have audited the non-consolidated balance sheet..."). The opinion paragraph will include, at the end, the words "... except that they are prepared on a non-consolidated basis, as explained in Note... ." Two points should be stressed with respect to this modification—first, the auditor must have previously reported on the company's consolidated financial statements for the year, and second, the financial statements must contain a note explaining that these financial statements are in addition to the consolidated financial statements. The auditor's report on the non-consolidated financial statements will normally be addressed to the board of directors.

Auditor's Report on Comparative Financial Statements

Most annual reports, in particular those prepared to meet the requirements of the Ontario Securities Commission, contain the current year's and the previous year's financial statements. In cases where the auditor has previously audited and issued a standard report on the financial statements for the prior year, the only modification will be to refer to the financial statements in plural and to identify the years. For example, the introductory sentence would read "I have audited the balance sheets... as at December 31, 2005 and 2006... ."

In other cases, such as where the current auditors gave an opinion with reservation in the preceding year, or where the preceding year's financial statements were audited and reported on, with or without reservation, by another auditor, the general rule is that the auditor should describe the circumstances in a separate paragraph after the opinion paragraph. Assurance and Related Services Guideline AuG-8, "Auditor's report on comparative financial statements," provides examples of the form of report to be used in such circumstances.

Auditor's Report on Financial Statements Prepared Using a Basis of Accounting Other Than Generally Accepted Accounting Principles

Section 5600 of the *CICA Handbook*, "Auditor's report on financial statements prepared using a basis of accounting other than generally accepted accounting principles," provides guidance in situations where specific users may require financial statements prepared using a basis of accounting other than generally accepted accounting principles to meet their information needs. The two acceptable situations identified in the *Handbook* are where the financial statements are prepared in accordance with regulatory requirements or where the financial statements are prepared in accordance with a buy/sell agreement. The words "specific users" in section 5600 are very important, as the section makes explicit that such statements are not acceptable as general purpose statements and that the auditors should confirm in writing the intended purpose(s), the specified user(s), and the basis of accounting used. As a result, an entity may, in keeping with the terms of an agreement or statute, prepare financial statements which are wholly or partially prepared in accordance with an appropriate disclosed basis of accounting other than generally accepted accounting principles. In such cases the auditor's report would replace "in accordance with generally accepting accounted principles" phrasing such as "in accordance with the basis of accounting required by... as disclosed in Note X to the financial statements." The note in the financial statements must fully disclose the authority under which such departure from generally accepted accounting principles is made.

Reservations in the Audit Report

LO 3⟩   The third reporting standard allows for the possibility that the auditor will be unable to issue a standard unqualified audit report on financial statements. There are three types of audit reports that depart from the unqualified audit report. The conditions for issuing such *reservations* are discussed next. Figure 16–1 presents an overview of the auditor's audit reporting decision.

FIGURE 16–1

An Overview of Audit Reporting

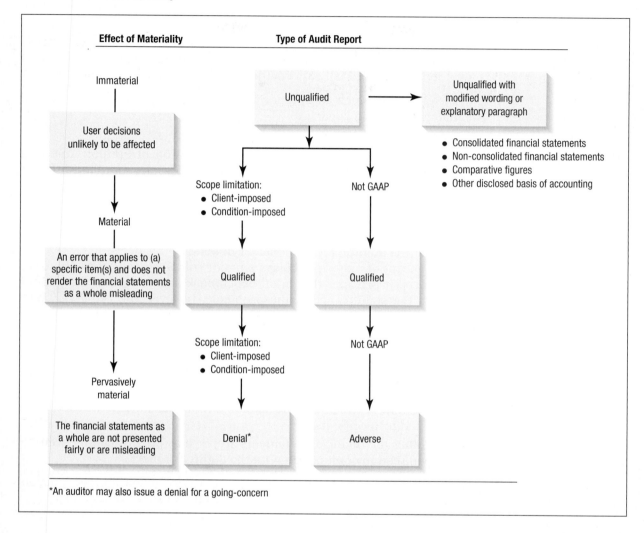

*An auditor may also issue a denial for a going-concern

Conditions for Departure	There are two basic reasons that an auditor may be unable to express an unqualified opinion:

1. **Scope limitation.** A scope limitation results from a lack of evidence, such as an inability to conduct an audit procedure considered necessary.
2. **Departure from GAAP.** The financial statements are affected by a departure from GAAP.

Other Types of Audit Reports	There are three types of reservations in the auditor's report:

1. **Qualified.** The auditor's opinion is qualified because of either a scope limitation or a departure from GAAP, but the overall financial statements present fairly.

2. ***Denial.*** The auditor denies an opinion on the financial statements either because there is insufficient competent evidence to form an opinion on the overall financial statements or because there is a lack of independence.

3. ***Adverse.*** The auditor's opinion states that the financial statements do not present fairly in conformity with GAAP because the departure materially affects the overall financial statements.

The choice of which audit report to issue depends on the condition and the materiality of the departure.

Factors Affecting the Form of Reservation

Once the auditor has determined that a reservation of opinion, due to a departure from generally accepted accounting principles, or a limitation in the scope of the examination, is appropriate, the next decision is whether a qualified opinion (GAAP- or scope-related), an adverse opinion (GAAP-related), or a denial of opinion (scope-related) should be given. *CICA Handbook*, section 5510, "Reservations in the auditor's report," discusses factors that the auditor should consider in making this decision.

The concept of materiality plays a major role in the auditor's choice of audit reports. It provides the initial benchmark against which the auditor can assess the significance of the problem. However, the *Handbook* also identifies additional qualitative criteria that the auditor should consider:

a. the degree to which the matter impairs the usefulness of the financial statements

b. the extent to which the effects of the matter on the financial statements can be determined

c. the extent to which the effects on the financial statements can be related to specific items

d. whether the financial statements are, or may be, misleading even when read in conjunction with the auditor's report

Assurance Guideline AuG-41, "Applying materiality and audit risk concepts in conducting an audit," also discusses the effect of misstatements on the financial statements and provides qualitative guidance in assessing those misstatements.

A qualified opinion for a departure from generally accepted accounting principles is normally considered adequate to inform readers. For example, the *Handbook* indicates that if the auditor, upon considering materiality and the qualitative factors identified above, judges that any departures do not impair the overall usefulness of the financial statements to the reader, and that the auditor's explanation allows the reader to assess the impact of any departures, a qualified opinion is appropriate. If one or other of those conditions is not met—in other words if the financial statements are misleading or virtually useless to the reader, even when read in conjunction with the auditor's report, an adverse opinion is the appropriate form of reservation.

In the case of a scope limitation, the auditor must be very careful in the exercise of professional judgement. The criteria are the same, but the difference in such cases is that since the auditor was unable to obtain sufficient evidence, he or she must base his or her decision on an assessment of the *potential* effects. Paragraph 5510.21 provides:

> Where the limitation in the scope of the auditor's examination is such that the auditor does not have sufficient evidence to conclude that the financial statements are prepared in accordance with generally accepted accounting principles, and he believes that the effect on the financial statements of possible departures from generally accepted accounting principles could be pervasive or significant, he would deny an opinion.

Discussion of the Auditor's Responsibility for Issuing Reservations of Opinion

Auditing-Related Deficiencies—Scope Limitation

LO 4⟩

A scope limitation results from an inability to obtain sufficient appropriate audit evidence about some component of the financial statements. This occurs because the auditor is unable to apply all the audit procedures considered necessary. Such restrictions on the scope of the audit may be imposed by the circumstances of the engagement or by the client. Auditors should be particularly cautious when a client limits the scope of the engagement. In such a situation, the client may be trying to prevent the auditor from discovering material misstatements. Auditing standards suggest that when restrictions imposed by the client significantly limit the scope of the engagement, the auditor should consider denying an opinion on the financial statements. However, if the auditor can overcome a scope limitation by performing alternative procedures, a standard unqualified audit report can be issued.

An example of a scope limitation due to circumstances of the engagement can occur with respect to opening inventory. Auditing standards require that the auditor observe inventory. However, circumstances may prevent the auditor from doing so. Suppose, for example, that the auditor is not engaged to conduct the audit until *after* year-end. In such a circumstance, the auditor may not be able to perform a number of audit procedures (like observing inventory). If such deficiencies in evidence cannot be overcome by other auditing procedures, the auditor will have to issue a qualified opinion or a disclaimer. Exhibit 16–2 is an example of a denial of opinion because of this type of scope limitation.

An example of a client-imposed scope limitation occurs when a client requests that the auditor not confirm accounts receivable because of concerns about creating conflicts with customers over amounts owed. If the auditor is satisfied that the client's reasons for not confirming are legitimate and is unable to apply alternative audit procedures to determine fairness of the receivables, he or she would qualify the opinion or deny an opinion.

Finally, the auditor may be unable to obtain audited financial statements for a long-term investment that is accounted for using the equity method. Exhibit 16–3 is an example of a qualified report for such a scope limitation.

Note that in both examples the paragraph that explains the scope limitation is presented *before* the opinion or denial paragraph.

EXHIBIT 16–2

Denial of Opinion—Scope Limitation

Auditor's Report

[*Standard wording for addressee*]
[*Standard wording for introductory paragraph*]

Except as explained in the following paragraph, I conducted my examination... [*standard wording for remainder of scope paragraph*].

Because I was appointed auditor of the company after year-end I was not able to observe the counting of physical inventories at the beginning or the end of the year, nor satisfy myself concerning those inventory quantities by alternate means. Also, my examination indicated serious deficiencies in internal control over inventory. As a consequence, I was unable to satisfy myself that all revenues and expenditures of the company had been recorded nor was I able to satisfy myself that the recorded transactions were proper. As a result, I was unable to determine whether adjustments were required in respect of recorded or unrecorded assets, recorded or unrecorded liabilities, and the components making up the statements of income, retained earnings, and cash flows.

In view of the possible material effects on the financial statements of the matters described in the preceding paragraph, I am unable to express an opinion whether these financial statements are presented fairly in accordance with Canadian generally accepted accounting principles.

EXHIBIT 16–3

Qualified Report—Scope Limitation

Auditor's Report

[*Standard wording for addressee*]
[*Standard wording for the introductory paragraph*]

Except as explained in the following paragraph . . . [*standard wording for remainder of scope paragraph*].

We were unable to obtain audited financial statements supporting the Company's investment in a foreign affiliate stated at $12,500,000 at December 31, 2006 or its equity in earnings of that affiliate of $1,200,000, which is included in net income for the year then ended as described in Note 10 to the financial statements; nor were we able to satisfy ourselves as to the carrying value of the investment in the foreign affiliate or the equity in its earnings by other auditing procedures.

In our opinion, except for the effects of such adjustments, if any, which I might have determined to be necessary had I been able to examine evidence regarding the foreign affiliate and earnings, these financial statements present fairly . . . [*same wording as for the remainder of the standard opinion paragraph*].

(signed) . . . .
CHARTERED ACCOUNTANT

City
Date

Accounting-Related Deficiencies— Statements Not in Conformity with GAAP

If the financial statements are materially affected by an unacceptable departure from GAAP, the auditor should express a qualified or adverse opinion. Examples of these types of departures are inappropriate accounting treatment, inappropriate valuation, and failure to disclose essential information.

When the financial statements contain an accounting principle that is not acceptable, the auditor should issue a qualified or adverse opinion depending on materiality. When the auditor expresses a qualified opinion, a separate explanatory paragraph should be added to the report *before* the opinion paragraph. The explanatory paragraph should disclose the effects of the departure on the financial statements. Exhibit 16–4 is an example of a report that has been qualified because of the use of an unacceptable accounting principle.

If the departure's effect is so pervasive that the financial statements taken as a whole are not presented fairly, the auditor should issue an adverse opinion. When an adverse opinion is issued, the auditor should add an explanatory paragraph that *precedes* the opinion paragraph. The explanatory paragraph should discuss the reasons for the adverse opinion and the effects of the departure on the financial statements. The opinion paragraph is modified to state that the financial statements *do not present fairly* in conformity with GAAP. Exhibit 16–5 is an example of an adverse report.

If a client fails to disclose information in the financial statements or notes that is required by GAAP, the auditor should issue a qualified or adverse report. The auditor should provide the information in the report, if practicable, unless omission is allowed by auditing standards. One situation in which the auditor would *not* have to provide the information is where a client who is required to include a statement of cash flows has declined to do so. Auditing standards do not require that the auditor prepare a statement when one has been omitted by the client. Exhibit 16–6 is a qualified report for inadequate disclosure.

Much of the value that users of an auditor's report place on the report is based on the assumption of an unbiased relationship between the auditor and the client. There are few situations in which an auditor would be engaged to audit a client and independence between the two parties would not exist. However, it is possible that an auditor could be engaged by a client, believing that all members of the audit team were independent of the client. At the end of the engagement, it might come to the audit partner's attention that a member of the audit team had a financial interest

EXHIBIT 16–4

Qualified Report—Not in Conformity with Generally Accepted Accounting Principles—Comparative Statements

Auditor's Report

[*Standard wording for the introductory and scope paragraphs*]

The Company has excluded, from property and debt in the accompanying balance sheets, certain lease obligations that, in our opinion, should be capitalized in order to conform with generally accepted accounting principles. If these lease obligations were capitalized, property would be increased by $7,500,000 and $7,200,000, long-term debt by $6,900,000 and $6,600,000, and retained earnings by $1,420,000 and $1,290,000 as of December 31, 2006 and 2005, respectively. Additionally, net income would be increased by $250,000 and $220,000 and earnings per share would be increased by $0.25 and $0.22, respectively, for the years then ended.

In our opinion, except for the effects of not capitalizing certain lease obligations as discussed in the preceding paragraph, these financial statements present fairly . . . [*same wording as for the remainder of the standard opinion paragraph*].

EXHIBIT 16–5

Adverse Opinion—Departure from Generally Accepted Accounting Principles

Auditor's Report

[Standard wording for the introductory and scope paragraphs]

As explained in Note 6 to the financial statements, commencing this year the company ceased to consolidate the financial statements of its subsidiary companies because it considers this basis to be inappropriate when there are substantial non-controlling interests. These investments are now accounted for on a cost basis. Under Canadian generally accepted accounting principles, the existence of such non-controlling interest is not an acceptable reason for not consolidating the financial statements of subsidiary companies with those of the reporting enterprise. Had consolidated financial statements been prepared, virtually every account in, and the information provided by way of notes to, the accompanying financial statements would have been materially different. The audited financial statements of the subsidiaries reveal that, while the company's proportionate share in the underlying book values is greater than cost, substantial losses have been incurred in the current year of which the company's share on consolidation would approximate $...

In our opinion, because the investment in subsidiary companies is not accounted for on a consolidated basis as explained in the preceding paragraph, these financial statements do not present fairly the financial position of the company as at..., 19... and the results of its operation and its cash flows for the year then ended in accordance with Canadian generally accepted accounting principles.

EXHIBIT 16–6

Qualified Report—Inadequate Disclosure—Comparative Statements

Auditor's Report

We have audited the balance sheets of O'Dea Company as of December 31, 2006 and 2005, and the related statements of income and retained earnings for the years then ended. These financial statements are the responsibility of the Company's management. Our responsibility is to express an opinion on these financial statements based on our audit.

[Standard wording for the scope paragraph]

The Company declined to present a statement of cash flows for the years ended December 31, 2006 and 2005. Presentation of such statement summarizing the Company's operating, investing, and financing activities is required by generally accepted accounting principles.

In our opinion, except that the omission of a statement of cash flows results in an incomplete presentation as explained in the preceding paragraph, these financial statements present fairly... *[same wording as for the remainder of the standard opinion paragraph]*.

---

in the client. In such circumstances, strictly speaking, the auditor should issue a denial of opinion, due to lack of independence. In practice, the auditor would probably resign from the engagement and the client would engage another auditor.

Going-Concern Reporting

Special circumstances exist with respect to the auditor's reporting responsibilities in situations where there are going concern issues. Chapter 15 discussed the auditor's responsibility to assess the client's ability to continue as a going-concern. Recall that if the auditor concludes that there is some question about the entity's ability to continue as a going-concern, he or she should assess whether there is adequate disclosure in the financial statements, sufficient to bring to the reader's attention the possibility that the enterprise may be unable to continue realizing its assets and discharging its obligations in the normal course of business. If the auditor concludes that the disclosure is sufficient to fully inform readers of the financial statements, the auditor can issue a standard audit report with no reservations.[1]

If management does not disclose the going concern issues or if, in the auditor's opinion, the disclosure is inadequate, the financial statements will not be in accordance with GAAP and the appropriate course of action would be for the auditor to issue a reservation or opinion. If the entity's disclosures with respect to the entity's ability to continue as a going concern are inadequate, a departure from GAAP exists and the auditor will issue a qualified or adverse opinion.

Other Related Information—Annual Reports, Interim Reports, and Other Public Documents

LO 5〉 Section 7500 of the *CICA Handbook*, "Auditor association with annual reports, interim reports, and other public documents," discusses the auditor's responsibilities in a number of areas, e.g., the additional information in annual reports as found in the Annual Information Form (AIF) and Management Discussion and Analysis (MD&A) prepared for filing with securities authorities. The auditor does not provide assurance on this additional information, but should ensure that the audited financial statements and the auditor's report are accurately reproduced in the annual report. With respect to any other information, the auditor should review this information for any inconsistencies with the financial statements on which the audit report is given.

If there is an error in the financial statements or in the audit report, the auditor should endeavour to have it corrected. If there is an inconsistency between the financial statements and the other information, and the inconsistency is in the other information, the auditor should request management to correct the inconsistency in the other information. In either case, if management will not amend the annual report to correct the problem, the auditor should formally notify the directors and consider what further action is appropriate, including seeking legal advice.

The auditor's responsibilities are quite broad in scope and include responsibility for documents transmitted to, or posted on, SEDAR, EDGAR, the entity's website, or any electronic site.

---

[1]When harmonization with International Auditing Standards is in place, the Canadian standard auditor's report may contain an "Emphasis on Matter" paragraph to supplement and draw attention to management's note disclosure. It is not to be interpreted as a qualification.

Special Audit Reports

LO 6>

In addition to audits of a complete set of financial statements, auditors may be engaged to express an opinion on a subset of that information, on an entity's compliance with the terms of an agreement, or on control procedures at a services organization. This section covers each of the three in more detail.

Financial Information Other Than Financial Statements

In some situations an auditor may be engaged to audit only part (specified elements, accounts, or items) of the financial statements. *CICA Handbook,* section 5805, "Audit reports on financial information other than financial statements," discusses the preparation of such a report. Examples include a report on rentals, royalties or profit participation. The basis of accounting for the elements, accounts, or items may be GAAP or a basis of accounting prescribed by a statute, contract, or agreement. An engagement to express an opinion on one or more specified elements, accounts, or items of a financial statement may be performed as a separate engagement or as part of an audit of financial statements. In engagements of this type, the auditor should comply with the general standard and the three examination standards.

Generally, an audit of an element, account, or item is more extensive than if the same information were considered as part of an audit of the overall financial statements. There are two reasons for this. First, the auditor should set materiality in the context of the element, account, or item being examined. This would constitute a smaller base against which to measure materiality, consequently reducing materiality to a smaller amount. Second, the auditor needs to consider interrelationships with other parts of the financial statements. For example, if the auditor was engaged to audit the entity's accounts receivable, other accounts such as sales and allowance for bad debts should also be considered.

Exhibit 16–7 is an example of a special report on gross sales for the calculation of rent. The introductory paragraph states that this specific account was audited. Similarly to the standard unqualified audit report, this paragraph states management's and the auditor's responsibilities. The second paragraph is the scope paragraph, which differs from the standard report only in that it references the account being audited. The third paragraph expresses the auditor's opinion on the account.

Compliance with Agreements, Statutes, and Regulations

CICA Handbook, section 5815, "Audit reports on compliance with agreements, statutes and regulations," covers situations where an auditor is engaged to report on an entity's compliance with certain contractual agreements or regulatory requirements related to audited financial statements. For example, loan agreements may include covenants such as restrictions on dividends or maintenance of certain levels for selected financial ratios. When engaged to perform such an examination, the auditor should comply with the general standard and the examination standards. Exhibit 16–8 is an example of a special report related to compliance with contractual provisions.

EXHIBIT 16–7

Special Report Relating to Gross Sales for the Calculation of Rent

Auditor's Report

We have audited the accompanying schedule of gross sales (as defined in the lease agreement dated March 4, 2004, between McGill Company, as lessor, and Asare Stores Corporation, as lessee) of Asare Stores Corporation at its Main Street store, Dunwoody, Nova Scotia, for the year ended December 31, 2006. This schedule is the responsibility of Asare Stores Corporation's management. Our responsibility is to express an opinion on this financial information based on our audit.

We conducted our audit in accordance with generally accepted auditing standards. Those standards require that we plan and perform the audit to obtain reasonable assurance about whether the schedule of gross sales is free of material misstatement. An audit includes examining, on a test basis, evidence supporting the amounts and disclosures in the schedule of gross sales. An audit also includes assessing the accounting principles used and significant estimates made by management, as well as evaluating the overall presentation of the financial information.

In our opinion, the schedule of gross sales referred to above presents fairly, in all material respects, the gross sales of Asare Stores Corporation at its Main Street store, Dunwoody, Nova Scotia, for the year ended December 31, 2006, in accordance with the terms of the lease agreement referred to in the first paragraph.

EXHIBIT 16–8

Report on Compliance with Contractual Provisions

To ABC Trust Company Limited:

I have audited Lynch Lumber Company Limited's compliance as at December 31, 2006 with the criteria established by the provisions of sections 6.1 to 6.14 inclusive of the Indenture dated July 21, 2001 with ABC Trust Company Limited and the interpretation of such indenture as set out in Note 1 attached. Compliance with the provisions of the indenture is the responsibility of management. My responsibility is to express an opinion on this compliance, based on my audit.

I conducted my audit in accordance with generally accepted auditing standards. Those standards require that I plan and perform an audit to obtain reasonable assurance whether Lynch Lumber Company Limited complied with the above criteria established by the provisions of the agreement referred to above. Such an audit includes examining, on a test basis, evidence supporting compliance, evaluating the overall compliance with the agreement and where applicable, assessing the accounting principles and significant estimates made by management.

In my opinion, as at December 31, 2006, Lynch Lumber Company Limited is in compliance in all material respects, with the criteria established by the provisions of sections 6.1 to 6.14 inclusive of the indenture with ABC Trust Company Limited.

Control Procedures at a Service Organization

Some companies have chosen to outsource certain of their operations to specialized providers of those specific services. Examples are payroll services and administration of company pension plans. The auditor's involvement may come about in one of two different ways. If the auditor's client is also a client of the service organization, as part of the audit of the client, the auditor will need to obtain evidence that the service organization has sufficient controls in place to safeguard the client's assets and provide timely and reliable information. The auditor may therefore audit the procedures that the service organization designed to do so.

It would be inefficient, and very detrimental to the operations of the service organization if the auditor of every one of their clients performed such an examination. Therefore an auditor may be hired by a service organization to perform an examination and give an opinion only once. The opinion will be provided to the auditors of the service organization's clients. The auditors of the service organization's clients may, upon appropriate consideration, rely on the opinion of the auditor of the service organization.

CICA Handbook, section 5970, "Auditor's report on controls at a service organization," provides guidance for the auditor. In such engagements, the auditor should comply with the general standard and with examination standards (i) and (iii). The reason for the omission of examination standard (ii) is that as it is stated, it relates to the study of internal control in the context of the audit of a set of financial statements. This examination focuses solely on the service organization's system of internal control so standard (ii) is really redundant in this case.

The auditor may issue one of two types of reports pursuant to this type of engagement. The first type of report, a Report on Controls Placed in Operation, results when the auditor is engaged to report on the design and existence of control procedures at a service organization. The auditor's procedures would include:

a. obtaining and reading the description of the stated internal control objectives of the system and the control procedures designed to achieve those objective;

b. verifying the existence of the control procedures at a point in time by such means as observation, enquiry, and tracing transactions through the system;

c. evaluating the suitability of the design of the control procedures by assessing their sufficiency and appropriateness to meet the stated internal control objectives of the system; and

d. obtaining written representation from management of the service organization as to the completeness and accuracy of the description.

The second type of report, a Report on Controls Placed in Operation and Tests of the Operating Effectiveness of Controls, results when the auditor is engaged to examine and report on, in addition, the continuity and effective operation of the control procedures throughout the specified period. In such an engagement the auditor must carry out tests to determine that the control procedures operated throughout the specified period and obtain written representation from management to that effect.

There are two major differences, both of which are indicative of the different scopes of the auditor's examinations. Firstly, the second report makes explicit reference to, and lists in a separate schedule, the tests that the auditor applied to obtain evidence about the effectiveness of controls. Secondly, the second type of report makes explicit reference to the period covered by the examination. The auditor explicitly states that the opinion refers only to that time period.

Financial Information Presented in Prescribed Forms or Schedules	Sometimes an entity has to file with an agency on a preprinted form or schedule and the auditor is asked to report using the prescribed form. Many of these forms are not acceptable for auditors because they do not conform to professional reporting standards. In such instances, the auditor may attach the prescribed separate form to a standard form auditor's report.

Reports on Agreed-Upon Procedures Regarding Internal Control over Financial Reporting

LO 7 ⟩ This form of report is contained in *CICA Handbook*, section 9110, "Agreed-upon procedures regarding the internal control over financial reporting." However, it is almost certain to be approved. While the report is not an audit report, it is included here because of its importance and because the special type of engagement that results in this report will almost certainly be part of a standard audit engagement for auditors when auditing publicly listed companies in Canada.

Recall from the discussion in Chapter 2 that in 2002, the US Congress passed the *Sarbanes-Oxley Act* (SOX). One of the provisions of SOX, applicable to publicly traded companies, is a requirement that senior management (CEOs and CFOs) report on the effectiveness of the company's internal control over financial reporting. The auditor's examination includes obtaining evidence about management's assertions regarding internal control over financial reporting and the standard auditor's report contains an opinion on its effectiveness.

The Canadian approach is somewhat different. In Canada, the Canadian Security Administrators' Multilateral Instrument 52–109 imposes a similar requirement for CEOs and CFOs of Canadian public companies to include matters pertaining to internal control over financial reporting in the certificates that are filed with Canadian securities regulators. In order to assist management, the public accountant may undertake an engagement to perform agreed-upon procedures related to the entity's system of internal control. The engagement will be performed as a public accountant rather than as an auditor and the resulting report, which will usually be addressed to the engaging party (normally management), will not provide an opinion, or any form of assurance. Instead it will report factually on the findings of having performed the procedures previously agreed upon with the engaging party. Unlike practice in the United States, the report is intended solely for the engaging party and it will not form part of the auditor's standard report. The final paragraph of the exposure draft example explicitly states that the report should not be distributed to other parties. Exhibit 16–9 provides a partial example of a Report on Agreed-Upon Procedures Regarding Internal Control over Financial Reporting.

EXHIBIT 16–9

Report of the Public Accountant's Findings on an Agreed-Upon Procedures Engagement Regarding Internal Control over Financial Reporting

To: CEO, ABC Company [or other engaging party]

We have performed the procedure specified by you and enumerated below. Our engagement was performed in accordance with Candian generally accepted standards for agreed-upon procedures engagements regarding internal control over financial reporting.

The procedures were performed solely to assist you in evaluating whether controls were operating effectively. The agreed-upon procedures and findings were as follows:

[insert complete list of agreed-upon procedures and findings]

This report is solely for the information and use of [addressee] in connection with your assessment of the [design, implementation, or operating effectiveness] of internal control over financial reporting [specific procedures, for example, component of internal control, segment of the entity, or control processes], and is not intended and should not be used for any other purpose. Consequently, the report should not be distributed to other parties without our prior written consent. Any use that a third party makes of this report, or any reliance or decisions made based on it, are the responsibility of such third party. We accept no responsibility for any loss or damages suffered by any third party as a result of decisions made or actions taken based on this report.

(signed) . . . .
CHARTERED ACCOUNTANT

City
Date

REVIEW QUESTIONS

LO 1 **16-1** Describe what is meant when an auditor is associated with a set of financial statements.

2 **16-2** Under what circumstances would the principal auditor refer to the other auditor in the audit report?

3 **16-3** How does the materiality of a condition that might lead to a departure affect the auditor's choice of audit reports?

3 **16-4** Give examples of a client-imposed and a condition-imposed scope limitation. Why is a client-imposed limitation generally considered more serious?

3 **16-5** How does a client's refusal to disclose information that is required by GAAP affect the auditor's report?

2 **16-6** In 2005 your firm issued an unqualified report on Tosi Corporation. During 2006 Tosi entered its first lease transaction, which you have determined is material and meets the criteria for a capitalized lease. Tosi Corporation's management chooses to treat the transaction as an operating lease. What types of reports would you issue on the corporation's comparative financial statements for 2005 and 2006?

5 **16-7** What are the auditor's responsibilities for other information included in an entity's annual report?

5 > **16-8** If the auditor determines that other information contained with the audited financial statements is incorrect and the client refuses to correct the other information, what actions can the auditor take?

4 > **16-9** If the auditor concludes that an entity will not continue as a going-concern, what type of audit report should be issued?

6 > **16-10** List three examples of special reports.

6 > **16-11** What type of special report does the auditor issue when reporting on an entity's compliance with contractual agreements?

MULTIPLE-CHOICE QUESTIONS FROM PROFESSIONAL EXAMINATIONS

Unless otherwise indicated, these multiple-choice questions were adapted from the CPA examinations, courtesy of the American Institute of Certified Public Accountants.

2 > **16-12** An entity changed from the straight-line method to the declining balance method of depreciation for all newly acquired assets. This change has no material effect on the current year's financial statements but is reasonably certain to have a substantial effect in later years. If the change is disclosed in the notes to the financial statements, the auditor should issue a report with a(n)

a. "Except for" qualified opinion.

b. Explanatory paragraph.

c. Unqualified opinion.

d. Piecemeal opinion.

3,4 > **16-13** Eagle Company's financial statements contain a departure from generally accepted accounting principles because, due to unusual circumstances, the statements would otherwise be misleading. The auditor should express an opinion that is

a. Unqualified but *not* mention the departure in the auditor's report.

b. Unqualified and describe the departure in a separate paragraph.

c. Qualified and describe the departure in a separate paragraph.

d. Qualified or adverse, depending on materiality, and describe the departure in a separate paragraph.

3,4 > **16-14** An auditor would issue an adverse opinion if

a. The audit was begun by other auditors who withdrew from the engagement.

b. A qualified opinion can *not* be given because the auditor lacks independence.

c. The restriction on the scope of the audit was significant.

d. The statements taken as a whole do *not* fairly present the financial condition and results of operations of the company.

3,4 > **16-15** In which of the following circumstances would an auditor usually choose between issuing a qualified opinion and issuing a denial of opinion?

a. Departure from generally accepted accounting principles.

b. Inadequate disclosure of accounting policies.

c. Inability to obtain sufficient competent evidential matter.

d. Unreasonable justification for a change in accounting principle.

3,4>   **16-16**   John King was engaged to audit the financial statements of Newton Company after its fiscal year had ended. King neither observed the inventory count nor confirmed the receivables by direct communication with debtors but was satisfied concerning both after applying alternative procedures. King's auditor's report most likely contained a(n)

a. Qualified opinion.

b. Denial of opinion.

c. Unqualified opinion.

d. Unqualified opinion with an explanatory paragraph.

1,2>   **16-17**   In which of the following situations would an auditor ordinarily issue an unqualified audit opinion without an explanatory paragraph?

a. The auditor wishes to emphasize that the entity had significant related-party transactions.

b. The auditor decides to refer to the report of another auditor as a basis, in part, for the auditor's opinion.

c. The entity issues financial statements that present financial position and results of operations but omits the statement of cash flows.

d. The auditor has substantial doubt about the entity's ability to continue as a going concern, but the circumstances are fully disclosed in the financial statements.

5>   **16-18**   Which of the following best describes the auditor's responsibility for "other information" included in the annual report to shareholders that contains financial statements and the auditor's report?

a. The auditor has *no* obligation to read the "other information."

b. The auditor has *no* obligation to corroborate the "other information" but should read the "other information" to determine whether it is materially inconsistent with the financial statements.

c. The auditor should extend the examination to the extent necessary to verify the "other information."

d. The auditor must modify the auditor's report to state that the other information "is unaudited" or "is not covered by the auditor's report."

3,4>   **16-19**   An auditor decides to issue a qualified opinion on an entity's financial statements because a major inadequacy in the entity's computerized accounting records prevents the auditor from applying necessary procedures. The opinion paragraph of the auditor's report should state that the qualification pertains to

a. A client-imposed scope limitation.

b. A departure from generally accepted auditing standards.

c. The possible effects on the financial statements.

d. Inadequate disclosure of necessary information.

6 > **16-20**   When an auditor is asked to express an opinion on the rental and royalty income of an entity, he or she may

    a. Not accept the engagement because to do so would be tantamount to agreeing to issue a piecemeal opinion.

    b. Not accept the engagement unless also engaged to audit the full financial statements of the entity.

    c. Accept the engagement provided the auditor's opinion is expressed in a special report.

    d. Accept the engagement provided distribution of the auditor's report is limited to the entity's management.

5 > **16-21**   The entity under audit has disclosed in the notes to its financial statements that it is experiencing severe difficulties and that there is doubt about its ability to continue as a going-concern. The appropriate form of auditor's report is:

    a. An unqualified report with an explanatory paragraph.

    b. An accounting-related reservation of opinion.

    c. An auditing-related reservation of opinion.

    d. An unqualified report.

PROBLEMS

2,3,4 > **16-22**   You are an audit manager with a mid-sized local public accounting firm. You have spent the last week reviewing various audit files and have noted the following **independent** items:

File 1: Audit field staff were unable to observe a material amount of inventory at a client's Kapuskasing location because the client claimed that the inventory was buried in snow. While you failed to obtain additional satisfactory evidence regarding the inventory existence, you do not feel that this lack of audit evidence prevents an audit opinion on the client's financial statements taken as a whole.

File 2: During the review of a client's legal records, a member of the audit team noted correspondence relating to a potential lawsuit against the company by a competitor in western Canada. After some discussion with your client's controller, the company agreed to add a note to the financial statements that outlines the nature of the contingency. Your audit staff member concluded that no financial statement adjustment was required and that the note disclosure was in accordance with generally accepted accounting principles (GAAP).

File 3: The audit team completed the examination of the client's records on May 5. On May 22, the company's vice president, finance, contacted the audit senior and advised her that one of the company's primary suppliers had declared bankruptcy. The client may be forced to obtain alternate inventory from an overseas supplier at a substantially higher price. No additional work was performed to May 22 except in relation to matters directly concerning the bankruptcy. The vice president, finance, agreed that the event was significant and would be disclosed in the notes to the financial statements in accordance with GAAP.

File 4: The audit senior noted that senior management would not provide the audit team with necessary information regarding a commitment to supply a non-resident company with a material amount of inventory at below-market prices, or to disclose this information in the financial statements in accordance with GAAP.

File 5: A member of the audit team noted that a lease for office computer equipment was recorded as an operating lease when in fact it was a capital lease. Your staff member noted the unadjusted errors and concluded the effect on all accounts was immaterial.

Required:

Assess and describe the significance of each of the above items on the auditors' report and, in each case, describe any changes necessary to the standard audit report.

(ICABC, adapted)

1,2,3,4 ▷   **16-23**   For each of the following independent situations, indicate the reason for and the type of audit report that you would issue. Assume that each item is significant.

a. Barfield Corporation, a wholly owned subsidiary of Sandy, Inc., is audited by another firm. As the auditor of Sandy, Inc., you have assured yourself of the other firm's independence and professional reputation. However, you are unwilling to take complete responsibility for their audit work.

b. The management of Gough Corporation has decided to exclude the statement of cash flows from their financial statements because they believe that their bankers do not find the statement to be very useful.

c. You are auditing Diverse Carbon, a manufacturer of nerve gas for the military, for the year ended September 30, 2006. On September 1, 2006, one of their manufacturing plants caught fire, releasing nerve gas into the surrounding area. Two thousand people were killed and numerous others paralyzed. The company's legal counsel indicates that the company is liable, but the company does not want to disclose this information in the financial statements.

d. During your audit of Cuccia Coal Company, the controller, Tracy Tricks, refuses to allow you to confirm accounts receivable because she is concerned about complaints from her customers. You are unable to satisfy yourself about accounts receivable by other audit procedures.

e. On January 31, 2007, Takeda Toy Manufacturing hired your firm to audit the company's financial statements for the year 2006. You were unable to observe the client's inventory on December 31, 2006. However, you were able to satisfy yourself about the inventory balance using other auditing procedures.

f. Gelato Bros., Inc., leases its manufacturing facility from a partnership controlled by the chief executive officer and major shareholder of Gelato. Your review of the lease indicates that the rental terms are in excess of rental terms for similar buildings in the area. The company refuses to disclose this relationship in the footnotes.

g. Mitchell Manufacturing Company has used the double-declining balance method to depreciate its machinery. During the current year, management switched to the straight-line method because they felt that it better represented the utilization of the assets. You concur with their decision. All information is adequately disclosed in the financial statements.

1,2,3,4 > **16-24** For each of the following independent situations, indicate the reason for and the type of audit report that you would issue. Assume that each item is significant.

a. International Mines, Corp., uses weighted average for valuing inventories held in Canada and FIFO for inventories produced and held in their foreign operations.

b. HiTech Computers is suing your client, Super Software, for royalties over patent infringement. Super Software's outside legal counsel assures you that HiTech's case is without merit.

c. In previous years, your client, Merc International, has consolidated its Panamanian subsidiary. Because of restrictions on repatriation of earnings placed on all foreign-owned corporations in Panama, Merc International has decided to account for the subsidiary on the equity basis in the current year.

d. In prior years Worcester Wool Mills has used replacement cost to value its inventory of raw wool. During the current year Worcester changed to FIFO for valuing raw wool.

e. Upon review of the recent history of the lives of their specialized automobiles, Gas Leak Technology changed the service lives for depreciation purposes on their autos from five years to three years. This change resulted in a material amount of additional depreciation expense.

f. During the 2006 audit of Brannon Bakery Equipment, you found that a material amount of inventory had been excluded from the inventory amount shown in the 2005 financial statements. After discussing this problem with management, you become convinced that it was an unintentional oversight.

g. Jay Johnson holds 10 percent of the stock in Koenig Construction Company. The board of directors of Koenig asks Johnson to conduct their audit. Johnson completes the audit and determines that the financial statements present fairly in accordance with generally accepted accounting principles.

h. Palatka Credit Union's financial condition has been deteriorating for the last five years. Most of their problems result from loans made to real estate developers in Saint Johns County. Your review of the loan portfolio indicates that there should be a major increase in the loan-loss reserve. Based on your calculations, the proposed write-down of the loans will put Palatka into violation of the province's capital requirements.

4▷   **16-25**   Darrell Hotels Inc. (DHI), a company located in Saskatchewan owns and operates a small hotel chain, Laze-Z-Daze Inns. The company has experienced financial difficulties over the past three years due to a decline in occupancy and poor management. Increasing losses and rapidly deteriorating working capital have adversely affected the company's ability to discharge its liabilities. It is doubtful whether the client will be able to refinance its long-term debt in the amount of $15 million, due this year. DHI does not want to disclose this information in the financial statements.

You are the auditor of Darrell Hotels Inc.

Required:

a. What are your *responsibilities* regarding the going-concern assumption?

b. What are your *concerns* pertaining to disclosing going-concern problems?

(ICABC, adapted)

2,3,4▷   **16-26**   Devon, Ltd., engaged Aaron Rao to examine its financial statements for the year ended December 31, 2006. The financial statements of Devon, Ltd., for the year ended December 31, 2005, were examined by Ron Jones, whose March 31, 2006, auditor's report expressed an unqualified opinion. The report of Jones is not presented with the 2006–2005 comparative financial statements.

Rao's working papers contain the following information that does not appear in footnotes to the 2006 financial statements as prepared by Devon, Ltd.:

- One director appointed in 2006 was formerly a partner in Jones's accounting firm. Jones's firm provided financial consulting services to Devon during 2004 and 2003, for which Devon paid approximately $1,600 and $9,000, respectively.

- The company refused to capitalize certain lease obligations for equipment acquired in 2006. Capitalization of the leases in conformity with generally accepted accounting principles would have increased assets and liabilities by $312,000 and $387,000, respectively, decreased retained earnings as of December 31, 2006, by $75,000, and decreased net income and earnings per share by $75,000 and $0.75, respectively, for the year then ended. Rao has concluded that the leases should have been capitalized.

- During the year, Devon changed its method of valuing inventory from the first-in, first-out method to the weighted average method. This change was made because management believes weighted average more clearly reflects net income by providing a closer matching of current costs and current revenues. The change had the effect of reducing inventory at December 31, 2006, by $65,000 and net income and earnings per share by $38,000 and $0.38, respectively, for the year then ended. The effect of the change on prior years was immaterial; accordingly, the change had no cumulative effect. Rao supports the company's position.

After completing the field work on February 29, 2007, Rao concludes that the expression of an adverse opinion is not warranted.

Required:

Prepare the body of Rao's report dated February 29, 2007, and addressed to the shareholders to accompany the 2006–2005 comparative financial statements.

(AICPA, adapted)

1,2,3,4⟩ 16-27 The audit report below was drafted by a staff accountant of Espinoza & Turner, CAs, at the completion of the audit of the financial statements of Lyon Computers, Corp., for the year ended March 31, 2006. It was submitted to the engagement partner, who reviewed matters thoroughly and properly concluded that Lyon's disclosures concerning its ability to continue as a going concern for a reasonable period of time were adequate.

Auditor's Report

To the Board of Directors of Lyon Computers, Inc.:
We have audited the accompanying balance sheet of Lyon Computers, Inc., as of March 31, 2006, and the other related financial statements for the year then ended. Our responsibility is to express an opinion on these financial statements based on our audit.

We conducted our audit in accordance with standards that require that we plan and perform the audit to obtain reasonable assurance about whether the financial statements are in conformity with generally accepted accounting principles. An audit includes examining, on a test basis, evidence supporting the amounts and disclosures in the financial statements. An audit also includes assessing the accounting principles used and significant estimates made by management.

The accompanying financial statements have been prepared assuming that the Company will continue as a going concern. As discussed in Note 7 to the financial statements, the Company has suffered recurring losses from operations and has a net capital deficiency that raises substantial doubt about its ability to continue as a going concern. We believe that management's plans in regard to these matters, which are also described in Note 7, will permit the Company to continue as a going concern beyond a reasonable period of time. The financial statements do not include any adjustments that might result from the outcome of this uncertainty.

In our opinion, subject to the effects on the financial statements of such adjustments, if any, as might have been required had the outcome of the uncertainty referred to in the preceding paragraph been known, the financial statements referred to above present fairly, in all material respects, the financial position of Lyon Computers, Inc., and the results of its operations and its cash flows in conformity with generally accepted accounting principles applied on a basis consistent with that of the preceding year.

Espinoza & Turner, CAs
April 28, 2007

Required:

Identify the deficiencies contained in the auditor's report as drafted by the staff accountant. Group the deficiencies by paragraph. Do *not* redraft the report.

(AICPA, adapted)

1,2,3,4 **16-28** For the year ended December 31, 2006, Friday & Co. ("Friday"), audited the financial statements of Kim Company and expressed an unqualified opinion on the balance sheet only. Friday did not observe the taking of the physical inventory as of December 31, 2005, because that date was prior to its appointment as auditor. Friday was unable to satisfy itself regarding inventory by means of other auditing procedures, so it did not express an opinion on the other basic financial statements that year.

For the year ended December 31, 2006, Friday expressed an unqualified opinion on all the basic financial statements and satisfied itself as to the consistent application of generally accepted accounting principles. The field work was completed on March 11, 2007; the partner-in-charge reviewed the working papers and signed the auditor's report on March 18, 2007. The report on the comparative financial statements for 2006 and 2005 was delivered to Kim on March 21, 2007.

Required:

Prepare Friday's audit report that was submitted to Kim's board of directors on the 2006 and 2005 comparative financial statements.

(AICPA, adapted)

DISCUSSION CASES

6 **16-29** You are a manager with the firm of Woo and Dunnit, a large regional firm that has offices across central and western Canada. You have just taken on the audit of a new client—SportsXtra (SX), a chain of sporting goods stores that has outlets in leased space in two dozen shopping malls, mostly located in western Canada. The lease for each store requires that the monthly rent be determined by a formula—a fixed amount plus a percentage of the store's revenue for the month. The lease agreements require the store to have its auditor issue a report to the lessor on the sales of the particular store covered by the lease. However, neither the nature of the auditor's examination nor the nature of the resulting report are specified by the lease agreement.

The annual financial statements aggregate the sales for each store into one figure and the previous auditors normally visited only some of the stores each year, generally the larger outlets, on a rotating basis. The previous auditors had issued each year a report for each store to be given to the lessor. Below is an example of such a report for the store at South Winnipeg Mall for last year:

As requested by SportsXtra, we report that the sales of the corporation's store in South Winnipeg Mall for the year ended September 30, 2006, are recorded in the amount of $3,505,000 in the general ledger sales account of the corporation.

Our examination of the corporation's financial statements for the year ended June 30, 2006 was not directed to the determination of sales of individual stores, nor have we examined the corporation's financial statements for the three-month period subsequent to June 30, 2006. We have not audited, and accordingly do not express an opinion on the amount of sales referred to in the preceding paragraph.

This year new ownership has taken over nine of the malls in which SportsXtra has stores. They have informed SportsXtra that they will no longer accept this report, stating that it provides them with no assurance that sales at individual stores are fairly stated. You, as the manager who will be responsible for the annual audit, have explained to the management of SportsXtra that it would cost considerably more in time and effort to provide an audit opinion on sales at each particular store location.

The management of SportsXtra is not very happy with the prospect of paying the extra cost for an audit of the sales at each location. The chief financial officer has said to you, "Why can't your firm provide some intermediate level of assurance between none, which is what the former auditors' report appears to indicate, and a full scope audit opinion?" In fact, he has proposed new wording as follows:

As requested by SportsXtra, we report that, in our opinion, the sales of the corporation's store in South Winnipeg Mall for the year ended September 30, 2006, in the amount of $3,505,000 are fairly stated in all respects material to the financial statements taken as a whole.

Required:

Identify and discuss the reporting approaches raised by the CFO of SportsXtra and any other reporting approaches that could satisfy both SportsXtra management and the new ownership of the malls.

(CICA, adapted)

1,2,3,4〉   **16-30**   Your client, Texter, Ltd., a publicly held shoe distributor, acquired 100 percent of Shoe-Rite in 2002. As a result, Texter owns approximately 30 percent of Armundi, S.A., an Italian shoe manufacturer, which is audited by an internationally recognized firm, Lafrance, Dematasco & Associates. Texter uses the equity method of accounting for its investment in Armundi.

Over the years, Texter's investment in Armundi has become a more substantial portion of its balance sheet. It originally accounted for 2 to 3 percent of Texter's total assets between 2002 and 2004 and for more than 5 percent by 2005. However, that investment has increased from about 8 percent of Texter's shareholders' equity in 2000 to approximately 39 percent of shareholders' equity in 2006. Further, Texter's share of Armundi's earnings has ranged from more than 5 percent of pretax earnings in 2000 to approximately 20 percent in 2006 and represents an average of approximately 14 percent of pretax earnings over the last five years except for one loss year. A weak Canadian dollar has magnified Armundi's contribution to earnings. Currently there are no business transactions (sales/purchases) between Texter and Armundi.

From an audit risk and reporting standpoint, Texter's increasing investment in Armundi and Armundi's increasing contribution to Texter's earnings raise the question of reliance on Armundi's auditors. Lafrance, Dematasco & Associates currently performs a full-scope audit of Armundi under GAAP/GAAS requirements in its country of domicile. This audit forms the basis for the Canadian GAAP compilation that Lafrance, Dematasco & Associates prepares for your purposes. Your discussions with Lafrance, Dematasco & Associates over the last several years have provided you with a level of assurance necessary to opine on Texter's consolidated financial statements. In prior years, you have also received letters from Lafrance, Dematasco & Associates about their independence of Texter and its affiliates.

Because Armundi's stock is not publicly traded, Texter is bound by restrictions on the sale of the stock that are set forth in Armundi's Articles of Association, which also give existing shareholders a right of first refusal on any shares offered for sale.

Texter has been receiving cash dividends from Armundi continuously since owning the stock. The cash is remitted to Texter without any problems. There are no significant exchange restrictions involving repatriation of earnings or proceeds from the sale of the stock.

During the past several years, Texter has attempted to increase its ownership percentage of Armundi through various means. Texter has worked closely with its counsel and Italian counsel and with Armundi's auditors, Lafrance, Dematasco & Associates, to structure a transaction that would give Texter a controlling interest in Armundi.

Required:

a. With respect to Texter's investment in Armundi, can you assume responsibility for the work performed by Lafrance, Dematasco & Associates?

b. What procedures should you perform?

c. Draft Texter, Inc.'s, audit report for the year ended 2006, assuming that you have decided to rely on Lafrance, Dematasco & Associates in the audit report. Assume that the audit report will cover only one year, 2006.

2,4> **16-31**   You are auditing the financial statements for your new client, Paper Packaging Corporation, a manufacturer of paper containers, for the year ended March 31, 2006. Paper Packaging's previous auditors had issued a going-concern opinion on the March 31, 2005, financial statements for the following reasons:

- Paper Packaging had defaulted on $10 million of unregistered debentures sold to three insurance companies, which were due in 2005, and the default constituted a possible violation of other debt agreements.

- The interest and principal payments due on the remainder of a 10-year credit agreement, which began in 2003, would exceed the cash flows generated from operations in recent years.

- The company had disposed of certain operating units. The proceeds from the sale were subject to possible adjustment through arbitration proceedings, the outcome of which was uncertain at year-end.

- Various lawsuits were pending against the company.

- The company was in the midst of tax proceedings as a result of an examination of the company's federal income tax returns for a period of 12 years.

You find that the status of the above matters is as follows at year-end, March 31, 2006:

- The company is still in default on $4.6 million of the debentures due in 2004 but is trying to negotiate a settlement with remaining bondholders. A large number of bondholders have settled their claims at significantly less than par.

- The company has renegotiated the 2004 credit agreement, which provides for a two-year moratorium on principal payments and interest at 8 percent. It also limits net losses ($2.25 million for 2005) and requires a certain level of defined cumulative quarterly operating income to be maintained.

- The arbitration proceedings were resolved in 2006.

- The legal actions were settled in 2006.

- Most of the tax issues have been resolved, and, according to the company's legal counsel, those remaining will result in a net cash inflow to the company.

At year-end Paper Packaging had a cash balance of $5.5 million and expects to generate a net cash flow of $3.2 million in the upcoming fiscal year.

The following information about Paper Packaging's plans for its operations in fiscal year 2007 may also be useful in arriving at a decision.

	Fiscal Year 2004 Budget	Fiscal Year 2006 Actual	Fiscal Year 2006 Budget
Net revenues	$66.2	$60.9	$79.8
Gross margin	34.7	33.6	45.6
Operating expenses	27.9	34.7	31.4
Interest—net	5.1	6.0	5.7
Other income (expenses)—net	(.8)	2.1	—
Earnings before income taxes and extraordinary items	1.5	(5.1)	(.2)
Cash flows:			
Receipts	69.9	79.7	
Disbursements	66.7	96.9	
Excess/deficit	3.2	(22.8)	

Required:

a. What should you consider in deciding whether to require Paper Packaging Corporation to discuss a going-concern uncertainty in its financial statement notes?

b. How much influence should the report on the March 31, 2005, financial statements have on your decision?

c. Should the notes to Paper Packaging Corporation's financial statements for the year ended March 31, 2006, include a discussion of a going-concern uncertainty? (In other words, what is your evaluation of the circumstances existing at March 31, 2006?)

Part VII PROFESSIONAL RESPONSIBILITIES

Ethics, Professional Conduct, and Quality Control ‹ Chapter 17

Learning Objectives

Upon completion of this chapter, you will be able to

1 Define ethics and professionalism.

2 Explain the three theories of ethical behaviour.

3 Deal with ethical dilemmas through an example situation.

4 Describe the framework for the Rules of Professional Conduct.

5 Explain the principles of professional conduct.

6 Outline some of the more important rules of professional conduct that apply to standards of behaviour expected of the auditor.

7 Describe how the Rules of Professional Conduct are interpreted and enforced.

8 Explain quality control systems, including the elements of quality control and how a firm monitors its quality control system.

RELEVANT ACCOUNTING AND ASSURANCE PRONOUNCEMENTS

General Standard for Firms—GSF-QC, General standards of quality control for firms performing assurance engagements

CICA Handbook, **section 5025**, Standards for assurance engagements

CICA Handbook, **section 5030,** Quality control procedures for assurance engagements

CICA Handbook, **section 5100,** Generally accepted auditing standards

CICA Handbook, **section 5135,** The auditor's responsibility to consider fraud

CICA Handbook, **section 5751,** Communication with those having oversight responsibility for the financial reporting process

Rules of Professional Conduct of the Provincial Institutes of Chartered Accountants

Rules of Professional Conduct of the Provincial Associations of Certified General Accountants

Rules of Professional Conduct of the Provincial Societies of Certified Management Accountants

PROFESSIONAL CONDUCT AND THE AUDITOR

PeopleSoft is a leading provider of software applications that assist companies in managing business activities. Ernst & Young LLP,* a Big 4 public accounting firm, was PeopleSoft's auditor from 1994 to June 2000. Besides earning almost $1.7 million for auditing PeopleSoft's financial statements from 1994 to 1999, Ernst & Young allegedly entered into a variety of lucrative business arrangements with the company. On April 16, 2004, a U.S. federal court found, among other things, that Ernst & Young engaged in improper professional conduct, violated applicable professional ethics standards, and engaged in conduct that was both reckless and negligent. The court also found that a reasonable investor who knew of Ernst & Young's and PeopleSoft's mutual interests in the business success of their joint efforts "would make an objective and pragmatic assessment that Ernst & Young would not be objective in its audit of PeopleSoft."

The court reiterated the importance of auditor independence:

---

* For full details on the case and the source of the above quotes, see *Initial Decision Release No. 249, Administrative Proceeding, File No. 3-10933, United States of America before the Securities and Exchange Commission in the Matter of Ernst & Young LLP* (www.sec.gov/litigation/aljdec/id249bpm.htm).

Auditors have been characterized as "gatekeepers" to the public securities markets that are crucial for capital formation. The independent public accountant performing this special function owes ultimate allegiance to the corporation's creditors and stockholders, as well as to the investing public. This "public watchdog" function demands that the accountant maintain total independence from the client at all times and requires complete fidelity to the public trust.

The judge ordered Ernst & Young to (1) "disgorge" $1,686,500, the amount of its fees for auditing PeopleSoft for fiscal years 1994 through 1999, along with a significant amount of prejudgment interest on those fees, (2) retain an independent consultant to work with the firm to ensure that the firm's leadership implemented policies and procedures to remedy the professional ethics violations found and come into compliance with rules on auditor independence, and (3) refrain from accepting additional audit engagements for new public audit clients for a period of six months. Of the three penalties, the sanction against accepting new clients was the most severe, as it had both significant reputation and revenue consequences.

An Ethical Framework

Ethics and Professionalism

LO 1⟩

Ethics refers to a system or code of conduct based on moral duties and obligations that indicates how an individual should behave. *Professionalism* refers to the conduct, aims, or qualities that characterize or mark a profession or professional person.[1] All professions establish rules or codes of conduct that define what is ethical (professional) behaviour for members of the profession. These rules exist so that (1) users of the professional services know what to expect when they purchase such services, (2) members of the profession know what is acceptable behaviour,

---

[1] S. M. Mintz, *Cases in Accounting Ethics and Professionalism*, 3d ed. (New York: Irwin/McGraw-Hill, 1997), p. 4.

and (3) the profession can use the rules to monitor the actions of its members. The accounting profession has a *Code of Professional Conduct* that guides the behaviour of accounting professionals, and monitors the actions of its professional members to ensure that they are in compliance with the Code.[2]

Theories of Ethical Behaviour

LO 2

When individuals are confronted with situations that have moral and ethical implications, they do not always agree on the issue at hand, which individuals or groups will be affected and how, or what solutions or courses of actions are available or appropriate for dealing with the situation. Such differences may be caused by differences in the individuals' concepts of fairness and different opinions about the right action to take in a particular situation.

S. M. Mintz has suggested that there are three methods or theories of ethical behaviour that can guide the analyses of ethical issues in accounting.[3] These theories are (1) *utilitarianism*, (2) a *rights-based approach*, and (3) a *justice-based approach*. No one approach is better than another. Elements of each theory may be appropriate for resolving ethical dilemmas.

Utilitarian theory recognizes that decision making involves tradeoffs between the benefits and burdens of alternative actions, and it focuses on the consequences of an action on the individuals affected. The theory proposes that the interests of all parties affected, not just one's self-interest, should be considered. One form of utilitarianism holds that rules have a central position in moral judgement. This approach may have significance for auditors who are expected to follow the Code of Professional Conduct in carrying out their responsibilities. One disadvantage in applying the utilitarian theory to ethical dilemmas is that it is difficult to measure the potential costs and benefits of the actions to be taken. It may also be difficult to balance the interests of all parties involved when those interests conflict with one another.

The theory of rights assumes that individuals have certain rights and other individuals have a duty to respect those rights. Thus, a decision maker who follows a theory of rights should undertake an action only if it does not violate the rights of *any* individual. An obvious disadvantage of the theory of rights is that, as with utilitarianism, it may be difficult or impossible to satisfy all rights of all affected parties, especially when those rights conflict. The theory of rights is important to auditors because of their public-interest responsibility. In conflicting situations, the rights of some individuals may not be satisfied in order that the primacy of the public-interest obligation of auditors may be maintained. According to the concept known as the "moral point of view," auditors must be willing, at least sometimes, to put the interests of other stakeholders, such as investors and creditors, ahead of their own self-interests and those of their firm. Thus, if a difference of opinion with top management exists over an accounting or reporting issue, the auditor should emphasize the interests

---

[2]Each of the accounting designations in Canada (e.g., CA, CGA, CMA) has its own code or rules of professional conduct. To simplify the exposition, they will be referred to in the singular.

[3]See S. M. Mintz, *Cases in Accounting Ethics and Professionalism*, 3rd ed. (New York: Irwin/McGraw-Hill, 1997), for a more detailed discussion of each of these models.

of the investors and creditors in deciding what action to take, even if it means losing the client.

The theory of justice is concerned with issues such as equity, fairness, and impartiality. Mintz indicates that decisions made within this theory should fairly and equitably distribute resources among those individuals or groups affected. There may be difficulty in trying to apply this theory in practice because the rights of one or more individuals or groups may be affected when a better distribution of benefits is provided to others; affirmative action programs are one example of the difficulty in applying the theory of justice. While none of these theories by itself can provide a perfect ethical framework, each can be useful in helping an auditor to solve dilemmas by providing an ethical perspective for resolving the dilemma.

Example—An Ethical Dilemma

LO 3>

Consider how an auditor might act given the following simplified situation.

CANADIAN SHIELD CREDIT UNION

Pine, Johnson & Associates has recently been awarded the audit of Canadian Shield Credit Union for the year ended December 31, 2006. Canadian Shield is now the largest client of Pine, Johnson & Associates, and the fees from this engagement represent a significant portion of the firm's revenues. Upon accepting the Canadian Shield engagement, the firm incurred additional costs by hiring several new employees and a new manager from a larger firm. In bidding on the engagement, Sam Johnson knew that the first-year fees would be just enough to cover the actual cost of the first year's audit, but he hoped that future audit fee increases and fees for other services might lead to a long-term, profitable engagement. Based on his discussions with the predecessor auditors, Johnson knew that there were possible problems with Canadian Shield's loans because of the collateral used for security. Johnson was also concerned that there might be problems with the loan-loss reserves due to the effects of the economic slowdown on the tourist industry in Canadian Shield over the last two years. However, Johnson felt that these problems were manageable.

During the current year, the amount included in the loan-loss reserves (i.e. provision to bad debts) account was $675,000, approximately the same as the figure for the prior year. Canadian banks are subject to federal regulations and the regulations require that an amount equal to 1.5 percent of the loans outstanding be included as a reserve against losses. The $675,000 was slightly above the statutory requirement. However, the audit staff identified two large loans, aggregating to $15 million, that appeared not to be collectible in full. The working papers disclosed that each loan had originated during the current year and that both had been in default for four months. Additionally, the collateral used to secure the loans was worth considerably less than the amount of the loans and was not in accordance with Canadian Shield's loan policy procedures. Based on this information, the staff estimates that about 40 percent of the $15 million,

(continued)

CANADIAN SHIELD CREDIT UNION *(concluded)*

or $6 million, will not be collected. The staff has also determined that these loans are to entities owned by Patricia Cabot, Canadian Shield's CEO, and some of her business associates.

When Johnson met with Cabot to discuss the two delinquent loans, Cabot tried to convince Johnson that the loans would be paid in full. She told Johnson that the loans had been properly made and that as soon as the economy picked up, payments would be made on the loans. She indicated that no additional reserves were needed and that if Johnson requires such adjustments, his firm might be replaced.

What ethical and professional concerns should Johnson consider in deciding on a course of action?

If Johnson follows a utilitarian approach, he should consider the consequences (benefits and costs) of his actions on all affected parties and whether any rules exist that might require a particular action. The benefits of requiring the increase in the reserve may be full and accurate disclosure of the facts as assessed by the audit team. Another benefit may arise from the time-honoured convention of conservatism. Costs need to be assessed in terms of Canadian Shield shareholders, Cabot's reputation, and the situation of the public accounting firm. For example, Johnson might consider that if he requires an additional reserve amount for the loans, the price of Canadian Shield shares might decline and the shareholders would suffer losses. By forcing Canadian Shield to increase the reserves, he might also damage Cabot's reputation if the loans are eventually paid. On the other hand, if Cabot is inappropriately using Canadian Shield funds for personal gain, the shareholders are being harmed by her actions. Finally, Johnson might consider how the loss of Canadian Shield as a client would affect his firm. If the client is lost, the newly hired personnel may need to be terminated. While Johnson knows that the reserve is in accordance with the federal statutory rule on loan losses, from a rules perspective he also knows that generally accepted accounting principles require that the loans be presented in the financial statements at net realizable value. Given the facts in this case and using a utilitarian approach, Johnson may conclude that the loan-loss reserves should be adjusted by the $6 million.

The theory of rights requires that Johnson consider whose rights would be violated if he does not require an increase in the loan-loss reserves because, based on the evidence, generally accepted accounting principles would require an adjustment. The shareholders' right to fair and accurate information for decision-making purposes is being violated. If Cabot has entered into loans at the expense of the shareholders, they will not have received accurate information about Canadian Shield profitability, liquidity, and so on. If Johnson does not require the adjustment and the loans eventually become uncollectible, the shareholders' rights will be violated and Johnson may be in violation of GAAP, GAAS, and other professional standards. Thus, under a rights approach, Johnson is likely to conclude that he has a duty to require the adjustment to the financial statements.

The theory of justice requires that Johnson's decisions impartially consider the interests of the shareholders, Cabot, the depositors, and the government, which is insuring the deposits. Johnson should therefore avoid favouring the interest of any individual or group. The theory of justice might lead Johnson to consider all interests without being biased toward any one. However, auditors are supposed to represent the public interest. This would likely lead Johnson to the conclusion that an adjustment should be made for the $6 million. The potential loss of the client may severely test Johnson's impartiality in this case. But integrity and objectivity would require that Johnson not subordinate his judgement to that of the client or place his own self-interest ahead of the public interest.

If Johnson follows the moral point of view, he should first consider the interests of Canadian Shield shareholders. This would result in Johnson requiring the client to book the $6 million adjustment for the delinquent loans.

In this case, Johnson's professionalism is likely to be tested. While he realizes that the loan-loss reserves probably should be increased, he is also likely to be concerned about the possibility of losing this valuable client and the significant investment in new personnel that the firm has made. While it seems fairly clear what action should be taken (requiring the client to adjust the reserve), the question becomes—as it so often does—does the auditor (Johnson) have the moral fortitude to do what is right?

Auditors frequently face such ethical dilemmas in their practice. It is important that auditors develop sound moral character so that they can respond appropriately in such situations. Mintz points out that auditors who possess certain "virtues" or traits of character are more capable of adhering to the moral point of view.[4] Examples of such virtues include honesty, integrity, impartiality, faithfulness, and trustworthiness. These are similar to the Principles of Professional Conduct discussed later in the chapter. The next section presents a model of moral development which can be used to demonstrate how Johnson's moral judgement should have developed to the point where he should require the credit union to provide additional reserves for the loans.

Professional Conduct

LO 4>   The way in which the Rules of Professional Conduct have been promulgated differs slightly across the Canadian professional accounting bodies. For instance, formally, each provincial institute of CAs has the responsibility for the determination and administration of its own Rules of Professional Conduct. However, the CICA has provided a skeleton framework for the provincial institutes and they have harmonized their rules of professional conduct so that any differences tend to be minor. (Harmonization facilitates the movement of members from one part of the country to another.) CGA-Canada has established one code across Canada with the responsibility for administration of the code (and the right to amend or augment the national code for specific circumstances) delegated to the provincial

---

[4]S. M. Mintz, "Virtue, Ethics, and Accounting Education," *Issues in Accounting Education* (Fall 1995), pp. 24–31.

associations. CMA Canada's Rules of Professional Conduct are under provincial jurisdiction. The professional associations and institutes also offer confidential assistance to their members in resolving ethical dilemmas in the members' professional practices.

Although the terminology and the format differ somewhat across the profession, substantively, the similarities between the professional bodies and across provinces are far greater than any differences. The following discussion deals with the important aspects of the rules of conduct for all professional accountants in Canada. If an individual is interested in becoming a member of a particular professional organization (e.g., CA, CGA, CMA), he or she should become familiar with the specifics of the rules for that organization in the specific locality.

Proceeding from the more general to the more specific, there are three main components to the Code of Professional Conduct:

- principles of Professional Conduct
- rules of Professional Conduct
- interpretations of the Rules of Professional Conduct

In addition, a fourth component is the published (summarized) rulings of the disciplinary committees or tribunals. Figure 17–1 provides a pictorial representation of the four parts of the Code of Professional Conduct.

Principles of Professional Conduct

LO 5⟩ The highest level in the hierarchy is the principles of professional conduct. Table 17–1 presents the definition of each principle. They are stated at a

FIGURE 17–1

Code of Professional Conduct

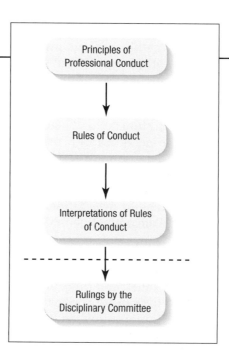

Table 17–1	**Principles of Professional Conduct**

- *Responsibilities:* In carrying out their responsibilities as professionals, members should exercise sensitive professional and moral judgements in all their activities.
- *The public interest:* Members should accept the obligation to act in a way that will serve the public interest, honour the public trust, and demonstrate commitment to professionalism.
- *Integrity:* To maintain and broaden public confidence, members should perform all professional responsibilities with the highest sense of integrity.
- *Objectivity and independence:* A member should maintain objectivity and be free of conflicts of interest in discharging professional responsibilities. A member in public practice should be independent in fact and appearance when providing auditing and other attestation services.
- *Due care:* A member should observe the profession's technical and ethical standards, strive continually to improve competence and the quality of services, and discharge professional responsibility to the best of the member's ability.
- *Scope and nature of services:* A member in public practice should observe the Principles of the Code of Professional Conduct in determining the scope and nature of services to be provided.

conceptual level and are meant to establish ideal standards of conduct. These principles of ethical conduct are not enforceable.

The first two principles address a "pubic accountant's responsibilities to exercise professional and moral judgement in a manner that serves the public interest." These principles reinforce the conviction that the public accountant role in society is to serve the public. The profession's public includes clients, creditors, employers, employees, governments, investors, and other members of the business and financial community—all the groups discussed in Chapter 1.

These groups rely on public accountant's integrity, objectivity, and independence when providing high-quality services. Integrity requires that a public accountant be honest and candid and honour both the form and the spirit of ethical standards. Thus, a public accountant should make judgements that are consistent with the theories of rights and justice. When faced with an ethical dilemma, the public accountant should ask, "What actions would an individual with integrity take, given these facts and circumstances?" Objectivity and independence are hallmarks of the public accounting profession. The principle of objectivity requires the public accountant to be impartial and free of conflicts of interest. Independence requires that the public accountant avoid relationships that would impair his or her objectivity. When a public accountant provides auditing- or attestation-related services, independence in both fact and appearance must be maintained. If a public accountant is perceived not to be independent, the various groups mentioned will not place much value on the services provided. The fifth principle, due care, requires that the public accountant perform his or her professional responsibilities with competence and diligence. While the performance of professional services must take into account the interests of the client, the public's interest is more important when the two interests conflict. The last principle requires that the public accountant determine that the services to be rendered are consistent with acceptable professional behaviour for public accountants. This principle also requires that the public accountant have internal quality control procedures to ensure that services are delivered competently and that no conflict of interest exists.

Main Rules of Professional Conduct

LO 6 There are four main dimensions to the Rules of Professional Conduct— general, standards of conduct affecting the public interest, relations with other individuals in public accounting, and organization and conduct of a professional practice. Each section addresses a different dimension of the public accountant's responsibilities. Table 17–2 reproduces in part the table of contents of the Rules of Professional Conduct of the Institute of Chartered Accountants of Ontario (the full version may be found at www.icao.on.ca/ Resources/Membershandbook/rules web.pdf) and for expositional purpose the following discussion uses those rules as a point of reference. For CGA-Canada's rules of professional conduct, the reader should visit www. cga-online.org/servlet/portal/library/About+Us/About+the+Association/ca ceproc v2-6.pdf. For an example of a set of provincial rules for CMAs, visit www.cmabc.com/pdf/Rulesprofconduct.pdf. Before proceeding to a discussion of the rules, here are a number of important definitions.

Client—Any person or entity that engages a member or member's firm to perform professional services or a person or entity with respect to which professional services are performed.

Enterprise—Synonymous with the term *client* for purposes of the code.

Financial statements—Statements and footnotes related thereto that purport to show financial position that relates to a point of time or changes in financial position that relate to a period of time, and statements that use cash or another incomplete basis of accounting.

Firm—A form of organization permitted by provincial law or regulation that is engaged in the practice of public accounting, including the individual owners thereof.

Member—A member of the CICA, CGA-Canada or CMA Canada.

Practice of public accounting—The performance for a client, by a member or a member's firm, of the professional services of accounting, tax, personal financial planning, litigation support services, and those professional services for which standards are promulgated by bodies designated by their respective councils.

Professional services—All services performed by a member for a client.

General

The rules in the general section relate primarily to the character and good reputation of the profession. For example, the member is required to comply with all the bylaws, regulations, and Rules of Professional Conduct of the Institute. Additionally, members are required to report any disciplinary action

Table 17–2 — Rules of Professional Conduct of the Institute of Chartered Accountants of Ontario

Section 100—GENERAL

101	Compliance with bylaws, regulations, and rules
102.1	Conviction of criminal or similar offences
102.2	Reporting disciplinary suspension, expulsion or restriction of right to practice
103	False or misleading applications
104	Requirement to reply in writing

Section 200—STANDARDS OF CONDUCT AFFECTING THE PUBLIC INTEREST

201.1, .2 & .03	Maintenance of reputation of profession
201.4	Advocacy services
202	Integrity and due care
203.1	Professional competence
.2	Co-operation with practice inspections and conduct investigations
204	Independence
.1	Assurance and specified auditing procedures engagements
.2	Identification of threats and safeguards
.3	Documentation
.4	Specific prohibitions, assurance, and specified auditing procedures engagements
.5	Members must disclose prohibited interests and relationships
.6	Firms to ensure compliance by partners and professional employees
.7	Independence: insolvency engagements
.8	Disclosure of impaired independence
205	False or misleading documents or oral representations
206	Compliance with professional standards
207	Unauthorized benefits
208	Confidentiality of information
209	Borrowing from clients
210	Conflict of interest
211	Duty to report breach of rules of professional conduct
212.1	Handling of trust funds and other property
.2	Handling property of others
213	Unlawful activity
214	Fee quotations
215	Contingent fees
216	Payment or receipt of commissions
217.1	Advertising and promotion
.2	Solicitation
.3	Endorsements
218	Retention of documentation and working papers

Section 300—RELATIONS WITH FELLOW MEMBERS AND WITH NON-MEMBERS LICENCED TO PRACTISE PUBLIC ACCOUNTING

302	Communication with predecessor
303	Co-operation with successor
304	Joint engagements
305	Communication of special engagements to incumbent
306.1	Responsibilities on accepting engagements
.2	Responsibilities on referred engagements

(continued)

Table 17–2	*(concluded)*

Section 400—**ORGANIZATION AND CONDUCT OF A PROFESSSIONAL PRACTICE**	
401	Practice names
402	Use of descriptive styles
403	Association with firms
404	Operation of members' offices
405	Office by representation

from any other province. Members must also promptly report any conviction for a criminal or similar offence related to their professional activities.

Standards of Conduct Affecting the Public Interest

As the title indicates, this section contains those Rules of Professional Conduct concerned with safeguarding the public interest. Rule 201.1 states:

> A member or student shall conduct himself or herself at all times in a manner which will maintain the good reputation of the profession and its ability to serve the public interest.

Specific actions the professional accountant should undertake include such things as:

- sustaining his or her professional competence (This may be accomplished on a firm-wide level by industry specialization groups. On an individual level, both the CICA and CGA-Canada require that their members engage in continuing professional education.)
- not becoming associated with any misleading documents or misleading representations
- disclosing any relationships that, while not being in contravention of the Rules of Professional Conduct, might cause an external observer to suspect impairment of the member's objectivity
- not acting as an advocate for an assurances services client or acting in any manner that would be perceived by an external observer as tending to impair objectivity
- reporting to the discipline committee any breaches of the Rules of Professional Conduct by other members (after informing the member of the intent to report)

The rules concerning integrity and due care, and professional competence, reinforce and elaborate on the general standard of generally accepted auditing standards (GAAS). A reputation for integrity is one of the most important assets that a professional accountant possesses. He or she must scrupulously protect this integrity in all dealings with clients, colleagues, employees, and employers.

It is also crucial that an auditor exercise due care in all facets of the exercise of his or her profession. The standard of behaviour implied by the term *due care* means the performance of his or her responsibilities with the level of care and skill that could be expected of a person with his or her level of expertise. As the next chapter will discuss, interpretation of this concept in specific circumstances has been a question of law for many years.

The rules regarding independence have undergone significant expansion and revision. The focus of the earlier version of the Canadian rule was objectivity. For example, the auditor was required to "... hold himself or herself free of any influence...which...impairs the member's professional judgement or objectivity or which, in the view of a reasonable observer, would impair the member's professional judgement or objectivity." Independence from the client, financial or relational, was the externally observable way in which objectivity was ensured.

In the wake of the financial failures of Enron, Global Crossings, WorldCom, and others, there was significant pressure, externally from the Canadian Public Accountability Board (CPAB) an organization created to oversee the practice of public accounting in Canada, and whose membership draws from the professional accounting bodies, securities regulators, and lay representatives, and internally from the profession itself, to strengthen the standards governing auditor objectivity. The new wording enunciates a proactive framework that requires members and firms, for each engagement, to:

a. consider independence before and throughout each assurance engagement
b. consider whether any "threats" to independence (e.g., the provision of non-audit services) exist
c. where threats are identified, consider whether there are any "safeguards" that exist or may be applied to eliminate the threat or reduce it to an acceptable level
d. where safeguards are found to be inadequate, decline or discontinue the engagement
e. notwithstanding the analysis of threats and safeguards, consider whether there are any "prohibitions" (Rule 204.4) that would preclude the undertaking or completion of the proposed engagement

If an auditor is not independent of the client it is unlikely that a user of the financial statements will place much reliance on his or her audit report. The profession must be concerned with independence in fact and independence in appearance. Independence in fact refers to the state of mind of the auditor, and as such, is unobservable. Therefore, other Rules of Professional Conduct in this section identify activities or relationships which, if undertaken by the auditor, could give an observer reason to think that there might be a lack of independence resulting in impairment of the auditor's objectivity. For example, this section also contains rules regarding potential conflicts of interest, the auditor's handling of trust funds, and a prohibition on accepting contingency fees.

The Rules of Professional Conduct may be supplemented by Council Interpretations, which often proscribe and prescribe what activities the auditor may undertake. A partial list of proscribed activities includes the following:

- direct or indirect ownership by the member, or his or her family, of an interest in an assurance client
- economic dependence on an assurance client
- indebtedness to an assurance client
- performance of management functions for the client as an employee or through the provision of management advisory services

There are exceptions to these conditions for involvement with social clubs and religious or charitable organizations. However, the following quotation from the *Members' Handbook* of the Institute of Chartered Accountants of British Columbia stresses the care that members of the profession must exercise:

> Members are cautioned that the test of objectivity is to be judged in the context of both real and perceived impairments. Often it is the perception of impairment that poses the greatest challenge to members. In all situations, members should reflect upon the wording of the applicable rule to ensure compliance with its spirit and intent.

Many firms regard the Rules of Professional Conduct as a minimum standard and are even more stringent regarding their partners' (although not usually more junior professional employees') ownership of shares of audit clients or of shares of companies that own audit clients. Similarly, immediate or close family relationships where a related individual is a director or officer of an audit client are not allowed. In this context, the terms immediate and close have commonsense meanings—spouses, dependants, and other household members such as children, siblings, parents, and parents-in-law. An exception to the share ownership proscription exists where the partner or related individual owns shares in a public mutual fund that may own shares in a client.

In addition to the Rules of Professional Conduct, which are the professions' own self-regulating mechanisms, bodies external to the profession have a strong influence on professional conduct. One of the major threats to independence as identified by the SEC is the provision of non-audit services to audit clients. However, following Enron and the other "audit failures," the major firms in both Canada and the United States voluntarily withdrew from providing IT consulting services and internal auditing outsourcing services to their audit clients, which have now both been expressly prohibited by the *Sarbanes-Oxley Act* of 2002.

In addition, SEC registrants (the client firms) are required to disclose in their annual financial reports, the aggregate of fees paid to their audit firms for both audit and non-audit services. This additional disclosure is intended to provide information so that financial statement readers can evaluate for themselves whether there is a potential problem with lack of independence and impairment of objectivity.

In audits of public companies, the auditor's independence is enhanced by the existence of the *audit committee* of the board of directors. An audit committee is required by the *Canada Business Corporations Act* (CBCA) for all publicly held companies incorporated under the federal Act (provincially incorporated companies are similarly required by provincial incorporation statutes). The audit committee is a subcommittee of the board of directors, comprised of external as well as internal directors. The CBCA's only formal requirement of the audit committee is that it review the financial statements before they are issued, but in many cases the audit committee participates more actively in the audit by, for example, selecting the public accounting firm who is to perform the audit, determining and communicating to the auditors the scope of the audit, meeting with the auditors several times throughout the course of the audit and receiving the auditor's report. A CICA publication provides guidance for audit committees in discussing auditor independence matters with the auditor.[5]

The existence of this independent group, representing the interests of the shareholders to whom the auditors can voice any concerns they have during the audit (recall the previous discussions of *Handbook*, sections 5135 and 5751) provides a liaison that helps to maintain the auditor's independence from undue influence of management.

Other rules in this section deal with confidentiality and confidential information. Except in limited circumstances, (e.g., defending against a lawsuit; in connection with an investigation of a possible breach of the Rules of Professional Conduct) the auditor should not voluntarily disclose to a third party any confidential information concerning the affairs of a client or former client. The relationship between an auditor and client is not privileged as is a lawyer-client relationship, and as a result an auditor is legally required to disclose information if subpoenaed or if requested to do so in a court proceeding. However, a 1970 ruling by the Supreme Court of Ontario recognized the notion of confidentiality by stating that an auditor in such circumstances should bring to the attention of the court the duty to endeavour to preserve the confidence of the client.

Confidentiality concerns can be problematic for auditors, as a well-known US court case some years ago against the now-disbanded Arthur Andersen firm illustrates. Arthur Andersen was the auditor of Fund of Funds Ltd. and King Resources Company, firms on both sides of a real estate transaction. King Resources, the vendor, was misrepresenting the property to Fund of Funds and overcharging for it. In the course of the audit of King Resources, Arthur Andersen became aware of facts that showed this to be the case, but did not disclose it to Fund of Funds. When the misrepresentation was subsequently discovered, Fund of Funds sued Arthur Andersen for not disclosing the information to them. The court did not accept Arthur Andersen's argument that client confidentiality precluded such disclosure and awarded Fund of Funds a sizeable settlement.

The last rules in the section concern acceptable and unacceptable forms of advertising and promotion. The rule is intended to prevent any advertising that could be perceived as unseemly and unprofessional. Specifically, if the advertising makes false or misleading claims (or a claim that the professional accountant should know to be false or misleading), makes claims that cannot be substantiated, or denigrates, directly or indirectly, the competence of another professional accountant, it is not acceptable. Advertising should inform the reader of available services, but it should be in professional good taste.

---

[5]Canadian Institute of Chartered Accountants, *Guidance for Audit Committees: Discussing Auditor Independence Matters with Your Auditor* (Toronto, Ontario: CICA, 2000).

Relations with Fellow Members and with Non-Members Engaged in Public Accounting

Two of the more important rules in this section govern relations between predecessor and successor auditors. A successor auditor, before accepting a new client, is required to contact the client's predecessor auditor (also required by the CBCA) and the predecessor auditor is required to respond to the successor auditor.

Organization and Conduct of a Professional Practice

The rules in this section are more procedural and deal with such things as acceptable forms of firm names, the appropriate forms of firm organization (e.g., proprietorships, partnerships, limited partnerships, etc.) and the carrying-on of business-related functions.

In summary, the Rules of Professional Conduct are extensive; this has been an overview only of some of the more important aspects of those rules. If you wish more detailed information you should consult the actual rules of the relevant professional body in the relevant jurisdiction.

Interpretation of the Rules of Professional Conduct and Enforcement

LO 7>

In order to make the CICA Rules of Professional Conduct more specific and understandable, they are supplemented by Interpretations. These Interpretations are produced by the councils of the provincial institutes and provide more detailed guidance to members in complying with the Rules of Professional Conduct. The greater specificity provided by the council Interpretations also makes enforcement of the rules more straightforward. In Canada, authority for enforcement has also been delegated to the provincial institutes. It is important to stress that the profession is self-regulating. In order to preserve this ability to self-regulate it is important that the public not perceive the profession's disciplinary process as lax or too lenient. The profession has taken steps to guard against this. First, the penalties are serious, often many thousands of dollars in fines and/or costs, and suspension of the right to practice. Second, Disciplinary Committees may include representatives from outside the profession. Third, information from Disciplinary Committee hearings regarding the findings and penalties imposed (and sometimes even the names of the parties involved) is made available to the public.

Before concluding the discussion of the Rules of Professional Conduct, it is important to reiterate that all professional accountants must comply with GAAP and the relevant standards for the type of examination in which they are engaged, e.g., GAAS for an audit examination. This is the standard of the profession and it is reinforced by the *Canada Business Corporations Act*, many provincial acts of incorporation, and policies of securities exchange commissions and stock exchanges in Canada.

Quality Control

LO 8>

A firm's system of quality control encompasses its organizational structure and the policies adopted and procedures established to provide the firm with reasonable assurance of conforming with professional standards. A firm's system of quality control, however, has to be tailored to its size, the nature of its practice, its organization, and cost–benefit considerations. For a sole practitioner or small firm, a system of quality control is likely to be much less formal than one for a national or international firm. However, as discussed below, there are CICA standards applicable to all firms.

System of Quality Control

The *CICA Handbook* contains two standards on quality control, applicable to assurance engagements in both the private and public sectors. Consistent with the movement towards international harmonization, the standards are comparable to international standards. They are to be read in conjunction with the existing rules of professional conduct or code of ethics, for example, reinforcing the stress on independence.

The "firm" standard, "GSF-QC, General standards of quality control for firms performing assurance engagements," provides guidelines for firms that perform assurance engagements. The firm standard is extremely comprehensive—among other things, it requires firms to:

- have quality control policies and procedures in place to provide reasonable assurance that professional standards and legal requirements are being met
- have policies and procedures to provide reasonable assurance that the firm maintains independence as required by the rules of professional conduct
- establish criteria for considering when rotation of the practitioner and other members of the assurance team is necessary
- have policies and procedures to identify the potential risks associated with a client relationship for both continuing and prospective engagements
- have policies and procedures for consultation with others, particularly on difficult or contentious matters
- monitor both the appropriateness and application of the firm's quality control policies and procedures on a continuing basis
- establish policies and procedures to provide evidence of the operation of each element of its system of quality control

The standard goes into considerable detail to specify how firms are to comply with its requirements.

The engagement standard, "Quality control procedures for assurance engagements," published as *CICA Handbook* Recommendations, section 5030, provides guidance concerning the specific quality control procedures to be performed by a practitioner in an assurance engagement. Examples of the requirements are for the practitioner to:

- obtain sufficient information to be able to evaluate whether there are threats to independence
- be satisfied that appropriate procedures have been performed concerning acceptance and continuance of the client and the engagement
- be satisfied that the assurance team has the necessary competence to perform the engagement

- consult on a timely basis on difficult or contentious matters
- ensure that an engagement quality control review is completed before issuance of the practitioner's report for engagements where such a review is to be performed

Some of the individual requirements above are elaborations of the existing standards for assurance engagements, for example the requirement that the assurance team has the necessary competence, but these requirements go beyond the standards elsewhere in the *Handbook*.

Monitoring Quality Control

The main mechanism by which quality control is monitored is through practice inspections. In addition to the inspections mandated and performed by the provincial institutes, practice inspections are now carried out for CPAB registrants by an independent national inspection body under the authority of the Canadian Public Accountability Board (CPAB), and will include public annual reporting of results. In order to perform audits of firms with securities listed on a public exchange, public practice firms that perform 50 or more audits of public clients per year will undergo inspection each year and firms with less than 50 public clients will be inspected every three years.

Firms are required to remedy any significant potential weaknesses identified in the board inspection report. If the firm has not satisfactorily addressed the identified weakness(es), the board has the authority to make public the portion of the report identifying the weakness(es) and the fact that the firm has failed to respond adequately.

Within the firm, monitoring involves the ongoing consideration and evaluation of the effects of the firm's management philosophy and the environment in which the firm practices and its clients operate on (1) the relevance of and compliance with the firm's policies and procedures, (2) the adequacy of the firm's guidance materials and practice aids, and (3) the effectiveness of professional development programs. Table 17–3 provides some selected examples of the types of policies or procedures a firm can implement to create a sound system of quality control. Procedures that let the firm identify and communicate circumstances that may necessitate changes and improvements to the firm's policies and procedures contribute to the monitoring function. Procedures for monitoring include:

- inspection procedures
- pre-issuance and post-issuance review of selected engagements
- analysis and assessment of
  - new professional pronouncements
  - results of independence confirmations
  - continuing professional education and other professional development activities undertaken by firm personnel
  - decisions related to acceptance and continuance of client relationships and engagements
  - interviews of firm personnel

Table 17–3	Selected Quality Control Policies and Procedures

Independence, Integrity, and Objectivity
- Inform personnel of the firm's independence policies and procedures and advise them that they are expected to be familiar with these policies and procedures.
- Obtain from personnel annual, written representations stating that they are familiar with the policies and procedures and that prohibited investments are not held and were not held during the period.

Personnel Management
- Plan for the firm's personnel needs at all levels and establish quantified hiring objectives based on current clientele, anticipated growth, personnel turnover, individual advancement, and retirement.
- Identiy the attributes to be sought in hirees, such as intelligence, integrity, honesty, motivation, and aptitude for the profession.

Acceptance and Continuance of Clients
- Establish procedures for evaluating prospective clients such as (1) obtaining and review of available financial information regarding the prospective clients and (2) enquiry of third parties about any information regarding the prospective client and its management.
- Designate an individual or group, at appropriate management levels, to evaluate the information obtained and to make the acceptance decision.

Engagement Performance
- Provide adequate supervision at all organizational levels, considering the training, ability, and experience of the personnel assigned.
- Develop guidelines for review of working papers and for documentation of the review process.

Monitoring
- Determine the inspection procedures necessary to provide reasonable assurance that the firm's other quality control policies and procedures are operating effectively.
- Inspect practice units, functions, or departments.

- determination of any corrective actions to be taken and improvements to be made in the quality control system
- communication to appropriate firm personnel of any weaknesses identified in the quality control system or in the level of understanding or compliance therewith
- follow-up by appropriate firm personnel to ensure that any necessary modifications are promptly made to the quality control policies and procedures

The manner in which this self-monitoring is performed varies across firms. For example, a sole practitioner with three professional staff members may use a simple checklist to monitor his or her firm's compliance with professional standards. On the other hand, a large international firm may develop very specific in-house procedures and assign full-time staff to ensure compliance with the firm's quality control system.

REVIEW QUESTIONS

LO 2>   **17-1**   Briefly describe the three theories of ethical behaviour that can be used to analyze ethical issues in accounting.

4>   **17-2**   What is the most important section of the Rules of Professional Conduct? What additional guidance is provided for applying the Rules of Conduct?

5>   **17-3**   Describe the six Principles of Professional Conduct.

5>   **17-4**   The prohibition against indebtedness to assurance clients does not apply to bank loans obtained under "normal commercial terms." Comment.

6,7>   **17-5**   Why are the Rules of Professional Conduct regarding independence of auditors so important?

6,7>   **17-6**   Describe how actual or threatened litigation may affect independence.

7>   **17-7**   Generally a public accountant should not disclose confidential client information without the consent of the client. Identify two circumstances that are exceptions to this rule.

9>   **17-8**   Advertising is allowed by the Rules of Professional Conduct as long as it is in professional good taste. Identify three types of claims or statements that would not be allowed under the rules.

8>   **17-9**   Who conducts practice inspections? What is their purpose?

8>   **17-10**   What is the purpose of a public accounting firm's establishing a system of quality control? List the five elements of quality control and provide one policy or procedure that can be used to fulfil each element.

8>   **17-11**   How are GAAP and GAAS quality control mechanisms?

MULTIPLE-CHOICE QUESTIONS FROM PROFESSIONAL EXAMINATIONS

Unless otherwise indicated, these multiple-choice questions were adapted from the CPA examinations, courtesy of the American Institute of Certified Public Accountants.

6>   **17-12**   A violation of the profession's ethical standards is most likely to occur when a public accountant

a. Compiles the financial statements of a client that employs the public accountant's spouse as a bookkeeper. ⌄

b. Receives a fee for referring audit clients to a company that sells limited partnership interests.

c. Purchases the portion of an insurance company that performs actuarial services for employee benefit plans.

d. Arranges with a financial institution to collect notes issued by a client in payment of fees due.

6>   **17-13**   A violation of the profession's ethical standards is *least* likely to occur when a public accountant

a. Purchases another public accountant's accounting practice and bases the price on a percentage of the fees accruing from clients over a three-year period.

b. Receives a percentage of the amounts invested by the public accountant's audit clients in a tax shelter with the clients' knowledge and approval.

c. Has a public accounting practice and also is president and sole shareholder of a corporation that engages in data processing services for the public.

d. Forms an association—*not* a partnership—with two other sole practitioners and calls the association "Adams, Betts & Associates."

6〉   **17-14**   After beginning an audit of a new client, William Larkin discovers that the professional competence necessary for the engagement is lacking. Larkin informs management of the situation and recommends another public accountant, and management engages the other public accountant. Under these circumstances,

a. Larkin's lack of competence should be construed to be a violation of generally accepted auditing standards.

b. Larkin may request compensation from the client for any professional services rendered to it in connection with the audit.

c. Larkin's request for a commission from the other public accountant is permitted because a more competent audit can now be performed.

d. Larkin may be indebted to the other public accountant because the other public accountant can collect from the client only the amount the client originally agreed to pay Larkin.

6〉   **17-15**   Joe Green is asked to render an opinion on the application of accounting principles by an entity that is audited by another public accountant. Green may

a. Not accept such an engagement because to do so would be considered unethical.

b. Not accept such an engagement because Green would lack the necessary information on which to base an opinion without conducting an audit.

c. Accept the engagement but should form an independent opinion without consulting with the continuing public accountant.

d. Accept the engagement but should consult with the continuing public accountant to ascertain all the available facts relevant to forming a professional judgement.

1,2,4〉   **17-16**   Which of the following statements best explains why the public accounting professions have found it essential to promulgate ethical standards and to establish means for ensuring their observance?

a. Vigorous enforcement of an established code of ethics is the best way to prevent unscrupulous acts.

b. Ethical standards that emphasize excellence in performance over material rewards establish a reputation for competence and character.

c. A distinguishing mark of a profession is its acceptance of responsibility to the public.

d. A requirement for a profession is to establish ethical standards that primarily stress responsibility to clients and colleagues.

6> **17-17**   Without the consent of the client, a public accountant should *not* disclose confidential client information contained in working papers to a

a. Voluntary quality control review board.

b. Public accountant firm that has purchased the public accountant's accounting practice.

c. Federal court that has issued a valid subpoena.

d. Disciplinary body created under statute.

8> **17-18**   One of a public accounting firm's basic objectives is to provide professional services that conform with professional standards. Reasonable assurance of achieving this basic objective is provided through

a. A system of quality control.

b. A system of peer review.

c. Continuing professional education.

d. Compliance with generally accepted reporting standards.

8> **17-19**   In connection with the element of personnel management, a public accounting firm's system of quality control should ordinarily provide that all personnel

a. Have the knowledge required to enable them to fulfill the responsibilities assigned to them.

b. Meet the profession's independence rules.

c. Seek assistance from persons having appropriate levels of knowledge, judgement, and authority.

d. Demonstrate compliance with peer review directives.

8> **17-20**   A public accounting firm's quality control procedures pertaining to the acceptance of a prospective audit client would most likely include

a. Enquiry of management as to whether disagreements between the predecessor auditor and the prospective client were resolved satisfactorily.

b. Consideration of whether sufficient competent audit evidence may be obtained to afford a reasonable basis for an opinion.

c. Enquiry of third parties, such as the prospective client's bankers and lawyers, about the prospective client and its management.

d. Consideration of whether the internal control system is sufficiently effective to permit a reduction in the extent of required substantive tests.

8> **17-21**   A public accounting firm should establish procedures for conducting and supervising work at all organizational levels to provide reasonable assurance that the work performed meets the firm's standards of quality. To achieve this goal, the firm would most likely establish procedures for

a. Evaluating prospective and continuing client relationships.

b. Reviewing engagement working papers and reports.

c. Requiring personnel to adhere to the applicable independence rules.

d. Maintaining personnel files containing documentation related to the evaluation of personnel.

PROBLEMS

1,4,5,6 ⟩   17-22   Ron Wood was auditing the financial statements of his continuing client, OS Industries. OS is a publicly held company whose shares are traded on the Toronto Stock Exchange. In discussing the property, plant, and equipment accounts with the controller, who is also a professional accountant, the auditor learned that a new building costing $25,000,000 (a material amount) was constructed for the company during the year by an affiliated firm, of which the president of OS is the sole shareholder.

To obtain audit evidence for this transaction, the auditor examined a contract signed by the president on behalf of OS and an invoice from the affiliated firm for $25,000,000, which was stamped "paid," along with a cancelled cheque for that amount, signed by the controller. He also examined a memo from the president to the controller of OS authorizing the payment of the invoice. Given the sensitivity of the matter, in the memo, the president of OS further instructed the controller neither to discuss the matter with anyone nor to disclose the nature of the transaction in the company's financial statements.

After his conversation with the controller, the auditor telephoned a friend who is a general manager of a large construction company, described the situation to him as well as the nature of the building project, and asked for a rough estimate of the cost of such a building. The friend said that "it would be about $10,000,000, maximum." Armed with this information, the auditor sent a letter to the president of OS resigning immediately from the engagement, along with his bill for the cost of audit work completed to date. He then telephoned officials at the Toronto Stock Exchange alleging fraud in the preparation of OS Industries' financial statements.

Required:

a. Did the controller behave ethically in this situation? Explain.

b. Did the auditor behave ethically in this situation? Explain.

c. Describe the specific actions the auditor should have taken after his conversation with the controller.

(CGA-Canada, adapted)

5,6> **17-23** You are having dinner with a fellow professional accountant and you overhear the following conversation taking place at the table behind you between two diners that you recognize as two other professional accountants from your Continuing Professional Development courses.

> Diner 1: *I'm sure glad we attended that PD course on starting your own practice. It will really help us when we start our practice next month. Did you buy those shares of Sunrise Industries Ltd. for us?*

> Diner 2: *Yes, I bought them this morning. Are you sure the share split is going to happen?*

> Diner 1: *Absolutely, the partner and I had a meeting with the VP Finance this afternoon to confirm the details and to discuss the final stage of the audit. I'll miss these hot stock tips when I leave the firm at the end of the Sunrise audit.*

> Diner 2: *Me too. Is that the last Professional Development course we have to attend? Those things are so time consuming.*

> Diner 1: *It's the last one that I'm attending. The Institute sends you those forms and you can just fill them out saying you did some personal PD. It's not like they check or anything. That old professional integrity!*

> Diner 2: *Sounds good to me. By the way, I printed up our new business cards. I hope you like the name, "Good and Cheap, Ltd." I thought it was catchy, yet got our message across.*

> Diner 1: *It's perfect. I'll need those business cards because I have already started talking to some of the firm's clients, especially those that just get their personal tax return completed by us. The firm is so expensive, I'm sure they will bring their business to us once they hear about our flat fee structure.*

> Diner 2: *I have also placed a few flyers in some of the waiting rooms around town to bring in some business. Hopefully no one from the Institute notices that we're not licensed.*

> Diner 1: *How do you find the time to get all these things done while you are still working?*

> Diner 2: *This audit client I am on now is so easy and nothing ever changes so I just copy last year's files and I'm done in half the time. It's the only way to get it done.*

> Diner 1: *I'll have to try that, but my supervisor is all over me. Where is your supervisor?*

> Diner 2: *Like I said, it's an easy job so my work is going straight to the file and into the filing cabinet.*

> Diner 1: *Sounds great, let's go.*

Required:

Prepare a memo discussing what actions you should take regarding the above discussion.

(ICABC, adapted)

3,5,6 ⟩   **17-24**   You are an audit senior working for a local firm. The firm has recently been engaged to perform a first-time audit for a contractor that installs ductwork for central heating/cooling systems in new housing developments. While reviewing cash disbursement transactions during the interim audit, you notice a number of unusual payments to individuals without adequate documentation. After giving you several unsatisfactory, ambiguous explanations, the controller finally explains that these are actually bribes paid to municipal building inspectors to obtain their approval of company work on completed housing projects. He further states that, were the bribes not paid, the inspectors would probably allege that the work was defective, requiring the company to incur additional costs.

The next day, you discuss your findings with the partner in charge of the engagement, who says that "bribes in this business are a fact of life, and, anyway, the amounts are immaterial so it's not our concern." He also tells you not to mention this issue in the working papers, and not to "waste any more time investigating this matter." Reflecting on the situation, you don't know what to do. You would like to disassociate yourself from this engagement, but doing so could mean being dismissed by your employer.

Required:

a. If you decide to go along with the partner and drop the matter, would your audit examination comply with generally accepted auditing standards? Explain fully.

b. Discuss how you would attempt to resolve your problem of deciding what action(s) to take in this situation.

(CGA-Canada, adapted)

3,5 ⟩   **17-25**   You have been approached by a potential new client, a closely held company, and asked to submit a bid to perform the audit for next year. The client is replacing its current audit firm because of a disagreement over the valuation of inventories that led the auditor to issue a qualified opinion on last year's financial statements.

The company manufactures small tools and related items for the "do-it-yourself" consumer market. Last year, the company's assets were $50,000,000, sales were $75,000,000, and net income was $5,000,000. After discussions with management and other client personnel and a visit to the company's plant, you believe the predecessor auditor's position on the inventory values may have been too harsh. Also, you estimate that the first year's audit will require 500 hours of staff and partner time. Your firm's normal average billing rate for this mix of time would be about $150 per hour. You are aware that several other public accounting firms are interested in the job because the client will likely also obtain tax and consulting services from its audit firm in the future. Moreover, the client's treasurer has hinted that the company has already received a proposal from a local firm to do the audit for $20,000 next year.

Required:

Discuss the ethical and business issues you should consider in developing a proposal for this audit engagement.

(CGA-Canada, adapted)

6▷   **17-26**   During a lunchtime shopping trip you meet your friend, Paul, who informs you that he is excited over the new audit his firm has obtained. The new client is Cleartaste Inc., a bottled water company. Cleartaste is in its development stages and is going to issue an initial public share offering within the next few weeks, just prior to the latest confidential marketing surveys becoming public.

Paul tells you to be sure to buy some shares as they will definitely increase in price once the surveys become public knowledge. One of the surveys indicates that Mexico has agreed to buy large amounts of the water, which should really get the company up and running. He tells you that he already has purchased 10 percent of the shares.

He also tells you that he thinks Cleartaste's previous auditors should be "kicked out" of the profession. He says that he has been reviewing the deferred development costs and that the amounts are incorrect. Cleartaste has been deferring both research and development costs for three years and the auditors have yet to catch it. Also, Cleartaste's president runs all his personal expenses through the company and buries them in the expense accounts.

You ask him if he told the previous auditors about these items and he looks at you like you are crazy and says "are you kidding, This client is going to make me a wealthy man. I'm not jeopardizing that for anything."

As you leave, he tells you to be sure to tell your friends to buy the shares quickly as he has told his entire family to buy as many as possible.

When you arrive back at your job as controller of Fineline Inc., a men's wear designer clothing company, you get a phone call from another friend, Roger, who says he has just started up his own practice and is wondering whether he can set up a meeting to make a bid on your audit for a set fee of $2,000 and to arrange to pay you, secretly, for client referrals. You tell him that you are happy with your existing auditors and that he better be careful. He just laughs and hangs up.

You decide you've had enough for one day and go out to your car to find a flyer advertising the services of a public accounting firm who will prepare personal tax returns for $40 or 50 percent of the difference between your calculation and theirs.

You shake your head and wonder what is happening to the profession.

Required:

Within the context of the Rules of Professional Conduct, discuss the issues raised above and what you should do about them.

(ICABC, adapted)

5,6 > **17-27**   Susan Savage has been asked by a nonpublic company audit client to perform a nonrecurring engagement involving implementing an IT information and control system. The client requests that, in setting up the new system and during the period prior to conversion to the new system, Savage

- Counsel on potential expansion of business activity plans.
- Search for and interview new personnel.
- Hire new personnel.
- Train personnel.

In addition, the client requests that, during the three months subsequent to the conversion, Savage

- Supervise the operation of the new system.
- Monitor client-prepared source documents and make changes in basic IT-generated data as Savage may deem necessary without the concurrence of the client.

Savage responds that she may perform some of the services requested but not all of them.

Required:

a. Which of these services may Savage perform, and which of them may Savage not perform?

b. Before undertaking this engagement, Savage should inform the client of all significant matters related to the engagement. What are these significant matters?

c. If Savage adds to her staff an individual who specializes in developing computer systems, what degree of knowledge must Savage possess in order to supervise the specialist's activities?

(AICPA, adapted)

5,6 > **17-28**   Archie Goodwin, a public accountant, and Paul Jensen, a banker, were the trustees of the Moore Family Trust. The trust, which was created as a spendthrift trust, provided for distribution of income annually to the four Moore adult children for life, with the principal to be distributed to their issue after the death of the last income beneficiary. The trust was funded with commercial and residential real estate and a stock portfolio.

Goodwin, in addition to being a trustee, was lawfully employed as the trust's accountant. As the trust's accountant, Goodwin prepared and signed all trust tax returns, kept the trust's accounting records, and supervised distributions to the income beneficiaries.

In 2005 Goodwin and Jensen, as trustees, sold a building owned by the trust for $400,000, its fair market value. The building had been valued at $250,000 when acquired by the trust. The $150,000 gain was allocated to income. In addition, the trust had rental, interest, and dividend income of $1,500,000 in 2005. Expenses for taxes, replacement of plumbing fixtures, roof repairs, utilities, salaries, and fees and commissions totalled $1,050,000.

On December 31, 2005, Goodwin and Jensen prepared and signed four $150,000 trust account cheques and sent three of them to three of the income beneficiaries and the fourth one to a creditor of the fourth beneficiary. This beneficiary had acknowledged that the creditor was owed $200,000.

In February 2006 Goodwin discovered that Jensen had embezzled $200,000 by secretly selling part of the trust's stock portfolio. Goodwin agreed not to reveal Jensen's embezzlement if Jensen would pay Goodwin $25,000.

In April 2006 Goodwin prepared the 2005 trust income tax return. The return was signed by Goodwin as preparer and by Jensen and Goodwin as trustees and was filed with CRA. Goodwin also prepared the 2005 income tax returns for the income beneficiaries. In an attempt to hide the embezzlement, Goodwin, in preparing the trust's tax return, claimed nonexistent losses and improper credits. The beneficiaries' returns reflected the same nonexistent losses and improper credits. Consequently, the beneficiaries' taxes were underpaid. As a result of a CRA audit, the nonexistent losses and improper credits were disallowed and the beneficiaries were assessed additional taxes, penalties, and interest.

Required:

Discuss each of the possible violations of the Rules of Professional Conduct by Goodwin.

(AICPA, adapted)

DISCUSSION CASES

3,6> 17-29 Refer back to the Canadian Shield Credit Union case presented at the opening of the chapter and consider each of the following independent situations:

a. Suppose that Pina, Johnson & Associates also audited one of the entities who had received one of the large loans that are in dispute. Sam Johnson is not involved with auditing that entity. Is it ethical for Johnson to seek information on the financial condition of that entity from the auditors in his firm? What are the rights of the affected parties in this instance, and what are the costs and benefits of using such information?

b. Suppose that Johnson has determined that one of the entities that owes a disputed loan is being investigated for violating environmental laws and may be sued by the Environmental Protection Agency. Can Johnson use this information in deciding on the proper loan-loss reserve? What are the ethical considerations?

3,6,7> 17-30 Wall Precision Tool Company is a large, publicly held manufacturer of precision-tooled parts with five subsidiaries located across Canada. On January 15, 2006, the company entered into negotiations to sell one of its subsidiaries to Tough-Nut Tool Corporation.

The sale was contingent on numerous events, including a complete physical inventory that was to be taken on January 31, 2006. The physical inventory, which was observed by Tough-Nut's auditors, indicated that the inventory of the subsidiary at January 31, 2006, had been overstated by 25 percent, or $10.5 million. When the inventory shortage was discovered, Tough-Nut withdrew from the negotiations.

Surprisingly, Wall's auditors, Arte & Sensor (A&S), had just observed the taking of the physical inventory at that location on December 31, 2005, as part of Wall's annual audit. Enquiries by Wall's management and its internal auditors disclosed that A&S's audit procedures for the inventory observation at the subsidiary had been deficient. In particular, A&S personnel had not obtained adequate control of the inventory tags, and they had not investigated certain inventory items that represented material amounts of inventory.

The following year, Wall and A&S agreed that an extensive study of Wall's inventory controls and management information system would be conducted. A&S offered to perform the study at 50 percent of normal billing rates. Wall demanded that A&S perform the work for free because the firm had failed to detect the inventory shortage. A&S eventually agreed to perform the work free of charge.

Late in 2006, Wall retained legal counsel to determine if it had grounds for a lawsuit against A&S. The board of directors met on February 1, 2007, and voted to initiate a lawsuit against A&S. This decision was not recorded in the board's minutes. On February 7, 2007, A&S issued an unqualified report on Wall's financial statements. A week later, Wall notified A&S of its intention to file a $10 million lawsuit for damages due to the inventory shortage.

On February 28, 2007, Wall's management and A&S met to negotiate a settlement. A&S agreed to pay Wall $2.5 million and to provide an additional $2 million in professional services at no cost. The $2.5 million payment was disclosed to the public when the suit was settled. No mention of the free professional services was announced.

When the agreement was reached, Wall requested that the two parties meet with the Ontario Securities Commission (OSC) to discuss the arrangement. Wall was concerned about whether the agreement with A&S would be viewed by the OSC as affecting A&S's independence.

Required:

a. Did A&S act ethically when agreeing to study Wall's inventory control and management information system for free? If not, what actions should A&S have taken at that time?

b. When A&S learned of Wall's lawsuit, should A&S have withdrawn from the engagement? Justify your answer.

6,8 >   **17-31**   Walter Schoeck is considering leaving a position at a major public accounting firm to join the staff of a local financial institution that does write-up work, tax preparation and planning, and financial planning.

Required:

a. What are the ethical issues for Schoeck in deciding whether to make this career change?

b. Are the Rules of Conduct applied differently to professionally designated accountants that work for a local financial institution as compared to a major public accounting firm?

c. Do you think the rules should be applied differently to professionally designated accountants depending on the type of entity they work for?

INTERNET ASSIGNMENT

8> **17-32** Visit the website of the Canadian Public Accountability Board (www.cpab-ccrc.ca) and follow the links to their annual reports of inspections done on audit firms of publicly traded companies. For each of the three reports released thus far, prepare a brief summary of the board's conclusion on the results of their inspections.

Legal Liability

Learning Objectives

Upon completion of this chapter, you will be able to

1 Describe the current legal environment for auditors.

2 Define key legal terms.

3 Outline the auditor's liability to clients under common law.

4 Outline the auditor's liability to third parties under common law.

5 Discuss the influence of important US statutes such as the *Securities Act* of 1933, the *Securities Exchange Act* of 1934, and the *Sarbanes-Oxley Act* of 2002, on the legal environment for Canadian auditors.

6 Explain how an auditor can be held criminally liable.

7 Discuss the various approaches that the public accounting profession and firms can take to minimize legal liability.

RELEVANT ACCOUNTING AND ASSURANCE PRONOUNCEMENTS

CICA Handbook, **section 5135,** The auditor's responsibility to consider fraud

CICA Handbook, **section 5136,** Misstatements—Illegal acts

CICA Handbook, **section 5750,** Communication of matters identified during the financial statement audit

CICA Handbook, **section 5751,** Communications with those having oversight responsibility for the financial reporting process

---

This chapter outlines auditors' legal liability. The current legal environment is presented first because in recent years auditors have been subjected to increased liability for their work product. This is followed by a brief overview of the types of legal liability an auditor may encounter. Auditors' liability under common law to clients and third parties is discussed first. Statutory liability for both civil and criminal complaints is presented next. The last section discusses a number of actions that auditors can undertake to minimize their exposure to legal liability.

AUDITOR LEGAL LIABILITY—A CAUTIONARY TALE

The $500 million accounting fraud at Phar-Mor, Inc., in the 1990s led to the bankruptcy of one of the largest private companies in the United States. As a result of the company's fraud and subsequent failure, charges were filed against both Phar-Mor's management and the company's auditors. Phar-Mor's former management was collectively fined just over $1 million, and two former members of Phar-Mor management received prison sentences. Even though neither Phar-Mor's management, the plaintiffs' attorneys, nor anyone else associated with the case ever alleged the auditors *knowingly* participated in the Phar-Mor fraud, on February 14, (Coopers) 1996, a jury found Coopers & Lybrand LLP liable under a fraud claim. The crux of the fraud charge was that Coopers made representations recklessly without regard to whether they were true or false, which enabled the plaintiffs to successfully sue the auditors for fraud under statutory and common law.

The plaintiffs acknowledged that the incidence of management fraud did not, by itself, prove there was an audit failure. Moreover, they did not allege that Coopers knowingly participated in the Phar-Mor fraud; nor did they allege Coopers was liable just because it did not find the fraud. Rather, the plaintiffs alleged that Coopers made fraudulent representations in its audit opinions. The two key alleged misrepresentations were Coopers' statements that its audits of Phar-Mor were performed in accordance with generally accepted auditing standards (GAAS) and the audited statements of Phar-Mor were in conformity with generally accepted accounting principles (GAAP).

Here is an excerpt from the plantiff's larger's opening statement:

> So the question, ladies and gentlemen, is not whether Coopers could have discovered the fraud. The question is whether Coopers falsely and misleadingly stated that it conducted a GAAS audit and falsely and misleadingly told [plaintiffs] that Phar-Mor's worthless financial statements were fairly presented. And the answer to that question is yes. (Sarah Wolf, Attorney for Sears)

The jury agreed and found coopers & Lybrand guilty.

Adapted with permission from "Finding Auditors Liable for Fraud: What the Jury Heard in the Phar-Mor Case," David Cottrell and Steven Glover, *CPA Journal* (July 1997).

The Legal Environment

LO 1 The issue of legal liability has been for some time one of the most potentially dramatic negative aspects of the profession, and recent events have only served to emphasize that impact. Through the early 1990s, it was estimated that in the US, the Big 6 (now the Big 4) spent up to 12 percent of their accounting and auditing revenues settling and defending lawsuits.[1] The amounts at stake have increased in the decade since then. In the US, by the mid-1990s, the profession's aggregate liability was estimated to be $30 billion, and the lawsuits against Arthur Andersen alone as a result of the recent collapse of Enron total approximately $25 billion. In Canada, estimates put the dollar amount of outstanding lawsuits against auditors

---

[1] *Accounting Today* (January 24, 1994).

at close to $3 billion by the early 2000s. While it is often the case that such suits are settled for less than the plaintiff's initial claim for damages, the amounts involved are still in the many millions of dollars.

Canadian Characteristics

The situation is not as dire in Canada as in the US for a number of reasons, related to the different legal and regulatory environments in the two countries.[2] Some of the differences are:

- **Trial by judge versus trial by jury.**   In the US, civil suits against auditors are before a jury. In Canada, they are usually before a judge who is more knowledgeable and presumably less easily swayed by appeals that might be effective with a jury.
- **Imposition of costs.**   In Canada, judges have been more willing to "reprimand" plaintiffs who bring frivolous lawsuits against auditors by requiring them to pay some or all of the defendant's costs if the case is decided in favour of the defendant. In the US, since lawyers charge contingent fees, and the imposition of costs is rare, bringing a lawsuit is essentially a costless procedure for the plaintiff, resulting in lawsuits of dubious validity.
- **Size of damage awards.**   Damage awards tend to be less in Canada. Juries in the US often award punitive damages far in excess of compensatory damages. One reason for this may be that the jury effectively grosses up the amount of the award in order to award the plaintiff what the jury considers to be a sufficient settlement after the lawyers' contingent fee of 35 percent of the award or more.
- **Class action suits.**   In Canada, the rules regarding class action suits, where a small group of plaintiffs brings suit on behalf of a much larger group or "class," are more restrictive, resulting in fewer suits of this type.
- **Regulatory system.**   In the US, both the regulatory environment (as exemplified by the SEC regulations) and the legislative environment (as exemplified by the *Foreign Corrupt Practices Act*, the *Racketeer Influenced and Corrupt Organizations Act*, and the *Sarbanes-Oxley Act*) create a harsher environment for auditors, although recent changes in Ontario securities legislation (described later in this chapter) have moved closer to the US regime.

However, notwithstanding the differences between Canada and the US, legal liability is of paramount concern in Canada. The trend in Canada is in the direction of the US, and the sums of money are sizeable. In particular, Canadian auditors of companies listed on the US exchanges are as subject as are US CPA firms to the provisions of the SEC and the above-mentioned acts.

You will note that many of the precedent cases cited and/or discussed are from countries other than Canada—to some extent the United Kingdom

---

[2]For more detail, see M. Pashell-Meade, "What Liability Crisis?" *CAMagazine* (May 1994), pp. 42–43.

Table 18–1	**Definition of Key Legal Terms**
• *Privity*	Absent a contractual or fiduciary relationship, the accountant does not owe a duty of care to an injured party.
• *Breach of contract*	Occurs when the client or auditor fails to meet the terms and obligations established in the contract, which is normally finalized in the engagement letter. Third parties may have privity or near privity of contract.
• *Tort*	A wrongful act other than a breach of contract for which civil action may be taken.
• *Ordinary negligence*	An absence of reasonable or due care in the conduct of an engagement. Due care is evaluated in terms of what other professional accountants would have done under similar circumstances.
• *Gross negligence*	An extreme, flagrant, or reckless departure from professional standards of due care. This is also referred to in the US as *constructive fraud*.
• *Fraud*	Actions taken with the knowledge and intent to deceive.

and to a greater extent the United States. The legal systems of all three countries have their roots in English common law (except for the province of Quebec which follows French civil law). Although judges are not bound to pay attention to decisions in other jurisdictions, a judgement will often make reference to prior decisions in those other jurisdictions as a basis for the current decision. Both the UK and the US have exerted, and will continue to exert, significant influence on the legal environment facing the auditor in Canada.

Overview[3]

LO 2 > In the current legal environment, auditors can be held liable for a number of types of actions. Table 18–1 defines key legal terms, and Table 18–2 summarizes the auditor's liability by type of liability and actions resulting in liability.

Under common law, an auditor can be held liable to clients for breach of contract, negligence or gross negligence, and fraud. The auditor's liability to third parties under common law represents one of the more perplexing areas of litigation. While the overall trend in this area has been to hold auditors liable to an expanded group of third parties, the problem is complicated by the fact that the outcomes of many cases have been determined by the location in which the case is tried. Some courts have followed a strict privity rule on lawsuits by third parties against auditors, while others have adopted a liberal interpretation of auditors' liability to third parties under common law.

---

[3]A number of excellent sources provide more detailed coverage of issues related to legal liability. The reader is referred to M. J. Epstein and A. D. Spalding, *The Accountant's Guide to Legal Liability and Ethics* (Homewood, IL: Business One Irwin, 1993); and R. S. Kay and D. G. Searfoss, *Deloitte & Touche Professor's Handbook*, chap. 34 (Boston: Warren, Gorham & Lamont, 1992 update). See also P. J. Ostling, "Accountants' Legal Liability—A Historical Perspective," *Auditing Symposium VIII: Proceedings of the 1986 Touche Ross/University of Kansas Symposium on Auditing Problems* (Lawrence: University of Kansas, 1986), for an excellent historical overview of auditors' legal liability.

Table 18–2	**Summary of Types of Liability and Auditors' Actions Resulting in Liability**

Type of Liability	*Auditors' Actions Resulting in Liability*
Common law—clients	Breach of contract Negligence Gross negligence/constructive fraud Fraud
Common law—third parties	Negligence Gross negligence/constructive fraud Fraud
Civil liability under provincial securities acts (e.g., OSC)	Negligence Gross negligence/constructive fraud Fraud
Criminal liability under federal jurisdiction (e.g., Criminal Code of Canada)	Wilful violation of federal law

Another area of liability for the public accountant, fiduciary[4] liability, may have been opened up by the some or the new assurance services offered by the professional bodies. While under the current interpretation of fiduciary duty, such a duty would not arise in normal auditor–client relationships, the conditions identified as creating a fiduciary relationship—where the fiduciary has the authority to unilaterally exercise discretionary powers and where the beneficiary is particularly vulnerable, would clearly be present in engagements such as Eldercare offered by the CAs and CGAs.

In Canada, the statutes of the Criminal Code of Canada govern auditors' potential criminal liability for knowingly issuing an incorrect auditor's report. In the US, major potential sources of legal action against auditors are found in US federal and state criminal statutes, as well as statutes of the *Securities Act of* 1933, the *Securities Exchange Act* of 1934, the *Racketeer Influenced and Corrupt Organizations Act* of 1970, the *Foreign Corrupt Practices Act* of 1977, and the *Sarbanes-Oxley Act* of 2002. Although they tend to be high-profile cases, for example, the criminal prosecution of Arthur Andersen in the wake of the Enron failure, there have been relatively few instances of major criminal actions against auditors. The main legal threat to the profession is from actions under common, rather than criminal, law. The next section will discuss this in more detail.

Common Law—Clients

LO 3> Common law does not require that the auditor guarantee his or her work product. It does, however, require that the auditor perform professional services with due care. This requires that the auditor perform his or her

---

[4]See the definition of *fiduciary responsibility* in the glossary. Also see M. Paskell-Meade, "Fiduciary Duty," *CAMagazine* (April 2004), pp. 43–44, 49.

professional services with the same degree of skill, knowledge, and judgement possessed by other members of the profession. When an auditor fails to carry out contractual arrangements with the client, he or she may be held liable for breach of contract or negligence. Under common law, the auditor is also liable to the client for gross negligence and fraud.

Breach of Contract

Breach-of-contract liability is based on the auditor's failing to complete the services agreed to in the contract with the client. As discussed in Chapter 5, an engagement letter should establish the responsibilities for both the auditor and the client. In performing an audit, the auditor's obligation is to examine the client's financial statements and issue the appropriate opinion in accordance with professional standards. The contract between the client and the auditor stipulates the amount of fees to be charged for the designated professional services, and deadlines for completing the services are normally indicated or implied in the contract. If the client breaches its obligations under the engagement letter, the auditor is excused from his or her contractual obligations. If the auditor discontinues an audit without adequate cause, he or she may be liable for economic injury suffered by the client (see Exhibit 18–1). Similarly, other issues (such as timely delivery of the audit report or failure to detect a material defalcation) can lead to litigation by the client against the auditor.

One issue that has given rise to client suits for breach of contract is confidentiality of client information, particularly when it conflicts with other obligations of professional conduct. Two US cases in the early 1980s illustrate clearly the problematic nature of this conflict. In *Consolidata Services Inc. v. Alexander Grant & Co.* (1981), the auditors determined that Consolidata Services Inc. (a payroll service) was insolvent. The auditors informed those customers of Consolidata who were also its clients and advised them not to provide any more funds to Consolidata. Consolidata sued and was awarded $1.3 million on the grounds that the auditors breached their contract by disclosing confidential information.

In *The Fund of Funds Ltd. v. Arthur Andersen & Co.* (1982), the situation was almost the reverse. Arthur Andersen was the auditor of companies on both sides of a transaction to sell and purchase land. In fact some of the same audit personnel were on both engagements. As auditors of King Resources Company (the seller), the auditors became aware that the price being charged to The Fund of Funds was substantially inflated over prices being charged for comparable sales to other customers of King Resources in spite of a written agreement between King Resources and The Fund of Funds to the contrary. When management of The Fund of Funds subsequently found out about this, they sued Arthur Andersen for not disclosing the information. The court found in favour of the plaintiff and awarded the shareholders of The Fund of Funds $80 million (later reduced on appeal).

A case in Canada (Supreme Court of BC and Court of Appeal for BC) quite strongly upholds the concept of confidentiality between the auditor and its client. In this case, *Transamerica Commercial Financial Corporation Canada V. Dunwoody & Company and F. S. Hintle* (1996), Transamerica Commercial Financial Corporation, was financing an automobile dealership, Robin Hood Holdings Ltd. The dealership was engaging in cheque

EXHIBIT 18–1

Deloitte & Touche's Withdrawal from Medtrans Audit Upheld

Medtrans, an ambulance service provider, retained Deloitte & Touche to audit its financial statements. Medtrans needed capital and sought $10 million in financing from an outside investor. Medtrans gave the potential investor *unaudited* financial statements showing profits of $1.9 million. Deloitte & Touche was in the process of completing its audit during Medtrans negotiations with the outside investor. Deloitte & Touche proposed adjustments that resulted in Medtrans's financial statements showing a $500,000 loss. Prior to Deloitte & Touche proposing the adjustments, the company's CFO resigned after indicating that he could not sign the management representation letter. When presented with the proposed adjustments, Medtrans's CEO threatened to get a court order forcing Deloitte & Touche to complete the audit. Deloitte withdrew from the engagement. Medtrans retained two other CPA firms, both of which were either discharged or withdrew. A third firm issued an unqualified audit report that contained the adjustments proposed by Deloitte & Touche.

Medtrans alleged that Deloitte & Touche's wrongful withdrawal resulted in the company's failure to complete the financing, and that the subsequent sale of the company was for significantly less than its true value. At trial Medtrans asserted that, under California law, a CPA firm could not, under any circumstances, withdraw from an engagement if it unduly jeopardized the interest of the client. Deloitte & Touche argued that the approved California jury instructions on the duration of a professional's duty were contrary to professional standards, which authorize the auditor to resign. The jury in this case ruled in favour of Medtrans and awarded the company nearly $10 million.

In March 1998 the California Court of Appeals reversed the decision, holding that judges should instruct juries about the profession's standards. The court held that an auditor, by auditing financial statements, assumes a public responsibility that transcends any employment relationship with the client. This decision is significant because it held that an accountant's duty of care can be based on professional standards rather than rules of law that are contrary to professional standards. It also upheld the auditor's right to withdraw from an engagement when the client requests conduct that is not consistent with GAAP or GAAS.

Sources: National Medical Transportation Network v. Deloitte & Touche, 98 D.A.R., 2850, March 23, 1998; and "Court Rules on Importance of GAAP and GAAS," Journal of Accountancy (June 1998), p. 24.

kiting and claiming nonexistent inventory to cover up its deteriorating financial position. The auditors became aware of both practices and directed Robin Hood to cease. However, they did not inform Transamerica. Ultimately the auditors, on the advice of their lawyers, resigned from the audit. Transamerica Commercial Financial Corporation carried out its own investigation and discovered the misrepresentations. It put Robin Hood into receivership, operated the dealership itself for a time, and eventually sold it. Transamerica sued the auditors for losses estimated at $1 million. They were unsuccessful. Both the trial court and the appeal court said that the auditor owed a professional duty of confidentiality to its client, Robin Hood.

Negligence

A tort is a wrongful act other than a breach of contract for which civil action may be taken. If an engagement is performed without due care, the auditor may be held liable for an actionable tort in negligence. Liability for negligence represents a deviation from a standard of behaviour that is consistent with that of a "reasonable person." When an individual such as a professional accountant possesses special skills and knowledge, ordinary reasonable care is not sufficient. An oft-cited quote from Cooley's *Torts*[5] indicates the responsibility of those offering special skills:

> In all those employments where particular skill is requisite, if one offers his services, he is understood as holding himself out to the public as possessing the degree of skill commonly possessed by others in the same employment, and if his pretensions are unfounded, he commits a species of fraud upon every man who employs him in reliance on his public profession. But no man, whether skilled or unskilled, undertakes that the task he assumes shall be performed successfully, and without fault or error; he undertakes for good faith and integrity, but not for infallibility, and he is liable to his employer for negligence, bad faith, or dishonesty, but not for losses consequent upon mere errors of judgement.

Thus, the auditor has the duty to conduct an engagement using the same degree of care that would be used by an ordinary, prudent member of the public accounting profession. The requisite elements required for establishing an auditor's liability for negligence are (1) the duty to conform to a required standard of care, (2) failure to act in accordance with that duty, (3) a causal connection between the auditor's negligence and the client's damage, and (4) actual loss or damage to the client.

Suits by clients against auditors often allege that the auditors did not detect some type of fraud or defalcation. The client can generally prove the existence of a duty of care based on the engagement contract. However, the auditor may be able to argue successfully that the client's loss was due not to any negligence on his or her part but rather to fraudulent actions committed by an employee or manager of the client. In such circumstances, there is *contributory negligence* by the client, and the court may reduce any damages awarded to the plaintiff accordingly. A case involving such circumstances was *H.E. Kane Ltd. v. Coopers & Lybrand*.[6] Exhibit 18–2 presents a summary of the case. In this instance, the client (the father) alleged that Coopers & Lybrand was negligent for not having uncovered the son's fraudulent actions. The court ruled that there was contributory negligence on the part of the father and reduced the damages awarded by 50 percent.

Another well-known US case that alleged negligence by an accountant is the *1136 Tenants' Corp. v. Max Rothenberg & Co.*, which relates to unaudited financial statements and a CPA's failure to communicate suspicious circumstances to the client. Exhibit 18–3 presents a summary of the case. The *1136 Tenants'* case established a duty on the part of a public accountant doing work on unaudited financial statements to communicate to the client any circumstances that give reason to believe that fraud may exist.

In Canada, professional accountants can take some comfort in the more recent case of *466715 Ontario Limited (Multi Graphics Print & Litho) v. Helen Proulx and Doane Raymond*.[7] Exhibit 18–4 summarizes this case.

---

[5]D. Haggard, *Cooley on Torts*, 4th ed., p. 472.

[6]For further details, see H. Rowan, QC, "Giving Credit Where Credit's Not Due, Part I," *CAMagazine* (June 1983), pp. 69–71; H. Rowan, QC, "Giving Credit Where Credit's Not Due, Part II," *CAMagazine* (August 1983), pp. 97–102; H. Rowan, QC, "When Fault is Divided," *CAMagazine* (August 1986), pp. 84–87.

[7]See also P. Kulig, "Doane Raymond Absolved of Wrongdoing," *The Bottom Line* (Nov. 1, 1998), p. 14.

EXHIBIT 18–2

> ### *H.E. Kane Agencies Ltd. v. Coopers & Lybrand* (1983)
>
> H.E. Kane had been an audit client of Coopers & Lybrand for several years. Harold Kane was the owner-operator, and his son, Charles, was an employee. In 1967, Charles persuaded his father to expand into the travel agency business and Kane Agencies became an agent for Air Canada.
>
> Harold Kane did not like credit and from 1967 to 1974 the travel agency aspect of the business was run almost exclusively as a cash business. Tickets were sold, usually on a cash basis to a wide clientele. When credit was extended, the sale was not recorded until the cash was received from the customer.
>
> In 1974 Kane acquired a large client, Trade Resources (International) Limited. The accounting procedure to recognize sales revenue was changed—an invoice was prepared when payment was received, rather than when the ticket or tickets were sold.
>
> As a result, there came to exist a large receivable from Trade Resources for tickets issued to them, but which was not recorded. More importantly, at the same time, there was a large payable to Air Canada for those same tickets. Charles Kane was the only individual who was aware of this practice.
>
> When Trade Resources declared bankruptcy in 1976 they owed Kane Agencies more than $250,000. Kane senior sued Coopers & Lybrand for negligence for not discovering the deception that Charles had perpetrated on him and Air Canada. Coopers & Lybrand argued that Charles Kane had concealed the unreported ticket sales from them and that Harold Kane was guilty of contributory negligence for not monitoring the operations of Charles and the travel division more closely.
>
> The judge accepted Coopers & Lybrand's arguments. The award was established at $87,599 but was then reduced by 50 percent due to the contributory negligence of H.E. Kane.

Fraud

An auditor can be held liable for fraud when he or she acted with knowledge and intent to deceive. Generally, however, actions alleging fraud result from lawsuits by third parties and thus are discussed in more detail in the next section.

Common Law—Third Parties

LO 4 Under common law, auditors can be held liable to third parties for negligence and fraud. However, this area of liability is very complex, and court rulings are not always consistent across federal and provincial judicial jurisdictions.

Negligence

When an auditor fails to conduct an engagement with due care, he or she can be held liable for negligence to third parties (plaintiffs). To prevail in a suit alleging negligence, the third party must prove that (1) the auditor had a duty to the plaintiff to exercise due care, (2) the auditor breached that duty by not following professional standards, (3) the auditor's breach of due care was the proximate cause of the third party's injury, and (4) the third party suffered an actual loss as a result. The main difficulty faced by third parties in proving negligence against an auditor is showing that the auditor's duty to exercise due care extended to them. Three standards have evolved for defining the extent of the auditor's liability to third parties: *privity, foreseen persons or classes,* and *reasonably foreseeable third parties.*

EXHIBIT 18–3

1136 Tenants' Corp. v. Max Rothenberg & Co. (1967)

Jerome Riker was a powerful New York City businessman with extensive business interests in the real estate industry. During the early 1960s, Riker diverted money from a number of trust funds of cooperatives that he managed for use in a personal real estate investment.

One of the cooperatives that was involved in the embezzlement was the 1136 Tenants' Corporation. Riker had misappropriated approximately $130,000 of the cooperative's funds. When the cooperative was unable to recover the funds from Riker, it filed a civil suit against the public accounting firm, Max Rothenberg & Company, which had prepared the annual financial statements and tax return. The plaintiffs alleged that the accounting firm should have discovered the embezzlement of funds by Riker.

One issue that arose during the trial was the contractual agreement between the public accounting firm and the 1136 Tenants' Corporation. There was no written engagement letter, only an oral agreement between one of the firm's partners and Riker. The cooperative alleged that the firm had been retained to do an audit, while the firm alleged that it had been retained only to prepare the tax return and perform "write-up" services. Another issue was the fact that the firm had identified some missing invoices and had not investigated these items further. The working papers detailed $44,000 of expenses for which no supporting documentation could be located. These were fictitious expenses used by Riker to extract funds from the cooperative.

The court ruled that even if the firm had agreed to provide only write-up services, it had an obligation to notify the tenants about the suspicious nature of the missing invoices. Damaging to the firm's defence was the admission by one of its partners that the engagement had been more extensive than that called for by a normal write-up engagement. The income statement also included a line item labeled "audit." The court ruled in favour of the tenants and awarded them damages of more than $230,000. The decision was upheld upon appeal by the New York appellate court. The size of the judgement was far in excess of the fee of $600 paid to the firm.

This court decision resulted in two significant changes in the profession:

- It reinforced the need by firms to have *written* engagement letters.
- It led to the issuance by the AICPA of Statements on Standards for Accounting and Review Services.

Privity   The traditional view held that, under common law, auditors had no liability to third parties who did not have a privity relationship with the auditor. *Privity* means that the obligations that exist under a contract are between the original parties to the contract, and failure to perform with due care results in a breach of that duty only to those parties. The landmark decision in this area, *Ultramares v. Touche, et al.*, held that the auditor was not liable to third parties who relied on a negligently prepared audit report. Exhibit 18–5 provides a summary of the *Ultramares* case. The rationale for this finding by the New York Court of Appeals is summarized in a famous quote by Judge Cardozo:

> If a liability for negligence exists, a thoughtless slip or blunder, the failure to detect a theft or forgery beneath the cover of deceptive entries, may expose accountants to a liability in an indeterminate amount for an indeterminate time to an indeterminate class. The hazards of a business on these terms are so extreme as to enkindle doubt whether a flaw may not exist in the implication of a duty that exposes to these circumstances.

In 1985, the New York Court of Appeals reaffirmed the privity rule in the case of *Credit Alliance v. Arthur Andersen & Co.* In this lawsuit, Credit

EXHIBIT 18–4

466715 Ontario Limited v. Helen Proulx and Doane Raymond

466715 Ontario Limited (operating name Multi Graphics Print & Litho) was a long-time review client of Doane Raymond (now Grant Thornton). The accounting function was solely handled by the bookkeeper, Helen Proulx. The concentration of duties was exacerbated by the adoption of the computerized ACCPAC Bedford system. Helen Proulx, who had sole signing authority, commenced her fraudulent activities in 1988 by preparing cheques to herself, recording them as payment of supplier accounts payable or reimbursement of petty cash, then signing and cashing them. She also diverted money received for C.O.D. orders, issued fictitious invoices, and recorded payments from customers at less than the amounts actually received, pocketing the difference when she deposited the cheques. The owners only signed cheques over $1,000 and did not monitor any of her other activity in any way. She eventually stole over $100,000.

Upon discovering the fraud, Multi Graphics sued Doane Raymond for negligence. The suit claimed that the auditors should have known of the potential problems with the nonexistent internal controls and should have informed management about the potential danger. Doane Raymond argued that the nature of the engagement was to provide review services, not an audit. They had signed engagement letters that explicitly described the nature of the review services, including that they were not responsible for considering internal controls or detecting fraud. They were not consulted about internal controls, the choice of the computerized accounting system, or the fact that Helen Proulx was made sole signing authority.

The plaintiff's action failed. The court held that Doane Raymond had fulfilled their professional and contractual obligations, particularly in light of the engagement letters that explicitly stated that they were not responsible to detect fraud and error.

EXHIBIT 18–5

Ultramares v. Touche, et al. (1931)

Fred Stern & Company imported and sold rubber during the 1920s. This industry required extensive working capital, and the company used borrowings from banks for its financing activities. In 1924 Stern requested a $100,000 loan from Ultramares Corporation. Before deciding to make the loan, Ultramares requested that Stern provide an audited balance sheet. Touche, Niven & Company had just issued an unqualified audit report on the December 31, 1923, balance sheet.

Stern's management asked Touche to provide 32 serially numbered copies of the audit report. Touche had audited Stern for three years and knew that the audit reports were being used by Stern to obtain external debt financing. Touche, however, did not know which specific banks or finance companies would be given the reports. The balance sheet showed assets of $2.5 million. Ultramares provided the $100,000 loan and two additional loans totaling $65,000. In addition, Stern obtained bank loans of approximately $300,000 by providing the December 31, 1923, balance sheet audited by Touche.

In 1925 the company declared bankruptcy. It came to light during the trial that Stern had already been bankrupt in 1923 and that false accounting record entries had concealed the company's problems. Ultramares alleged that Touche had been both negligent and fraudulent in its audit of Stern. This case was viewed as a test case for third parties seeking damages from auditors. At that time, legal doctrine required that a contractual relationship exist between the auditor and a third party before losses could be recovered.

The jury in the case dismissed the fraud charges against Touche but ruled that Touche had been negligent and awarded approximately $186,000 in damages. The trial judge overturned the jury's verdict on the grounds that Ultramares had not been in privity with Touche. The appellate division of the New York Supreme Court voted 3 to 2 in favour of Ultramares, ruling that the judge had inappropriately overruled the jury verdict. Touche's attorneys appealed the decision to the court of appeals, which ruled unanimously in favour of Touche, therefore upholding the privity doctrine. The quote included in the text by Judge Cardozo, the chief justice of the court, summarizes the court's decision.

Alliance alleged that the auditor had known that the plaintiff was the client's principal lender and had frequently communicated with the plaintiff regarding the audited financial statements. The court upheld the lender's claim that Arthur Andersen had known that Credit Alliance was relying on the financial statements prior to extending credit. The court also ruled that there had been direct communication between the lender and the auditor regarding the client. The *Credit Alliance* case lists the following tests that must be satisfied for holding auditors liable for negligence to third parties: (1) the accountant must be aware that the financial statements are to be used for a particular purpose or purposes, (2) in the furtherance of which a known party or parties was intended to rely, and (3) there must have been some conduct on the part of the accountants linking them to that party or parties, which evinces the accountants' understanding of that party or parties' reliance.

In a 1992 case, *Security Pacific Business Credit, Inc. v. Peat Marwick Main & Co.,* the New York Court of Appeals ruled in favour of Peat Marwick because the plaintiff's reliance was based on one telephone call to the firm's audit partner. Based on this case, it appears that a critical test established in the *Credit Alliance* case is element 3, the requirement that the third party be known to the auditor and that the auditor has directly conveyed the audit report or acted to induce reliance on the audit report.

Foreseen Persons or Classes   While the *Ultramares* decision held to a strict privity standard, a number of subsequent court decisions in other jurisdictions have eroded this precedent. Many courts have reexamined the notion of *caveat emptor* ("buyer beware") and substituted the concept of public responsibility. Among the reasons that have been advanced by the courts for extending the privity standard are (1) the increased liability of other professionals to nonprivity users of their services, (2) the lack of fairness of imposing the burden of economic loss on innocent financial statement users, (3) the assumption that expanded liability will cause auditors to improve their auditing procedures, (4) the ability of auditors to obtain insurance against the increased risks, and (5) the ability of the auditors to pass the increased audit costs and insurance premiums on to their clients.

The application of the concept of privity began to change in 1963 with a landmark decision in the UK, *Hedley Byrne & Co. Ltd. v. Heller & Partners.* Although the case was British, and although Hedley Byrne was an advertising agency and Heller & Partners was a bank, the implications of the decision have strongly impacted the accounting profession. Hedley Byrne, before providing advertising services for Easipower Ltd., enquired of Heller, Easipower's bankers, regarding Easipower's financial condition. Heller said that Easipower's financial position was sound. Hedley entered into business with Easipower who subsequently went into liquidation owing Hedley a substantial sum. Hedley sued Heller for negligence.

The majority opinion of the law lords (this case was ultimately decided by the House of Lords, another reason for its importance) was that Heller (the banker) should have foreseen that Hedley Byrne would rely on their

EXHIBIT 18–6

Rusch Factors, Inc. v. Levin (1968)

In this case, the plaintiff, Rusch Factors, Inc., had requested audited financial statements as a prerequisite for providing a loan to a Rhode Island corporation. Levin audited the financial statements, which showed the company to be solvent when it was actually insolvent. Rusch Factors loaned the corporation $337,000 based on the audited financial statements. When the company went into receivership, Rusch Factors sued Levin for a loss of $121,000.

The federal district court, sitting in Rhode Island, denied Levin's motion to dismiss for a lack of privity. In finding Levin liable for negligence, the court concluded that the *Ultramares* doctrine was inappropriate and relied heavily on the Restatement (Second) of the Law of Torts. The court stated that the auditor had known that his certification was to be used and relied upon by Rusch Factors, and therefore he could be held liable for financial misrepresentations relied upon by *foreseen and limited classes of persons.*

statement about their client. The ultimate decision was in favour of the defendant because Heller, in its communications with Hedley, had explicitly disclaimed responsibility for its opinion. However, in spite of the ultimate outcome, the principle of an implied duty of care to third parties was clearly enunciated in this judgement.

This expansion of the auditor's responsibility to third parties was recognized in 1968 by a US federal district court decision in *Rusch Factors, Inc. v. Levin*. The judge's decision upheld the principle, annunciated in 1963, in *Hedley Byrne v. Heller*, that the auditor owes a duty of care to certain third parties. Exhibit 18–6 provides a summary of the case.

In Canada, a somewhat narrower interpretation was provided in 1976 in another landmark case that went all the way to the Supreme Court of Canada. In deciding *Gordon T. Haig v. Ralph Bamford et al.*, the court ruled that the appropriate criteria to apply was whether the defendants had actual knowledge of the limited class of persons who would rely on the audited information.

Reasonably Foreseeable Third Parties   A third and more expansive view of auditors' liability to third parties can be termed the "reasonably foreseeable third parties" approach. During the same time period that *Haig v. Bamford* was wending its way through the courts, another case, *Toromont Industrial Holdings Limited v. Thorne, Gunn, Helliwell, and Christensen*, was being heard in Ontario. Exhibit 18–7 discusses the case in more detail. In that instance, the court ruled that the auditor did owe a duty of care to Toromont. The facts of the case were different from *Haig v. Bamford*, and the judgement made reference to both *Hedley Byrne v. Heller* and to a lower court decision in *Haig v. Bamford* but the interpretation of the ruling in *Toromont v. Thorne* is that the judgement did broaden the auditor's liability to third parties. In the US in *H. Rosenblum, Inc. v. Adler*, the New Jersey Supreme Court ruled that Touche Ross & Co. was responsible for damages incurred by all reasonably foreseeable third parties who had relied on the financial statements. Exhibit 18–8 provides more details on this case.

EXHIBIT 18–7

Toromont Industrial Holdings Ltd. v. Thorne, Gunn, Helliwell, and Christensen (1975)

Toromont was negotiating with Cimco Ltd. to acquire all of the shares of Cimco for cash and Toromont shares. The purchase price was to be based on the values in Cimco's financial statements as of December 31, 1968. At the time of negotiating, the financial statements were in draft form, to be audited by Thorne. There had even been discussions between Toromont management and the Thorne partner on the audit, about the work that Thorne had done so far. This is an important point because it clearly shows that Thorne knew of Toromont's interest in Cimco's financial statements.

Subsequent to the transaction, Toromont became aware of some accounting practices used by Cimco that they felt had inflated the purchase price and sued Thorne for negligence for not informing them.

The results of the legal action were interesting. The court found that Thorne did owe a duty of care to Toromont and that they had been negligent in carrying out that duty. In fact the judgement specifically identified instances of negligence, from insufficient testing of the system of internal control to overreliance on management representations. However, the court found that Toromont did not show that they suffered a loss as a result of the negligence and they did not win the suit.

Notwithstanding the ultimate outcome this clearly signalled that auditors could be held liable to third parties.

As a result of this case, the profession issued more definitive standards on reviewing subsequent events.

EXHIBIT 18–8

H. Rosenblum, Inc. v. Adler (1983)

The Rosenblum family agreed to sell its retail catalogue showroom business, H. Rosenblum, Inc., to Giant Stores in exchange for Giant common stock. The Rosenblums relied on Giant's 1971 and 1972 financial statements, which had been audited by Touche Ross & Co. A year later, it was revealed that Giant Stores's financial statements contained material misstatements. Giant Stores filed for bankruptcy, and the company's stock became worthless. The Rosenblums sued Touche, alleging negligence. Touche did not know the Rosenblums and had not known that the financial statements would be relied on during merger negotiations.

The lower courts in this case did not allow the Rosenblums' claims against Touche, on the grounds that the Rosenblums did not meet either the *Ultramares* privity test or the Restatement (Second) of the Law of Torts' "foreseen third parties" test. The New Jersey Supreme Court overturned the lower courts' decisions. The court held that the auditor had "a duty to all those whom the auditor should reasonably foresee as recipient from the company of the statements for its proper business purposes, provided that the recipients rely on the statements." Thus the court concluded that auditors should be liable to all reasonably foreseeable third parties who rely on the financial statements. The court indicated that the auditor's function had expanded from one of a watchdog for management to that of an independent evaluator of the adequacy and fairness of the financial statements presented by management to third parties. The court also cited the accountant's ability to obtain insurance against third-party claims.

Another important case that followed this approach was *Citizens State Bank v. Timm, Schmidt & Company* (1983). In this case, the bank sued the public accounting firm after relying on financial statements for one of its debtors that had been audited by Timm, Schmidt & Company. The

Wisconsin court extended the scope of third parties to include all reasonably foreseeable users. The court used a number of the reasons just cited for extending auditors' liability beyond privity. The following quote from this case demonstrates the court's thoughts.

> If relying third parties, such as creditors, are not allowed to recover, the cost of credit to the general public will increase because creditors will either have to absorb the cost of bad loans made in reliance on faulty information or hire independent accountants to verify the information received. Accountants may spread the risk through the use of liability insurance.

One difficulty with this approach is that, in the current legal environment, public accounting firms may no longer be able to secure sufficient liability insurance, or the cost of such insurance may be exorbitant.

Following decisions such as *Toromont v. Thorne* and *Rosenblum v. Adler* (see Exhibit 18–8), the picture did not look overly optimistic for the public accounting profession. However, since that time, other decisions have tended to go "back and forth" on the issue of auditor liability to third parties.

In 1989, two cases, in England, *Caparo Industries PLC v. Dickmans* and *Al Saudi Banque et al. v. Clark Pixley*, and a Canadian case, *Dixon v. Deacon, Morgan, McEwan, Eason et al.*, somewhat retreated from this ever-broadening perspective. This was reinforced by a Supreme Court of Canada decision of 1997 in *Hercules Management Ltd. v. Ernst & Young*, a case that had been dismissed originally, and on appeal, in Manitoba, and was ultimately appealed to the Supreme Court. Basically, the court said that the auditor was not liable to shareholders for any reductions in the value of their investment. However, this is clearly not the end of the debate on auditor liability to third parties, as the two following items demonstrate.

In the same year as the Supreme Court decision on *Hercules v. Ernst*, a prominent case involving what appear to be similar issues, *Kripps v. Touche Ross*, was decided in favour of the plaintiffs by the BC Court of Appeal. The unsuccessful defendants were not given leave to appeal to the Supreme Court of Canada). Exhibit 18–9 provides additional details on this case.

Fraud

If an auditor has acted with knowledge and intent to deceive a third party, he or she can be held liable for fraud. The plaintiff (third party) must prove (1) a false representation by the accountant, (2) knowledge or belief by the accountant that the representation was false, (3) that the accountant intended to induce the third party to rely on the false representation, (4) that the third party relied on the false representation, and (5) that the third party suffered damages. However, it is difficult for a plaintiff to establish knowledge and (especially) intent on the part of the auditor.

Courts have held that fraudulent intent may be established by proof that the accountant acted with knowledge of the false representation or

EXHIBIT 18–9

Kripps v. Touche Ross (1997)

Steven Kripps, along with five other individuals who were investors in Victoria Mortgage Corporation Ltd., sued Touche Ross & Co. (now Deloitte & Touche) over losses they sustained when the company failed in 1985. In 1984 Victoria Mortgage Corporation Ltd. issued a prospectus that included financial statements audited by Touche Ross (who were their auditors from 1980 to 1984). The plaintiffs argued that they had based their investment decisions on the financial statements in the prospectus and that those financial statements were misleading, specifically in that they did not disclose that loans totalling $3.5 million were in default over 90 days, nor provide an adequate allowance for losses on the loan portfolio.

The original action was brought against Touche Ross in 1986. It was dismissed. The first trial judge did not believe that the investors had relied on the financial statements to make their investment decisions.

In 1997, the BC Court of Appeals reversed the original decision. They accepted that Touche Ross owed a duty of care to the investors and that they had breached that duty. Touche Ross's rebuttal was that according to GAAP the financial statements were not required to disclose the loans and that therefore their unqualified opinion was appropriate.

The reasons given for the majority (two out of the three judges) decision in favour of the plaintiffs are highly interesting. Although the judges agreed that GAAP did not explicitly require disclosure of the loans, the decision went on to say that the phrase "present fairly" overrides the specific provisions of GAAP and fair presentation should be the ultimate criterion. This is notice to the profession that following GAAP without concern for whether it results in fair presentation may not be a sufficient defence (and it should be noted that *CICA Handbook*, section 1000, also makes it clear that fair presentation takes precedence over the specific provisions of GAAP).

with reckless disregard for its truth (referred to as *scienter*) but to establish gross negligence (characterized as negligence that is flagrant, extreme, or reckless) is much more demanding than establishing ordinary negligence. As a result, civil actions for fraud are rare, especially in Canada. A past case in the US, *State Street Trust v. Ernst* (in 1938), is an example of a case where a plaintiff pursued this avenue successfully.

In this case, the auditors issued an unqualified opinion on their client's financial statements, knowing that State Street Trust Company was making a loan based on those financial statements. A month later, the auditors sent a letter to the client indicating that receivables had been overstated. The auditors, however, did not communicate this information to State Street Trust Company, and the client subsequently went bankrupt. The New York court ruled that the auditor's actions appeared to be gross negligence and that "heedless and reckless disregard of consequences may take the place of deliberate intention."

In summary, it is clear that the issue of auditor liability to third parties is still very much undecided. Prudence dictates that the auditor be cognizant of the most negative possible interpretations by the courts and resulting possible outcomes and act accordingly.

Statutory Liability under Securities Legislation

The Canadian Environment—Bill 198

LO 5>

In Canada, statutory liability is not as important a factor in auditor liability for negligence. The Ontario Securities Commission (OSC), the senior securities regulator, has in the past been much less interventionist. However, Ontario Bill 198 creates statutory liability for auditors for damages suffered as a result of secondary trading. There is now a statutory right of action if a misrepresentation exists. A person who acquires or disposes of securities is deemed to have relied on the misrepresentation. The plaintiff does not have to prove reliance on the statements and the burden of proof is on the auditor to prove he or she conducted a reasonable investigation and had no reasonable grounds to believe there was a misrepresentation.[8] This is very much a rejection of the principle established by the courts in Hercules v Ernst. Similar provisions already exist with respect to prospectuses, but extending the provisions to the secondary market would dramatically increase the auditor's potential liability to third parties.

Ontario securities legislation extension of the boundaries of auditor liability to third parties fortunately also contains changes that will provide some relief to auditors. One of these is a change from *joint and several liability to proportionate liability*. This is be a very significant change and warrants elaboration.

One of the reasons for the escalating dollar amounts in the lawsuits against auditors is the concept of joint and several liability. Joint and several liability means that the auditors are liable to the plaintiffs for all of the damages, even if they are responsible for only a small part of them. Since the auditors are considered to have "deep pockets" (and the client company is often bankrupt or insolvent) this makes them the prime target for lawsuits.

The fundamental shift to proportionate liability means that each defendant is liable solely for the portion of the damages that corresponds to the percentage of responsibility of that defendant, although joint and several liability may still exist where the defendant is found to have knowingly violated securities laws. However, proportionate liability may discourage "deep-pockets" lawsuits where plaintiffs hope to pressure defendants to settle out of court because the legal costs to fight the lawsuit may be greater than the costs to settle. The actual determination of the percentage of responsibility to be assigned to the auditors will no doubt prove to be a contentious legal process, but the change from joint and several liability to proportionate liability is a significant one.

Notwithstanding the recent changes mentioned above for Canadian-listed companies that reflect the same influences that exist in the US for SEC-regulated companies, the Canadian approach has historically been, and still is, less legislative. For example, the new Canadian rules on independence and the extensive recommendations regarding quality control were developed by the CICA to respond to the same set of concerns that in the US led to the sections of the *Sarbanes-Oxley Act* dealing with independence. Also in Canada the CICA, jointly with representatives of other professional accounting bodies and regulators formed the Canadian Public Accountability Board to monitor firms' compliance with the provisions of the independence and quality control rules and regulations.

---

[8]See B. Morgan, "New Liabilities," *CAMagazine* (June/July 2003), pp. 34–36.

The US Environment

A brief look at the US environment is warranted for two reasons. First, changes have occurred that move Canada in the direction of the regime that exists in the US (see the preceding discussion of the new Ontario legislation affecting OSC-registered companies). Second, a Canadian auditor would come under the jurisdiction of the Securities Exchange Commission if the company it audited, or the parent of the company it audited, was listed on the NYSE, AMEX, or NASDAQ.

The SEC

The Securities and Exchange Commission (SEC) in the US is a very powerful regulatory agency. It administers the provisions of the *Securities Act* of 1933, the *Securities Exchange Act* of 1934, and the *Sarbanes-Oxley* Act of 2002. The SEC has powers of monitoring, enforcement, and sanction and has used those powers to temporarily suspend individuals and firms from auditing SEC registrants. It was under SEC rules that Arthur Andersen was going to be suspended from audits of SEC-registered companies. However, Arthur Andersen's total loss of client base and resulting demise were much more devastating than SEC sanctions.

Securities Act of 1933

This statute generally regulates the disclosure of material facts in a registration statement for a new public offering of securities. Section 11 of the *Securities Act* of 1933 imposes a liability on issuers and others, including auditors, for losses suffered by third parties when false or misleading information is included in a registration statement.

In contrast to the situation under common law, the plaintiff does not have to prove negligence or fraud, reliance on the auditor's opinion, a causal relationship, or a contractual relationship; the plaintiff need only prove that a loss was suffered by investing in the registered security and that the audited financial statements contained a material omission or misstatement. The misstatement can be the result of mere ordinary negligence. Thus, section 11 is more favourable for plaintiffs than is common law because the auditor must prove that he or she was not negligent.

Securities Exchange Act of 1934

This statute is concerned primarily with ongoing reporting by companies whose securities are listed and traded on a stock exchange or that meet certain other statutory requirements. Typical reporting requirements under the 1934 act include the quarterly filing of a 10Q Form, the annual filing of a 10K Form, and the filing of an 8K Form whenever a significant event takes place that affects the entity.

Section 18 imposes liability on any person who makes a material false or misleading statement in documents filed with the Securities and Exchange Commission (SEC). The auditor's liability can be limited if the auditor can show that he or she "acted in good faith and had no knowledge that such statement was false or misleading." However, a number of cases have limited the auditor's good-faith defence when the auditor's action has been judged to be grossly negligent.

Sarbanes-Oxley Act of 2002

As a direct result of events surrounding the collapse of Enron, the US Congress passed the *Sarbanes-Oxley* Act in mid-2002. The *Sarbanes-Oxley* Act creates a five-member panel known as the Public Company Accounting Oversight Board (PCAOB), which has the authority to set and enforce auditing, quality control, and ethics (including independence) standards for auditors of public companies. It also has the right to inspect the operations of public accounting firms that audit public companies and impose sanctions for violations of the boards securities laws, and professional accounting and auditing standards.

Some of the other provisions of the act

- require the rotation of the lead audit partner and reviewing partner every five years
- extend the statute of limitations for discovery of fraud
- impose harsh penalties for securities law violations, corporate fraud and document shredding (a direct reference to Arthur Andersen and Enron)
- identify eight types of services that are "unlawful if provided to a publicly held company by its auditors": bookkeeping, information systems design and implementation, appraisals and valuation services, actuarial services, internal auditing, management and human resources services, broker/dealer in investment banking services, and legal or expert services related to audit services

The provisions of the *Sarbanes-Oxley* Act are highly relevant to Canadian auditors—section 106 of the Act requires all foreign accounting firms who audit a US company, including audits of foreign branches or subsidiaries of US parent companies, to register with the Public Accounting Oversight Board (PCAOB), and be subject to the provisions of the Act. There is much more of relevance to the *Sarbanes-Oxley* Act. You can find a summary of its provisions at www.aicpa.org/info/sarbanes-oxley_summary.htm.

Racketeer Influenced and Corrupt Organizations Act

Although the *Racketeer Influenced and Corrupt Organizations Act* (RICO) was enacted by Congress in 1970 to combat the infiltration of legitimate businesses by organized crime, it has been used against auditors. RICO provides civil and criminal sanctions for certain types of illegal acts. A major factor in bringing an action under RICO is that the law provides for treble damages in civil RICO cases. Racketeering activity includes a long list of federal and state crimes, with mail fraud and wire fraud the most common acts alleged against auditors.

Foreign Corrupt Practices Act

The Foreign Corrupt Practices Act (FCPA) was passed by Congress in 1977 in response to the discovery of bribery and other misconduct on the part of more than 300 American companies. The act was codified in 1988 as an amendment to the *Securities Exchange Act* of 1934. The FCPA prohibits corporate officers from knowingly participating in bribing foreign officials to obtain or retain business. The external auditor may detect activities that violate the FCPA; such violations should be communicated to management immediately. Failure to do so may result in the auditor being subject to administrative proceedings, civil liability, and civil penalties under the FCPA.

Criminal Liability in Canada

LO 6 Section 338 of the Criminal Code of Canada is the section under which an auditor could be prosecuted by the Crown for fraud. It is important to stress that a criminal action for fraud brought by the Crown could be concurrent with a civil action for fraud brought by a client or third party.

There have been practically no Canadian criminal prosecutions for fraud. However, in addition to the recent Enron case, there have been some very high profile criminal fraud cases in the US. Because such cases impact the reputation of auditors in Canada as well as the US, and because they are fascinating, they are important reading for anyone intending to enter the auditing profession in Canada as well as the US. You will find a summary of significant US case law on the companion website to this text. Included among these cases are Continental Vending (*United States v. Simon*), National Student Marketing (*United States v. Natelli*), Equity Funding (*United States v. Weiner*), and ESM Government Securities, Inc. (*In re Alexander Grant & Co. Litigation*). Note that, in addition to criminal prosecution of the auditors, the auditors' firms faced civil liability for violating various statutes and paid large sums to settle the cases.

Because of its recency (the lawsuits are still ongoing) and its impact (it resulted in the demise of the venerable US firm of Arthur Andersen), a discussion of the audit-related legal issues involved in the Enron collapse is presented following. Refer to the Chapter 3 opening box on page 66 for a chronology of the rise and fall of Enron.

Enron (*United States v. Arthur Andersen LLP*, 2002)

Arthur Andersen's demise as a result of its involvement in Enron's failure in the fall of 2001 is an example of how the auditor may attract legal liability from more than one source for the same set of actions. The firm was named in civil lawsuits by investors and creditors of Enron for a total of approximately $25 billion. It was also charged, on March 15, 2002, with criminal obstruction of justice for allegedly shredding documents relating to the criminal investigation of Enron, Inc. The US Justice Department's obstruction of justice charges against Arthur Andersen went to trial in May 2002. The engagement partner was charged individually with obstruction of justice and pled guilty in April 2002. In June 2002, a jury found the firm guilty of obstruction of justice. The jury indicated that although they were in agreement on the verdict, they were not in complete agreement as to the actual person(s) responsible. Arthur Andersen appealed on those grounds and asked the judge to set aside the verdict. The appeal was unsuccessful—the judge upheld the jury's verdict in a decision in September 2002, and in October 2002, sentenced Arthur Andersen to a $500,000 fine and five years' probation. Arthur Andersen had earlier agreed to abide by an SEC prohibition and had stated that it would no longer audit public companies as of August 31, 2002. However, the prohibition was unnecessary, by this time Arthur Andersen's client base had evaporated as public clients sought to end their association with Arthur Andersen. Arthur Andersen's conviction was overturned in May 2005 because the Appeals Court held that there had been procedural irregularities in the original trial but by that time the firm had effectively ceased to exist.

At the same time, settlement negotiations were ongoing with the many civil plaintiffs. It is reported that at one time the SEC was demanding Arthur Andersen pay $500 million in compensation and Arthur Andersen was offering $350 million. During the impasse in negotiations, as Arthur Andersen's client base dwindled, so did the firm's resources. After protracted negotiations, in November 2003, the same judge who had presided at the obstruction of justice trial gave court approval to settlement by Andersen Worldwide SC (the worldwide "umbrella" organization) of $40 million. At this time, the civil litigation against Arthur Andersen is still ongoing, and probably will be for many years to come.

Approaches to Minimizing Legal Liability

LO 7 > Everyone involved with the public accounting profession has an interest in minimizing auditors' exposure to legal liability. Lawsuits against auditors not only result in direct financial effects such as large settlement costs but also impact the profession and society in other ways. For example, many firms have seen their costs of defending such lawsuits, including management time and their insurance premiums, increase dramatically in recent years. The firms have also suffered significant blows to their reputations through the negative publicity arising from litigation.

One recent change to the laws governing the legal organization of public accounting firms has provided some reduction in risk to the individual members of a partnership. British Columbia, Ontario, Alberta, and Saskatchewan now allow partnerships to be organized as *Limited Liability Partnerships* (LLPs). In the usual general partnership form of organization, if one partner is sued, the suit encompasses all partners and all partners are personally liable to the extent of their partnership and personal assets. In an LLP, partners who are not directly involved in the suit (for example, in a suit against an auditor for negligence, partners who were not involved in the audit of that client) are liable only to the extent of their partnership assets.

However, the risk of financial and reputational damage to a partnership is not reduced by the change to a limited liability form of organization. As a result, many public accounting firms now practice active risk reduction, including avoiding clients that operate in certain industries or that are considered high risk. Some small to medium-size public accounting firms are limiting or abandoning their audit practices. A number of steps can be taken by the profession and by individual firms to minimize legal liability.

At the Profession Level

The public accounting profession, through federal and provincial institutes and associations, can do a number of things to reduce its exposure to legal liability. These include

- **Continue to lobby for changes in laws.** The changes brought about by Ontario Bill 198 are positive changes to the profession, but continued lobbying to have those changes adopted by other jurisdictions is still needed.

- *Establishing stronger auditing and attestation standards.* While adherence to GAAS (and GAAP) is a minimum defence against lawsuits, the profession should strive to issue standards that require the best form of practice.[9] This includes revising standards to address practice problems that are revealed through litigation.
- *Continually updating the Codes of Professional Conduct and sanctioning members who do not comply with it.* The profession should continually revise the Codes of Professional Conduct to reflect acceptable practices that meet users' needs. Members who do not comply with the Codes should be sanctioned. Such sanctions will demonstrate to the profession's constituency that the profession is willing to discipline members who act unprofessionally.
- *Educating users.* In recent years, the profession has undertaken a number of actions to close the "expectation gap," including revision of a number of important auditing standards. These revisions clarified auditors' responsibilities for issues such as errors and fraud, illegal acts, and going-concern evaluation. The wording in the auditor's report was also revised so as to better communicate to users what an audit entails. The profession needs an ongoing program to educate the public about auditors' activities.

At the Firm Level

Individual public accounting firms can also take steps to avoid litigation. These include

- *Following professional standards.*   All professional personnel in the firm should follow the standards set out in the *CICA Handbook*. In fact they should be encouraged to treat the *CICA Handbook* standards as the minimum acceptable standards for performance of any assurance engagements.
- *Instituting sound quality control and review procedures.* A system of quality control and review can give the firm reasonable assurance of conforming with professional standards. Chapter 17 provided detailed coverage of quality control and review.
- *Ensuring that members of the firm are independent.* Members of the firm must be independent in both fact and appearance. A review of legal cases indicates that on numerous occasions auditors did not maintain a sufficiently high level of "professional scepticism" and accepted a client's responses without investigating the facts adequately.
- *Following sound client acceptance and retention procedures.* Auditors need to be very careful in accepting new clients. If a client is known to lack integrity, the likelihood increases that its management will take actions that are detrimental to user groups, including management fraud.
- *Being alert to risk factors that may result in lawsuits.* A number of important risk factors seem to lead to litigation. These include

---

[9]An example of this is *CICA Handbook*, section 5135, "The auditor's responsibility to consider fraud." Refer to Chapter 3 for a detailed discussion of this section.

the presence of management fraud, the commission of illegal acts, insolvency, disagreements between auditors and management, first-year audits, and acquisition audits. For example, when management fraud occurs, auditors are usually subject to litigation, and such cases are more costly to resolve.[10] Some audit deficiencies have also been noted in the litigation against public accounting firms. These include incomplete client acceptance or retention procedures, unrealistic risk assessments given the client's circumstances, staff that is inadequately trained to audit specialized industries, inadequate documentation of difficult decisions, insufficient partner and manager participation in resolving key issues, and excessive reliance on management representations.

- ***Performing and documenting work diligently.*** A quality audit involves following relevant professional standards and includes (1) planning properly, (2) understanding the client's internal control adequately, (3) obtaining sufficient competent evidence as to financial assertions, (4) having experienced personnel review the work done, and (5) issuing an appropriate audit report.

The threat of legal liability serves to prevent or limit inappropriate behaviour on the part of auditors. However, auditors cannot be expected to guarantee the accuracy of either financial statements or the financial health of a business entity. The auditor's responsibility is to provide reasonable assurance that there are no material misstatements in the financial statements.

REVIEW QUESTIONS

LO 1 **18-1** Describe the current legal environment for auditors.

2 **18-2** What is meant by *proportionate liability?* Contrast this legal doctrine with the doctrine of *joint and several liability.*

3 **18-3** For what types of actions are auditors liable to a client under common law? Why would a client prefer to sue the auditor for a tort action rather than for a breach of contract?

3 **18-4** Liability for negligence represents a deviation from a standard of behaviour that is consistent with that of a "reasonable person." What behaviours constitute a "reasonable person" in this context?

3 **18-5** What elements must a client prove to maintain an action against an auditor for negligence?

3 **18-6** What significant changes occurred for the public accounting profession as a result of the 1136 *Tenants'* case?

4 **18-7** Distinguish among the three standards that have evolved for defining auditors' liability to third parties under common law. Why is this area of auditors' liability so complex?

4 **18-8** When an auditor is accused of fraud, what must the third party plaintiff prove?

[10]A review of over 1000 auditor-related lawsuits by Z. V. Palmrose, "Empirical Research on Auditor Litigation: Considerations and the Data," *Studies in Accounting Research* (23) Sarasota, FL: American Accounting Association, 1999, provides detailed data on the incidence and resolution of litigation against auditors in the US.

5> **18-9** Distinguish between the *Securities Act* of 1933 and the *Securities Exchange Act* of 1934. Why is it easier for a plaintiff to sue an auditor under the *Securities Act* of 1933?

5> **18-10** Briefly contrast the Canadian versus US approaches to dealing with the issues of auditor independence.

5> **18-11** Briefly describe how the *Proceeds of Crime Act* can affect an auditor's liability.

5> **18-12** Briefly describe the *Racketeer Influenced and Corrupt Organizations Act* and why plaintiffs might seek to sue auditors under this statute.

6> **18-13** What actions can result in an auditor being held criminally liable under statutes and regulations?

7> **18-14** Identify steps that can be taken at the profession level and individual level to minimize legal liability against auditors.

MULTIPLE-CHOICE QUESTIONS FROM PROFESSIONAL EXAMINATIONS

Unless otherwise indicated, these multiple-choice questions were adapted from the CPA examinations, courtesy of the American Institute of Certified Public Accountants.

2,3,4> **18-15** Cable Corporation orally engaged Drake & Company to audit its financial statements. Cable's management informed Drake that it suspected the accounts receivable were materially overstated. Though the financial statements Drake audited included a materially overstated accounts receivable balance, Drake issued an unqualified opinion. Cable used the financial statements to obtain a loan to expand its operations. Cable defaulted on the loan and incurred a substantial loss. If Cable sues Drake for negligence in failing to discover the overstatement, Drake's best defence would be that Drake did *not*

a. Have privity of contract with Cable.

b. Sign an engagement letter.

c. Perform the audit recklessly or with an intent to deceive.

d. Violate generally accepted auditing standards in performing the audit.

3> **18-16** Which of the following best describes whether an auditor has met the required standard of care in auditing a client's financial statements?

a. Whether the client's expectations are met with regard to the accuracy of audited financial statements.

b. Whether the statements conform to generally accepted accounting principles.

c. Whether the auditor conducted the audit with the same skill and care expected of an ordinarily prudent auditor under the circumstances.

d. Whether the audit was conducted to investigate and discover all acts of fraud.

3,4> **18-17** Sun Corporation approved a merger plan with Cord Corporation. One of the determining factors in approving the merger was the financial statements of Cord, which had been audited by Frank & Company. Sun had engaged Frank to audit Cord's financial statements. While performing the audit, Frank failed to discover fraud that later caused Sun to suffer substantial losses. For Frank to be liable under common-law negligence, Sun at a minimum must prove that Frank

a. Knew of the fraud.

b. Failed to exercise due care.

c. Was grossly negligent.

d. Acted with scienter.

4 >   **18-18**   Brown & Company issued an unqualified opinion on the financial statements of its client, King Corporation. Based on the strength of King's financial statements, Safe Bank loaned King $500,000. Brown was unaware that Safe would receive a copy of the financial statements or that they would be used by King in obtaining a loan. King defaulted on the loan.

If Safe commences an action for negligence against Brown and Brown is able to prove that it conducted the audit in conformity with GAAS, Brown will

a. Be liable to Safe, because Safe relied on the financial statements.

b. Be liable to Safe, because the Statute of Frauds has been satisfied.

c. Not be liable to Safe, because there is a conclusive presumption that following GAAS is the equivalent of acting reasonably and with due care.

d. Not be liable to Safe, because there was a lack of privity of contract.

2,3,4 >   **18-19**   In general, the third-party (primary) beneficiary rule as applied to the auditor's legal liability in conducting an audit is relevant to which of the following causes of action against the auditor?

	Fraud	*Constructive Fraud*	*Negligence*
a.	Yes	Yes	No
b.	Yes	No	No
c.	No	Yes	Yes
d.	No	No	Yes

Question 19-20 and 19-21 are based on the following information:

While conducting an audit, Larson Associates failed to detect material misstatements included in its client's financial statements. Larson's unqualified opinion was included with the financial statements in a registration statement and prospectus for a public offering of securities made by the client. Larson knew that its opinion and the financial statements would be used for this purpose.

3,4 >   **18-20**   In a suit by a purchaser against Larson for common-law negligence, Larson's best defence would be that the

a. Audit was conducted in accordance with generally accepted auditing standards.

b. Client was aware of the misstatements.

c. Purchaser was *not* in privity of contract with Larson.

d. Identity of the purchaser was *not* known to Larson at the time of the audit.

3,4 > **18-21** In a suit by a purchaser against Larson for common-law fraud, Larson's best defence would be that

a. Larson did *not* have actual or constructive knowledge of the misstatements.

b. Larson's client knew or should have known of the misstatements.

c. Larson did *not* have actual knowledge that the purchaser was an intended beneficiary of the audit.

d. Larson was *not* in privity of contract with its client.

3 > **18-22** Which of the following is the best defence an audit firm can assert to a suit for common-law fraud based on its unqualified opinion on materially false financial statements?

a. Lack of privity.

b. Lack of scienter.

c. Contributory negligence on the part of the client.

d. A disclaimer contained in the engagement letter.

5 > **18-23** How does Bill 198, which imposes civil liability on auditors for misrepresentations or omissions of material facts in a publicly available document, expand auditors' liability to purchasers of securities beyond that of common law?

a. Purchasers have to prove only that a loss was caused by reliance on audited financial statements.

b. Privity with purchasers is *not* a necessary element of proof.

c. Purchasers have to prove either fraud or gross negligence as a basis for recovery.

d. Auditors are held to a standard of care described as "professional scepticism."

4 > **18-24** If an auditor recklessly departs from the standards of due care when conducting an audit, the auditor will be liable to third parties who are unknown to the auditor based on

a. Negligence.

b. Gross negligence.

c. Strict liability.

d. Criminal deceit.

PROBLEMS

4,6 > **18-25** Martini & Rossi (MR) has performed the audit of the financial statements of Advanced Technology Ltd. (AT) for the last five years and has always rendered an unqualified opinion. Over the past five years AT has grown to be a very large producer of computer components and peripherals. In fact, the partner in charge of the MR audit learned that AT was intending, during the next year, to issue debentures of $15,000,000 to raise capital for expansion of its production facilities.

Unbeknownst to MR, several very large accounts receivable shown on AT's books represented goods that the "purchasers" had actually accepted from AT on consignment. William Cooke, the president of AT, had somehow persuaded the companies involved to sign the receivable confirmations for the amounts shown. AT also had a large inventory of semi-conductor chips that it carried at full value even though the chips were "old technology" and not marketable at full price. The combined result of these misrepresentations was to show a net profit of $2,000,000 instead of a loss of $2,500,000 and a positive net worth instead of a negative net worth.

The current year's audit proceeded smoothly and MR issued an unqualified report on the financial statements. The following year, AT issued the debentures. Unfortunately the expanded production facilities came on stream just in time for the severe downturn in the technology sector and AT, facing a declining market and high debt load, went bankrupt.

Required:

a. Could the investors succeed in a negligence suit against MR?

b. What defence or defences could MR use?

c. Several of the investors were wiped out financially, and are so angry at MR that they wish to proceed with a fraud action. What is the difference between fraud and negligence? Given the precedents in common law and the facts of this case, what would be your advice to them?

(CGA-Canada, adapted)

5 > 18-26   Sleek Corporation is a public corporation whose stock is traded on a national securities exchange. Sleek hired Garson Ames to audit Sleek's financial statements. Sleek needed the audit to obtain bank loans and to offer public stock so that it could expand.

Before the engagement, Fred Hedge, Sleek's president, told Garson's managing partner that the audited financial statements would be submitted to Sleek's banks to obtain the necessary loans.

During the course of the audit, Garson's managing partner found that Hedge and other Sleek officers had embezzled substantial amounts of money from the corporation. These embezzlements threatened Sleek's financial stability. When these findings were brought to Hedge's attention, Hedge promised that the money would be repaid and begged that the audit not disclose the embezzlements.

Hedge also told Garson's managing partner that several friends and relatives of Sleek's officers had been advised about the projected business expansion and proposed stock offering and had purchased significant amounts of Sleek's stock based on this information.

Garson submitted an unqualified opinion on Sleek's financial statements, which did not include adjustments for or disclosures about the embezzlements and insider stock transactions. The financial statements and audit report were submitted to Sleek's regular banks, including Knox Bank. Knox, relying on the financial statements and Garson's report, gave Sleek a $2 million loan.

Sleek's audited financial statements were also incorporated into a registration statement prepared under the provisions of the *Securities Act* of 1933. The registration statement was filed with the SEC in conjunction with Sleek's public offering of 1,000,000 shares of its common stock at $10 per share.

An SEC investigation of Sleek disclosed the embezzlements and the insider trading. Trading in Sleek's stock was suspended, and Sleek defaulted on the Knox loan.

As a result, the following legal actions were taken:

- Knox sued Garson.
- The general-public purchasers of Sleek's stock offering sued Garson.

Required:

Answer the following questions and give the reasons for your conclusions.

a. Would Knox recover from Garson for fraud?

b. Would the general-public purchasers of Sleek's stock offerings recover from Garson

 1. Under the liability provisions of the *Securities Act* of 1933?

 2. Under the *Securities Exchange Act* of 1934?

(AICPA, adapted)

2,3,4 **18-27** Becker, Inc., purchased the assets of Bell Corporation. A condition of the purchase agreement was that Bell have its financial statements audited. The purpose of the audit was to determine whether the unaudited financial statements furnished to Becker fairly presented Bell's financial position. Bell retained Salam & Company to perform the audit.

While performing the audit, Salam discovered that Bell's bookkeeper had embezzled $500. Salam had some evidence of other embezzlements by the bookkeeper. However, Salam decided that the $500 was immaterial and that the other suspected embezzlements did not require further investigation. Salam did not discuss the matter with Bell's management. Unknown to Salam, the bookkeeper had, in fact, embezzled large sums of cash from Bell. In addition, the accounts receivable were significantly overstated. Salam did not detect the overstatement because of Salam's failure to follow its audit program.

Despite the foregoing, Salam issued an unqualified opinion on Bell's financial statements and furnished a copy of the audited financial statements to Becker. Unknown to Salam, Becker required financing to purchase Bell's assets and furnished a copy of Bell's audited financial statements to City Bank to obtain approval of the loan. Based on Bell's audited financial statements, City loaned Becker $600,000.

Becker paid Bell $750,000 to purchase Bell's assets. Within six months, Becker began experiencing financial difficulties resulting from the undiscovered embezzlements and overstated accounts receivable. Becker later defaulted on the City loan.

City has commenced a lawsuit against Salam based on the following causes of action:

- Constructive fraud
- Negligence

Required:

In separate paragraphs, discuss whether City is likely to prevail on the causes of action it has raised. Set forth reasons for each conclusion.

(AICPA, adapted)

4> 18-28 You are a recently promoted manager in your firm. The partner for whom you work most often has told you that you have a "legal mind" (meant as a compliment, she assures you) and that she wants you to give a presentation to the firm's junior staff on auditor liability. She particularly wants you to focus on the concepts of privity and duty of care.

Required:

Prepare a draft of your presentation to the firm's junior staff explaining what is meant by the two terms and illustrating with precedent cases, how the standards of privity and duty of care have evolved and changed over the past three decades.

3,4,5> 18-29 Astor Electronics, Corp., markets a wide variety of computer-related products throughout Canada. Astor's officers decided to raise $1 million by selling shares of Astor's common stock. In connection with the offering, Astor engaged Apple & Company to audit Astor's financial statements. The audited financial statements, including Apple's unqualified opinion, were included in the offering memorandum given to prospective purchasers of Astor's stock. Apple was aware that Astor intended to include the statements in the offering materials.

Astor's financial statements reported certain inventory items at a cost of $930,000 when in fact they had a fair market value of less than $100,000 because of technological obsolescence. Apple accepted the assurances of Astor's controller that cost was the appropriate valuation, despite the fact that Apple was aware of ongoing sales of the products at prices substantially less than cost. All of this was thoroughly documented in Apple's working papers.

Musk purchased 10,000 shares of Astor's common stock at a total price of $300,000. In deciding to make the purchase, Musk had reviewed the audited financial statements of Astor that accompanied the other offering materials and had been impressed by Astor's apparent financial strength.

Shortly after the stock offering was completed, Astor's management discovered that the audited financial statements reflected the materially overstated valuation of the company's inventory. Astor advised its shareholders of the problem.

Upon receiving notice from Astor of the overstated inventory amount, Musk became very upset because the stock value was now substantially less than what it would have been had the financial statements been accurate. In fact, the stock was worth only about $200,000.

Musk has commenced an action against Apple, alleging that Apple is liable to Musk based on the following causes of action:

- common-law fraud
- negligence

During the litigation Apple has refused to give to Musk its working papers pertaining to the Astor audit, claiming that these constitute privileged communications. The state in which the actions have been commenced has no accountants' privileged communication statute.

The law applicable to this action follows the *Ultramares* decision with respect to accountants' liability to third parties for negligence or fraud. Apple has also asserted that the actions should be dismissed because of the absence of any contractual relationship between Apple and Musk, that is, a lack of privity.

Required:

Answer the following, setting forth your reasons for any conclusions stated.

a. Will Apple be required to give Musk its working papers?

b. What elements must be established by Musk to support a cause of action based on negligence?

c. Is Apple's assertion regarding lack of privity correct with regard to Musk's causes of action for negligence and fraud?

(AICPA, adapted)

DISCUSSION CASES

4,5> **18-30**   Conan Doyle & Associates (CD&A) served as the auditors for both Lestrad Corporation and Watson Corporation, publicly held companies traded on NASDAQ. Watson recently acquired Lestrad Corporation in a merger that involved swapping 1.75 shares of Watson for 1 share of Lestrad. In connection with that merger, CD&A issued an unqualified report on the financial statements and participated in the preparation of the pro forma unaudited financial statements contained in the combined prospectus and proxy statement circulated to obtain shareholder approval of the merger and to register the shares to be issued in connection with the merger. Watson prepared the required filing documents in connection with the merger. Shortly thereafter, financial disaster beset the merged company, resulting in large losses to the shareholders and creditors. A class action suit on behalf of shareholders and creditors has been filed against Watson and its management. In addition, it names CD&A as co-defendants, challenging the fairness, accuracy, and truthfulness of the financial statements.

Required:

Discuss CD&A's potential civil liability in common law to the shareholders and creditors of Watson as a result of issuing an unqualified report on the audited financial statements of Watson and Lestrad and having participated in preparing the unaudited financial statements required in connection with the merger.

(AICPA, adapted)

4,6>   **18-31**   Transnational Precious Metals Ltd. (TPM), a company primarily engaged in exploration and development of potential gold mining properties, has been a problem for its auditor, Hal Holton, for several years. The company is listed on the Toronto Venture Exchange and company management is constantly concerned about keeping reported earnings high to support the share price. At the end of each audit, Holton faced an argument with the vice president of finance who would resist recording any of Holton's proposed adjustments by claiming they were not individually material. TPM was a lucrative client with the promise of even bigger things to come and Holton, against his better judgement, acceded to the vice president's wishes. As a result, each year the net income was overstated by 3 to 5 percent.

This year, Holton was concerned about a $10 million investment in leases in mining property in South-East Asia that TPM had carried on its books for the past five years. During the audit, Holton came across a report indicating that the property was "mined out" and that the leases were worthless. The report also indicated that this had been the case for the past two years. Holton confronted the vice president of finance who suggested a compromise of writing the investment off in equal instalments over the next 10 years. He pointed out that this would prevent the impact on net income from being too drastic in any one year, and would also prevent embarrassment or liability to Holton for having to acknowledge that the past years' financial statements were misstated. The vice president said that recognition of the total loss in the current year would mean bankruptcy for TPM and certain liability for Holton.

Required:

Discuss what course of action you would tell Holton to take, including discussing what liability Holton would face if he accepts the vice president's proposal and what liability he would face if he does not accept the vice president's proposal.

Part VIII ACCOUNTING SERVICES, ATTEST ENGAGEMENTS, AND ASSURANCE SERVICES

Accounting Services, Attest Engagements, and Assurance Services

Chapter **19**

Learning Objectives

Upon completion of this chapter, you will be able to

1 Explain the accountant's responsibilities in a review engagement.

2 Explain the accountant's responsibilities in a compilation engagement.

3 Describe an attest engagement and be familiar with some examples of attest engagements.

4 Outline the auditor's involvement with, and reporting on, prospectuses.

5 Report on future oriented financial information.

6 Define assurance services and explain why there is a demand for assurance services.

7 Define other professional services such as forensic auditing, environmental auditing, and business performance measurement.

8 Describe the transition of Canadian auditing Standards to harmonization with International Standards.

RELEVANT ACCOUNTING AND ASSURANCE PRONOUNCEMENTS

CICA Handbook, Introduction to assurance and related services

CICA Handbook, **section 4250,** Future oriented financial information

CICA Handbook, **section 5025,** Standards for assurance engagements

CICA Handbook, **section 5805,** Audit reports on financial information other than financial statements

CICA Handbook, **section 5815,** Audit reports on compliance with agreements, statutes, and regulations

CICA Handbook, **section 5970,** Auditor's report on controls at a service organization

CICA Handbook, **section 7050,** Auditor review of interim financial statements

CICA Handbook, **section 7110,** Auditor involvement with offering documents of public and private entities

CICA Handbook, **section 7115,** Auditor involvement with offering documents of public and private entities—current legislative and regulatory requirements

CICA Handbook, **section 8100,** General review standards

CICA Handbook, **section 8200,** Public accountant's reviews of financial statements

CICA Handbook, **section 8500,** Reviews of financial information other than financial statements

CICA Handbook, **section 8600,** Reviews of compliance with agreements and regulations

CICA Handbook, **section 9100,** Report on the results of applying specified auditing procedures

to financial information other than financial statements

CICA Handbook, **section 9200,** Compilation engagements

AuG-6, Examination of a financial forecast or projection included in a prospectus or other offering document

AuG-16, Compilation of a financial forecast or projection

It should be stressed that this chapter does not cover every type of engagement that a professional accountant might undertake, but attempts to present a representative sample of some of the more frequent types of engagements.

FOCUSING ON WILLIS & ADAMS

EarthWear EarthWear is one of Willis & Adams' most important clients, but Willis & Adams has many other clients as well and offers many other types of services to those clients. For example, many clients of Willis & Adams are small-to-medium business enterprises and are not required by law to have their annual financial statements audited. They will most likely have Willis & Adams, as accountants rather than auditors, perform a *review engagement* of their financial statements and obtain a *review engagement report*. In a review engagement, the public accountant will use procedures such as enquiry, observation, and analysis with the objective of determining whether the financial statements are "plausible in the circumstances." Such a report may be required by the business's bank as a condition of a loan to the business. Many of Willis & Adams' clients may not even wish to have a review engagement. An accounting service that Willis & Adams may provide for these clients is a *compilation*. These are often performed for businesses that do not have an in-house accounting function. In such an engagement, Willis & Adams will take the accounting records and other information supplied by the management of the business and compile that information into financial statements. The calculation of taxable income for a business begins with the business's financial statement net income and many small businesses engage Willis & Adams to both compile their financial statements and prepare their income tax filing for CRA.

As well as review engagements and compilations, Willis & Adams can provide many other auditing and accounting services to clients. Reports on financial information other than on the full set of financial statements, reports on future-oriented financial statements, reports on internal control, and reports relating to the issuance of debt or equity securities, are all additional types of engagements that Willis & Adams may undertake for their clients. This chapter discusses some of the more common of the engagements in order to give a flavour of the broad scope of activities provided by public accounting firms.

The chapter ends with a brief look ahead. The public accounting profession in Canada is in the midst of substantial change. Over the period of time between now and 2011, the Canadian standards governing all aspects of assurance engagements will move to concordance with international standards. The chapter will end with a brief discussion of how that process is expected to transpire.

Review Engagements

Reviews of Financial Statements

LO 1 ▷

Many entities do not need an audit of their financial statements. An alternative for these entities is to engage a public accountant to perform a review of their financial statements. Sections 8100 and 8200 of the *CICA Handbook* detail the accountant's responsibilities in a review of an entity's annual financial statements and section 7050 covers the accountant's responsibilities for interim financial statements (note that the practitioner performs the engagement as an accountant rather than as an auditor).

A review is less extensive, and provides less assurance than an audit, but a company may not need to provide audited financial statements—for example the statutory requirement to produce audited financial statements is not applicable to nonpublic companies. A lending institution such as a bank may wish to see a review engagement report before advancing an applicant a loan—but if they require additional information the bank can ask the company directly. The company, since they are applying to the bank for a loan, will generally be willing to supply the requested additional information.

Standards Applicable to Review Engagements

In performing a review engagement the accountant must comply with generally accepted review standards (GARS). With important exceptions, these standards are very similar to GAAS. One obvious difference is that the general standard refers to "review" rather than "audit." The examination standards (called review standards in this context) differ more significantly. Three differences in particular are:

- The accountant's objective is to assess whether the information is plausible in the circumstances.
- There is no requirement to study internal control.
- The recommended examination techniques are enquiry, analytical procedures, and discussion.

The reporting standards differ in that they require that the report explicitly state that no audit was performed and that no opinion is expressed, and that the accountant express limited or negative assurance about the results of the examination. In other words the accountant states that nothing has come to his or her attention that causes him or her to believe that the statements are not, in all material respects, in accordance with generally accepted accounting principles. Table 19–1 presents the generally accepted review standards.

Review Engagement Procedures

A review consists of enquiry, analytical procedures, and discussion in order to provide the accountant with a reasonable basis for expressing negative assurance. In conducting a review, the accountant's work involves the following:

- obtaining knowledge of the accounting principles and practices of the industry in which the entity operates and an understanding of the entity's business

Table 19–1	Standards Applicable to Review Engagements

General Standard

The review should be performed and the review engagement report prepared by a person or persons having adequate technical training and proficiency in conducting reviews, with due care and an objective state of mind.

Review Standards

The work should be adequately planned and properly executed. If assistants are employed, they should be properly supervised.

The public accountant should possess or acquire sufficient knowledge of the business carried on by the enterprise so that intelligent enquiry and assessment of information obtained can be made.

The public accountant should perform a review with the limited objective of assessing whether the information being reported on is plausible in the circumstances within the framework of appropriate criteria. Such a review should consist of:

- enquiry, analytical procedures, and discussion; and
- additional or more extensive procedures when the public accountant's knowledge of the business carried on by the enterprise and the results of the enquiry, analytical procedures, and discussion cause him or her to doubt the plausibility of such information.

Reporting Standards

The review engagement report should indicate the scope of the review. The nature of the review engagement should be made evident and be clearly distinguished from an audit.

The report should indicate, based on the review:

- whether anything has come to the public accountant's attention that causes him or her to believe that the information being reported on is not, in all material respects, in according with appropriate criteria; or
- that no assurance can be provided.

The report should provide an explanation of the nature of any reservations contained therein and, if readily determinable, their effect.

- obtaining a general understanding of the entity's organization, its operating characteristics, and the nature of its assets, liabilities, revenues, and expenses (this would include general knowledge of the entity's production, distribution, and compensation methods, types of products and services, operating locations, and material transactions with related parties)
- asking the entity's personnel about some of the items noted in Table 19–2
- performing analytical procedures to identify relationships and individual items that appear to be unusual (the process followed for conducting analytical procedures is similar to the one described for audits in Chapter 5)
- reading the financial statements to determine if they conform to GAAP
- obtaining reports from other accountants, if any, who have audited or reviewed the financial statements or significant components thereof
- obtaining a representation letter from management (generally, the chief executive officer and chief financial officer should sign the representation letter)

Note that a review engagement does not require the accountant to obtain an understanding of internal control, test accounting records,

Table 19–2	Examples of Enquiries Made during a Review Engagement

1. Enquiries concerning the client's accounting principles and practices.

2. Enquiries concerning the client's procedures for recording, classifying, and summarizing accounting transactions.

3. Enquiries concerning actions taken at shareholders', board of directors', and other committee meetings.

4. Enquiries of persons responsible for the financial statements concerning

   • Whether the statements are in accordance with GAAP.

   • Changes in the client's business activities or accounting principles.

   • Any exceptions arising from other analytical procedures.

   • Subsequent events having a material effect on the statements.

or corroborate enquires, as would normally be done on an audit. However, if the accountant becomes aware of information that is incorrect, incomplete, or misleading based on the work performed, he or she should perform any additional procedures necessary to provide limited assurance that no material modifications to the financial statements are required.

Review Engagement Report

A standard review engagement report assumes that the financial statements are in accordance with generally accepted accounting principles or another comprehensive basis of accounting. This includes all necessary disclosures. The review report should be dated as of the completion of the accountant's enquiry and analytical procedures. Additionally, each page of the financial statements should be conspicuously marked "unaudited." Exhibit 19–1 is an example of the standard review report.

Conditions That May Result in Changes to the Review Engagement Report

When the accountant conducts a review, he or she may become aware of situations that require modification to the standard report. Two particular situations are (1) a departure from generally accepted accounting principles (or other appropriate criteria) and (2) inability to complete the review because there is a lack of information to allow the accountant to decide if the information is plausible. In such cases a reservation should be expressed in the review engagement report, although it is important to note that it is not a "reservation of opinion" as the review engagement report does not contain an opinion in the first place. Examples of reservations in review engagement reports are in Appendix B of *CICA Handbook,* section 8200.

Compilations

LO 2 > Compilation services, described in section 9200 of the *CICA Handbook,* are accounting services provided by public accounting firms. It is important to stress that an accountant performing a compilation engagement provides assistance to the client in preparing financial statements but does not provide any assurance about those financial statements, which may be a complete set of balance sheet, income statement, and statement of changes in financial position, or only part of that set. The standards for a compilation engagement, listed in Table 19–3 indicate the reduced level of involvement

EXHIBIT 19–1

Example of a Standard Review Report

We have reviewed the accompanying balance sheet of Sierra Company as of December 31, 2006, and the related statements of income, retained earnings, and cash flows for the year then ended. Our review was made in accordance with Canadian generally accepted standards for review engagements and accordingly consisted primarily of enquiry, analytical procedures, and discussion related to information supplied to us by the company. All information included in these financial statements is the representation of the management of Sierra Company.

A review does not constitute an audit and consequently we do not express an audit opinion on these financial statements.

Based on our review nothing has come our attention that causes us to believe that these financial statements are not, in all material respects, in accordance with Canadian generally accepted accounting principles.

Table 19–3   Standards for Compilation Engagements

Standards applicable to compilation engagements are as follows:

(i) the services should be performed and the communication should be prepared by a person or persons having adequate technical training and proficiency in accounting, and with due care; and

(ii) the work should be adequately planned and properly executed and, if assistants are employed, they should be properly supervised.

of the accountant. In particular note that (1) there is no requirement for the accountant to be independent and (2) there is no requirement for the accountant to apply any examination techniques whatsoever to the information supplied to him or her. The accountant signals his or her limited involvement to the reader by including with the financial statements a "Notice to Reader" that:

- states that the financial statements were compiled from information supplied by management
- states that the accountant did not perform an audit or a review and expresses no assurance
- cautions the reader that the information may not be suitable for their purposes
- each page of the compiled financial statements is clearly stamped "Unaudited—see Notice to Reader."

The intent is to make it clear to the reader that the accountant does not express any form of opinion or negative assurance and that none should be inferred from the accountant's association with the financial statements. Exhibit 19–2 presents an example of a Notice to Reader. If it is presented as a separate report, as shown in the figure, each page of the financial statements should be conspicuously marked "Unaudited—see Notice to Reader." Figure 19–1 illustrates the assurance levels resulting from an audit, a review engagement, and a compilation engagement.

EXHIBIT 19–2

Notice to Reader

On the basis of information provided by management, we have compiled the balance sheet of Calton Ltd., as at December 31, 2006, and the statements of income, retained earnings, and cash flows for the year then ended.

We have not performed an audit, or a review engagement in respect of these financial statements and accordingly, we express no assurance thereon. Readers are cautioned that these statements may not be appropriate for their purposes.

FIGURE 19–1

Assurance Levels for a Compilation, a Review, and an Audit

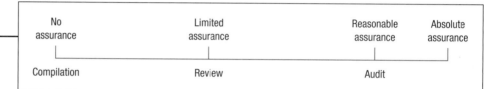

It is important to remember that even though compilation engagements do not provide assurance, the relationship between the accountant and the client, and the accountant's conduct, are still governed by the provisions of *CICA Handbook*, section 5020, "Association."

Because of this association, the public accountant has professional responsibilities with respect to the performance of a compilation engagement. While the financial statements do not necessarily have to be in accordance with generally accepted accounting principles (e.g., limited or no note disclosures, or cash basis) as long as they are appropriate for the users (such as management) who are aware of the limitations, the provincial rules of professional conduct clearly prohibit association by the public accountant with financial statements that he or she knows to be misleading. This may place the public accountant in a somewhat precarious position in that because of his or her very limited involvement in this type of engagement, it may be difficult to know if the financial statements are false or misleading. There is also the possibility of subsequent distribution of the compiled financial statements by management to third parties who may not be aware of or understand the very limited extent of the public accountant's involvement. The approach implicit in *CICA Handbook* section 9200 is for the public to exercise caution before association is established. The recommendations of paragraph 9200.12 of the *CICA Handbook* set out the criteria that the public accountant should apply in deciding whether to accept such a compilation engagement:

The public accountant should perform a compilation engagement only if at the time of accepting the engagement and during the conduct thereof:

(a) there is no reason to believe that the financial statements the public accountant has been engaged to compile are false or misleading, and;

(b) the public accountant believes that the client understands that:

(i) such statements may not be appropriate for general purpose use; and

(ii) uninformed readers could be mislead unless they are aware of the possible limitations of the statements, and of the public accountant's very limited involvement.

The appendix to section 9200 of the *Handbook* provides an example of an engagement letter to be obtained from the client for such an engagement. In addition to written documentation of the client's agreement and understanding of the conditions above, it requires management to acknowledge responsibility for the financial information provided to the accountant, lays out the form of the report (Notice to Reader) to be provided and explicitly states that it may not be appropriate for general use, and so on.

Finally, it directs that public accountant that if he or she becomes aware of matters that would cause the financial statements to be false or misleading, he or she should request additional or revised information and if management does not provide the requested information, the public accountant should not release the statements and should withdraw from the engagement.

The *Handbook* also identifies another type of engagement in section 9100 that provides no assurance to the reader—"Reports on the results of applying specified auditing procedures to financial information other than financial statements." The practitioner and the client will mutually agree upon the procedures to be performed, the practitioner will perform the specified procedures and report factually on the results. Exhibit 19–3 presents an example of a report following an engagement to apply specified audit procedures to the client's long-term debt. The report is often prepared for a third party but it is important to stress that it is for a specific stated purpose (only) and that it explicitly states that the practitioner is not expressing an opinion, simply factually stating the results of applying the procedure, and offers no positive or negative assurance.

Other Attest Engagements

LO 3> The *CICA Handbook* defines an attest engagement as one where the practitioner's conclusion will be on a written assertion prepared by the accountable party (an audit is a special form of attest engagement). Audits and review engagements clearly fit within this definition and are the two most commonly performed attest engagements. This section discusses some of the other attest engagements that public accountants may perform for their clients.

In the definition, *practitioner* refers to a professional accountant in the practice of public accounting. Because attest engagements are not audits as defined in GAAS, the attest standards use *practitioner* instead of *auditor*. The term *assertion* here refers to any declaration, or set of related

EXHIBIT 19-3

Example of a Report on Specified Auditing Procedures Carried Out on Long-Term Debt

To: Trustee Ltd.

Re: Client Ltd.

As specifically agreed, I have performed the following procedures in connection with the above company's certificate dated December 31, 2006, as to the amount of the company's Funded Obligations as at December 31, 2006.

[list of procedures]

as a result of applying the above procedures, I found [no/the following] exceptions [list of exceptions, if any]. However, these procedures do not constitute an audit of the company's Funded Obligations, and therefore I express no opinion on the amount of Funded Obligations as at December 31, 2006.

This letter is for use solely in connection with the closing on January 20, 2007, of the issue of subordinate debenture securities of the company.

FIGURE 19-2

The Three-Party Relationship in an Attest Engagement

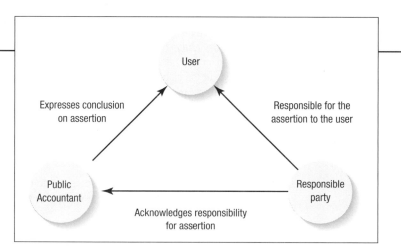

declarations, taken as a whole by a party responsible for it. An example of an assertion by management would be "EarthWear Clothiers maintains effective internal control over financial reporting."

Typically, an attest engagement involves three parties: a user or users; a party responsible for making the assertion, such as management; and a public accountant. Figure 19-2 depicts the relationship among the three parties to an attest engagement. Note the direction of the arrows in this figure. The responsible party is responsible for the assertion to the user and acknowledges that responsibility to the public accountant. The public accountant expresses a conclusion to the user on management's assertion. In some cases, the engagement may involve only two parties because the user and the responsible party are the same.

The practitioner should use an "attestation risk" model to meet the standards of field work in an attest engagement. Attestation risk is analogous to audit risk and is composed of the same three components (inherent risk, control risk, and detection risk) as audit risk discussed in Chapter 3. In the

EXHIBIT   19–4

Auditor's Report on the Effectiveness of the System of Internal Control over Financial Reporting

To the Shareholders of Tenco Ltd.:

We have audited management's assertion that Tenco Ltd. maintained an effective system of internal control over financial reporting as of December 31, 2006 in relation to the criteria described in the appendix to this report. Management's assertion is included in the accompanying report "Report on Effectiveness of Internal Control at Tenco Ltd." as of December 31, 2006. The maintenance of an effective system of internal control over financial reporting is the responsibility of management. Our responsibility is to express an opinion on management's assertion about the effectiveness of the internal control system based on our audit.

We conducted our examination in accordance with assurance standards established by the Canadian Institute of Chartered Accountants. Those standards require that we plan and perform the examination to obtain reasonable assurance that management's assertion is free from significant misstatements. The engagement also includes examining, on a test basis, evidence supporting the content and disclosure in management's assertion. An audit also includes assessing the criteria used and the significant judgements made by management, as well as evaluating the overall presentation of management's assertion.

In our opinion, management's assertion presents fairly, in all significant respects, the effectiveness of the system of internal control over financial reporting of Tenco Ltd. as of December 31, 2006 based on the criteria referred to above.

Because of the inherent limitations in any internal control system, errors or fraud and other irregularities may occur and not be detected. Also, projections of any evaluation of the internal control system over financial reporting to future periods are subject to the risk that the internal control system may become inadequate because of changes in conditions, or that the degree of compliance with the policies or procedures may deteriorate.

following sections, the text discusses a number of different attest engagements which the practitioner may undertake.

Examination of an Entity's Internal Control Over Financial Reporting[1] Prior to *CICA Handbook*, section 9110, an example of an attest examination providing a high level of assurance was an audit report on an entity's internal control over financial reporting. An example of the resulting report is shown in Exhibit 19–4. You can see the similarities between this report and the standard audit report, including the fact that the final paragraph begins with "In our opinion...." The assurance standards in Table 19–1 govern such an examination.

Examination of Financial Information Other Than Financial Statements This type of examination and report, covered in section 5805 of the *CICA Handbook,* was discussed in Chapter 16 and shown in Exhibit 16–7. A common example of this type of engagement occurs when the auditor's client is a shopping mall. Each of the individual stores is a tenant and pays rent to the mall. The contract terms often call for the store's rent to be based at least in part on its revenue. The contract will also provide for an audit of the store's reported revenue figure.

---

[1]An examination of financial information other than financial statements may also be performed as a review—such engagements are covered by section 8500 of the *CICA Handbook.*

Examination of Compliance with Contractual Agreements, Statutes, and Regulations   Section 5815 of the *CICA Handbook* discusses another type of examination leading to an auditor's opinion. Such a report results when an auditor is engaged to report on a client's compliance with a contractual agreement, statute, or regulation.[2] The auditor's responsibilities in this type of engagement were discussed in Chapter 16 and an example of such a report was presented in Exhibit 16–8.

Examination of Control Procedures at a Service Organization   The auditor may undertake an engagement to render an opinion on the control procedures at a service organization. This is covered in section 5970 of the *CICA Handbook*.[3] This type of examination was covered in Chapter 16 and an example of the resulting reports was presented in Exhibits 16–9 and 16–10.

Prospectuses

LO 4 >

In order to make a public offering of its securities, (e.g., debt, equity), an entity is required by securities legislation to provide to prospective investors information of a financial and nonfinancial nature to assist them in making informed decisions. Such information is contained in a prospectus. This section will briefly discuss the basic aspects of the auditor's involvement in the preparation of a *prospectus*. The auditor's involvement in a prospectus may be quite extensive, depending on the circumstances—readers desiring more information should refer to *CICA Handbook,* sections 7110, "Auditor involvement with offering documents of public and private entities" and 7115, "Auditor involvement with offering documents of public and private entities—current legislative and regulatory requirements."

Securities legislation usually requires a prospectus to include comparative balance sheets for two years and comparative statements of income, retained earnings, and cash flows for five years. The most straightforward situation is where an entity that is an ongoing audit client issues a prospectus within a specified future period, often 90 days, of its year-end. In such cases the prospectus contains an auditor's report on the financial statements for the most recent fiscal year (and, in the case of the balance sheet the preceding year; in the case of the income statement, statement of retained earnings, and cash flow statement, the preceding two years). The differences between the audit report to be included in the prospectus and the audit report issued for the year just completed, are that this report will be addressed to the directors, and will identify the multiple years of financial statements reported on.

The auditor will also transmit to the securities authority a letter consenting to the use of the audit report in the prospectus. Before signing and transmitting the letter of consent to the securities authority, the *CICA Handbook* recommends that the auditor:

---

[2]An examination of compliance with agreements and regulations may also be performed as a review—such engagements are covered by section 8600 of the *CICA Handbook.*

[3]See also R. J. Widdowson, Auditor Reports on Control Procedures at Service Organizations (Third Party Reports) (Toronto: CICA, 1990).

Consent Letter

JULY 23, 2007

ONTARIO SECURITIES COMMISSION

To Whom It May Concern:

Re: Algon Limited

I have read the prospectus of the above company dated June 22, 2007 relating to the sale and issue of 5,000,000 Class "A" common shares. I have complied with Canadian generally accepted standards for an auditor's involvement with offering documents.

I consent to the use in the above mentioned prospectus of my report dated February 23, 2007 to the directors of Algon Limited on the following financial statements:

Balance sheets as at December 31, 2006 and 2005;

Statements of income, retained earnings, and cash flows for each of the years in the three year period ended December 31, 2006.

City

Date   PUBLIC ACCOUNTANT

a. read the minutes of meetings of shareholders, the board of directors and appropriate committees for the period since the year-end, and enquire of official matters dealt with at those meetings for which minutes are not yet available.

b. read internal financial statements relating to the period since the year-end for the purpose of identifying and obtaining explanations for relationships and individual items that, based on the auditor's knowledge, appear to be unusual.

c. enquire of appropriate members of management (generally the chief executive officer and the chief financial officer) and the issuer's legal counsel concerning any significant events or changes during the period since the year-end and obtain written representations in this regard.

If the auditor's procedures identify no outstanding issues, the auditor will issue a consent letter as illustrated in Exhibit 19–5.

If the financial statements to be included in the prospectus have been audited by more than one auditor (e.g., the first year by one firm, after which time the entity switched to another auditor) the opinion of both the predecessor and the successor auditors will be included for the relevant financial statements and both would provide consent letters.

If the period of time between the end of the most recent audited financial statements and the prospectus exceeds the allowable "stub period," the prospectus will include unaudited interim financial statements for the stub period. In such cases the auditor's involvement becomes more extensive. When the prospectus includes unaudited interim financial statements, the auditor is normally required to provide a *comfort letter* to the securities authority. In order to provide a comfort letter, the auditor should perform a review of the unaudited interim financial statements. The standards for this review are similar to those for a review engagement under *CICA Handbook,*

Comfort Letter Expressing Negative Assurance

August 15, 2006

ALBERTA SECURITIES COMMISSION

To Whom It May Concern:

Re: Caltron Corporation Limited

I am the auditor of the above company and under date of February 20, 2006, I reported on the following financial statements in the prospectus relating to the sale and issue of 10,000,000 shares of common shares:

> Balance sheets as at December 31, 2004 and 2005;
>
> Statements of income, retained earnings, and cash flows for each of the years in the five year period ending December 21, 2005.

The prospectus includes the following unaudited interim financial statements:

> Balance sheet as at June 30, 2006;
>
> Statements of income retained earnings and cash flows for the six months ending June 30, 2006 and 2005.

I have not audited any financial statements of the company as at any date or for any period subsequent to December 31, 2005. Although I have performed an audit for the year ended December 31, 2005, the purpose and therefore the scope of the audit was to enable me to express my opinion on the financial statements as at December 31, 2005 and for the year then ended, but not on the financial statements for any interim period within that year.

Therefore, I am unable to and do not express an opinion on the unaudited balance sheet as at June 30, 2005 and the unaudited interim statements of income, retained earnings, and cash flows for the three months ended June 30, 2006 and 2005 nor on the financial position, results of operations, or cash flows as at any date or for any period subsequent to December 31, 2005.

I have, however, performed review procedures which meet the standards established by the Canadian Institute of Chartered Accountants relating to unaudited interim financial statements in prospectuses. Based on the results of these procedures, nothing has come to my attention which causes me to believe that the unaudited interim financial statements are not presented, in all material respects, in accordance with Canadian generally accepted accounting principles.

The procedures referred to in the preceding paragraph do not constitute an audit and would not necessarily reveal material adjustments which might be required to present fairly, in all material respects, the financial position of the company as at June 30, 2006 and the results of its operations and its cash flows for the three months ended June 30, 2006 and 2005 in accordance with Canadian generally accepted accounting principles.

This letter is provided solely for the purpose of assisting the securities regulatory authority to which it is addressed in discharging its responsibilities and should not be relied on for any other purpose.

> City
>
> Date   PUBLIC ACCOUNTANT

section 7050, "Auditor review of interim financial statements." The objective of the review is to allow the auditor to express negative assurance on the unaudited interim financial statements. Exhibit 19–6 is an example of a comfort letter expressing negative assurance.

Additional auditor involvement may be appropriate if there is a preliminary prospectus, or if the prospectus contains a financial forecast, projection, or pro forma financial statements. Refer to *CICA Handbook,* sections 7110 and 7115.

Future Oriented Financial Information

LO 5

Handbook section 4250, "Future oriented financial information" sets out accounting standards for such information. Future oriented financial information generally takes one of two forms, *forecasts* and *projections*. A forecast can be defined as future oriented financial information that represent the results of management's planned courses of action for the future period under (in management's opinion) the most likely economic conditions. A projection differs from a forecast in that as well as planned actions based on management's estimate of the most likely economic conditions, it is based on one or more assumptions that may not, in management's judgement, be the most likely.

Audit Guidelines in the assurance section of the *CICA Handbook* discuss two different sets of circumstances where this type of information may be presented. The first, AuG-6, issued in 1989, deals with the situation where future oriented financial information is included in a prospectus or other offering document. In this type of examination, the public accountant is reporting on three assertions:

a. Management's assertions are suitably supported and consistent with the plans of the entity, and provide a reasonable basis for the forecast.

b. The forecast reflects such assumptions.

c. The financial forecast complies with the presentation and disclosure standards established by CICA.

The public accountant's objective in conducting the examination is to obtain sufficient evidence that management has included all the assumptions necessary for the preparation of the future oriented financial information and whether the assumptions form a reasonable basis for the forecast or projection. Exhibit 19–7 presents an example of a report on a financial forecast. Note that although AuG-6 refers to "public accountant" rather than "auditor," and the standards that the public accountant is suggested to follow are similar to GARS, the resulting report does express an opinion.

The circumstances contemplated by AuG-16, issued in 1993, occur where management wishes to produce future oriented financial information but does not require the public accountant to provide any assurance regarding such information. In such cases the public accountant's involvement will be to assist in the compilation of the future oriented financial information. The public accountant should follow the standards similar to those for a compilation under *CICA Handbook* section 9200 and the resulting communication is not unlike the Notice to Reader of that section. Exhibit 19–8 presents an example of the appropriate communication when a public accountant assists in the compilation of a financial projection.

Assurance Services

LO 6

Figure 19–3 reproduces Figure 1–2 which presents the relationship of assurance services to attestation and auditing. As discussed in Chapter 1, assurance services include attestation and auditing services. The joint

EXHIBIT 19–7

Auditor's Report on Financial Forecast

To the Directors of Delgard Limited:

The accompanying financial forecast of Delgard Limited, consisting of a balance sheet as at December 31, 2006 and the statements of income, retained earnings, and cash flows for the period then ending, has been prepared by management using assumptions with an effective date of February 28, 2006. I have examined the support provided by management for the assumptions, and the preparation and presentation of the forecast. My examination was made in accordance with the applicable Assurance and Related Services Guideline issued by the Canadian Institute of Chartered Accountants. I have no responsibility to update this report for events and circumstances occurring after the date of my report.

In my opinion:

a. as at the date of this report, the assumptions developed by management are suitably supported and consistent with the plans of the Company, and provide a reasonable basis for the forecast;

b. this forecast reflects such assumptions; and

c. the financial forecast complies with the presentation and disclosure standards for forecasts established by the Canadian Institute of Chartered Accountants.

Since this forecast is based on assumptions regarding future events, actual results will vary from the information presented and the variations may be material. Accordingly, I express no opinion as to whether this forecast will be achieved.

Vancouver, BC
June 30, 2006   PUBLIC ACCOUNTANT

EXHIBIT 19–8

Notice to Reader on the Compilation of a Financial Projection

To the Directors of Entan Corporation:

I have compiled the financial projection of Entan Corporation, consisting of a balance sheet as at December 31, 2006 and statements of income, retained earnings, and cash flows for the period then ending using assumptions, including the hypothesis set out in Note 2, with an effective date of January 31, 2006, and other information provided by management. My engagement was performed in accordance with the applicable guidance on compilation of a financial projection issued by the Canadian Institute of Chartered Accountants.

A compilation is limited to presenting, in the form of a financial projection, information provided by management and does not include evaluating the support for the assumptions, including the hypothesis, or other information underlying the projection. Accordingly, I do not express an opinion or any other form of assurance on the financial projection or assumptions, including the hypothesis. Further, since this financial projection is based on assumptions regarding future events, actual results will vary from the information presented even if the hypothesis occurs, and the variations may be material. I have no responsibility to update this communication for events and circumstances occurring after the date of this communication.

Calgary, Alberta
July 31, 2007   PUBLIC ACCOUNTANT

FIGURE 19–3

The Relationship between Assurance Services, Attestation, and Auditing

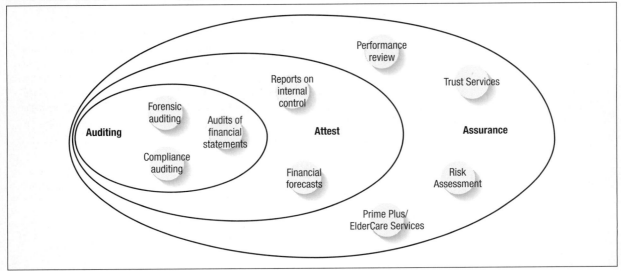

CICA/AICPA Special Committee on Assurance Services has defined assurance services as follows:

> **Assurance services** are independent professional services that improve the quality of information, or its context, for decision makers.

This definition captures a number of important concepts. First, the definition focuses on decision making. Making good decisions requires quality information, which can be financial or nonfinancial. Figure 19–4 presents a model for decision making and the role of information in decision-making activities. An assurance service engagement can help the decision maker to identify which pieces of information are relevant for the required decision. The second concept relates to improving the quality of information or its context. In the decision model shown in Figure 19–4, an assurance service engagement can improve quality through increasing confidence in the information's reliability and relevance. Context can be improved by the format in which information is presented.

The third important concept in the definition of assurance services is independence. As with the earlier discussions of financial statement auditing, independence is the hallmark of the profession. The last concept is professional services, which encompasses the application of professional judgement. The practitioner applies professional judgement to the information that is the subject of the assurance service. In summary, assurance services can capture information, improve its quality, and enhance its usefulness for decision makers.

The Demand for Assurance Services

Economic, social, and regulatory trends are changing the context in which public accountants provide services. These trends include the explosion

FIGURE 19–4

A Model for Decision Making and the Role of Information

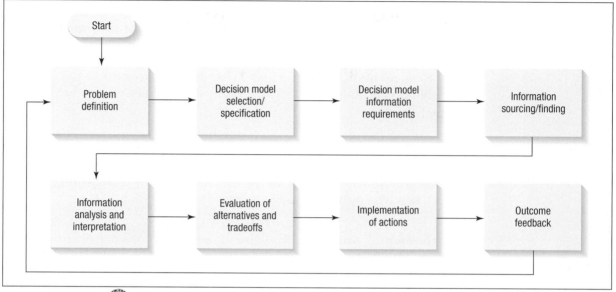

Source: http://www.aicpa.org/assurance/scas/comstud/relevance/pract.htm.

of information technology, increased competition for entities and public accounting firms, globalization of business, accountability of corporate managers, and aging of the population. For example, information technologies continue to advance at a tremendous pace and, generally, at a lower cost. The new technologies change the way entities and people work, and they increase the amount of information and the speed at which this information is available to users. While these changes may potentially threaten the traditional audit, they offer an enormous opportunity for public accountants to provide additional services. The generation of information will require assurance about its reliability, credibility, relevance, and timeliness. Another example is the aging of the population. Statistics Canada's figures indicate that by 2011 individuals over 65 will represent approximately 15 percent of the population and those between 45–65 will represent approximately 29 percent of the population. This increased number of older adults gives public accountants opportunities to provide additional services related to health care performance, personal financial planning, estate planning, pension plan audits, and fraud protection services.

Thus the demand for assurance services can be traced to two sources. First, clients and others have asked auditors to provide services that rely on the auditor's traditional competencies of independence, objectivity, and concern for the public interest. Second, in the face of flat revenue growth from traditional audits, the profession has sought to identify new services that can be delivered to existing and new clients.

Recall from the discussion in Chapter 2, that in response to the demand for expanded assurance services, the CICA and the AICPA formed a joint task force to develop a broader vision. In 1997, the CICA issued *Handbook* section 5025, "Standards for assurance engagements," containing the standards to be followed in assurance engagements.

The CICA has established task forces, some in conjunction with the AICPA, to identify new avenues for the development of assurance services and to develop and communicate guidance to its members who wish to provide those services. Two of the more recently developed services, CA Trust Services and CA Prime Plus/ElderCare are discussed in the companion Online Learning Centre, and a number of other services are covered briefly below.

Other Assurance Services

There are numerous forms of assurance services that a practitioner can provide to his or her clients. This section will review some of them briefly, in order to give you a flavour of the broader range of services that may be undertaken by a professional accountant.[4]

Environmental Auditing   The auditor needs to consider environmental issues in an audit of financial statements because of potential contingent liabilities. However, the auditor could undertake an engagement to examine compliance with specific environmental legislation, or assist organizations in developing or improving their own systems for monitoring compliance with such legislation.

Forensic Auditing   Auditors may specialize in forensic auditing. Forensic auditors assist in many types of criminal investigations, such as insurance fraud, credit card fraud, embezzlement, and money laundering. The CICA has recently concluded an agreement with the Association of Certified Fraud Examiners so that CAs may obtain their CFE designation and concentrate on this specialization.

Business Valuations   Another area of specialization is business valuation. A CA who is a Certified Business Valuator (CBV) can provide service in business valuations prior to sale or merger, estate valuations, or even property valuations in cases of marital breakdown.

Business Performance Reporting   The CICA is undertaking a number of new initiatives related to business performance reporting. *CA Performance View* is a service being developed by a joint CICA/AICPA task force, focusing on business performance measures. The objective is to identify measures that can be tracked over time to assess progress made in achieving specific targets linked to an entity's vision.

[4]The CICA has produced a number of publications in these areas. See, for example, *Environmental Auditing and the Role of the Accounting Profession* (Toronto: CICA, 1992); and *CA Performance View: A Practitioner's Guide to Performance Measurement Engagements* (Toronto: CICA, 2000).

The Canadian Performance Reporting Initiative   CPRI is an initiative of the CICA that currently has five projects underway to improve and enhance various dimensions of performance reporting. For example, *Integrated Performance Reporting* (Management Discussion and Analysis) has as its objective the production of a publication that outlines a framework for MD&A disclosures, including describing its components and how they can be prepared. Other projects of the CPRI underway at this time are *Intellectual Capital Management, Shareholder Value Creation, Environmental Performance Reporting, and Total Value Creation.*

A Look Ahead

LO 8⟩   The Canadian auditing profession is in the midst of major changes. In February 2007, the Auditing and Assurance Standards Board (AASB) of the CICA issued two documents that discuss how and when the new Canadian Auditing Standards (CASs), which are based on the International Auditing Standards (IASs), will replace the existing standards in the *CICA Handbook*. The first document is titled "Adopting International Standards on Auditing (ISAs)."

At this time the International Auditing and Assurance Standards Board (IAASB) is in the process of a major standards revision project called the Clarity Project which will result in all IASs being revised using new drafting conventions. The intent is that the Clarity Project will result in a complete set of auditing standards that are consistent in approach and presentation. The AASB will be very much involved in developing the proposed clarified IASs. The AASB intends to adopt the revised IASs and incorporate them into the new CASs. The AASB has indicated that it may modify the IASs when adopting them as CASs if it deems it appropriate to do so, and has produced guidelines for any modifications to be made.

The Exposure Draft procedure in Canada will be modified—an ED of a proposed CAS will have four elements: a link to the IAASB's exposure draft of the proposed ISA, discussion and explanation of the AASB's process for adopting the ISA and the proposed effective date of the new CAS, discussion of any significant changes to current Canadian Standards, and discussion of any significant proposed modifications to the ISA. The result of all this will be a *CICA Handbook* that is substantially different both in content and in format.

Along with the above-described document, the AASB also released a schedule of proposed adoptions for 2007 and 2008. This is a tentative schedule only, and will no doubt be modified with the passage of time, but it presents a timetable for the almost complete replacement of the current *Handbook* standards with new Canadian Auditing Standards based on International Auditing Standards. The IAASB expects that all of the final clarified ISAs will be approved by the fall of 2008 and that the earliest effective date for the new ISAs will be for periods beginning on or after December 15, 2008. The AASB has stated that it plans to issue its own ED of a proposed CAS at or near the same time as the corresponding IAASB is issued, and finalize the CAS as soon as possible thereafter. If the AASB's

plans are realized, the CASs could be effective for periods beginning as early as, say, the beginning of 2009. The interested reader is strongly encouraged to review the documents themselves, both of which can be accessed through the AASB's website, www.aasb.ca or directly at www.aasb.ca/index.cfm/ci_id/36185/la_id/1/document/1/re_id/0 (Adopting International Standards) and www.aasb.ca/index.cfm/ci_id/35435/la_id/1/document/1/re_id/0 (Project Schedule).

As a final comment, at the time of writing this book, the AASB has already issued 12 exposure drafts of proposed Canadian Auditing Standards (CASs). The current list of outstanding exposure drafts can be accessed at www.aasb.ca/index.cfm?ci_id=11265&1a_id=1.

REVIEW QUESTIONS

LO 6 **19-1** Define *assurance services*. Discuss why the definition focuses on decision making and information.

6 **19-2** Why did the public accounting profession issue assurance standards and promote assurance services?

6 **19-3** Identify and discuss the two sources for the demand for assurance services.

7 **19-4** What are the risks of electronic commerce?

6 **19-5** What are the major differences between assurance standards and generally accepted auditing standards?

3 **19-6** Define an attest engagement. List two conditions that are necessary in order to perform an attest engagement.

4,5,6,7,8 **19-7** What types of engagements can be provided as attest engagements? Identify four attest engagements.

4,5 **19-8** List two sets of criteria that can measure the effectiveness of internal control.

5 **19-9** What types of engagements are allowed for future oriented financial statements?

1,2 **19-10** What type of knowledge must an accountant possess about the entity in order to perform a compilation engagement? A review engagement?

1 **19-11** What type of assurance is provided by the accountant when a review engagement report is issued? How does this differ from the assurance in an audit report?

MULTIPLE-CHOICE QUESTIONS FROM PROFESSIONAL EXAMINATIONS

Unless otherwise indicated, these multiple-choice questions were adapted from the CPA examinations, courtesy of the American Institute of Certified Public Accountants.

6 **19-12*** An assurance report on information can provide assurance about the information's

a. Reliability.

b. Relevance.

c. Timeliness.

d. All of the above.

7> **19-13*** Which of the following is not a Trust Services Principle?

    a. Processing integrity.

    b. Availability.

    c. Digital certificate authorization.

    d. Online privacy.

3> **19-14** Which of the following professional services would be considered an attest engagement?

    a. A management consulting engagement to provide IT advice to a client.

    b. An engagement to report on compliance with statutory requirements.

    c. An income tax engagement to prepare federal and provincial tax returns.

    d. Compilation of financial statements from a client's accounting records.

1,2> **19-15** Jones Retailing, a nonpublic entity, has asked Winters & Co., to compile financial statements that omit substantially all disclosures required by generally accepted accounting principles. Winters may compile such financial statements, provided the

    a. Reason for omitting the disclosures is explained in the engagement letter and acknowledged in the management representation letter.

    b. Financial statements are prepared on a comprehensive basis of accounting other than generally accepted accounting principles.

    c. Distribution of the financial statements is restricted to internal use only.

    d. Omission is *not* undertaken to mislead the users of the financial statements and is properly disclosed in the accountant's report.

1,2> **19-16** The standard report issued by an accountant after reviewing the financial statements of a nonpublic entity states that

    a. A review includes assessing the accounting principles used and significant estimates made by management.

    b. A review engagement includes examining, on a test basis, evidence supporting the amounts and disclosures in the financial statements.

    c. The accountant is *not* aware of any material modifications that should be made to the financial statements.

    d. The accountant does *not* express an opinion or any other form of assurance on the financial statements.

2> **19-17** When compiling the financial statements of a nonpublic entity, an accountant should

    a. Review agreements with financial institutions for restrictions on cash balances.

    b. Understand the accounting principles and practices of the entity's industry.

---

* These questions were prepared by the author.

c. Enquire of key personnel concerning related parties and subsequent events.

d. Perform ratio analyses of the financial data of comparable prior periods.

1> **19-18** Which of the following procedures is *not* usually performed by the accountant during a review engagement of a nonpublic entity?

a. Enquiry about actions taken at meetings of the board of directors that may affect the financial statements.

b. Issuance of a report stating that the review was performed in accordance with standards established in the CICA.

c. Reading of the financial statements to determine if they conform with generally accepted accounting principles.

d. Communication of any material weaknesses discovered during the consideration of internal control.

1,2> **19-19** Which of the following statements is correct concerning both an engagement to compile and an engagement to review a nonpublic entity's financial statements?

a. The accountant does *not* contemplate obtaining an understanding of internal control.

b. The accountant must be independent in fact and appearance.

c. The accountant expresses *no* assurance on the financial statements.

d. The accountant should obtain a written management representation letter.

1,2> **19-20** Financial statements of a nonpublic entity that have been reviewed by an accountant should be accompanied by a report which states in part

a. The scope of the enquiry and the analytical procedures performed by the accountant have *not* been restricted.

b. The opinion is expressed on the financial statements.

c. A review includes examining, on a test basis, evidence supporting the amounts and disclosures in the financial statements.

d. A review is greater in scope than a compilation, the objective of which is to present financial statements that are free of material misstatements.

1,2> **19-21** During an engagement to review the financial statements of a nonpublic entity, an accountant becomes aware of a material departure from GAAP. If the accountant decides to modify the standard review report because management will *not* revise the financial statements, the accountant should

a. Express negative assurance on the accounting principles that do *not* conform with GAAP.

b. Disclose the departure from GAAP in a separate paragraph of the report.

c. Issue an adverse or an "except for" qualified opinion, depending on materiality.

d. Express positive assurance on the accounting principles that conform with GAAP.

PROBLEMS

7> 19-22 Your client, Rhett Corporation, a local sporting goods company, has asked your firm for assistance in setting up its website. Eric Rhett, the CEO, is concerned that potential customers will be reluctant to place orders over the Internet to a relatively unknown entity. He recently heard about companies finding ways to provide assurance to customers about secure websites, and Rhett has asked to meet with you about this issue.

Required:

Prepare answers to each of the following questions that may be asked by Rhett (see Appendix H).

a. Why are customers reluctant to engage in electronic commerce?

b. What type of assurance can your firm provide to his customers concerning the company's website?

c. What process will your firm follow in providing a Trust Services-CA/CPA *WebTrust*SM assurance service for Rhett's website?

4> 19-23 You have audited the financial statements of the Orange Grove Credit Union, a TSX-listed company, for the year ended December 31, 2006. Management is required to certify the effectiveness of Orange Grove's internal control over financial reporting. You have been engaged under section 9110 to support management's certification.

Required:

a. Prepare a draft of your report supporting management's certification of the effectiveness of the credit union's internal control. It is not necessary to list specific procedures.

4,5> 19-24 You are the manager of the examination engagement of the financial forecast of Honey's Health Foods as of December 31, 2006, and for the year then ended which they wish to include in their soon-to-be issued prospectus. The audit senior, Currie, has prepared the following draft of the examination report:

To the Board of Directors of Honey's Health Foods:

We have examined the accompanying forecast balance sheet and statements of income, retained earnings, and cash flows of Honey's Health Foods as of December 31, 2006, and for the year then ending. Our examination was made in accordance with standards for an examination of a projection and accordingly included such procedures as we considered necessary to evaluate the assumptions used by management.

In our opinion, the accompanying forecast is presented in conformity with guidelines for presentation of a forecast established by the Canadian Institute of Chartered Accountants, and the underlying assumptions provide a reasonable basis for management's projection. However, there will usually be differences between the projected and actual results because events and circumstances frequently do not occur as expected, and those differences may be material.

Wilson & Phillips, CAs

Required:

Identify the deficiencies in Currie's draft of the examination report. Group the deficiencies by paragraph.

2⟩ **19-25** The following report was drafted on October 25, 2006, by John Major at the completion of an engagement to compile the financial statements of Ajax Company for the year ended September 30, 2006. Ajax is a nonpublic entity in which Major's child has a material direct financial interest. Ajax decided to omit substantially all of the disclosures required by generally accepted accounting principles because the financial statements will be for management's use only. The statement of cash flows was also omitted because management does not believe it to be a useful financial statement.

To the Board of Directors of Ajax Company:

I have compiled the accompanying financial statements of Ajax Company as of September 30, 2006, and for the year then ended. I planned and performed the compilation to obtain limited assurance about whether the financial statements are free of material misstatements.

A compilation is limited to presenting information in the form of financial statements. It is substantially less in scope than an audit in accordance with generally accepted auditing standards, the objective of which is the expression of an opinion regarding the financial statements taken as a whole. I have not audited the accompanying financial statements and accordingly do not express any opinion on them.

Management has elected to omit substantially all of the disclosures required by generally accepted accounting principles. If the omitted disclosures were included in the financial statements, they might influence the user's conclusions about the company's financial position, results of operations, and changes in financial position.

I am not independent with respect to Ajax Company. This lack of independence is due to my child's ownership of a material direct financial interest in Ajax Company.

This report is intended solely for the information and use of the board of directors and management of Ajax Company and should not be used for any other purpose.

Major John

Required:

Identify the deficiencies contained in Major's report on the compiled financial statements. Group the deficiencies by paragraph where applicable. Do *not* redraft the report.

(AICPA, adapted)

4> **19-26** South Face Inc. (South) was incorporated in May 1999 and has been an audit client since incorporation. South has a fiscal year-end of December 31. The company originated as a small contractor supplying specific mountain climbing equipment to retailers. Recent years have seen South expand into retail operations for mountain climbing equipment. South was the vision of its sole founder and shareholder, Philip Logan.

It is now August 2007 and Philip is encouraged by 2006's strong sales and profit results. He has decided to take the company public. He wants to obtain a listing on a Canadian stock exchange. He has provided you with management statements for the stub period ending June 30, 2006.

Philip has no experience with offering documents and has contacted you to enquire about the process of going public. Philip is interested in knowing which of South's financial statements should be included in a prospectus. He would like you to give him a brief idea about what actions you must perform specific to the prospectus offering. The partner would like you to outline for Philip the steps that a public accountant must take before consenting to the use of his or her name in connection with financial information.

Required:

Respond to the partner's and Philip's requests.

(ICABC, adapted)

1,2> **19-27** It is May and Jane Martin, who just opened her own practice in January, has hired you as a summer intern. Jane was extremely busy during tax season, but expects that business may slow down during the summer. She has been marketing her practice during the past few months by attending various business luncheons and sponsoring a few charitable functions. She has followed the advertising and marketing guidelines established by the profession in all her endeavours.

Many of the people she has met during her activities have asked about the differences between her practice and those of the larger firms. Of course, from the perspective of existing and potential clients, fees are one of the main differences and Jane has discussed them in general with those who have asked. She is careful to not give any specific figures without being formally asked for a bid. However, Jane believes that for the most part, clients do not really understand what accountants offer and especially do not understand the differences in the amount of work and the results of an audit, review, and compilation engagement.

Required:

Prepare a summary for future summer interns that summarizes the differences between the three types of engagements so that they will be able to explain the differences to Jane's clients.

9> **19-28** Axen Manufacturing Limited consists of two operating divisions: Axen Plastics, which produces various plastic consumer products, and Axen Chemicals, which uses a by-product of Axen Plastics to produce various resins for sale to other companies for further processing.

As a result of increasing public concern about environmental issues, Donna Reed, president of Axen, has asked the audit engagement partner for Axen to provide her with a proposal to conduct an environmental audit of the Axen Plastics Division. The results will be used to provide an environmental "report card" for the division and will be included in the company's next annual report to its shareholders.

The partner has asked you to provide him with a memo that discusses the issues that you think are important to accepting this type of engagement. Your memo should include a discussion of the way in which you would approach an engagement such as this and the nature and content of the report that you would issue as result of this environmental audit.

Required:

Prepare the memo requested by the partner.

(CICA, adapted)

1,2,3>   19-29   SuperVac Ltd. produces and sells special bagless "tornado" vacuums under a licence agreement with Ronda Watson, who invented the unique process. The licence agreement calls for SuperVac to pay Watson $20 for each vacuum sold. Watson does not suspect SuperVac of any shady practices with respect to their obligations to her under the royalty agreement, but just to be on the safe side, she wishes to have some assurance regarding SuperVac's revenue from the tornado vacuum and their remittances to her as per the royalty agreement. She has heard that there are provisions in the *CICA Handbook* for examinations and reports of this kind. She has come to you to ask what kinds of examinations you can do and what kind of report you can provide.

Required:

Prepare a reply to Ronda Watson, informing her of what types of examinations you could undertake, a general description of what would be involved in your examinations, and the reports that you could provide as a result.

DISCUSSION CASE

6,7>   19-30   You are a newly promoted manager at your firm. On Monday you receive a phone call from one of the partners in your office, asking you to come see her. She recounts to you that on Saturday evening she had a discussion with Dave Clark, president of the Chamber of Commerce at a charity fundraiser she was attending. The topic of their discussion was the expansion of the traditional auditor's role to becoming a provider of "assurance services." He asked her if she would be willing to give a brief presentation to the next meeting of the Chamber of Commerce on that topic.

"You're good at thinking on your feet," she says to you. "I would like you to represent our firm and make the presentation. There are going to be a lot of senior businesspeople there and this could be a golden opportunity for the firm and for you to make some contacts for the future. I want you to prepare a presentation which will give these businesspeople a good understanding of assurance services—why the profession felt the need to offer them, the standards that govern the professional in performing assurance engagements, and some examples of the new services that are available. Dave Clark said that they would be particularly interested in services pertaining to e-commerce and IT. And oh yes, the meeting is Thursday night."

Required:

Draft your presentation along the lines suggested by the partner.

INTERNET ASSIGNMENTS

7> **19-31** The CICA and the AICPA have jointly developed an assurance service related to electronic commerce called Trust Services-CA/CPA *WebTrust*^SM. Visit the CICA's and AICPA's websites (www.cica.ca; www.aicpa.org) and examine their CA/CPA *WebTrust*^SM seals.

Required:

List the assertions made by the management of the CICA/AICPA. Who "signed" the management report on assertions? What time period is covered by the report?

7> **19-32** EarthWear has a number of competitors that sell goods over the Internet. Visit the website for any two of EarthWear's competitors. For example, visit Timberland (www.timberland.com), L. L. Bean (www.llbean.com), or Land's End (www.landsend.com).

Required:

a. Determine if any of the sites selected provides any type of assurance on its electronic commerce. Note that you may have to prepare to order a product before any assurances are presented on the site.

b. If any of the sites provides assurance on electronic commerce, compare the assurances provided with the CA/CPA *WebTrust*^SM Principles and Criteria.

Glossary

A

accounting data The books of original entry, related accounting manuals, and records such as worksheets and spreadsheets that support amounts in the financial statements. (129)

agreed-upon procedures Specific procedures performed on the subject matter of an assertion while a practitioner is engaged by a client to issue a report of findings. (214)

allowance for sampling risk The uncertainty that results from sampling; the difference between the expected mean of the population and the tolerable deviation or misstatement. (267)

analysis Analysis is the name given to the combination of individual analytical procedures that the auditor may use. Analytical procedures are evaluations of financial information made by a study of plausible relationships among both financial and nonfinancial data. (52)

application controls Controls that apply to the processing of specific computer applications and are part of the computer programs used in the accounting system. (224)

assertions Expressed or implied representations by management that are reflected in the financial statement components. (3)

assurance services Independent professional services that improve the quality of information, or its context, for decision makers. (1)

attestation A communication issued by a practitioner to express a conclusion about the reliability of an assertion that is the responsibility of another party. (7)

attribute sampling Sampling used to estimate the proportion of a population that possesses a specified characteristic. (268)

audit evidence Accounting data and all corroborating information that supports the amounts included in the financial statements. (6)

auditing A systematic process of (1) objectively obtaining and evaluating evidence regarding assertions about economic actions and events to ascertain the degree of correspondence between those assertions and established criteria and (2) communicating the results to interested users. (1)

auditor business risk The auditor's exposure to financial loss or damage to his or her professional reputation. (77)

audit committee A committee consisting of members of the board of directors, charged with overseeing the entity's system of internal control over financial reporting, internal and external auditors, and the financial reporting process. Typically must be independent of management. (15)

audit procedures Specific acts performed as the auditor gathers evidence to determine if specific audit objectives are being met. (18)

audit risk The risk that the auditor may unknowingly fail to appropriately modify his or her opinion on financial statements that are materially misstated. (36)

audit sampling The application of an audit procedure to less than 100 percent of the items within an account or class of transactions for the purpose of evaluating some characteristic of the balance or class. (263)

B

blank or zero balance confirmation A confirmation request on which the recipient fills in the amount or furnishes the information requested. (391)

board of directors Individuals elected by the shareholders of a corporation to oversee management and to direct the affairs of the corporation. (12)

breach of contract Occurs when the client or auditor fails to meet the terms and obligations established in the contract (engagement letter). (655)

business processes Processes implemented by management to achieve entity objectives. Business processes are typically organized into the following categories: revenue, purchasing, human resource management, inventory management, and financing processes. (33)

business risks Risks resulting from significant conditions, events, circumstances, actions or inactions that may adversely affect the entity's ability to execute its strategies and to achieve its objectives. (8)

C

classical variables sampling The use of normal distribution theory to estimate the dollar amount of misstatement for a class of transactions or an account balance. (287)

client business risk The risk that an entity's business objectives will not be attained as a result of the external and internal factors, pressures, and forces brought to bear on the entity and, ultimately, the risk associated with the entity's survival and profitability. (51)

compilation services The presentation, in the form of financial statements, of information that is the representation of management or owners without undertaking to express any assurance on the statements. (687)

compliance audit An audit that determines the extent to which rules, policies, laws, covenants, or governmental regulations are being followed by the entity. (11)

computer-assisted audit techniques Computer programs that allow auditors to test computer files and databases. (134)

confirmation The process of obtaining and evaluating direct communication from a third party in response to a request for information about a particular item affecting financial statement assertions. (37)

contingent liability An existing condition, situation, or set of circumstances involving uncertainty as to possible loss to an entity that will ultimately be resolved when some future event occurs or fails to occur. (563)

control activities The policies and procedures ensuring that necessary actions are taken to address the risks involved in achieving the entity's objectives. (83)

control deficiency A control, whether by design or operation, that does not allow management or employees, in the normal course of performing their assigned functions, to prevent or detect misstatements on a timely basis. (578)

control environment The tone of an organization, which reflects the overall attitude and actions of the board of directors, management, and owners influencing the control consciousness of its people. (79)

control procedures The policies and procedures that help ensure that management's directives are carried out. (79)

control risk The risk that material misstatements that could occur will not be prevented or detected by internal controls. (47)

corporate governance The oversight mechanisms in place to help ensure the proper stewardship over an entity's assets. Management and the board of directors play primary roles, and the external auditor plays a key facilitating role. (32)

corroborating audit evidence Written and electronic information such as cheques, records of electronic transfers, invoices, contracts, minutes, confirmations, and written representation; it also includes information obtained by the auditor through inquiry, observation, inspection, and physical examination. (129)

D

detection risk The risk that the auditor will not detect a material misstatement that exists in the financial statements. (80)

dual dating The auditor's report is dual dated when a subsequent event occurs after completion of field work but before the financial statements are issued. (570)

dual-purpose tests Tests of transactions that both evaluate the effectiveness of controls and detect monetary errors. (177)

due professional care A legal standard requiring that the auditor perform his or her professional services with the same degree of skill, knowledge, and judgement possessed by other members of the profession. (36)

E

electronic (Internet) commerce Business transactions between individuals and organizations that occur without paper documents, using computers and telecommunications networks. (8)

electronic data interchange The transmission of business transactions over telecommunications networks. (129)

engagement letter A letter that formalizes the contract between the auditor and the client and outlines the responsibilities of both parties. (51)

auditor business risk (engagement risk) The risk of the auditor's exposure to loss or injury to professional practice from litigation, adverse publicity, or other events arising in connection with financial statements audited and reported on. (77)

enquiry Seeking information, both financial and nonfinancial, of knowledgeable persons throughout the entity or outside the entity. (45)

enquiry letter An audit enquiry sent to the client's lawyers in order to obtain or corroborate information about litigation, claims, and assessments. (565)

errors Unintentional misstatements or omissions of amounts or disclosures. (70)

ethics A system or code of conduct based on moral duties and obligations that indicates how an individual should behave. (16)

expected misstatement The amount of misstatement that the auditor believes exists in the population. (280)

F

forecasts, financial Prospective financial statements that present an entity's expected financial position, results of operations, and cash flows. (696)

projections, financial Prospective financial statements that present, given one or more hypothetical assumptions, an entity's expected financial position, results of operations, and cash flows. (696)

forensic audit Auditing activities that focus on detecting or deterring a wide variety of fraudulent activities. (10)

forensic auditors Auditors that are employed by corporations, government agencies, public accounting firms, and consulting and investigative services firms. They are trained in detecting, investigating, and deterring fraud and white-collar crime. (13)

fraud Intentional misstatements that can be classified as fraudulent financial reporting and misappropriation of assets. (12)

G

general controls Controls that relate to the overall information processing environment and have a pervasive effect on the entity's computer operations. (224)

Generally Accepted Auditing Standards (GAAS) Measures of the quality of the auditor's performance. (32)

I

illegal acts Violations of laws or of government regulations. (43)

imprest cash (bank) accounts Bank accounts that contain a stipulated amount of money and are used for limited purposes. (530)

independence A state of objectivity in fact and appearance, including the absence of any significant conflicts of interest. (13)

independent (concurring) partner review A review by a second (non-engagement) partner of the financial statements and audit report of a publicly traded company. (574)

information asymmetry Refers to the fact that the manager generally has more information about the true financial position and results of operations of the entity than the absentee owner does. (4)

inherent risk   The susceptibility of an assertion to material misstatement, assuming no related internal controls.   (77)

internal control   A process affected by an entity's board of directors, management, and other personnel that is designed to provide reasonable assurance regarding the achievement of objectives in the following categories: (1) effectiveness and efficiency of operations, (2) reliability of financial reporting, and (3) compliance with applicable laws and regulations.   (8)

K

key business processes   The business processes (also called accounting or transaction cycles) of the entity that are critical to its success in attaining its strategic objectives. For instance, a financial institution in the business of providing commercial mortgage loans must have controls in place to monitor its approval process for mortgage applicants. The risk is that bad debt losses may become unmanageable—the risk to the financial statements is that the valuation of the loan portfolio may be overstated.   (10)

kiting   The process of covering a cash shortage by transferring money from one bank account to another and recording the transactions improperly on the client's books.   (537)

L

lapping   The process of covering a cash shortage by applying cash from one customer's accounts receivable against another customer's accounts receivable.   (324)

M

management advisory services   Consulting services that may provide advice and assistance concerning an entity's organization, personnel, finances, operations, systems, or other activities.   (18)

materiality   The magnitude of an omission or misstatement of accounting information that, in light of surrounding circumstances, makes it probable that the judgement of a reasonable person relying on the information would have been changed or influenced.   (41)

misstatement   An instance where a financial statement assertion is not in accordance with the criteria against which is audited (e.g., GAAP). Misstatements may be due to errors (unintentional), fraud (intentional) or other illegal acts such as noncompliance with laws and regulations (intentional and unintentional).   (2)

monetary-unit sampling   Attribute sampling techniques used to estimate the dollar amount of misstatement for a class of transactions or an account balance.   (280)

monitoring   The process that assesses the quality of internal control over time.   (4)

N

negative confirmation   A confirmation request to which the recipient responds only if the amount or information stated is incorrect.   (337)

nonsampling risk   The possibility that the auditor may use inappropriate audit procedures, fail to detect a misstatement when applying an audit procedure, or misinterpret an audit result.   (264)

nonstatistical sampling   Audit sampling that relies on the auditor's judgement to select the sample and evaluate the results for the purpose of reaching a conclusion about the population.   (264)

O

observation   Process of watching a process or procedure being performed by others.   (45)

operational audit   The systematic review of an organization's activities, or a part of them, in relation to the efficient and effective use of resources.   (11)

ordinary negligence   An absence of reasonable or due care in the conduct of an engagement.   (667)

P

positive confirmation   A confirmation request to which the recipient responds whether or not he or she agrees with the amount or information stated.   (286)

privity   A party's contractual or fiduciary relationship with the accountant.   (655)

professionalism   The conduct, aims, or qualities that characterize or mark a profession or professional person.   (624)

professional scepticism   An attitude that includes a questioning mind and a critical assessment of audit evidence. The auditor should not assume that management is either honest or dishonest.   (22)

projected misstatement   The best estimate of the population mean based on the sample.   (76)

proof of cash   A statement used to reconcile the cash receipts and disbursements recorded on the client's books with the cash deposited and disbursed from the client's bank account for a specified period.   (537)

Q

quality control   A firm's organizational structure, policies, and procedures established to provide the firm with reasonable assurance of conforming to professional standards.   (23)

R

reasonable assurance   A term that implies some risk that a material misstatement could be present in the financial statements without the auditor detecting it.   (2)

relevance of evidence   Whether evidence relates to the specific audit objective being tested.   (130)

relevant assertions   Assertions that have a meaningful bearing on whether the account is fairly stated.   (235)

reliability of evidence   The diagnosticity of evidence; that is, whether the type of evidence can be relied on to signal the true state of the assertion or audit objective.   (9)

reliance strategy   The auditor's decision to rely on the entity's controls, test those controls, and reduce the direct tests of the financial statement accounts.   (225)

reportable conditions   Significant deficiencies in the design or operation of internal control that could adversely affect the organization's ability to record, process, summarize, and report financial data consistent with management's assertions.   (88)

representation letter A letter that corroborates oral representations made to the auditor by management and documents the continued appropriateness of such representations. (161)

review engagement The performance of inquiry and analytical procedures that give the accountant a reasonable basis for expressing limited assurance that no material modifications should be made to the statements in order for them to conform to GAAP. (685)

risk assessment The identification, analysis, and management of risks relevant to the preparation of financial statements that are fairly presented in conformity with GAAP. (8)

risk of assessing control risk too high The risk that the assessed level of control risk based on the sample is greater than the true operating effectiveness of the control structure policy or procedure. (266)

risk of assessing control risk too low The risk that the assessed level of control risk based on the sample is less than the true operating effectiveness of the control structure policy or procedure. (266)

risk of incorrect acceptance The risk that the sample supports the conclusion that the recorded account balance is not materially misstated when it is materially misstated. (266)

risk of incorrect rejection The risk that the sample supports the conclusion that the recorded account balance is materially misstated when it is not materially misstated. (266)

risk of material misstatement The risk that the entity's financial statements will contain a material misstatement whether caused by error or fraud. (45)

S

safeguarding of assets Those policies and procedures that provide reasonable assurance regarding prevention or timely detection of unauthorized acquisition, use or disposition of the company's assets that could have a material effect on the financial statements. (216)

sampling risk The possibility that the sample drawn is not representative of the population and that, as a result, the auditor reaches an incorrect conclusion about the account balance or class of transactions based on the sample. (264)

sampling unit The individual member of the population being sampled. (271)

scanning Reviewing accounting data to identify significant or unusual items; including identification of anomalous individual items within account balances or other client data in entries in transaction listings, suspense accounts, reconciliations, and other detailed reports. (132)

scope limitation A lack of evidence, such as an inability to conduct an audit procedure considered necessary. (572)

significant weakness in internal control A condition in which the design or operation of one or more specific internal control components does not reduce to a relatively low level the risk that errors or fraud in amounts material to the financial statements being audited might occur and not be promptly detected by employees performing their normal assigned functions. (91)

statistical sampling Sampling that uses the laws of probability to select and evaluate the results of an audit sample, thereby permitting the auditor to quantify the sampling risk for the purpose of reaching a conclusion about the population. (263)

subsequent event An event or transaction that occurs after the balance sheet date but prior to the issuance of the financial statements and the auditor's report that may materially affect the financial statements. (53)

substantive strategy The auditor's decision not to rely on the entity's controls and to directly audit the related financial statement accounts. (234)

substantive tests Audit procedures performed to test material misstatements in an account balance, transaction class, or disclosure component of the financial statements. (52)

substantive tests of transactions Tests to detect errors or fraud in individual transactions. (176)

T

tests of account balances Tests that concentrate on the details of amounts contained in an account balance. (177)

tests of controls Procedures that evaluate the effectiveness of the design and operation of internal controls. (52)

tests of details of account balances and disclosures Substantive tests that concentrate on the details of items contained in the account balance, and disclosure. (177)

tolerable deviation rate The maximum frequency of deviation from a prescribed control that the auditor is willing to accept without altering the planned assessed level of control risk. (275)

tolerable misstatement The amount of the preliminary judgment about materiality that is allocated to a financial statement account. (76)

tort A wrongful act other than a breach of contract for which civil action may be taken. (658)

W

walkthrough The auditor's tracing of a transaction from origination through the entity's information system until it is reflected in the entity's financial reports. It encompasses the entire process of initiating, authorizing, recording, processing, and reporting individual transactions and controls for each of the significant processes identified. (176)

working papers The auditor's record of the work performed and the conclusions reached on the audit. Also referred to as audit documentation. (18)

Index